Land Law

Second Edition

Chris Bevan

BA(Hons)(Cantab), MA(Cantab)
Barrister (Middle Temple)
Associate Professor in Property Law
Durham Law School, Durham University

OXFORD
UNIVERSITY PRESS

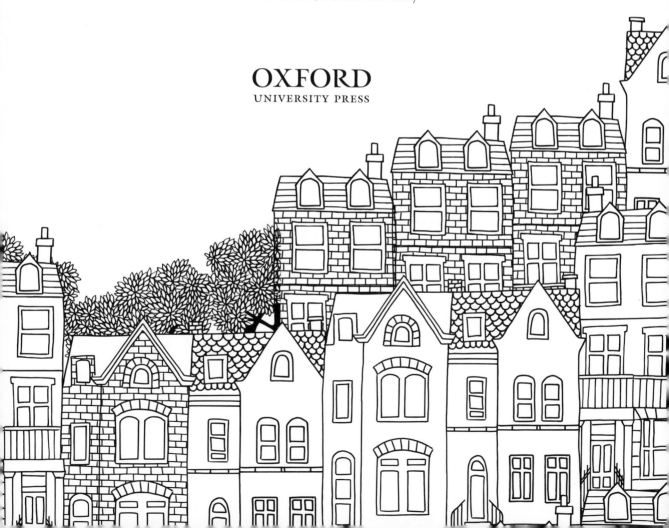

OXFORD
UNIVERSITY PRESS

Great Clarendon Street, Oxford, OX2 6DP,
United Kingdom

Oxford University Press is a department of the University of Oxford.
It furthers the University's objective of excellence in research, scholarship,
and education by publishing worldwide. Oxford is a registered trade mark of
Oxford University Press in the UK and in certain other countries

First Edition 2018
Second Edition 2020
Impression: 4

Published in the United States of America by Oxford University Press
198 Madison Avenue, New York, NY 10016, United States of America

British Library Cataloguing in Publication Data
Data available

Library of Congress Control Number: 2020932786

ISBN 978–0–19–884032–9

Printed in Great Britain by
Bell & Bain Ltd., Glasgow

Land Law

Brief Contents

Detailed Contents

Preface

For students coming to the subject for the first time, land law can appear tricky and unfamiliar. This may be unsettling but worry not, this initial apprehension is entirely normal. Land law owes a lot to its historical past and, in particular, draws heavily on terminology and language that often feels antiquated to a modern audience. What's more, there is a commonly peddled misconception that land law cannot compete with the sexiness of, say, the criminal law, with its feverish, fast-paced depiction in televised dramas. In fact, land law is not dry at all but is a deeply stimulating and vital body of law which reaches into many of the most important moments in life. Land is the stage on which our lives play out. Land law provides the scaffolding which supports that stage. But land law is about much more than just soil and boundary fences. It is about people. It is about relationships. It is about you and me. It is about that essential cry: 'this is mine and not yours'. It is important to us all, so when you lean into this subject and embrace the colours and flavours that it has to offer, you will thrive. That is where this book comes in.

This book serves to blast away any worries you may have, tear down barriers to understanding, and cast a searching and energizing spotlight over the complexities and uncertainties of the law. This book offers a clear, vibrant, and readily understandable study of the key land law principles across its 14 chapters to prepare you for success. The aim is to provide as concise as possible an account of the law without, of course, imagining that its some 686 pages can possibly cover everything. The focus is on helping you to understand and apply the legal principles rather than delivering an encyclopaedic treatment of the law. In this book, I have adopted a more informal writing style to help you in this endeavour and to invite you into this exciting subject. I have also offered case citations using case names and dates only so as not to clog up the text, but please do remember to stick to formality in your land law essays, both in terms of writing style and making use of full case citations where appropriate (see the Table of Cases for the full citations for this book). For me, land law is a fresh, modern, and inclusive discipline, so to reflect this I have made broad use of female pronouns in contrast to the traditional textbook's male preference. Beyond this, the book includes a number of further features designed to aid your understanding:

- Key cases in each topic area are displayed distinctly in case boxes so that you can easily identify the most seminal court judgments. Note, however, that this is no substitute for reading case law in full which, naturally, you are strongly encouraged to do. It is in the reading of judgments that cases really come alive.

- Important academic thinkers are identified, further reading suggestions made, and extracts from journal articles drawn out clearly in the text.

- Frequent, carefully constructed diagrams, flowcharts, and tables help you visualize and absorb the more complex aspects of the law.

- Generous use of headings, subheadings, and bulleted and numbered lists break down the text and make for a more digestible read.

- A 'Future directions' section at the close of each chapter explores hot debates in the topic area and considers where the law may be going next.

- A comprehensive glossary is included at the end of the book as a reference tool to dip into to help you grasp important land law concepts and terminology.

- Extensive online resources (www.oup.com/uk/bevan2e/) as detailed on page xv, to help you to check your understanding and revise, answer essay questions, stay updated on developments in land law since publication, and engage even further with the debates and cases covered in the book.

Of course, like other areas of the law, land law has its fair share of fascinating complexities, depths, and nuances which cannot and should not be overlooked. Whilst seeking to offer clarity, this book therefore does not shy away from exploring these thornier issues which will help you to gain a comprehensive and rounded understanding of the law. At all times, however, my aim in writing this book has been to provide a lively, thought-provoking yet readable text that motivates, enthuses, and engages you, as students of land law, in the joys of this great subject. I hope that once you have read the book, you will share my passion for land law—on which note, please don't hesitate to get in touch with me directly if you have any questions or feedback: my email address is: christopher.w.bevan@durham.ac.uk.

Enjoy it!

Acknowledgements

As I have discovered in writing this book, there is much more to the exercise than merely putting words on the page. Rather, the process has involved genuine collaboration and I have drawn real support from a whole raft of sources. In this vein and for this second edition, I remain sincerely grateful to the outstanding team at OUP who have shown me nothing but brimming enthusiasm, energy and encouragement at all stages of the production of this book. In particular, I express my keenest gratitude to Lucy Read and Emma Sheffield who have walked every step of the project with me. I thank also those academic colleagues who provided invaluable feedback on the first edition which, as a result, I am in no doubt, have resulted in this edition being a better work.

A textbook is a living, breathing and shifting creature and, as this the 2nd Edition is published I am indebted to my students past and present who are easily the most rewarding aspect of my job. It is for them that this book is written and it is they who unwittingly sound in and have shaped every page and who are a continued inspiration to strive to make the book as clear and effective as it can possible be.

Once again to those who are, it seems to me, all too-often underacknowledged when books are written: family. To Mum, Bill & Claire, I thank you for the unswerving belief and confidence you always have in me when I do not. To Andy, I thank you for your unending and sustaining support, for keeping me sane in ways no one else can and, above all, for being the light of my life. Finally, to two great friends to whom this book remains dedicated: Eddie & Dennis.

Chris Bevan
Durham
September 2019

New to this Edition

New cases explored in this second edition include:

- On overreaching: *Mortgage Express v Lambert* (2016); *Baker v Craggs* (2018)
- On adverse possession: *Thorpe v Frank* (2019); *Rashid v Nasrullah* (2019)
- On resulting trusts and the family home: *Curran v Collins* (2015); *Marr v Collie* (2017)
- On proprietary estoppel: *Henry v Henry* (2010); *Davies v Davies* (2016); *James v James* (2018); *Dobson v Griffey* (2018); *Thompson v Thompson* (2018); *Gee v Gee* (2018); *Moore v Moore* (2018); *Habberfield v Habberfield* (2019)
- On leases: *Watts v Stewart* (2016); *Gilpin v Legg* (2017); *Camelot Property Management Ltd v Roynon* (2017); *Camelot Guardian Management Ltd v Khoo* (2018)
- On easements: *Donovan v Rana* (2014); *Gore v Naheed* (2017); *Regency Villas Title Ltd v Diamond Resorts (Europe) Ltd* (2018); *Churston Golf Club Ltd v Haddock* (2019); *Parker v Roberts* (2019)
- On freehold covenants: *Davies v Jones* (2010); *Birdlip v Hunter* (2016)
- On leasehold covenants: *Anders v Haralambous* (2013); *Telchadder v Wickland Holdings Ltd* (2014); *Pineport v Grangeglen* (2016); *Golding v Martin* (2019)
- On mortgages: *Philbin v Davies* (2018)
- On land law and human rights: *FJM v UK* (2018)*; Vrzic v Croatia* (2018)

New Legislation and Law Commission Reports explored in this second edition:

- Tenant Fees Act 2019 and Homes (Fitness for Human Habitation) Act 2018
- Law Commission Report No. 380, Updating the Land Registration Act 2002 (2018)

Further updates to the content in this second edition:

- Separate, dedicated chapters for licences; proprietary estoppel; leasehold covenants
- Additional and improved figures and flowcharts

Guide to using this book

ELEVATE YOUR LEARNING WITH *LAND LAW*

Chris Bevan's *Land Law* offers a rich learning experience, which brings the law to life in order to support a detailed understanding of the subject area. Outlined here are the key features and tools included in the book and the online resources to ensure you understand each topic, how the law applies in practice, and where the law might go in future.

 www.oup.com/uk/bevan2e/

UNDERSTAND AND CONTEXTUALIZE the topic at hand

Chapter introductions outline the topic, and prompt questions that will be at the forefront of your learning throughout each chapter.

KEY CASES demystified

Directing you towards a better analysis of the law, each key case is set out clearly from the main text. Broken down into sections covering 'Facts', 'Legal issue' and 'Judgment', the significance of the cases is made plain, enabling you to see the evolution of the law and how it has been applied. Online, you can find links which take you direct to the judgments themselves, making it easy to read the law for yourself.

REVISE AND MEMORISE WITH OVER 95 diagrams and visual aids

Consolidate your learning through diagrams and flowcharts (with audio walk-throughs on some flowcharts accessible online) that explain key concepts or legislation in a digestible way. Maps and related questions are also online to help visualise concepts. Keep these to hand while revising by downloading them for quick-fire ways to retain important information.

GO FURTHER WITH YOUR LEARNING by considering the future of land law and wider debates

Each chapter is summarised with a 'Future directions' section which prompts investigative thought and asks you to consider how land law might develop over time. This is accompanied by further reading within the text with additional links online to external sources of information.

TEST YOUR KNOWLEDGE with self-test and scenario-style questions

Online, topics within the book are accompanied by self-test questions which provide instant feedback on important facts and legislation. You can also practice scenario questions for every chapter, enabling you to engage practically with the content. These questions, accompanied by notes on what a good answer would cover and how it might be structured, will help you develop your essay-writing techniques and improve your performance in coursework and exams.

WATCH, LISTEN, AND LEARN from the author

Videos and audio podcasts (with transcripts) are available online, allowing you to hear direct from the author as he helps with assessment preparation and discusses the importance of key topics in their wider context.

RELATE TO THE LAW by learning from professionals in the field

Exclusive to this book, you can watch Chris Bevan in conversation with leading barristers who appeared in seminal land law cases such as *Stack v Dowden* (2007), *Wood v Waddington* (2015) and more. Complementing the books extensive use and analysis of case law, these videos bring the judgments to life, giving you a greater and more nuanced understanding of land law.

INTERACT AND INTEGRATE your learning through tasks

Matching exercises and interactive timelines available online offer a different way of revising topics and testing your understanding.

REVISE KEY TERMS and definitions in the glossary

Throughout the text, words emboldened with colour signal key legal terms. You can learn the definitions to accompany these by accessing the glossary at the end of the book.

Table of Cases

International

European Court of Human Rights

European Court of Justice

National Cases

Australia

Canada

Hong Kong

Table of Legislation

Introduction to Land Law

1.1 Introduction

So here we go … Welcome to your study of land law. Shake off any preconceptions you might have. Land law is an exciting, rich subject that offers intense rewards to those willing to embrace it. Land law is 'proper' law—a perfect amalgam of statute, common law, and policy. It is the site of some of society's most important developments and helps answer some of the most fundamental questions: who owns what and whose land is that? It goes to that ancient, essential cry of 'this is *mine* and not yours'. In short, land law matters because land matters. Land is all around us. It is beneath your feet and all around you right now as you read this. Land is the stage for life's most pivotal events. It can offer security, safety, and a sanctuary in the form of the family home. Land can equally be the site of division, oppression,[1] deprivation of one's culture,[2] and violation of human rights.[3] Figure 1.1 muses on why land is so special.

Figure 1.1 captures land's distinct status which necessitates distinct rules to govern it—this is what we call land law. Let's unpack its special features:[4]

1. Land is permanent: Land is fixed. For the most part, it is not going anywhere. This degree of permanence gives land a stability, a durability, and a longevity which means that dealings with it offer a sense of security, long-termism, and commitment. This also explains why investment in land is often seen as a 'safe option'. A key feature of land's permanence is our ability to deal with it: we can hold land for ourselves but also pass it on to others for their use or benefit and even to our heirs on death. More than this, we can split the enjoyment of land: for example, you might be the owner of a piece of land but decide to **rent** it out to your neighbour.

---

[1] For a feminist perspective on land law, see amongst others, H. Lim and A. Bottomley (eds.), *Feminist Perspectives on Land Law* (Abingdon: Routledge-Cavendish, 2007).

[2] For example, the land grabs from indigenous peoples around the world.

[3] We explore the relationship between land law and human rights in Chapter 14.

[4] See B. McFarlane, *The Structure of Property Law* (Oxford: Hart, 2008), 7.

Figure 1.1 The features that make land special

2. Land is in limited supply: Land is a finite resource. There is only so much of it available. You cannot make more land in the way that, for example, if there is a shortage of cars, we can manufacture more. Limited availability means that land is valuable, expensive, in demand. It means that most of us can only hope to own land with the aid of a **mortgage** from the bank. For land lawyers, the limited supply means land must be freed up, made available, be marketable so that its maximum potential can be realized. We want land to be unlocked, without **encumbrances**, and not over-burdened or constrained.[5]

3. Land is connected: A parcel of land never exists in isolation. In almost every case, it will be connected to at least one other piece of land, maybe more, and this means that understanding the rights and relationships operating on land often involves considering the rights of adjoining landowners. Interconnectedness and disputes between adjoining plots of land are therefore an unavoidable feature of dealing with land.

4. Land is unique: Every piece of land is distinct, a one-off; making it is expensive. Even two apparently identical plots of land are different—each having a unique physical place which no other parcel of land shares. The many property shows on the television where couples seek their 'perfect home' are premised on the very idea of land's uniqueness, that each plot of land has its own magic. The distinctiveness of land can create a personal attachment which makes deprivation of that land by, for example, repossession or eviction difficult to accept. This in turn can lead to bitter legal wranglings which land law must resolve. Uniqueness is also a price inflator.

---

[5] In Chapter 2, we will explore how a system of land registration contributes to this goal.

5. Land is socially and economically important: **Billions of pounds are loaned to individuals and businesses in the UK to purchase land. Land is one of several vital pillars supporting the British economy. Evidence of this is all around us; you need only think of the concerns in the media of a 'housing bubble',[6] of rising house prices, or of irresponsible mortgage lending to see that land is a key protagonist in the story of our economy's rise and fall. But land is also socially important. Land is much more than the sods of earth that comprise it: consider the purchase of a property as a home.[7] Socially, land gives us somewhere to live, somewhere to build a family, somewhere to be active citizens—it provides the blank canvas against which we shape our lives and our businesses.**

6. Land is capable of supporting multiple interests: **This is land's *pièce de résistance*, its showpiece, but also the source of most disputes over it. Land is able to sustain simultaneous, multiple uses and interests. Let's take an example: Armita buys a parcel of land but cannot afford the full asking price. She therefore takes out a mortgage loan. In return for the loan, the bank enjoys an interest in the land. Imagine that when Armita purchases the land she promises the neighbours that she will not run a business from the site. She gives another neighbour, Ben, the right to walk over her land and park his car and, finally, she rents out part of her land to Cai who becomes her** tenant. **Armita, the bank, Ben, and Cai all have rights concerning the use of the land. The law allows for these rights to coexist simultaneously, maximizing the use-value of land. With multiple interests, however, come risks. Chief among them is what land lawyers call the 'enforceability' or 'priority question'. In other words, whose interest wins? Who takes priority when a dispute arises between these competing claims? It is this question of enforceability and priority between right holders that is the very essence of land law.**

Land's special features mean that a body of rules has developed around it: this is land law.

 Visit the online resources to watch a video introducing the topic of land law.

1.2 The scope of contemporary land law: What is land law?

English law draws a distinction between 'real' and 'personal' property. In its most straightforward sense, real property consists of land and personal property is all other property that is not land. Land law is the law concerning 'real property' or **realty** rather than personal property, or **personalty** as it is called. Birks explains the difference between real and personal property in the following passage:[8]

> If a lay person hears 'real property' or 'real estate' or 'realty', what will come to mind will be an image of land. For most lawyers the effect will be the same … 'Personal property' or 'personalty' similarly evoke cars, cows, televisions, crockery, pictures, money and a host of other moveable things … A judgment in money can be called personal because it gives the victorious claimant no right in or to any particular thing but merely a right that a person, the defeated defendant, pay the sum in

---

[6] A housing bubble occurs where land prices rise inexorably and thus so do house prices in a manner that is unsustainable and ultimately the bubble bursts as prices decline.

[7] We consider in Chapter 6 what makes land a home and how you acquire an interest in it.

[8] P. Birks, 'Before We Begin: Five Keys to Land Law' in S. Bright and J. Dewar (eds.), *Land Law: Themes and Perspectives* (Oxford: Oxford University Press, 1998), 470.

question … in some actions, you could recover the thing itself. Those actions came to be called 'real actions', 'real' meaning 'thing-related' in the simplest sense that the person claiming would recover the very thing claimed. The subject matter of real actions then became real property.

Land law is the law of real property. It is 'that part of the general law which governs the allocation of rights and responsibilities in relation to "real" or "immoveable" property'.[9] As Birks explains, the word 'real' indicates that we are concerned with rights *in rem*, which is Latin for rights *in the thing*. The real/personal distinction is ancient and historically described the nature of the remedy available when legal proceedings were brought: an action *in rem* involved seeking recovery (i.e. return) of the land, for example, where the true owner had been dispossessed. In contrast, an action *in personam* consisted of an action against a wrongdoer personally, and for which the remedy would be compensation in the form of damages. Today, this real/personal distinction endures but represents largely a historical overhang from the early development of the law. Most of the rights we encounter in this book are regarded as real property as they would have been protected by actions *in rem*.

Land law is about rights in things; in other words, rights in the land rather than rights which are merely personal to the people who created them. But land law is also about responsibilities and crucially, about relationships. Land does not exist in a vacuum and land law must also be regarded as the body of law governing the *relationship* between the thing and the owner of that thing. More specifically, land law creates a framework in which a variety of relationships between people and land can operate. Land law is concerned with the nature, creation, and protection of rights in land and, also the content of those rights. If you rent a parcel of land, for example, what rights do you have? If the land is sold or disposed of without your consent, what forms of redress do you have? How can you protect your position?[10] These are all questions to which land law attempts to provide the answers.

1.3 What is land?

The traditional starting point is the definition of 'land' in s. 205(1)(ix) of the Law of Property Act 1925 (LPA 1925) which provides that:

> 'Land' includes land of any tenure, and mines and minerals, whether or not held apart from the surface, buildings or parts of buildings (whether the division is horizontal, vertical or made in any other way) and other corporeal hereditaments; also a manor, an advowson, and a rent and other incorporeal hereditaments, and an easement, right, privilege, or benefit in, over, or derived from land.

Section 205 offers a rather confounding statutory definition but it serves a vital function. It tells us that land law is about more than just physical, tangible property such as trees and coal (so-called **corporeal hereditaments**): it also concerns intangible rights in land (so-called **incorporeal hereditaments**). These intangible rights are those which are not necessarily visible on the land but are extremely important, and include such rights as **leases**, **easements**, **covenants**, and **mortgages**.[11] Land, under s. 205, is defined as including both

---

[9] K. Gray and S. F. Gray, *Elements of Land Law*, 5th edn (Oxford: Oxford University Press, 2008), 3.

[10] These are issues concerning leasehold land which we cover in Chapter 9.

[11] All of which we consider later in this book in Chapters 9, 10, 11, and 13 respectively.

Figure 1.2 The expansive meaning of land

the physical aspects of land as well as those rights of enjoyment of land that cannot be seen. When we talk of 'land'—what do we mean and what does 'land' include?

1.3.1 The expansive meaning of 'land'

Land enjoys an expansive meaning. At common law, the following sixteenth-century maxim (though very old) really sums up the breadth of interpretation given to land: *Cuius est solum, eius est usque ad coelom ad inferos*—the owner of the soil also owns everything up to the sky and down to the centre of the earth. What this maxim tells us is that land involves much more than just rights to the surface level of the soil and can encapsulate rights both above and below the surface: see Figure 1.2. But just how far upwards and downwards do these rights extend?[12] As we will discover, the extent of your rights has been delimited and qualified by both common law developments and statutory intervention.

- Airspace: It has never been the case that an owner of land owns the entire airspace above her property, reaching infinitely up into the heavens. The common law has long distinguished between two different strata: the lower stratum and the upper stratum. The lower stratum refers to airspace 'to such height as is necessary for the ordinary use

---

[12] For a fulsome analysis of the question, see K. Gray, 'Property in Thin Air' (1991) 50 CLJ 252.

and enjoyment of . . . land and the structures upon it'.[13] The upper stratum refers to the airspace above this height. A landowner's rights are limited to those of the lower stratum. Section 76 of the Civil Aviation Act 1982 offers further help in explaining this:[14]

> The lower stratum is unlikely to extend beyond an altitude of much more than 500 or 1,000 feet above roof level, this being roughly the minimum permissible distance for normal overflying by any aircraft.

The development of technology has meant that qualifications and restrictions were needed on landowners' rights. Where the lower stratum is intruded upon or invaded in some way, the landowner may be able to bring an action for trespass and seek an injunction irrespective of whether any damage has been caused to the landowner.[15] Examples include: overhanging jibs or booms of cranes used for construction on adjacent land,[16] the branches of neighbours' trees dangling over into a piece of land,[17] overhanging eaves,[18] advertising signs,[19] and cables.

- Subsoil: The owner of land will usually also own any man-made and natural space below the land which is actually capable of being owned. These subsurface spaces will normally be so owned even if they have been created by another party and even where the landowner is not in fact able to access them.[20]

- Mines and minerals: At common law, an owner of land is said to be entitled to 'all mines and minerals' within the land.[21] This was codified in s. 205(1)(ix) of the LPA 1925 (look back at the extract in section 1.3), but this position has been qualified by the court and by statute which have carved out certain exceptions. Any coal, natural gas, and oil beneath the land, for example, are deemed by statute to be property of the Crown.[22] The same is true of any unmined gold or silver found in mines on or under land.[23]

- Water: The position as to water is rather technical. Water which passes over or flows through land cannot be owned. If you own land which is, in part, covered with water, you also do not own this water. There can be ownership only as to very small volumes of water for agricultural or domestic, household purposes. If you wish to extract greater volumes of water, you need a licence granted by the National Rivers Authority.[24]

- Flora and fauna—trees, plants, flowers and wild animals: Land is taken to include all the trees, plants, hedges, and flowers growing, whether they have been cultivated by the landowner or have sprouted up and grown wild on the property.[25] Perhaps macabrely, the position for wild animals depends on whether they are alive or dead. When wild animals are alive, the landowner has only 'qualified' **property rights** over them. This gives the landowner

---

[13] *Bernstein v Skyviews and General Ltd* (1978), per Griffiths J.

[14] See also Sch. 1 and s. 3(5) of the Rules of the Air Regulations 2007.　　[15] *Kelsen v Imperial Tobacco Co.* (1957).

[16] *Graham v K. D. Morris & Sons Pty Ltd* (1974).　　[17] *Lemmon v Webb* (1895).

[18] *Baten's Case* (1610).　　[19] *Gifford v Dent* (1926).

[20] *Metropolitan Railway Co. v Fowler* (1893) (which involved a railway tunnel); *Grigsby v Melville* (1972) (which involved a cellar).

[21] Note, however, the vibrant debate around changes to trespass law under the Infrastructure Act 2015 which, subject to conditions, permits fracking firms to drill under homes without prior permission.

[22] Coal Industry Act 1994, s. 9; Petroleum Act 1998, s. 2.

[23] *Case of Mines* (1567); *Attorney-General v Morgan* (1891).

[24] Water Resources Act 1991, ss. 24 and 27.　　[25] *Stukeley v Butler* (1615).

the right to catch and kill the animals on their land. Once wild animals have been caught and killed, the animals become the absolute property of the landowner.[26]

- Items found in or on land: If an item, say a gold bracelet, is found on a piece of land, who owns it? This involves asking who has superior title i.e. a superior claim to the item. We need to distinguish between three different scenarios: (1) finder vs true owner disputes; (2) finder vs dispossessor disputes; and (3) finder vs occupier disputes. In finder-true owner disputes, if an item is found but the true owner comes forward, that true owner can reclaim it: *Moffatt v Kazana* (1969). A finder-dispossessor dispute is where one person (the finder) finds the item but hands it to another person (the dispossessor) who perhaps refuses to return it to the finder. In finder v dispossessor disputes, the finder has a better title than anyone who interferes with and takes the item e.g. dispossessor. The finder has a superior claim to the property save for the true owner of the item: *Armory v Delamirie* (1722). Here, a chimney sweep's boy found a ring and took it to a jeweller who would not return it. The court held in the boy's favour. A finder-occupier dispute is where one person (the finder) finds an item on land which is occupied (but not owned) by another and that occupier claims title to the item. In such cases, Donaldson L.J. held that the occupier can only claim superior title to the finder if the occupier can demonstrate: (a) that she has exercised sufficient control over the item, and (b) can demonstrate an intention to exercise this control. In *Parker*, a finder of a gold bracelet on an airport floor acquired title over the item; British Airways could not demonstrate sufficient control of lost property. Beyond this, if an item is found *in* or *attached to* land, the general rule is that it belongs to the landowner: in *Elwes v Brigg Gas Company* (1886), a prehistoric boat found some 6 feet beneath the soil was held to belong to the landowner. In *Waverley Borough Council v Fletcher* (1995), a metal-detector enthusiast who found a gold brooch while searching through council land also failed in his claim to ownership of the item. The brooch, said the court, belonged to the council who owned the land.

- Where an item found amounts to 'treasure' under the provisions of the Treasure Act 1996,[27] the item belongs to the Crown. The definition of 'treasure' is provided in s. 1 of the 1996 Act.

- 'Treasure' excludes single coins but otherwise includes: any object at least 300 years old with at least 10 per cent precious metal; more than one coin at least 300 years old with at least 10 per cent precious metal; or one of more than ten coins in the same find which are at least 300 years old (in this latter example there is no requirement of 10 per cent precious metal). Other items, at least 200 years old, may also be considered treasure as defined by the relevant Secretary of State. A person finding items she reasonably believes to be treasure has a duty to notify the coroner.

- Buildings: Any building constructed on land which has its foundations set into the ground will almost certainly form part of the land.[28] Where there are no foundations, whether the building is part of the land will depend on the rules governing so-called 'fixtures', which we discuss in section 1.3.2.

---

[26] This has been confirmed for both wild animals such as game: *Blades v Higgs* (1865); as well as fish: *Nicholls v Ely Beet Sugar Factory Ltd (No. 2)* (1936).

[27] For a discussion of the 1996 Act see J. Marston and L. Ross, 'Treasure and Portable Antiquities in the 1990s Still Chained to the Ghosts of the Past: The Treasure Act 1996' [1997] Conv 273; the Government undertook a consultation in 2019 on revising the definition of 'treasure' under the 1996 Act to ensure greater protection for archaeological finds. Keep an eye out for any proposed changes. [28] As confirmed in *Elwes*.

- Fixtures: Any **fixture** is deemed to form part of the land. This much is simple. What is less straightforward is determining what is and is not a fixture. Fixtures are governed by a series of distinct legal principles and therefore warrant their own separate consideration. We turn to this now.

1.3.2 **Fixtures**

According to the Latin maxim *Quicquid plantatur solo, solo credit*, whatever is attached to the soil becomes part of it. What this means is that any 'chattel'—in other words, an item of movable, personal property such as a piece of furniture—which becomes attached or fixed to the land takes on the status of a 'fixture' and then forms part of that land. It is important to be able to distinguish between a chattel and a fixture because a fixture, forming part of the land, will belong to the owner of the land whereas a chattel may belong to another person who is not the landowner. The chattel/fixture distinction is particularly significant in the following contexts:

1. Where land is transferred or sold to a new owner. Any fixtures will belong to that new owner and pass with the land; chattels will not. A new owner will therefore want to argue that items are fixtures and attached to their newly acquired land.

2. Where a bank or building society advances money by way of mortgage and their interest is secured against the borrower's land. The bank or building society may seek to argue that items are fixtures to increase the value of its security.

3. Where land is leased by a landlord to a tenant. Any items which are fixtures belong to the landlord at the end of the lease so a landlord will want to be clear as to which items fall into which category.

KEY CASE *Elitestone Ltd v Morris* (1997)

Facts: Elitestone Ltd purchased land on which Mr Morris' bungalow was situated and 26 other properties had been built. Elitestone intended to demolish all the properties and redevelop the land. Elitestone therefore brought possession proceedings against all the property owners. Mr Morris defended the claim by arguing that he was a protected tenant of the bungalow under the Rent Act 1977 which extended protection to tenants of 'dwelling houses'. If Mr Morris were a protected tenant, Elitestone would only have been able to seek possession on very narrow grounds—none of which was available on the facts. Elitestone argued that the bungalow was not a dwelling-house because it did not form part of the land as the bungalow rested by its own weight on concrete pillars and was not physically attached to the ground.

Legal issue: Was Mr Morris a tenant of a dwelling-house? Was the bungalow sufficiently attached to the land that it would attract the protection of the Rent Act?

Judgment: At first instance, the court held that the bungalow was part of the land. In the Court of Appeal, this result was reversed on the basis that the bungalow rested on concrete pillars without attachment to the land. The bungalow was therefore a chattel and Mr Morris was not a protected tenant under the Rent Act. Mr Morris appealed to the House of Lords.

The House of Lords found for Mr Morris, holding that the bungalow was to be regarded as part of the land. This meant Mr Morris could resist the possession claim. In particular, Lord Lloyd:

→

---

1. Affirmed the approach of Blackburn J in *Holland v Hodgson* (1872) that in determining whether a chattel has become a fixture there are two key factors:

   The answer to the question . . . depends on the circumstances of each case, but mainly on two factors, the degree of annexation to the land, and the object [purpose] of the annexation.

2. Noted that the importance of annexation (physical attachment to the land) varied from object to object but, in the case of a large object such as a house, physical attachment to the land 'goes without saying'.

3. Identified that many tests had been put forward when considering the purpose of the annexation; for example, whether the item had been fixed for the better enjoyment of the object as a chattel or whether to effect a permanent improvement of the land. In the case of Mr Morris' bungalow, it had been built in a way that the only means of removing it was demolition. It was not therefore intended as a chattel even though the property had no physical attachment to the soil.

4. Held that the intention of the parties (to be assessed objectively) was relevant to the issue of the degree and purpose of the annexation and formed part of an enquiry into all the circumstances of the case.

1.3.2.1 When will a chattel become a fixture?

No single test has been developed for determining whether a chattel has become a fixture. Instead, a series of factors are taken into account by the court. A key starting point is the House of Lords' decision in *Elitestone Ltd v Morris*. As with all important land law cases, this decision really should be read in full: the case extracts provided throughout this book are here not as a substitute for reading the cases but merely to allow you to get an overview of the issues. You must read the key cases in their totality if you want to really understand the subject. The case of *Elitestone* tells us that two key factors will be relied upon by the court to determine whether a chattel has become a fixture. These factors are: (1) the degree of annexation; and (2) the purpose of annexation. In practice today, far greater weight is placed on the purpose of annexation than on the degree of annexation but we will consider both factors in turn.

The degree of annexation

This factor looks to whether the item or object is merely resting on land by the fact of its own weight or whether it is annexed, i.e. fixed or attached to the land. Under the court's more traditional approach, an item 'no further attached to the land, than by its own weight' was generally presumed to be a mere chattel[29] unless this was rebutted by evidence of the purpose of annexation.[30] In *Holland*, mill looms were attached to a stone floor by nails. The mortgage lender claimed it was entitled to the looms as they had become fixtures. Blackburn J held that the looms had indeed been affixed to the floor and had therefore become fixtures. In considering the degree of annexation, the mode of affixing the item to the land can therefore prove particularly significant. In *Leigh v Taylor* (1902) valuable tapestries were stretched across boards and attached to the walls of a mansion using nails. The court was called upon to decide if the tapestries were chattels or fixtures belonging to the owners of the mansion and it held

---

[29] *Holland*, per Blackburn J affirming the approach taken in *Wiltshear v Cottrell* (1853).

[30] We discuss the purpose of annexation in the next section.

that the tapestries, despite their being affixed to the walls, were chattels. The Earl of Halsbury presiding over the case explained that the tapestries did not form part of the house. This was:[31]

> evident from the very nature of the attachment, the extent and degree of which was as slight as the nature of the thing attached would admit of. Therefore, I come to the conclusion that this thing, put up for ornamentation and for the enjoyment of the person while occupying the house, is not, under such circumstances as these, part of the house.

In more contemporary cases, however, the method of annexation is no longer the decisive factor—we saw in *Elitestone*, that a wooden bungalow resting on its own weight and not affixed to the ground was nevertheless held to amount to a fixture. In that case, the fact that only demolition would have allowed removal of the bungalow was key. In *Leigh*, the fact the tapestries were held to the wall by nails (that could be readily removed and taken town) meant there was only a 'slight' attachment so the tapestries were chattels. It is apparent that the ease with which an item can be removed from the land is a vital aspect when considering the degree of annexation. In *Mew v Tristmire* (2011), a houseboat resting on wooden platforms in a harbour was held to amount to a chattel. *Elitestone* was distinguished on the basis that the houseboat, unlike Mr Morris' bungalow in *Elitestone*, could be easily removed without demolition of the item. In the same vein, in *Caddick v Whitsand Bay Holiday Park Ltd* (2015), a holiday bungalow was also a chattel as expert evidence showed that the bungalow could be removed without demolition.

The purpose of annexation

As technology has developed, it has become far easier to affix and remove items from land, even buildings, meaning less and less weight has been attached to the means by which an item is annexed to the land, so the purpose of annexation has become the more important

---

KEY CASE *Berkley v Poulett* (1977)

Facts: Lord Poulett sold the Hinton St George Estate at an auction in August 1968 to Effold Ltd. Effold Ltd had agreed that were it successful at auction, it would sell a house situated on the estate and part of the estate grounds to Mr Berkley. Mr Berkley planned to transform the house into a tourist attraction. The sale was delayed, completion not taking place until November 1968. During this delay, Lord Poulett sold a number of items connected with the house to third parties. Mr Berkley brought an action against Lord Poulett's executors, arguing that these sold items (including objets d'art) were fixtures as opposed to chattels and therefore should have formed part of the sale to him. These items included: a series of paintings set into oak panelling, a marble statue resting on a solid plinth and a sundial.

Legal issue: Were these items chattels belonging to Lord Poulett's estate or fixtures which had therefore passed to the purchaser of the house and gardens when the sale was completed?

Judgment: The Court of Appeal held that none of the items were fixtures. The court underlined and affirmed the two-factor test which considered the degree of annexation and the purpose of annexation. Lord Scarman elaborated on the test:

→

---

[31] *Leigh*, 161.

> [A] degree of annexation which in earlier times the law would have treated as conclusive may now prove nothing. If the purpose of the annexation be for the better enjoyment of the object itself, it may remain a chattel, notwithstanding a high degree of physical annexation . . . If an object cannot be removed without serious damage to, or destruction of, some part of the realty, the case for its having become a fixture is a strong one . . . If there is no physical annexation there is no fixture . . . Nevertheless, an object, resting on the ground by its own weight alone, can be a fixture, if it be so heavy that there is no need to tie it into a foundation, and if it were put in place to improve the realty. Prima facie, however, an object resting on the ground by its own weight alone is not a fixture. Conversely, an object affixed to realty but capable of being removed without much difficulty may yet be a fixture, if, for example, the purpose of its affixing be that 'of creating a beautiful room as a whole' (Neville J in *In Re Whaley* [1908] 1 Ch 615 at p 619).
>
> Today, so great are the technical skills of affixing and removing objects on land or buildings that the second test is more likely than the first to be decisive. Scarman LJ concluded that the paintings had been hung for their better enjoyment and were not part of a composite design (they could be switched and changed), and the sundial and statute were never fixed to the land even if the plinth had itself been annexed. None of the items were therefore fixtures.

factor. This point was made plain in *Berkley v Poulett*. The purpose of annexation 'test' holds whether an item has become a fixture is determined by examining the object or purpose for which the item was attached or affixed to the land. At its simplest, if the item was annexed merely to increase the enjoyment of it, it will retain its chattel status.[32] If, however, the purpose of annexation was to permanently improve *the land*, the chattel will have become a fixture.[33]

Post-*Berkley* we must ask: was the item in question intended to constitute a permanent, lasting improvement to *the land* or was it attached merely temporarily for the purpose of increasing or making more convenient the use and enjoyment of *the item*? If the former is true, the item is a fixture; if the latter, it will amount to a chattel. This line between permanent improvement to land and increased enjoyment of the item is, however, not an easy one to draw. It can prove elusive. As the court noted in *Credit Valley Cable TV/FM Ltd v Peel Condominium Corp. No. 95* (1980), in a sense, every chattel affixed to a building could be said to improve the building or else it would not have been affixed.

So, where does this leave us? The law governing the distinction between chattels and fixtures is regrettably inconsistent and, at times, unpredictable. Some have questioned whether there is any discernible principle at all governing the area. This is made worse by the more recent trend towards taking an extremely fact- and case-sensitive approach to the issue. Several summarizing observations are provided here to guide you in getting to grips with the current state of the law:

1. Whilst as a general rule there must be some degree of annexation for a chattel to have become a fixture, physical annexation alone is no longer a conclusive factor. Physical attachment of an item to land can be overruled by considerations of the purpose of the annexation, that being the more persuasive of the two factors.

---

[32] *Leigh.*   [33] *D'Eyncourt v Gregory* (1866).

2. Where an item has an element of permanency and increases the enjoyment and use of the *land*, it will be a fixture. Where an item is annexed to land simply to increase enjoyment or use of the *item*, it will be a chattel. Certain items, for example, can only be used if they are affixed to land: tapestries,[34] display cases for stuffed birds,[35] curtains and blinds.[36] These items will be chattels.

3. Some items which rest on their own weight and are not annexed to the land may still be classified as fixtures:

    (i) Where the item is so heavy there is 'no need to tie it into a foundation'[37] or affix it to the land (for example, heavy lion statues[38]), provided the item is part of a permanent architectural design or part of a composite design scheme,[39] or

    (ii) Where the item (for example, a building) is not fixed to the ground, as in *Elitestone*, but the removal of the item would require its demolition.[40]

4. In *Botham v TSB* (1996), the court was called upon to determine the status of a series of everyday household items. If they proved to be fixtures, the mortgage lender who had brought possession proceedings against Mr Botham would be able to sell the land to a new purchaser with the fixtures included. Any chattels would belong to Mr Botham. Table 1.1 brings together the key findings of the court.

5. Roch LJ in *Botham* set out a series of considerations that will be relevant to the court when deciding whether a chattel has become a fixture:

    • whether the item is ornamental and attachment is simply to enable the item to be enjoyed: this will indicate a chattel: e.g. a picture or painting;

    • the damage that removal of the item would cause: the greater the damage, the more likely the item is a fixture;

Table 1.1 The classification of everyday household items: Chattel or fixture?

ITEM	CHATTEL OR FIXTURE?
Kitchen appliances and white goods	CHATTELS
Curtains and blinds	CHATTELS
Light fittings	CHATTELS
Decorative fire-places	CHATTELS
Carpets	CHATTELS
Bathroom fittings such as taps and plugs	FIXTURES
Bathroom mirrors and marble fixed to wall	FIXTURES
Towel rails, toilet roll holder, soap dishes	FIXTURES

[34] *Leigh.*   [35] *Viscount Hill v Bullock* (1897).   [36] *Palumberi v Palumberi* (1986).
[37] *Berkley,* per Scarman LJ.   [38] *D'Eyncourt v Gregory* (1866).
[39] *Re Whaley* (1908): a tapestry and picture were classified as fixtures because they formed part of a specimen, mock-up of an Elizabethan house.   [40] *Elitestone.*

- the lifespan of the item: the more limited the lifespan, the more likely the item is a chattel: for example, a free-standing cooker;
- the type of person who installed or attached the item to the land: a builder is more likely to install a fixture; a contractor or landowner is more likely to install a chattel.

Botham establishes the classification of some everyday items found in most homes. Yet, beyond this, it serves to demonstrate the arbitrariness of the distinction between chattels and fixtures. How is it, for example, that bathroom taps and plugs constitute fixtures yet light fittings do not? Is this defensible? Equally, how far is the type of person installing the item any reliable indicator of the item's status?

1.3.2.2 The right of removal of a fixture

In what circumstances can a fixture be removed or severed from the land? We need to distinguish three key scenarios: where the owner of land wishes to sever a fixture; where the owner of land is selling her land to a purchaser; and where a landlord–tenant relationship comes to an end.

1. Where the owner of land wishes to sever a fixture: When a chattel has become a fixture, the landowner is entirely within her rights to sever that fixture from the land and so return its status to that of a mere chattel. This is because the landowner is the only person with a claim to the fixture. We call this the right of removal or severance of a fixture.

2. Where the owner of land is selling her land to a purchaser: Where land is being sold, the position is a little more complicated. In most sales today, the parties enter specific agreements (contracts) clarifying which items will and will not be included when the land is sold. The effect of this is to supersede the rules on the chattel/fixture distinction as the express terms of the agreement trump these principles. If the selling party (the vendor) does not wish for a fixture to be included within the sale, she easily can ensure the contract is drafted to reflect this. From the moment the contract of sale is made, the vendor can only remove or sever fixtures from the land as is provided for in the contract. To do otherwise will be a breach of the agreement. Any fixtures which are not covered by the terms of the contract will pass automatically upon the sale.[41]

3. Where a landlord-tenant relationship comes to an end: Where a tenant has leased land from a landlord, it is quite common for that tenant to bring chattels onto the land which subsequently become fixtures. During the lifetime of the lease, the tenant is free to remove these fixtures from the land. When the landlord–tenant relationship comes to an end, at common law, the starting point is that any fixture belongs to the landlord.[42] Certain exceptions have developed, however, which relax the strictness of this rule and to encourage tenants to improve the leased property during the lifetime of the lease which they might not otherwise have been minded to do if any benefit would only accrue to the landlord at the termination of the lease. There are three exceptions which provide for circumstances when a tenant is able to remove or sever a fixture:

---

[41] This is the effect of s. 62 of the LPA 1925.   [42] *Re Roberts ex parte Brook* (1878); *R v Smith* (1974).

- Exception 1: The removal or severance of trade fixtures: A tenant is able to remove so-called 'trade fixtures' which she installed during the lifetime of her lease.[43] In *Mancetter Developments v Garmanson Ltd* (1986), for example, tenants were permitted to remove an extractor fan at the end of their **tenancy** (lease) as the fan had been installed as part of the running of a chemicals business from the leased land.
- Exception 2: The removal or severance of ornamental and domestic fixtures: Items installed in the property for an ornamental, decorative, or domestic purpose can also be removed when the tenancy comes to an end but only if removal is possible without causing irreparable damage to the property. In *Spyer v Phillipson* (1931), a tenant installed antique wooden panelling and fireplaces to the leased property in order to recreate a Jacobean-style design. The court held that the tenant was entitled to remove the fixture when the tenancy came to an end as the items were ornamental, decorative fixtures. The items were only affixed with screws and could therefore be removed with ease.
- Exception 3: The right of agricultural tenants to remove or sever fixtures: Under the Agricultural Holdings Act 1986,[44] an agricultural tenant is able to remove fixtures installed during the lifetime of the lease at the time of the termination of the lease or within two months of the lease coming to an end.[45] An agricultural tenant can only remove fixtures when certain conditions have been satisfied.[46]

A tenant can only remove a fixture, in any event, if it can be done without inflicting lasting structural damage to the property. Where any damage is caused, the tenant is under a duty to compensate the landlord for any loss caused.[47]

1.4 The personal/proprietary divide

We turn now to examine the foundations of land law. First and foremost is one of the subject's most fundamental distinctions: the personal/proprietary divide. What really sets rights in land apart from, say, rights arising under a contract, is that they are *proprietary* in nature as opposed to being merely *personal* to the parties. This personal/proprietary divide runs like an artery throughout the entirety of land law. The key point is this: **proprietary rights** are capable of binding, in other words, being enforceable against third parties

---

[43] *Poole's Case* (1703). Trade fixtures are those fixtures necessary for the purpose of carrying on a business or trade and include petrol pumps: *Smith v City Petroleum* (1940); theatre seating: *New Zealand Government Property Corp. v HM & S Ltd* (1982); and even light fittings and carpets where there was a discernible link between these items and a business or trade: *Young v Dalgety plc* (1987).

[44] Section 10 of the 1986 Act.

[45] Farm tenants have similar rights under s. 8 of the Agricultural Tenancies Act 1995.

[46] One month's notice must be given to the landlord; any rent falling due must have been paid and there must be no damage caused by the fixture's removal.

[47] This was confirmed in *Mancetter Developments* where removal of the extractor fan led to holes in the wall where the screws had affixed the fan; but see also *Re de Falbe* (1901) where Rigby LJ explained that the duty to make good any damage did not extend to the mere redecoration of a wall from which a fixture had been removed.

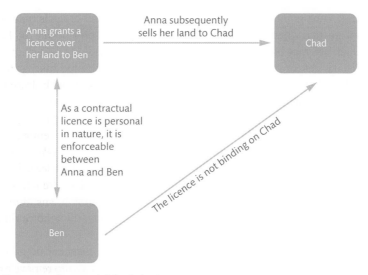

Figure 1.3 The nature of personal rights in land

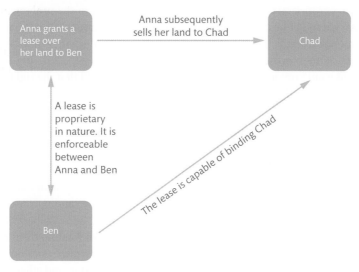

Figure 1.4 The nature of proprietary rights in land

whereas **personal rights** bind only the parties that created the rights.[48] It is this proprietary character which gives interests in land their potency. Two examples will help you to grasp the significance of the personal/proprietary distinction: see Figures 1.3 and 1.4.

In Figure 1.3, Anna grants a contractual **licence** over her land to Ben. Contractual licences are personal interests in land (subject to some exceptions[49]). This means that when Anna sells her land to Chad, this personal right is incapable of binding Chad. Ben will not be able to assert his rights against Chad.

---

[48] This personal/proprietary divide is particularly important when distinguishing licences from leases. We consider precisely how this distinction is made in detail in Chapter 9.

[49] We consider these exceptions in Chapter 7 on licences.

In Figure 1.4, Anna grants a lease over her land to Ben. Leases are proprietary rights in land.[50] This means that when Anna sells her land to Chad, this proprietary right is capable of binding Chad. Ben may be able to assert his right against Chad.

The proprietary status of a right is crucial and goes to the enforceability/priority question identified in section 1.1. The evident power of proprietary rights means that the categories of rights which are regarded as proprietary must be clearly defined.[51] If the categories of proprietary right were not controlled and almost any right concerning land enjoyed proprietary status then land would be overburdened, use and enjoyment of the land would be severely curtailed, and, ultimately, its value would be diminished. Strictly speaking, there is therefore a difference between a right *in* land which is proprietary and rights more generally operating *in relation to* land which will not have proprietary status: a postwoman crossing your land to deliver a parcel enjoys a permission, a right *in relation to* your land allowing her to lawfully reach your front door but this will not be a right *in* your land. It is a personal permission only.

A good starting point for determining whether a right is personal or proprietary is the judgment of Lord Wilberforce in *National Provincial Bank v Ainsworth* (1965). Lord Wilberforce was called upon to determine whether a wife living in a former matrimonial home enjoyed a proprietary right, despite not owning any part of the property. If the right was proprietary, it might be capable of being binding on the National Provincial Bank, who had loaned money towards the purchase of the property, and the wife would be able to defeat the bank's claim to possession of the land. If the right was personal only, it would not be binding and would not affect the bank. Lord Wilberforce held that the right was merely personal in nature, explaining that:[52]

> Before a right or an interest can be admitted into the category of property, or of a right affecting property, it must be definable, identifiable by third parties, capable in its nature of assumption by third parties, and have some degree of permanence or stability. The wife's right has none of these qualities, it is characterized by the reverse of them.

Lord Wilberforce established the traditional four-step test for proprietary status. According to Wilberforce, a right will be proprietary and potentially binding on third parties when it is 'capable in its nature of assumption by third parties'. Lord Wilberforce seems to suggest that a right will bind third parties when it is capable of binding third parties. The test is horribly circular and largely unhelpful. What Lord Wilberforce does do, however, is remind us that proprietary rights are those rights that are rooted in and affixed to the land such that they can survive changes in ownership or occupation. With no definitive list of proprietary rights, it has been left to case law to determine where the dividing line is drawn and on which side of the line different rights fall. As we will explore in Chapter 9, the dividing line between personal and proprietary rights is particularly hotly contested when distinguishing between licences[53] and leases.[54] Keep the personal/proprietary divide very much in the front of your mind as we move through the book.

---

[50] We explore leases in detail in Chapter 9 and, in particular, an intriguing exception to the rule that leases are proprietary: *Bruton* tenancies.

[51] As you will discover in section 1.8, certainty is a key driving force in land law.   [52] *Ainsworth*, 1243.

[53] Licences are personal permissions to be on or do something on another's land.

[54] Leases are proprietary and involve a right of exclusive possession of another's land for a certain period of time.

1.5 Tenure, estates, and interests in land

Land law is very much a historical subject and a measure of historical context is necessary if you are to fully grasp the essential foundations of the subject. Three building blocks must be considered:

- **tenure;**
- **estates** in land; and
- interests in land.

1.5.1 Tenure

Much of our modern land law finds its origins in the reforms to the feudal system imposed by William the Conqueror following 1066.[55] In the reforms post-1066, it was determined that all land was owned by the King. If the King's subjects were to enjoy rights in land, they did so, essentially, as tenants of the monarch and were required to provide services to the King in return. Under these arrangements, there was no transfer of ownership in land from the King to his subjects. The King retained ownership. The terms on which rights in land were enjoyed was called *tenure* and, in practice, this described the supply of services desired by the King. Tenure took many forms depending on the nature of the services provided:

- Knight's Service: where armed horsemen were provided for battles.
- Grand Sergeant: where personal services were provided such as taking up State office or the blowing of horns.
- Frankalmoign or divine service: where religious services were provided, for example prayers said for the soul of the king.
- Socage: where agricultural services were provided.

Today, the doctrine of tenure has very little practical importance but remains the theoretical basis on which land is held. So, whilst the practical effect of tenure has been removed, the underlying doctrine persists. Today, the only tenure that remains is the free tenure of common socage.[56] The word tenure comes from the French verb *tenir*, 'to hold', and speaks to the basis on which land is held. If we were to be completely accurate, when we say 'I own my home' what we really should be saying is 'I have tenure'. All land today is still held directly from the Crown and consequently if a landowner dies without having made a will, and there are no relatives, the land passes back to the Crown. This sometimes surprises students but is evidence of the historical hang-over of land law's feudal past.

---

[55] See generally A. W. B. Simpson, *A History of the Land Law* (Oxford: Oxford University Press, 1986).

[56] The Tenures Abolition Act 1660 effectively ended feudal tenures in England.

1.5.2 **Estates in land**

An 'estate' in land describes how long a person is entitled to enjoy rights of use and possession of that land. As Megarry and Wade explain: an estate is an 'interest in land for some particular duration'.[57] An estate reflects 'a time in the land, or land for a time'.[58] The type of estate will determine the length of time that rights of use and possession can be enjoyed. Today, under s. 1 of the LPA 1925, there are only two types of legal estate: (1) the **freehold** estate and (2) the **leasehold** estate. Before 1926, a far wider variety of estates existed. Important amongst these were:

- The fee tail: The fee tail is no longer recognized as a legal estate in land.[59] The fee tail operated to keep land in the family. It worked like this: the owner of the land under a fee tail was entitled to the land for his lifetime. When he died, the land could only be passed to direct or lineal descendants and not to all possible heirs. When there were no lineal descendants left, the land could be claimed by the Crown. Examples can be seen in famous novels including Austen's *Pride and Prejudice*, Waugh's *Brideshead Revisited*, and even made an appearance in television's *Downton Abbey*.

- The life estate: Again, the life estate is no longer recognized as a legal estate in land.[60] The essence of the life estate was that the owner could use and enjoy the land but only for the duration of the estate holder's life. When the estate holder died, the estate came to an end and the land reverted to the original grantor (person granting the estate). It was entirely possible for the life estate holder to transfer the land during his lifetime but even where this was done the estate would still come to an end when the original estate owner died making it a rather precarious prospect.

Don't forget that today, at law, there are only two types of legal estate: freehold and leasehold.

1.5.2.1 **The freehold estate or fee simple**

The freehold estate or 'estate in **fee simple absolute in possession**', to give it its full title, is the closest thing to absolute ownership of land that is recognized in land law today. The person holding the freehold is known as the 'freeholder' or 'freehold owner'. When someone buys a house and says they 'own' the property, what they actually mean is that they own the freehold estate. Let's break this down a little:

- Fee simple: Means that the freeholder has the right to use and enjoy the land for the duration of her life and can transfer the land to others either during her lifetime (as a gift or by sale) or on her death under a will. Where land is transferred or passes to a third party, that person becomes the new estate owner and can themselves enjoy the land for their lifetime, and pass the land to their heirs and so on.

---

[57] C. Harpum, S. Bridge, and M. Dixon, *Megarry and Wade: The Law of Real Property*, 8th edn (London: Sweet & Maxwell, 2012).   [58] *Walsingham's Case* (1573).

[59] The fee tail can still exist as an equitable interest: s. 1(3) of the LPA 1925 notes that, outside s. 1(1) and (2): 'All other estates, interests, and charges in or over land take effect as equitable interests.' The fee tail falls into this category.

[60] Like the fee tail, however, a life estate can exist as an equitable interest: s. 1(3) of the LPA 1925.

- Absolute: Means that the freeholder's rights are neither conditional nor liable to be brought to an end on the occurrence of some event (for example when a certain age is reached).

- In possession: Means that the freeholder enjoys an immediate right to occupy and enjoy the land.

While freehold ownership is an estate in land which is theoretically limited in time, freehold ownership can last for generation after generation as the land is passed from heir to heir. It is this which gives freehold ownership the characteristics of outright, permanent ownership even though technically the land is ultimately 'owned' by the Crown.

1.5.2.2 The leasehold estate

The only other legal estate that can exist today is the leasehold estate also known as the **'term of years absolute'** or simply as the lease.[61] The person holding the leasehold estate is known as the 'leaseholder', **'lessee'**, or 'tenant'. The party granting the lease is the landlord also known as the **'lessor'**. A leaseholder is entitled to use and enjoyment of the land exclusively for *a certain period of time* and can transfer or sell (**'assign'**) the leasehold to a third party provided the term of the lease has not come to an end. It is this limited duration which sets apart the leasehold from the freehold estate. The language of 'term of years' indicates this—'term' reminding us that the leasehold estate must be of a definable duration. This period may be long, say 99 years or it may be short, say one month or a few days. During that defined period, the leaseholder is taken as exercising rights akin to a temporary owner.[62] A leasehold estate arises by being carved out of another estate in land provided that the leasehold is for a duration less than that of the larger estate.[63] For example, a one year leasehold could be carved out of a freehold estate or, alternatively, out of a longer leasehold estate of, say, seven years' fixed duration.[64]

1.5.3 Interests in land

A further building block to grasp is that of interests in land. An interest in land is a property right which does not confer any rights of ownership. An interest in land describes a right that someone enjoys over another's land. The classic example is where one person enjoys a right of way across another's land. This is known as an easement.[65] Other examples of interests in land include mortgages,[66] **options**,[67] and **restrictive covenants**.[68] The key

---

[61] The Government in 2017 said it was to consult on whether to ban the sale of new homes to would-be buyers under leasehold arrangements. This practice, which has been used widely by developers, means purchasers essentially are buying a right to occupy the land only and are faced with often large 'ground rents' and other associated fees not payable when purchasing the freehold. Watch this space as to how far the Government's promise to consult translates into meaningful action.

[62] See *Street v Mountford* (1985), 816, per Lord Templeman. We explore this important case in Chapter 9.

[63] In Chapter 9, we also explore the controversial decision in *Bruton v London and Quadrant Housing Trust* (2000) which suggests that a new form of 'non-proprietary' lease can also arise which is not carved out of an estate in land.

[64] We consider the law of leasehold in detail in Chapter 9.

[65] We consider the law of easements and profits in Chapter 10.

[66] A debt secured against the debtor's land: we consider the law of mortgages in Chapter 13.

[67] A right to buy another's land during a particular time period.

[68] A right preventing use of land in a specified manner: we consider the law of freehold covenants in Chapter 11.

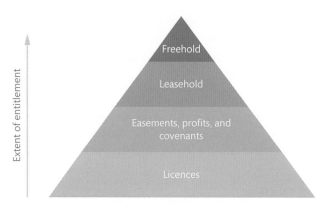

Figure 1.5 Hierarchy of rights in and over land

feature of interests in land is that they are proprietary. We saw in Figure 1.4 that proprietary rights are capable of binding third parties, for example, purchasers of land. As a result, they are enforceable not just between the original parties but also potentially against third parties, such as later owners of the land over which they operate. Personal rights including licences are not (subject to a few exceptions) binding on third parties.

What emerges from our discussion of estates and interests is a hierarchy of entitlement of rights in and over land ranging from the most powerful and enduring rights of the freehold estate at the top of our hierarchy to the second tier, the leasehold estate, to the third tier of non-possessory (i.e. rights not involving possession of land) but proprietary interests in land (including easements, profits and covenants) to the purely personal, non-proprietary licence at the bottom tier: see Figure 1.5. We will encounter and discuss all of these rights and interests from leases, easements and profits, covenants and licences as we move through the book.[69]

1.6 The legal/equitable distinction

Just like the personal/proprietary divide, there is another fundamental facet of land law which runs through the heart of this book: the legal/equitable distinction. Whether a right is legal or **equitable** concerns a right's status and quality, not its substantive content. Understanding not only when rights will be legal and when they will be equitable but also why this matters for modern land law is crucial if you want to get to grips with the subject. We therefore reflect on this a little further here.

1.6.1 Law and equity: A very brief history

Historically, there were two distinct systems for adjudicating legal disputes.[70] The particular court in which a dispute was heard determined the nature of the remedy that could be awarded. The King's Court, or common law court, awarded remedies to those able to make

---

[69]   In Chapters 9, 10, 11, 12 and 7 respectively.

[70]   For a full account of the development of the courts of the common law and of equity, see C. Harpum, S. Bridge, and M. Dixon, *Megarry and Wade: The Law of Real Property*, 8th edn (Sweet & Maxwell, London, 2012), [5–003].

out their case 'at law' which involved satisfying strict formality requirements and bringing the case in a prescribed, rigid way. A remedy was only available if the correct procedure and **writ** for the legal grievance had been used. The common law court was great at developing consistency in the law but was dreadfully slow and soon became overburdened with a backlog of unheard cases. In addition, the common law court's insistence on form meant it was unable to adapt to determine more novel grievances. The common law came to be seen as deficient in a variety of ways as set out in Figure 1.6.

Disgruntled claimants with no formalized route to appeal had to petition the King directly to seek redress. The result was that the King became overloaded with cases and so passed them to his Lord Chancellor to adjudicate. The Lord Chancellor, a man of religion, approached the task by applying principles of fairness and flexibility, guided by the conscience of the parties involved in a dispute. In time, a separate court emerged, the Court of Chancery, which was prepared to award *equitable* remedies—including granting **injunctions** and orders for **specific performance** of contracts—even where the necessary common law formalities were not satisfied. The Court of Chancery recognized new forms of right including equitable rights such as mortgages and the **trust**.[71] The result was two distinct,

Figure 1.6 Deficiencies of the common law system

[71] We consider the trust in section 1.6.3 and mortgages in Chapter 13.

separate jurisdictions; one applying legal principles, the other applying the more flexible equitable principles. The existence of these two separate courts came to be seen as profligate and so, under the Judicature Acts 1873–75, the two systems were fused. Since then, any court has been free to apply both legal and equitable rules. Just how 'fused' the two systems really are remains the subject of much debate. As is often said, 'the two streams ... though they run in the same channel run side by side and do not mingle their waters'.[72] Importantly, the historical division of law and equity continues to resonate in the modern law.

1.6.2 When will a right be legal or equitable?

Determining whether a right is legal or equitable requires us to consider two separate issues: first, 'the capacity question': is the right *capable* of being legal and/or equitable? Secondly, 'the creation question': *how* was the right created? See Figure 1.7.

1.6.2.1 The capacity question: Is the right capable of being legal and/or equitable?

Not all rights can be legal. Section 1(2) of the LPA 1925 offers a complete list of the rights that are *capable* of being created at law. If a right is not covered by s. 1(2), it can only take effect as an *equitable* interest. Section 1(2) is a vital starting point when determining the status of rights in land: see Table 1.2.

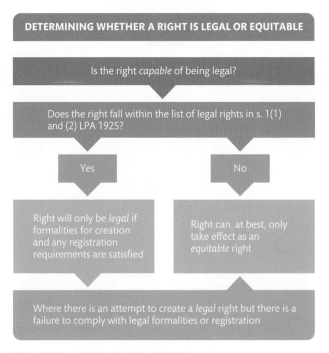

Figure 1.7 Determining whether a right is legal or equitable

---

[72] W. Ashburner, *Principles of Equity*, 2nd edn (London: Butterworths, 1933), 18.

Table 1.2 The categories of rights in land capable of being legal and equitable

Legal Estates	Freehold; leasehold
Legal Interests	Easements; profits; mortgages; rights of re-entry contained in a legal lease; rentcharges
Equitable Interests	All other interests not provided for in s. 1 of the LPA 1925: fee tail, life estate, restrictive covenants, options

Section 1(2) only takes us so far, though. It tells us only that a right is *capable* of existing at law. We must proceed to the next stage of our analysis, the creation question, to determine whether a right is *in fact* legal or equitable.

1.6.2.2 The creation question: How was the right created?

In general, for a right to be legal, it must have been created in full compliance with formality requirements. Equity, by contrast, is prepared to permit far greater informality.[73]

Creation of legal rights

Most legal rights must be created by **deed**.[74] A deed is, in essence, a very formal, written contract that complies with certain strict formality requirements. Under s. 1(2) of the Law of Property (Miscellaneous Provisions) Act 1989 (LP(MP)A 1989), an instrument is not a deed unless:

- it is made in writing;
- it makes it clear on its face that it is intended to be a deed by the person making it or, as the case may be, by the parties to it (whether by describing itself as a deed or expressing itself to be executed or signed as a deed or otherwise); and
- it is validly executed (signed and witnessed) as a deed by that person or, as the case may be, one or more of those parties.[75]

In addition to the need for a deed, for some rights they can only operate at law if they have been registered.[76] We consider registration in detail in Chapter 2. For now, it suffices to appreciate that if a right is required to be registered to operate at law and is not registered, it cannot be legal. Failure of registration will mean that the right is equitable only.

Creation of equitable rights

A right will be equitable:

1. if it is a right which is not capable of being legal under the provisions of s. 1 of the LPA 1925; or

---

[73] This has obvious resonances with the historical development of equity as a reaction to the deficiencies and rigidity of the common law.

[74] Not every right attracting legal status is required to be created by deed, including short leases of a duration of three years or less and easements arising by long use. We explore these in Chapters 9 and 10.

[75] 'Execution by deed' means that the deed is signed and witnessed.

[76] Under s. 27 of the LRA 2002. These are called 'registrable dispositions' and include all freehold estates, all leasehold estates of more than seven years' duration, all legal mortgages, and all expressly created easements.

2. if there has been an attempt to create a legal right but there has been a failure of formalities, for example, not making use of a deed; or

3. if there has been an attempt to create a legal right but there has been a failure to register the right when required.

Not concerned with or insisting on the same degree of formality as the common law, equity does nevertheless generally[77] require that writing be used for the creation of rights in land: either a written contract (albeit not a deed) complying with the provisions of s. 2 of the LP(MP)A 1989[78] or under s. 53 of the LPA 1925. The requirement for writing recognizes that, although the right may be equitable and not legal, it still carries proprietary force. Even equity, with its more flexible approach, acknowledges the need for some measure of formality where the precious and unique commodity of land is involved.

1.6.3 The trust

In considering the legal/equitable divide, we cannot ignore the trust—easily the most significant contribution of equity. According to Maitland:[79]

> Of all the exploits of equity the largest and most important is the invention and development of the trust ... it is an 'institute' of great elasticity [and] forms the most distinctive achievement of English lawyers. It seems to us almost essential to civilization, and yet there is nothing quite like it in foreign law.

The trust is said to have its origin in the era of the crusades, though it took a very different form then to that which modern land law recognizes and its precise beginnings are hotly debated. In fact, it is likely that the crusades allowed for contact between legal systems, in particular those of England and the Middle East where a similar device to the trust, the Islamic *waqf*, was already developing.[80] At the time of the crusades, a large number of landowners were called up to fight. Naturally, they were required to leave their land for, on occasion, years at a time. They required someone to manage and protect their land while they were away. The solution was to transfer the land to a friend with an agreement that the land would revert to its true owner when they returned from fighting. Any income derived from the land was to go to the family of the crusading knight. On returning from the crusades, however, some refused to return the land to its rightful owner. When the matter came before the court, the strict common law rules refused to recognize the knights' claims as they were no longer the legal owners of the land. Legal **title** to the land had been transferred to another prior to their departure. The Chancellor, however, was prepared to recognize a division of ownership and that, in practice, the land had been transferred to a friend but ultimately for the use and benefit of the knight. This was the first recognition of what we, today, call the trust. It was originally termed the 'use'.

---

[77] There are exceptions when an equitable right in land can be created where no writing is present. The most important of these are rights arising under an implied trust and claims under the doctrine of proprietary estoppel. These are covered in Chapters 6 and 8 respectively.

[78] Before the 1989 Act, equitable interests could be created by oral contract.

[79] F. W. Maitland, *Equity: A Course of Lectures* (Cambridge: Cambridge University Press, 2011), 23.

[80] See, for example, G. Makdisi, *The Rise of Colleges* (Edinburgh: Edinburgh University Press, 1984), who argued that the English trust emerged as a result of interaction with the Islamic law of the *waqf*.

The trust allows for ownership to be split into ownership at law and ownership in equity so that there can be more than one owner of land. The result is that one person holds the legal title whilst another is able to hold the equitable title. The trust allows for a single parcel of land to have a legal owner and a separate equitable owner. The legal owner (also known as the '**trustee**') holds the land on trust for the equitable owner (also known as the *cestui que trust* or '**beneficiary**', i.e. that person holding the **beneficial interest**). See Figure 1.8. The effect is that the trustee acts almost as the manager of the land and holds the land for the benefit of the equitable owner, who is entitled to its benefits. It is this capacity to divide or split ownership that is so novel to the English legal system and is now found in other common law jurisdictions.

The trust has developed into an extremely flexible device used across a range of contexts and for a variety of different purposes including to guarantee efficient dealings with land, in complex business dealings, and to reduce tax liabilities.[81] Trusts can be expressly created (i.e. created deliberately and formally (**express trusts**)),[82] can also arise by implication by the court (**implied trusts**);[83] and, in some cases, will be imposed, for example, whenever there is **co-ownership** of land.[84] We will be returning to consider the operation of trusts in greater detail as we move through the book.

1.6.4 The significance of the legal/equitable distinction: Why does it matter?

The significance of the legal/equitable distinction comes into sharp focus when deciding if a third party acquiring land—for example, a purchaser—is bound by pre-existing property rights operating over that land: we identified this in section 1.1 as the 'enforceability or priority' question. Equitable interests are far more precarious than their legal counterparts

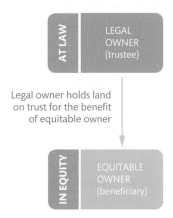

Figure 1.8 The basic idea of the 'trust of land'

---

[81] See generally R. Pearce and W. Barr, *Trusts and Equitable Obligations* (Oxford: Oxford University Press, 2014).

[82] Express trusts of land must satisfy formality requirements. They must be 'manifested and proved by some writing' under s. 53(1)(b) of the LPA 1925.

[83] We consider express and implied trusts in Chapter 6.   [84] We consider co-ownership in Chapter 5.

and are less likely to bind third parties, though this has to some degree been diluted as a result of the fully fledged land registration system, governed by the Land Registration Act 2002 (LRA 2002), which now largely determines how far a purchaser of land will be bound by pre-existing rights.[85] Generally, under the LRA 2002, the holder of an equitable interest must take more steps to ensure their interest is protected and binding on third parties. We will return to precisely this issue in Chapter 2 and as we discuss the various interests in land that are covered in the remaining chapters of this book.

On 1 January 1926, a raft of property law legislation—often referred to as 'the 1925 legislation'—came into force which marked a significant shift in the way interests in land law operated. Before the introduction of land registration (discussed in section 1.7 and in depth in Chapter 2) which began with this 1925 legislation, the legal/equitable distinction was of even greater significance. It is helpful to consider this period briefly here.

Before the 1925 legislation came into force, *legal* rights in land were binding against the world. This meant that anyone who owned the land or later became owner of it, any squatter, or even anyone receiving the land as a gift was bound by those legal rights.

Before the 1925 legislation came into force, *equitable* rights in land were binding against any person to whom the land was transferred except a *bona fide purchaser of a legal estate for value without notice of the* equitable right—known as '**Equity's Darling**'. The classic statement of this **bona fide** purchaser test (also called the '**doctrine of notice**') was laid down by James LJ in *Pilcher v Rawlins* (1872). This test continues to play a very limited role today in **unregistered land** (but is helpful in understanding the wider implications of land registration) and is explored in Chapter 3 in our discussion of unregistered land. To introduce it here: under the bona fide purchaser rule, if a purchaser is to 'take free' of any pre-existing equitable rights, several requirements have to be satisfied. These can be summed up as follows:

1. Bona fide: This means 'acting in good faith'.[86] It is said that 'he who comes to equity must do so with clean hands'. Equity will not assist someone who has acted dishonestly or fraudulently or otherwise in a manner which is considered by the court to be unconscionable.

2. Purchaser: 'Purchaser' is not given a narrow meaning and includes those acquiring land under a will as well as those buying land. It must, however, be a voluntary act rather than by operation of law[87]—squatters and adverse possessors[88] of another's land are not regarded as 'purchasers'.[89] 'Purchaser' here means that something of value must have been transferred.

3. For value: This means that consideration must be given for receiving the land. Consideration must be more than nominal[90] though need not be commensurate with the value of the land. It must be 'money or money's worth'.

4. Of legal estate: The purchaser must purchase a legal estate in the land and not an equitable interest only. The legal estate purchased could be but need not necessary be the freehold: purchase of a legal lease, for example, will also suffice.[91]

---

[85] The LRA 2002 system is introduced in section 1.7 and considered in detail in Chapters 2 and 3.
[86] See *Midland Bank Trust Co. v Green* (1981).   [87] *Inland Revenue Commissioners v Gribble* (1913).
[88] We consider adverse possession in Chapter 4.   [89] *Re Nisbit and Potts' Contract* (1906).
[90] Section 205(1)(xxi) LPA 1925.   [91] *Wilkes v Spooner* (1911).

5. Without notice of the equitable right: The purchase must have been made without notice of the equitable right. Three forms of notice have been identified for this purpose:

- *Actual notice*—a purchaser is taken as having actual notice of everything within their knowledge. Actual notice is determined by the particular state of mind of the purchaser. The effect is that there will be no notice if a purchaser once knew of the equitable right but has subsequently forgotten all about it.[92]
- *Imputed notice*—where a purchaser employs an agent (for example a solicitor), any notice—whether actual or constructive—which that agent has, will be imputed to the purchaser (this is logical as otherwise a purchaser could employ an agent as a device for avoiding the enforceability of equitable interests).
- *Constructive notice*—under s. 199(1)(ii)(a) of the LPA 1925, a purchaser has constructive notice of those matters that would have come to his notice had he made inquiries and inspections that a reasonable and prudent purchaser would have made. But, what inquiries are these? The case law establishes that a reasonable and prudent purchaser would: (1) investigate the documents of title going back 15 years;[93] and (2) go to physically inspect the land: *Hunt v Luck* (1902); *Kingsnorth Finance Co. Ltd v Tizard* (1986).

The 1925 legislation heralded the first steps towards and set the tone for the land registration system in place today under the LRA 2002.

1.6.5 The 1925 legislation: Setting the tone for modern land law

Before 1 January 1926, there were a series of defects, problems, and pitfalls in the law of real property. Particularly problematic for purchasers of land was that they very often found themselves bound by equitable rights of which they knew nothing. This was, in large part, down to the broad interpretation given to the 'doctrine of notice' (the bona fide purchaser test just discussed in section 1.6.4). In addition, the process of buying land was cumbersome and risky. For purchasers, it involved investigating whether the party selling land actually had a right to sell. Reform was needed. On 1 January 1926, a tranche of property legislation across six different Acts of Parliament came into force which set the tone for the development of land law in the contemporary era: we focus on the Law of Property Act 1925, the Land Charges Act 1925, and the Land Registration Act 1925. Even today, in large part, the 1925 legislation remains the bedrock of our modern law.

The 1925 legislation did not replace the core basis upon which land law had previously operated but consolidated some 40 years of reforms, from 1882 to 1922, as well as rationalizing and simplifying land law concepts and the conveyancing process (i.e. the buying and selling of land) with a view to making land more **alienable**—in other words, more capable of being sold or transferred from one party to another. The aims of the 1925 reform scheme included:

1. facilitation of the investigation and acquisition of ownership rights in order to promote the alienability of land so that, when a purchaser acquired land, she would know that she was getting good title;

---

[92] *Re Montagu's Settlement* (1987), per Megarry V-C.
[93] Section 44(1) of the LPA 1925 as amended by s. 23 of the LPA 1969.

2. facilitation of the investigation and discovery of third party interests affecting land so that a purchaser buying land would be fully aware of the rights that would bind that land and restrict her enjoyment of it;

3. protection of third party interests in land so that, as the position of purchasers was strengthened, those holding rights over the land would not lose out.

These essential aims were achieved by:

- Reclassification of estates and interests in land: Before the 1925 legislation was enacted, the fee simple could be fragmented into a series of estates[94] and if a purchaser wished to acquire the fee simple, she had to identify *all* the owners of any estate in the land to be purchased and seek their agreement to the sale. This had a stifling effect on conveyancing. The LPA 1925 addressed this by reducing the number of legal estates to two (freehold and leasehold) and by making the fee simple absolute in possession the essential basis of conveyancing in England. In addition, the number of interests in land that were capable of being legal was reduced.[95]

- Statutory machinery for the protection of interests in land: The second major problem pre-1926 concerned equitable rights binding purchasers of land. Before the 1925 legislation, this was a question of notice: a purchaser with notice of the equitable right would be bound by it. Notice was given a wide interpretation and many purchasers found themselves bound by rights of which they had no knowledge at the time of the purchase. The response of the 1925 legislation was two-pronged.

First, the legislation provided for a statutory mechanism under which a purchaser could ensure that when they bought land that they took the land free from certain equitable interests. This is called 'overreaching'[96] and we discuss its operation in section 2.6. Overreaching allows a purchaser to take free of any equitable, non-commercial, family rights (the most important for our purposes being rights under a trust) that may exist over the land they are acquiring by detaching the equitable rights and converting them into monetary compensation for the interest holder.

Secondly, the legislation introduced the statutory machinery for registration. The Land Registration Act 1925 (LRA 1925)—now replaced entirely by the Land Registration Act 2002—ushered in a new system under which title to land and certain interests over land could be recorded on a **register** held by Land Registry. In fact, various attempts had been made to begin the move towards registration some years earlier but mostly without success, as Pottage explains:[97]

> The idea of registration … had been familiar for decades before the first effective scheme of registration [under] the Land Transfer Act 1897. There are a number of reasons why it took so long … First, a good deal of time was wasted on experiments with deeds registration. Secondly, there

---

[94] See section 1.5.2.

[95] Section 1(2) of the LPA 1925 as discussed in section 1.6.2.1.

[96] In fact, overreaching had been developing incrementally since the 1882 legislation, but the 1925 statute put it beyond doubt.

[97] A. Pottage, 'Evidencing Ownership' in S. Bright and J. Dewar (eds.), *Land Law: Themes and Perspectives* (Oxford: Oxford University Press, 1998), 142.

were some outstanding technological problems to overcome, not least that of finding an effective method of identifying and indexing landholdings. Most contentious and most important, there is the question of [the conveyancing profession's] economic self-interest.

A new system of registration was heralded. For land that was unregistered, a system of limited registration of commercial interests as 'land charges' was also introduced under the Land Charges Act 1925.[98] We discuss both of these systems in Chapters 2 and 3 but provide an overview in section 1.7. The aim was to bring greater clarity and certainty to conveyancing while giving right holders the opportunity to register their interests, protecting their position against future purchasers. Pre-1926, the State was not involved in the conveyancing process, there was no comprehensive record of dealing in land: title to land was established by referring to the paper title deeds and a series of other bulky, dusty, and voluminous documents which were kept by the owners of land. The 1925 legislation was therefore an important moment. The LRA 2002—which came into force on 13 October 2003—replaced the LRA 1925 and provides the modern framework for land registration in England.

1.7 Introduction to registered and unregistered land

The final and crucial building block to be grasped before we delve further into the detail of land law is between registered and unregistered land. There are two separate systems for demonstrating title to land, in other words, ways of proving ownership. These two systems are known as registered and unregistered land. Different rules for proving ownership apply depending on whether land is registered or not. Quite different regimes apply to each.[99] Registered land is subject to the provisions of both the LPA 1925 and the LRA 2002. Unregistered land is subject to the provisions of the LPA 1925 and the LCA 1972 which replaced the LCA 1925)) as we discussed in section 1.6.5). So, when we say that land is 'registered' or 'unregistered' what do we mean? See Figure 1.9.

1.7.1 Registered land

If land is 'registered', this means the land has been registered (recorded) at Land Registry.[100] When this is done, each title is provided with a unique title number and information concerning the owners of that land is also recorded. Once a person is registered as the proprietor, the State guarantees their ownership.[101] When the land is sold, the new owner must register the transfer at Land Registry and they will then become the new registered proprietor. Registered land today is governed chiefly by the LRA 2002 which presents a scheme for registration of estates and interests in land. To help understand how this scheme works, we can view the LRA regime as falling into four broad 'groups'. These groupings are not

---

[98] Today, the system is governed by the Land Charges Act 1972 which we consider in greater detail in section 3.4.
[99] Note that overreaching applies equally to registered and unregistered land.
[100] Note: 'Land Registry' is referred to without the definite article 'the'.   [101] Section 58 of the LRA 2002.

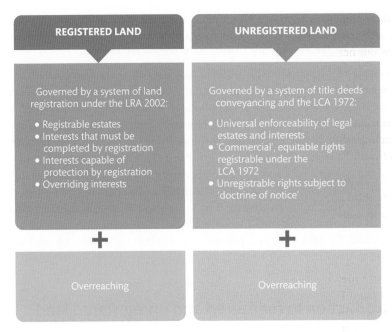

Figure 1.9 Registered and unregistered land

perfect and some interests fall outside them but it helps to get a sense of the scaffolding or framework of the 2002 Act and this grouping system can help with that. We will be revisiting this in greater detail in Chapter 2:

- Group 1—Substantively registrable estates: The LRA 2002 allows for the legal fee simple and leasehold estates of more than seven years' duration to be substantively registered. In other words, these estates will each generate a separate title with their own title number at Land Registry.

- Group 2—Interests which though not substantively registrable must be completed by registration to be legal:[102] The 2002 Act calls these 'registrable **dispositions**' and they only operate at law if they are completed by registration. Examples include: transfers of registrable estates, expressly created easements,[103] and legal **charges** (mortgages).[104]

- Group 3—Interests capable of protection on the register: These interests are not required to be registered but registering them against the title they affect will mean they take priority (i.e. are binding). If not registered (by entering a 'notice'[105]) they may lose priority and may not be enforceable against a purchaser of the land over which they operate. Very many property interests in land can be protected in this way, except a few listed,

---

[102] Ibid., s. 27.   [103] We explore easements in Chapter 10.   [104] We explore mortgages in Chapter 13.

[105] You must draw a distinction between this 'notice', which is entered on the register, and the 'doctrine of notice' which we discussed in section 1.6.4 in respect of unregistered land.

excluded interests[106] which may nevertheless be protected either by entering what is called a 'restriction'[107] or may fall within a category known as **'overriding interests'** covered by our next group: Group 4.

* Group 4—'Overriding interests': Not to be confused with the concept of overreaching (see section 2.6), these are interests which although do not appear on the register (i.e. are not registered) are binding on a purchaser of the land or even a non-purchaser to whom the land is transferred provided particular statutory provisions are satisfied.[108] These interests include: short leases, legal easements, and the interests of people in 'actual occupation' of land.[109]

The crux of land registration under the LRA 2002 is that whether a proprietary right is binding on third parties acquiring the land is determined by reference to that right's registration status under the provisions of the 2002 scheme.

1.7.2 **Unregistered land**

By contrast, 'unregistered land' means that title to the land has not been registered (recorded) at Land Registry. With just 14 per cent of total land mass in England and Wales unregistered,[110] the unregistered principles are fast-becoming redundant. As already noted, in unregistered land, title is not to be found on any register but rather contained in the traditional, paper title deeds which comprise a bulk of documents kept by the current owner and a purchaser has to search through these title deeds to investigate the 'root of title' to be sure of what they are buying. The unregistered land 'scheme' (if we can call it that) is examined in Chapter 3 and operates, in summary, as follows:

* Legal rights which 'bind the whole world': Legal rights in unregistered land enjoy universal enforceability and will bind a purchaser whether she is aware of their existence or not.

* Equitable 'commercial' rights which are land charges and registrable under the LCA 1972: These rights must be registered under the LCA 1972 against the name of the owner of the land if they are to be binding on a purchaser of that land. If they are not registered, they will be void against a purchaser.[111]

* Equitable 'family' rights which are covered neither by LCA 1972 nor the doctrine of notice but which are 'overreachable': These 'family' rights including equitable interests under a trust are capable of being 'overreached' and if they are overreached will not bind a purchaser. The right holder's interest is converted into a proportionate share of the purchase price paid for the land.

---

[106] Examples of excluded interests include: interests under a trust of land, short leases of three years or less, and restrictive covenants between landlord and tenant.

[107] Not all excluded interests can be the subject of a restriction but interests under a trust of land are, for our purposes, the most important example of interests that can.

[108] The interests defined as 'interests that override' are provided for in Schs. 1 and 3 of the LRA 2002.

[109] Do not worry about what 'actual occupation' means at this point; we return to this in section 2.7.4.2.

[110] HM Land Registry (2019 estimate): https://www.gov.uk/government/publications/registering-local-authority-land-and-property-with-hm-land-registry/register-local-authority-land-and-property.

[111] Section 4 of the LCA 1972.

- Equitable rights which are not overreached and not covered by the LCA 1972: For this very limited group of rights,[112] whether they bind a purchaser is governed by the 'doctrine of notice'. This is the only instance where the doctrine of notice remains operative today.

A number of preliminary points can be made about the unregistered land scheme:

- The position in unregistered land is rather more inefficient and unsatisfactory than in registered land under the LRA 2002.
- The problematic 'doctrine of notice' continues to play a role in unregistered land (albeit a minuscule one).
- The legal/equitable distinction remains particularly important in unregistered land whereas it is less so (although still relevant) in registered land.
- The doctrine of overreaching applies in *both* registered and unregistered land.
- The LRA 2002 provides for a series of 'events' which trigger compulsory registration.[113] The effect is that more and more plots of unregistered land are being pulled into the registered land scheme. The scale and significance of unregistered land is therefore dwindling and, in the not too distant future, may be of only historical rather than practical interest.

1.8 Bringing it all together: Land law as a puzzle

Land law is a rewarding subject and you are encouraged to see it as a puzzle; not a perplexing Rubik's cube but a puzzle of interlocking, interrelated parts which come together to form the discipline as a whole. You will really grasp this puzzle by appreciating from the outset that land law is driven by a series of impulses which ultimately guide and shape the law. If you grasp these impulses now, it can only make your understanding of the topics outlined in the chapters that follow a far smoother ride. We have already encountered some of these, including the personal/proprietary divide, the legal/equitable distinction, and the 'enforceability' or 'priority' question. But, beyond this, what are the drivers of land law? Birks argues that there are 'five keys' to understanding how land law works: *duality, reality, formality, space*, and *time*.[114]

There is also 'one pervasive theme' which he terms 'facilitation'. Birks explains that each of the five keys can be seen as operating to 'facilitate' the achievement of goals which people routinely wish to achieve in relation to land—whether that be ownership of land, renting land, allowing others rights over your land, or restricting how land is used. Birks explains:[115]

(1) It is the business of land law to say what property rights can exist in land. A property right is a real right, a right *in rem*. It has special characteristics, which distinguish it from a personal right, a right *in personam* . . .

---

[112] Including restrictive covenants and equitable easements created before 1926.

[113] The triggers for compulsory registration are examined in section 2.4.2.2.

[114] P. Birks, 'Before We Begin: Five Keys to Land Law' in Bright and Dewar (eds.), *Land Law: Themes and Perspectives* (Oxford: Oxford University Press, 1998), 470–1.   [115] Ibid., 470.

(2) English law has an inheritance of duality ... there is the duality between law and equity. The real rights which land law recognises can be legal or equitable ... equitable rights might be called 'weak' proprietary rights. That is the price of equity's more relaxed attitude to 'reality'.

(3) The value of legal certainty, which the equitable jurisdiction seems on occasion to undermine, is in general reinforced by insistence on the rigour of formality ... formality has meant writing in one form or another, but nowadays it means above all the public registration of real rights in land.

(4) The surface of a piece of land is a cross-section of a space. Every space has the potential for multiple uses ...

(5) Land law continues to facilitate dealing in slices of time, most obviously through the lease ... The days have gone when land law's principal mission was to structure wealth and power.

Keep these driving forces at the front of your mind as we navigate the subject. These are the impulses and impetuses that have moulded the law and continue to influence it today and will help you unlock the puzzle of land law. So, as we embark, do so with an open mind to the myriad colours and flavours that land law has to offer and, above all else, enjoy it.

Further reading

- P. Birks, 'Before We Begin: Five Keys to Land Law' in Bright and Dewar (eds.) *Land Law: Themes and Perspectives* (Oxford: Oxford University Press, 1998).

- S. Blandy, S. Bright, and S. Nield, 'The Dynamics of Enduring Property Relations in Land' (2018) 81(1) MLR 85.

- S. Bridge, 'Part and Parcel: Fixtures in the House of Lords' (1997) 56 CLJ 498.

- S. Bright, 'Of Estates and Interests: A Tale of Ownership and Property Rights' in S. Bright and J. Dewar (eds.), *Land Law: Themes and Perspectives* (Oxford: Oxford University Press, 1998), 529.

- E. Cooke, *Land Law* (Oxford: Oxford University Press, 2012), Chapters 1 and 2.

- K. Gray, 'Property in Thin Air' (1991) 50 CLJ 252.

- K. Gray and S. Gray, 'The Idea of Property Law' in Bright and Dewar (eds.), *Land Law: Themes and Perspectives* (Oxford: Oxford University Press, 1998), 15.

- M. Haley, 'The Law of Fixtures: An Unprincipled Metamorphosis?' [1998] Conv 137.

- J. W. Harris, 'Legal Doctrine and Interests in Land' in J. M. Eekelaar and J. Bell (eds.), *Oxford Essays in Jurisprudence*, 3rd series (Oxford: Oxford University Press, 1987).

- H. Lim and A. Bottomley (eds.), *Feminist Perspectives on Land Law* (Oxford: Routledge-Cavendish, 2007).

- J. Marston and L. Ross, 'Treasure and Portable Antiquities in the 1990s Still Chained to the Ghosts of the Past: The Treasure Act 1996' [1997] Conv 273.

- J. Marston and L. Ross, 'The Treasure Act 1996, Code of Practice and Home Office Circular on Treasure Inquests' [1998] Conv 252.

- M. Thompson, 'Must a House Be Land?' [2001] Conv 417.

Online resources

Access the online resources at www.oup.com/uk/bevan2e/ to test yourself with self-test questions and scenario problems relevant to the topics in this chapter. You can also view additional supporting material, including:

- *Videos*
- *Audio podcasts*
- *Maps, diagrams, and flowcharts*
- *Interactive exercises*
- *Examples of real-life legal documentation*

2 Registered Land

2.1 Introduction

In land law, concepts do not get much more fundamental than land registration. You were first introduced to registration in outline in Chapter 1.[1] As we found, registration sits as a central foundation of land law. This chapter offers an overview of the Land Registration Act 2002 (LRA 2002) which governs land registration today, its objectives, mechanics, as well as exploring when land can and must be registered. This chapter therefore first serves to clarify and cement in your minds *the idea, the concept* of registration before turning to examine more closely the nuts and bolts of how our contemporary registration system functions.[2]

As of 2019, 86 per cent of titles in England and Wales were registered; that's over 25 million registered titles, leaving just 14 per cent of titles unregistered.[3] The significance of this is that, by quite some way, the majority of dealings with land now engage registered land principles. Imagine that you and a partner decide to purchase a first house together. The land will likely be registered, so the steps you must follow to 'own' the land or, as we say, 'acquire title to the property' and to determine whether you will be bound by any pre-existing rights affecting that land will be governed by the registered land regime. When we speak of 'title to land' here we are referring to that bundle of rights that makes you 'owner' of land—note the obvious connection to the word *entitlement*. Being 'title holder' of a parcel of land brings with it the right to keep strangers out, to determine how the land is put to use, and to decide how it is disposed of i.e. dealt with.

---

[1] See section 1.7.

[2] We will return to land registration throughout the book as we consider the different rights affecting land from easements, to covenants, to mortgages.

[3] HM Land Registry (2019 estimate): https://www.gov.uk/government/publications/registering-local-authority-land-and-property-with-hm-land-registry/register-local-authority-land-and-property; unregistered land is diminishing year on year.

When we talk of land being 'registered', what we mean is that title to land (in other words, the 'estate' in land) has been recorded in a register that is maintained, controlled, and overseen by Land Registry, a State institution officially named 'Her Majesty's Land Registry' which is charged with administering the register. Our registration system is more precisely a system of *title registration* rather than registration of *land* per se. Why does this matter? Because it means that more than one title can be registered in relation to a single piece of land—the freehold estate in land can be registered and so too, for example, can a leasehold estate over the same plot (we encountered the concept of estates and freehold and leasehold in section 1.5.2 of Chapter 1). Where a freehold and leasehold are registered over the same land, the register will reflect both titles so that a purchaser of the freehold or leasehold would be made aware of the other title affecting the land. Our title registration regime derives from the 'Torrens' title system of registration devised by Sir Robert Torrens introduced in Southern Australia from 1858 and which proved so successful that it soon spread throughout much of the Commonwealth nations. It's interesting that Torrens has never met with widespread success in the United States[4] with only certain states fully embracing this system of title registration. The reasons for this are complex but the high costs of initial registration (in many states, court proceedings were needed before title registration could take place) and opposition from other title assurance providers in the US have been blamed. There is just insufficient public outcry in the US for the Torrens system for it to be implemented nationally.[5]

What is the idea of the register? The idea is that the register should provide as comprehensive an account as possible of ownership of land titles in England and Wales and the interests which bind that land. The registration system seeks to tidy up and improve upon the old system, known as 'title deeds conveyancing' (which we touched on in Chapter 1), whereby land ownership was determined by whoever held the physical, paper copy title deeds to the land in question. 'Title deeds conveyancing', as this old system is known, does retain a role today for those titles which are not yet registered and is examined in Chapter 3. It involves the purchaser searching through the physical documents relating to the land to discover any interests that might burden it. The modern system of land registration system replaces this. Title deeds conveyancing had significant drawbacks: it was described in *Williams & Glyn's Bank v Boland* (1981) as a 'wearisome and intricate task' involving investigation of paper documentation which, as Lord Westbury noted, may be 'difficult to read, impossible to understand and disgusting to touch'.[6] Just imagine what those paper documents look and smell like after many decades! Importantly, in unregistered land, documentation recording rights over land are held by the right holder themselves and not by any centrally administered authority. This makes investigation of the title deeds a time-consuming, expensive, and repetitive exercise. Title registration removes this problem by providing a centralized register.

---

[4] Mapp described that other than the US, he knew of no other jurisdiction where Torrens was known to have failed to take hold: T. W. Mapp, *Torrens' Elusive Title: Basic Legal Principles of an Efficient Torrens' System* (Edmonton: University of Alberta, Faculty of Law, 1978).

[5] For an interesting take on why the US has not embraced Torrens see J. L. McCormack, 'Torrens and Recording: Land Title Assurance in the Computer Age' (1992) 18(1) William Mitchell Law Review 61.

[6] C. H. S. Fifoot, *Pollock and Maitland* (Glasgow: University of Glasgow Publications, 1971), 15.

In contrast to title deeds conveyancing, the fundamentals of title registration are strikingly straightforward: the register should represent as clear and comprehensive as possible a picture of the land and the interests affecting it.[7] Every title is given a unique title number. Gray and Gray explain how the register operates:[8]

> Each substantive registered title number effectively identifies a major interest around which are clustered register entries relating to a range of minor interests. The operative distinction is therefore between large forms of estate ownership (which are recorded substantively under unique title numbers) and all other kinds of interest in the land which enhance, diminish or qualify such ownership.

Today, the LRA 2002 (which came into force in October 2003) is the primary source for our title registration system and it provides the statutory framework for the modern law, supplemented by Land Registration Rules which add flesh to the bones of the Act. Registration has, however, been around far longer than you might think. Today's system is the product of a series of incremental developments in statute from the Acts of 1862, 1875, and 1897[9] to the Land Registration Acts of 1925 and 1997:[10]

- The Land Registry Act 1862 heralded a measure of registration on a strictly voluntary basis and was bolstered by the Land Transfer Act 1875.

- The Land Transfer Act 1897 introduced compulsory registration of title for dealings with land but was geographically restricted to London.

- Only with the Land Registration Act 1925 (LRA 1925) were great strides made towards a comprehensive, nationwide system of registration through a combination of voluntary and compulsory registration.

Even under the LRA 1925, land registration spread sluggishly across the country and exhibited something of an 'experimental' character.[11] It was not until 1 December 1990[12] that it was made compulsory across the entirety of England and Wales that, on sale of land, all unregistered titles in England and Wales must be registered. The LRA 1925 continued to supply the framework for registration until the 2002 Act, bringing many pieces of land onto the register, but it was flawed. The Law Commission noted that the 1925 statute was 'both badly drafted and lacking in clarity' and whilst it had been 'made to work', this was in spite of rather than as a result of its legislative structure.[13] The upshot was that, the Law Commission together with the Land Registry, embarked on years of work resulting ultimately in a draft bill which was adopted by Parliament in a near-unamended form and became the LRA 2002. In 2016, the Law Commission launched a fresh consultation into

---

[7] The register is held by the Chief Land Registrar in London but is accessible through 18 district land registries across the country and electronically online meaning that, for a small fee, anyone can view and investigate a registered title from their computer.

[8] K. Gray and S. F. Gray, *Elements of Land Law*, 5th edn (Oxford: Oxford University Press, 2009), 189.

[9] The 1875 Act introduced the concept of a single Land Register and the 1897 legislation made registration on sale of land in London compulsory.

[10] For an account of history of the LRA 1925 in particular see J. Stuart Anderson, *Lawyers and the Making of English Land Law 1832–1940* (Oxford: Clarendon Press, 1992).

[11] See T. B. Ruoff and R. B. Roper, *Registered Conveyancing* (London: Stevens and Sons Ltd, 1986), [1–05].

[12] By way of the Registration of Title Order 1989.

[13] Law Commission Report No. 254, *Land Registration for the Twenty-First Century: A Consultative Document* (1998), [1.3].

updates and improvements that can be made to the 2002 regime.[14] This reported in 2018 and we will consider its recommendations in section 2.9.

A key component of the 2002 Act and a marker of the statute's significance was the further expansion it introduced in the categories of 'triggering events' for registration.[15] The categories of triggering events are now extremely broadly drawn and are designed to catch many transactions involving land beyond sale, thus bringing ever more unregistered land onto the register. Unregistered land is thus becoming an increasingly rare specimen. All this is not to say that 100 per cent registration of land titles in England and Wales is the inevitable outcome of the registration project. It is the view of the Law Commission that whilst movement should be made towards 'total registration' this will take time and there are reasons for proceeding cautiously.[16] In particular, the Commission emphasized that there will be those with no intention to conduct any dealings with their land and these people should not be compelled to register their land. Equally, there are a small number of—admittedly rather obscure—examples of land that is likely to remain unregistered; largely because none of the triggering events for first registration will arise.[17]

 Visit the online resources to watch a video on wider debates in registered land.

2.2 The system of registered land: Aims and objectives

In probing the aims and objectives of the system of registered land, we draw a distinction: first, we consider the general aims of a land registration system and, secondly, the particular objectives of the LRA 2002 regime.

2.2.1 The general aims of a system of registered land

The concept of registration is not unique nor confined to the legal sphere or land law more specifically. You will find examples of registers and registration of interests in many other fields and walks of life, from registers of company assets or shareholdings to marriages. All registers have a central objective in mind, namely providing a clear and comprehensive account of the interests they seek to record. McFarlane has described this general aim as one of 'publicity' and cites birth and death registers as examples where the publicity or publication of these registers gives interested parties the opportunity to discover important information about a community.[18] The same is true in the context of land registration. A land register provides interested parties, including those intending to purchase a parcel of land with the opportunity to find out more about a particular plot of land and to determine whether the party selling has the power to do so and whether the land to be

---

[14] Law Commission Consultation Document No. 227, *Updating the Land Registration Act 2002: A Consultation Paper* (2016).

[15] See generally s. 2 of the LRA 2002.

[16] Law Commission Report No. 271, *Land Registration for the 21st Century: A Conveyancing Revolution* (2001), [2.10]–[2.12].

[17] For example, land held by the Church and sizeable rural estates that have remained in the same family for generations.

[18] B. McFarlane, *The Structure of Property Law* (Oxford: Hart, 2008), 82.

purchased will be acquired free from or encumbered by pre-existing rights operating over it. In addition to publicity, registration allows interested parties to mitigate or guard against risks in dealings with land.

Registration holds an especially prominent role in relation to land. This reflects the economic, social, and cultural value that attaches to land in our society. Land is not like other property. The qualities that make land special were explored in section 1.1. These same qualities that make land unique provide justification for the certainty and clarity which a land register can provide. When land is purchased, we want to know that what we are buying is free from other unwelcome rights such as mortgages, rights of way, or other individuals' rights that may burden it. Registration of land therefore serves as a form of protection for purchasers and interest holders, and this notion of registration as protection can be expanded as we consider the wider advantages of a system of registered land. The following are benefits and aims of land registration:

1. To provide a complete and accurate reflection of the state of land at any given time so that title to land can be investigated with the minimum of additional enquiries and inspections: This is said by the Law Commission to be the 'fundamental objective'[19] of a land registration system.

2. To remove the cost and drudgery of investigation of the root of title and documents of title under title deeds conveyancing: In unregistered land, a purchaser must search through the vendor (seller's) documents of title. The vendor must demonstrate at least 15 years of good title which the purchaser must then inspect. Deeds may be lost, concealed, or even forged, and a purchaser may find herself bound by interests affecting the land about which she knew nothing when completing the sale. A system of registration removes much of this uncertainty. Rather than requiring purchasers to search through years of dealings with land and through often incomplete or soiled paper documentation, in a registered system a purchaser can easily search the register electronically thereby vastly reducing expense and delay, speeding up and simplifying dealings with land.

3. To reduce the risk of fraud and protect a purchaser from acquiring land from a vendor who does not have good title to the land: Registered titles are far easier to investigate, search, and verify, which reduces the likelihood of fraud, and a purchaser of registered land can rest assured that the land has been investigated by Land Registry before being duly recorded on the register thus guaranteeing the validity of the title. Importantly, in a registered land system, it is the fact of registration that guarantees title rather than the dusty, bulky title deeds under title deeds conveyancing.

4. To alert potential purchasers to any property rights that burden the land: As well as providing a description of the nature of a title, a land register also records rights and interests that affect the land. This is vital as these rights may be enforceable, i.e. binding against a potential purchaser. By flagging up these rights and interests that burden the land, potential purchasers can make a fully informed decision as to whether to proceed with the sale or not and whether to negotiate a lower purchase price in view of these encumbrances. Subject to certain caveats,[20] what a purchaser sees on the register is what she gets.

---

[19] Law Commission Report No. 271, [1.5].

[20] In particular, the so-called 'overriding interests' which are interests which although not registered nevertheless can be binding on purchasers. We consider these interests in greater detail in section 2.7.

5. **To standardize, clarify, and generally improve the conveyancing process:** Land registration provides an opportunity for improvements to the nature of the conveyancing process to be implemented, including encouraging the creation of more accurate plans of plots of registered land (i.e. plans which reflect the true extent of land, reductions in transaction costs, and streamlining in the resolution of disputes over land).[21]

6. **To support the market and benefit the economy:** O'Connor identifies that beyond the advantages of simplifying and streamlining of the conveyancing process, land registration is a market-supporting mechanism and has enormous economic benefits as greater security of title leads to the facilitation of land transfer, encouraging investment and growth.[22] As O'Connor explains, 'laws that ensure the security and transferability of property establish the framework of incentives that enable the creation of new wealth from existing assets'. So, if landowners feel that their land is secure, they are more likely to invest in improving it. Purchasers will also find it easier to access mortgages on favourable terms to fund the purchase and ultimately transaction costs fall.

Security of title is, however, an 'elusive ideal'[23] and, in examining this, Demogue distinguishes between a view of land as *static* security and as *dynamic* security: the former holds that owners should not be deprived of their rights by the acts of third parties without their consent while the latter seeks to protect purchasers' reasonable expectation of acquiring land free of unknown burdens and defects. A land registration system seeks to achieve both static and dynamic security in the trade-off between owners and purchasers of land. It is for you, as we move through the chapter, to assess where the law draws the line and how successfully this tension is navigated.

2.2.2 The aims and objectives of the LRA 2002 regime

We have seen that a system of land registration 'ultimately aims to reduce or eliminate complexity and uncertainty in conveyancing'.[24] Here, we examine the essential guiding principles and specific policy objectives of the 2002 legislation.

2.2.2.1 Three foundational principles

Both the LRA 2002 and the LRA 1925 which it repealed were guided by three core principles. These seminal principles were identified by Ruoff as being: the mirror principle, the curtain principle, and the insurance principle.[25] See Figure 2.1.

These principles apply to any system of registered title wherever it operates throughout the world and provide a means of assessing or examining the efficacy and priorities of systems of title registration. These three principles are essentially policy aspirations rather

---

[21] Note, however, that land registry plans are not conclusive as to boundaries and disputes may arise warranting adjudication.

[22] P. O'Connor, 'Registration of Title in England and Australia' in E. Cooke (ed.), *Modern Studies in Property Law*, Vol. 2 (Oxford: Hart, 2003), 84; see also Mapp, *Torrens' Elusive Title: Basic Principles of an Efficient Torrens System*.

[23] Mapp, *Torrens' Elusive Title: Basic Principles of an Efficient Torrens System*, 63.

[24] Law Commission Consultation Paper No. 277, *Updating the Land Registration Act 2002* (2016), [2.7].

[25] T. B. F. Ruoff, *An Englishman Looks at the Torrens System* (Sydney: Law Book Co. of Australasia, 1957).

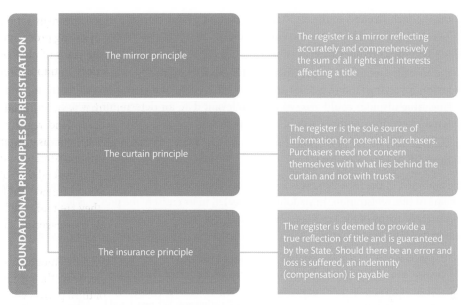

Figure 2.1 Ruoff's three foundational principles of a system of registered title

than delivered outcomes: they serve as a useful barometer or analytical tool to help us better understand registration but do not represent the totality of the story. You are advised to use these principles with caution and to view them as a starting point for assessing, at a macro level, the success of the LRA 2002 regime. As you will discover, in practice, in legislating for the 2002 Act, a series of compromises had to be made which to a larger and lesser extent undermine aspects of Ruoff's seminal principles owing to issues of pragmatism, practicality, and countervailing policy impulses.[26] Indeed, Ruoff himself acknowledged that the three principles sit, to some extent, in conflict with one another and are far from a perfect descriptor of the ambitions of a system of title registration, noting that 'in this imperfect world the mirror does not invariably give a completely reliable reflection'.[27] By way of example, why would an insurance principle even be necessary if the mirror and curtain principles operated as intended? Ruoff's work offers an imperfect but helpful analytical guide and should be employed with care.

2.2.2.2 The stated aims of the LRA 2002

The Law Commission had in its 1998 Consultation Paper[28] identified a number of deficiencies with the LRA 1925 including:

- the complexity of the LRA 1925 legislative scheme and the multitude of accompanying land registration rules;

---

[26] The most obvious example being the extent to which overriding interests undermine the mirror principle. These compromises also go to the static/dynamic security debate outlined at section 2.2.1.

[27] Ruoff, *An Englishman Looks at the Torrens System*, 9.   [28] Law Commission Report No. 254, [1.3].

- the inconclusiveness of the register as a result of a large category of interests—so-called 'overriding interests' that were enforceable against purchasers even though they were not recorded on the register;
- the so-called 'registration gap'; namely the gap that existed between the date of a transaction involving land (e.g. sale) and the eventual date of registration of that transaction (meaning disputes could arise as to the relevant date for determining whether unregistered 'overriding interests' would be enforceable);
- the antiquity of the legislation (in particular, the LRA 1925 took no account of modern methods of conveyancing).

The ambition of the LRA 2002 was to introduce a strengthened, simplified, and modernized scheme of title registration. In so doing, it repealed in its entirety the previous legislation but, importantly, many of the key ideas and principles of the 1925 scheme endure. The Commission in its 2001 Report signalled what it regarded as the crux of the proposed new system:[29]

> The purpose of [the Land Registration] Bill is a bold and striking one. It is to create the necessary framework in which registered conveyancing can be conducted electronically. The Bill will bring about an unprecedented conveyancing revolution within a comparatively short time. It will also make other profound changes to the substantive law that governs registered land. These changes, taken together, are likely to be even more far-reaching than the great reforms of property law that were made by the 1925 property legislation.

The Law Commission therefore indicated a shift in approach from the raft of legislation that came before it which had largely proceeded on the basis that registration should not bring about any change to the substantive law:[30]

> Largely because of the rather tortuous history of the Land Registration Act 1925, it has always been accepted that the principles of registered land should, so far as possible, be the same as they are where title is unregistered. The Land Registration Act 1925 has been perceived as mere machinery for translating those principles into a registered format . . . In most legal systems within the Commonwealth that have adopted a system of title registration, it has been recognised that registered and unregistered systems *are* different. At its most fundamental level, the basis of title to unregistered land is possession, whereas . . . the basis for registered title is the fact of registration . . . there seems little point in inhibiting the rational development of principles of property law by reference to a system that is rapidly disappearing.

The development of registered land principles should not, therefore, be constrained by attempting to keep registered and unregistered land aligned. The Commission also foresaw a change of attitude, a conveyancing revolution which would see realization of a central, 'fundamental objective':[31]

> The fundamental objective of the [Land Registration] Bill is that, under the system of electronic dealing with land that it seeks to create, the register should be a complete and accurate reflection of the state of the title to land at any given time.

The move towards e-conveyancing was the core objective of the Commission's work and the Draft Land Registration Bill sought to establish the statutory framework for achieving

---

[29] Law Commission Report No. 271, [1.1].   [30] Law Commission Consultation Paper No. 254, [1.5].
[31] Law Commission Report No. 271, [1.5].

this. This, said the Commission, was merely a reflection of the general development of e-commerce and the 'legitimate public expectation' for a more expeditious and 'less stressful system of dealing with land'.[32] The Commission envisaged that 'within a comparatively short time' both the creation and transfer of interests in registered land would be completed electronically. Significantly, the creation, transfer, and registration of interests in land would then take place at the click of a button in one single process, whether that be transferring land to a purchaser, granting a mortgage over land, or creating a third party right such as a right of way.[33] Paper dealings with land would, ultimately, cease to be effective. In truth, progress towards this objective has been extremely slow and no date for implementation of e-conveyancing has been announced. In fact, the Commission acknowledged this in its 2018 report on updating the LRA 2002 in which it recommended that e-conveyancing in the form anticipated by the 2002 Act was not, at present, an achievable goal and that a retreat was necessary from the original aspiration of the simultaneous creation and registration of interests in land.[34]

In addition to the fundamental objective of introducing e-conveyancing, the scheme under the LRA 2002 should be seen as responding to a series of stated aims and impulses. Chief among them are:

1. A recognition that unregistered land has 'had its day' and therefore the triggers for first registration of unregistered land should be expanded, bringing the remaining unregistered titles onto the register. As far as possible this would allow investigation of title to land by reference to the register 'with the minimum of additional enquiries and inspections'.[35]

2. A refocus on ensuring the register is, as far as possible, a complete and accurate reflection of the state of land titles at a given point in time. This would involve a reduction in the number of 'overriding interests' which were binding even though they had not been recorded on the register.

3. A recognition of the need for the State to guarantee the accuracy of the register. The register must guarantee title—in other words, guarantee the truth of what the register records. This should be reinforced by the provision of an indemnity. If the register is incorrect, it must be capable of being rectified and any loss suffered compensated.

4. Bringing about a 'change in attitude' in relation to registration and a necessary shift in the public perception as to title to land. A widely held view had developed that it was unreasonable to expect people to register their rights in land. This, said the Commission, was puzzling in light of the growth of registered land and because registration was not an unduly onerous process.

---

[32] Ibid.

[33] This button would, of course, be clicked by solicitors and conveyancers with training and licensed from Land Registry.

[34] The Commission had already in 2011, after spending £41 million, abandoned its plans to introduce e-transfers of land due to widespread concerns as to the security of the scheme and the risk of hacking. We return to the status of e-conveyancing in section 2.9.

[35] Law Commission Report No. 271, [1.5].

2.3 The Land Registration Act 2002: An overview

We have explored the general aims of a registered system and the specific objectives of the LRA 2002. Before we turn to the nuts and bolts of the scheme, this section provides a short overview of how the LRA works.[36] This overview should allow you to fully grasp the discussion of the mechanics of the LRA 2002 which follows. In this section, we focus on two key issues:

* the non-application of the doctrine of notice in registered land;
* the four-group categorization of proprietary rights under the LRA 2002.

2.3.1 Non-application of the doctrine of notice in registered land

Under the LRA 2002 regime, notice is no longer the means of determining the enforceability of proprietary rights in registered land.[37] Put differently, the doctrine of notice which we encountered in Chapter 1 (and return to in Chapter 3) plays no role in the registered land system.[38] Recall that under the doctrine, a bona fide purchaser of a legal estate for value will take the land free of prior unregistered equitable interests provided she does not have notice (actual, constructive, or imputed) of those interests. In registered land, this doctrine has no application and is irrelevant. It is the *fact of registration* which determines enforceability. In other words, a purchaser of registered land takes that land subject to the estates, rights, and interests recorded in the register: whether or not a purchaser is bound by a preexisting interest is to be determined by reference to the registered principles laid down in the 2002 Act and is not determined by how far the purchaser had knowledge or notice of that interest. Equally, whether she acted in good faith is also irrelevant. This aligns directly with the aims of the 2002 Act to reduce to a minimum the need to make inquiries and inspections of land, and with the ambitions of e-conveyancing, which are clearly incompatible with the doctrine of notice.

2.3.2 The four-group categorization of proprietary rights under the LRA 2002

To understand how the LRA 2002 regime functions, you need to be aware of a four-group categorization of proprietary rights inherent in the scheme. You were first introduced to this in section 1.7. You will not find express reference to this categorization on the face of the 2002 Act itself: this classification of rights is offered as a useful guide for you to understand how the scheme of the statute hangs together. Importantly, overlap between the groups of rights is possible; for example, an **option to purchase** land or a short legal lease is capable of protection by way of entry of a notice (group 3) but can also amount to an overriding interest (group 4). Equally, certain rights are also excluded from falling into group 3

---

[36] For a general overview, see Law Commission Report No. 271, [2.1]–[2.58].

[37] As we will note the regime does make references to 'knowledge' and draws on the concept of discoverability in a limited number of cases, in particular, as to overriding interests. This was not, however, intended to import the doctrine of notice and should not be interpreted as such. See generally Law Commission Report No. 271, [5.16].

[38] As to the doctrine of notice see section 1.6.4 and section 3.4.5.

by s. 33 of the LRA 2002 but can nevertheless be protected by entry of a restriction and/or may also fall into group 4 as overriding interests; for example, equitable interests under a trust. We outline this four-group categorization here: see Figure 2.2.

2.3.2.1 Group 1—Substantively registrable estates

Only legal estates are capable of being substantively registered. Substantive registration means that these estates are registered in their own right, generate a separate title, and are provided with their own distinct title number. According to the scheme of the LRA, there are two legal estates which are capable of substantive registration: the legal fee simple (free-hold) and the legal term of years (leasehold) granted for more than seven years.[39] Where land is unregistered, the transfer of freehold land or the grant out of that unregistered land of a lease of more than seven years will constitute a 'triggering event' and the title must be registered.[40] Where land is already registered, a transfer of a freehold estate or the granting of a lease of more than seven years out of the registered estate will constitute a 'registrable disposition' and the disposition must be completed by registration if it is to operate at law.[41] Failure to complete with registration will mean the transferee can only obtain an equitable title in the land.[42] We explore registrable dispositions in more detail in section 2.4.3.1. As you will gather, the LRA 2002 chooses 'seven' as the key duration for leasehold and for trig-gering registration requirements. This represents a reduction from the position under the 1925 legislation which provided for registration of leases granted for more than 21 years.

2.3.2.2 Group 2—Interests which although not substantively registrable must be completed by registration to be legal

Section 27 of the LRA 2002 Act lists a series of dispositions (dealings with land) which are 'required to be registered'. These are dispositions of an estate or charge which has already been registered. The statute calls these 'registrable dispositions' and these dispositions can

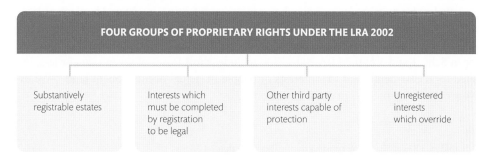

FOUR GROUPS OF PROPRIETARY RIGHTS UNDER THE LRA 2002

| Substantively registrable estates | Interests which must be completed by registration to be legal | Other third party interests capable of protection | Unregistered interests which override |

Figure 2.2 The four-group categorization of proprietary rights under the LRA 2002

---

[39] See ss. 2, 3, 4, and 27 of the LRA 2002.

[40] Section 4 of the LRA 2002. You should also note that the grant of a lease which is to take effect more than three months after its grant must also be registered however long its duration: s. 4(1)(d).

[41] We consider registrable dispositions, first registration, and compulsory registration in more detail in section 2.4.

[42] Section 7 of the LRA 2002.

only operate *at law* if they are completed by registration and the 'relevant registration requirements are met'.[43] These registration requirements are provided in Sch. 2 of the Act. Examples of registrable dispositions include: the transfer of a registered estate, the grant out of a registered estate of a lease of more than seven years, or an expressly created legal easement or legal charges (mortgage).[44]

2.3.2.3 Group 3—Other third party interests capable of protection on the register

These are interests which are not required to be registered, cannot be substantively registered but can, nevertheless, be protected by registering them against the estate they affect. By 'protection' we mean that, if registered, these interests will take priority—in other words, will be binding against successors. Under the LRA 1925, these interests were named 'minor interests'. This terminology was very unhelpful and thankfully the LRA 2002 abandons it as it suggested that these 'minor' rights were insignificant. Not so. In fact, some of the most important rights affecting land fall into Group 3 of 'interests capable of protection' including many easements and covenants, as well as options to purchase. So, how do you 'protect' these interests? Protection is achieved by entering a '**notice**' which ensures the priority of the right.[45] If not registered, they will lose priority and will not be enforceable against a purchaser of the land they affect. Pretty much all property interests in land can be protected in this way except a few listed, excluded interests including interests under a trust; leases granted for three years, or less; and restrictive covenants between a lessor and lessee.[46] The LRA 2002 saw an expansion in the number of third party rights that could be protected by entry of a notice as part of the statute's wider strategy to increase the rights reflected on the register.[47] We explore further the mechanics of the 'notice' in section 2.5.

2.3.2.4 Group 4—'Unregistered interests which override'

These are interests which, although not registered and not appearing on the register, are nonetheless binding on any person who acquires an interest in registered land whether on first registration of land (voluntary or compulsory) or where there has been a registrable disposition of a registered estate completed by registration.[48] These interests are provided for in Schs. 1 and 3 of the LRA 2002[49] and include: short leases of seven years or less, implied legal easements, and the interests of people in 'actual occupation' of land.[50] We explore overriding interests in detail in section 2.7.

---

[43] Ibid., s. 27(1).   [44] We consider this further in section 2.4.3.1.

[45] This 'notice' which is entered on the register is not to be confused with the doctrine of notice which as we noted is irrelevant to the registered land scheme.

[46] Section 33 of the LRA 2002.

[47] See Law Commission Report No. 271, [2.19]; there was also a simultaneous reduction in the scope of overriding interests.

[48] For discussion, see Law Commission Report No. 271, [2.24].

[49] Schedule 1 contains 'interests which override first registration' and Sch. 3 'interests which override registered dispositions'—mostly identical but some differences.

[50] Do not worry about what 'actual occupation' means at this point, we return to this in section 2.7.

2.3.3 **The conveyancing process for registered land: A brief overview**

So how does buying and selling registered land take place? A very brief overview is offered here:

- The first stage in the purchase/sale of registered land is the pre-contract or negotiations stage at which the buyer makes an offer and the seller accepts. Once agreed, the seller's solicitor will obtain an up-to-date copy of the title from Land Registry. The buyer's solicitors will commission a survey of the land and commence investigation into the title of the property including local authority searches, checking the legal title, and raising any pre-contractual enquiries. Solicitors for both sides will finalize the terms of the contract for sale which is then signed by both parties.

- The second stage is exchange of contracts which, today, generally takes place over the phone according to one of three formulae approved by the Law Society. Most commonly, this involves solicitors for the parties confirming they each hold a contract signed by their client and that the buyer has provided a deposit. Each side agrees to send the contracts to the other in the post that same day along with the buyer's deposit to the seller's solicitor. The parties are now legally tied to the sale. Withdrawing now will result in significant costs.

- The next stage is pre-completion. The buyer's solicitor will carry out a land registry search against the title to be acquired (if not already done) and a search of the bankruptcy register. The buyer's solicitor prepares the draft transfer deed (in most cases this means using a Land Registry 'TR1 Form'[51]) and sends it to the seller's solicitor for approval. The transfer document is then signed by both parties. Financing and stamp duty will also be confirmed at this stage.

- The final stage is completion. On the agreed date, the buyer's solicitor will send to the seller's solicitor the funds to complete the sale and keys will be handed over to the new owner. Arrangements will be made for the purchase to be registered at Land Registry. A transfer of a registered estate only takes effect at law once it had been completed by registration (see section 2.4.3.1). Until that time the seller remains the legal owner of the land, though the buyer is the owner in equity from the moment the contracts are exchanged. Once Land Registry has completed the registration, the buyer will receive a copy of the registered title from Land Registry.

Having now considered the LRA scheme and conveyancing process in outline, we move in the remainder of the chapter to examine the mechanics of the LRA 2002 regime—in other words, how the system functions in practice.

2.4 Titles in registered land

Registration under the LRA 2002 involves registration of *titles* as opposed to registration against names as in unregistered land. We need to unpack this further. The following issues warrant a little more thought:

- the nature of the register;
- first and compulsory registration under the LRA;
- subsequent dealings with registered titles.

---

[51] You can find these forms on the Gov.uk website.

2.4.1 **The nature of the register**

Although we refer to 'the register', the register is made up of three distinct registers known as the Property Register, the Proprietorship Register, and the Charges Register each of which contains slightly different information about a plot of land: see Figure 2.3. At Land Registry, if you log on electronically to search a particular title, you will see a single file or 'register' which comprises the three distinct sections or registers outlined in Figure 2.3. To help you visualize this, Figure 2.4 provides a sample of an official register held at Land Registry.

2.4.2 **First and compulsory registration of title: Bringing previously unregistered land onto the register**

First registration of a title describes the moment when previously unregistered land becomes registered. First registration under the LRA is provided for in two ways: voluntary first registration under s. 3 of the 2002 Act and compulsory first registration under s. 4.

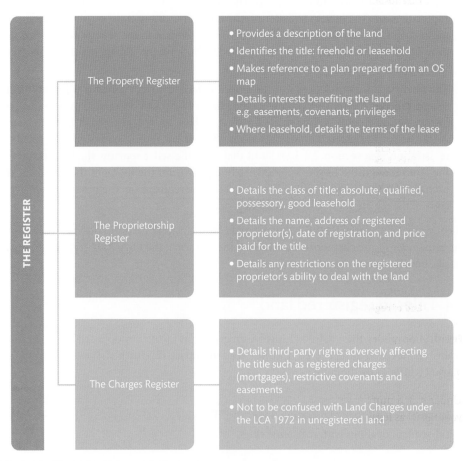

Figure 2.3 Details of the register held by Land Registry

REGISTER EXTRACT

Title Number	: CS72510
Address of Property	: 23 Cottage Lane, Kerwick, PL14 3JP.
Price Paid/Value Stated	: £128,000
Registered Owners	: PETER ANDREW BARTRAM of 23 Cottage Lane, Kerwick
Lender	: Ilkingham Building Society

A. Property Register

This register describes the land and estate comprised in the title.

CORNSHIRE: MARADON

1. (29 August 1974) The Freehold land shown edged with red on the plan of the above Title filed at the Registry and being 23 Cottage Lane, Kerwick, (PL14 3JP).
2. (29 August 1974) The land tinted yellow on the title plan has the benefit of a right of way on foot over the passageway to Cottage land.
3. The land has rights of drainage under adjoining land.

B. Proprietorship Register

This register specifies the class of title and identifies the owner. It contains any entries that affect the right of disposal.

Title absolute

1. (18 December 2001): PROPRIETOR: PETER ANDREW BARTRAM and SUSAN HELEN BARTRAM of 23 Cottage Lane, Kerwick, (PL14 3JP).
2. (18 December 2001) The price stated to have been paid on 3 December 2001 was £128,000.
3. (18 December 2001) Except under an order of the registrar no disposition by the proprietor of the land is to be registered without the consent of the proprietor of the charge dated 3 December 2001 in favour of the Ilkingham Building Society referred to in the Charges Register.

C. Charges Register

This register contains any charges and other matters that affect the land.

1. (29 August 1974) A Conveyance of the land tinted pink on the title plan dated 14 February 1965 made between (1) Archibald Henry Dawson (Vendor) and (2) Thomas Yorke (Purchaser) contains the following covenants:-

   "THE Purchaser hereby covenants with the Vendor so as to bind the land hereby conveyed into whosoever hands the same may come that the Purchaser and his successors in title will not use the premises hereby conveyed for the retail sale of grocery or as a butchers shop."
2. (29 August 1974) A Transfer of the land in this title dated 21 August 1974 made between (1) Henry Smith and (2) David Stanley Charles and Susan Charles contains restrictive covenants.
3. (20 December 2001) REGISTERED CHARGE dated 3 December 2001 to secure the moneys including the further advances therein mentioned.
4. (20 December 2001) PROPRIETOR: Ilkingham Building Society of 101 Cambridge Street, Ilkingham IL1 3FC.

End of register

Figure 2.4 Sample register

2.4.2.1 Voluntary first registration under s. 3 of the LRA 2002

Under s. 3, a number of proprietary rights taking effect as legal interests can be registered *voluntarily* as legal estates. These are given in s. 3(1) and include:

- rentcharges[52]
- franchises[53]
- *profits à prendre*.[54]

An unregistered freehold can also be voluntarily registered, as can an unregistered lease-hold provided that it still has more than seven years of its term unexpired.[55] Land Registry has introduced incentives to encourage voluntary registration of titles including reducing registration fees.

2.4.2.2 Compulsory first registration under s. 4 of the LRA 2002

Section 4 of the LRA 2002 contains a number of events that 'trigger' compulsory regis-tration of previously unregistered titles and these cover some of the most common deal-ings with land. This is entirely intentional as a means of capturing as many unregistered titles and so drawing as much unregistered land as possible into the registered system. The events triggering compulsory registration are so widely drawn that *any* dealing with an un-registered legal estate will engage compulsory registration. Only where unregistered land remains static and is not subject to any dealing of any kind will it escape the tentacles of compulsory registration. Under s. 4, the following are the principal triggering events:[56]

- the transfer of an unregistered freehold or transfer of leasehold with more than seven years to run;[57]
- the grant of a lease for a term of more than seven years;
- the grant of a reversionary lease for any term where the lease is to take effect more than three months after the grant;
- the grant of a protected, first legal mortgage.

When a triggering event takes place, registration must be completed within a period of two months from the relevant transaction.[58] Section 7 provides the consequences of a failure to register within this time period.

2.4.2.3 The effect of first registration: Conclusiveness of title

First registration of a previously unregistered title signals a new chapter; a break from the old unregistered regime. Registration confers a new statutory title on the registered pro-prietor and, from then on, this forms the basis for all subsequent dealings with the land.

---

[52] A rentcharge is an annual sum paid by the owner of freehold land to another person who has no other legal interest in the land.

[53] A franchise in this sense is a right granted by the Crown, such as a right to hold a market or fair, which does not carry with it any ownership of physical land.

[54] A *profit à prendre* (Middle French for 'right in taking') is a right to take something from the land of another. 'In gross' means that the right is exercisable by the right holder without that person having any ownership of any particular piece of land. The right holder may own no land at all.

[55] Section 3(3) of the LRA 2002. Provision is also made for the voluntary registration of Crown land.

[56] The Lord Chancellor is endowed under s. 5 with the power to extend the categories of triggering events still further. See section 2.9.1 of this chapter for a discussion of the recommendations made by the Law Commission in its latest report, *Updating the Land Registration Act 2002*, on changes it proposes including compulsory triggers for registration in dispositions involving mine and mineral estates.

[57] Under the LRA 1925, only transfer and grant of leases exceeding 21 years was a triggering event.

[58] Section 6(4) of the LRA 2002. This period can be extended on an application to the Land Registrar (the person responsible for overseeing the register) if there are good grounds for so doing: s. 6(5) of the LRA 2002.

Under s. 58 of the LRA 2002, the 'conclusiveness' of title is guaranteed. Section 58 provides that if a person is entered in the register as the registered proprietor of a legal estate, registration has the effect of vesting the legal estate in her. Section 58 has been described by the Law Commission as 'one of the most fundamental principles of registered conveyancing'.[59] It is central to the operation of the LRA 2002 in that it confirms that registration is 'constitutive'; in other words, it is the fact of registration which confers title—a system of title *by* registration as opposed to registration *of* title.[60]

Registration confers title on the registered proprietor even where there has been no **conveyance** of the legal estate to that proprietor. This means that even if a person is registered as proprietor in error as a result of fraud or if there has been a conveyance of the legal estate but it is intrinsically void, the proprietor can rely on s. 58 to assert that title has conclusively vested in them.[61] The registered proprietor may, however, then be subject to a claim to rectify the register. Where this happens, the party registered in error is likely to be entitled to an indemnity payment to compensate any loss suffered as a result of the changes made to the register. We consider alteration and **rectification** of the register in section 2.8. A consideration of the recent case of *Walker v Burton* will bring to life the significance of the protection of s. 58 of the LRA 2002.

KEY CASE *Walker v Burton* (2013)

Facts: A dispute arose between angry villagers of Ireby in Lancashire and the Burtons who had recently moved into the area. The matter concerned a fell near the village. The fell had been unclaimed, unregistered land used by villagers for the purposes of grazing and recreational activities. Having purchased a neighbouring farmhouse, the Burtons registered a claim to Lordship of the Manor (i.e. the right to call oneself Lord of the land), claimed title to the fell, and were duly registered as proprietors of the land.

Legal issue: The villagers challenged the Burtons' claim to the land. The villagers argued that the 'Lordship of the Manor' had long been extinct and, on this basis, brought an action under the LRA 2002, Sch. 4 to have the register altered on the grounds of mistake and have the title 'Lordship of the Manor' and title to the fell both closed.

Judgment: The Deputy Registrar found that the Burtons had no claim to Lordship of the Manor and that this title should be closed. Regarding title to the fell, however, he held that although the Burtons had been registered as proprietors by mistake, the title should not be closed. The fact of their registration as proprietors vested title in the Burtons under the guarantee of title in s. 58 of the LRA 2002. The villagers appealed ultimately to the Court of Appeal which upheld the decision of the Deputy Registrar. The villagers could not demonstrate that it would be unjust to refuse to alter the register under Sch. 4 as the Burtons had invested 'time, effort and money on improving the Fell and its management had discouraged harmful practices, such as tipping waste and use of motorised vehicles'. In addition, the Burtons were in possession of the fell and there was no evidence of fraud or lack of due care on their part. It was relevant that the villagers, while challenging the Burtons' claim to the fell, were not themselves asserting title to the land. Had they done so, the case may have been decided differently. No other party had come forward to claim title to the land.

---

[59] Law Commission Report No. 271, [9.4].
[60] Confirmed by the Law Commission as a key feature of the LRA 2002 regime in its Report No. 271, [1.10].
[61] *Walker*.

Despite a series of legal challenges to the forerunner provision to s. 58 of the LRA (s. 69 of the LPA 1925) in *Malory Enterprises Ltd v Cheshire Homes (UK) Ltd* (2002) and challenges to the present provision of s. 58 itself in *Park v Kinnear Investments* (2012), the Court of Appeal has recently confirmed the operation of the current conclusiveness principle in *Swift 1st v Chief Land Registrar* (2015) holding that:[62]

> It is registration rather than the quality of the prior disposition which creates and constitutes the proprietor's title to the registered estate or charge: see s. 58(1) LRA 2002. This is certainly the view of the editors of *Ruoff & Roper on the Law and Practice of Registered Conveyancing* (see paragraph 47-006) and it was the view of the Law Commission when it produced its report on land registration which led to the passing of the LRA 2002.

In summary, case law confirms the conclusive effect of registration under s. 58. Registration guarantees title, subject to claims to alteration and rectification of the register. The point is this: whether a claim to rectification succeeds is to be decided by reference to the specific provisions on rectification (discussed in section 2.8) and, succeed or fail, the register is conclusive unless and until it is altered.

2.4.2.4 The effect of first registration: Four classes of title

When an application for first registration is made, the party seeking to be registered as proprietor will send the title deeds to the land along with the appropriate Land Registry forms and application fee to their nearest Land Registry office. The Registrar will investigate the root of title, consider the validity of the application for registration, and determine which *class of title* is to be granted depending on the nature of the documentation available and by considering the wider factual circumstances. At the same time, the Registrar will enter on the register any interests affecting the land that are discovered. There are four classes of title from which the Registrar can choose:

1. Absolute title: The 'gold standard' of title, **absolute title** is available for both freehold and leasehold land: absolute freehold, absolute leasehold.
2. Qualified title: Where there is some defect in the title, a qualified title may be registered: see s. 9(4) of the LRA 2002 as to freehold and s. 10(3) as to leasehold.
3. Possessory title: Where there is insufficient documentary evidence of title (whether leasehold or freehold) on an application for first registration, a possessory title may be registered: see s. 9(5) of the LRA 2002 as to freehold and s. 10(6) as to leasehold.
4. Good leasehold: Absolute leasehold title requires the Registrar to be able to verify the landlord/lessor's title from which the lease was granted. This may not always be straightforward, particularly in cases of very long leases. As such, good leasehold title may be registered: see s. 10(3) of the LRA 2002.

The four classes of title represent a hierarchy with absolute title and good leasehold title being the stronger, more secure titles; qualified and possessory being the weaker. Section 62 of the LRA 2002 allows for the upgrading of title where the proprietor has not been

---

[62] *Swift*, [26], per Patten LJ; see generally E. Lees, 'Registration and Make-Believe and Forgery: *Swift 1st Ltd v Chief Land Registrar*' (2015) 131 LQR 515.

registered with absolute title. Under this provision, the Registrar can subsequently upgrade the class of title from, say, qualified or possessory title where the requirements of the superior class of absolute title have been met. This would be appropriate where, for example, missing title documentation (limiting title to possessory title) is subsequently found or where a defect in the title (limiting title to qualified title) is no longer operating.[63]

2.4.3 Subsequent dealings with registered land

Once first registration has taken place, the title is registered and subject to the regime of the LRA 2002. Crucially, any subsequent transactions with that land will be governed by the principles on dealings with registered land. We can call these dealings 'registrable dispositions' and we consider these in this section. For the sake of absolute clarity, when we talk about 'dealings with registered land' what we mean is circumstances where registered land is, for example, sold; transferred to a third party; a lease is granted out of a registered estate or mortgaged.

2.4.3.1 The meaning of 'registrable disposition': Section 27 of the LRA 2002

As we saw in section 2.2, it is key to a registered land system that the register is as accurate and up-to-date as possible. To assist in this, the LRA 2002 provides that subsequent dealings with registered land must be completed by registration. S. 27 of the LRA 2002 lists the following as registrable dispositions:

- the transfer of a registered fee simple;
- the transfer of a registered lease (of any duration);
- the grant out of a registered estate of a lease for a term exceeding seven years;
- the grant out of a registered estate of a lease to take effect after three months from the date of grant—a so-called 'reversionary lease';
- the grant out of a registered estate of a discontinuous lease;[64]
- the grant or reservation of a legal easement;
- the grant of a legal charge/mortgage.

Registrable dispositions must be completed by registration. The requirements for registration are provided in Sch. 2 of the LRA 2002. Section 27(1) sets out the consequences of a failure to complete with registration: the disposition will not operate at law. In other words, the disposition will have no effect at law until registration is complete and, at best, will take effect in equity.

An inevitable consequence of s. 27 is a hiatus, the so-called 'registration gap', between the time when the disposition is completed (for example, a transfer of registered land) and the time that the disposition is registered at Land Registry. So, why does this matter? In

---

[63] It is also possible for good leasehold to be upgraded to absolute leasehold where the landlord's title is verified and for qualified titles to be upgraded to good leasehold. For a more fulsome discussion, see Law Commission Report No. 271, [9.17]–[9.27].

[64] A discontinuous lease is a lease where the tenant's right to possession is not for a single continuous period. Most commonly, discontinuous leases arise as to holiday properties and are often called 'timeshare leases'.

this registration gap, the purchaser of registered land is exposed to the possibility that third party rights may arise or other dealings with the land might take place that will bind the land being acquired.[65] Now, this registration gap would be eliminated if e-conveyancing as originally conceived when the LRA 2002 was enacted, were to be implemented because the making of a disposition and its registration would take place simultaneously thereby closing the gap. However, e-conveyancing has stalled and the Law Commission in 2018 recommended stepping back from simultaneous completion and registration.[66] The effect is that even if this new and more limited form of e-conveyancing were to be implemented, the registration gap would remain a live and significant issue. In response to the registration gap, the Commission takes the view that personal liability offers an adequate sticking plaster solution.[67]

2.4.3.2 The effect of registrable dispositions: Conclusiveness of the register

We considered the issue of conclusiveness of title in section 2.4.2.3 as to first registration but conclusiveness is equally important when there are subsequent dealings with registered land. Once a registrable disposition is completed by registration, s. 58 of the LRA confirms that if the legal estate is not otherwise vested in the registered proprietor, it is deemed to be conclusively vested. Section 58(2) makes plain, however, that if the registration requirements have not been satisfied, the legal estate will not be vested in the disponee (the person to whom a registrable disposition is made), underlining again that a registrable disposition must be completed by registration if it is to operate at law.[68]

2.4.3.3 The effect of registrable dispositions: The powers of registered proprietors

A key feature of the LRA regime is the clarification it provides on the powers enjoyed by registered proprietors. This clarification is a further attempt to ensure the comprehensiveness and accuracy of the register as part of the move towards the introduction of e-conveyancing. As the Law Commission explained in its 2001 report:[69]

> The register must . . . provide all the necessary information about the title. One ground on which a disposition of land might be challenged is that the party who made it was acting outside his or her powers in some way . . . The present law is not entirely clear on this point. However, it has been assumed that a registered proprietor is to be taken to have all the powers of disposition that an absolute owner of a registered estate or charge would have under the general law, unless there is some entry in the register . . . which limits those powers.

The LRA 2002 gives statutory effect to this assumption in ss. 23 and 24. These provisions confirm that a person registered as the registered proprietor is entitled to exercise all the powers of a legal owner in relation to the estate including the power to make dispositions of the land or to grant a charge over it. Any limitation on these 'owner's powers' should be clearly reflected on the register. No such provision existed in the old 1925 legislation.

---

[65] For examples of this problem, see *Abbey National Building Society v Cann* (1991); *Brown & Root Technology Ltd v Sun Alliance and London Assurance Co.* (1996).

[66] Law Commission Report, *Updating the Land Registration Act 2002*, chapter 20.

[67] On which, see Law Commission Report No. 271, [1.20] and section 2.5.5.1.

[68] See discussion of s. 58 in this context in *Barclays Bank plc v Guy* (2008).   [69] At [2.15].

2.4.3.4 The effect of registrable dispositions: The protection for purchasers of registered land

Section 23 of the LRA is buttressed by s. 26 which offers clarification of the protection afforded to a disponee (remember: this is the person to whom a registrable disposition is made, for example a purchaser of the registered title). It provides that, as a general principle, a disponee's right to exercise owner's powers in relation to a registered title is unlimited unless there is some entry in the register or imposed under the 2002 Act. In effect, s. 26 operates to prevent the title of the disponee being questioned. Any dealings with the land in contravention of these limitations will not affect title to the land, though they may result in personal liability. That said, as s. 26(3) makes clear, if a disposition is unlawful, it will not be rendered lawful by its registration.

Let's take an example to clarify how s. 26 works. Imagine that Anita and Bilal are registered proprietors of land which they hold on trust. It is a term of the trust that the consent of a third party, Carol, is needed before the land can be sold. This is a limitation on Anita and Bilal's powers as owners and could be entered on the register. Imagine that this has not been done. Under s. 26, if Anita and Bilal sell the land to Dev without obtaining Carol's consent and act in contravention of the limitation, Dev's title is protected even though the disposition was unlawful. Crucially, registration of Dev as the new owner does not render the disposition lawful. Anita and Bilal have committed a breach of trust and can be sued personally by Carol but Dev's title is—thanks to s. 26—unimpeachable.[70]

One controversial issue has been the effect of a forged disposition of registered land. In particular, where the transferor pretends to be the registered proprietor and transfers the land to a purchaser, how far can that purchaser gain the protection of s. 26? In *Malory*, under s. 69 of the LRA 1925, the forerunner to s. 26 of the LRA 2002, the Court of Appeal held that a forged disposition gave the transferee the legal title but not the equitable title. *Malory* was subsequently followed in *Fitzwilliam v Richall Holding Services* (2013), a case decided under the provisions of the LRA 2002. In a recent decision, however, *Swift*,[71] the Court of Appeal held that *Malory* had been decided *per incuriam*[72] and the court could depart from the judgment. The court in *Swift* held that a forged disposition transfers both legal and equitable title to the transferee in spite of the forgery. When the register is later altered to rectify the mistake, the innocent transferee is entitled to an indemnity under Sch. 8 of the LRA 2002.[73]

2.4.3.5 The effect of a registrable disposition: The priority rules

This is the really important stuff! The LRA 2002 simplifies the rules on the priority of interests in registered land in ss. 28 and 29. Section 28 lays down the 'basic rule' of priority which provides that whether an interest affecting registered land is binding is determined

---

[70] Dev may be liable in equity for assisting in a breach of trust or for knowing receipt of trust property subject to what Dev knew of the trust and Anita and Bilal's actions.

[71] On which see R. Smith, 'Forgeries and Indemnity in Land Registration' 74(3) CLJ 401; P. Milne, 'Guarantee of Title and Void Dispositions: Work in Progress' [2015] Conv 356.

[72] A case decided *per incuriam* is one which fails to engage with contradictory, relevant or earlier binding authority (or statute) and therefore is regarded as wrong or not authoritative in law.

[73] We consider the operation of Sch. 8 of the LRA 2002 in section 2.8.

according to its date of creation: earlier-created interests take priority over later dispositions. Section 29 provides for a significant exception to the s. 28 basic rule of priority:

(1) If a registrable disposition of a registered estate is made for valuable consideration, completion of the disposition by registration has the effect of postponing to the interest under the disposition any interest affecting the estate immediately before the disposition whose priority is not protected at the time of registration.

(2) For the purposes of subsection (1), the priority of an interest is protected—

(a) in any case, if the interest—

(i)   is a registered charge or the subject of a notice in the register,

(ii)   falls within any of the paragraphs of Schedule 3, or

(iii) appears from the register to be excepted from the effect of registration . . .

Section 29(1) and (2) work like this: if there is a registrable disposition of a registered estate and that disposition is made for valuable consideration (i.e. money is paid) and the disposition is completed by registration, that disposition will take priority over any pre-existing proprietary rights affecting the land *except* (1) those pre-existing interests which are protected by the entry of a notice on the register[74] and (2) any overriding interests under Sch. 3.[75] As you can see, s. 29 consists of a series of moving or constituent parts. Figure 2.5 will help you visualize the operation of this vital provision.

The exception in s. 29 to the basic rule in s. 28 is highly significant and will apply in many of the most frequent transactions involving registered land: wherever there is a registrable disposition of a registered estate for valuable consideration. This will include the transfer of a registered estate, the grant out of a registered estate of a lease of seven or more years' duration, and the creation of a legal charge/mortgage. Importantly, s. 29(4) also makes clear that where a lease of seven years or less is granted—in other words, a lease which would not constitute a registrable disposition under s. 27—this lease is, nevertheless, given the protection of s. 29.

For s. 29 to operate it has to be shown that there is:

1. a registrable disposition;

2. of a registered estate;

3. for valuable consideration;

4. completed by registration.

In a problem question, for example, you must make sure all of these elements are present before you conclude that s. 29 applies. If these are not met, we fall back on the basic rule of priority in s. 28.

We have already explored what constitutes a registrable disposition in section 2.4.3.1[76] and the scope of registered estates.[77] The remaining two requirements for s. 29 to apply are that the disposition has been made for valuable consideration and completed by registration. According to s. 132(1) of the LRA 2002, valuable consideration does not include

---

[74] We explore the entry of notices in the register in section 2.5.

[75] We examine overriding interests in section 2.7.   [76] Section 27 of the LRA 2002.

[77] Ibid., ss. 2, 3, 4, and 27.

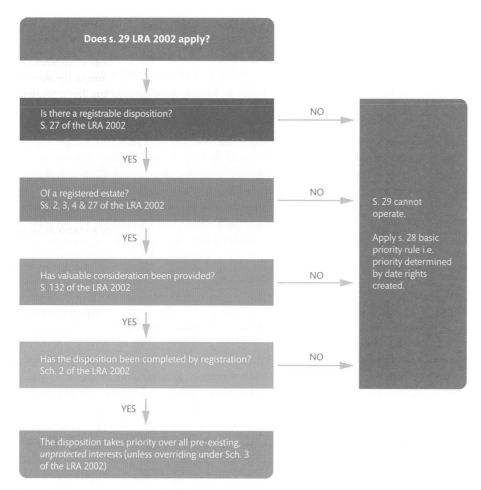

Figure 2.5 The operation of s. 29 of the LRA 2002

marriage consideration or a nominal consideration in money.[78] Clearly, transactions taking the form of gifts fall outside s. 29. As for 'completion by registration', as we noted earlier, we must look to Sch. 2 of the LRA 2002 which lays down the requirements here. These are quite technical and depend on the nature of the disposition but, by way of example, for disposition of a registered estate, Sch. 2 requires that the transferee's name (the person to whom the estate is transferred) be entered in the register as the new proprietor.

If all four elements of s. 29 are satisfied, the disponee (person to whom the disposition is made) takes the land free of *unprotected*, pre-existing interests[79] but will be bound by any earlier interest protected by entry of a notice or any interests which amount to an overriding

---

[78] In *Peffer v Rigg* (1977), £1 was held to amount to nominal consideration; note the Law Commission, in its 2018 report *Updating the Land Registration Act 2002*, recommends removing the exclusion of nominal consideration in s.132 LRA 2002—but we wait to see if Government implements this.

[79] Section 30 of the LRA 2002 makes similar provision as to dispositions of registered charges.

interests under Sch. 3. It is important to grasp that s. 29 does not mean the registered disposition takes priority over all pre-existing interests but rather takes priority over those prior *unprotected* interests only. Do note that, if operative, the protection of s. 29 applies 'at the time of registration' against pre-existing rights arising 'immediately before the disposition'.[80] This means that no protection is provided to rights arising in the registration gap.

Note the language of 'postponement' in s. 29. The significance of this language is open to discussion. In particular, what is the effect of postponement on those pre-existing, unprotected rights? This remains somewhat unclear. Norris J in *Halifax plc v Curry Popeck* (2008) supported the view that 'all [s. 29] . . . did was to destroy the subsistence of those interests as interests in land, leaving them capable of enforcement as personal rights'.[81] Dixon has argued, however, that s. 29 changed the pre-LRA 2002 law and that 'postponement' suggests that the pre-existing, unprotected interests lose priority but retain their proprietary character. Rather than wiping the slate clean, the interests remain proprietary and have the potential to take priority against rights not deriving from the registrable disposition.[82]

2.5 Notices and restrictions

It is an essential goal of the LRA that, in order to ensure the register is comprehensive and accurate, as many proprietary rights affecting a registered title as is feasible should be recorded on the register. Yet there is a category of interests which are neither registrable estates nor registrable dispositions, nor do they amount to overriding interests.[83] This category of interests can usefully be termed 'interests capable of protection by registration'. They consist largely of non-possessory proprietary rights and include interests such as options to purchase, restrictive covenants, and easements. The LRA 2002 sought to simplify and streamline the scheme for protection of these third party interests[84] and where previously there were four methods for protecting these interests,[85] today there are only two: the notice and the restriction. Notices protect the priority of rights where a disposition is made under s. 29 of the LRA 2002 whereas restrictions limit the circumstances in which a s. 29 disposition can be made at all. We explore notices and restrictions in this section.

2.5.1 What are notices and how do they work?

Notices are very straightforward. According to s. 32 of the LRA 2002, a notice is defined as 'an entry in the register in respect of the burden of an interest affecting a registered estate or charge'. Notices are entered in the Charges Register[86] against the registered title they affect and there are two principle types of notices: agreed notices and unilateral notices.

---

[80] Ibid., s. 29(1).   [81] *Halifax plc v Curry Popeck*, [49].

[82] M. Dixon, 'Priorities under the Land Registration Act 2002' (2009) 125 LQR 401.

[83] There are a small number of exceptions, e.g. a six-year legal lease which amounts to an overriding interest under Sch. 3, para. 1 but is, alternatively, also capable of protection by registration.

[84] See Law Commission Report No. 271, Part VI.

[85] Under the LRA 1925 protection was offered by way of four methods: notices, restrictions, cautions, and inhibitions.

[86] Land Registration Rules 2003, r. 84.

Remember that whether a notice has been entered is important when considering the effect of s. 29 of the LRA 2002, which, as you will recall, provides that an interest subject to the entry of a notice will take priority over a subsequent registered disposition of a registered estate.

As the name suggests, once entered the notice alerts any party acquiring the land to the interests affecting the title. Notices are entered in anticipation of the land they burden later being sold. A notice is like a post-it note, flagging up to potential purchasers of the registered title those interests which will be binding on them. Whether the notice is a unilateral notice or an agreed notice, it confers priority of the interest subject to the notice against transferees of the registered title. Importantly, the notice does not guarantee the validity of the interest.[87] The entry of a notice to protect, say, a right of way (easement) does not mean that the easement was validly created. The effect instead is that if the easement has been validly created, it will be binding on transferees. Cooke explains that notices should be viewed as 'recording' interests rather than guaranteeing them.[88]

So, which rights can be protected by the entry of a notice? Rather than provide a complete list of rights capable of protection by the entry of a notice, the LRA 2002 takes an exclusionary approach: s. 33 of the LRA 2002 specifies which interests *cannot* be protected by entry of a notice. The key interests for which a notice *may not* be entered are as follows:

- interests under a trust[89]—these interests can, however, be protected by entry of a restriction;[90]
- leases granted for a term of three years or less—but these interests are protected and will be enforceable as overriding interests;[91]
- restrictive covenants made between a lessor and lessee—these interests are governed by a distinct statutory regime outside the LRA 2002.[92]

Bearing in mind these exclusions, you will appreciate that a very broad range of interests *can* therefore be the subject of a notice. Of these, perhaps the most important are:

- easements (legal or equitable);
- leases of more than three years (but less than seven);[93]
- family home rights under the Family Law Act 1996;[94]
- **estate contracts;**
- restrictive covenants (other than those between landlord and tenants);
- rights arising from a claim to **proprietary estoppel**.[95]

---

[87] Section 32(3) of the LRA 2002.

[88] E. Cooke, *The New Law of Land Registration* (Oxford: Hart, 2003), 4.

[89] Interests under a trust are protected by way of overreaching which was introduced in section 1.6.6.2 and we explore in detail in this chapter in section 2.5.

[90] We discuss restrictions in section 2.5.4.   [91] Schedule 3, para. 1 of the LRA 2002. See section 2.7.4.

[92] Landlord and Tenant (Covenants) Act 1995.

[93] Remember that leases of more than seven years constitute registrable dispositions which must be completed by registration to operate at law.

[94] We discuss these in Chapter 6.   [95] We discuss proprietary estoppel in Chapter 8.

2.5.2 How do you get a notice on the register and what type of notice should it be?

A party wishing to have a notice entered on the Charges Register may make an application under s. 34 of the LRA 2002 but only those who 'claim to be entitled to the benefit of an interest affecting a registered estate or charge' can apply to the Registrar for this purpose and only if the interest in question is not excluded under s. 33. The application must specify whether the notice sought is an agreed notice or unilateral notice. Both types function in the same way in conferring priority; the difference turns on whether the registered proprietor consents to the notice being entered.

2.5.2.1 Agreed notices

An agreed notice will be entered by the Registrar if one of three circumstances listed in s. 34(3) is met:

1. the applicant is the registered proprietor or the person entitled to be registered as proprietor of the title affected by the interest which is to be the subject of the notice, or

2. the registered proprietor gives consent for the notice to entered, or

3. the Registrar is satisfied as to the validity of the applicant's claim.

Some interests can only be protected by an agreed notice and not by a unilateral notice. These are provided for in the Land Registration Rules 2003, r. 80 and include home rights under the Family Law Act 1996 and notices in respect of orders under the Neighbouring Land Act 1992, but do not concern yourself too much with the detail here. In applying for an agreed notice, the applicant must provide evidence accompanying their application. This will usually take the form of written proof of the registered proprietor's consent or written evidence of the creation of the right which would satisfy the Registrar of the validity of the applicant's claim.[96]

2.5.2.2 Unilateral notices

A unilateral notice will be entered in circumstances where the consent of the registered proprietor is not given, there is some measure of hostility or disagreement between the parties, or the validity of the applicant's claim cannot be verified.[97] The applicant must, nevertheless, produce some evidence that the interest that is to be subject of the notice actually exists.

When a unilateral notice is entered, the Registrar must notify the registered proprietor of the title to which the notice relates.[98] This notification gives the proprietor an opportunity to apply for cancellation of the notice and for the applicant to prove her interest.[99] A unilateral notice must identify itself as such and indicate who is the beneficiary of the notice—in other words, who benefits from it.[100]

---

[96] See Land Registration Rules 2003, r. 81(1)(c)(ii).

[97] In other words, where none of the conditions in s. 34(3) of the LRA 2002 is met.

[98] Ibid., s. 35(1).   [99] We discuss cancellation of notices in section 2.5.3.

[100] Section 35(2) of the LRA 2002.

2.5.2.3 Land Registrar's powers to enter a notice

In addition to agreed and unilateral notices, the Registrar also has a free-standing power, under s. 37 of the LRA 2002, to enter a notice relating to interests which are overriding on first registration of title, fall within a list provided in Sch. 1, and are not excluded from being protected by notice under s. 33.[101] If you look closely at the words of the section, you will see that the Registrar *may* but is not compelled to enter a notice under s. 37. The Registrar is, however, under a *duty* to enter a notice on the title of an estate burdened by an interest created by certain registrable dispositions. For example, the express grant of a legal easement over registered title is a registrable disposition under s. 27(2)(d). On registration, the Registrar will enter a notice against the registered title reflecting the burden of this easement.

Do not lose sight of the significance of a notice having been entered. In particular, recall that an interest subject to a notice will bind a subsequent registered proprietor under s. 29 of the LRA 2002 under the exception to the basic priority rule. Of course, if the interest subject to the notice is proved to be invalid, a registered proprietor will not be bound by it.[102]

2.5.3 **How do you cancel a notice on the register?**

Generally, agreed notices are not cancelled as, by their very nature, they have been entered with the consent of the parties and are rarely subject to challenge. The Land Registration Rules 2003 do, however, provide for a mechanism to cancel an agreed notice where there is evidence that the interest that is the subject of the notice has come to an end.[103]

Far more antagonistic are unilateral notices and it is here that issues of challenge and cancellation are most alive. This is understandable as unilateral notices, by their nature, do not have the consent of the registered proprietor. We need to separate two distinct issues: (1) removal of a unilateral notice and (2) cancellation. The beneficiary of a unilateral notice can apply, under s. 35(3) of the LRA 2002, for the notice to be removed. If the Registrar is satisfied that the application is 'in order', he will remove the notice. Cancellation of a unilateral notice[104] is a more contentious matter and involves a challenge to the validity of the interest subject to the notice. Cancellation is governed by s. 36 of the LRA which, through the Land Registration Rule 2003, sets out the full cancellation procedure: see Figure 2.6. In particular, note that only the registered proprietor of the estate affected by the notice or a person entitled to be registered as proprietor can apply to cancel a unilateral notice. The cancellation process essentially provides the beneficiary of the notice with an opportunity to demonstrate the validity of their interest and, if they do not do so, the notice will be cancelled.

---

[101] These are sometimes referred to as 'Registrar's Notices'.

[102] This is confirmed by s. 32(3) of the LRA 2002.

[103] Under Land Registration Rules 2003, r. 87.

[104] See section 2.9.1 of this chapter for a discussion of the recommendations made by the Law Commission in its latest report, *Updating the Land Registration Act 2002*, on changes it proposes to the process for cancellation of unilateral notices.

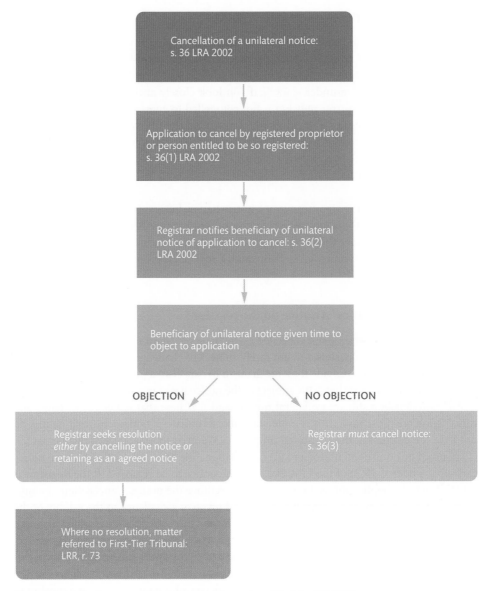

Figure 2.6 Application to cancel a unilateral notice under s. 36 of the LRA 2002

2.5.4 **Restrictions: What are they and how are they different from notices?**

As the name suggests, a restriction provides for limitations on the powers of disposition of the registered proprietor in relation to the registered estate. Put differently, restrictions limit the ability to deal with the land, for example selling it. Section 40 of the LRA defines a restriction as 'an entry in the register regulating the circumstances in which a disposition of a registered estate or change may be the subject of an entry in the register'. In practice, a restriction operates by restraining the proprietor in some way and by preventing entries on the register unless certain conditions are met.[105] These conditions may relate to the occurrence of an event, to a particular time period, or the requirement for consent of parties to deal with land.[106] Restrictions are entered in the Proprietorship Register.

Let's take the most common practical scenario in which restrictions arise: sale of registered land that is held under a trust. Here, a restriction may have been entered requiring that, if the land is to be sold, purchase money is paid to at least two trustees in order that overreaching take place with the result that equitable interests (e.g. those under a trust) are detached from the land and the purchaser takes the land free of these burdens. We encountered overreaching in Chapter 1 and examine it in detail in section 2.6 in this chapter. The relationship between overreaching and overriding interests (which we have already briefly discussed and return in section 2.7) is a common pitfall for students and a source of confusion. Overreaching is concerned with the detachment of equitable interests from land. It is most commonly relied upon as a defence by *purchasers* as a means of proving or guaranteeing that they have acquired the land free from beneficial interests under a trust. Overriding interests, on the other hand, are asserted by *interest holders* to argue they have an interest which is binding on a purchaser despite that interest not having been protected on the register. Much of the confusion in students' minds stems from the fact that interests which are *capable* of being overreached but which have *not been overreached* (e.g. for failure to meet the conditions for overreaching) can despite this still bind a purchaser by amounting to an overriding interest. We explore overreaching in more detail in section 2.6 and overriding interests in section 2.7.

Where a restriction has been entered, only where the conditions of that restriction are met will the Registrar register the purchaser as the new proprietor of the registered title.[107] As you can see, a restriction regulates dealings with registered land and is quite distinct from a notice which confers priority simply by its very entry in the register. In truth, restrictions are not directly concerned with the protection of third party interests in the way notices are.

Under s. 42(1) of the LRA 2002, the Registrar has the *power* to enter a restriction if it appears to him to be necessary or desirable to prevent invalid or unlawful dispositions of a registered estate, to enable overreaching to take place on disposition of a registered estate, or to otherwise protect a right or claim to a registered estate. Where he does so of his own initiative, the Registrar must notify the registered proprietor who is then given an opportunity to object. In one circumstance, the Registrar is under a duty and *must* enter a restriction. This is where two or more persons are registered as proprietors of a registered estate.[108] It is important not to exaggerate the protection offered by the entry of a restriction. In fact, in some circumstances, the perceived protection of a restriction is nothing more than illusory. The case of *City of London Building Society v Flegg* (1988) (which we

---

[105] Section 41 of the LRA 2002. The Registrar has a power, on an application by an interested party, to disapply the limitations in a restriction but this is very rarely exercised.

[106] Land Registration Rules, Sch. 4 provides a series of 'standard form' restrictions which might be used in the most commonplace circumstances.

[107] We explore overreaching in more detail in section 2.6. Restrictions are also very common in the bankruptcy context to avoid dealings with a bankrupt's registered title that would serve to defeat the interests of creditors.

[108] See s. 44 of the LRA 2002. The terms of this restriction are such as to ensure overreaching on disposition of the registered title.

explore fully in section 2.6.2.2) provides a perfect example of this. In this case, even if the Fleggs had entered a restriction in relation to their contribution-based equitable interest under a trust, this would not have altered the outcome in the case as the bank advancing mortgage funds had, in any event, paid the monies to two trustees thereby complying with the requirements for overreaching to take place. In addition, in *Flegg*, the trustees to whom the mortgage loan had been paid had spent the money and so the Fleggs received nothing. *Flegg* offers an important reminder that restrictions do not prevent dealings with land, do not confer priority (like notices) but rather, as the name indicates, merely restrict or limit these dealings. In most instances, it is relatively simple to comply with the terms of the restriction and so side-step the apparent protection restrictions offer—protection which is revealed as rather thin.

2.5.5 Failure to protect a third party interest by entry of a notice

The effect of s. 29 of the LRA 2002 is that third party interests which are not protected by the entry of a notice (and which do not amount to overriding interests[109]) lose priority to the interest of the registered disposition. That said, there are several caveats, qualifications to this position, which must be borne in mind. These represent instances where unregistered interest may, nevertheless, take priority despite not having been protected:

1. An unregistered interest will take priority where it amounts to an overriding interest under Sch. 3 of the LRA 2002.

2. An unregistered interest will take priority where the registered title has been transferred to a non-purchaser, for example, where the land is transferred as a gift or under a will.[110] Here, s. 29 cannot operate and the basic priority rule in s. 28 takes over. The donee of a gift or devisee under a will therefore takes subject to the pre-existing, unregistered interest.

3. An unregistered interest will take priority where there is a registrable disposition of a registered estate but the new owner does not register their title as required under s. 27 of the LRA 2002. In such a case, the new owner acquires an equitable title only. Falling outside the operation of s. 29, the basic rule of priority in s. 28 applies and, again, the new owner takes the land subject to pre-existing, unregistered interests.

4. An unregistered interest will take priority where the purchaser is seeking to rely on the statute as an instrument of fraud.[111] So, if a purchaser relies on the strict operation of s. 29 to argue that she is not bound by pre-existing, unprotected interests affecting the title in furtherance of some fraudulent activity, the court may uphold the validity and priority of that interest and the purchaser may, despite the lack of registration, be bound.

2.5.5.1 Avoiding the effects of loss of priority under s. 29

In addition to the qualifications outlined, a number of further avenues for escaping the effects of the loss of priority under s. 29 have been attempted where there has been a failure to protect an interest by entering a notice. It must be said that these attempts have met with varying degrees of success. We explore three of these here.

---

[109] Discussed in section 2.7.   [110] As confirmed in *Halifax plc v Curry Popeck*.
[111] For an example of this principle more broadly, see *Binions v Evans* (1972).

Arguments based on bad faith and notice

Might it be possible to argue that an unregistered interest may nevertheless be binding on a purchaser of the registered title on the basis of bad faith or notice of that unprotected interest? Attempts to mount arguments based on bad faith and notice are best captured by the case of *Peffer v Rigg*.

KEY CASE *Peffer v Rigg* (1977)

Facts: Mr Peffer and Mr Rigg who had married two sisters purchased together a house to provide a home for their shared mother-in-law. The house was, however, in Mr Rigg's sole name. He held it on trust for himself and Mr Peffer in equity. When Mr Rigg's marriage broke down, he transferred the house to his wife for just £1. Mr Peffer sought a declaration against Mrs Rigg that she held the property on trust for herself and Mr Peffer.

Legal issue: Was Mrs Rigg bound by Mr Peffer's beneficial interest in the house? Mrs Rigg, who knew of Mr Peffer's interest under the trust, argued, that Mr Peffer's interest was not binding on her under the provisions of s. 59 of the LRA 1925, which provided that purchasers were not to be concerned with matters not entered on the register 'whether he has or has not notice therefore, express, implied or constructive'. Section 3 of the LRA 1925 defined a 'purchaser' as 'purchaser in good faith for valuable consideration'.

Judgment: Graham J held that when the house was transferred to Mrs Rigg she knew the property was held on trust for Mr Peffer and that, as a result she could not be considered to have acted 'in good faith' for the purposes of s. 3 of the LRA 1925 as she had notice of something affecting the title.

Peffer, decided under the old law, is a heavily criticized judgment.[112] While many might agree with the result, the reasoning on the issue of notice has been lambasted as being entirely inconsistent with the philosophy of land registration and incompatible with the express provisions of the LRA 1925, which made plain that notice was irrelevant. In particular, the decision was attacked for equating Mrs Rigg's knowledge of Mr Peffer's interest with bad faith and for overlooking the plethora of obiter statements of the court on the irrelevance of notice to registered land regimes.[113] The Law Commission in its work leading to the LRA 2002 put beyond doubt that issues of good faith and notice were irrelevant and that the reasoning of Graham J in *Peffer* could 'cannot be supported'.[114] The Commission had initially proposed that a statutory statement be included in the 2002 Act to confirm that the doctrine of notice had no application but this ultimately was dropped. It is worth noting that some property academics (though a minority) support a role for notice as part

---

[112] See, for example, E. Cooke and P. O'Connor, 'Purchaser Liability to Third Parties in the English Land Registration System: A Comparative Perspective' (2004) 120 LQR 640, 653–4.

[113] See, amongst others, dicta of Cross J in *Strand Securities Ltd v Caswell* (1965), [30] that 'it is vital to the working of the land registration system that notice of something which is not on the register of the title in question shall not affect a transferee unless it is an overriding interest'.

[114] Law Commission Report No. 254, [3.44].

of a registration scheme in order to bring a fairer, more equitable and ethical element into the issue of priority in registered land.[115] One voice weighing the arguments is Smith:[116]

> One can readily comprehend the argument that a purchaser who is aware of an unprotected right should not be able to take advantage of a failure to register it. Whilst one of the most important benefits of registration is the ouster of constructive notice, protection of purchasers who are aware of unprotected interests is less easy to defend. As has been observed time and time again, the courts strive to find means of holding these purchasers bound: judges obviously feel that justice points in that direction. That may be reasonable on the facts of a particular case, but the question facing the law reformer is whether it causes an unacceptable level of uncertainty for purchasers generally.

Despite some proponents arguing for a continued role for notice under the LRA 2002, the doctrine of notice plays no role under the 2002 legislation. The Commission was at pains to note, additionally, the 'safety valve' offered by the possibility of personal remedies where the transferor or transferee of registered land has acted unreasonably. We discuss these later.

Arguments based on constructive trust

Arguments founded on the principles of '**constructive trust**' have proved more successful in permitting unprotected, unregistered interests to enjoy priority against purchasers of a registered title. We will examine constructive trusts in the family home context in Chapter 6, but for now, it suffices to know that a constructive trust is an **implied trust** (i.e. there is no express declaration of trust between the parties) so the trust is, if you like, 'constructed' by the court having regard to the actions and intentions of the parties. In short, a constructive trust is implied where a purchaser has promised to give effect to an interest over registered title and the court is satisfied that the purchaser's conscience is affected such that it would be inequitable to allow her to deny the validity of the interest. A personal constructive trust will be imposed ensuring priority of that interest: *Lyus v Prowsa* (1982); *Lloyd v Dugdale* (2001). That said, the courts have been keen to restrain this avenue so that only in very limited circumstances will a constructive trust be established successfully.

KEY CASE *Lyus v Prowsa* (1982)

Facts: A development company, Pennock, was the registered proprietor of a parcel of land which had been charged by way of mortgage to a bank. The company entered into a contract with the claimants, Mr and Mrs Lyus, under which it agreed to build a house on a plot of land and then sell the land to them on completion. Before the house was built, the company became insolvent and was wound up. The bank, as **mortgagee**, decided to sell the plot of land to Prowsa Developments 'subject to and with the benefit of' the contract entered into between Mr and Mrs Lyus and Pennock. The transfer itself, however, made no mention of the contract.

Legal issue: Could Mr and Mrs Lyus enforce the terms of the contract with Pennock against Prowsa on the basis that Prowsa had acquired the land 'subject to' the contract even though there was no

→

---

[115] See, amongst others, G. Battersby, 'Informal Transactions in Land, Estoppel and Registration' (1995) 58 MLR 637; J. Howell, 'Notice: A Broad and a Narrow View' [1996] Conv 34; R. Smith, 'Land Registration: Reform at Last' in P. Jackson and D. Wilde (ed.), *The Reform of Property Law* (Dartmouth: Ashgate, 1997), 129.
[116] Smith, 'Land Registration: Reform at Last', 136.

> →
>
> entry of this on the register and no mention in the transfer? Mr and Mrs Lyus sought a declaration that the contract was binding, enforceable, and an order for specific performance.
>
> Judgment: Dillon J ordered specific performance of the contract. Prowsa had acquired the land in the full knowledge of Mr and Mrs Lyus's contract and, therefore, it would be wrong to allow the registration regime of the LRA 1925 to be used as an instrument of fraud and to permit Prowsa to disregard the contract and gain priority. It would be inequitable for Prowsa to renege on the undertaking it had made, so a constructive trust was imposed with the result that the contract was binding on Prowsa.

In *Lloyd*, the broad approach to constructive trust adopted in *Lyus* was narrowed significantly. In this case, Sir Christopher Slade made plain that:[117]

> There is no general principle which renders it unconscionable for a purchaser of land to rely on want of registration of a claim against registered land, even though he took with express notice. A decision to the contrary would defeat the purpose of the legislature in introducing a system of registration . . .

Sir Christopher Slade laid down the circumstances in which a constructive trust would arise, noting:[118]

- Even where sale of land is made subject to possible incumbrances or prior interests, there is no general rule that a constructive trust will be imposed to give priority to those interests.[119]
- The court will only impose a constructive trust if satisfied that the conscience of the newly registered proprietor is affected so that it would be inequitable to allow him to deny the claimant's interest in the property.
- In determining whether conscience is affected, of crucial importance is whether the newly registered proprietor has 'undertaken a new obligation, not otherwise existing, to give effect to the relevant incumbrance or prior interest'. Only where such a new obligation is undertaken will a constructive trust be imposed. One example of a new obligation is proof of a reduced purchase price agreed on the basis that the new proprietor will give effect to the prior interest.

In requiring evidence of a 'new obligation', *Lloyd* represents a clear brake on the *Lyus* authority. A constructive trust will not be imposed 'in reliance on inference from slender materials'.[120] *Lyus* and *Lloyd* were considered more recently in *Chaudhary v Yavuz* (2013).[121] In *Chaudhary*, a contract for sale of land made general, non-specific references to 'incumbrances on the property'. The issue was whether an unprotected right of way (easement) was binding on the new owner. The Court of Appeal held that *Lyus* was correctly decided

---

[117] *Lloyd*, [50].   [118] Ibid., [52].

[119] See dicta of Dillon J in *Lyus* at 1054 (approved by Fox LJ in *Ashburn Anstalt v Arnold* (1989)) and on which Sir Christopher Slade drew in reaching this view.

[120] *Ashburn Anstalt v Arnold*, per Fox LJ, [26].

[121] On which see B. McFarlane, 'Eastenders, Neighbours and Upstairs Downstairs' [2013] Conv 74.

but did not apply on the facts. There were, said the court, three key differences between *Lyus* and this case because in *Lyus*:

1. The third party rights in question were specifically identified in the contract for sale.

2. The bank's mortgage already took priority so there was no need for the bank to protect itself as regards enforcement of the Lyus' contract.

3. There was nothing more by way of registration that Mr and Mrs Lyus could have done to ensure a purchaser from the bank would be bound by their contract.[122]

By contrast, in *Chaudhary* the contract was in general terms only and a notice could have been entered in the Charges Register to ensure protection of the right of way. Lloyd LJ added that *Lyus* was 'a very unusual case, and is not likely to be followed in more than a few others'.[123] The decisions in *Lloyd* and *Yavuz* put strict limits on when a constructive trust will be imposed so as to give priority to a prior, unregistered interest. This supports the primacy of title registration but also seeks to ensure that Parliament's intentions in legislating are not undermined.

Personal claims

The Law Commission has recognized that an interest which is unprotected and which has lost priority under s. 29, may, nevertheless, give rise to 'a wide range of personal remedies'[124] either against the party transferring the land or the party acquiring it, the transferee 'who in some way behaves improperly'.[125] The precise nature of these claims depends entirely on the circumstances of each case; however, the following gives a flavour of the potential scope of personal liability:

- breach of contract;
- misrepresentation or undue influence;
- breach of trust (where registered land held under a trust is transferred to a third party in breach of the terms of that trust);
- knowing receipt of trust property (where registered land held under a trust is transferred to someone knowing of the breach).

As Cooke and O'Connor note:[126]

> *In personam* liability now becomes the one vehicle available for the courts when faced with sharp conduct, on the part of a purchaser, of a kind that should disentitle him to the protection of the registration system. It is therefore to be expected that *in personam* liability will be developed rather further than the Law Commission perhaps anticipated.

The imposition of personal liability is not, however, without controversy as the availability of personal liability has the very real potential to undermine fundamental aspects

---

[122] They had entered a caution to protect their position against purchasers from the original development company, Pennock, but this did not affect sale by the bank to a purchaser.

[123] *Chaudhary*, [61].

[124] Law Commission Report No. 254, [3.48]; see also M. Thompson, 'Registration, Fraud and Notice' (1985) 44(2) CLJ 280.

[125] Law Commission Report No. 254, [3.48].

[126] Cooke and O'Connor, 'Purchaser Liability to Third Parties in the English Land Registration System', 666.

of the registration regime—in particular, the conclusiveness of the register and the protections afforded to purchasers. Equally, these claims might be seen as reintroducing aspects of constructive notice into a scheme designed specifically to exclude these considerations.

2.6 Overreaching

You were introduced to overreaching in Chapter 1[127] and we have already touched on it in this chapter. Overreaching is essentially a 'defence mechanism'[128] facilitating conveyancing, assisting purchasers, and ensuring efficient dealings with land. Overreaching achieves this by allowing a purchaser to acquire land free of certain equitable interests by detaching those interests from the land so that the purchaser takes the land unencumbered of these burdens. Whilst this is of clear advantage to the purchaser, equitable interest holders are not entirely unrewarded. An attempt is made to balance the protection for purchasers against the rights of those enjoying equitable interests in the land. In this way, overreaching goes to wider debates encircling land law (i.e. the tension between a view of land as 'static security', on the one hand, and as 'dynamic security', on the other). We touched on the static/dynamic dichotomy in section 2.2.1.[129] O'Connor explains it as follows:[130]

> [S]tatic security . . . protects the rights of existing owners [and interest holders] at the expense, if necessary, of purchasers . . . Conveyancing rules based on static security suited a society emerging from feudalism where land ownership was confined to the privileged few, and was rarely traded. By the mid-19th century, England [was] developing market economies in which value id captured through exchange. The enactment of registration of title legislation in mid-19th century England and Australia decisively shifted the conveyancing law towards the opposing principle of dynamic security. Dynamic security is provided by legal rules that protect the reasonable expectations of those who purchase in good faith . . . by reducing or eliminating the risk that the purchaser's title will be the subject to unknown prior claims and title defects. This lowers transaction costs by limiting the inquiries that purchasers need to make . . . De Soto explains that, while the law in Western countries seeks to promote both types of security, dynamic security is favoured because of its greater economic importance.

In this section, we explore more precisely what overreaching actually is and how it fits into the scheme of the LRA 2002. As we go, keep the static/dynamic debate in mind. Owen has argued that overreaching favours too strongly dynamic security and the interests of purchasers at the expense of beneficiaries and should be reformed to redress this imbalance.[131] Do you agree?

---

[127] In section 1.6.5.

[128] See J. G. Owen and D. Cahill, 'Overreaching—Getting the Right Balance' [2017] Conv 26.

[129] See O'Connor, 'Registration of Title in England and Australia'; R. Demogue, 'Security' in A. Fouillée et al. (eds.), *Modern French Legal Philosophy* (Boston: The Boston Book Co., 1916).

[130] O'Connor, 'Registration of Title in England and Australia', 85–6.

[131] See, most recently, Owen and Cahill, 'Overreaching—Getting the Right Balance'.

2.6.1 **The nature and effect of overreaching**

The concept of overreaching is not a creation of the LRA 2002 nor of the LRA 1925 and applies equally to unregistered land as it does to registered titles.[132] So what is it? Overreaching describes the process under which particular equitable interests in land (practically speaking we mean equitable interests under a trust) that might otherwise potentially bind a purchaser of that land are detached from the land and are translated into the proceeds of sale. We say that the interests 'sound' in or are 'commuted' into their equivalent monetary value in the proceeds of sale. In essence, overreaching operates where there is a conveyance of land (e.g. sale of land) and serves to substitute for money certain equitable interests affecting that land.

Where overreaching takes place, those pre-existing equitable interests are said to have been 'overreached' and the purchaser acquires the land entirely free of those interests: the interests are wiped clean from the land. This is clearly a very useful device for the purchaser as a means of avoiding being fixed with land subject to unwanted proprietary burdens. At the same time, a compromise is achieved by providing the equitable interest holder with money—in other words, compensation in return for the loss of their interests: see Figure 2.7. How far the balance is fairly struck is open to some debate. In particular, do interest holders want money? Perhaps they have a particular attachment to the land that no amount of money could compensate. Equally, overreaching can take place without the consent of the interest holder. Generally speaking—and as O'Connor notes—modern land law favours the view of land as dynamic security protecting purchasers in order to ensure the free alienability of land. Overreaching can be seen as evidence of just that.

2.6.2 **The requirements for overreaching**

For overreaching to operate, two requirements must be satisfied:

1. There must be an equitable interest which is *capable* of being overreached.

2. The statutory conditions for overreaching must be met: ss. 2 and 27 of the LPA 1925.

We will look at each in turn.

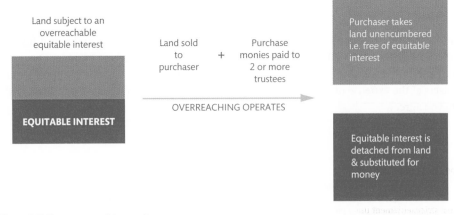

Figure 2.7 How overreaching works

---

[132] We consider overreaching in unregistered land in section 3.4.4.

2.6.2.1 Requirement 1: There is an equitable interest capable of being overreached

Not all interests in land are 'overreachable'—in other words, capable of being overreached. Section 2 of the LPA 1925 tells us which interests can be overreached and which interests under s. 2(3) are excluded; for example, an equitable lease, equitable easement or estate contract can never be overreached.[133] For our purposes, we can think of overreaching as applying principally to equitable interests under a trust.[134] For interests that cannot be overreached, their priority is determined by applying the usual rules on priority under ss. 28 and 29 as discussed in this chapter.[135]

2.6.2.2 Requirement 2: The statutory conditions for overreaching are met

In addition to the requirement for an overreachable interest, the statutory machinery of the LPA 1925 must also be fulfilled. These statutory conditions for overreaching are provided in ss. 2 and 27 of the LPA 1925:

- There must be 'a conveyance to a purchaser of a legal estate in land' (s. 2(1) of the LPA 1925).
- Purchase/mortgage monies must be paid to at least two trustees or a trust corporation (s. 27 of the LPA 1925).

As to the first condition, s. 205(1)(ii) defines a 'conveyance' as including 'a mortgage, charge, lease . . . ' and we know that reference to 'a legal estate' includes both freehold and leasehold land. Commonly, overreaching will operate where land subject to a trust is sold or mortgaged. In the family home context,[136] those enjoying equitable interests under a **trust of land** will often also be the holders of the legal title. This means that if the land is sold (for which all legal co-owners must consent), overreaching will take place without any difficulty. The problems arise where those holding the legal title are different people to those with beneficial interests in the land under a trust. It is this situation which is most frequently encountered when studying overreaching as part of a land law course so we confine our discussion to this scenario in this section.[137] To demonstrate how overreaching works in practice, we can look to one of the leading cases: *Flegg*.

KEY CASE *City of London Building Society v Flegg* (1988)

Facts: Mr and Mrs Maxwell Brown purchased a property, Bleak House, in 1977 for £34,000 with half the purchase monies being advanced by Mr and Mrs Flegg, Mrs Maxwell Brown's parents. The property was registered in the names of Mr and Mrs Maxwell Brown. This gave rise to a trust. In 1982, the

→

---

[133] See s. 2(3) of the LPA 1925 as to excluded interests. [134] See, for an example, *Flegg*.

[135] As to equitable interests, this usually comes down to the question of whether a notice has been entered to protect the equitable interest or whether it constitutes an overriding interest under Schs 1 or 3.

[136] We explore trusts of land and the family home context in Chapters 5 and 6.

[137] Under s. 2(1) of the LPA 1925 overreaching can also take place where there is a conveyance of land subject to a strict settlement under the Settled Land Act 1925; a conveyance by a mortgagee or personal representative in exercise of his paramount powers in relation to a deceased owner's land, and where there is a conveyance made under order of the court.

> ➜
>
> Maxwell Browns mortgaged the property in favour of the City of London Building Society in the sum of £37,500. Mr and Mrs Flegg were entirely unaware of the mortgage. The Maxwell Browns defaulted on mortgage payments and the Building Society brought proceedings to recover possession of the property. The Fleggs, who were living in the property, sought to defend the action by arguing they had acquired a beneficial interest as a result of their contribution and that this was binding on the Building Society as an overriding interest.
>
> Legal issue: Had the Fleggs' equitable, contribution-based interest in the property been overreached when the Building Society advanced mortgage monies?
>
> Judgment: In the House of Lords, the Fleggs' interest was found to have been overreached and therefore took effect in the proceeds of sale only. The interest was overreachable and mortgage monies had been advanced to two trustees, Mr and Mrs Maxwell Brown. Overreaching therefore operated to detach the Fleggs' interest from the land. There was no longer any interest capable of being binding on the Building Society.

In *Flegg*, overreaching took place and the interests under the trust were detached from the land. However, on the facts, Mr and Mrs Maxwell Brown had no money from which Mr and Mrs Flegg could be compensated. Therefore, the Fleggs walked away with nothing despite the operation of overreaching. It is in this result that the protection of overreaching for beneficiaries might be said to be illusory and the results can be harsh and unjust. Note also that overreaching operates without the beneficiaries' consent. In *Baker v Craggs* (2018),[138] the Court of Appeal confirmed that the grant of an easement did not satisfy the requirement, under s. 2 of the LPA 1925, for a 'conveyance of a legal estate in land' for the purposes of overreaching. In this case, Mr and Mrs Charlton sold part of farmland they owned to Mr Craggs in January 2012. The transfer was not registered until May 2012 and, in the interim period between sale and registration, the Charltons transferred other land to the Bakers. The conveyance purported to grant the Bakers a right of way over the land already sold to Mr Craggs. The transfer to the Bakers was registered prior to that of Mr Craggs. Falling into the registration gap, Mr Craggs would therefore be bound by the right of way unless he could show he was in actual occupation[139] when the right was granted and that his interest had not been overreached. The High Court held that whilst Mr Craggs had been in actual occupation, the grant of the easement amounted to conveyance of a legal estate in land and Mr Craggs' interest had indeed been overreached when the Bakers paid the purchase price to two trustees. However, the Court of Appeal disagreed; holding that while an easement was a legal estate, it was not, for the purposes of s. 2 of the LPA 1925, a 'conveyance of a legal estate in land' because, under s. 1 of the LPA 1925, the only estates capable of subsisting or being conveyed at law were freehold and leasehold estates. Accordingly, overreaching could not operate. If those drafting the overreaching provisions had intended s. 2 to extend to the granting of a legal easement, said the court, this would have been made clear. Mr Craggs' interest had therefore not been overreached.

---

[138] For a discussion of this case, see P. Sparkes, 'Overreaching, trust breaking and underreaching' (2019) 1 Conv 14.
[139] Thereby amounting to an overriding interest under Sch. 3, para. 2 of the LRA 2002.

A number of further observations can be made about the operation of overreaching:

1. Where purchase/mortgage monies are paid to just a single trustee, overreaching will not take place and the equitable interest will remain enforceable against the purchaser/mortgagee: *Boland*. Purchasers or mortgagees will often insist on the appointment of a second trustee if none is present to guarantee that the effects of overreaching are realized.

2. Where there is fraud, overreaching cannot take place: *HSBC v Dyche* (2009). Here, Mr Collelldevall owned a property but became bankrupt. An order for sale as well as a possession order were granted but not enforced. Subsequently, the property was transferred to Mr Collelldevall's daughter, Mrs Dyche and her husband for a significant undervalue of £25,000 (with the **trustee in bankruptcy's** consent) in order to allow the Collelldevalls to remain living there. This was facilitated by the Dyches taking out a mortgage of the property. The court accepted Mr Collelldevall's assertion that there had been an agreement that once the mortgage has been discharged (the Collelldevalls having agreed to pay the instalments), the Dyches would re-transfer the property back into Mr Collelldevall's name. On this basis, the Dyches were said to hold the property on constructive trust for the Collelldevalls.

   Mrs Collelldevall later died and Mr Collelldevall remained in occupation. Mrs Dyche subsequently divorced her husband and transferred the property herself into her sole name (paying Mr Dyche £5,000 in divorce proceedings). She then remortgaged the property to HSBC Bank. In the application form, she claimed to be landlord of the property and that Mr Collelldevall was her tenant by forging the latter's signature. She fell into arrears on the mortgage and HSBC sought possession. Mr Collelldevall, who knew nothing of the remortgage, argued, in an attempt to defeat of the possession proceedings, that his beneficial interest (under the constructive trust) coupled with his actual occupation of the property gave him an overriding interest binding on HSBC. HSBC argued that his interest had been overreached when the mortgage had been granted. The High Court held that Mrs Dyche had no intention of re-transferring the property back to her father once the mortgage had been discharged. She had acted in breach of trust (i.e. ultra vires) in transferring the property to herself and dishonestly in remortgaging it through forgery. Overreaching of Mr Collelldevall's interest did not take place as loan monies had been paid to Mrs Dyche only, a single trustee, and she could not be said to have been purchasing 'in good faith' within the definition of purchaser in s. 205(1)(xi) of the LPA 1925. Mr Collelldevall's interest was therefore overriding and the property was to be re-transferred to him free of the HSBC mortgage. The decision is problematic, however, because there is nothing in the overreaching provisions of ss. 2 or 27 LPA 1925 to suggest that 'good faith' is a requirement for overreaching. *Dyche* is perhaps best interpreted, then, as authority for the proposition that where there is fraud, overreaching cannot take place.

3. Where no capital monies are raised on the conveyance (e.g. a mortgage to discharge debt or secure future debt), there is no requirement for payment to two or more trustees (s. 27 of the LPA 1925) for overreaching to operate: *State Bank of India v Sood* (1997).[140] In *Sood*, two members of the Sood family mortgaged the family home, which was

---

[140] For a discussion of the case, see M. Thompson, 'Overreaching Without Payment' [1997] Conv 134.

subject to a trust of land, in order to discharge present and future indebtedness relating to their family textile business. When mortgage payments were not met, the bank sought possession of the home and argued that the equitable interests of the wider Sood family who lived in the premises had been overreached. The Soods argued that, as no capital monies had been paid, the statutory conditions for overreaching under s. 27 of the LPA 1925 had not been satisfied. The court held that this requirement of payment to two or more trustees only applied where the conveyance gave rise to capital monies. If no capital monies arose, there was no requirement to pay two or more trustees. Overreaching had therefore taken place.

4. In *Shami v Shami* (2012) in the High Court, the approach taken in *Sood* was affirmed. The court at first instance in *Shami* appeared to go even further in supporting (obiter only) the view that overreaching could operate where there was a conveyance involving just a single trustee. This may be a difficult argument to sustain given that s. 2(1) of the LPA 1925 references 'trustees of land' in the plural. Equally, it may not be desirable if we accept that the requirement of payment to 'two or more' trustees is designed to offer a counterbalance against the 'forcible translation of interests into (possibly non-existent) capital money by the act of a person acting alone'.[141]

5. In *Mortgage Express v Lambert* (2016),[142] the Court of Appeal held that a mere equity arising from an unconscionable bargain amounted to a proprietary right (by reason of s. 116 LRA 2002) and that this is a right capable of being overreached. Ms Lambert owned the leasehold of a flat worth £120,000. She was in financial difficulty and so agreed that two fraudsters could buy the leasehold for £30,000. The fraudsters took out a mortgage against the flat, defaulted on repayments, and the lender sought possession of the property. In a decision which stretches the concept of overreaching, the Court of Appeal confirmed that Ms Lambert had a right to set aside the sale on the grounds that it was an unconscionable bargain, and that this right was a 'mere equity' which, under s. 116 LRA 2002, amounted to a proprietary right. This right was one capable of being overreached and had been overreached by payment of the mortgage monies to the two fraudsters. Mere equities (along with interests arising by estoppel: *Birmingham Midshires Mortgage Services Ltd v Sabherwal* (2000)) are therefore overreachable including those arising from unconscionable bargains. *Lambert* suggests that overreaching is not as narrow a concept as may have been thought.

2.6.2.3 What if the requirements for overreaching are not met?

Where the two conditions for overreaching are not satisfied, overreaching cannot operate. This means those equitable interests remain attached to the land. Most commonly this arises where there is a failure of payment to two or more trustees or a trust corporation. The question becomes whether these non-overreached interests are binding on a third party acquiring the land. Consider the following three scenarios:

---

[141] See M. Dixon, 'Reaching Up for the Box in the Attic' [2013] Conv 165.

[142] For a discussion of this interesting case, see M. Dixon, 'Priority, Overreaching and Surprises under the Land Registration Act 2002' (2017) 133 LQR 173.

- Overreaching has not taken place and the third party acquiring the land is a purchaser (i.e. provides consideration): If a purchaser registers her title and overreaching has not taken place, under s. 29 of the LRA 2002, that purchaser will take the land free of pre-existing, non-overreached equitable interests that are not otherwise protected on the register under s. 29 of the LRA 2002.[143]

- Overreaching has not taken place and the third party acquiring the land is a non-purchaser (i.e. provides no consideration): If a non-purchaser acquires the land (e.g. by way of gift), under the basic priority rule in s. 28 of the LRA 2002, the third party will be bound by the pre-existing but non-overreached interest according to the date of creation of the interests.

- Overreaching has not taken place yet an overriding interest can be established: If despite a failure of overreaching, the non-overreached interest nevertheless amounts to an overriding interest under Sch. 3 of the LRA 2002, that equitable interest will still bind the purchaser of the land under the operation of s. 29 of the LRA 2002. This happens more frequently than you might think as, for example, in *Boland* where, despite no overreaching taking place, Julia Boland was able establish an overriding interest as a result of her actual occupation of the home.[144]

Remember: do not confuse overreaching with overriding interests. As we noted in section 2.5.4, they are quite different and must be kept firmly separate in your mind. To avoid confusion, start your analysis by considering if overreaching is possible and whether it has, in fact, taken place. If overreaching cannot take place or has failed, move to consider whether the non-overreached interest could nonetheless amount to a binding overriding interest. Let's explore overriding interests.

2.7 Unregistered interests that override

We turn now to consider those interests which do not appear on the register but nevertheless are binding on purchasers and others acquiring registered land. Quite unavoidably, the very existence of a category of unregistered interests which are enforceable despite non-registration is a direct affront to the very objective of the registration project. As the Law Commission has noted:[145]

> Overriding interests ... present a very significant impediment to one of the main objectives of the [Land Registration] Bill, namely that the register should be as complete a record of the title as it can be, with the result that it should be possible for title to land to be investigated almost entirely on-line.

Before we explore the scope of these 'overriding interests', we begin by considering the rationale for this category of unprotected yet enforceable rights.

---

[143] Unless an overriding interest can be established.

[144] We examine actual occupation and return to the case of *Boland* in section 2.7.

[145] Law Commission Report No. 271, [2.24].

2.7.1 **The nature and rationale for overriding interests**

Overriding interests are nothing new and existed under the LRA 1925. The category is preserved under the LRA 2002 regime yet it is worth asking why? The operation of overriding interests might be seen as deeply unfair to purchasers who, without enquiries and inspection of the land, may know nothing of the existence of these rights yet be bound by them. The Law Commission identified a number of reasons to preserve the status of overriding interests, noting that 'most overriding interests do have one shared characteristic . . . namely that it is unrealistic to expect a person who has the benefit of the right to register it'.[146] In addition, overriding status offers a protection to those interests which arise informally, including rights under a trust of land (protected by actual occupation), and those interests for which it would prove overly burdensome and inconvenient to expect registration, such as short leases. As Jackson notes:[147]

> The rationale that underpins the informal acquisition of interests in land would be defeated by a prescriptive method of ensuring their priority against a purchaser. The rationale is relatively straightforward: a category of overriding interests must be retained as it is unreasonable to expect these particular interests to be registered. Of course, as Cooke has observed, whilst the rationale is easily stated, the effect of retention of the category has wider consequences for the registration project and the static/dynamic security debate; clearly any suggestion of a fully comprehensive and complete register must be regarded as 'a myth'.[148]

2.7.2 **Overriding interests under the LRA 2002**

Whilst the category of overriding interests was preserved under the LRA 2002, the new scheme nevertheless employed a series of strategies to restrict the impact of these interests:

- A number of interests previously overriding under the LRA 1925 would lose overriding status.[149]

- The ambit of certain overriding interests would be tightened (e.g. rights of those in actual occupation under Sch. 3, para. 2).

- A number of interests previously overriding under the LRA 1925 would be phased out over a period of ten years following the entry into force of the 2002 Act.[150]

- A new duty of disclosure[151] would be introduced under which a person applying to be registered as title owner would be required to provide to Land Registrar information of any unregistered interests affecting the estate so that they could be registered.

---

[146] Law Commission Report No. 254, [4.4].

[147] N. Jackson, 'Title by Registration and Concealed Overriding Interests: The Cause and Effect of Antipathy to Documentary Proof' (2003) 119 LQR 660.

[148] E. Cooke, *Land Law* (Oxford: Oxford University Press, 2012), 76.

[149] These include: rights of chancel repair liability, rights acquired under the Limitation Act 1980, and rights of persons in receipt of rent and profits.

[150] These included: franchises, manorial rights, Crown and corn rents, and lost overriding status at midnight on 12 October 2013.

[151] Under s. 71 of the LRA 2002.

- There would be a simplification in the protection of third party interests by entry of a notice[152] and expansion in the third party rights capable of being so protected.

Despite these measures, the category of 'unregistered interests that override' survives and, as a result, continues to seriously undermine the registered land project and the mirror principle, in particular. This residual bundle of rights, retained on the grounds of policy (both social and economic) creates a deep 'crack in the mirror'[153] that the register is said to represent. So long as this category exists, a measure of inspection and inquiry of land beyond a mere electronic search of the register will be necessary. Is this not precisely the exercise that the registration project sought to avoid?

Under the scheme of the LRA, overriding interests operate in two contexts:

- unregistered interests which override first registration: Sch. 1 of the LRA 2002, and
- unregistered interests which override a registered disposition—in other words, disposition of an already registered title: Sch. 3 of the LRA 2002.

Overriding interests provided for in Schs. 1 and 3 are very similar in nature but, understandably, those overriding first registration under Sch. 1 are slightly broader in scope. This is to ensure that when previously unregistered land is first brought onto the register the first registered proprietor is not able to rely on registration as a way of escaping the effect of rights that were previously binding on her. An application for registration should not be a means of avoiding being bound by rights in land. Whilst Sch. 1 is clearly an important provision, we will focus our attention in this chapter on Sch. 3 which, with the diminishing incidence of unregistered land, will increasingly be the first port of call for an assessment of overriding interests. Where there are differences between Sch. 1 and Sch. 3 these will, however, be flagged up.

2.7.3 Unregistered interests which override first registration: Sch. 1 of the LRA 2002

When a person becomes a first registered proprietor of freehold or leasehold land, they take that land subject to the overriding interests listed in Sch. 1:[154]

- paragraph 1: legal leases granted for a term of seven years or less[155]
- paragraph 2: interests of persons in actual occupation
- paragraph 3: legal easements and *profits à prendre*
- paragraph 4: customary rights[156]

---

[152] This was achieved by abolishing two of the existing forms of protection: cautions against dealings and inhibitions.

[153] D. Hayton, *Registered Land*, 3rd edn (1981), 76.

[154] See s. 11 of the LRA 2002 as to freehold and s. 12 as to leasehold.

[155] Recall, legal leases granted for more than seven years are registrable titles, trigger compulsory first registration, and are to be substantively registered: ibid., s. 4.

[156] Customary rights are those enjoyed by all inhabitants in a particular locality.

- paragraph 5: public rights[157]
- paragraph 6: local land charges.[158]

Paragraphs 1–3 are, by some way, the most important rights which override first registration and those of persons in actual occupation of land have the greatest capacity to override first registration. We explore actual occupation and what it entails in some detail as we turn now to discuss Sch. 3.

2.7.4 Unregistered interests which override a registered disposition: Sch. 3 of the LRA 2002

The interests which override a registered disposition of land are listed in Sch. 3 and appear remarkably similar to—though, in fact, are less extensive than—those under Sch. 1. Recall that a registrable disposition includes a transfer of a registered title, sale, grant of a lease of more than seven years, or mortgage. Where there is a registrable disposition of a registered title, the registered proprietor takes that land subject to the overriding interests listed in Sch. 3:[159]

- paragraph 1: legal leases granted for a term of seven years or less
- paragraph 2: interests of persons in actual occupation—subject to exceptions not applicable under Sch. 1
- paragraph 3: legal easements and *profits à prendre*
- paragraph 4: customary rights
- paragraph 5: public rights
- paragraph 6: local land charges.

We will say no more of customary and public rights nor of local land charges. We do, however, need to unpack a little further Sch. 3, paras. 1–3—in particular, actual occupation, which is by far the most important class of overriding interest.

2.7.4.1 Short legal leases as overriding interests: Sch. 3, para. 1

Short leases are important in land law because they are extremely commonplace and are the arrangement under which an increasing number of people now establish a stable home life as home-ownership rates in the country fall. As the Law Commission explained in its work leading to the LRA 2002, the policy behind short leases enjoying overriding status stems from their 'short duration and the risk that they would clutter the register'.[160] It was also felt unreasonable to expect those with short leases to register them. Under the old law,

---

[157] Public rights are rights exercisable by anyone, whether they own land or not, merely by virtue of the general law and include: rights of passage along the highway, rights of passage in navigable waters, rights of fishing, and rights to discharge into a public sewer.

[158] Quite distinct from Land Charges in unregistered land title deeds conveyancing, local land charges concern rights as to planning, highways, and other local authority matters.

[159] See s. 11 of the LRA 2002 as to freehold and s. 12 as to leasehold.

[160] Law Commission Report No. 271, [8.9].

legal leases of 21 years or less were overriding.[161] The Commission consulted on reducing the length of lease that would be overriding and, today, legal leases granted for seven years or less are overriding under Sch. 3, para. 1 of the LRA 2002.[162]

Leases for a duration of more than seven years are registrable titles which must be registered substantively. No further conditions, beyond the short duration, are stipulated and, as such, short leases are overriding interests and automatically binding on the registered proprietor.[163] Importantly, only *legal* leases amount to overriding interests under this paragraph.[164] Equitable leases are not covered and must be protected by the entry of a notice if they are to bind the registered proprietor. Equitable leases, may however also constitute an overriding interest under Schs. 1 and 3, para. 2 if the tenant is in actual occupation of the land. Certain special case leases are provided for in Sch. 3, para. 1. First, certain leases are excluded from overriding status. These include, amongst others, leases granted under the right to buy provisions of the Housing Act 1985, the grant of discontinuous leases,[165] and leases to take effect in possession more than three months after the grant. Secondly, a 'relevant social housing tenancy' under the Localism Act 2011 is endowed with overriding status regardless of its duration.[166] It is envisaged that the duration of leases given overriding status will be reduced further in time—in particular, if and when e-conveyancing is introduced, making it 'possible to register shorter leases very easily and to ensure that they are removed on expiry'.[167]

2.7.4.2 Interests of those in actual occupation: Sch. 3, para. 2

This class of overriding interest has been described as 'the most notorious—and most litigated' and it is doubtless the most important and controversial of all overriding interests. It strikes directly at the core of the mirror principle underpinning land registration and has played a key role in enforcing, in particular, equitable interests under a trust of land against purchasers and mortgagees (mortgage lenders such as banks) where overreaching has not taken place. Whilst Schs. 1 and 3 both make provision for actual occupation as an overriding interest, Sch. 3 is far narrower in scope and sets up a series of qualifications or exceptions which restrict when overriding status is conferred. These qualifications centre, as you will see, on issues of discoverability (which was not a requirement under the previous law of the LRA 1925) and inquiry. Before we turn to consider the hoops that must be jumped through for an interest to enjoy overriding status on the basis of actual occupation, we will explore briefly the overriding status of legal easements and profits.

---

[161] Under s. 70(1)(k) of the LRA 1925.

[162] Schedule 1, para. 1 of the LRA 2002 contains an almost identical provision. Note: as more and more unregistered titles are brought onto the register, it is anticipated that the duration of legal leases endowed with overriding status will likely be reduced again: ibid., s. 118.

[163] Under ibid., s. 29.

[164] This was confirmed in *City Permanent Building Society v Miller* (1952) where the court noted that reference to the word 'granted' could only signify legal and not equitable leases.

[165] Recall that a discontinuous lease is a lease where the tenant's right to possession is not for a single continuous period.

[166] Schedule 3, para. 1A of the LRA 2002 and s. 157 of the Localism Act 2011.

[167] Law Commission Report No. 271, [8.9].

2.7.4.3 Legal easements and profits: Sch. 3, para. 3

Schedule 3, para. 3 provides for the overriding status of legal easements and profits. In large part, it recreates the position adopted under the old law provision of s. 70(1)(a) of the LRA 1925. Be warned, however, as the language of Sch. 3, para. 3 is ripe for misunderstanding and catches out many a student on first, if not second, reading.

You must take a very close look at the wording of para. 3 if you are to grasp it. Unlike Sch. 1, para. 3 which provides for automatic overriding status to legal easements and profits, Sch. 3 lists a number of qualifications on when a legal easement or profit will and will not constitute an overriding interest. It is important to understand, at a broad level, what para. 3 is seeking to achieve. Schedule 3, para. 3 is far narrower in scope than its Sch. 1 relation. The basic idea is that by including qualifications and conditions on overriding status under Sch. 3, a smaller number of easements and profits will amount to overriding interests, hence contributing to the comprehensiveness of the register. With that in mind, a number of observations can be made:

1. Any easement that took effect as an overriding interest before the LRA 2002 came into force continues to enjoy overriding status no matter how it was created.[168] Outside this transitional position, only legal easements (that satisfy the qualifications set out in point 4) enjoy overriding status under Sch. 3.

2. All legal easements and profits *expressly* granted out of a registered estate after the coming into force of the LRA 2002 amount to registrable dispositions under s. 27(2)(d) of the LRA 2002 and must be completed by registration to operate at law and do not constitute overriding interests under Sch. 3.

3. Equitable easements are clearly excluded by the words of Sch. 3, para. 3 which makes explicit reference to 'legal' easements and profits only. Equitable easements and profits must be protected by entry of a notice.

4. Chiefly, the only new legal easements and profits that will amount to overriding interests will be those implied easements created under s. 62 of the LPA 1925, under the rule in *Wheeldon v Burrows* (1879) or impliedly created by necessity, common intention, or **prescription**.[169] Even here, these implied easements or profits will only be overriding if they satisfy any one of the following qualifications in para. 3:

   - The easement is registered under Part 1 of the Commons Act 2006.
   - The easement or profit is 'within the actual knowledge of the person to whom the disposition is made'.
   - The easement or profit, judged objectively, would have been 'obvious on a reasonably careful inspection of the land'.
   - The person entitled to the easement or profit 'proves that it has been exercised' in the last 12 months ending on the day of the disposition.

This final qualification is crucial because, in practice, most legal easements or profits will have been exercised within the last 12 months, ending with the date of disposition.

---

[168] Schedule 12, para. 9 of the LRA 2002: this will catch legal easements and also some equitable easements also.
[169] We explore the law of easements and implied creation in Chapter 10.

Therefore, provided the easement or profit is not a registrable disposition, most implied legal easements and profits will be caught by this provision and will be overriding.

2.7.5 'Actual occupation' under Sch. 3, para. 2: Rationale, requirements, and definitions

Now we return to actual occupation. So important is actual occupation that we dedicate the remainder of this section of the chapter to it, considering why special protection is afforded to those in actual occupation, what actual occupation is, and how it is shown to exist.

2.7.5.1 The rationale for actual occupation

Not a new invention, the need for a category to protect those in occupation of land can be traced back to the Report of the Royal Commission on the Land Transfer Acts in 1911 which noted that, 'there should be provision that the rights of parties actually in occupation . . . should not be affected by registration . . . '[170] Under the old law, s. 70(1)(g) of the LRA 1925, an interest of a person in actual occupation was given overriding status. Discussing this provision, Lord Denning in *Strand Securities Ltd v Caswell* (1965) noted:[171]

> Fundamentally, its object is to protect a person in actual occupation of land from having his rights lost in the welter of registration. He can stay there and do nothing. Yet he will be protected. No one can buy the land over his head and thereby take away or diminish his rights. It is up to every purchaser before he buys to make the inquiry on the premises. If he fails to do so, it is at his own risk.

As part of its wide-ranging work into reform the LRA 1925, the Law Commission considered whether actual occupation as a class of overriding interest should be abandoned but roundly rejected this view; recommending retention of the category albeit in a newly restricted form. The Law Commission offered two grounds for maintaining the class, explaining that:[172]

> [First] it is unreasonable to expect all encumbrances to register their rights, particularly where those rights arise informally, under (say) a constructive trust or by estoppels . . . to require their registration would defeat the sound policy that underlies their recognition. [Secondly], when people occupy land they are unlikely to appreciate the need to take the formal steps of registering their occupation . . . the retention of this category of overriding interests is justified . . . because this is a very clear case where protection against purchasers is needed but where it is 'not reasonable to expect nor sensible to require any entry on the register'.

So, actual occupation survives under the LRA 2002 albeit in Sch. 3 in a circumscribed—if nevertheless significant—formula. What are the essential requirements or elements of actual occupation? Put differently, what must be proved for an interest to enjoy overriding status as a result of actual occupation? This enquiry must be broken down into two parts:

1. the general requirements for actual occupation—which, in practice, apply to both Schs. 1 and 3 and must be satisfied under both schedules; and

2. the exceptions to actual occupation which apply only to Sch. 3.

---

[170] CD 5483 (1911), [81]. [171] *Strand Securities Ltd*, 979.
[172] Law Commission Report No. 254, [5.61] (in part quoting from earlier in report at [4.17]).

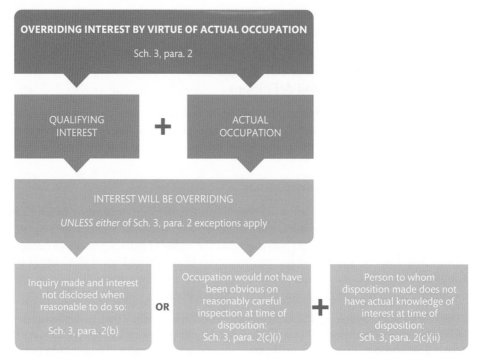

Figure 2.8 Establishing an overriding interest by virtue of actual occupation under Sch. 3, para. 2.

Figure 2.8 depicts diagrammatically how an overriding interest under Sch. 3, para. 2 is established.

2.7.5.2 The general requirements for actual occupation

A person claiming an overriding interest under either Sch. 1 or 3 on the basis of actual occupation must satisfy two general requirements: *qualifying interest + actual occupation*. The result is simple: where there is actual occupation but no qualifying interest or a qualifying interest without actual occupation, there can be no overriding interest.[173]

What constitutes a 'qualifying interest'? Several points can be made about this requirement:

1. Only proprietary interests rather than purely personal rights are 'qualifying interests': *Scott v Southern Pacific Mortgages Ltd* (2014). Whilst there is no statutory statement and no provision in the LRA 2002 to this effect, the need for a proprietary interest is now widely accepted and was confirmed by Wilberforce LJ in *National Provincial Bank v Ainsworth* (1965).[174] On this basis, on the facts of *Ainsworth*, a wife's personal right to occupy the matrimonial home was incapable of constituting an overriding interest under the old

---

[173] *Flegg*, per Lord Oliver, [74]; this was confirmed by the Supreme Court in *Scott v Southern Pacific Mortgages* (2014).

[174] *Ainsworth*, [1261]; see also Law Commission Report No. 254, [4.36].

law s. 70(1)(g) of the LRA 1925. Overriding status cannot be generated on the basis of a personal right such as a contractual licence or a family home right under the Family Law Act 1996.

2. Any (non-excluded) proprietary right can amount to a 'qualifying interest' for the purposes of actual occupation: Unless expressly exempted by statute,[175] any proprietary interest in land can, in theory, amount to a 'qualifying interest'. The most commonly encountered qualifying interests are:

- equitable interests under a trust of land[176]
- leases[177]
- options to purchase[178]
- rights arising by proprietary estoppel and mere equities.[179]

Other, less familiar rights that constitute 'qualifying interests' include: right to have a transaction rectified,[180] rights to have a transaction set aside on the grounds of undue influence,[181] and a right to seek alteration of the register.[182] Do not forget that any 'qualifying interest' must also be accompanied by actual occupation to amount to an overriding interest.

3. Interests which are capable of being protected on the register can enjoy a 'dual status' and also amount to overriding interests if coupled with actual occupation: The court in *Boland*, confirmed that an interest which could be protected, for example, by the entry of a restriction or notice, but was not so protected could, nevertheless, still amount to an overriding interest.[183]

4. Interests which have been overreached do not constitute qualifying interests: Whilst interests can enjoy dual status as both 'overreachable' and overriding interests (as in *Boland*) once an interest has, in fact, been overreached, it cannot also amount to an overriding interest as a qualifying interest when coupled with actual occupation.[184]

2.7.5.3 The meaning of 'actual occupation'

It is not enough to identify a qualifying interest; that interest must also be coupled with actual occupation. Given the importance and controversial nature of this requirement, there are a number of different aspects and factors of which you should be aware. We will consider them here.

The relevance of pre-LRA 2002 case law

The LRA 2002 provides no definition of what constitutes 'actual occupation'. So, we turn to case law for assistance. In so doing, the pre-LRA 2002 case law is a useful tool. In fact, the old case law is taken as the starting point for interpretation of actual occupation under

---

[175] Interests under a settlement under the Settled Land Act 1925 are excluded from amounting to overriding interests under Sch. 1, para. 2; Sch. 3, para. 2(a); legal leases taking effect in possession after three months from date of grant are expressly excluded as overriding interests under Sch. 3, para. 2(d) as are home rights under Family Law Act 1996, s. 31(10)(b).

[176] See, for example, *Boland*.   [177] *Trevallion v Watmore* (2016).   [178] *Webb v Pollmount* (1966).

[179] Confirmed as having proprietary effect by s. 116 of the LRA 2002; see also *Lloyd*.

[180] *Blacklocks v J. B. Developments*; *Malory*.   [181] *Thompson v Foy* (2009); *Link Lending v Bustard* (2010).

[182] *Malory*.   [183] Dual status of interests was confirmed in *Webb v Pollmount*, [599–603].

[184] Confirmed by the House of Lords in *Flegg*.

the 2002 Act. In *Link Lending v Bustard* (2010),[185] Mummery LJ explained the relevance of old case law:

> The construction of the earlier equivalent provisions by the House of Lords is binding on this court. The trend of the cases shows that the courts are reluctant to lay down, or even, suggest, a single test for determining whether a person is in actual occupation.

A plain English interpretation of 'actual occupation'

Lord Wilberforce in *Boland* called for a reading of the actual occupation provision 'for what it says':[186]

> 'Actual occupation'? These words are ordinary words of plain English, and should, in my opinion, be interpreted as such . . . I do not think that the word 'actual' was intended to introduce any additional qualification, certainly not to suggest that possession must be 'adverse': it merely emphasises that what is required is physical presence, not some entitlement in law.

This important case rewards closer attention.[187]

KEY CASE *Williams & Glyn's Bank v Boland* (1981)

Facts: Michael Boland was the sole registered legal owner of Ridge Park, a matrimonial home which he shared with his wife, Julia. Michael secured a loan against the property from Williams & Glyn's Bank by way of mortgage to finance his building company. He subsequently fell into arrears and defaulted on the repayments. The bank sought possession of the property. Julia, who had made a substantial financial contribution to the purchase price of the home, argued that she thereby enjoyed a contribution-based equitable interest under a trust of land and that, because she was occupying the home, the bank was bound by her interest which amounted to an overriding interest.

Legal issue: Does a spouse with a contribution-based equitable interest in a matrimonial home but who is not a registered legal owner of that property have an overriding interest which is binding on a mortgagee (bank)? Was Julia Boland in actual occupation for the purposes of the then-applicable provision: s. 70(1)(g) of the LRA 1925 (the forerunner to today's Sch. 3, para. 2 of the LRA 2002)?

Judgment: In the Chancery Division, Templeman J held that Julia was not in actual occupation within s. 70(1)(g) on the basis that the occupation of a spouse with no legal interest in the property forms part of the occupation of the legal owner and did not therefore amount to actual occupation in its own right. On appeal, the Court of Appeal reversed this decision finding that Julia was in actual occupation under s. 70(1)(g) and enjoyed an overriding interest which was binding on the bank. Lord Denning MR, delivering the leading judgment, rejected the view (advanced in *Caunce v Caunce* and *Bird v Syme-Thomson*) that a wife could not be in actual occupation when her husband was the sole legal owner of the property. These views, he added, 'would have been true a hundred years ago when the law regarded husband and wife as one: and the husband as that one. But they are not true today.' The bank appealed. In the House of Lords, the Court of Appeal decision was upheld. Julia

→

---

[185] *Bustard*, [27].   [186] *Boland*, 504.

[187] For a discussion of the case see R. Smith, '*Williams and Glyn's Bank Ltd v Boland* (1980): The Development of a System of Title by Registration' in N. Gravells (ed.), *Landmark Cases in Land Law* (Oxford: Hart, 2013).

→

enjoyed a proprietary interest in the land coupled with actual occupation. Her interest had not been overreached as mortgage monies were advanced to just one trustee. Discussing the meaning of 'actual occupation', Lord Wilberforce urged that the words be given their plain English interpretation and that what was required was evidence of 'physical presence' on the land. Any suggestion that a wife's occupation was a mere shadow of her husband's occupation was an outmoded view and 'heavily obsolete'. The court also rejected the bank's assertion that, to fall within s. 70(1)(g), occupation had to be inconsistent with the title of the legal owner, here Michael. This suggestion was 'unacceptable' and amounted to a 'rewriting of the paragraph'. Instead the paragraph should be read 'with common sense . . . for what it says'. The bank's charge on the Bolands' matrimonial home was therefore subject to Julia's binding overriding interest. The court confirmed that an interest capable of protection on the register (here by way of a restriction) but which had not been so protected could nevertheless still amount to an overriding interest.

It may be hard to grasp today but, at the time, the decision in *Boland* caused a real stir, controversy in financial quarters and even fear. *Boland* revealed the scope and breadth of the old law s. 70(1)(g) and the susceptibility of purchasers and banks to being bound by overriding interests. There were calls for legislation to change the law on overriding interests and to limit the scope of overreaching. A special Law Commission report put forward these proposals but they were not implemented due to strong opposition. Instead of changes to the law, conveyancers amended their practices to minimize the fall-out of the decision by, for example, requiring anyone occupying land to provide prior consent to any dealings with the property. For many, *Boland* shifted the balance too far in favour of occupiers and too far against purchasers and banks. In part, this was redressed by the House of Lords in *Flegg*, which, as we saw in section 2.6.2.2, reasserted the true power of overreaching and can be taken as restoring a balance between static and dynamic security. Nevertheless, *Boland* let something out of the box which could not be so easily put back. It underscored a shift towards greater acceptance and recognition of informally created rights in land and heralded a looser approach to actual occupation and a preoccupation, some might say, with overriding interests.

The factors to be weighed by the judge in determining actual occupation

The Court of Appeal in *Thompson v Foy* (2009)[188] and subsequently in *Bustard* engaged in an analysis of the meaning of actual occupation. Mummery LJ in *Bustard* offered the following by way of a précis of the key factors that will be relevant when examining if a person is in actual occupation of land:[189]

> The degree of permanence and continuity of presence of the person concerned, the intentions and wishes of that person, the length of absence from the property and the reason for it and the nature of the property and personal circumstances of the person are among the relevant factors.

Assessing whether a person is in actual occupation therefore engages a wide-ranging evaluation of the factual circumstances of each individual case. That said, there are a number of circumstances that commonly crop up and we cover those in the remaining part of this section.

---

[188] *Bustard*, [127].   [189] Ibid.

What degree of permanence is required? The problem of merely preparatory acts

We have seen that the most straightforward way to demonstrate actual occupation is to show that a person was physically present, residing in the property, as in *Boland* itself where Julia Boland was actively living in the home. Not all cases are so simple, however. A key authority addressing the necessary 'degree of permanence and continuity' is *Abbey National v Cann*.

KEY CASE *Abbey National v Cann* (1991)

Facts: In May 1984, Mr Cann applied to Abbey National Building Society for a loan of £25,000 to be secured by way of mortgage against a property he wanted to buy. He claimed the property would be for his sole occupation but, in fact, he intended that he, his mother, and her partner would all occupy the property. Abbey National agreed to the loan. On 13 August completion of the purchase and the charge took place. Thirty-five minutes before completion, Mr Cann and his mother's partner arrived at the property with carpet-layers and to unload furniture, at all times with the vendor's consent. Mr Cann's mother was abroad on holiday. Mrs Cann returned from her holiday and all three began occupying the property. On 13 September the property was registered in Mr Cann's sole name with Abbey National as proprietor of the charge. Mr Cann subsequently defaulted on mortgage payments and Abbey National brought proceedings seeking possession of the property. In resisting this action, Mr Cann's mother argued that she enjoyed an equitable interest in the property by reason of her contribution and assurances made by Mr Cann that she would always have a roof over her head. She argued that this interest was overriding by way of actual occupation which took priority over Abbey National's charge.

Legal issue: Could Mrs Cann demonstrate actual occupation of the property despite being physically out of the country on the date of completion of the purchase? The Building Society accepted that Mrs Cann was in occupation after 13 September but argued that she had not been in occupation at the relevant date.

Judgment: The House of Lords confirmed that a party seeking to demonstrate an overriding interest based on actual occupation must be able to point to that occupation *at the date of completion*. At the date of completion, Mrs Cann was not personally in the country let alone in occupation of the property. The acts of Mr Cann and Mrs Cann's partner 35 minutes before completion were 'merely preparatory' to actual occupation, which only followed after completion. This could not give rise to an overriding interest in Mrs Cann's favour. Lord Oliver added that actual occupation must involve 'some degree of permanence and continuity which would rule out mere fleeting presence'. A purchaser who goes into a property to plan decoration work or to measure for furnishing would not, 'in ordinary parlance, be said to be occupying it, even though he might be there for hours at a time'.

Interruptions to occupation and absences from the land:
The importance of an intention to return

The case of *Cann* demonstrates that acts merely preparatory of occupation will not suffice to prove actual occupation. A greater degree of permanence and continuity is required. That said, case law has shown that the law will permit a finding of actual occupation where there are interruptions to occupation or absences from the land. Where a person is not physically present on land, actual occupation will however only be demonstrated where the court is satisfied that there is a clear and *continuing intention to return*. This requires evidence of an ongoing connection to the land and that, despite periods of temporary absence, in no sense occupation of the land been abandoned. There are a number of contrasting authorities which can usefully be considered here and which indicate the line the courts have drawn in determining when an absence is too lengthy and will prove fatal to a finding of actual occupation.

In *Chhokar v Chhokar* the court considered the effect of a short hospital stay.

KEY CASE *Chhokar v Chhokar* (1984)

Facts: Mr and Mrs Chhokar were married in 1975 and had a child. In 1977, a property was purchased in Mr Chhokar's sole name but both parties contributed to the purchase price and upkeep of the home. Following a trip to India in 1978, Mr Chhokar abandoned his wife and, without informing her, made preparations for sale of the family home. In early 1978, while Mrs Chhokar was in hospital giving birth, sale of the property was completed and Mr Chhokar fled to India with the proceeds. When Mrs Chhokar returned home, she found herself locked out of the property.

Legal issue: Among other issues, the court was asked to consider whether Mrs Chhokar could be taken as having been in actual occupation of the premises during her temporary absence in hospital.

Judgment: The court held that Mrs Chhokar had an interest in the home by way of her contribution to the purchase price and was in actual occupation despite her absence. Mrs Chhokar kept her possessions such as furniture in the house and she had every intention of returning home after the birth of her child.

In *Bustard* the court was called on to consider whether actual occupation could be established where there was a longer period of *involuntary* detention in a psychiatric unit.

KEY CASE *Link Lending v Bustard* (2010)

Facts: Mrs Bustard owned a property in which she lived as her home. She suffered from a severe mental illness which impacted on her abilities of comprehension and judgment. In 2004, she transferred the property to Mrs Hussein who had fraudulently taken advantage of Mrs Bustard's vulnerable position. Mrs Hussein secured a loan against the property. At no time did Mrs Bustard receive any money for the transfer or from the loan. In 2007, whilst remaining in occupation of the property, Mrs Bustard was sectioned under the Mental Health Act 1983 and was detained in a psychiatric hospital. As part of her detention, Mrs Bustard was unable to permanently return home but was permitted to visit once a week to check post and to pay household bills. Mrs Hussein secured a further, bridging loan against the property with Link Lending but subsequently defaulted on the mortgage payments. Link Lending brought proceedings for possession of the property.

Legal issue: Was Mrs Bustard in actual occupation despite her involuntary, long-term detention in a psychiatric hospital? Link Lending argued that Mrs Bustard could not be in actual occupation as she was not physically present at the property at the date of the bridging loan and had not been permanently resident at the house for over a year.

Judgment: The Court of Appeal held that whether Mrs Bustard was in actual occupation was a matter of fact. The trial judge had been justified in finding that Mrs Bustard was in actual occupation of the property. Mrs Bustard kept all her belongings and furniture in the house, received her post there, her incarceration had been involuntary and, importantly, there was evidence of Mrs Bustard's continuing intention to return home once recovered as demonstrated by her regular visits to the property.

In two further cases, the court established when a period of absence would prove fatal to a finding of actual occupation: *Stockholm Finance Ltd v Garden Holdings Inc.* (1995) and *AIB v Turner* (2016). In *Stockholm Finance*, the court held that a Saudi princess who had been living abroad with her mother for 14 months was not in actual occupation of her fully furnished London home in which she had not 'set foot' in over a year. Walker J (as he was at this time), explained that:[190]

> Whether a person's intermittent presence at a house . . . should be seen as continues occupation or a pattern of alternating periods of presence and absence is a matter of perception which defies deep analysis. Not only the length of any absence but also the reason for it, may be material (a holiday or business trip may be easier to reconcile with continuing and unbroken occupation than a move to a second home, even though the duration of the absence is the same in each). But there must come a point at which a person's absence from his house is so prolonged that the notion of continuing to be in actual occupation of it becomes unsupportable.

In *Turner*, the court held that Mrs Turner who owned a home in Derbyshire but lived in Barbados was not in actual occupation of the UK property as she lived out of the country for prolonged periods of time and only returned to the UK very occasionally. There was nothing 'actual' about her occupation and this was not altered by insistence it was her 'primary residence'. There was also evidence that Mrs Turner had made a positive decision to live permanently outside the UK which was inconsistent with her actual occupation of the Derbyshire house.

We can see from these examples that much turns on the precise facts of each case but shorter absences in hospital (*Chhokar*) or involuntary, forced absences with evidence of a clear intention to return (*Bustard*) will not prevent a finding of actual occupation. More protracted, prolonged periods of absence and evidence of a settled, second home in another jurisdiction will likely prove fatal (*Stockholm Finance*; *Turner*). Where there is evidence of a positive decision not to return to the property, this positive intention will also preclude a finding of actual occupation (*Thompson v Foy*).[191]

How far should intentions and wishes be determining factors of actual occupation?

It may seem entirely logical for the court to consider a person's intentions and wishes but, in taking account of intentions, the recent case law seems to echo the considerations usually associated with questions of **adverse possession** and possession more generally in property law. This is significant because the test is 'actual occupation' and not 'actual possession', and a key, stated ambition of the LRA 2002 was to minimize inspections and inquiries beyond the register. A purchaser cannot protect herself if the test for actual occupation draws on the vagaries of the subjective intentions and wishes of those occupying land. The relevance of intentions and wishes in determining actual occupation has drawn academic attention. Bogusz, for example, argues that:[192]

> The not insignificant judicial weight being increasingly apportioned to these largely unverifiable and opaque subjective intentions can be identified as a sea change with regard to how the courts

---

[190] *Stockholm Finance.*

[191] In *Thompson v Foy*, Mrs Thompson had made a clear decision that she wished to live permanently in Spain. This was a key ground on which an argument based on actual occupation failed.

[192] B. Bogusz, 'The Relevance of "Intentions and Wishes" to Determine Actual Occupation: A Sea Change in Judicial Thinking?' [2014] Conv 27, 27–32.

are prepared to interpret what constitutes 'all the circumstances of the case' . . . The positioning of the 'intention and wishes' of the person within the rubric devised by Mummery L.J. [in *Bustard*] cannot be dismissed as merely imprecise judicial language. It is arguably used strategically as the second factor for consideration by the courts, following on from 'the degree of permanence and continuity of presence' . . . By reference to the intentions and wishes of a party in his statement, Mummery L.J. has formally acknowledged these as relevant factors that the courts should take into consideration . . . However, the use of intentions and wishes is not without difficulty, not least because the effect of the court employing these imprecise intentions in its reasoning may result in what can be termed 'occupation creep'. That is to say, the existence of actual occupation may be extended to a person in circumstances where the facts alone are vague with regard to whether Sch. 3 para. 2 is satisfied. The latent result of confirming the existence of actual occupation by reference to a person's intentions is that it could have a significant and unexpected impact upon the rights of legal owners or third parties, for example mortgagees, who are bound by an interest which, factually, may not have been unequivocally established nor anticipated.

There is an argument that the court's greater recourse to intentions and wishes is at odds with decided case law and, more fundamentally, sits in conflict with the overarching aims of the LRA 2002 which we discussed in section 2.2.2. In my own work,[193] I have argued that this threatens to undermine the registration project more generally and sets overriding interests on a new, expansive footing rather than diminishing and restricting the category as the Law Commission and Parliament intended when legislating:

> In the absence of the introduction of a comprehensive e-conveyancing system, the courts are left to incrementally develop the law in that space; a space that was never intended by the Law Commission to be quite so wide . . . observations of those such as Pascoe and Dixon that overriding interests were entering their final days, and that 'the 2002 Act lays the axe to the tree with some vigour' require re-evaluation after *Link Lending*, *Thompson* and *Thomas*. The actual occupation principles appear more vigorous, more expansive and more subjective than ever. Such an approach runs the risk of undermining the very foundations of the 2002 Act, a statute that has been described as a masterclass in property law draughtsmanship. Seemingly, the words of Roger Smith in 1990 are as apposite today as they were when first committed to paper, that 'overriding interests in registered land continue to justify their reputation as the most controversial and difficult part of the system'.

I question the court's mandate to adopt a more subjective, intentions-based analysis and call for a return to a less expansive, more faithful rendering of the statutory language of the actual occupation provisions.[194]

The nature and context of the land

Whether the land is residential or commercial in nature and its physical state are also relevant factors for the purpose of establishing actual occupation: *Lloyds Bank v Rosset* (1989). Quite clearly, where property is purchased with the purpose of providing a home, actual occupation is logically to be equated with residence. In other words, a person found to be 'residing' on a plot of land should have no difficulty persuading a court that she is in actual

---

[193] C. Bevan, 'Overriding and Over-Extended? Actual Occupation: A Call to Orthodoxy' [2016] Conv 104, 117.

[194] For more on the court's more expansive, reflexive approach to actual occupation see generally ibid and B. Bogusz, 'Defining the Scope of Actual Occupation under the LRA 2002: Some Recent Judicial Clarification' [2011] Conv 268.

occupation of that land. But what of commercial land where actual occupation cannot be equated with residence? Arden LJ In *Malory* explained:[195]

> What constitutes actual occupation of property depends on the nature and state of the property in question . . . If a site is uninhabitable . . . residence is not required, but there must be some physical presence, with some degree of permanence and continuity.

The effect of this is that for non-residential land, the emphasis is on physical presence and evidence of control of the property rather than residence:

- Storing goods and erecting a perimeter fence on derelict and uninhabitable land can suffice as evidence of actual occupation: *Malory*.[196]

- Erecting a barn on farmland can suffice: *Blacklocks v J. B. Developments* (1982).

- Regularly parking a car on land can suffice: *Kling v Keston Properties Ltd* (1983); *Saeed v Plustrade Ltd* (2001).[197] Should it suffice?

- Daily visits to a derelict property to oversee building and decoration works can suffice: *Rosset*.

Is the presence of furniture evidence of actual occupation?

The presence of belongings, possessions such as furniture, on land seems not to amount to actual occupation. In *Strand Securities Ltd*, Russell LJ doubted whether the depositing of furniture could give rise to actual occupation. Whilst insufficient in itself, where the presence of furniture forms evidence of a wider intention to return to premises after an absence or interruption, it can, nevertheless, be relevant: *Bustard*.[198]

Actual occupation *and not actual use of the land*

A distinction must be drawn between actual *occupation* and *use* of the land. The court is looking for actual *occupation* of the land and not merely actual *use* or exercise of a proprietary right affecting land. This point was made plain in *Chaudhary*. Mr Chaudhary attempted to argue that exercise of a right of way (an easement) over a metal staircase as a means of access to two flats constituted actual occupation. This was rejected by the court. Use of the staircase could not amount to occupation for the purposes of Sch. 3.

Actual *and not* exclusive *occupation*

A person claiming an overriding interest based on their *actual* occupation of land need not demonstrate that they occupy the land to the *exclusion* of others. In fact, it is entirely possible for more than one person to be in actual occupation of the same parcel of land at the same time. Take the example of co-owned land. Here, there may very well be multiple occupiers of the land all of whom may be able to assert an interest by virtue of actual occupation. The test is one of *actual* and not exclusive occupation.

---

[195] *Malory*, [80].

[196] Maintaining a compost heap on a parcel of land and depositing waste does not amount to actual occupation however: *Bhullar v McArdle* (2001).

[197] Contrast with the earlier decision in *Epps v Esso Petroleum* (1973).

[198] In this case the property was filled with the claimant's belongings, furniture, and paperwork despite periods of absence while in treatment at the psychiatric unit.

Relevant date for actual occupation

The relevant date on which actual occupation must be proved was addressed in *Cann* in which it was held that actual occupation must be demonstrated at the date the transaction (the registrable disposition) is completed.[199] To find otherwise, said Lord Oliver, would be to introduce a conveyancing absurdity in that, after completion but before registration, a third party could come forward to claim actual occupation. If the date of registration were the relevant date for actual occupation, overriding interests could be created by the party transferring land (the vendor, for example) in breach of contract which would bind purchasers. The wording of Sch. 3, para. 2 appears to lend support to the result reached in *Cann* in that overriding status extends to an interest '*at the time of the disposition* to a person in actual occupation',[200] and makes no mention of the date of registration.

The matter of the relevant date was again considered in *Thompson v Foy* in which Lewison J confirmed the approach taken in *Cann* but recognized the argument that one interpretation of s. 29 of the LRA 2002 required actual occupation to be present at *both* the date of completion and the date of registration. These comments were obiter however and Lewison J noted that the leading texts were against this interpretation and left the issue to be resolved in a case which expressly required that a determination be made. Of course, if simultaneous completion and registration was implemented through e-conveyancing, the 'registration gap' would be closed, completion and registration would take place at the same moment, and the debate on the relevant date for actual occupation would vanish. However, in view of the recent 2018 Law Commission's recommended retreat from simultaneous completion and registration, this problem will seemingly persist even if e-conveyancing is introduced. For now, and for the avoidance of any doubt, the relevant date is the date of completion.[201]

Actual occupation through an agent or proxy

It is possible for a third party, acting as an agent, to be in actual occupation on behalf of the interest holder. The actual occupation of, for example, an employee, a representative of a company, or a caretaker will suffice to provide the interest holder with an overriding interest provided that the third party is in occupation as the principal's agent and not as a licensee:[202]

- In *Rosset*, the Court of Appeal accepted that builders carrying out decoration works on a property were in actual occupation on behalf of their client, Mrs Rosset.[203]
- In *Lloyd*, Mr Dugdale used commercial premises as managing director of a company. He was held to be in actual occupation on behalf of the company in which he was majority shareholder.

Actual occupation by minors

The leading authority on minors is *Hypo-Mortgage Services Ltd v Robinson* (1997)[204] in which the Court of Appeal held that minors living with their parents (the parents enjoying

---

[199] This was confirmed by the Supreme Court in *Scott v Southern Pacific Mortgages*.
[200] Italics added for emphasis.   [201] For a critique of this choice of date, see R. Smith (1988) LQR 507.
[202] Confirmed in *Strand Securities Ltd*; *Turner* in the High Court.
[203] See also *Thomas v Clydesdale Bank plc* (2010).
[204] For a discussion of the case, see P. H. Kenny, 'Children Are Spare Ribs' [1997] Conv 84; E. Cooke, 'Children and Real Property: Trusts, Interests and Considerations' (June 1998) Fam Law 349.

interests in the land) cannot be in actual occupation of that property for the purposes of overriding interests. Nourse LJ explained:

> [I]t as axiomatic that minor children of the legal owner are not in actual occupation . . . the minor children are there because their parent is there. They have no right of occupation of their own . . . they are there as shadows of the occupation of their parent.

This result was justified by Nourse LJ on two grounds: first, that if children could to be regarded as being in actual occupation, mortgagees' securities could easily be undermined by parents routinely arguing their children were in occupation and, secondly, making inquiries of children is inherently difficult. This is, in practice, an application of the 'shadow doctrine'[205] applied in the children context according to which children are regarded merely as shadows of their parents and so cannot be in actual occupation in their own right. The shadow doctrine has long been rejected in the spousal context of husband and wife, which should give us pause for thought as to its application in relation to children. Lord Wilberforce, in *Boland*, held quite emphatically that wives do not occupy property as shadows of their husbands. This must cast doubt on the pertinence of the doctrine as to children.

The extent of actual occupation: Part-occupation of the land?

How far does actual occupation extend? Put differently, will occupation of just part of a larger plot of land generate an overriding interest over the entirety? There has been a change of the law in this area. Prior to the enactment of the LRA 2002, the leading authority on this question was *Ferrishurst v Wallcite* (1999), in which the Court of Appeal held that, provided a party holds a right that operates over the whole land (here, an option to purchase), actual occupation of part of the land generates an overriding interest as to that whole land. The decision was regarded by the Law Commission as leading to a 'strange result' in that it appeared to place a heavier burden on purchasers of registered land to inspect the land than applied if land was unregistered.[206] This ran counter to the objectives of the proposed legislative regime and, under the LRA 2002, the decision in *Ferrishurst* was reversed. Both Sch. 1, para. 2 and Sch. 3, para. 2 make explicit that overriding status only extends 'so far as relating to land of which he is in actual occupation'. The effect of this is that if a person has a proprietary interest in the whole land but is only in actual occupation of part of the land, the overriding interest extends only to the land of which she is in actual occupation.[207]

Actual occupation and the absolutism/constitutionalism debate

In understanding how actual occupation works, Hayton has advanced two 'views' of actual occupation: the absolutist view and the constitutionalist view.[208] Both approaches have attracted judicial support.

According to the absolutist view, actual occupation is a question of pure fact. A person is absolutely bound by the rights of every person in actual occupation and it is irrelevant whether or not it is unreasonably difficult to discover the occupation. The high watermark

---

[205] See *Bird*, per Templeman J.   [206] Law Commission Report No. 271, [8.57].
[207] See discussion in *Thompson v Foy*, [128]–[129].   [208] Hayton, *Registered Land*, 87–91.

of support for the absolutist view was undoubtedly the judgments of Lords Wilberforce and Scarman in *Boland* where Julia Boland, through her contribution to the purchase price of property, acquired an equitable interest which, when coupled with her actual occupation of the land, was binding on a mortgagee as an overriding interest. In adopting the absolutist approach, Lord Wilberforce in *Boland* noted:[209]

> I do not accept the argument . . . that, in applying s 70(1)(g) LRA 1925, we should have regard to and limit the application of the paragraph in light of the doctrine of notice . . . this would run counter to the whole purpose of the Act. The purpose, in each system [unregistered and registered] is the same, namely, to safeguard the rights of person in occupation, but the method used differs. In the case of unregistered land, the purchaser's obligation depends upon what he has notice of—notice actual or constructive. In the case of registered land, it is the fact of occupation that matters. If there is actual occupation, and the occupier has rights, the purchaser takes subject to them. If not, he does not. No further element [of notice] is material.

Remember that s. 70(1)(g) was the old law, forerunner provision to today's Sch. 3, para. 2 of the LRA 2002.

According to the constitutionalist view, which grew out of the doctrine of notice under the rule in *Hunt v Luck* applicable to unregistered land, a person is bound by the rights of those in actual occupation according to traditional conveyancing principles such as constructive notice. On this view, a purchaser would only be bound if there was a degree of discoverability to the occupation. Sparkes (1989)[210] has written in support of this approach arguing that the absolutist view in *Boland* is overstated and that 'discoverability' is an inherent assumption in the formulation of the law of actual occupation. Judicial support for the constitutionalist view and rejection of the absolutist view is seen most clearly in the Court of Appeal in *Rosset*.[211] Purchas LJ explained that:[212]

> The provisions of [s. 70(1)(g) of the LRA 1925] clearly were intended to import into the law relating to registered land the equitable concept of constructive notice. Thus, a purchaser or a charge acquiring the title to or an interest in the land where the vendor was not in actual possession in order to protect his interest has to make appropriate inquiries if he found someone else in occupation of the property . . . in order for the wife's interest in the property to qualify as an overriding interest . . . two things must be established: (a) was she in actual occupation? And (b) would appropriate inquiries made by the bank have elicited the fact of her interest?

Mustill LJ added:[213]

> [Although s. 70(1)(g)] does not actually say the acts constituting actual occupation must be such that a purchaser who went to the land and investigated would discover the fact of occupation and thereby be put on inquiry, the closing words of the paragraph are at least a hint that this is what Parliament principally has in mind.

---

[209] *Boland*, 504.

[210] P. Sparkes, [1989] Conv 342; P. Sparkes, *A New Land Law*, 2nd edn (Oxford: Hart, 2003), 281.

[211] In the Court of Appeal, Mrs Rosset was found to have been in actual occupation through the agency of independent contractors who were carrying out works on the property. When the matter reached the House of Lords, Mrs Rosset was found to have no proprietary interest in the property and therefore no qualifying interest on which a claim to actual occupation could be based.

[212] *Rosset*, 403–4.   [213] Ibid., 397.

It will not have escaped you that these authorities concern the old law under the LRA 1925. As we will explore in section 2.7.5.4, the LRA 2002 in Sch. 3, para. 2 imports new qualifications and exceptions not present under the old law: for example, a reasonable inspection qualification in para. 2(c). The effect is to move away from the absolutist view of actual occupation towards embracing a more constitutionalist approach whilst, crucially, engaging elements of both approaches. So, while the meaning of actual occupation itself remains a question of fact (absolutist), the reasonable inspection qualification imports constitutionalist notions of discoverability. This can be described as a 'third way' or 'hybrid approach'.[214]

2.7.5.4 The exceptions to actual occupation under Sch. 3, para. 2

Schedule 3 contains certain additional qualifications which, if applicable, prevent an overriding interest arising on the grounds of actual occupation. These conditions, which are more accurately described as 'exceptions', provide for circumstances when, if the conditions are met, overriding status will be lost even though there is a qualifying interest and actual occupation has been established according to the principles outlined in section 2.7.5.2: see Figure 2.8. These exceptions did not exist under the old law and do not apply to Sch. 1. Under Sch. 3, para. 2, there are two exceptions to consider. Let's consider each now.

Exception 1: Rights of persons whose occupation is not apparent

Schedule 3, para. 2(c) provides that the interest of a person in actual occupation will not override a registered disposition where two conditions are met:

1. the interest holder's *occupation* of the land would not have been obvious on a reasonably careful inspection at the time of the disposition, and

2. the person to whom the disposition is made does not actually know of the *interest* at the time of the disposition.

The object of this exception is to protect purchasers (and other registered disponees) in cases where the fact of occupation is neither subjectively known to them nor readily apparent nor discoverable. A number of general points can be made on the operation of this exception:

- There are two conditions or two limbs to satisfy and they are cumulative: *both* must be satisfied if the exception is to be activated to deprive overriding status. Students often mistakenly apply just one of the conditions.

- The first limb concerns the obviousness of *occupation* whilst the second limb concerns knowledge of the *interest*.

- The exception is not concerned with the doctrine of notice and is not to be seen as introducing questions of notice into the registration scheme, as the Law Commission explained:[215]

---

[214] See Bogusz, 'The Relevance of "Intentions and Wishes" to Determine Actual Occupation: A Sea Change in Judicial Thinking?', 28.

[215] Law Commission Report No. 254, [5.72].

The doctrine of notice should not be introduced into registered land . . . the test is whether the [occupation] is apparent on a reasonable inspection of the land, not whether the right would have been discovered if the purchaser had made all the enquiries which ought reasonably to have been made.

Limb 1 (obviousness of occupation) concerns the question of whether occupation would not have been obvious on a reasonably careful inspection. This is not the same as whether the purchaser had notice of the occupation. Whilst in most cases, a physical inspection of the land will have taken place, as explained in *Thompson v Foy*, this first limb 'is a relevant hypothetical question . . . [and] does not require an actual inspection . . . it asks what *would* have been obvious if an inspection had been made'.[216] There is, as yet, very little case law on Sch. 3, para. 2(c). The leading authority is *Thomas v Clydesdale Bank plc* (2010) in which Ramsey J explained that: 'what has to be obvious is the relevant visible signs of occupation upon which a person who asserts an interest by actual occupation relies'.[217] The phrase 'reasonably careful inspection' is an objective test and does not take account of any subjective characteristics of the purchaser.[218] Jackson has argued that this objective test may produce unfair results in that:[219]

> [A] purchaser may end up being bound by an interest that was objectively apparent to the legally minded officious bystander but which was undiscoverable to the purchaser if only because he did not know what he was looking for.

As Ramsey J explained, under the second limb (actual knowledge of interest), the purchaser must have 'actual knowledge of the facts giving rise to the alleged interest'. Remember that the limbs are cumulative so if occupation would have been obvious, knowledge becomes irrelevant as the first limb is not satisfied. In *Trevallion v Watmore* (2016), Ms Watmore's cursory inspection of land she was purchasing involved a failure to peer behind a particularly luscious fuchsia bush. Had she done so, she would have seen the neighbour's fencing of a triangular parcel of land and thus discovered the Trevallions' occupation. A reasonably careful inspection would have revealed this and therefore the Trevallions' rights were overriding and binding on Ms Watmore.

Exception 2: Rights not disclosed on reasonable inquiry

Schedule 3, para. 2(b) provides that the interest of a person in actual occupation will not override a registered disposition where inquiry was made of that person before the disposition and that person failed to disclose the interest when she could reasonably have been expected to disclose it. A series of points can be made:

1. This exception is a reformulation of an exception applicable under the old law provision of s. 70(1)(g) of the LRA 1925.[220] What is new is the reference to 'reasonableness'. The exception only operates to deprive overriding status where an interest could reasonably be expected to be disclosed. This appears to indicate that those who do not know they have an interest in land cannot be expected to disclose it and their interest retains the

---

[216] *Thompson v Foy*, [132], per Lewison J. [217] *Thomas*, [38]. [218] Ibid., [40].
[219] Jackson, 'Title by Registration and Concealed Overriding Interests', 666.
[220] Section 70(1)(g) read: 'save where enquiry is made of such person and the rights are not disclosed'; see also *Hodgson v Marks* (1971).

protection of overriding status. In the absence of case law, the introduction of 'reasonableness' must be seen as importing a dose of uncertainty into the law.[221]

2. The exception is only relevant—in other words, is only activated—*if* inquiries are actually made. Hypothetical responses to hypothetical inquiries or any assumptions about what might or might not have been revealed are irrelevant.[222]

3. The exception operates as a form of estoppel so that if operative, the exception will mean that an interest holder is estopped from asserting the priority of her undisclosed interest.[223]

4. In the absence of recent case law, we might look for guidance (with necessary caution) to the old law. A number of points of clarification of the inquiry provision under the LRA 1925 offer some useful direction:

   - Inquiries are only relevant if addressed to the interest holder or her solicitor rather than the vendor.[224]
   - Inquiries are only relevant if they concern the rights of an occupier generally as opposed to an inquiry as to a specific right.[225]
   - Inquiries need not be made personally by the purchaser; for example, they can be made on her behalf.

Finally, note the importance of '**waiver**' of priority. It is now commonplace for mortgage lenders when advancing mortgage monies to ask any other people occupying the land being charged to sign a waiver. A waiver generally takes one of two forms and arises most commonly in respect of occupiers. Under the first form of waiver, an occupier confirms that she has no rights, estate, or interest in the property or in the proceeds of sale—here the occupier will not later be able to assert priority based on her actual occupation as the lender is taken as having made reasonable inquiries and the occupiers rights have not been disclosed. Under the second form of waiver, the occupier agrees that the lender's mortgage on the property has priority over any right, estate, or interest that the occupier may have—here the occupier has consented to postponing her interest to that of the lender. Waiver is a key mode of protection for lenders against overriding interests based on actual occupation.

We have now concluded our discussion (sections 2.5–2.7) of the priority of third party interests in registered land. In order to summarize the position, Figure 2.9 explores diagrammatically when a third party interest will be binding on a purchaser of registered land.

Figure 2.10 offers a flowchart which brings together the material covered so far in this chapter to help you gain a better understanding and to visualize how the issues explored connect with one another and how to approach the priority of interests in registered land.

---

[221] M. Dixon, 'The Reform of Property Law and the Land Registration Act 2002: A Risk Assessment' [2003] Conv 136, 147.

[222] Confirmed in *Thompson v Foy*, [132], per Lewison J.

[223] As explained by the Law Commission in its Report No. 271, [8.60].

[224] *Winkworth v Edward Baron Development* (1986).   [225] Noted in *Bank of Scotland v Hussain* (2010).

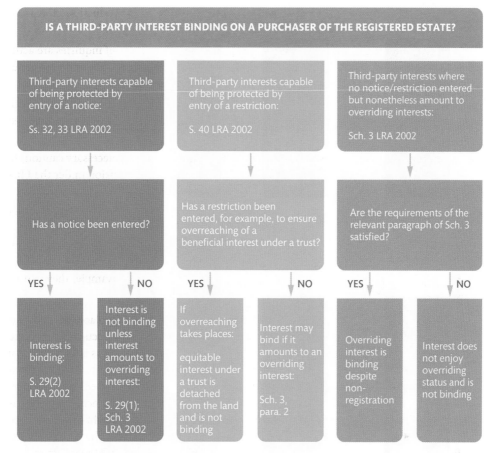

IS A THIRD-PARTY INTEREST BINDING ON A PURCHASER OF THE REGISTERED ESTATE?

Third-party interests capable of being protected by entry of a notice: Ss. 32, 33 LRA 2002	Third-party interests capable of being protected by entry of a restriction: S. 40 LRA 2002	Third-party interests where no notice/restriction entered but nonetheless amount to overriding interests: Sch. 3 LRA 2002
Has a notice been entered?	Has a restriction been entered, for example, to ensure overreaching of a beneficial interest under a trust?	Are the requirements of the relevant paragraph of Sch. 3 satisfied?

YES / NO — YES / NO — YES / NO

YES	NO	YES	NO	YES	NO
Interest is binding: S. 29(2) LRA 2002	Interest is not binding unless interest amounts to overriding interest: S. 29(1); Sch. 3 LRA 2002	If overreaching takes places: equitable interest under a trust is detached from the land and is not binding	Interest may bind if it amounts to an overriding interest: Sch. 3, para. 2	Overriding interest is binding despite non-registration	Interest does not enjoy overriding status and is not binding

Figure 2.9 The priority of third party rights in registered land

2.8 Alteration of the register and indemnity

If the core objective of the LRA to provide a complete and accurate register is to be achieved, provision must be made for the eventuality of error, mistake, and fraud.[226] Though relatively rare, the wrong person, for example, may be registered as proprietor.[227] Where the register is not a fair or true reflection of the rights and interests affecting the land, the register must be corrected. Under the LRA 2002, this is known as alteration of the register and is governed by Sch. 4. The forerunner to the 2002 Act, the LRA 1925, did allow for changes to be made to the register but the system was heavily criticized for its

---

[226] See section 2.9.1 of this chapter for a discussion of the recommendations made by the Law Commission in its latest report, *Updating the Land Registration Act 2002*, on changes it proposes to the rules on alteration, rectification and indemnity.

[227] Whether as a result of fraud, deliberate error, or merely negligence.

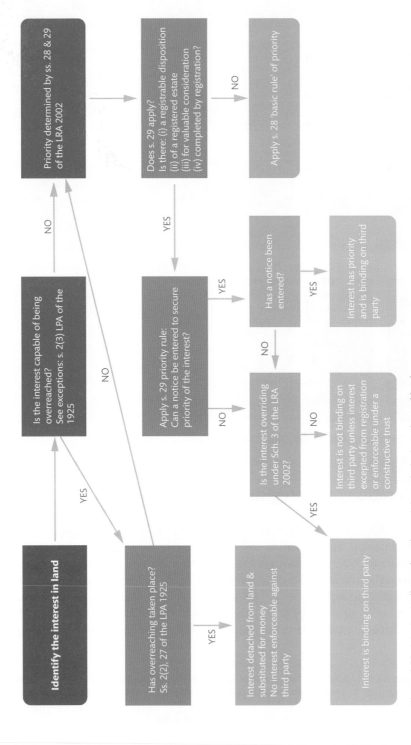

Identify the interest in land

Has overreaching taken place?
Ss. 2(2), 27 of the LPA 1925

YES →

Interest detached from land & substituted for money
No interest enforceable against third party

Is the interest capable of being overreached?
See exceptions: s. 2(3) LPA of the 1925

NO →

Priority determined by ss. 28 & 29 of the LRA 2002

Does s. 29 apply?
Is there: (i) a registrable disposition (ii) of a registered estate (iii) for valuable consideration (iv) completed by registration?

NO →

Apply s. 28 'basic rule' of priority

YES ↓

Apply s. 29 priority rule:
Can a notice be entered to secure priority of the interest?

YES →

Has a notice been entered?

YES →

Interest has priority and is binding on third party

NO ↓

Is the interest overriding under Sch. 3 of the LRA 2002?

NO →

Interest is not binding on third party unless interest excepted from registration or enforceable under a constructive trust

YES →

Interest is binding on third party

Figure 2.10 Bringing it all together: determining priority in registered land

obscurity and the LRA 2002 brings about a much-needed clarification of the terminology in this area. Under the LRA 1925, all changes to the register were termed '**rectifications**'. This was considered misleading and, today, under the LRA 2002, the term 'alteration' is used for all changes to the register with the exception of a narrow category which make use of the term 'rectification'. A rectification now refers to just one example of an alteration: an alteration which prejudicially affects the title of a proprietor.[228]

In certain, defined circumstances, where a party has suffered loss as a result of a mistake in the register, compensation in the form of an indemnity is available. This is governed by Sch. 8. In this section, we explore when the register can be altered, when rectified, and the circumstances in which an indemnity is payable.

2.8.1 Alteration of the register

Alterations under the LRA 2002 can be seen as falling into two categories: administrative alterations and rectifications. Administrative alterations are, essentially, those changes to the register which do not prejudice the title of the registered proprietor; in other words, which do not affect the registered proprietor's rights. Schedule 4 of the LRA 2002 provides for the circumstances in which administrative alterations of the register are possible either by an order of the court[229] or at the discretion of the Registrar.[230] There are three such circumstances: see Table 2.1.

In addition, the Registrar is given a power to remove superfluous entries on the register.[231]

Rectifications, by contrast, are alterations to the register to correct mistakes where the alteration will or could prejudicially affect the title. Given this, distinct rules apply. Whether an administrative alteration or a rectification is sought is particularly important for another reason; namely, that rectification of the register is a key ground on which an

Table 2.1 Administrative alterations to the register

CIRCUMSTANCE	EXAMPLE
To correct a mistake	• Where a third party interest is entered against the wrong registered title, it can be deleted and entered against the appropriate estate.
To bring the register up to date	• Where a lease affecting a registered estate has terminated or been brought to an end by court order, the entry may be removed; or • Where third party interests have arisen but which are not yet recorded on the register, an entry may be made to reflect this.
To give effect to an estate, right, or interest excepted from the effect of registration	• Where, for example, an entry is made relating to a qualified, possessory, or good leasehold title.

---

[228] Schedule 4, para. 1.   [229] Ibid, para. 2(1).   [230] Ibid, para. 5(1).

[231] Ibid, para. 5(1)(d); see also the case of *Stein v Stein* (2004) where a superfluous restriction was removed from the register under this power.

indemnity or compensation for loss suffered may be claimed.[232] Under Sch. 4, para. 1, for a rectification to arise, two conditions must be met:

- the alteration involves correction of a mistake, and
- this alteration prejudicially affects the title of the registered proprietor.

Several questions spring from this, so we will address each one by one.

2.8.1.1 Who can order a rectification?

Rectification can be ordered by the court but also can be made by the Registrar.[233]

2.8.1.2 What constitutes a mistake?

'Mistake' is given a broad interpretation. Let's take an example. Imagine that Amel purchases land from Brian and is registered as proprietor of the land. If, later, it is discovered that Brian had himself acquired the land by means of fraud from Cai, there will have been a mistake in the register—both that the register wrongly recorded Brian as registered proprietor and, subsequently, that Amel was registered as new proprietor. Here, Amel is an entirely innocent party but there is, nevertheless, a mistake in the register which may be rectified.

A leading decision in this area is *Baxter v Mannion* (2011). In this case, Mr Baxter made an application under Sch. 6 of the LRA 2002 to be registered as proprietor of a field owned by Mr Mannion, claiming to have been in adverse possession of the land since 1985. Mr Mannion was notified of Mr Baxter's claim but, due to difficulties instructing a solicitor and health concerns, Mr Mannion failed to object to the application within the prescribed 65-day period. Mr Baxter was therefore registered as the new proprietor of the field. Mr Mannion later requested an extension to the time in which to object but was informed that he must make an application to rectify the register which he did. The Deputy Adjudicator hearing the matter held that Mr Baxter had, in fact, failed to meet the statutory requirement of ten years' adverse possession[234] and had not therefore been entitled to apply and be registered as the new proprietor. Mr Baxter appealed to the High Court which upheld this result. He appealed again and the matter was heard by the Court of Appeal. Here, the court held that there had indeed been a mistake that could be rectified and that 'mistake' should not be construed narrowly so as to extend only to official errors at Land Registry (as counsel for Mr Baxter had argued). Despite Mr Mannion's failure to object to the application within the original time frame, Mr Baxter would not have been registered as proprietor of the field had all the facts been available to the Registrar at the relevant time. Mr Baxter's registration amounted to a mistake that it would be unjust not to correct.

A far trickier type of mistake arises where three parties are involved. Imagine that land belonging to Amel is transferred to Brian as a result of Brian forging the transfer documents and, subsequently, Brian transfers that land to Cai (an entirely innocent third party).

---

[232] We examine indemnity in section 2.8.2.

[233] Schedule 4, para. 3 as to court ordered rectifications; Sch. 4, para. 6 as to Registrar ordered rectifications.

[234] We explore adverse possession in Chapter 4.

When that transfer is registered, does this registration in Cai's favour amount to a mistake? Essentially, three views have emerged:

- View 1—the narrower view of mistake: The effect of ss. 58 and 23 of the LRA 2002 is that when Brian is registered as proprietor of Amel's land, his title is conclusive and he enjoys all the powers of an owner of the land. Brian can lawfully and effectively transfer that land to Cai. It is therefore not a mistake for Cai to be registered as proprietor of the land. There can be no rectification and no indemnity. The decision in *Barclays Bank plc v Guy* (2008) supported this interpretation and, it can be seen as reinforcing dynamic security in that Cai, who has purchased in good faith and relied on the register, is protected. The loser, on this view, is Amel.

- View 2—the broader view of mistake: In spite of ss. 58 and 23, it may still be a mistake for Cai to be registered as proprietor. This is naturally a rejection of the narrower view of mistake (view 1). Support for this view can be found in *Odogwu v Vastguide* (2009) and in the dicta of Lord Neuberger MR in a subsequent appeal in the *Guy*. Here Lord Neuberger offered two grounds on which the broader view could be made out:[235] (a) that the removal of, in our scenario, Amel's name from the register was a mistake, and to correct that mistake, Cai's name must also be removed; or alternatively (b) the registration of Cai as proprietor flows as 'part and parcel' of the mistake of registering Brian as proprietor. Cai's name may therefore be removed. Cooper has described this broader approach as 'long-arm rectification' as the law reaches beyond the mistaken entry of Brian, in our scenario, as proprietor and on to subsequent registered proprietors such as Cai.[236] Judges, particularly in recent decisions, have shown themselves more likely to adopt this broader view of mistake, to protect the original proprietor (Amel) and subsequent, innocent registered proprietors (Cai) in rejecting the narrower view of mistake. The court is keen to ensure that original, registered proprietors are not deprived of their land without their consent.

- View 3—the discredited view: A final view (heavily criticized in *Swift*) holds that when Brian in our scenario transfers the land to Cai, only the legal title to the land is transferred. Amel therefore remains the beneficial owner of the land throughout. Should Amel have remained on the land through the transfer to Brian and to Cai, she may be able to assert an overriding interest binding on Brian and Cai on the basis of her actual occupation. The decisions in *Malory* and *Fitzwilliam* supported this view which reinforces static security. The key difficulty with this approach is that it side-steps altogether the rectification rules. The court in *Swift* heavily discredited the *Malory/Fitzwilliam* construction, holding it to be *per incuriam* and wrong. This third view of mistake will therefore not be applied.

2.8.1.3 When will the alteration prejudicially affect the title of the registered proprietor?

Alterations which involve the removal of a registered proprietor, the addition of a new proprietor, or which impact upon the value of the registered title will be prejudicial. Not every correction of a mistake will be prejudicial, however. An alteration which is made to reflect an overriding interest which was already binding on the registered proprietor will not be prejudicial to the title and cannot amount to a rectification: *Re Chowood's Registered Land* (1933).

---

[235] *Guy*, [35].   [236] S. Cooper, 'Resolving Title Conflicts in Registered Land' (2015) 131 LQR 108, 111.

2.8.1.4 When will rectification be ordered?

There are a several rather technical hurdles to overcome before rectification can be ordered: see Figure 2.11.

First, rectification is only possible where the alteration satisfies the two limbs outlined: correction of a mistake and prejudice to the title of the registered proprietor.

Secondly, where rectification is made and the registered proprietor is in possession of the land,[237] an additional obstacle must be overcome. Here, rectification is only possible where one of three statutory conditions is met. These conditions are that either (i) the registered proprietor consents to rectification, or (ii) the registered proprietor caused or substantially contributed to the mistake by fraud or lack of proper care, or (iii) it would be unjust not to make the alteration. This reflects a tightening of the law compared with the position of the LRA 1925. Most problematic is the third catch-all condition and, in particular, determining when it will be unjust not to make the alteration. The problem must surely be that, in the natural course of events, it would be unjust not to correct any and all mistakes in the register. In *Rees v Peters* (2011), a restrictive covenant had not been entered into the Charges Register of a registered title. The court held compensation alone would not be adequate and it would be unjust not to order rectification.[238]

Finally, where rectification is not against a proprietor in possession or, if the proprietor is in possession but one of the statutory conditions is met, the court or the Registrar

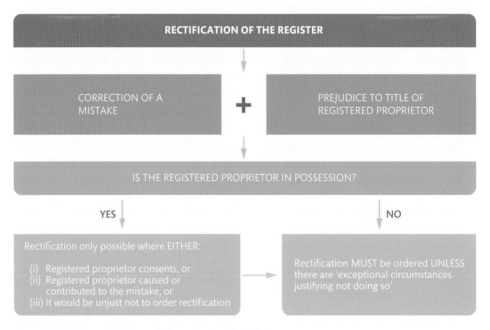

Figure 2.11 When rectification will be ordered under Sch. 4

---

[237] Possession here involves physically possessing the land or possession via agents: s. 131 of the LRA 2002 and confirmed in *Walker*.

[238] In contrast, the old law decision of *Pinto v Lim* (2005) offers an example were rectification was refused as the registered proprietor was held to have acted entirely innocently, was in settled possession, and had been for over four years, occupying the land as a home.

must order rectification and can only refuse to do so if there are exceptional circumstances justifying not doing so.[239] 'Exceptional' means just that and is taken as reflecting a higher standard than merely unusual circumstances. It has been suggested, for example, that rectification might be refused in cases of registered proprietors with severe disabilities or medical conditions who have made significant adjustments to property and alteration of the register would cause particular and disproportionate hardship. In *MacLeod v Gold Harp Properties* (2014),[240] the court refused to accept as 'exceptional' the lengthy delay in applying for rectification. In *Derbyshire CC v Fallon* (2007),[241] alteration of the register to amend the boundary line between two properties was refused on the basis that the registered proprietors, the Fallons, had already built on the land according to the old boundary and that, even if the boundary were to be altered, it was very unlikely the Council would be able to recover the land in any event.[242]

If the necessary hurdles are surmounted, the Registrar will take the required steps to correct the mistake and alter the register. The effects of rectification may be wide-ranging and can, for example, have a significant impact on the priority of interests in land. In *MacLeod*, the court rectified the register to re-enter a lease against the title that had been mistakenly removed. The effect of rectification was that the new proprietor found itself bound by a lease of which it knew nothing when acquiring the land.

2.8.2 **Indemnity**

Just as an effective registration system must make provision for alterations to the register, so too must it allow for the payment of compensation (an indemnity) where loss is suffered. This is the very idea behind Ruoff's 'insurance principle'. Yet, it is not that simple. Importantly, the availability of an indemnity is far more restricted than many students first think. It is certainly not the case that compensation is available whenever the register is altered.

2.8.2.1 When is an indemnity payable?

Under Sch. 8, para. 1, a person is entitled to an indemnity if loss is suffered by reason of:

- rectification of the register;
- failure to rectify the register;
- removal of an innocent registered proprietor from a title as a result of a forgery;
- a mistake in an official search, an official copy, in copy documents kept by the Registrar and referred to in the register;

---

[239] Schedule 4, paras. 3(3) and 6(3) as to court ordered alterations and Registrar ordered alterations respectively. As to what constitutes exceptional circumstances, see *Paton v Todd* (2012).

[240] On which, see R. Smith, 'Land Registration: Rectification and Purchasers' (2015) 74(1) CLJ 10; A. Goymour, 'Resolving the Tension between the Land Registration Act 2002's "Priority" and "Alteration" Provisions' [2015] Conv 253.

[241] Not strictly a rectification case as there was found to be no prejudice to the Fallons in that any alteration of the register would merely be to reflect the real, true boundary of the property.

[242] The Fallons would be able to mount a strong claim to an estoppel to resist any action by the Council; a point conceded by Derbyshire County Council.

- the loss or destruction of documents lodged at Land Registry;
- a mistake in the cautions register;[243]
- failure by the Registrar to perform his s. 50 duty.[244]

No indemnity is payable for other alterations falling outside the listed circumstances. For our purposes, the first three categories of Sch. 8, para. 1 are the most important and all concern the availability of an indemnity where loss is suffered in connection with rectification. Remember that there can be no indemnity in the first place unless the conditions for rectification, outlined in section 2.8.1 are satisfied: correction of a mistake where the alteration has affected or could prejudicially affect the title of the registered proprietor. Let's look a little more closely at these three categories:

1. Loss caused by reason of the rectification itself:[245] An indemnity is payable where a mistake has been corrected and loss has been suffered as a result of that correction—for example, where rectification involves removal of a registered proprietor who, as a consequence, is deprived of title to land.

2. Loss caused by a failure to rectify a mistake:[246] An indemnity is payable where a mistake justifying rectification has arisen but that mistake is not corrected and, in consequence, loss is suffered—for example, where a charge is not registered and the land is subsequently sold to an innocent purchaser who takes possession. Most likely rectification will not be ordered as none of the statutory conditions for rectification where proprietors are in possession will be met. Here, the failure to rectify will cause loss to the chargee (person in whose favour the charge was granted) as it cannot be enforced against the new proprietor and an indemnity may be payable.

3. Loss caused to innocent proprietor by reason of a forgery:[247] An indemnity is payable where an innocent party, acting in good faith, is registered as proprietor of a registered estate on the basis of what transpires to have been a forged disposition. When this proprietor is removed from the register, she is regarded as having suffered loss as a result of this rectification: *Swift*.

In *Swift*, a charge was granted to Swift 1st Ltd against property without the owner's knowledge by way of forgery. When no payments were made, Swift sought possession and the mistake was revealed. The court ordered that the charge be removed from the register and Swift claimed an indemnity. The Registrar argued no indemnity should be paid and that the alteration had not prejudicially affected the title of the registered proprietor, Swift, as the chargee, had always been subject to the landowner's right to have the forged disposition set aside, which was itself an overriding interest binding on Swift. To justify its claim to an indemnity, Swift relied on Sch. 8, para. 1(2)(b) under which the proprietor of a registered charge claiming in good faith under a forged disposition is deemed to have suffered loss. The Registrar raised the authority of *Chowood* (1933) in defence where the court held that

---

[243] This concerns mistakes in the register of cautions against first registration of land.

[244] This concerns the duty of the Registrar under which, when registering a person as proprietor of a statutory charge that has priority over a prior charge entered on the register, the Registrar must notify the prior chargee of that statutory charge.

[245] Schedule 8, para. 1(1)(a).   [246] Ibid., para. 1(1)(b).   [247] Ibid., para. 1(2)(b).

no loss justifying an indemnity had been suffered where the register had been rectified in order to give effect to a long-standing overriding interest binding on the registered title. Having analysed the history of the old law and the present provision paragprah 1(2)(b), the court concluded that 'the application of *Chowood* in the present case would lead to the conclusion that there has been no loss which [was] directly contrary to the statutory presumption under paragraph 1(2)(b)'. Had a different result been intended by Parliament it would have legislated for this more clearly. Swift was therefore entitled to its indemnity.

2.8.2.2 Limitations on the right to an indemnity

Under Sch. 8, there are a number of limitations on the right to an indemnity:

- There is no right to an indemnity if the claimant's loss was caused wholly or in part as a result of her own fraud.[248]
- Right to an indemnity is lost if the claimant's loss was caused wholly as a result of her own lack of proper care.[249]
- Where the claimant's lack of proper care contributed in part to the loss suffered, the indemnity payable will be reduced to such extent as is fair having regard to her share of the responsibility for that loss.[250]
- The right to apply to the court to secure an indemnity will be lost if not brought within six years from the date on which the claimant knew or ought to have known of her claim.[251]
- In cases concerning mines and minerals, no indemnity is payable unless there is an entry on the register indicating that the title to the registered estate included mines and minerals.[252]

2.8.2.3 The measure of the indemnity: How much will be paid?

Where an indemnity is claimed, how much is paid is determined by the value of the estate or interest that has been lost. How this is valued is governed by Sch. 8, para. 6, which tells us:

- Where the indemnity is claimed on the basis of loss suffered as a result of rectification the indemnity payable must not exceed the value of the estate or interest lost immediately before rectification of the register.[253]
- Where the indemnity is claimed on the basis of loss suffered as a result of a failure to rectify the register the indemnity payable must not exceed the value of the estate or interest at the time when the mistake was made which caused the loss.[254]

---

[248] Ibid., para. 5(1)(a): fraud committed by predecessors in title to the claimant (i.e. those holding the land before the claimant) will be treated as fraud of the claimant unless the claimant paid for the registered estate in respect of which the loss was suffered.

[249] Ibid., para. 5(1)(b): lack of proper care of predecessors in title to the claimant will be treated as carelessness of the claimant unless the claimant paid for the registered estate in respect of which the loss was suffered.

[250] Ibid., para. 5(2).

[251] Ibid., para. 8. Most claims to an indemnity proceed on the basis of negotiation between the claimant and the Registrar and no court order is sought.

[252] Ibid., para. 2.   [253] Ibid., para. 6(a).   [254] Ibid., para. 6(b).

The result is that an indemnity is likely to be more favourable under the first head as opposed to the second given that an indemnity payable by reference to the value of the estate or interest immediately prior to rectification will take account of any increase in property prices therefore leading to a larger compensation award. By contrast, under the second head, an indemnity determined by the date of the mistake will not take account of such rises and may reflect a far lower property value. In the event of any dispute concerning the measure of the indemnity payable, a claimant can apply to the court for judicial determination of the matter.[255]

2.9 Future directions

It is hard to overstate the importance and impact of land registration on land law. Its influence has been seismic and it has reshaped and reframed our appreciation of what land law is and how it works. In this section, we pause to reflect on the possible direction of travel for the registration project.

2.9.1 Updating the Land Registration Act 2002

In 2018, the Law Commission produced its recommendations for changes to the LRA 2002 in its report, *Updating the Land Registration Act 2002*. It is important to note that, in spite of these recommendations, for the purposes of your land law course, the changes are mostly technical fixes (which importantly the Government is yet to signal it will implement). Despite the recommendations, the foundational structure of the LRA 2002 explored in this chapter, and its guiding principles, remain intact. You might wish to dip into the 2018 report (and the 2016 consultation paper in particular that gave rise to it) if, for nothing else, to get a helpful summary of the current law. Here, we capture the key reforms recommended by the Law Commission:

- Mines and minerals: Currently not required to be registered with their own titles, the Commission recommends that dispositions of mine and mineral estates should be subject to compulsory registration just like other estates in land.

- Reducing registered land fraud: Fraud is a big problem with criminals impersonating and assuming the identify of owners of land, selling it and disappearing with the proceeds. Land Registry (essentially us as tax payers!) through the guarantee of title, rectification, and indemnity effectively underwrite this loss. Therefore, the Commission recommends changes as to how decisions on the alteration of the register are made including:

    - When a proprietor is removed by mistake, the law should be weighted in favour of returning the land to the innocent party so that, where the proprietor of a registered estate has been removed or omitted from the register by mistake, the proprietor should be restored to the register if she is in possession of the land, unless it would be unjust to do so.

    - The protection afforded to the proprietor of a registered estate who has been removed or omitted from the register by mistake should not be confined to situations where

---

[255] Ibid., para. 7. The court can determine a claimant's entitlement to an indemnity under this provision.

her possession of the land has been continuous, as long as she is the proprietor in possession when the Sch. 4 procedure is applied.

- A 'longstop' should be introduced so that after ten years rectification of the register would generally cease to be possible (though an indemnity would still be available).
- Where a charge (mortgage) is registered by mistake the chargee should not be able to oppose rectification of the register (confined only to an indemnity).
- Where, through a mistake, an interest in land that is granted out of another interest or estate (e.g. a lease granted from a freehold estate) loses priority (and so no longer binds the land), the register should be able to be altered to restore the priority of that interest (the ten-year longstop would also apply here).
- In cases where more than one person is registered as proprietor of the same land—so-called 'multiple registration'—this should be resolved through the scheme for alteration and rectification, applying the above principles (rather than, for example, through the law of adverse possession).

- E-conveyancing: There should be a retreat from the ambition of the LRA 2002 for simultaneous completion of dispositions and their registration in order to facilitate a speedier move towards mandated e-conveyancing (though simultaneous completion and registration should remain the ultimate goal).

- Unilateral notices: Those enjoying interests in land and wishing to protect them by entry of a notice will still be able to do so under the reforms recommended; however, if an application is made (e.g. by the registered proprietor of land) to have the notice cancelled, the Commission recommends that the interest holder will be obliged to provide evidence that shows, on its face, that the interest actually exists. Currently, evidence need only be adduced once the matter has reached a tribunal. The reforms would require evidence to be presented far earlier in the cancellation process.

- Adverse possession: No changes are recommended to the legal principles of adverse possession but rather to clarify the procedure by which a claim is made including:

  - An adverse possessor should be prevented from making a further application under Sch. 6 when a previous application has been rejected under Sch. 6, para. 5.
  - Where a claimant relies on the condition in Sch. 6, para. 5(4), she must apply within 12 months of when her reasonable belief that the land belonged to her came to an end.
  - An adverse possessor of unregistered land should not be able to apply for first registration with possessory title until the unregistered proprietor's superior title has been extinguished under the Limitation Act 1980.
  - An adverse possessor of registered land should not be able to apply for first registration of any legal estate acquired by adverse possession (since the coming into force of the LRA 2002) except through the procedure in Sch. 6.

- Valuable consideration: The Commission recommends that the definition of valuable consideration under s. 132 LRA 2002 be amended to remove the exclusion of 'nominal consideration in money' therefore permitting nominal consideration.

- Owner's powers: Various recommendations are made but chief among them is that the LRA 2002 should be clarified so that, in the case of a person entitled to be registered as the proprietor, owner's powers are not limited by reason only of the fact that the person is not yet registered as the proprietor and so merely has an equitable, rather than a legal title.

- The jurisdiction of the Land Registration Division of the First-Tier Tribunal: The Commission recommends giving the Tribunal a clear statutory power to determine where a boundary line lies in boundary disputes (currently it is somewhat unclear if it has this power), and the power to make declarations on (i) how an equity by estoppel should be satisfied and (ii) the extent of a beneficial interest in land.

The 2018 Report is a major piece of work—we wait to see if Government implements the reforms recommended—but you should not lose sight of the fact that it does not change the fundamental pillars of land registration discussed in this chapter. The project was only ever intended to reflect on and recommend technical (albeit important) tweaks to improve the efficiency and clarity of the registration system.

Putting to one side the Law Commission's recent work, where might land registration be headed?

2.9.2 The future of e-conveyancing

The fundamental objective of the LRA 2002 was not just to get more titles registered but was about delivering what Gardner has termed 'constitutive registration'[256]—in other words, that the creation and disposition of interests in land was to be 'constituted' by registration and was to happen simultaneously. Gardner explains that 'the establishment of registration arrangements was not the end in itself, but a means to deliver the Act's real key aspiration, namely that all conveyancing would take place via a prescribed form of electronic transaction'.[257] If the end-game was e-conveyancing, in looking to the future we must ask whether the e-conveyancing project is in rude health or in trouble?

Despite clear assertions that the LRA 2002 was to be the vehicle for delivering an e-conveyancing revolution and introduction of electronic dealings with land was 'the most important single function' of the legislation,[258] it is fair to say the march towards electronic dealings with registered land has stalled. The project was officially put 'on hold' by Land Registry in 2011,[259] for which three reasons were given: (1) fraud: concerns that levels of fraud would be increased; (2) timing: the global, economic downturn had reduced appetite for take-up; (3) practical difficulties with delegating to conveyancers the power to provide e-signatures for dispositions on their clients' behalf.[260] After spending many millions of pounds on the project, it seemed the Land Registry had (perhaps understandably) lost its nerve. The Law Commission in its 2016 Consultation acknowledged the barriers to the introduction noting that, 'in light of these concerns, simultaneous completion and registration does not provide a practical way forward at this time. We feel that for electronic conveyancing to become a reality it is necessary to step back from the goal.'[261] The Commission has now recommended removal of provision for simultaneous completion and registration under the LRA 2002, with the result that the 'registration gap' will endure and the possibility of equitable

---

[256] S. Gardner, 'The Land Registration Act 2002—the Show on the Road' (2014) 77(5) MLR 763, 764.
[257] Ibid.   [258] Law Commission Report No. 271, [13.1].
[259] Land Registry Report on Responses to E-Conveyancing Secondary Legislation Part 3, [5.2].
[260] Ibid., [5.1].   [261] Law Commission Consultation Paper No. 227, [2.20].

interests arising between completion of dealings with land and their registration remains real.[262] We are, without doubt, seeing the dilution of the ambition of e-conveyancing (certainly in the short term) and the sound is very much of the can being kicked down the road. E-conveyancing feels, if anything, further off on the horizon than it did when the buzz around e-dealings with land was first fizzing when the 2002 Act joined the statute books. Should we care? Well, yes, if we want to close the registration gap. Beyond this, there are financial as well as efficiency arguments in favour of e-conveyancing and, as Gardner argues, even citizens' autonomy is at stake by the failure or 'lapse' in the e-conveyancing project:[263]

> Without e-conveyancing, parties do not have the same control over the registration events that constitutively adjust their title. Instead, these events are brought about by the Registry staff. This is the reason for viewing the lapse of e-conveyancing as diminishing the parties' autonomy. However, the argument is less clear-cut than it may seem. With e-conveyancing, registration events would not normally have been brought about by the parties in person: rather by their lawyers, following their instructions. Without e-conveyancing, the parties instruct their lawyers, who instruct the Registry staff, who bring about the events. There appears no reason to think that the Registry staff are more often delinquent in following their instructions than the parties' lawyers themselves, so the insertion of this additional link in the chain probably makes little practical difference (other than as a source of delay, as already discussed). On the other hand . . . the parties select their own lawyers, whereas they by no means select the Registry officer who deals with their matter . . . It is surely fair to say that in none of these respects is the present regime, without e-conveyancing, intolerable. Certainly, their significance is less practical (normally) than symbolic. But in at least some degree they represent ways in which the lapse of e-conveyancing leaves the regime less supportive of autonomy than it would otherwise have been, and as such render this lapse regrettable.

Yet e-conveyancing may not be all sunlit uplands. There may be unintended consequences including the facilitation of fraud. It is far easier to commit fraud electronically than to forge a signature on paper.[264] It has also been suggested that e-conveyancing could result in an explosion of proprietary estoppel claims where there has been non-compliance with the e-regime—for example, if an attempt is made to create or deal with a property right outside the electronic conveyancing system.[265] As Cooke has indicated, estoppel in this context places in the hands of the court 'the power to sabotage the new system'.[266] Perhaps the 'evaporation'[267] of the promise of e-conveyancing is to be cautiously welcomed as providing space to step back to reflect on the best way to proceed.

2.9.3 The future of the concept of overreaching

As long ago as 1989,[268] the Law Commission recommended that in cases involving the family home, overreaching should only be possible with the consent of those enjoying beneficial interests in the home, in occupation, of full age and with capacity. The aim of the

---

[262] Ibid., [2.23]–[2.24]. Simultaneous creation and registration remains an 'ultimate, if long term, goal'.

[263] Gardner, 'The Land Registration Act 2002—the Show on the Road', 770–1.

[264] See Cooke, *The New Law of Land Registration*, 164.

[265] M. Dixon, 'Proprietary Estoppel and Formalities in Land Law and the Land Registration Act 2002: A Theory of Unconscionability' in E. Cooke (ed.), *Modern Studies in Property Law*, Vol. 2 (Oxford: Hart, 2003), 165.

[266] Cooke, *The New Law of Land Registration*, 164.

[267] As Gardner describes the failure to deliver on the e-conveyancing revolution: Gardner, 'The Land Registration Act 2002—the Show on the Road', 779.

[268] Report No. 188, 'Transfer of Land, Overreaching: Beneficiaries in Occupation' (1989).

consent requirement was to ensure purchasers made further enquiries when buying property consisting of a family home and to offer greater protections to those with interests in the home. This recommendation was not adopted by the government, however.[269] The government's rejection of the proposal indicated that property as investment, alienability, and the interests of purchasers of land trump considerations of interest holders.

Owen has recently called for significant reform to (though not abandonment of) the concept of overreaching. Owen draws on experience from Australia to argue that beneficiaries should be able to register their interests under a reformed LRA 2002 regime. Currently, they can enter a restriction to ensure overreaching but cannot enter a notice. Owen explains that, under his scheme, only where beneficiaries have not registered their interests could overreaching take place.[270] At present, there are no indications that reform along these lines is on the cards but should we look again at overreaching? Is overreaching, for example, human-rights compliant? This issue was raised but not fully litigated in the cases of *Birmingham Midshires Mortgage Services v Sabherwal* (2000) and *National Westminster Bank plc v Malhan* (2004) but the challenge on human rights grounds was rejected on the basis that Art. 8 did not have retrospective effect and could not, therefore, be pertinent in either case. Despite this, there is surely force in the argument that the automatic operation of overreaching on the payment to two or more trustees under s. 27 of the LPA 1925 without room for the personal circumstances of the parties to be balanced against those of the purchaser is vulnerable to an Art. 8 challenge.[271] We await a test case. The Law Commission did not, as part of its 2016–18 project *Updating the Land Registration Act 2002*, review the law on overreaching, arguing that overreaching rested largely on the provisions of the LPA 1925 and therefore fell outside its consultative focus on the 2002 Act.[272]

2.9.4 Should a fully complete and accurate register really be the ambition of the LRA 2002?

As we have seen, the completeness and accuracy of the register is a key goal of the registration project and yet this ambition is heavily undermined in a number of ways by the LRA 2002, particularly by the retention of the category of overriding interests which are binding despite not appearing on the register.[273] Given that the scope of overriding interests falls outside the remit of the Law Commission's latest review and no significant change to the law of overriding interests is anticipated anytime soon, has the moment not arrived that the ambition of comprehensiveness be abandoned? As Gardner has noted, an approach to registration of 'the more the better' may be an unsafe strategy for devising a

---

[269] 1998 587 HL Deb WA213.

[270] J. G. Owen, 'A New Paradigm for Overreaching: Some Inspiration from Down Under' [2013] Conv 377, 391; see also J. G. Owen, 'A New Model for Overreaching: Some Historical Inspiration' [2015] Conv 226; Owen and Cahill, 'Overreaching—Getting the Right Balance'.

[271] McFarlane, *The Structure of Property Law*, 404.

[272] See, however, N. Jackson, 'Overreaching in Registered Land Law' (2006) 69(2) MLR 214, who has argued (in reference to the LRA 1925 provisions) that the registration legislation contains its own overreaching machinery and not under the LPA 1925.

[273] Equally, the guarantee of title under s. 58 of the Act is qualified by the broad power to rectify the register to correct 'mistakes'.

functioning registration regime.[274] Much rhetoric surrounded the enactment of the 2002 Act, giving rise to an impression of an unstoppable march or of an ambition of 100 per cent registration of rights in land. Surely this was wholly unrealistic. The tenor of the debate encircling overriding interests, in particular in the work leading to the 2002 Act, portrayed overriding interests as the unfortunate, 'unsatisfactory' blight or canker on an otherwise gleaming registration system. Perhaps this tone and the insistence on a 'conveyancing revolution' was too feverish and over-enthusiastic and, after almost two decades of the LRA 2002 being in force, the time is now to reflect on whether it will *always* be desirable that the Julia Bolands of this world triumph despite non-registration of their interests. This drive to evermore registration should, on this view, be revisited. Certainly, the tension which land law is called upon to resolve between static/dynamic security, between occupiers whose interests have not been registered on one side and banks and purchasers on the other, is not going anywhere. That is not to say that we disembark wholesale from the registration train but perhaps we should accept the long-term, meaningful, and entirely justified role for overriding interests within the registration regime.

Further reading

- C. Bevan, 'Overriding and Over-Extended? Actual Occupation: A Call to Orthodoxy' [2016] Conv 104, 117.
- B. Bogusz, 'Defining the Scope of Actual Occupation under the LRA 2002: Some Recent Judicial Clarification' [2011] Conv 268.
- B. Bogusz, 'The Relevance of "Intentions and Wishes" to Determine Actual Occupation: A Sea Change in Judicial Thinking?' [2014] Conv 27, 27–32.
- E. Cooke, 'Children and Real Property: Trusts, Interests and Considerations' (June 1998) Fam Law 349.
- E. Cooke, *Land Law* (Oxford: Oxford University Press, 2012), chapter 6.
- E. Cooke, 'The Register's Guarantee of Title' [2013] Conv 344.
- E. Cooke and P. O'Connor, 'Purchaser Liability to Third Parties in the English Land Registration System: A Comparative Perspective' (2004) 120 LQR 640.
- S. Cooper, 'Regulating Fallibility in Registered Land Titles' (2013) 72 CLJ 341.
- R. Demogue, 'Security' in A. Fouillée et al. (eds.), *Modern French Legal Philosophy* (Boston: The Boston Book Co., 1916).
- G. Ferris and G. Battersby, 'General Principles of Overreaching and the Reforms of the 1925 Legislation' (2002) 118 LQR 270.
- G. Ferris and G. Battersby, 'The General Principles of Overreaching and the Modern Legislative Reforms 1996–2002' (2003) 119 LQR 94.
- A. Goymour, 'Mistaken Registrations of Land: Exploding the Myth of "Title by Registration"' (2013) 72(3) CLJ 617.
- C. Harpum and J. Bignall, *Land Registration* (Bristol: Jordans, 2004).

---

[274] Gardner, 'The Land Registration Act 2002—the Show on the Road', 779.

- D. Hayton, *Registered Land*, 3rd edn (London: Sweet and Maxwell, 1981).
- N. Jackson, 'Title by Registration and Concealed Overriding Interests: The Cause and Effect of Antipathy to Documentary Proof' (2003) 119 LQR 660.
- N. Jackson, 'Overreaching in Registered Land Law' (2006) 69 MLR 214.
- E. Lees, 'Title by Registration: Rectification, Indemnity and Mistake and the Land Registration Act 2002' (2013) 75 MLR 62.
- E. Lees, 'Registration and Make-Believe and Forgery: *Swift 1st Ltd v Chief Land Registrar*' (2015) 131 LQR 515.
- B. McFarlane, 'Eastenders, Neighbours and Upstairs Downstairs' [2013] Conv 74.
- P. O'Connor, 'Registration of Title in England and Australia' in E. Cooke (ed.), *Modern Studies in Property Law*, Vol. 2 (Oxford: Hart, 2003).
- J. G. Owen, 'A New Paradigm for Overreaching—Some Inspiration from Down Under' [2013] Conv 377.
- J. G. Owen, 'A New Model for Overreaching—Some Historical Inspiration' [2015] Conv 226.
- J. G. Owen and D. Cahill, 'Overreaching—Getting the Right Balance' [2017] Conv 26.
- T. B. F. Ruoff, *An Englishman Looks at the Torrens System* (Sydney: Law Book Co. of Australasia, 1957).
- P. Sparkes, 'The Discoverability of Occupiers in Registered Land' [1989] Conv 342.

 ## Online resources

Access the online resources at www.oup.com/uk/bevan2e/ to test yourself with self-test questions and scenario problems. You can also view additional supporting material relevant to the topics in this chapter, including:

- *Videos*
- *Audio podcasts*
- *Maps, diagrams, and flowcharts*
- *Interactive exercises*
- *Examples of real-life legal documentation*

3 Unregistered Land

3.1 Introduction

As we saw in Chapter 2, we are on a march towards ever greater numbers of titles in England and Wales joining the register and becoming part of the registered land system governed by the Land Registration Act 2002. We also noted in section 2.1 that just 14 per cent of the titles in England and Wales remains unregistered and this is diminishing year on year. Why, then, devote a chapter to unregistered land? Why bother? Well, there are two reasons: first, unregistered land, like it or not, continues to play a residual role in modern land law and, although its influence is dwindling,[1] there remains a core clutch of land for which, for the foreseeable future, there will be no trigger for compulsory registration and will therefore remain unregistered. Secondly, an appreciation of the principles of unregistered land gives you, as students of the subject, a better insight into and a more informed angle on the principles of registered land and their effectiveness. Almost 100 years after the 1925 raft of legislation—much of which was designed to facilitate land registration—unregistered land principles retain a significance. In this short chapter, we consider how dealings with unregistered land known as 'title deeds conveyancing' operate.

 Visit the online resources to watch a video on why we study unregistered land.

3.2 Unregistered title deeds conveyancing: An overview

We start with what might seem like an obvious question, yet is a fundamental one: what actually is unregistered land? When we speak of 'unregistered land', what we are referring to is land whose title is not to be found on the register held and managed by Land Registry. This means that in unregistered land, title to or, put differently, ownership of land has to be *proved* in the old-fashioned way—in other words, by investigating the conveyancing history of the land. This involves trawling through the physical title documents: bundles of conveyances, deeds, and other papers which offer an account of how the land has been

---

[1] Encouraged by Land Registry through voluntary registration and incentives such as reduced registration fees.

dealt with and through whose hands it has passed. As we touched upon in Chapter 2, dealings with unregistered land are called 'title deeds conveyancing' and are quite different to dealings with registered land where proving title involves a simple inspection of the register, much of which can now be done online. In section 3.3, we consider how a would-be purchaser of unregistered land investigates title.

When a person acquires unregistered land, what they want to know is whether they are bound by any pre-existing interests burdening the land they have purchased. Third-party rights exist in unregistered land just as they do in registered land: leasehold estates, easements, covenants, and so on. What differs is how the 'enforceability' or 'priority' question is addressed. As we explore in section 3.4, in unregistered land the enforceability of third-party rights is determined by asking a series of questions. In summary, this means we begin by asking: what is the nature of the right? Is it legal or equitable? Is the right a 'commercial' right or a 'family' right? Can it be overreached or does it falls outside these categories? For rights which are commercial in character, there exists a limited scheme of registration under the Land Charges Act 1972 (LCA 1972).[2]

It is vital from the outset that you keep title deeds conveyancing completely separate in your mind from the registered land regime we encountered in Chapter 2. In particular, you need to draw a clear distinction between the partial system of registration that exists in unregistered land under the LCA 1972 from the far more substantial registered land regime under the LRA 2002. Try to avoid allowing registered principles to bleed into discussion of unregistered land and vice versa. Do note, however, that the doctrine of overreaching applies to both registered land and unregistered land. To understand the system of title deeds conveyancing, we must therefore examine in more detail, first, how title is proved and what we understand by investigating title before turning to consider the steps we must follow to determine the enforceability of third-party rights in unregistered land.

3.3 Investigation of title

Although the precise mechanics of the purchase/sale of unregistered land are not of direct concern to us in this book, a little background is helpful particularly in understanding when and how investigation of title to unregistered land fits into this broader picture:

- The first stage in the purchase/sale process is pre-contractual negotiations[3] (sometimes called pre-exchange) during which the purchaser and vendor agree, amongst other matters, on the price to be paid for the land.

- Then comes the second stage: the 'exchange of contracts' stage during which contracts for sale of the land are signed and passed between the parties. When contracts have been exchanged, a binding contract (known as an 'estate contract' which can be protected by registration under the Land Charges Act 1972)[4] exists between the parties.

---

[2] The 1972 legislation's forerunner, the LCA 1925, was introduced as part of the raft of important legislation introduced in 1925. We explored this in Chapter 1.

[3] There is also a 'local land charges' search. Local land charges are restrictions on a piece of land which limit its use—for example, relating to planning or road decisions, tree or other conservation orders.

[4] We explore registration of estate contracts under the LCA 1972 and its significance in section 3.4.3.

From then on, should either side back out of the deal (i.e. withdraw from the contract), they will commit a breach of contract and the wronged party may be able to seek a remedy such as specific performance of the contract. It is after the exchange of contracts that the title to the land will be investigated. Investigation of title requires the vendor to produce an 'abstract of title' which consists of a bundle of deeds recording previous dealings with the land. From this, the purchaser must establish 'good root of title' going back at least 15 years.[5] A good root of title is evidence of an unbroken chain of ownership of the land ending with the current owner, the vendor. This is usually demonstrated by providing documentation showing any relevant conveyances of the estate.[6] This proves that the party selling the land actually owns it and is entitled to sell it. If the vendor cannot produce evidence from which 15 years' good root of title can be proved, the purchaser is entitled to withdraw the contract for sale of the land. Once investigation of title has taken place and at least 15 years of 'good title' established, the purchaser will make a physical inspection of the land as well as searching the register of land charges (we discuss this in section 3.4).

- The final step in the process is the 'completion stage' which involves the formal conveyance of the land by deed[7] to the new owner and payment of any outstanding sums. Keys are handed over and the new owner takes possession of the land.

3.4 The enforceability of third-party rights in unregistered land

For a person acquiring unregistered land, a key question is whether she will be bound by any pre-existing third-party interests affecting that land. We explore this 'enforceability question' in this section. The enforceability of third-party interests in unregistered land is determined by the nature of the right in question: see Figure 3.1.

3.4.1 Legal third-party rights

Under the principle of universal enforceability, legal rights in unregistered land are binding on the world—in other words, are enforceable whether or not any purchaser has notice or knowledge of the right. In practice, this means that a purchaser of unregistered land will take the land subject to all pre-existing legal rights including, for example, legal leases or legal easements whether or not she knew of them prior to or at the time of the sale. There is an exception to this position: so-called **puisne mortgages** which are second legal

---

[5] Prior to 1970, the vendor was required to provide the purchaser with an abstract of title going back 30 years but this was reduced to 15 under s. 23 of the Law of Property Act 1969 (LPA 1969).

[6] See the classic definition of 'good root of title' in T. C. Williams and J. M. Lightwood, *A Treatise on the Law of Vendor and Purchaser*, 4th edn (London: Sweet & Maxwell, 1936), 47: an instrument of disposition which 'must deal with or prove on the face of it, without the aid of extrinsic evidence ownership of the whole legal and equitable estate and interest in the property; contain a description by which the property can be identified; and show nothing to cast any doubt on the title of the disposing parties'.   [7] As required by s. 52(1) of the LPA 1925.

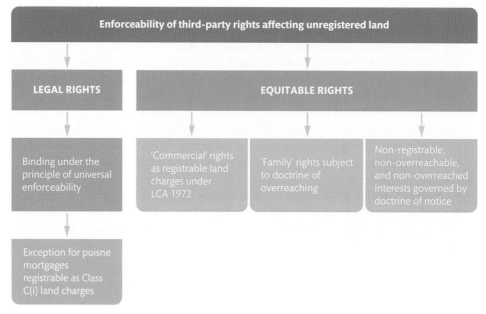

Figure 3.1 Enforceability of third-party rights in unregistered land

mortgages and are registrable as Class C(i) land charges under s. 2(4)(i) of the LCA 1972[8] and not universally enforceable despite being legal rights.

3.4.2 **Equitable third-party rights**

The position of equitable rights is less straightforward. It helps to draw a distinction between three categories of equitable rights:

- 'commercial' interests which are registrable as land charges under the LCA 1972
- 'family' interests which are not registrable as land charges but are subject to the doctrine of overreaching
- non-registrable, non-overreachable, and non-overreached rights which are governed by the doctrine of notice.

These are not categories that you will find written down in statute but help you to understand now the law works in this area and this categorization has been used by the courts. Before 1926, all equitable interests were subject to the traditional doctrine of notice (which we discuss in section 3.4.5) but a limited scheme of land charges registration was introduced by the LCA 1925. This regime did not and never was intended to provide for registration of all equitable rights. Those rights falling outside the scheme were to remain subject to the doctrine of notice. This position is unchanged today albeit now governed by the current legislation, the LCA 1972. As Robert Walker LJ clarified in *Birmingham Midshires v Sabherwal* (2000) 'the essential distinction is, as the authors of Megarry and Wade note,

---

[8] Section 2(4)(i) of the LCA 1972. We discuss puisne mortgages in section 3.4.1.

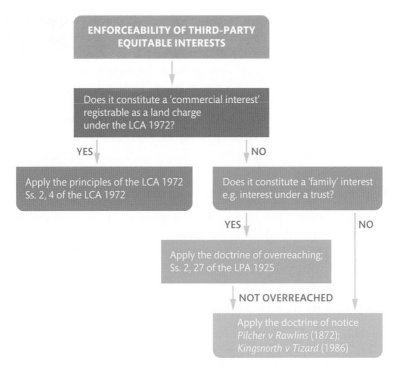

Figure 3.2 Enforceability of equitable rights in unregistered land

between commercial and family interests'.[9] Commercial interests are those registrable as land charges under the LCA 1972. Family interests (or non-commercial interests) are those not registrable under the LCA 1972 and include (most importantly for our purposes) equitable interests under a trust. Interests under a trust are, however, offered a degree of protection by way of the doctrine of overreaching.[10] Figure 3.2 summarizes the position. It is only where an interest is non-commercial and not overreached that the doctrine of notice becomes operative in a residual capacity.

In assessing the enforceability of equitable rights in unregistered land, there are therefore three categories to consider: (1) commercial rights; (2) family rights; and (3) non-commercial, non-overreachable, and non-overreached rights. Let's take a closer look at each of these.

3.4.3 Commercial interests registrable as land charges under the LCA 1972

As we noted in the Introduction, the LCA 1925 introduced a partial system of registration for certain categories of third party equitable interests,[11] which are called 'land charges'. This is quite distinct from the wholesale title registration system of the LRA 2002 applicable in registered land. It may seem rather odd to talk of 'registration' in unregistered land

---

[9] *Sabherwal*, [28].   [10] See section 3.4.2.

[11] With one exception: puisne mortgages, which are legal interests registrable as land charges under the LCA 1925 and now as Class C(i) land charges under the LCA 1972.

but do remember that this is a very curtailed, limited scheme and still very much forms part of the system of title deeds conveyancing. As Megarry and Wade note, the aim of the land charges Act 1925, replaced by the LCA 1972, was to allow registration of 'numerous everyday transactions',[12] to reduce the application of the doctrine of notice which was regarded as generating unacceptable uncertainty, and to replace it with a form of statutory notice. Put simply, where registered as a land charge, a right is binding on a purchaser irrespective of whether that purchaser would or would not have had notice of it under the old doctrine of notice principles. We need to unpack the LCA 1972 regime a little further. A number of issues require our attention.

3.4.3.1 Which interests can be registered as land charges?

Section 2 of the LCA 1972 provides for a list of interests which are registrable as land charges. These interests are divided into six 'classes' and certain classes are then further subdivided. For our purposes, Classes C(i), C(iv), D(ii), D(iii), and F are by far the most important: see Table 3.1.

3.4.3.2 Which interests are excluded from registration?

Aside from those exclusions provided for by statute (pre-1926 restrictive covenants and easements (see Table 3.1)), there are further interests which are 'commercial' in nature but cannot be registered as land charges including: rights arising from an estoppel,[13] rights of re-entry for breach of a covenant in a lease,[14] and 'family' interests which are capable of being overreached.[15]

3.4.3.3 How does land charges registration work?

Under s. 3(1) of the LCA 1972, when a land charge is registered, it is registered against the *name* of the owner of the unregistered estate at the time of registration and not against the *title* itself. The Land Charges Register under the LCA 1972 is therefore a register of names rather than titles. A purchaser, after exchanging contracts and investigating the title, will then move to search the Land Charges Register via either a personal search (very rare and risky) or by requisitioning an official search (more common and advantageous)[16] to discover what interests affect the land. Names-based registration can, however, pose difficulties.[17] Why? Well, clearly the effectiveness of the Land Charges Register rests on the interest being recorded against the correct name and searches being made against the correct name also. What could go wrong? Consider the following:

---

[12] *Megarry and Wade: The Law of Real Property*, ed. C. Harpum, 6th edn (London: Sweet & Maxwell, 2000), [5–086].   [13] *E. R. Ives Investments v High* (1967).

  [14] *Shiloh Spinners Ltd v Harding* (1973).   [15] We discuss 'family' interests in section 3.4.4.

  [16] An official search is carried out against name(s) provided to the Land Registry by the purchaser or purchaser's representative. An official search is the preferred option as, under s. 10(4) of the LCA 1972, a search certificate is generated which is taken as conclusive; provides for protection to purchasers against any interests registered between search and completion of the sale (under a 'priority period') and any errors give rise to an action in negligence against Land Registry.

  [17] See H. W. R. Wade, 'Land Charges Revisited' (1956) 14(2) CLJ 216 who described the system as akin to Frankenstein's monster.

Table 3.1 Classes C, D, and F land charges under s. 2 of the LCA 1972

CLASS OF LAND CHARGE	INTEREST
Class C(i)	**Puisne mortgages** • This is the only legal interest registrable as a land charge under the LCA 1972 and an exception to the principle of universal enforceability of legal rights in unregistered land. • A **puisne mortgage** is defined in s. 2(4)(i) as a 'legal mortgage which is not protected by deposition of documents relating to the legal estate affected'. • Puisne mortgages are usually second or subsequent mortgages since the first legal mortgagee (lender) will generally be holding the title deeds and so registration offers protection to the second/subsequent mortgagee with whom no deeds are deposited.

Class C(iv)	**Estate contracts**
	• Arguably the most important and broadest class of land charge, estate contracts are contracts to convey or create any legal estate or interest (defined in s. 2(4)(iv)). Common examples include:
	  – contracts for the sale of freehold land (discussed in section 3.3)
	  – contracts to grant a lease
	  – contracts granting an option to purchase
	  – contracts to create a mortgage
	  – contracts to create an easement.

Class D(ii)	**Restrictive covenants** • Not all restrictive covenants can be registered: only those (i) entered into after 1 January 1926 and (ii) relating to freehold land are registrable land charges. • Pre-1926 restrictive covenants are subject to the doctrine of notice.
Class D(iii)	**Equitable easements** • Not all easements can be registered: only those (i) which are equitable in nature (legal easements are universally enforceable) and (ii) created on or after 1 January 1926. • Pre-1926 equitable easements are subject to the doctrine of notice. • An attempt by Lord Denning in *E. R. Ives Investments v High* (1967) to import a narrow interpretation of Class D(iii) land charges as extending only to easements that would have been legal had they been created before 1926 has been criticized as artificial and should not be followed: *Shiloh Spinners Ltd v Harding* (1973). All equitable easements created on or after 1 January 1926 are registrable as Class D(iii) land charges.
Class F	**Statutory home rights of occupation in matrimonial/civil partnership home** • Rights of occupation of matrimonial/civil partnership homes conferred under Part IV of the Family Law Act 1996 on spouses and civil partners not owning legal title to the property are registrable as Class F land charges. • Registration is unlikely as parties very rarely aware of this avenue of protection for their rights to occupation. • Home rights (discussed in Chapter 6) are not to be confused with the question of beneficial interests under a trust or 'family' interests.

• where the interest was registered against the wrong name, but an official search is made against the correct name: This will naturally not reveal any interests. The purchaser will have a defence against the wrongly-registered interest which will not be binding on her: *Diligent Finance v Alleyne* (1972).

- where the interest was registered against the correct name but an official search is made against the wrong name: The purchaser will be bound by the interest that the search failed to divulge.
- where vendors go by several different names or make common use of a nickname: the court expects purchasers to search against all common variations and versions of the vendor's name and will be bound if they fail to do so and the interest was registered against such a common variation in name: *Oak Co-operative Building Society v Blackburn* (1968).[18]
- where the purchaser does not know or has not been given the full name of the vendor or the full names of all previous owners against which to search: the purchaser will be unable to conduct a fulsome search to discover all interests potentially binding on her.

Fortunately, every year more and more titles are joining the registered land system we explored in Chapter 2 and so the problems and pitfalls of names-based registration are quickly becoming less and less important. More recent cases have also attempted to take a common-sense approach, clarifying that it is the name provided in the conveyancing documentation which is regarded as the 'fixed point of reference'.[19]

3.4.3.4 What is the effect of registration?

It was a central aim of the LCA 1925 that the doctrine of notice be replaced with statutory notice for those interests registrable as land charges. This position is confirmed by s. 198(1) of the LPA 1925 which provides that registration of a land charge under the LCA 1972 'shall be deemed to constitute actual notice' of the interest to all persons and for all purposes. This means that once registered, everyone in the world (!) is deemed as knowing of the interest's existence. Purchasers will, as such, be bound by the interest.

3.4.3.5 What is the effect of non-registration?

Section 4 of the LCA 1972 sets out the effect of non-registration. In general terms, a registrable interest (i.e. one capable of registration) that is, nevertheless, not registered will be rendered void as against a purchaser of the land. Particular statutory provisions apply depending on the precise class of land charge in issue.

Non-registration of a class C(iv) or class D land charge

Under s. 4(6) of the LCA 1972, if not registered, an interest of these classes is rendered void against a purchaser for money or money's worth of a legal estate in the land. Such a purchaser therefore takes the land free of these non-registered interests. Non-purchasers for example those receiving land by way of a gift or purchasers other than for money or money's worth will nevertheless take the land subject to the non-registered interest.

---

[18] See *Oak Co-operative Building Society v Blackburn* (1968) where the court held that purchasers should search against all common forms of the name of a vendor—for example, Frank, Francis, etc.

[19] *Standard Property Investment plc v British Plastics Federation* (1985).

Non-registration of other classes of land charge

As to all other classes of land charge, non-registration will result in the interest being void as against a purchaser for 'valuable consideration' of any interest in the land.[20] Such a purchaser therefore takes the land free of these non-registered interests. Again, non-purchasers or purchases other than for valuable consideration will take subject to the non-registered interest.

The key distinction between non-registration of Classes C(iv) and D land charges and non-registration of all other classes is therefore twofold: first, in the former category, interests are void as against purchaser for 'money or money's worth' whereas for all other classes interests are void against purchasers for 'valuable consideration' as within the definition of a purchaser under the 1972 Act.[21] Valuable consideration embraces a wider definition than money or money's worth and includes marriage consideration. Secondly, non-registration of Classes C(iv) and D land charges will only render the interest void against purchasers of a legal estate. Non-registration of all other classes renders the interest void against purchasers of any interest in the land—for example, equitable interests.

3.4.3.6 Attempts to circumvent the consequences of non-registration

A series of arguments have been advanced in an attempt to avoid the consequences of non-registration under the LCA 1972. We explore five of these arguments here.

Argument 1: Where a purchaser has actual notice of the non-registered interest

The limited system of registration under the LCA 1972 appeared to close the door on any argument based on the doctrine of notice. Section 199(1) of the LPA 1925 provides that notice of any interest which is rendered void by a provision of the Land Charges Act 1925

KEY CASE *Midland Bank Trust Co. Ltd v Green* (1981)

Facts: Walter was the freehold owner of farmland. In 1961, He granted to his son, Geoffrey, who was actively farming the land, an option to purchase the land. Under the LCA 1925 in force at the time, this option to purchase land, as an estate contract, was registrable as a Class C land charge. Geoffrey failed to register the option. There followed a significant breakdown in familial relations and Walter wished to revoke the option. In 1967, in order to defeat the unregistered option, Walter sold the farmland to his wife, Evelyne, for just £500 (the land was worth in the region of £40,000). At all times, Evelyne had actual notice (i.e. actually knew) of the option to purchase that Walter had granted to Geoffrey.

Legal issue: Was Geoffrey entitled to a declaration from the court that the option was still binding and an order for specific performance or was the option unenforceable as a result of his failure to register it under the LCA? What relevance should be attached to Evelyne's actual notice of the option and her and Walter's apparent bad faith in conspiring to sell the land to defeat the option?

Judgment: At first instance, the trial judge rejected Geoffrey's claim arguing that the conveyance of the farmland to Evelyne had been a genuine sale and fell squarely within the definition of a sale to a purchaser for money or money's worth as defined by the LCA 1925. On this basis, the option was

→

---

[20] See s. 4(2), (5), (8) of the LCA 1972.
[21] Ibid., s. 17.

→

unenforceable. Geoffrey appealed and was successful. The Court of Appeal, reversing the trial judge's decision, held that the sale to Evelyne did not constitute a sale for 'money or money's worth' as, on the findings of the trial judge: (1) the sale was calculated to defeat Geoffrey's option; and (2) the £500 paid for the land was a 'grotesque undervalue'. In these circumstances, Evelyne was not, for the purposes of the legislation, to be considered a purchaser. Evelyne's estate appealed to the House of Lords. In the House of Lords, it was held, per Lord Wilberforce:

1. There was no requirement under the definition of a 'purchaser' under the LCA 1925 or indeed anywhere in the legislative scheme that such a person must be acting in good faith. To write in these words would be 'bold' and this omission from the legislation was to be understood as deliberate. To insert a good faith requirement would involve an inquiry into the purchaser's subjective state of mind. This was not intended by the LCA and would involve a violent departure from the language of the statute.

2. This case was 'a plain one and the Act . . . clear and definite'. The option was entered into after 1 January 1926, Evelyne had provided monetary consideration for the land, and the option had not been registered. The option was therefore void as against Evelyne. The statute should not be 'read down or glossed: to do so would destroy the usefulness of the Act'.

3. The LCA required that money or money's worth be provided. This was intended to exclude marriage consideration but was not intended to require consideration that was more than nominal. The sale at an undervalue amounted to monetary consideration and no inquiry into the adequacy of this consideration was permitted. Any references to a requirement of more than nominal consideration under the LPA 1925 definition of a 'purchaser' could not be extended to apply to the LCA 1925. To do so would be to rewrite the statute.

4. An action in the tort of conspiracy did, however, exist against Walter and Evelyne.

or later enactment is irrelevant. Nevertheless, in *Midland Bank Trust Co. Ltd v Green*,[22] an attempt was made to argue that a purchaser with actual knowledge or notice of a registrable but non-registered interest should nevertheless be bound by that interest.

The effect of *Green* in the House of Lords may, at first, seem rather harsh to poor Geoffrey. However, it is nothing more than an assertion by the court of the primacy of registration and a strong endorsement and confirmation of the strict and clearly worded provisions of the LCA. The Law Commission in its Report No. 158 in 1987 had initially made its feelings plain that 'the consequences of omitting a good faith element do not seem to us acceptable'.[23] However, by the time of its Report No. 254 in 1998, the Commission had resiled from this view. Any attempt to add a gloss to the words of the statute on the basis of good faith or a purchaser's actual notice of a non-registered interest is therefore untenable.[24] As Megarry and Wade note,[25] the clarity of this approach comes at a price:

Convenience [under the LCA 1925] was bought at the price of injustice in cases where the owners of registrable interests did not realise that they should register them . . . and so suffered loss. To allow the defeat of a prior interest by a later transaction is a failure on the part of the law . . .

---

[22] See, generally, M. Thompson, '*Midland Bank v Green* (1980): Maintaining the Integrity of Registration Systems' in N. Gravells (ed.), *Landmark Cases in Land Law* (Oxford: Hart, 2013).

[23] Law Commission Report No. 158, *Third Report on Land Registration* (1987), [4.15].

[24] See also *Coles v Samuel Smith Old Brewery and Rochdale* (2007) in which a similar argument based on a purchaser's actual knowledge of an unregistered option to purchase again failed.

[25] *Megarry and Wade: The Law of Real Property*, [5–120].

the House of Lords [in *Midland Bank v Green*] has now [however] reasserted the stark policy of 1925, unethical and uncompromising but clear and simple, at least for those who are aware of it.

Argument 2: Where there is a fraudulent transaction

In *Green*, the House of Lords refused to accept that Evelyne had acted fraudulently but rather was relying on her statutory rights under the LCA. This does, however, leave open the possibility that the effects of non-registration of a registrable interest may be avoided if there has been fraud or other deliberate wrongdoing going beyond asserting statutory rights. The court is, for example, unlikely to find void a non-registered interest against a purchaser who owes a fiduciary duty to that non-registered interest holder or where a purchase is instigated through a shell or sham company where the purchaser and landowner are essentially one and the same person.

Argument 3: Where the interest holder is in possession or in actual occupation

A further argument advanced to circumvent the effects of non-registration rests upon the somewhat puzzling provision of s. 14 of the LPA 1925 which provides that '[t]his Part of this Act shall not prejudicially affect the interest of any person in possession or in actual occupation of land to which he may be entitled in right of such possession or occupation'. It has therefore been suggested that a registrable but non-registered interest should not be void where the interest holder is in possession or actual occupation of the land. There are, however, problems with this argument. First, s. 14 expressly makes reference to 'this part of this Act', namely Part 1 of the LPA 1925. The provisions on the effect of non-registration are given in s. 4 of the LCA 1972 and not in Part 1 of the LPA 1925. This must, surely, close down any argument in reliance on s. 14, or does it? Friend and Newton note that s. 14 may in fact have been included in Part 1 of the LPA 1925 in error.[26] They argue that the forerunner to s. 14, s. 33 of the LPA 1922, should have appeared in the body of the LCA 1925 but for an 'error in the final stages of drafting'. Building on this, we might say that s. 14 should apply to the LCA 1972 today. Be that as it may, it is hard to accept that an error in drafting has remained unremedied ever since. Were this to have been Parliament's intention, would this error not have been addressed? Perhaps the inclusion of s. 14 in Part 1 of the LPA 1925 is no error at all? This remains an unresolved issue.

Argument 4: Estoppel

Another argument is that despite non-registration of a registrable interest under the LCA, the purchaser may nevertheless be estopped from relying on that non-registration. We discuss proprietary estoppel in Chapter 8. For now, let's see how estoppel might work in the context of non-registration. Imagine a purchaser represents to the holder of a registrable but non-registered land charge that the interest is enforceable and the interest holder reasonably relies on the representation to her detriment; the purchaser may be estopped i.e. prevented from relying on the non-registration of that interest. This possibility was supported by Danckwerts and Winn LJJ in *E. R. Ives Investments v High* (1967) and Oliver J in *Taylors Fashions Ltd v Liverpool Victoria Trustees Co. Ltd* (1982).

---

[26] M. Friend and J. Newton [1982] Conv 213, 215–17.

Argument 5: Where there is an independent interest enforceable against the purchaser

In *Lloyds Bank plc v Carrick* (1996), an argument was attempted that where a separate interest independent of the non-registered land charge is established, that interest may be binding on a purchaser and the effects of non-registration, consequently, side-stepped. In *Carrick*, Mrs Carrick entered a specifically enforceable contract with her brother-in-law, Mr Carrick, under which she agreed to purchase a maisonette property held by Mr Carrick under a long lease. Mrs Carrick sold her own house, paid Mr Carrick the agreed £19,000, and moved into the maisonette. The contract between the parties constituted an estate contract and was therefore registrable as a Class C(iv) land charge but had not been registered. The interest was therefore void. In the Court of Appeal, Mrs Carrick argued that her interest was enforceable either under a constructive trust or by virtue of proprietary estoppel. Sadly, for Mrs Carrick, these grounds were roundly rejected. Mrs Carrick's claim both under trust and to an estoppel were founded on the contract between herself and Mr Carrick—the very contract that was void for non-registration. Constructive trust and estoppel could not be raised to 'correct' a failure of registration under the LCA 1972. *Carrick* therefore adopts a strict approach to the effects of non-registration under the LCA. The result can be challenged in particular for its unduly harsh line on constructive trusts which, by their very nature, as we explore in Chapter 6, operate flexibly and outside the usual formality constraints of property law.

3.4.4 Family interests and overreaching

Having considered 'commercial' equitable interests which are registrable as land charges under the LCA 1972, the second category of equitable rights in unregistered land for us to consider is 'family' interests. Essentially these are interests which are non-commercial and *cannot* be registered as land charges under the LCA 1972. Family interests are chiefly, for our purposes, equitable interests arising under a trust of land. These interests are protected in unregistered land, first and foremost, by the doctrine of overreaching. We encountered overreaching in section 2.6 and the doctrine operates in the same way in unregistered land. There is, therefore, no need for us to repeat the issues. Suffice to say that, as you will recall, for overreaching to take place there must (1) be an interest capable of being overreached, and (2) the statutory requirements for overreaching must be satisfied.[27] Where overreaching takes place, the equitable interest is detached from the land and is translated into the purchase price monies paid by a purchaser of the land: a 50 per cent equitable ownership interest will, for example, equate to 50 per cent of the proceeds of sale.

There is, however, one important point of difference between overreaching in registered land and its operation in unregistered land. This relates to interests which are capable of overreaching—in other words, are 'overreachable' but which have not, in fact, been overreached (e.g. for a lack of payment of purchase monies two trustees). Unlike in registered land, in unregistered land, the enforceability of overreachable interests which have not been overreached falls to be determined by the doctrine of notice which we discuss in section 3.4.5.

---

[27] Sections 2(1), 27 of the LPA 1925.

3.4.5 **Non-registrable, non-overreachable, non-overreached interests: The doctrine of notice**

The third category of equitable rights to be considered comprises those rights that are either (1) non-registrable under the LCA 1972; (2) non-overreachable rights; or (3) those family rights that are overreachable but have not been overreached. Enforceability of rights falling into this residual category is governed by the doctrine of notice, an old equitable doctrine which grew out of jurisdiction of the court of Equity with its focus on conscience and good faith. You were introduced to the doctrine of notice in Chapter 1. According to this doctrine, a purchaser will take land free from earlier equitable rights if certain conditions are satisfied—namely, that there is a purchase of a legal estate for value without notice. This purchaser is known as 'Equity's Darling' and is provided with an 'absolute, unqualified and unanswerable defence'[28] against equitable rights affecting the land prior to the purchase. Pre-1926, the doctrine of notice played a far greater role than it does today but for this residual group of rights, its operation remains important. There are a number of aspects to consider:

- the rights governed by the doctrine
- the constituent elements of the doctrine
- the effect of the doctrine on those equitable rights that lose out in the priority battle.

3.4.5.1 **Which rights are governed by the doctrine?**

The most important rights governed by the doctrine of notice are:

- equitable interests under a trust of land which have not been overreached;[29]
- restrictive covenants and easements entered into or created pre-1926 which are excluded from registration under s. 2(5)(ii) and (iii) of the LCA 1972;
- restrictive covenants between a lessor and lessee which are also excluded from registration under s. 2(5)(ii) of the LCA 1972;
- equitable mortgages which are protected by deposit of title deeds;
- a right of re-entry[30] contained in an equitable lease;[31]
- interests arising through operation of the doctrine of proprietary estoppel.[32]

3.4.5.2 **The constituent elements of the doctrine**

The classic statement of the doctrine of notice was provided by James LJ in *Pilcher v Rawlins* (1872)[33] who confirmed the four constituent elements that must be satisfied. Figure 3.3 depicts these four conditions diagrammatically and adds a little further detail on how these elements are satisfied.

---

[28] *Pilcher v Rawlins* (1872), 269, per James LJ.

[29] Confirmed in *Kingsnorth Finance Co. Ltd v Tizard* (1986), discussed in section 3.4.5.2.

[30] Such an interest gives a landlord the right to re-enter leased property and terminate the lease when there has been a breach of a leasehold covenant.

[31] Confirmed in *Shiloh Spinners*.　　[32] See *E. R. Ives Investments v High*.　　[33] *Pilcher v Rawlins*, 268–9.

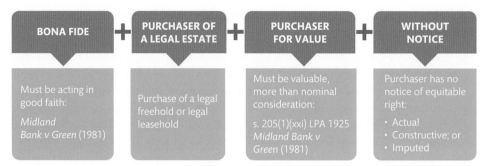

Figure 3.3 The four constituent elements of the doctrine of notice

Bona fide

The first element is that the doctrine will only operate where the purchaser acts bona fide, in other words, 'in good faith'. A purchaser acting dishonestly (e.g. to defeat another's equitable rights) would fall foul of this. There has been much discussion as to whether this requirement for 'good faith' reflects a separate element from the absence of notice (element 4 which we will shortly explore). However, in *Green*, Lord Wilberforce made plain that bona fides very much remains a discrete test in the doctrine of notice:[34]

> My Lords, the character in the law known as the bona fide (good faith) purchaser for value without notice was the creation of equity. In order to affect a purchaser for value of a legal estate with some equity or equitable interest, equity fastened upon his conscience and the composite expression was used to epitomise the circumstances in which equity would or rather would not do so. I think that it would generally be true to say that the words 'in good faith' related to the existence of notice. Equity, in other words, required not only absence of notice, but genuine and honest absence of notice. As the law developed, this requirement became crystallised in the doctrine of constructive notice which assumed a statutory form in the Conveyancing Act 1882, s. 3. But, and so far I would be willing to accompany the respondents, it would be a mistake to suppose that the requirement of good faith extended only to the matter of notice, or that when notice came to be regulated by statute, the requirement of good faith became obsolete. Equity still retained its interest in and power over the purchaser's conscience. The classic judgment of James L.J. in *Pilcher v. Rawlins* (1872) is clear authority that it did: good faith there is stated as a separate test which may have to be passed even though absence of notice is proved. And there are references in cases subsequent to 1882 which confirm the proposition that honesty or bona fides remained something which might be inquired into.

Purchaser of legal estate

Secondly, the doctrine only comes to the aid of and offers protection to a purchaser acquiring a legal estate: either a legal freehold or a legal leasehold. This means that the doctrine will not operate where an equitable estate (e.g. an equitable lease) is purchased.

Purchaser for value

Valuable consideration must have been provided. This includes payment of a purchase price below the market value of the property and also includes non-monetary consideration such as marriage consideration. Nominal consideration will not suffice: s. 205(1)(xxi)

---

[34] *Green*, 528.

of the LPA 1925. It is clear, however, that the doctrine will not operate where a legal estate is acquired by adverse possession,[35] otherwise by operation of law,[36] or where property is acquired as a gift because 'equity will not assist a volunteer' (in other words, a person who has not provided consideration). Note: the definition of 'purchaser' extends beyond those acquiring the freehold or leasehold estate to also include mortgagees and lessees.

Without notice

By far the most important element of the doctrine is the requirement that the purchaser must have no notice of the equitable right. Notice can take one of three forms: actual, constructive, or imputed notice. The 'absence of notice' requirement neatly captures the essence of the doctrine in that equity responds to the conscience of the purchaser. If she knew of a right and nevertheless proceeded with the purchase, she ought to be bound by it. If not, she should be afforded equity's protection and not be bound.

The most straightforward form of notice, actual notice, means that a purchaser is consciously aware and has knowledge of the existence of the equitable right. How the purchaser came upon that notice is irrelevant and knowledge of the right need not stem from the interest holder herself. Note the word 'consciously'. According to Megarry V-C in *Re Montagu's Settlement* (1987),[37] a person is not taken as having actual notice of a right if, despite once enjoying clear and distinct knowledge of the right, she has since genuinely forgotten all about it.

By far the most contentious form of notice is constructive notice. It is this type of notice which makes the entire doctrine so fraught with uncertainty and, arguably, places too high a burden of inspection on purchasers. What is constructive notice? Section 199(1)(ii)(a) of the LPA 1925 defines the scope of constructive notice making reference to those matters that 'would have come to [a purchaser's] knowledge if such inquiries and inspections had been made as ought reasonably to have been made by him'. Practically speaking, this means that a purchaser will be 'fixed' with constructive notice of matters that a reasonable and prudent purchaser would have discovered. This is an objective test and so it does not matter if the purchaser did not inspect the land and did not discover the rights affecting the land. The question is straightforward: what *would* a reasonable and prudent purchaser have discovered after inquiries and inspection of the land? The purchaser will be bound by any interests that such reasonable inquiries and inspections would have revealed.

In general terms, a reasonable purchaser is expected to do three things: (1) inspect the title documents, (2) physically inspect the land, and (3) make any inquiries arising from that inspection. As you might imagine, however, a key battleground has been identifying what amounts to reasonable and prudent inquiry and inspection of land. In *Hunt v Luck* (1902), the court established that a reasonable and prudent purchaser would not only inspect title deeds but also inspect the land itself, looking for adverse interests affecting the property. This included a duty to ask those in occupation of the land who were not the vendor (seller) if they enjoyed any interest in the property. If the freehold owner was not in occupation, however, this did not extend to asking questions of those occupying the

---

[35] *Re Nisbit and Pott's Contract* (1906).   [36] *Inland Revenue Commissioners v Gribble* (1913).

[37] *Re Monatagu's Settlement*, 284.

land as tenants (i.e. leasing the land). The so-called 'rule in *Hunt v Luck*' was explained by Williams LJ:[38]

> [I]f a purchaser or a mortgagee has notice that the vendor or mortgagor is not in possession of the property, he must make inquiries of the person in possession . . . and find out from him what his rights are, and if he does not choose to do that, then whatever title he acquires . . . will be subject to the title or right of the [party] in possession.

In *Caunce v Caunce* (1969)[39]—a controversial decision, which has never been overruled but is today not followed—a narrower approach was adopted. The issue was how far a bank was to be fixed with notice of a wife's equitable interest. Both Mr and Mrs Caunce had contributed to the purchase price of the matrimonial home but title was in Mr Caunce's sole name. Mrs Caunce therefore enjoyed an equitable, contribution-based interest under a trust. Mr Caunce took out three loans using the home as security and, subsequently, became bankrupt. In an action for possession of the home, Mrs Caunce argued that the bank had constructive notice of her equitable interest as a result of her occupation. Stamp J held that the bank was not fixed with notice as Mrs Caunce's occupation was 'wholly consistent with the title offered' by Mr Caunce to the bank. The same would have been true, said Stamp, had the vendor's Uncle Harry or Aunt Matilda been in occupation. The presence of a wife, uncle or aunt 'implies nothing to negative the title offered' and it was not in the public interest that banks be snoopers or busybodies making inquiries into the wife that would be 'embarrassing' and 'intolerable'.

Caunce therefore established that a purchaser would only be fixed with constructive notice where occupation was inconsistent with the vendor's title. *Caunce* has been strongly criticized as outmoded in suggesting a wife is a mere shadow of her husband (under the unity of husband and wife doctrine). As we saw in Chapter 2, this argument was held to be 'heavily obsolete' in *Boland*. To import a requirement of 'inconsistency with title' into the question of notice was an unjustified rewriting of the statute. Where a wife was in occupation, said the House of Lords, inquiry should be made of her. *Caunce*, whilst never overruled, is clearly out-of-step with contemporary, social attitudes and is unlikely to ever be followed. Today, a far broader interpretation is given to 'reasonable inquiries' as demonstrated by the leading authority on constructive notice: *Kingsnorth Finance Co. Ltd v Tizard*.

KEY CASE *Kingsnorth Finance Co. Ltd v Tizard* (1986)

Facts: Title to a family home was held in Mr Tizard's sole name but with Mrs Tizard enjoying an equitable interest in the property. After marriage breakdown, Mrs Tizard stopped living permanently at the property but did sleep at the house when Mr Tizard was away. Mrs Tizard visited the house every day to care for the children both in the mornings and the evenings even when she did not sleep there overnight and her belongings remained in the home. Unbeknown to Mrs Tizard, Mr Tizard took out a loan secured by way of mortgage against the house, using the money to emigrate to America. The

→

---

[38] *Hunt*, 433.   [39] A case we encountered in Chapter 2 in our discussion of *Boland*: see section 2.7.5.3.

➔

space for a spouse's signature on Mr Tizard's mortgage application had been left blank and Mr Tizard had described himself as single on the form. An agent for the bank, Mr Marshall, had visited the house prior to advancing the loan to value the property. Mr Tizard had arranged the visit for a particular day and time, a Sunday afternoon, when he was sure that Mrs Tizard and children would be out of the house. Despite claiming to be single, Mr Tizard told Mr Marshall that he had separated from his wife who lived elsewhere. Mr Marshall whose inspection did not involve opening cupboards, could see evidence of the children's occupation but not that of Mrs Tizard. Mr Tizard defaulted on the loan, disappeared, and the bank sought possession of the house.

Legal issue: Could Mrs Tizard defend the application for possession by arguing that the bank was fixed with constructive notice of and therefore subject to her interest in the property?

Judgment: The bank was held to have constructive notice of Mrs Tizard's interest and its action for possession failed. John Finlay QC held:

1. Mr Tizard's description as 'single' when coupled with references in Mr Marshall's report to a 'son and daughter' and to his having been 'separated' from his wife should have alerted the bank to make further inquiries. These inquiries were not made but, had they been, would have revealed Mrs Tizard's interest.

2. It was material that Mr Tizard had clearly orchestrated the inspection by Mr Marshall to take place at a pre-arranged date and time to allow the concealment of his wife's interest. If the object of the inspection is to ascertain who is in occupation, a pre-arranged visit to suit the vendor does not meet this objective.

3. What amounted to a 'reasonable' inspection was dependent on all the circumstances of each case. It would, however, not be reasonable to expect cupboards to be opened and drawers riffled.

4. The bank was therefore limited to enforcing its rights against Mr Tizard's share in the property.

Ultimately, despite the court's ruling, Mrs Tizard agreed to the sale of the property and the bank took Mr Tizard's share of the proceeds to discharge the debt it was owed. The effect of *Tizard* is a broadening of the concept of occupation from that seen in *Hunt* and in *Caunce* as well as a clarification of the steps that a reasonable and prudent purchaser must take to avoid being fixed with constructive notice. This is welcome but the decision can be criticized: first, for an over-emphasis on Mrs Tizard's occupation rather than on notice of her interest. The focus of the doctrine of notice is, as the name suggests, on the *notice* of equitable rights and not on occupation. This is a key distinction between the doctrine and the test for actual occupation under Sch. 3 para. 2 of the LRA 2002 in registered land where the obviousness and discoverability of occupation is in issue. Secondly, we might ask whether *Tizard* places too hefty a burden on purchasers to make inquiries. Are purchasers, as Thompson considers,[40] expected to become 'private detectives' in view of the judgment? Thompson also argues that the court went too far in attaching so much weight to Mr Tizard's pre-arrangement of the inspection.[41] Thompson would place less emphasis on the arrangements for the inspection and offers an important reminder to us that the test is objective: the question is what would reasonable inquiries divulge?

[40] M. Thompson, 'The Purchaser as Private Detective' [1986] Conv 283.   [41] Ibid., 286.

Clearly, an inspection of the property should take place. If the mortgagor says this can take place at the weekend, can it really be supposed that the . . . agent must insist on calling at an alternative, unannounced time to check whether the mortgagor is lying? . . . such behaviour goes beyond what are reasonable inquiries. It is suggested that the onus on a purchaser . . . is not this heavy. It is necessary that a vendor should be asked whether he shares the house with anyone else. Additionally he should be asked if he either is or was married. If the answers reveal the existence of anybody, then inquiries where possible should be made of that person. Further, an inspection of the property should be carried out. If such an inspective gives no cause to suspect adverse rights . . . even if this inspection was performed at a time arranged with the vendor, the purchaser should be held to have done all that is required of him . . . to insist on doing more carries the inevitable implication that he suspects the vendor of deceit. Such demands should not be considered to be within the scope of reasonable inquiries.

However far you agree or disagree with the result in *Tizard*, it clarifies that where ambiguities and factual inconsistencies are raised, a reasonable purchaser should investigate further. As we have seen, the burden is on the purchaser to make inquiries and an inspection of the land. There is one situation, however, where the priority of an interest may be lost as a result of the *interest-holder's* failure to disclose their interest. In *Midland Bank Ltd v Farmpride Hatcheries Ltd* (1980), the court held that an equitable interest holder, acting fraudulently, had 'set up a smoke-screen designed to hide even the possible existence' of his interest from the bank who advanced him a loan by way of mortgage. In the circumstances, the interest holder's claim that the bank had constructive notice of the interest was rejected and he was estopped from relying on the priority of his interest.[42]

The third and final form of notice is imputed notice.[43] Where a purchaser engages an agent to act on its behalf for the purposes of the sale, any actual or constructive notice of that agent is imputed to the purchaser (who is known as 'the principal' in this agency relationship). Imputed notice is provided for in s. 199(1)(ii)(b) of the LPA 1925 which makes clear that only notice acquired by an agent in the same transaction can be imputed to the purchaser. The upshot of this is that any notice acquired by an agent in separate transactions cannot be imputed. We saw an illustration of imputed notice in *Tizard* where the constructive notice of Mr Marshall (agent of the bank) was then imputed to the bank servicing the loan to Mr Tizard. Imputed notice is practically very important as agents are commonly employed by purchasers and banks. It would be unacceptable if the law sanctioned the engagement of agents as a means of evading the enforceability of equitable interests under the doctrine of notice.

3.4.5.3 What is the effect of the doctrine of notice if all four elements are satisfied?

Where all four constituent elements of the doctrine of notice are satisfied, the purchaser takes the land free from the equitable interest; the equitable interest loses out in the priority battle. Once defeated, that equitable interest cannot be revived even if subsequent purchasers have notice of the interest. This is the effect of the decision in *Wilkes v Spooner* (1911). What this means is that once a bona fide purchaser has acquired the land free from an equitable interest, that interest cannot be resurrected to bind successive purchasers even

---

[42] See *Farmpride Hatcheries*, 497, per Shaw LJ.
[43] See generally S. Nield, 'Imputed Notice' [2000] Conv 196.

if those successors have notice of the equitable right. This demonstrates the true power of the doctrine.[44]

Figure 3.4 offers a flowchart which brings together diagrammatically the material covered in this chapter to help you gain a better understanding and to visualize how the issues explored connect with one another and how to analyse the enforceability of third party interests in unregistered land.

3.5 **Future directions**

In this short chapter, we have explored the principles and machinery of the law of unregistered title deeds conveyancing. In this final section, we consider the continuing significance of unregistered land and in so doing reflect upon the pitfalls and problems of the system.

The future for unregistered land is one in which the principles of title deeds conveyancing play an ever-diminishing role. For many this is cause for optimism. In particular, the expansion in the triggering events for first registration of previously unregistered land under the LRA 2002 (see section 2.4.2) has had the effect that almost any dealing with unregistered land will compel registration: sale, mortgage, or leaving land as an inheritance to an heir. In time, the result will be that the only unregistered land that endures will likely be land belonging, for example, to the Crown, the Church, and universities which remains static and is not dealt with, transferred, or otherwise disposed of (which would trigger registration). The favourable terms and incentives on which voluntary registration is offered by Land Registry may also entice registration even in these more atypical circumstances.

Soon, unregistered land will fade into land law's historical hinterland. Few will shed a tear but what is really so wrong with the unregistered system? In fact, quite a lot:

- The partial system of registration under the LCA 1972 provides protection but only for those commercial equitable rights that are registrable under s. 2. Not all rights in unregistered land are registrable.

- Speaking of the LCA 1972, the regime is not a system of title registration but a names-based scheme opening up the very real possibility of errors stemming from searching against an incorrect name. This risks purchasers being bound by interests registered against names that they have no way of discovering. This cannot surely be how dealings with such a precious and unique resource, land, should operate.

- The court in *Green* emphasized the primacy of the statutory language of the LCA 1972. On one view, the court went too far in adopting a strict reading of the effects of non-registration at the expense of any role for the actual, subjective intentions of the parties.

- Finally, the enforceability of equitable rights falling outside the limited regime of the LCA 1972 (and overreaching) ultimately collapses back on the uncertainty, ambiguity, and general 'fuzziness' of the doctrine of notice with its inherently vague and problematic parameters, in particular, as to what constitutes and does not constitute constructive notice.

---

[44] Successors may, nevertheless, potentially be bound by way of an estoppel if they have made an express promise to that effect or if they act as part of a fraud.

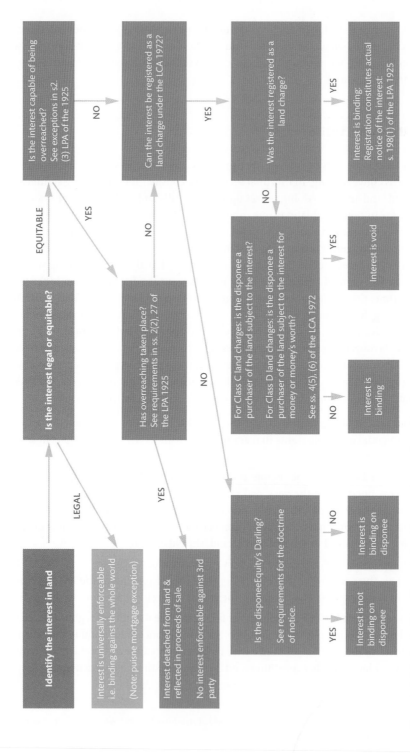

Figure 3.4 Bringing it all together: priority of interests in unregistered land

By contrast, in registered land the system is founded on registration of *titles* avoiding the problems of searches against *names*. There is no role for the unpredictable doctrine of notice; rather the enforceability of interests in registered land is determined by priority rules (ss. 28 and 29) and protection through entry of a notice (subject to the residual category of overriding interests of Schs. 1 and 3). The registered land regime offers a more comprehensive, straightforward, and secure regime for dealings with land than its unregistered cousin. Having now examined registered and unregistered land, you should take some time to reflect on the differences and connections between the two systems. Will you miss unregistered land when it has all but vanished from the legal landscape?

Further reading

- J. Howell, 'The Doctrine of Notice: An Historical Perspective' [1997] Conv 431.
- S. Nield, 'Imputed Notice' [2000] Conv 196.
- M. Thompson, 'The Purchaser as Private Detective' [1986] Conv 283.
- M. Thompson, '*Midland Bank v Green* (1980): Maintaining the Integrity of Registration Systems' in N. Gravells (ed.), *Landmark Cases in Land Law* (Oxford: Hart, 2013).
- H. W. R. Wade, 'Land Charges Registration Reviewed' (1956) 14(2) CLJ 216.

 ## Online resources

Access the online resources at www.oup.com/uk/bevan2e/ to test yourself with self-test questions and scenario problems. You can also view additional supporting material relevant to the topics in this chapter, including:

- *Videos*
- *Audio podcasts*
- *Maps, diagrams, and flowcharts*
- *Interactive exercises*
- *Examples of real-life legal documentation.*

4 Adverse Possession

4.1 Introduction

In order to acquire an interest in land, generally certain formality requirements have to be satisfied.[1] Legal estates and interests cannot, in the normal course, be acquired informally.[2] In this chapter, however, we explore one rather curious exception to this position: the law of adverse possession.

A claim to adverse possession is a claim brought by a trespasser or squatter who has been in possession of another's land for a long period of time (often called 'long user'). Land law recognizes other rights arising after use over a protracted period—for example, easements by prescription[3]—but adverse possession is quite different, mostly due to its effects. If successful, the trespasser or squatter becomes the legal owner of the land. The law of adverse possession is, as you might imagine, controversial because, if the claim is made out, it operates negatively,[4] meaning that the trespasser becomes the new owner of the land and the title of the previous owner of the land is lost. You may have read some of the more colourful reports in the papers of squatters gaining rights in land via this route. Some even see it as land-theft engaging human rights' arguments.[5] The essential features for establishing a claim to adverse possession apply whether the land in question is registered or not, but, distinct rules do exist for the separate registered and unregistered land systems when it comes to the effects of the doctrine.

---

[1] There are exceptions—for example, the granting of short leases of three years or less under s. 52(2) of the LPA 1925 and implied trusts, on which see Chapter 6.

[2] Of course, there are exceptions including implied legal easements explored in section 10.4.

[3] We discuss easements in Chapter 10 and prescription more specifically in section 10.4.5.

[4] Unlike the law of prescription which operates positively to generate easements on which see Chapter 10.

[5] We return to the interplay of human rights and adverse possession in section 4.9 and in Chapter 14.

Today, however, the significance of the law of adverse possession in registered land has been dramatically diluted as a result of the provisions of Schedule 6 of the LRA 2002 which set down a wholly new regime and procedure for adverse possession claims. The effect of this new regime is that far fewer claims will now succeed. That said, with 14 per cent of land titles still unregistered, the law of adverse possession remains very much alive and well; not to mention that it is one of the more vibrant areas of land law . . . .

 Visit the online resources to watch a video on how the LRA 2002 has changed the law of adverse possession.

4.2 The basis for adverse possession

'*Long user*' forms the fundamental basis for the informal acquisition of title on the grounds of adverse possession, but why? Why should possession for a long period by a trespasser or squatter of another person's land give rise to ownership of that land? How far is this justified? Howard and Hill have argued the fact that a squatter has enjoyed a cost-free benefit of another's land for a lengthy period is not sufficient justification to allow continuation of that right.[6] Another point must be appreciated the essential fact that adverse possession has, at its very core, a 'wrong' (i.e. it is based on trespass or squatting on land belonging to another). We might say it rewards those stealing another's land. The Law Commission has raised just this argument noting:[7]

> It is, of course, remarkable that the law is prepared to legitimise such 'possession of wrong' (Nourse LJ in *Buckinghamshire County Council v Moran* (1990)) which, at least in some cases, is tantamount to sanctioning a theft of land. So sweeping a doctrine requires strong justification.

The Law Commission identified what are widely seen as the four classic justifications for the right to acquire land of another by adverse possession:

1. The law of adverse possession is as an aspect of the law on limitation of actions. The policy objectives for the statutory provisions limiting when legal claims can be brought (under the Limitation Act 1980) can be seen as explaining the rationale for adverse possession including protecting defendants from stale claims and encouraging claimants not to sleep on their rights.

2. If land ownership and the reality of possession (i.e. who owns land and who is in control of it) are out of kilter, the land in question is rendered unmarketable—for example, where the true owner has disappeared and the squatter has been in possession of the land for a considerable period. This is the socio-economic argument for recognizing adverse possession. On this view, given that land is a unique and scarce resource, the law should encourage the most productive and efficient use of this special commodity.

3. In cases of mistake, the law of adverse possession can actually prevent hardship, if, for example, a squatter enters land believing she owns it and incurs expense in reliance on this mistaken belief as to her entitlement.

---

[6] M. Howard and J. Hill, 'The Informal Creation of Interests in Land' (1995) 15 LS 356.

[7] Law Commission Report No. 254, *Land Registration for the Twenty-First Century: A Consultative Document* (1998).

4. Regarded by the Commission as the 'strongest justification', adverse possession in unregistered land is said to offer the clearest example of the principle of the 'relativity of title' that has been a foundation of land law since feudal times. According to this principle, title to land is relative, is never absolute, and depends ultimately on possession and who can assert the best claim to the property. The person with best title to the land will be the person with the best right to possession of it. Building on this view and drawing on the work of famous American jurist Oliver Wendell Holmes Jr,[8] the law of adverse possession can be justified as responding to the psychological attachment of a person (including trespassers) to land:

> The connection is further back than the first recorded history. It is in the nature of man's mind. A thing which you have enjoyed and used as your own for a long time, whether property or an opinion, takes root in your being and cannot be torn away without your resenting the act and trying to defend yourself, however you came by it. The law can ask no better justification than the deepest instincts of man.

Gray and Gray expand on this by locating:[9]

> a deeply anti-intellectual streak in the common law tradition which cares little for grand or abstract theories of ownership, preferring to fasten on the raw organic facts of human behaviour . . . Accordingly, the crude empiricism of this outlook leaves the recognition of property to rest upon essentially intuitive perceptions of the degree to which a claimant successfully asserts *de facto* possessory control over land.

Adverse possession therefore stems from a historical fixation of property law on factual possession of land. On this view, the law of adverse possession exudes a 'curative effect'[10] by which the informal acquisition of title by a squatter or trespasser is simply a reflection in law of the reality on the ground of possessory control.

So, what does this review of the oft-cited justifications for the law of adverse possession tell us? In fact, it tells us quite a lot. It exposes an important truth: that adverse possession operates most meaningfully in the context of unregistered land. Today with the dominance of land registration and the increasing number of unregistered titles caught by the events triggering first registration under the LRA 2002, the justifications for adverse possession are significantly undermined. Though still possible to mount a claim to adverse possession over registered land, as we explore in section 4.6, the likely success of this claim is greatly diminished under the new regime. Put another way, the law of adverse possession is largely incompatible with the central tenets of land registration where the fact of registration is the basis of title rather than the fact of possession.

4.3 Analysing a claim to adverse possession

The best way to approach analysis of an adverse possession claim is to break it down into two fundamental questions or two stages: (1) has a claim to adverse possession been established? and (2) what is the effect of the adverse possession on the original landowner? See Figure 4.1.

---

[8] O. W. Holmes, 'The Path of the Law' (1897) 10 Harv LR 457.

[9] K. Gray and S. F. Gray, 'The Idea of Property in Land' in S. Bright and J. Dewar (eds.), *Land Law: Themes and Perspectives* (Oxford: Oxford University Press, 1998), 18.

[10] M. J. Goodman, 'Adverse Possession of Land: Morality and Motive' (1970) 33 MLR 281.

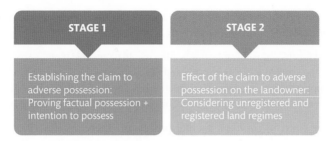

Figure 4.1 The two stages for analysing a claim to adverse possession

At stage 1, we are concerned with how a claim to adverse possession is made out. Here, the common law has developed a single set of rules which apply equally to unregistered as to registered land. Establishing a claim requires proof that 'the essential features' of adverse possession are present (as affirmed in the leading case of *J. A. Pye (Oxford) Ltd v Graham* (2002)). At stage 2, we are focused on how adverse possession affects the original land-owner. At stage 2, very different principles apply depending on whether the land is un-registered or registered. For unregistered land, the rules of limitation of actions under the Limitation Act 1980 operate while, in registered land, the new, more stringent statutory regime under Schedule 6 of the LRA 2002 applies.

4.4 Stage 1: Establishing a claim to adverse possession—the essential elements

Irrespective of whether the land is unregistered or registered, a claimant wishing to acquire title over another person's land on the grounds of adverse possession must begin by estab-lishing their claim. This means satisfying two essential requirements:

1. the claimant is in *factual possession* of the land,[11] and
2. the claimant exhibits the requisite *intention to possess* to the land.[12]

The law on establishing a claim to adverse possession is not found in statute but instead has developed incrementally by the courts. The result is a significant measure of elasticity. For-tunately, the House of Lords in the leading case on adverse possession, *Graham*, offered a long-overdue and welcome clarification of many of the key principles in this area—we con-sider this case in detail later. This has made advising on the law (and studying it!) a far more straightforward exercise. *Graham* confirmed the two essential elements of adverse posses-sion: factual possession and the intention to possess. We unpack these in this section.

4.4.1 Factual possession of the land

Plainly, understanding what is required in terms of factual possession is fundamental to the very notion of 'adverse possession'. For some considerable time, the courts grappled (not altogether coherently) with how to make sense of it. Helpfully, to a large extent, this

---

[11] *Graham; Powell v McFarlane* (1979).   [12] *Graham; Buckinghamshire CC v Moran* (1990).

complexity has now been swept aside by the more common-sense approach of the House of Lords in *Graham* where Lord Browne-Wilkinson noted:[13]

> In my judgment much confusion and complication would be avoided if reference to adverse possession were to be avoided so far as possible and effect given to the clear words of the Acts. The question is simply whether the defendant squatter has dispossessed the paper owner by going into ordinary possession of the land for the requisite period without the consent of the owner.

According to the court in *Graham*, 'factual possession' therefore describes a claimant entering into possession of another's land without that landowner's permission. In clarifying this test of factual possession, the court was heavily influenced by the case of *Powell v McFarlane* (1979) where Slade J explained the meaning of 'factual possession' in the following terms:[14]

> Factual possession signifies an appropriate degree of physical control. It must be a single and [exclusive] possession, though there can be a single possession exercised by or on behalf of several persons jointly. Thus an owner of land and a person intruding on that land without his consent cannot both be in possession of the land at the same time. The questions what acts constitute a sufficient degree of exclusive physical control must depend on the circumstances, in particular the nature of the land and the manner in which land of that nature is commonly used or enjoyed ... Everything must depend on the particular circumstances, but broadly, I think what must be shown ... is that the alleged possessor has been dealing with the land in question as an occupying owner might have been expected to deal with it and that no-one else has done so.

Factual possession therefore requires evidence that the squatter is in possession of the land as an occupying owner might deal with the land, exhibiting physical control of the land without the landowner's consent. Several important additional observations can also be made:

1. What constitutes factual possession is determined by the *nature and character of the land* in question.
2. Factual possession must be *exclusive*.[15]
3. Possession must be *adverse*.
4. Possession must be *open*.

4.4.1.1 The nature and character of the land

In *Lord Advocate v Lord Lovat* (1880), Lord O'Hagan explained that:[16]

> Possession ... must be considered in every case with reference to the peculiar circumstances. The character and value of the property, the suitable and natural mode of using it, the course of conduct which the proprietor might reasonably be expected to follow with a due regard to his own interests—all these things, greatly varying as they must, under various conditions, are to be taken into account in determining the sufficiency of a possession.

---

[13] *Graham*, 434.   [14] *Powell*, 471.   [15] See comments ibid., 469–71.
[16] *Lord Advocate v Lord Lovat*, 288.

The recent case of *Thorpe v Frank* (2019) highlights the importance that is placed on the nature and character of the land in issue. *Thorpe* concerned two neighbouring bungalows: No. 8 and No. 9. The owner of No. 9 claimed to have acquired a triangular piece of land in front of the two houses by way of adverse possession, arguing that she had paved the area in 1986 without objection from No. 8 and had fenced it off in 2013. The Upper Tribunal overturned the First-Tier Tribunal's decision, holding that the owner of No. 9 had not demonstrated factual possession as the paving works amounted to a temporary act of trespass (lasting only a fortnight). However, in the Court of Appeal, the appeal was allowed. In determining adverse possession claims, the nature and character of the land in question was crucial. The particular land here had been open-plan in nature and the paving of the area with a permanent new surface amounted to a clear assertion of factual possession. The Upper Tribunal had overly concentrated on the absence of steps to exclude others until the fencing of 2013 when it should have asked what an occupying owner might have been expected to do when dealing with the land. No clear authority existed that paving of land alone could amount to adverse possession but physical changes to land could give rise to such claims. It was not disputed that intention to possess existed. *Thorpe* therefore confirms that paving of another's land may be sufficient to demonstrate factual possession of it; fencing is not always needed and, in addition, what constitutes a sufficient degree of exclusive physical control will very much depend on the nature and character of the land and the manner in which that land is commonly used or enjoyed.

4.4.1.2 Factual possession must be exclusive

This means that the squatter or trespasser must possess the land in question to the *exclusion* of the landowner and any other person enjoying rights over the land. If possession is shared with the true owner, the claim will fail.[17] In *British Waterways Board v Toor* (2006), a claim to adverse possession of an alleyway was rejected in circumstances where the alleged possessor had allowed others to park their vehicles along it. Equally, there will be no adverse possession where land is occupied by temporary, non-permanent structures such as catering or refreshment vehicles, customer tables and chairs which are not fixed to the land, are removed for cleaning purposes or cleared away overnight.[18]

4.4.1.3 Possession must be adverse

Possession must be *without the consent of the landowner* and, in this sense, adverse to the interests of the true landowner.[19] A claim to adverse possession will fail if the claimant has permission to be present on the land, either as a tenant[20] or under a licence.[21] As Slade LJ explained in *Buckinghamshire CC v Moran* (1990):[22]

---

[17] *Sava v SS Global Ltd* (2008).   [18] *Balevents Ltd v Sartori* (2011).   [19] *BP Properties v Buckler* (1987).

[20] *Colchester BC v Smith* (1991).

[21] See *BP Properties v Buckler* where a squatter had been given a licence to remain on the land by the landowner but it had neither been accepted nor rejected by the squatter, meaning her possession could not be described as 'adverse'. The court held possession may have been adverse had the licence been rejected.

[22] *Moran*, 636.

Possession is never 'adverse' if it is enjoyed by lawful title. If, therefore, a person occupies or uses land by licence of the owner and his licence has not been duly determined, he cannot be treated as having been in 'adverse possession'.

What starts as lawful possession may become adverse, however, if the claimant exceeds any permission or consent granted to be present on the land—for example, remaining in possession after the expiry of a licence or after the termination of a lease. In *Allen v Matthews* (2007), a scrap-metal merchant succeeded in his claim for adverse possession in circumstances where the Court of Appeal found that a granted, limited permission of storage had been clearly exceeded in both nature and degree.

It is clear, however, that possession will clearly not be adverse where the court implies a licence in the alleged possessor's favour thus giving her permission to be present on the land. An important decision here is *Wallis's Cayton Bay Holiday Camp Ltd v Shell Mex & BP Ltd*.

> **KEY CASE** *Wallis's Cayton Bay Holiday Camp Ltd v Shell Mex & BP Ltd* (1975)
>
> Facts: The claimants owned a holiday camp which fronted onto a main road. The defendant petroleum company owned adjoining land for which they had plans, sometime in the future, to be the site of a petrol station once a new road had been built. That new road was never built. The claimant company used the land for various purposes including farming and extending its caravan park. The defendant company took no steps to prevent this use of the land. The claimant company claimed title to the land on the grounds of adverse possession.
>
> Legal issue: Would the claimant succeed in its claim to adverse possession in circumstances where the true owner of the land had not used the land for 12 years but had an expressed intention as to a future purpose to which the land would be put?
>
> Judgment: Lord Denning MR held that the true owner intended to use the land for a particular, future purpose and so had left the land unoccupied. The use of the land by the claimant was under an implied licence and, as it did not contradict the landowner's intended future use for the property, this meant that the possession was not adverse and did not defeat the defendants' title. The claim to adverse possession failed.

Lord Denning's 'implied licence theory' proved extremely controversial as it appeared to slam shut the door to many claims of adverse possession over unoccupied land. Later described as 'an original heresy' by Nourse LJ in *Moran*, Parliament intervened in the form of s. 15(6) and Sch. 1 para. 8(4) of the Limitation Act 1980 to reverse the decision on this point. Schedule 1, para. 8(4) provides:

> For the purpose of determining whether a person occupying any land is in adverse possession of the land it shall not be assumed by implication of law that his occupation is by permission of the person entitled to the land merely by virtue of the fact that his occupation is not inconsistent with the latter's present or future enjoyment of the land. As Jackson[23] and McCormack[24] have argued, it is important to note what this provision does and does not do. The provision reverses the decision in *Wallis's* but, crucially, it does not prevent a court from finding an implied licence if

[23] N. Jackson (1980) 96 LQR 333.   [24] G. McCormack [1986] Conv 434.

the appropriate circumstances of the case justify it. That said, for an implied licence to arise, there must first be an overt act or non-verbal communication intended to be understood as granting permission to do something which would otherwise amount to a trespass and, secondly, it must be such that a reasonable person would appreciate that permission had been granted.[25]

The court is prepared, for example, to imply a licence where there are negotiations for the purchase or lease of land and the purchaser or tenant is in occupation of the land. In *Colin Dawson Windows Ltd v King's Lynn & West Norfolk BC* (2005), the Court of Appeal found that an implied licence had been granted in favour of squatters claiming adverse possession where the squatters had been allowed to occupy land during negotiations for purchase of a parcel of land. The vendor had made clear that the potential purchasers would have to vacate the property if the sale did not go through. This, held the court, was evidence that there had been permission during the negotiations to be present on the land. The squatter's claim to adverse possession therefore failed. Can a landowner unilaterally turn an adverse possessor into a licensee, for example, by writing to them informing them that they regard the adverse possessor as occupying under a licence? This was considered in *BP Properties Ltd v Buckler* (1987) where the Court of Appeal held that a unilateral communication to the adverse possessor could create a licence though not if the adverse possessor wrote back contesting the licence. This unilateral licence analysis has been criticized[26] but was approved in *Colin Dawson Windows Ltd* and relied upon by Hart J in *Clowes Developments (UK) Ltd v Walters* (2006).

4.4.1.4 Possession must be *open*

Possession must be open, in other words, not be concealed from the landowner. The law will not allow the informal acquisition of title where there is evidence of deliberate concealment, fraud, or other deception on the part of the claimant adverse possessor.[27] That said, while possession must be exclusive and adverse, it seems it does not need to have been 'obvious' to the true landowner.[28]

Particular issues have arisen in relation to fencing off or enclosure of land as evidence of physical control in an adverse possession claim. The leading case here is, *Graham*. It is summarized in this section but you really must read it in full if you are to fully grasp its significance.

KEY CASE *J. A. Pye (Oxford) Ltd v Graham* (2002)

Facts: Pye was the proprietor of development land which adjoined a farm owned by the Grahams. The Grahams had purchased the farm in 1982 and a year later, in 1983, had entered into a short grazing agreement to make use of the development land in return for £2,000 paid to Pye. Pye subsequently

→

---

[25] *Chambers v London Borough of Havering* (2011); *Colin Dawson Windows Ltd v King's Lynn & West Norfolk BC* (2005).

[26] See, for example, H. Wallace (1994) Conv 196.

[27] *Beaulane Properties Ltd v Palmer* (2006).   [28] *Wretham v Ross* (2005).

→

refused to renew the grazing agreement as he wanted to apply for planning permission and took the view this would be more likely to be granted if the land was not in use. Pye requested that the Grahams vacate the land and cease using it for the purpose of grazing. The Grahams continued in their occupation and use of the land and did, for a time, make repeated requests for renewal of the grazing agreement. When there was no correspondence from Pye, the Grahams persisted in using the land as they had previously. The land was enclosed by a series of hedges and accessed via a gate for which only the Grahams had a key. Additionally, the Grahams maintained the hedges and boundary fencing and ditches every year. In 1999, Pye issued legal proceedings seeking possession of the land. In response, the Grahams claimed adverse possession of the land.

Legal issue: Had the Grahams demonstrated the necessary factual possession of the land (and intention to possess) to succeed in their claim to title of the land?

Judgment: The House of Lords confirmed that in order to establish a claim for adverse possession there were two essential elements which were to be considered separately:

1. A sufficient degree of physical custody and control of the land ('factual possession'), and

2. An intention to exercise such custody and control of the land on one's own behalf and for one's own benefit ('intention to possess').

As to the first, the House of Lords held that Pye's claim to possession was defeated by the Grahams' factual possession of the land. The Grahams had demonstrated factual possession of the land as they both occupied and had exclusive physical control of the property. Important to this finding was evidence that Pye was excluded from the land by enclosing hedges and as a result of Pye lacking an access key.

As to the second, the necessary intention to possess the land was satisfied by evidence that the Grahams had farmed the land in precisely the same manner they farmed their own land. It was irrelevant that the Grahams were aware of Pye's proposed use of the land for development. This did not prevent the finding of the requisite intention to possess.

Hedges or enclosures which exclude the true owner will be important evidence of physical control and possession of the land. In *Seddon v Smith* (1877), Cockburn CJ noted enclosure is the strongest possible evidence of adverse possession.[29] A further, useful, and must-read illustration is provided by the case of *Moran*.

There have, however, been cases where fencing has proved insufficient to establish factual possession.[30] In *Boosey v Davis* (1988), a mesh fence erected by the Booseys was held

---

KEY CASE *Buckingham CC v Moran* (1990)

Facts: In 1995, Buckingham Council acquired a plot of land neighbouring several houses in order to carry out a planned road diversion and road-widening works. The Council left the property unoccupied for many years. The Council had fenced off the land from the property surrounding it but there had been no fence between the land and Mr Moran's house and garden. The predecessors in title to Mr Moran had been using the Council's land since 1967, mowing the lawn, tending the hedges, and

→

---

[29] *Seddon v Smith*, 168.   [30] *Basildon DC v Manning* (1975).

> ➥
>
> otherwise using it as their own land including parking a horse-box. Mr Moran purchased the land in 1971 and in 1976 even wrote to the Council expressing his genuinely held belief that he was permitted to use of the land until the Council had need for it. The Council finally brought possession proceedings in 1985 at which time Mr Moran claimed he had acquired title by adverse possession.
>
> Legal issue: Was Mr Moran entitled to the freehold on the grounds of adverse possession?
>
> Judgment: The Court of Appeal upheld the decision at first instance that Mr Moran was entitled to the freehold on the basis of adverse possession. In using the land as an extension of his own garden, maintaining the hedges and fences, as well as installing a new gate and lock, Mr Moran had established factual possession of the land and, additionally, had demonstrated the requisite intention to possess.

to be insufficient evidence of factual possession as the fence was intended to keep a grazing goat in and not to keep out or exclude the true owner. Equally, fences or enclosures erected on a temporary basis and later removed will most likely not be enough. In *Marsden v Miller* (1992), an alleged possessor failed in his action for adverse possession in a case where a fence he had erected was subsequently removed 24 hours later by the true landowner. Finally, while sufficient to evidence factual possession, fencing or enclosures are not necessary in order to establish a claim to adverse possession. In *Pilford v Greenmanor* (2012), the court held that it was not necessary for a claimant to establish that land was completely enclosed to the exclusion of others. All that is required is that a claimant can demonstrate physical custody and control of the land.

Figure 4.2 brings together some of the most common examples of factual possession.

4.4.1.5 Factual possession of land which you are registered proprietor

Can you be in adverse possession of land of which you are the registered owner? This question was addressed recently in *Rashid v Nasrullah* (2019). The First-Tier and Upper Tribunals said no; the Court of Appeal said yes. The facts of the case were complex and, what's more, two of the parties had the very same name (Mohammed Rashid) so were referred to as MR1 and MR2 by the court. In summary, MR2 was the registered proprietor of land until 1989 when MR1 perpetrated a fraud and transferred the land to himself and was registered as proprietor. In 1990, R (MR1's son), who was complicit in the fraud, was gifted the land and was registered as the new proprietor. In 2013, MR2 who had returned to the UK after a lengthy period in Pakistan sought to have the register rectified to correct the mistake and reflect himself as the true owner. R objected arguing that he had been in adverse possession of the land for over 20 years—this, despite the fact the register already reflected that R was the registered proprietor (even if it was as a result of fraud!). MR2 sought to rely on the authority of *Parshall v Bryans* (2013) which had held that time for adverse possession cannot run in favour of an adverse possessor where they are the registered owner. Lewison LJ rejected this argument, however, finding *Parshall* to be incompatible with *Pye v Graham*. Quite simply, held Lewison LJ, the relevant question for adverse possession was whether one person had taken possession of the land of another without that other's consent for the required period of time. Whilst the court had sympathy for MR2 as the victim of MR1 and R's 'brazen fraud', R's claim to adverse possession succeeded. As the court underlined, what made R's claim good was not the fraud itself but the fact of

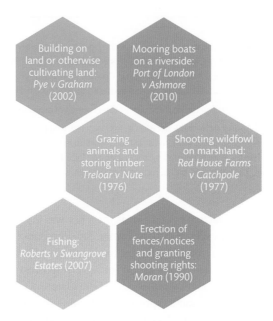

Figure 4.2 Common examples of factual possession

his possession of the land for the required length of time without MR2's consent. *Rashid* is therefore a cautionary tale; a stark warning to landowners that 'you snooze; you lose' if, when faced with adverse possession, you fail to take action. Even in a case of fraud and where the claimant is already registered as the owner of the land, if the elements of adverse possession are made out, a claim can succeed.

4.4.2 The requisite intention to possess

Factual possession is not the end of the story. The court will not permit the informal acquisition of another's land based on factual possession alone. In addition, there must be the requisite intention to possess that other's land—sometimes referred to by the Latin phrase **animus possidendi**. In this section, we get to grips with what is meant by this required 'intention to possess', how the courts have interpreted this element, and how this intention might be demonstrated.

4.4.2.1 What does 'intention to possess' mean and how is it demonstrated?

Historically, 'intention to possess' was understood as requiring that a trespasser actually intended to *own* the land in question.[31] This was, however, rejected by the Court of Appeal in *Moran* and confirmed in *Graham*[32] where Lord Browne-Wilkinson expressed regret at the confusion that this element had caused. Certainly, the shift from 'intention to own' to an 'intention to possess' is significant and broadens the scope of the doctrine. Consider the

---

[31] *Littledale v Liverpool College* (1900); *George Wimpey & Co. Ltd v Sohn* (1967).
[32] For the counter viewpoint, see L. Tee, 'Adverse Possession and the Intention to Possess' [2000] Conv 113.

facts of *Moran* and *Graham*. In *Moran*, Mr Moran was all too aware that the land in dispute was owned by the Council and had even written a letter confirming this belief. In *Graham*, the Grahams had sought to renew the grazing agreement thereby acknowledging the true owner's right to the land. In neither case could it be said that there was any intention to own the disputed land on the part of the adverse possessor and both Mr Moran and the Grahams knew of the purpose to which the true owners intended the land to be put. Nevertheless, on the wider 'intention to possess' formulation, their respective claims to adverse possession succeeded. Lord Browne-Wilkinson in *Graham* held that in considering 'intention to possess' the court's focus is on the intention of the claimant and not the intention of the true owner. To focus on the latter's intention would be 'heretical and wrong'. Only in exceptional circumstances would a claimant's knowledge of the intended, future purpose to which the land was to be put prevent a finding of intention to possess:[33]

> [I]f the squatter is aware of a special purpose for which the paper owner uses or intends to use the land . . . that may provide some support for a finding as a question of fact that the squatter has no intention to possess the land in the ordinary sense but only an intention to occupy it until needed by the paper owner. For myself, I think there will be few occasions in which inference could properly be drawn in cases where the true owner has been physically excluded from the land. But it remains a possible, if improbably, inference in some cases.

How then is 'intention to possess' demonstrated? The court in *Graham* approved the test laid down in *Powell* where Slade J explained:[34]

> What is really meant, in my judgment, is that, the *animus possidendi* involves the intention, in one's own name and on one's own behalf, to exclude the world at large, including the owner with the paper title . . . so far as is reasonably practicable and so far as the processes of the law will allow.

'Intention to possession' therefore means showing that the adverse possessor had an intention to exclude the world at large and to put the land to her own particular use and for her own benefit, irrespective of whether she knew of the true landowner's rights.

As you can appreciate, evidence of an intention to exclude the world at large will often overlap significantly with the requirement for factual possession. Take the issue of fencing off and enclosure of land. In *Moran*, the Court of Appeal noted the wealth of case law demonstrating that enclosure by a claimant adverse possessor 'itself prima facie indicates the requisite animus possidendi',[35] yet also provides evidence from which factual possession can be established. In the case of *Marshall v Taylor* (1895) Lord Halsbury LC indicated that once land is enclosed, it is undeniable that the true landowner cannot gain access in the ordinary sense and therefore the landowner and the world can be seen as excluded. In *Graham*, the House of Lords found the requisite intention to possess on the grounds that the Grahams made use of the land, 'for all practical purposes . . . as their own and in a normal way for an owner to use it'.[36] The court will therefore place great weight on the claimant's actions in seeking to locate the necessary intention to possess. The unavoidable result is that whilst factual possession and intention to possess are said to be separate requirements, to an extent and in some cases, they will inevitably collapse into a single issue.

---

[33] *Graham*, 438.   [34] *Powell*, 471.

[35] *Moran*, 641, per Slade LJ referencing *Seddon v Smith*; *George Wimpey & Co. Ltd v Sohn*.

[36] *Graham*, 443–4.

Thus, in *Moran* the erection and maintenance of fencing and enclosures provided evidence of *both* factual possession and the *animus possidendi*. The same is true in *Graham*, where the grazing of cattle on land enclosed by hedges and gate was used to satisfy both essential elements of the adverse possession claim.

Where does this leave us? It seems that where the claimant adverse possessor is able to establish factual possession, an intention to possess will frequently be assumed or, at least, will likely be determined by reference to the very same facts or circumstances. In *Powell*, the court recognized one instance when this would not be the case, however: where the adverse possessor's use of another's land is 'equivocal in the sense that it did not necessarily, by itself, betoken an intention on his part to claim the land as his own and exclude the true owner'.[37] Where the use of land is equivocal, 'compelling evidence' of an intention to possess will be needed. One example would be where a trespasser crosses neighbouring land belonging to another to access her own property. Here, whilst this may give rise to a right of way[38] in the trespasser's favour, without clear evidence of an intention to possess the neighbouring land, it will likely not be enough to establish an adverse possession claim. An interesting and recent example of how the court will approach the issue of 'equivocal use' is the case of *King & Blair v The Incumbent of Newburn* (2019). Church authorities wanted to sell off an old and long-closed church to allow for the land to be converted into a house. The descendants of those buried in a burial vault beneath the church objected and, in response, one argument advanced by church authorities was that title to the burial vault (which had vested in the descendants of those buried) had passed to the church through adverse possession. The First-Tier Tribunal found in the church's favour, holding that, since 2004, the church had been closed, the doors locked, and so, after 12 years, title had been lost through adverse possession. However, the Upper Tribunal allowed the appeal finding that since no one from the church authorities had ever entered the vault, they could not have been in control or possession of it and that locking the church was 'equivocal' as it was not directed at excluding the public in general nor at excluding the descendants of those buried. Finally, the descendants were never put on notice that they were being excluded from the vault and had been granted access whenever they requested it. Neither factual possession nor intention to possess had therefore been demonstrated.

4.5 Terminating or interrupting a period of adverse possession

As Figure 4.3 depicts, in certain circumstances, a period of adverse possession may be interrupted or terminated. Do bear in mind, however, that where one period of adverse possession comes to an end, it is entirely possible for a new period of adverse possession to subsequently begin over the same land. Let's take a closer look at each potential terminating event.

---

[37] *Powell*, 476, per Slade J cited with approval in *Graham*.
[38] This is a classic example of an easement and we consider easements in Chapter 10.

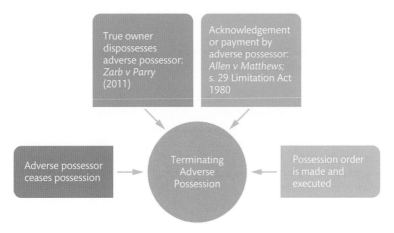

Figure 4.3 Means of terminating or interrupting a period of adverse possession

4.5.1 Adverse possessor ceases possession

Where the adverse possessor ceases possession of the disputed land, quite obviously any adverse possession is brought to an end and the continuity of that adverse possession is broken. Should the adverse possessor re-enter into possession of the land, the adverse possession clock will restart from this time.

4.5.2 True owner dispossesses adverse possessor

Where the true owner dispossesses the adverse possessor either by eviction or by taking back possession of the disputed land, the continuity of that period of adverse possession is broken. If the adverse possessor subsequently remains in possession, a new period of adverse possession will begin. The leading decision here is *Zarb v Parry* in which the court considered what action would suffice to constitute interruption of adverse possession.

KEY CASE *Zarb v Parry* (2011)

Facts: There was a dispute between the Zarbs and the Parrys as to a strip of land that was part of the Parrys' garden. The Zarbs' predecessor in title, Mr Little had sold part of his garden to the Ceens, predecessors in title to the Parrys. The Ceens had always considered the boundary between the two properties as being marked by a hedge. The Zarbs contended that the boundary was actually 12 feet further north of the hedge. In 2007, the Zarbs entered onto the disputed strip of land, cut down a tree, uprooted the existing fence, and placed new fence posts where they believed the boundary was located. The Zarbs made use of surveyor's tape to mark out what they considered to be the true boundary. The Parrys returned home and challenged the Zarbs. The confrontation lasted 20 minutes. The Zarbs subsequently sought a declaration from the court that the boundary was as they asserted. In defence, the Parrys claimed adverse possession over the disputed land. The trial judge held that the Parrys had been in adverse possession of the strip of land for over ten years and had obtained title to the land as a result. The Zarbs appealed.

→

➜

Legal issue: On appeal, the Zarbs argued that the period of adverse possession by the Parrys had been interrupted by the Zarbs' attempt to fence off the strip of land and that, consequently, time had started running again.

Judgment: The Court of Appeal rejected the Zarbs' ground of appeal holding that for the Parrys' adverse possession to have been interrupted, the Zarbs had to establish that the possession has been brought to an end. Whilst intending to regain possession of the strip of land, the Zarbs did not retake possession 'in any meaningful way'. They had withdrawn part-way through the endeavour due to the protests from the Parrys. The planting of new fence stakes and the use of surveyor's tape were symbolic acts and insufficient to take possession of the strip. Adverse possession by the Parrys had not therefore been interrupted.

The decision in *Zarb* establishes that acts which are merely preparatory, such as the use of surveyor's tape or cutting down trees, will not be sufficient to retake possession or terminate adverse possession even when coupled with a clear intention to do so. Further, as the court established in *Bligh v Martin* (1968), merely setting foot on the disputed land it is not enough to recover possession. Equally, neither oral demands for possession[39] nor those committed to writing[40] will be sufficient to dispossess the adverse possessor or recover possession. Finally, while concurrent possession by the true owner and the claimant adverse possessor will prevent the adverse possession clock from starting,[41] subsequent concurrent possession will be ineffective to dispossess an adverse possessor and therefore insufficient to terminate a period of adverse possession that has already begun.[42]

4.5.3 Possession order is made and executed

Where the true landowner brings a successful action in the courts for a possession order, this naturally terminates the period of adverse possession. Interestingly, the court in *Higgs v Leshel Maryas Investment Co.* (2009) appears to go further in suggesting that the adverse possession clock will stop running when proceedings other than possession proceedings are initiated where those proceedings affirm the true owner's title.

4.5.4 Acknowledgement or payment by adverse possessor

Under s. 29 of the Limitation Act 1980, if the adverse possessor acknowledges the title of the true landowner, any period of adverse possession is interrupted and the adverse possession clock is reset and starts running again from this time. As to what constitutes an acknowledgement of title, it is worth noting the following:

1. Section 30 of the 1980 Act requires that the acknowledgement be in writing and signed by the adverse possessor if it is to be effective.

---

[39] *Zarb.*   [40] *Mount Carmel Investments v Peter Thurlow* (1988).
[41] *Sava v SS Global Ltd.*   [42] *Strachey v Ramage* (2008).

2. Whether or not a particular piece of writing amounts to an acknowledgement of the true owner's rights is determined by construing the document in all the surrounding circumstances. As to what the court is looking for here, in *Allen v Matthews*, it was noted:[43]

> [A]ll that is required is that, as between himself and the owner of the paper title, the person in possession acknowledges that the paper owner is entitled to better title to the land.

3. Where there is a claim to adverse possession over land which is subject to a mortgage, a payment of a sum towards the cost of that mortgage by the adverse possessor serves as an acknowledgement of the true owner's title and therefore interrupts any period of adverse possession that might have accrued prior to the payment.[44]

4. The court engaged in a close analysis of the operation of ss. 29 and 30 of the Limitation Act 1980 in *Ofulue v Bossert* (2008). The House of Lords established that:

- Statements in court pleadings are capable of constituting an acknowledgement of title for the purposes of s. 29 of the Limitation Act 1980.
- An acknowledgement operates at the time it is made and, in the absence of a fresh or re-served acknowledgement, is not generally to be treated as a continuing acknowledgement of the true owner's title.
- 'Without Prejudice' correspondence does not constitute an acknowledgement of title.

4.6 Stage 2: The effect of adverse possession

Once the claim to adverse possession has been established, it falls to determine, at stage 2 of our enquiry, what the effect of that adverse possession will be on the title of the original or true landowner. We need to draw a distinction between three scenarios:

- the effect of adverse possession in unregistered land, which is governed by the Limitation Act 1980;
- the effect of adverse possession in registered land, which is now governed by Schedule 6 of the LRA 2002; and
- the effect of adverse possession in registered land before the 2002 Act came into force, which is governed by the Limitation Act 1980 and transitional provisions under the LRA 2002.

Figure 4.4 will help you visualize and better understand how we decide which regime should be applied and when.

4.6.1 The effect of adverse possession: Unregistered land

The rules governing the effect of adverse possession in unregistered land are by far the most straightforward to grasp. Under s. 15 of the Limitation Act 1980, an adverse possessor will acquire title after adversely possessing the disputed land for a period of 12

---

[43] *Allen v Matthews*, 454.
[44] *National Westminster Bank plc v Ashe* (2008); see also s. 29(3) of the Limitation Act 1980.

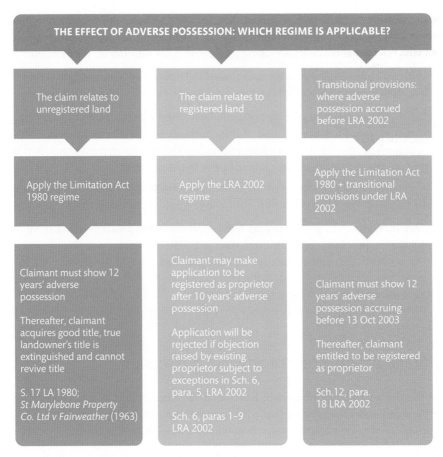

Figure 4.4 The effect of adverse possession: The different regimes

years or more. Section 15 operates by barring the true landowner from bringing an action against the adverse possessor once this period of 12 years' adverse possession has accrued. Section 17 confirms that once that minimum of 12 years has accrued, the true owner's title is extinguished! Importantly, the claimant must be able to point to a 12-year period of *continuous* adverse possession. If the period was interrupted (in the ways discussed in section 4.5), the adverse possession clock restarts from the point at which the interruption came to an end. Provided there is no break in the chain of possession, it is possible, then, for the 12-year period of adverse possession to be accrued by *more than one* adverse possessor.

Let's take an example to bring this to life. Imagine that Manish enters adverse possession of Nina's land in 2002. In 2007, Nina recovers possession of her land from Manish. In 2013, a third party, Oleg, enters adverse possession of Nina's land. In this scenario, Oleg, the second adverse possessor, will be unable to acquire good title to the land through adverse possession as he will be unable to point to a *continuous or uninterrupted* period of 12 years' possession because Nina recovered possession in 2007. However, if Oleg had entered into adverse possession *immediately* after Manish (and Nina had not recovered possession)

Oleg would then be able to *add together* Manish's period of adverse possession with his own in order to demonstrate over 12 years' continuous possession.

The effect of adverse possession in unregistered land was explained neatly in the case of *St Marylebone Property Co. Ltd v Fairweather* (1963) where the court clarified the nature of the title acquired by the adverse possessor. Lord Radcliffe explained that:[45]

> [The adverse possessor] is not at any stage of his possession a successor in title of the man he has dispossessed. He comes in and remains in always by right of possession, which in due course becomes incapable of disturbance as time exhausts the one or more periods allowed by statute for successful intervention. His title, therefore, is never derived through but arises always in spite of the dispossessed owner.

You should note that whilst the claimant adverse possessor must be able to point to 12 years' continuous, uninterrupted possession, there is no requirement that she be in possession of the land at the time the claim to title of the land is made.[46] What happens, however, in the case of an adverse possessor who can demonstrate 12 years' continuous possession but the true landowner has sold the land to a third party? In this context, the transfer of the unregistered land will trigger first registration under the provisions of the LRA 2002. Under s. 11 of the LRA 2002, the third party purchaser will be registered as the new owner and will only be bound if the adverse possessor is in actual occupation of the land.[47]

The effect of s. 11 of the LRA 2002 is that if an adverse possessor can demonstrate 12 years or more of adverse possession but the land was sold by the original owner to a third party, and the adverse possessor has subsequently moved out or left the land, the new registered owner may very well take free of the adverse possessor's rights. Where an adverse possessor successfully acquires title of disputed land but there are pre-existing proprietary rights (such as rights of way) over the land, the adverse possessor will take the land subject to all these pre-existing property interests. This is because the adverse possessor is not a purchaser of the land for value.[48]

4.6.2 The effect of adverse possession: Land Registration Act 2002

The LRA 2002 ushered a new regime for adverse possession claims in registered land which marked a significant departure from both the position in unregistered land and under the previous registered land scheme of the Land Registration Act 1925 (LRA 1925). The new scheme makes no attempt to align registered land with the law of adverse possession as it operates unregistered land. In fact, as s. 96 of the LRA 2002 makes perfectly plain, ss. 15 and 17 of the Limitation Act 1980 which provide for the 12-year limitation period and extinguishment of the true owner's title after 12 years of adverse possession in unregistered land, have no application whatsoever to registered land.

Under the LRA 2002, an adverse possessor has no automatic entitlement to title of the disputed land merely because she has possessed the land for a particular period of time. Instead, the 2002 Act replaces limitation periods and extinguishment of title with an application

---

[45] *St Marylebone Property Co. Ltd v Fairweather*, 535. [46] *Hounslow v Minchinton* (1997).
[47] LRA 2002, Sch. 1, para. 2. [48] *Re Nisbet and Potts' Contract* (1906).

process. This procedure is set out in Sch. 6 of the 2002 Act.[49] Under this procedure, the burden rests squarely on the claimant adverse possessor *to apply to be registered* as the new proprietor of the land in question. An application can only be made if: (1) there has actually been adverse possession (i.e. the essential elements of factual possession and intention to possess as we discussed in section 4.4 are satisfied) and (2) the claimant can point to at least 10 years' adverse possession ending on the date of the application. The existing proprietor is then given an opportunity to object to the application. Before examining the new regime in greater detail, it is worth pausing to consider the motivations behind the new scheme. The Commission in its Report No. 271 explained that:[50]

(1) Registration should of itself provide a means of protection against adverse possession, though it should not be unlimited protection. Title to registered land is not possession-based as is title to unregistered land. It is registration that vests the legal estate in the owner and that person's ownership is apparent from the register. The registered proprietor and other interested persons . . . are given the opportunity to oppose an application by a squatter to be registered as proprietor.

(2) If the application is not opposed . . . the squatter will be registered as proprietor instead. This ensures that land which has (say) been abandoned by the proprietor, or which he or does not consider to be worth the price of possession proceedings, will remain in commerce.

(3) If the registered proprietor (or other interested person) opposes the registration, then it is incumbent on him or her to ensure that the squatter is either evicted or his or her position regularized within two years. If the squatter remains in adverse possession for two years after such objection has been made, he or she will be entitled to apply once again to be registered, and this time the registered proprietor will not be able to object. In other words, the scheme provides a registered proprietor with one chance, but only one chance, to prevent a squatter from acquiring title to his or her land. The proprietor who fails to take appropriate action following his or her objection will lose the land to the squatter.

(4) Consistently with the approach set out above, a registered proprietor who takes possession proceedings against a squatter will succeed, unless the squatter can bring him or herself within some very limited exceptions.

It is clear from this summary that one of the essential features of the scheme is that it aims to produce a decisive result. Either the claimant is evicted or otherwise ceases to be in adverse possession, or he or she is registered as the new proprietor of the land.

The real change made by the 2002 regime is therefore that the onus is very much on the adverse possessor to positively *apply* for registration and not on the landowner to protectively defend his land. Thus, while a ten-year period of adverse possession is a prerequisite for an application to be registered as new owner, it is the act of registration that confers title on the adverse possessor and not the fact of having accrued a fixed period of possession. The new system was therefore intended to both reflect the logic of title registration and to strike an appropriate balance between the landowner and the adverse possessor.[51] Let's delve a little deeper into the 2002 regime.

---

[49] See section 2.9 to learn more of the Law Commission's latest recommendations for how the adverse possession procedure in Sch. 6 might be reformed.

[50] Law Commission Report No. 271, *Land Registration for the Twenty-First Century: A Conveyancing Revolution* (2001), [14.6].

[51] Law Commission Report No. 271, [14.4].

4.6.2.1 The LRA 2002 regime unpacked

An adverse possessor wishing to become the new registered proprietor of disputed land must follow the procedure set out in Sch. 6, paras. 1–4 of the LRA 2002. The essence of this process is that the adverse possessor must apply to be registered as proprietor and the land-owner is given an opportunity to respond and object to the application. This is a significant change in the law and dramatically reduces the likelihood of an adverse possessor acquiring title. Figure 4.5 depicts step-by-step how the new procedure works.

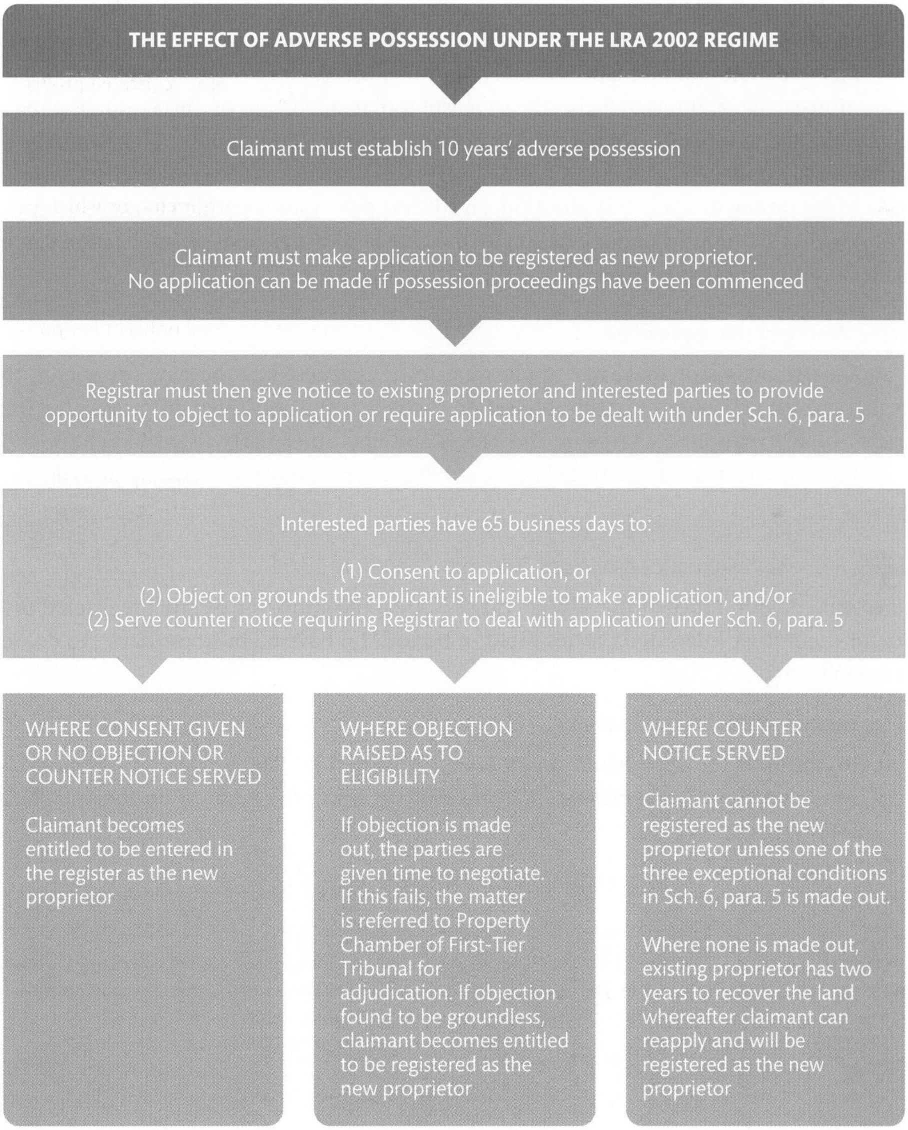

THE EFFECT OF ADVERSE POSSESSION UNDER THE LRA 2002 REGIME

Claimant must establish 10 years' adverse possession

Claimant must make application to be registered as new proprietor.
No application can be made if possession proceedings have been commenced

Registrar must then give notice to existing proprietor and interested parties to provide opportunity to object to application or require application to be dealt with under Sch. 6, para. 5

Interested parties have 65 business days to:

(1) Consent to application, or
(2) Object on grounds the applicant is ineligible to make application, and/or
(2) Serve counter notice requiring Registrar to deal with application under Sch. 6, para. 5

WHERE CONSENT GIVEN OR NO OBJECTION OR COUNTER NOTICE SERVED	WHERE OBJECTION RAISED AS TO ELIGIBILITY	WHERE COUNTER NOTICE SERVED
Claimant becomes entitled to be entered in the register as the new proprietor	If objection is made out, the parties are given time to negotiate. If this fails, the matter is referred to Property Chamber of First-Tier Tribunal for adjudication. If objection found to be groundless, claimant becomes entitled to be registered as the new proprietor	Claimant cannot be registered as the new proprietor unless one of the three exceptional conditions in Sch. 6, para. 5 is made out. Where none is made out, existing proprietor has two years to recover the land whereafter claimant can reapply and will be registered as the new proprietor

Figure 4.5 The new regime under Sch. 6 of the LRA 2002

The 2002 regime therefore consists of a series of distinct steps. We will take a look at each in turn. Be warned, these steps can seem rather procedural and technical.

Step 1: Adverse possessor's application

An adverse possessor wishing to acquire title must make an application to the Registrar to be registered as the new proprietor. This application can only be made once the claimant has been in adverse possession for at least ten years ending on the date of application.[52] If an adverse possessor is registered as the legal proprietor of the land but has not satisfied the ten-year requirement, this will constitute a mistake in the register and the register can be altered (*Baxter v Mannion* (2011);[53] *The Chief Land Registrar v Franks* (2011)). We discussed the case of *Baxter* in Chapter 2. In this decision, the Court of Appeal strongly rejected Mr Baxter's argument that the Sch. 6 procedure was a 'once and for all' system and that, after Mr Mannion had failed to object in time, Mr Baxter's registration as proprietor was unimpeachable. It rejected also the suggestion that correction of mistakes in the register was limited to official errors in the examination of Sch. 6 applications. This would be an invitation to fraud.

As to the timing of a Sch. 6 application, an adverse possessor is entitled to make an application within six months of her eviction by the true landowner[54] but no application can be made once the landowner has begun possession proceedings.[55]

Step 2: Notice of the application

If an adverse possessor makes an application to be registered as the new proprietor, the Registrar must give notice[56] of the application to the existing registered proprietor, the proprietor of any registered charge on the estate, and any other party listed in Sch. 6, para. 2(1). The aim is to alert all interested parties to the adverse possessor's claim and to the new proprietor.

Step 3: Responding to notice of the application

Once served with notice of the adverse possessor's application, the existing registered proprietor (and other interested parties listed in para. 2(1)) have 65 business days[57] to do one of the following:

(i)   to consent to the application;

(ii)   to object to the application under s. 73(1) of the LRA 2002. Such an objection asserts that the adverse possessor is *ineligible* to make the application for one of the following reasons:

- The adverse possessor cannot demonstrate ten years' adverse possession.[58]

---

[52] Schedule 6, para. 1(1) of the LRA 2002. Note: an application cannot be made against an existing registered proprietor who is suffering from a mental disability. Equally, applications concerning Crown foreshore land can be made only after a period of 60 years of adverse possession: paras. 8(2) and 13 respectively.

[53] See discussion in section 2.8.1.   [54] Schedule 6, para. 1(2)(a) of the LRA 2002.

[55] Ibid., Sch. 6, para. 1(3).

[56] Ibid., Sch. 6, para. 2. This will be posted to the address of the existing registered proprietor and other interested parties held at Land Registry.

[57] Land Registration Rules 2003, r. 189.

- The land is subject to a possession order or there are proceedings underway to obtain a possession order over the land.[59]
- The existing registered proprietor suffers from a mental disability.[60]

(iii) to serve a counter-notice to the Registrar requiring the Registrar to deal with the application under Sch. 6, para. 5;

(iv) to object to the application on the grounds of the claimant's ineligibility and serve a counter-notice requiring the application be dealt with under Sch. 6, para. 5;

(v) to do nothing: neither consent, nor object, nor serve a counter-notice.

Step 4: Where the existing proprietor consents to the application

After 65 business days have elapsed and consent to the application has been granted, the claimant adverse possessor becomes entitled to be entered in the register as the new proprietor of the estate and therefore acquires title to the land.[61]

Step 5: Where an objection asserting the claimant's ineligibility is raised

If an objection is raised, a written statement signed by the party or parties objecting must be delivered to the Registrar detailing the grounds for the objection (as just noted) with the objector's full name and address. Where an objection is raised, the claimant adverse possessor's application cannot be determined until the objection is dealt with appropriately. If the Registrar finds the objection groundless, the Registrar will proceed to register the adverse possessor as the new proprietor.[62] If the Registrar finds the objection has merit, notice of the objection will be served to the adverse possessor[63] requesting that all parties seek to negotiate a settlement. Where no agreement is possible, the Registrar must refer the case to the Property Chamber of the First-Tier Tribunal for adjudication.[64]

Step 6: Where a counter-notice is served requiring the application be dealt with under Sch. 6, para. 5

If the existing proprietor or other interested party asserts that the adverse possessor's application is required to be dealt with under Sch. 6, para. 5, the claimant adverse possessor will only be entitled to be registered as the new proprietor if one of three listed, exceptional 'conditions' in para. 5 is satisfied:[65]

- Condition 1: It would be unconscionable as a result of an estoppel for the existing registered proprietor to seek to dispossess the adverse possessor and so the applicant ought to be registered as the new proprietor.
- Condition 2: The applicant is 'for some other reason' entitled to be registered as the proprietor of the estate.

---

[58] Sch. 6, para. 2(1) of the LRA 2002.   [59] Ibid., Sch. 6, para. 1.
[60] Ibid., Sch. 6, para. 8.   [61] *Balevents Ltd v Sartori.*
[62] Section 73(5) and (6) of the LRA 2002.   [63] Ibid., s. 73(5).
[64] Ibid., s. 73(7).   [65] Ibid., Sch. 6, para. 5(1).

- Condition 3: The application relates to a boundary dispute and the adverse possessor reasonably believed that the land she possessed belonged to her.

Conditions 1 and 2 provided for in para. 5(2) and (3) respectively and are mostly straightforward. Condition 1, the estoppel condition, will be satisfied, for example, in circumstances where the existing proprietor has assured the adverse possessor either that she is the true landowner or that she will not be dispossessed and the adverse possessor has relied upon this assurance to her detriment. Do not worry about estoppel at this stage; we cover this topic in some detail in Chapter 8. Condition 2 will be engaged, for example, where the adverse possessor has agreed to purchase the land, advanced purchase monies, entered possession but the transfer simply has not been completed.[66]

Condition 3 is easily the most significant exception and requires closer attention. Schedule 6, para. 5(4) provides:

The third condition is that—

(a) the land to which the application relates is adjacent to land belonging to the applicant,

(b) the exact line of the boundary between the two has not been determined under rules under section 60,

(c) for at least ten years of the period of adverse possession ending on the date of the application, the applicant (or any predecessor in title) reasonably believed that the land to which the application relates belonged to him, and

(d) the estate to which the application relates was registered more than one year prior to the date of the application.

Looking at para. 5(4), two key questions warrant further thought:

1. What is meant by 'reasonable belief'? and

2. At what time is reasonable belief determined?

The question of what constitutes 'reasonable belief' was considered by the Court of Appeal in *IAM Group plc v Chowdrey* which held that an honest belief held by an adverse possessor of entitlement to the land was insufficient; the word 'reasonable' was crucial.

KEY CASE *IAM Group plc v Chowdrey (2012)*

Facts: Mr Chowdrey purchased the freehold of commercial retail premises which he had previously leased. During the lease, Mr Chowdrey had made use of two floors contained within the neighbouring property which were accessible through his tenanted premises. Mr Chowdrey did not know, on purchasing the freehold, that the two floors of the neighbouring property were not included in the sale. Mr Chowdrey had used the two floors in the neighbouring property for well over ten years without complaint from the claimants, Iam Group. Subsequently, Iam issued possession proceedings against Mr Chowdrey.

→

---

[66] As you can see, where either condition 1 or 2 might apply, the claimant will have other remedies available to them to protect their position.

→

Legal issue: In construing the requirement for 'reasonable belief' under Sch. 6, para. 5(4) whose belief was relevant and what was the nature of the belief required by this provision?

Judgment: The Court of Appeal held that it was the adverse possessor's belief that was in issue and the court was 'not here concerned with knowledge in the context, which frequently arises, of imputing an agent's knowledge to the principal. We are here concerned with the requirement as to the reasonable belief of a particular person. In this case, it is the respondent, but generally it is the person who is seeking to apply for registration of title by virtue of adverse possession. What is in issue therefore is not imputed knowledge but rather whether that particular person—here the respondent—was reasonable in holding the belief that he or she did in all the circumstances.' The court therefore rejected the argument advanced by Iam that Mr Chowdrey's solicitors ought to have known of the scope of the sale and that *this* knowledge was imputed to Mr Chowdrey. Etherton LJ clarified that, for the purposes of para. 5(4), the question was whether the adverse possessor was 'reasonable in holding the belief that he or she did in all the circumstances'. In assessing reasonableness, the court should consider whether the adverse possessor should have made enquiries of his solicitors or otherwise. In the circumstances, Mr Chowdrey had used the two floors of the neighbouring property for nearly 18 years without objection including during his period as a tenant. His belief that he was entitled to the two floors of the neighbouring property was reasonable. The mere fact that Iam had challenged Mr Chowdrey's belief of ownership including in letters sent to him did not render his continuing belief of entitlement unreasonable.

As for the timing of reasonable belief, para. 5(4)(c) requires that the adverse possessor reasonably believed the land to belong to him 'for at least ten years of the period of adverse possession ending on the date of the application'. The provision is open to several interpretations as Milne has argued.[67] Does it require a reasonable belief of ownership be held for at least ten years and that persists at the time of the application? Alternatively, does it require the belief be held for ten years at any point during the period of adverse possession irrespective of whether or not it has ended by the time of the application? The issue was addressed by Arden LJ in *Zarb*, who suggested that the adverse possessor's belief of ownership does not have to endure up to the date of the application provided it does not end more than a short time before the application is made. Lord Neuberger MR appeared to disagree in suggesting that the belief must be continuous up to the time of the application. Though not finally settled, the view of Arden LJ is surely preferable as otherwise an adverse possessor who has held an honest and reasonable belief of ownership for ten years would be defeated if she were to be provided with evidence at the very last moment before an application of her non-entitlement.

In the event that none of the three exceptional 'conditions' listed in Sch. 6, para. 5 is made out, the existing registered proprietor then has two years within which to commence possession proceedings against the adverse possessor. If no possession proceedings are initiated within this period, the adverse possessor is entitled to make a fresh application to be registered as the new proprietor provided that she has continued in adverse possession for an additional two years.[68] The adverse possessor will automatically be entitled to be registered as the new proprietor of the estate.[69]

---

[67] P. Milne, 'Mistaken Belief and Adverse Possession—Mistaken Interpretation? *Iam Group plc v Chowdrey*' [2012] Conv 343.

[68] Schedule 6, para. 6(1) of the LRA 2002.   [69] Ibid., Sch. 6, para. 7.

Step 7: Where an objection is raised and a counter-notice is served

A prudent registered proprietor served with notice of the claimant adverse possessor's application will most likely want to both object to the application (asserting the claimant's ineligibility, for example, on the basis that she has not proved factual possession or intention to possess for the required ten-year period) *and* take advantage of the Sch. 6, para. 5 process. The existing registered proprietor would be wise to exploit both routes here because if the proprietor raises an objection but fails to also require the application to be dealt with under Sch. 6, para. 5, they will lose the right to have the matter considered under this provision once the 65-business-day period has elapsed.

Step 8: Where the registered proprietor does nothing: neither consents, nor objects, nor serves a counter-notice

Here, after the 65-business-day period has elapsed, the adverse possessor becomes entitled to be entered in the register as the new proprietor of the estate.[70] This is the case even if notice of the application served by the Registrar never reached the original proprietor.

Step 9: The effect of registration of the adverse possessor as the new proprietor

Where the claimant is registered as the new proprietor of the registered estate, Sch. 6, para. 9 clarifies that the registration does not affect the priority of any interests affecting the estate.[71] Under para. 9, the adverse possessor therefore takes the land subject to all interest affecting the land except any registered charge. Importantly, an adverse possessor who is registered as proprietor under any of the three conditions in Sch. 6, para. 5 takes subject to all interests affecting the land *including* registered charges. This is because a mortgage lender will have been unable to object to the registration of the adverse possessor as proprietor where any of these three exceptional conditions are met and therefore it would be unfair to allow the adverse possessor to escape liabilities towards the lender (chargee) in these circumstances.

4.6.2.2 The LRA 2002 regime: A brief critique

We noted earlier that the motivation behind the new scheme was to strike a balance between the rights of the existing proprietor and the adverse possessor. How far does the LRA 2002 regime achieve this? Two principal viewpoints emerge.

Viewpoint 1: The new regime renders almost irrelevant the law of adverse possession in registered land

- Cooke has argued that the effect of the LRA 2002 scheme is to render registered land 'virtually squatter proof',[72] a view shared by Dixon who is even more dramatic in his assessment of the LRA 2002, describing the 'emasculation of adverse possession'.[73]

---

[70] Ibid., Sch. 6, para. 4.

[71] There is an exception as regards registered charges. A registered chargee that fails to object to the adverse possessor's application to be registered as proprietor is unable to enforce its charge against the adverse possessor once she is registered as the new proprietor.

[72] E. Cooke, *The New Law of Land Registration* (Oxford: Hart, 2003), 139.

[73] M. Dixon, 'The Reform of Property Law and the Land Registration Act 2002: A Risk Assessment' [2003] Conv 136, 150.

According to this viewpoint, adverse possession is reduced to a minimal, vanishing role governing mostly boundary disputes in unregistered land and land which has clearly been abandoned by the registered proprietor.

- The effect of the changes under the LRA 2002 scheme is that, putting the issue of consent and objection on the grounds of ineligibility to one side, unless a claimant adverse possessor is able to demonstrate one of the three exceptional circumstances in Sch. 6, para. 5, an existing proprietor has two years within which to commence possession proceedings. These proceedings are straightforward to initiate and will prove successful by merely demonstrating the existing proprietor's title. It is for this reason that it might be said that new regime is weighted heavily in the registered proprietor's favour.

- Cobb and Fox argue that the LRA reflects a clear policy choice to sure up and secure the position of registered land and to support the principles of land registration. It is another incentive for those owning unregistered land to seek first registration in order to unlock the greater protections that the new scheme offers in comparison to the more generous approach to adverse possessors we see in the unregistered context.

- Much depends on the degree to which landowners engage with the system of notification under Sch. 6 of the LRA 2002. If the notice served by the Registrar is not received, not read by the registered proprietor, or not responded to, the protection is rendered useless and the new scheme bites hard in entitling the claimant adverse possessor to be registered as the new proprietor. Could it be argued, though, that such an unconcerned, careless (?) and absent landowner would have little ground for complaint in these circumstances?

Viewpoint 2: The new regime is a welcome affirmation that the fact of registration and not possession is the basis of our registered land system

- According to this view, the land registration project is only strengthened by ensuring an accurate register and this requires restriction of the law of adverse possession. On this view, adverse possession makes far less sense today in a contemporary society where land ownership is so highly prized and where far less land is abandoned.

- Bogusz has argued that:[74]

  The economic reality of land being an important commercial commodity, that is freely and widely traded, makes adverse possession appear to be a very outdated concept. In this sense the LRA 2002 has very much lived up to the objective of the Law Commission's Consultation Document of 1998 and as far as adverse possession is concerned, brought land registration into the twenty-first century.

Which, if either, viewpoint do you share?

4.6.3 The effect of adverse possession: Transitional provisions

There is a third and final scenario for us to consider: where the period of adverse possession has accrued in registered land but before the coming into force of the new regime under the LRA 2002, in other words, before 13 October 2003. In this situation, both the

---

[74] B. Bogusz, 'Bringing Land Registration into the Twenty-First Century: The Land Registration Act 2002' (2002) 65 MLR 556, 563.

Limitation Act 1980 and the transitional provisions under Sch. 12, para. 18 of the LRA 2002 are activated. In short, this works as follows: an adverse possessor will be entitled to be registered as the new owner of the land if she can demonstrate that two conditions are met. These conditions are:

1. That, as at 13 October 2003, the land over which she claims adverse possession, was registered, and

2. That there had been adverse possession of the land (factual possession + intention to possession) for the 12 years' limitation period as provided for under the Limitation Act 1980 accruing before 13 October 2003.

If these conditions are satisfied, the adverse possessor is entitled to be registered as the new owner of the land in question.

The LRA 1925, the forerunner to the LRA 2002, had sought to bring the law of adverse possession as it applied to registered land into line with the law in unregistered land. It did so by applying the Limitation Act 1980 limitation periods as they operated in unregistered land (in other words, requiring 12 years' adverse possession) into the registered land sphere. However, there was one key change. Under s. 75(1) of the LRA 1925, the estate of the registered proprietor rather than being extinguished at the end of the limitation period was instead deemed to be held on trust for the adverse possessor. The effect was to provide the adverse possessor with the right to apply for registration as the new registered proprietor.[75] The imposition of this trust has been described as 'the English lawyer's natural response to a situation where true ownership and paper title diverge'.[76] The Law Commission in 1998 examined the operation of adverse possession in registered land and criticized the imposition of the trust under s. 75 of the LRA 1925 arguing that:[77]

> All that was required was to provide . . . that once the limitation period has expired, the squatter should be entitled to be registered as proprietor of the land . . . unfortunately, this simple solution was not adopted. Instead, the draftsman added a further and (in our view) quite unnecessary layer of complexity to the scheme . . . the statutory trust [under s. 75 of the LRA 1925]. This provision gives rise to many difficulties, not least of which is whether the 'trust' imposed on a registered proprietor by section 75(1) of the Land Registration Act 1925 can be regarded as having the normal characteristics of a trust . . . it gives rise to a number of odd consequences.

A principal criticism of this statutory trust was that it resulted in a windfall to the adverse possessor who was able to elect between a proprietary remedy or, additionally, a personal remedy against the original landowner.[78] The Law Commission concluded that:[79]

> The most fundamental criticism of the present law is the uncertainty and confusion that is created by the introduction of the concept of a trust into the law of adverse possession. We are unable to see why such a trust is necessary, because we consider that it would be perfectly possible to reflect the way in which adverse possession operates in unregistered land without having recourse to it.

---

[75] Land Registration Act 1925, s. 75(2); *Central London Commercial Estates Ltd v Kato Kagaku Co. Ltd* (1998).
[76] Cooke, *The New Law of Land Registration*, 136.   [77] Law Commission Report No. 254, [10.29].
[78] For further discussion see E. Cooke, 'Adverse Possession: Problems of Title in Registered Land' (1994) 14 LS 1.
[79] Law Commission Report No. 254, [10.40].

As a consequence, the Commission recommended that the statutory trust be abolished and that an adverse possessor should be able to simply apply to be registered as proprietor after the requisite period of possession has accrued. These proposals found voice in the new regime under the LRA 2002, which we have explored, but also in the transitional provisions. As to the transitional provisions, Sch. 12, para. 18(1) clarifies that, where prior to the enactment of the new regime, land was held on trust for an adverse possessor, that adverse possessor is entitled to be registered as the proprietor of the estate.

One final but crucial point must be grasped: where the period of 12 years' adverse possession is *not* completed before the 13 October 2003, the new regime under Schedule 6 of the LRA 2002 (just discussed) will operate. This is important because, as we have seen, the scheme under the LRA 2002 offers a far less generous route for adverse possessors than that in unregistered land.

4.7 Adverse possession and leasehold land: In brief

So far in this chapter, we have considered the position of adverse possession involving freehold land but adverse possession can also arise in relation to leasehold land. In fact, many of the same principles apply. In particular, the essential elements needed to establish an adverse possession claim (factual possession and an intention to possess) apply equally. Beyond this, in the distinctly leasehold context, we must distinguish between two different situations: (1) a claim by an adverse possessor to acquire the leasehold estate—in other words, a claim to be entitled to a lease existing over land; and (2) a claim by an adverse possessor to acquire title to the freehold—in other words, a claim to be entitled to the freehold land out of which a lease was carved: see Figure 4.6.

4.7.1 Claim to the leasehold estate

A squatter taking possession of land which is subject to a lease is able to acquire the leasehold estate on the grounds of adverse possession. This means that the adverse possessor, if successful, will take the place of the lessee or tenant under the lease. When the lease expires or is terminated so too, however, will the new lessee and the adverse possessor's rights come to an end. We must distinguish registered leasehold estates and those which are unregistered. Where title to the lease is registered, the provisions of Sch. 6 of the LRA 2002 apply as discussed in section 4.6.2. Here, where the claimant accrues ten years' adverse possession she is able to make an application to be registered as the new titleholder of the leasehold estate. Where title to the lease is unregistered, the unregistered land regime under the Limitation Act 1980 applies. Here, as we found in section 4.6.1, the claimant will acquire the leasehold estate if she can demonstrate 12 years' adverse possession.

4.7.2 Claim to freehold land subject to a lease

Can a adverse possessor claim title to the freehold which is subject to—that is to say, out of which a lease was carved? For as long as the lease remains in force, any adverse possession will only be adverse to the existing tenant and will not be adverse to the freeholder (the landlord).

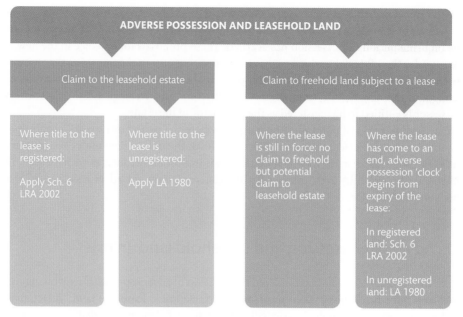

Figure 4.6 Claims to adverse possession concerning leasehold land

Therefore, the adverse possessor can only acquire the freehold by way of adverse possession once the lease has come to an end. The claimant adverse possessor must therefore demonstrate accrual of the required period of adverse possession after the expiry of the lease. In registered land this means that a claimant must demonstrate ten years' adverse possession and make an application under Sch. 6 of the LRA 2002 to be registered as the new proprietor of the freehold land. In unregistered land, this means the claimant must demonstrate 12 years' continuous, uninterrupted adverse possession in order to acquire the freehold. If the existing tenant wishes to bring a claim to the freehold by way of adverse possession, once again, the adverse possession 'clock' does not start running until the lease has come to an end. Thereafter, the effect of the adverse possession is determined according to the rules as apply to unregistered or registered land as explored in this chapter.

4.8 Criminalizing residential squatting

Adverse possession may, in some circumstances, engage the criminal law. In the introduction, it was noted that some may regard adverse possession as sanctioning 'land theft'. Today there are three key criminal offences which might be activated by adverse possession:

1. Section 6 of the Criminal Law Act 1977 states that an offence is committed by 'any person who, without lawful authority, uses or threatens violence for the purpose of securing entry into any premises' subject to a defence where entry to premises is sought by a 'displaced residential occupier'[80] or 'protected intending occupier'.[81]

---

[80] See the definition in s. 12(3)–(5) of the Criminal Law Act 1977.   [81] See the definition ibid., s. 12A.

2. Section 7 of the Criminal Law Act 1977 states that an offence is committed by a person who is on any premises as a trespasser and fails to leave on being required to do so by or on behalf of a displaced residential occupier or a protected intending occupier.

3. Section 144 of the Legal Aid, Sentencing and Punishment of Offenders Act 2012 (LASPO 2012) created the new offence of 'squatting in a residential building'.[82] A person commits an offence under s. 144 where she lives or intends to live in a residential building which she entered as a trespasser and she knew or ought to have known she was a trespasser.[83]

The relationship between criminalization of squatting under s. 144 and adverse possession was explored in the case of *Best v Chief Land Registrar* (2015). Mr Best took possession of an empty (and abandoned) house in 1997 on learning that the owner had died. He carried out considerable renovation to the property and in January 2012 moved in permanently. Mr Best applied under Sch. 6 of the LRA 2002 to be registered as proprietor of the house but the Registrar rejected his application on the grounds that his possession of the property had amounted to a criminal offence and could not therefore be relied upon. The matter reached the Court of Appeal where the Registrar argued that the public interest in ensuring a person did not benefit from committing a crime outweighed the public policy of the law of adverse possession. The Registrar's appeal failed and the court confirmed that just because an act of adverse possession may amount to a crime does not prevent an application to be registered as proprietor under the LRA 2002. Sales LJ explained that Sch. 6 of the 2002 Act involved a careful balancing act between protection of registered proprietors from losing title to their land and the public interest in ensuring meaningful use and marketability of land. Section 144 of LASPO 2012 was designed to provide deterrence and practical help to homeowners to remove those squatting on their land and was not intended to 'produce any collateral effect' on the law of adverse possession nor to rebalance the competing interests of registered proprietors and squatters. Had this been the intention, LASPO 2012 would have made it plain on its face.

The court also engaged in a wide-ranging discussion of the doctrine of illegality concluding that there was no 'blanket' illegality rule applicable in every context but rather a series of distinct rules adapted to particular contexts.[84] For example, illegality may nevertheless act as a bar to an adverse possession claim in extreme cases such as murder of the true owner by an adverse possessor or bribes of the police not to take enforcement action.

4.9 Adverse possession and human rights

We discuss the relationship between land law and human rights in Chapter 14. However, here we consider the particular interaction of adverse possession and human rights arguments. Where a claim to adverse possession is successful, it results in the existing

---

[82] The offence came into force on 1 September 2012.

[83] For more detail on the law of squatting which falls outside the scope of this book, see L. Fox O'Mahony, D. O'Mahony, and R. Hickey (eds.), *Moral Rhetoric and the Criminalisation of Squatting: Vulnerable Demons?* (Abingdon: Routledge, 2014).

[84] See discussion at [64]–[80], per Sales LJ.

proprietor of land being, in essence, stripped of their property. It is in this way that an argument is raised that the effect of a successful adverse possession claim is in breach of the European Convention on Human Rights (ECHR) as incorporated into domestic law by the Human Rights Act 1998. This was precisely the argument advanced by Pye following its loss in *J. A. Pye Ltd v Graham* in the House of Lords.[85] Pye brought proceedings in the European Court of Human Rights contending that the deprivation of its land by way of adverse possession infringed Art. 1 of Protocol 1 of the ECHR and that it should be awarded compensation from the British government for its loss, which Pye argued amounted to some £10 million.

The European Court sitting as a chamber of seven judges originally allowed Pye's case, finding by 4:3 that the deprivation of property as a result of adverse possession infringed Art. 1 of Protocol 1 of the ECHR.[86] On appeal, the Grand Chamber reversed this decision by 10:7.[87] The Grand Chamber accepted that Art. 1 of Protocol 1 was engaged and considered closely the justification for the law of adverse possession, in particular, whether it served a legitimate aim. In issue was the LRA 1925 regime (and not the later enacted LRA 2002 scheme) and the Grand Chamber found that the principles struck a fair balance between the rights of individuals and the public interest:[88]

> Even where title to real property is registered, it must be open to the legislature to attach more weight to lengthy, unchallenged possession than to the formal fact of registration. The Court accepts that to extinguish title where the former owner is prevented, as a consequence of the application of the law, from recovering possession of land cannot be said to be manifestly without reasonable foundation.

The Chamber was not persuaded that the scale of Pye's loss and the windfall enjoyed by the Grahams played any role in determining whether the adverse possession regime was ECHR-compliant. The Chamber held that if the limitation periods were to fulfil their stated purpose then they must apply irrespective of the extent of any loss that could result from their operation. Those seven dissenting in the Grand Chamber did so on a number of different grounds. Five of the seven dissentient voices argued that the principle of adverse possession under the LRA 1925 did not strike a fair balance between the individual interest and the public interest on the grounds that, in registered land, as opposed to unregistered land, title depends not on possession but on registration. The LRA 1925 (unlike the LRA 2002) regime did not provide sufficient protection to existing registered proprietors. Two further judges dissented on the basis that the principles of adverse possession under the LRA 1925 did not serve a legitimate function and were disproportionate.

Where does *J. A. Pye (Oxford) Ltd v UK* leave us? While the decision of the Grand Chamber was concerned with human rights arguments as to the LRA 1925 regime, it has been argued by Jones that it must be implicit in the reasoning of the Chamber that the LRA 2002 is also human rights-compliant given that the new scheme under the 2002 legislation contains greater safeguards and protections for existing registered proprietors than is the case under the 1925 regime.[89] As we have examined, even five of the seven dissenting

---

[85] Human rights arguments were not raised before the House of Lords as the case was heard before the coming into force of the Human Rights Act 1998.   [86] *J. A. Pye (Oxford) Ltd v UK* (2008).

[87] Ibid.   [88] Ibid., [74].

[89] O. Jones, 'Out with the Owners! The Eurasian Sequels to *JA Pye (Oxford) Ltd v United Kingdom*' (2008) 27 CJQ 260.

judges appeared to acknowledge this. As a matter of legal precedent, the decision of the Grand Chamber is not strictly binding on the domestic courts. However, the Court of Appeal in *Ofulue*[90] followed the Grand Chamber's decision in holding that the Ofulues' deprivation of property by way of adverse possession was not a violation of Art. 1 of Protocol 1 of the ECHR. *Ofulue* therefore seems to put beyond doubt that the law of adverse possession is human rights-compliant. Accepting this means that the best advice to landowners is to ensure that their titles are registered and therefore subject to the more protective Sch. 6 regime under the LRA 2002.

4.10 Future directions

The enactment of the LRA 2002 and the new adverse possession regime introduced under Sch. 6 has significantly limited the impact of adverse possession in modern land law. Provided an existing registered proprietor is reasonably prudent in responding to a claimant adverse possessor's application to be registered as the new proprietor, in every likelihood the vast majority of adverse possession claims will now fail. Additionally, following *J. A. Pye (Oxford) Ltd v UK* and *Ofulue*, the door to human rights challenge of the principles of adverse possession appears to have been firmly slammed shut. This does not mean that adverse possession is an academic graveyard, however. Certainly not. A number of issues remain live. In particular, the introduction of the new criminal offence of squatting in a residential building under s. 144 of LASPO 2012 has incited much debate.

The s. 144 offence of squatting in residential buildings has led to calls for the offence to be extended to cover commercial premises. Largely, this call has come from business owners and Members of Parliament affiliated to the Conservative Party. The case for extending the law runs like this: squatters fearing prosecution will and are already making the move out of residential buildings into abandoned or empty business premises to escape prosecution under the new s. 144 offence. *The Guardian* newspaper has suggested that squatters have begun to move to possessing abandoned pubs as the crisis in the pub trade has coincided with the criminalization of residential squatting.[91] Would extending the offence constitute a fair development of the law or an attack on society's vulnerable who have nowhere else to go?

Another debate centres around the argument put forward by Cobb and Fox that, in adopting the new regime for adverse possession under the LRA 2002, the Law Commission and Parliament have identified squatters as morally blameworthy and have failed to properly examine:[92]

> the complexities involved in striking a balance between advertent squatters and neglectful landowners, as well as failing to take account of the knock-on effect of squatting for the property market and housing market . . . and [appear] to have closed off any prospect of further debate

---

[90] Human rights' arguments were not raised when the case was appealed to the House of Lords.

[91] O. Bowcott, 'Criminalise Squatting in Commercial Premises say Tory MPs', *The Guardian*, 30 November (2012): http://www.theguardian.com/society/2012/nov/30/criminalise-squatting-commercial-property.

[92] N. Cobb and L. Fox, '"Living Outside the System?" The (Im)morality of Urban Squatting after the Land Registration Act 2002' (2007) 27 LS 236, 259.

on the subject. Yet reports indicating significant increases in the incidences of urban squatting suggest the converse: that it is now apposite to reconsider the wide range of issues surrounding urban squatters, from the philosophical and moral construction of the squatter to the social, cultural, economic and housing implications of deliberate unlawful occupation in empty residential properties.

Cobb and Fox conclude that the new LRA 2002 scheme incentivizes squatters to operate 'outside the system' and to ensure continued possession of properties by avoiding making an application to be registered as proprietor.[93] This is because applications are largely 'doomed to fail', argue the authors, and necessarily trigger notification of their possession to the existing proprietor. Schedule 6 of the LRA 2002 attempts to both protect registered proprietors as well as providing a procedure by which adverse possessors are able to acquire title. If the result is a growing number of squatters operating outside the system and not engaging with the LRA 2002 scheme, this could signify the failure of the new regime.

A third and fascinating perspective on the law of adverse possession concerns our emotional reaction to its operation. Conway and Stannard have explored the 'emotional paradoxes' that lie at the foundation of the doctrine which they argue help us understand precisely why adverse possession is so divisive and visceral in its impact. The authors identify three central paradoxes: (1) something which is essentially a wrong becomes a right— a tortious act becomes the basis of the acquisition of title; (2) the clash of the emotional responses to adverse possession from those viewing it as an 'attack' or a 'theft' and those who see the doctrine as rewarding effort, initiative, and resourcefulness in occupying often abandoned land; (3) the response of the legislature and judiciary which appears to be motivated by the need to respond to the general public's emotional response to adverse possession.[94] Conway and Stannard's work raises an interesting question as to the moral dimensions of adverse possession. How far have law-makers been influenced by contemporary, social attitudes to adverse possession in legislating for the LRA 2002? Fundamentally, how do you regard the doctrine: as sanctioning land theft or as compensating those unlocking abandoned or under-used land?

Further reading

- N. Cobb and L. Fox, 'Living Outside the System?' The (Im)morality of Urban Squatting after the Land Registration Act 2002' (2007) 27 LS 236.

- H. Conway and J. Stannard, 'The Emotional Paradoxes of Adverse Possession' (2013) 64 NILQ 75.

- E. Cooke, *The New Law of Land Registration* (Oxford: Hart, 2003), chapter 7.

- D. Cowan, L. Fox O'Mahony, and N. Cobb, *Great Debates in Property Law* (Basingstoke: Palgrave, 2012), chapter 6.

- M. Dockray, 'Why Do We Need Adverse Possession?' [1985] Conv 272.

- L. Fox O'Mahony, D. O'Mahony, and R. Hickey (eds.), *Moral Rhetoric and the Criminalisation of Squatting: Vulnerable Demons?* (Abingdon: Routledge, 2014).

---

[93] H. Conway and J. Stannard, 'The Emotional Paradoxes of Adverse Possession' (2013) 64 NILQ 75.
[94] Ibid., 89.

- C. Harpum and O. Radley-Gardner, 'Adverse Possession and the Intention to Possess: A Reply' [2011] Conv 155.

- O. Jones, 'Out with the Owners! The Eurasian Sequels to *JA Pye (Oxford) Ltd v United Kingdom*' (2008) 27 CJQ 260.

- L. Tee, 'Adverse Possession and the Intention to Possess' [2000] Conv 113.

- L. Tee, 'Adverse Possession and the Intention to Possess: A Reply to Harpum' [2002] Conv 50.

Online resources

Access the online resources at www.oup.com/uk/bevan2e/ to test yourself with self-test questions and scenario problems. You can also view additional supporting material relevant to the topics in this chapter, including:

- *Videos*
- *Audio podcasts*
- *Maps, diagrams, and flowcharts*
- *Interactive exercises*
- *Examples of real-life legal documentation*

5 Co-ownership

5.1 Introduction

Co-ownership is the name given to the situation where two or more people own land at the same time. This land may be freehold or it may be leasehold. In this way, we say that ownership is 'concurrent' (rather than successive) by which we mean that the ownership rights enjoyed by those co-owners are enjoyed simultaneously: see Figure 5.1.

Co-ownership is very common and, in practice, extremely useful. Co-ownership means that more than one person at a time can enjoy the benefits that ownership of land offers. Just imagine how inflexible our land law system would be if only one person at a time could own property. Co-ownership allows loved ones (married or unmarried), friends, neighbours, family members to come together to purchase and take the benefit of land. The family home, for example, will often be co-owned by partners in a romantic relationship. It also allows for business people setting out on a joint commercial venture to share entitlement in land. At some stage and in some degree or other co-ownership will impact us all. It can arise expressly where parties purposely set out to formally create a co-ownership arrangement. Equally, it can arise impliedly.[1]

With the great advantages that concurrent ownership brings, there are unsurprisingly also challenges and disputes. The body of law that had developed in this area has therefore had to react to the problems that can occur when co-owners fall out, their relationships break down, or where one or more of the co-owners wishes for the land to be sold. This involves a fine balancing act of all the parties' interests and may also mean weighing up the interests of co-owners against any creditor who, for example, has a security interest in the co-owned land. The law must also respond when one or more co-owners becomes bankrupt. All of these issues we consider in this chapter. As you will see, the law of co-ownership represents an amalgam of common law rules and statutory provisions, most notably under

---

[1] This takes place under an implied trust. We consider these in Chapter 6.

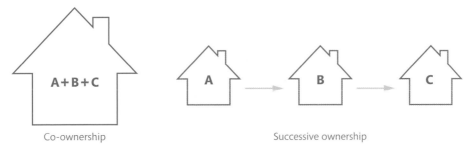

Figure 5.1 Distinguishing concurrent co-ownership from successive ownership

the provisions of the LPA 1925 and the Trusts of Land and Appointment of Trustees Act 1996 (TOLATA 1996). Importantly, the law on co-ownership must strive to keep pace with shifting social attitudes and changes in the way couples, in particular, manage their affairs. As Crown observed:[2]

> Co-ownership is one of the most common forms of land holding in England and Wales and indeed in most common law countries. It has formed part of the legal system since the earliest times. One might therefore be forgiven for assuming that legal problems relating to the nature and effect of co-ownership had been worked out long ago.

This chapter therefore tracks the path of these problems which reflect some of the biggest battles in land law: how does the law get to grips with disputes over the family home where spouses face relationship breakdown often with one partner wishing to remain in the home, perhaps with children? Whose interest prevails, the individual or the bank, when a co-owner finds herself in serious debt? Creditors want a law that is robust, clear, and certain. Non-creditors want a softer, more fact-sympathetic approach that recognizes the importance of property as a home. Who wins in this co-owner versus creditor clash? Where does and should the law draw that line? Do creditors, as Brown argued, 'always win in the end'?[3] We consider these fascinating questions here. Before we embark upon an examination of how co-ownership operates in modern land law, however, two fundamental features of co-ownership must be grasped:

1. First, the distinguishing feature of co-ownership is what we call 'the unity of possession'. This means that each co-owner enjoys an entitlement to possess the co-owned land. This sits as a fundamental and irreducible core of the co-ownership idea. If there is no unity of possession, quite simply, there can be no co-ownership.

2. Secondly, under English law, all forms of shared ownership must operate behind a trust.[4] This means that wherever there is co-ownership, a trust will arise. As we saw in Chapter 1, the trust is a device which involves the separation of the formal legal title to land from the underlying, equitable ownership of the land called the 'equitable' or 'beneficial' interest'. Those holding the legal title are known as trustees whilst those enjoying the

[2] B. C. Crown, 'Severance of Joint Tenancy of Land by Partial Alienation' (2001) 117 LQR 477, 477.
[3] D. Brown, 'Insolvency and the Matrimonial Home—Sins of the Fathers: *In Re Citro (A Bankrupt)*' (1992) 55 MLR 284, 288.
[4] You were introduced to the concept of the trust in section 1.6.3.

equitable interest in the land are known as 'beneficiaries'. In a nutshell, the trustees can be seen as the 'managers' of the land whilst the beneficiaries (as the name suggests) enjoy the benefit of ownership of the land. This benefit may involve the right to occupy the land, take profits from the land, and/or a right to the proceeds of any sale of the land. The imposition of a trust wherever there is co-ownership carries an important significance for our study of this area. As the trust device necessarily involves the fragmentation of the legal and equitable titles, practically, this means that in every co-ownership scenario there is a need for us to consider (1) how the property is held at law; and (2) how the property is held in equity. As we will see in section 5.2, this is a vital step in our analysis of co-ownership.

   Visit the online resources to watch a video on the topic of co-ownership.

5.2 The two forms of co-ownership

There are only two forms of co-ownership recognized in English law today: the **joint tenancy** and the **tenancy in common**. Whilst both forms can be described as constituting shared or co-ownership, in practice, they operate quite differently. We will look at each in turn.

5.2.1 Joint tenancy

Where co-ownership operates under a joint tenancy, each co-owner is regarded as being wholly entitled to the land. No single co-owner has any 'share' in the co-owned land and, collectively, all co-owners are treated as constituting a single unit. As Coke famously noted:[5]

> [E]ach joint tenant holds the whole and holds nothing, that is, he holds the whole jointly and nothing separately.

Imagine a married couple who are co-owners of a house under a joint tenancy. They are both wholly entitled to the land. It would be quite inappropriate to speak of either having a 'share' in the land. Equally, irrespective of how much each party may have contributed to the purchase price of the house, still we say that each is wholly entitled. As to who owns the house, we say that together they own the whole of the house. They are one single owner. The language of 'shares' has no place in relation to a joint tenancy. For the sake of absolute clarity, if there is an express declaration of joint tenancy, this will give rise to a joint tenancy even if the contributions to the purchase price are unequal.

5.2.1.1 The four unities

A joint tenancy can only exist where what we call the 'four unities' are present. We have already encountered one of the four unities in the introduction when we noted that co-ownership can only arise where there is unity of possession. For a joint tenancy to exist, all four of the unities must be found. If any of the four unities are missing, no joint tenancy can exist. So, what are they? See Table 5.1.

---

[5] *Coke Upon Littleton*, 19th edn (London: Hargrave and Butler, 1832), 186a.

Table 5.1 The four unities

The Unity of Possession	• Co-owners must enjoy an entitlement to possess the whole of the co-owned land. • No single co-owner is permitted to exclude another from either part or the entirety of the co-owned land (*Wiseman v Simpson* (1988)). If they are so entitled, there will be no unity of possession.
The Unity of Interest	• Co-owners must each hold the same, identical interest in the land, e.g. freehold. • If one co-owner holds the freehold and another a leasehold interest only, there will be no unity of interest.
The Unity of Title	• Co-owners must acquire their identical interests from the same act, transaction or same document, e.g. from the same conveyance or transfer, or from adverse possession.
The Unity of Time	• Co-owners must all have acquired their interest at the same time. • If one co-owner acquired their interest at a later date, there will be no unity of time.

5.2.1.2 Survivorship

The most important, practical significance of co-ownership under a joint tenancy as opposed to co-ownership under a tenancy in common (the other recognized form of co-ownership) is that, as between co-owners that are joint tenants, the doctrine of survivorship (also known as *ius accrescendi*) operates. The doctrine of survivorship has been described as the 'grand and distinguishing'[6] feature of the joint tenancy. Let's take a closer look at how survivorship operates.

The crux of the doctrine is that when one joint tenant dies, her interest automatically passes to or 'survives to' the remaining joint tenants. As we recognized in section 5.2.1, joint tenants are wholly entitled to the co-owned land and do not enjoy a 'share' in that land. It therefore makes logical sense that, on the death of one joint tenant, the deceased simply disappears from the picture and the surviving joint tenants continue to be wholly entitled to the co-owned land. Despite there now being one less co-owner, the position of the surviving joint tenants has, essentially, not changed: they remain wholly entitled to the land.

Survivorship operates automatically on death. Under a joint tenancy, co-owners are unable to bequeath their interest in the co-owned land in a will and, should they die intestate (i.e. without having made a will), their interest will also not pass under the intestacy rules. This is because individually each joint tenant owns nothing or, at least, nothing that they can point to as representing their own particular 'share' to pass on to their heirs. On their death, survivorship will automatically operate as just described and their interest will survive to the remaining joint tenants. This means that survivorship takes precedence over the terms of a will.[7]

When all but one joint tenant has deceased, that single remaining joint tenant is no longer a co-owner and instead becomes absolutely entitled to the land. As the saying goes, 'the winner takes it all'. At this point, co-ownership has clearly been terminated and the surviving party can do whatever she wishes with the land—she is the outright owner.

---

[6] See K. Gray and S. F. Gray, *Elements of Land Law*, 5th edn (Oxford: Oxford University Press, 2009), 914.
[7] Unless there are joint wills which provide for mutual agreement to sever the joint tenancy.

This leaves unresolved one final, beguiling question: what happens if the final surviving joint tenants seemingly die at the same moment? The effect of the doctrine of survivorship means it matters who died first. This ghoulish conundrum has been the subject of statutory intervention under s. 184 of the LPA 1925 which anticipated just this problem. Under s. 184:

> In all cases where, after the commencement of this Act, two or more persons have died in circumstances rendering it uncertain which of them survived the other or others, such deaths shall (subject to any order of the court), for all purposes affecting the title to property, be presumed to have occurred in order of seniority, and accordingly the younger shall be deemed to have survived the elder.

Although it is criticized, there are three key benefits to the operation of survivorship:

1. First, in the domestic context, it often reflects the wishes of the parties. Many couples, for example, make no provision for their property should one of them die. Survivorship ensures that, in the event, the surviving partner becomes entitled to the land.

2. Secondly, survivorship simplifies probate. Given that survivorship operates automatically on death, there is no need for co-owners to take the time or incur the cost of formally providing for the vesting of their interest in the surviving co-owners in the event of their death. Surviving co-owners need take no action when a fellow co-owner dies.

3. Finally, it simplifies purchases of co-owned land. As there will be only one title vested in several joint tenants, for a potential purchaser this makes the process of investigating title far simpler, quicker, and so less likely to delay the sale.

5.2.1.3 Introduction to severance

Where there is co-ownership under a joint tenancy, joint tenants can separate their interest from the other joint tenants by a process called **severance**. Where severance takes place, a joint tenant's interest in the co-owned land is transformed into a notional 'share' of the co-owned land and that co-owner becomes a tenant in common. The remaining co-owners will continue to be joint tenants unless and until such a time as they too decide to sever. As to the size of the share, this is calculated as a proportion of the total number of co-owners. Severance has important consequences. Where severance has taken place, the doctrine of survivorship will not operate in relation to that co-owner's interest but will continue to operate in relation to the remaining joint tenants' interests. As a result, on death, the interest of the tenant in common does not survive automatically to the remaining co-owners. Rather, having severed, this co-owner is free to bequeath her interest to her heirs. Equally, having severed, this co-owner or her estate is not then able to assert entitlement to benefit under survivorship. Survivorship does not operate under a tenancy in common.

We examine severance in greater detail in section 5.5 where you will discover that severance can only take place in equity. There can be no severance at law. As to *how* a co-owner severs their interest (i.e. the different methods of severance), we discuss this in full in section 5.5.2. Before then, we turn to consider the second form of co-ownership recognized in English law: the tenancy in common.

5.2.2 Tenancy in common

Unlike under a joint tenancy, a co-owner holding an interest in land as a tenant in common is seen as entitled to a notional or undivided share in the land. This does not mean that a tenant in common can point to a particular space or room in the co-owned property and say 'this belongs to me', nor can a tenant in common subdivide the co-owned property. No, the entitlement to a notional or undivided share reflects that the tenant in common is able to deal with their share in the co-owned land during their lifetime and, equally, may leave it to their heirs on their death. A tenant in common is therefore able to sell their share or even mortgage it. Crucially, a tenant in common is also able to draw up a will bequeathing their share. While for a joint tenancy to arise, all four of the four unities must be present, for a tenancy in common to arise only one is needed: the unity of possession (recall that without this unity of possession no co-ownership can exist at all!). The second key characteristic of the tenancy in common, as we noted in section 5.2.1.3, is that the doctrine of survivorship does not apply.

We identified in the introduction to this chapter that co-ownership operates under a trust of land, meaning that legal and equitable ownership are split. This means we have to examine separately how co-owned land is held at law and in equity. We do this in sections 5.3 and 5.4.

5.3 The position at law

When thinking about a co-ownership scenario, you need to be able to determine how the land is held (1) at law and (2) in equity. In other words, is there a joint tenancy or a tenancy at common? Importantly, the same piece of land can, and often is, held differently at law and in equity (e.g. there may be a joint tenancy at law but a tenancy in common in equity). In this section, we consider the position *at law*. Unlike the position in equity, which we explore in section 5.4, co-ownership of the legal title is far more restrictive. Several key points can be made:

1. At law, co-ownership can only exist under a joint tenancy. There can be no tenancy in common at law: s. 1(6) of the LPA 1925.

2. Logic dictates that, as there can be no tenancy in common at law, there can also be no severance of a joint tenancy at law: s. 36(2) of the LPA 1925. This does not, however, affect a joint tenant's ability to 'release' her interest to the other joint tenants and simply drop out of legal co-ownership of land.

3. Statute places a limit on the number of people who can exist as co-owners at law over a parcel of land. Under s. 34(2) of the LPA 1925, there can be no more than four legal co-owners. Where legal title is conveyed to more than four, s. 34(2) makes clear that it will be the first four people named in the conveyance who are of full age that will be registered as legal co-owners. Note: there is no limit to the number of co-owners that can exist nor any rule against co-owners who are under 18 *in equity*.

5.4 The position in equity

Once you've determined that co-ownership operates under a joint tenancy *at law*, you need to consider how the land is being held *in equity*. Unlike the more restrictive approach at law, co-ownership in equity is far more flexible. In equity, co-owners may be either joint tenants or tenants in common. How are we to know whether co-owners are joint tenants or tenants in common? In addressing this question, there are three key analytical tools we can use to help us:

1. any express declarations of trust;
2. the presence or otherwise of the four unities;
3. the application of various equitable presumptions.

5.4.1 Any express declarations of trust

Where a trust of land has been created expressly, an express declaration may indicate how the property is to be held in equity.[8] The declaration may, for example, make plain on its face that co-owned land is to be 'held on trust for A and B as legal and equitable joint tenants'. It may also indicate the share of the property that each party is to enjoy. Where there is an express declaration, this clear expression of intention will be conclusive of the issue and will not be usurped by any implication to be drawn on the facts.[9] This was confirmed by the court in *Goodman v Gallant*[10] and recently confirmed in *Pankhania v Chandegra* (2012). The case of *Goodman* in particular warrants reading in full.

> **KEY CASE** *Goodman v Gallant* (1986)
>
> Facts: In 1960, Mrs Goodman and her husband purchased a house which was conveyed into Mr Goodman's sole name. There was, despite this, an agreement between the couple that Mrs Goodman was entitled to a 50 per cent share in the beneficial interest in the property. In 1971, the marriage broke down. Mrs Goodman left her husband but remained in the property. Later, the defendant, Mr Gallant began living with Mrs Goodman. In 1978, Mr Goodman conveyed the freehold estate in the house to Mrs Goodman and Mr Gallant 'to hold the same unto the purchasers in fee simple as beneficial joint tenants'. In 1983, Mrs Goodman severed the joint tenancy and issued a court summons seeking determination of her and Mr Gallant's respective beneficial interests. Mrs Goodman argued that she was entitled to a three-quarters share of the beneficial interest and Mr Gallant to a one-quarter share only.
>
> ➡

---

[8] A declaration may be usurped by evidence of vitiating factors e.g. fraud. Such express declarations will either be done on the Form TR1 which is used to transfer registered property or separately on a Form JO (Joint Ownership). The TR1 form was introduced in 1997 and contains a box for transferees of registered land to declare whether they hold the land as joint tenants or tenancy in common in equity. Importantly, completion of this section of the form is, in practice, voluntary and a transfer remains valid even where the parties have not filled out this box.

[9] On which see C. Bevan, 'The Search for Common Intention: The Status of an Executed, Express Declaration of Trust Post-*Stack* and *Jones*' (2019) 135(4) LQR 660.

[10] On which see S. Gardner, 'Understanding *Goodman v Gallant*' [2015] Conv 199.

→

Legal issue: What was the status of the express statement in the conveyance to Mrs Goodman and Mr Gallant which provided that they held as joint tenants? Was Mrs Goodman entitled to a three-quarters share or did severance operate to provide her with a lesser entitlement?

Judgment: The Court of Appeal held that where a conveyance contains an express declaration of trust that makes clear the parties are to hold property as joint tenants, this express statement will be exhaustive and conclusive in the absence of evidence of fraud or a material change of circumstances. The court noted:

> In these circumstances the overwhelming preponderance of authority, including the three decisions of this court in *Wilson v. Wilson* [1963], *Leake (formerly Bruzzi) v. Bruzzi* [1974] and *Pink v. Lawrence*, in our judgment both entitle and oblige us to hold that, in the absence of any claim for rectification or rescission, the provision in the conveyance declaring that the claimant and the defendant were to hold the proceeds of sale of the property 'upon trust for themselves as joint tenants' concludes the question of the respective beneficial interests of the two parties in so far as that declaration of trust, on its true construction, exhaustively declares the beneficial interests.

The court held that the effect of severance of a joint tenancy in equity was to create a tenancy in common in equal shares. Mrs Goodman was therefore entitled to a 50 per cent share of the beneficial interest in the property and not the three-quarter share she claimed.

KEY CASE *Pankhania v Chandegra* (2012)

Facts: A property was purchased in the joint names of Pankania and his aunt, Chandegra. There was an express declaration that the property was to be held by the parties as tenants in common in equal shares in equity. The aunt sought to argue that, despite this express declaration, she was entitled to 100 per cent of the beneficial interest in the property on the basis that the transfer had been a sham and that it was always intended between the parties that she would be the sole beneficiary of the entire equitable interest.

Legal issue: Would the court be prepared to look beyond the express declaration of trust to consider the wider circumstances and find in favour of Chandegra?

Judgment: The High Court found for Chandegra holding that the transfer to Pankhania and Chandegra as tenants in common had been a sham devised in light of Chandegra's lack of sufficient income to secure a mortgage on the property. The High Court found that, in view of this, Pankhania had agreed to be jointly liable under the mortgage so that his salary would be taken into account thereby increasing the chances of a mortgage being granted. The judge found that there had never been an intention that Pankhania would reside in the property, nor derive any benefit from it. Chandegra held the entire beneficial interest in the property. Pankhania appealed. In the Court of Appeal, Pankhania succeeded. The Court of Appeal held that the express declaration as to how the property was to be held was conclusive. There was no room for the court to engage in an analysis founded on the implication of a constructive trust to usurp the express declaration. An express declaration would only not be conclusive if there was evidence of mistake, fraud, or undue influence. Nothing of this nature had been alleged or pleaded in this case. The High Court had, therefore, been wrong to look behind the express declaration of trust. The authorities of *Goodman* and *Pink v Lawrence* were to be followed.

Be clear: the effect of *Goodman* and *Pankhania* is that where there is an express declaration and it is not tainted by fraud or undue influence, the terms of that declaration as to how the land is held will be conclusive. There is no need to go on to consider our other analytical tools set out above: points (2) and (3) (the four unities and the application of equitable presumptions).

Where there is no express declaration as to how property is held in equity, the words used in the conveyance may indicate the nature of the co-ownership. In particular, we might look for 'words of severance' in the conveyance of land which will be indicative of the existence of a tenancy in common. Words of severance are those indicating a splitting of the equitable ownership which is inconsistent with a joint tenancy. Phrases such as 'to be divided'[11] or 'in equal shares'[12] will therefore give rise to a tenancy in common.

5.4.2 The presence or otherwise of the four unities

We have seen that for a joint tenancy to exist, all four of the unities must be present. We can therefore use the existence or otherwise of the unities as a means of determining how co-ownership is operating in equity. If all four unities are present, this may suggest that the land is held under a joint tenancy in equity. If the four unities are not present, it cannot be a joint tenancy and may indicate a tenancy in common. This is not alone determinative of the issue, however, and a tenancy in common may nevertheless still arise where all four of the unities are present . . . so be sure to make use of the other analytical tools.

5.4.3 The application of the equitable presumptions

Where there is no express declaration of trust, the court will look to a series of established equitable presumptions to determine whether property is held under a joint tenancy or a tenancy in common. Be aware however that these presumptions are just that; they are presumptions which are capable of being rebutted and, moreover, they can often work in quite a contradictory fashion.

5.4.3.1 Presumption 1: Equity follows the law

This general presumption means that, given there can only be a joint tenancy at law, it is presumed that there will also be a joint tenancy in equity. This presumption can, of course, be rebutted by evidence of contrary intention and is subject to being overridden by any of the other presumptions discussed. Following the important decisions of *Stack v Dowden* (2007) and *Jones v Kernott* (2011),[13] where a property is purchased in joint names as a family home, a strong but rebuttable presumption of an equitable joint tenancy arises even where there are unequal contributions to the purchase price. Rebutting this 'heavy' presumption, said Baroness Hale (as she then was) in *Stack*, will be 'very unusual'. In *Stack* evidence of a clear separation of financial affairs between domestic partners was sufficient to rebut this presumption.

5.4.3.2 Presumption 2: Equity prefers a tenancy in common

Quite in contrast to the first presumption, it is often said that equity prefers a tenancy in common. Why is this? An equitable maxim with which you may be familiar is that 'equality is equity'. When we say 'equity prefers a tenancy in common' what this really means is

---

[11] *Fisher v Wigg* (1700).   [12] *Payne v Webb* (1874).   [13] We discuss these important cases in Chapter 6.

that a tenancy in common is regarded as operating more fairly to the parties than a joint tenancy. This is largely on the basis that the doctrine of survivorship does not operate under a tenancy in common, a doctrine which, as we have seen, rewards the surviving co-owners and prevents the passing of an interest of joint tenants by will.

5.4.3.3 Presumption 3: Unequal contribution to the purchase price

Except in the domestic/family home context (where presumption 1 will operate),[14] where the legal owners of a property have contributed unequally to the purchase price, there is a presumption of a tenancy in common in equity. Here, the shares of each tenant in common will be proportionate to their contribution. In equity, a tenancy in common is seen as the fairest way to reflect the discrepancy in the size of the contributions. Naturally and by extension, where the contributions to the purchase price are all equal, there will be a presumption of joint tenancy in equity.

5.4.3.4 Presumption 4: Mortgage loans from two or more mortgagees

Where a mortgage loan is advanced to a **mortgagor** (the borrower) from two or more mortgagees (lenders), there is a presumption that those mortgagees hold an interest in the mortgaged property as tenants in common in equity.

5.4.3.5 Presumption 5: Commercial/business partnerships

Where business partners, as part of a commercial enterprise, acquire land jointly, there is a presumption that they hold the land as tenants in common in equity: *Lake v Craddock* (1732). This is because it is presumed that the commercial nature of their relationship is inconsistent with the operation of the doctrine of survivorship. Of course, commercial/business partners are able to hold land as joint tenants in equity but only where there is an express declaration of trust to this effect or, from all the surrounding circumstances, it is clear that the parties positively intended a joint tenancy.[15]

5.4.3.6 Presumption 6: Business tenants

Where there is a lease of business premises taken out by two or more businesses jointly at law to allow for distinct business purposes to be pursued, there is a presumption of tenancy in common in equity: *Malayan Credit Ltd v Jack Chia-MPH Ltd* (1986). In this case, two businesses took out a lease of a floor of an office block. A dispute arose and one of the businesses, Jack Chia, applied for sale of the lease, seeking an equal share of the proceeds. The key issue was whether the property was held under a joint tenancy or tenancy in common in equity. The court held that the businesses had agreed an unequal share of floor space and there was a meticulous and unequal division of liabilities as to rent and service charges between the two. On this basis, the court found a tenancy in common in equity in unequal shares.

---

[14] Which will be covered by the *Stack/Jones* presumption of equitable joint tenancy.

[15] A case in which such a clear intention to create a joint tenancy was found is *Bathurst v Scarborow* (2004).

Determining how co-owned property is held both at law and in equity is not, as we have seen, always entirely straightforward. Figure 5.2 offers a suggestion for how to visualize this information hanging together.

5.5 Severance

We have seen that co-owners hold land either as joint tenants or tenants in common. At law, there can only be a joint tenancy and this tenancy is, under statute, not capable of being severed. In equity, however, there can be either a joint tenancy or a tenancy in common. It is therefore in equity where the question of severance arises. You were introduced to severance in section 5.2.1.3. In this section, we consider what severance means, its consequences, and examine the different methods by which severance takes place.

5.5.1 The meaning and significance of severance

Severance describes the process by which a joint tenant is converted into a tenant in common. As Dillon LJ explained in *Harris v Goddard* (1983):[16]

> Severance . . . is the process of separating off the share of a joint tenant, so that the concurrent ownership will continue but the right of survivorship will no longer apply. The parties [who have severed] will hold separate shares as tenants in common.

Dillon LJ neatly captures the principal reason why joint tenants would wish to sever: to avoid the effects of survivorship and to enable them to access a 'share' in the co-owned land. Freed from the effects of survivorship, severance gives the severing co-owner the ability to deal with their interest (their share)—for example, by selling it or passing it on death under a will or, if no will is made, under the rules on intestacy. A number of points can be made about the operation and significance of severance:

1. Severance operates to convert a joint tenant in equity into a tenant in common in equity. Severance can only operate in equity as, under s. 36(2) of the LPA 1925, there can be no severance at law.

2. Where an equitable joint tenant severs, she becomes an equitable tenant in common. Severance *does not* have any effect on the remaining co-owners whose status remains unchanged unless and until such time as they sever.

3. Where an equitable joint tenant severs, she is entitled to a share of the co-owned land which is proportionate to the total number of joint tenants.[17] It is generally irrelevant that each co-owner initially contributed unequally to the purchase price of the property.[18] The position was clarified by Russell LJ in *Bedson v Bedson* (1965):[19]

---

[16] *Harris*, 1210.   [17] *Goodman*.

[18] The court in *Barton v Morris* (1985) and *Singla v Brown* (2007) recognized that severance can give rise to a share that is other than proportionate to the total number of joint tenants if there is a clear and unequivocal agreement to this effect between the parties.   [19] *Bedson*, 689.

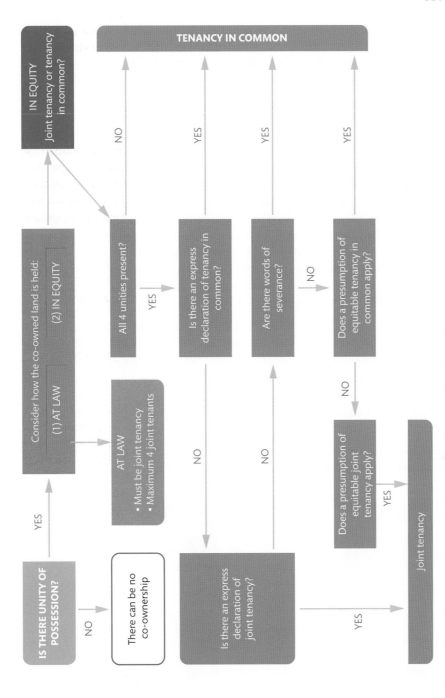

Figure 5.2 Bringing it all together—determining how co-owned land is held at law and in equity

On severance the beneficial joint tenancy becomes a beneficial tenancy in common in un-divided shares, and the right of survivorship no longer obtains. If there be two beneficial joint tenants, severance produces a beneficial tenancy in common in two equal shares. If there be three beneficial joint tenants and only one severs, he is entitled to one-third un-divided share and there is no longer survivorship between him and the other two, though the other two may remain inter se beneficial joint tenants of the other two-thirds.

Let's take an example: Anita, Ben, Cai, Dillon, and Eva are co-owners of a £350,000 house they have jointly purchased. Anita and Ben both contributed £100,000 to the pur-chase price while Cai, Dillon, and Eva contributed only £50,000 each. The terms of the conveyance contains an express declaration that they are joint tenants at law and in eq-uity. As the first four named in the conveyance, Anita, Ben, Cai, and Dillon are legal joint tenants. At law, they must be joint tenants as there can be no tenancy in common at law. They hold the property on trust for themselves and Eva as joint tenants in equity. Now imagine that Anita decides to sever. She remains a joint tenant at law but, in equity, she becomes a tenant in common with a one-fifth share of the equitable ownership in the house. Ben, Cai, Dillon, and Eva continue as joint tenants in equity of the remaining four-fifths unaffected by Anita's severance: see Figure 5.3.

4. Severance must take place before the death of the joint tenant. This is because the doc-trine of survivorship operates automatically on death. The effect of this is that severance cannot be effected by will (*Carr v Isard* (2007)) and must take place during the lifetime of the equitable joint tenant if it is to be effective.

5. It is for the joint tenant claiming to have severed to prove that effective severance has taken place. In other words, the burden of proof rests on the shoulders of the severing party.[20]

6. Severance cannot be reversed or undone. Once severance has taken place, the severing joint tenant will be a tenant in common and cannot rewind the clock.

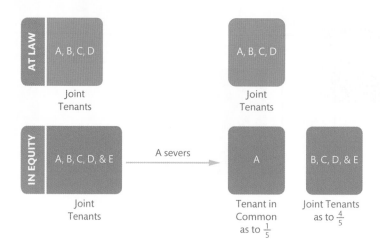

Figure 5.3 The effect of severance

[20] *Re Denny* (1947).

5.5.2 **The five methods of severance**

We have now explored the meaning and effect of severance and so it falls to consider how an equitable joint tenant goes about effecting severance. There are five principal methods of severance. As shown in Figure 5.4, an equitable joint tenancy can be severed by written notice or by **forfeiture,** or in three further ways that are together known as the 'Hensman catalogue' as they were laid down by the court in *Williams v Hensman* (1861).

You must appreciate that there is a clear overlap between the five methods. Indeed, it is quite common for a joint tenant who claims to have severed to argue several different methods in the alternative. In your own analysis of a severance scenario, it will serve you well to do the same. The starting point for a discussion of the different methods of severance is s. 36(2) of the LPA 1925. Section 36(2) provides that:

> [W]here a legal estate . . . is vested in joint tenants beneficially, and any tenant desires to sever the joint tenancy in equity, he shall give to the other joint tenants a notice in writing of such desire or do such other acts or things as would, in the case of personal estate, have been effectual to sever the tenancy in equity.

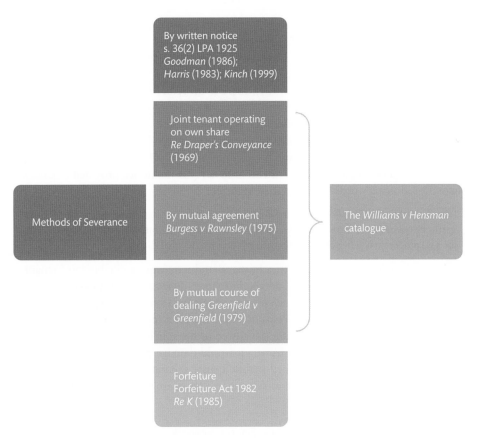

Figure 5.4 The methods of severance

Section 36 is important in two ways: (1) it provides the first method of severance for our consideration, severance by written notice, but also (2) it expressly preserves the other methods of severance already recognized by the common law. We begin with a closer look at severance by written notice.

5.5.2.1 Severance by written notice

Severance by written notice under s. 36(2) of the LPA 1925, or 'statutory severance' as it is also known, is one of two methods of severance that is entirely unilateral in nature.[21] This means that a joint tenant can sever by written notice without first gaining the consent of the other co-owners. The remaining modes of severance either involve all of the joint tenants[22] or involve severance by operation of law.[23] Perhaps in view of the unilateral nature of severance by written notice, certain restrictions or limitations have developed. Section 36 therefore makes plain that, in order to sever, a joint tenant must (1) make this desire to sever clear in a written notice, and (2) serve that notice on *all* other joint tenants. We need to unpack these requirements further. There are two aspects to consider:

- What amounts to an effective notice of severance?
- When is a written notice of severance served?

What amounts to an effective notice of severance?

The first thing to note is that there is no particular set form that this 'written notice' must take in order to give rise to effective severance under s. 36. In addition, as Plowman J confirmed in *Re Draper's Conveyance* (1969), there is no requirement in the wording of the statute for the written notice to contain any signature of a joint tenant. Importantly, the written notice must express *an immediate intention to sever* the joint tenancy: *Harris v Goddard* (1983). A written notice which discusses the possibility of severance or of severance potentially taking place at some future time will not suffice. A classic illustration of a clear and immediate, unequivocal intention to sever is the notice provided in *Goodman* where the following words were held to be sufficient:

> I hereby give you notice of my desire to sever as from this day the joint tenancy and equity of and in [the co-owned land] now held by you and me as joint tenants both at law and in equity so that the said property shall henceforth belong to you and me in equal shares.

In *Gore and Snell v Carpenter* (1990) a husband and wife were equitable joint tenants of two homes. The couple separated and the husband's divorce solicitor was instructed to draw up a separation agreement which contained references to severance. The draft agreement was served on the wife but it remained in draft form and was not formally accepted by both sides. The husband, rejecting the advice of his solicitor, refused to serve a written notice of severance on his wife fearing it would damage prospects for productive divorce negotiations. The husband died before a final separation agreement was reached and without having served a notice of severance. The court held that there was no clear,

---

[21] The other being acting on one's own share under the *Hensman* catalogue discussed in section 5.5.2.2.

[22] Severance by mutual agreement and by severance by mutual course of dealing discussed in sections 5.5.2.3 and 5.5.2.4.

[23] Severance by forfeiture discussed in section 5.5.2.5.

unequivocal, immediate intention to sever the joint tenancy. The effect of this was that the wife was entitled to 100 per cent of the equitable ownership in the properties under the doctrine of survivorship.

The two leading cases on what amounts to an immediate intention to sever are *Re Draper's Conveyance* and *Harris*. Again, do read these cases in their entirety.

KEY CASE *Re Draper's Conveyance* (1969)

Facts: A husband and wife were co-owners of their matrimonial home. They held the property as joint tenants at law and in equity. The marriage broke down and the couple divorced. The wife issued a summons under the Married Women's Property Act 1882 seeking a court order that the former matrimonial home be sold and that the proceeds be divided equally between the couple. The court made an order for sale of the property but, before the home was sold, the husband died.

Legal issue: Had severance taken place? If severance had taken place, the former wife would be entitled to a 50 per cent share of the proceeds of sale of the home. If severance had not taken place, she would be entitled, under survivorship, to the entire beneficial ownership of the property.

Judgment: Plowman J held that the equitable joint tenancy had been severed when the wife issued her summons to court accompanied by an affidavit in support. In the view of the court, taken together, this amounted to a written notice of severance which 'clearly evinced an intention on the part of the wife that she wished the property to be sold and the proceeds distributed, a half to her and a half to the husband'. The equitable joint tenancy had therefore been severed effectively before the husband's death and, as a result, on his death, survivorship did not operate in the wife's favour.

KEY CASE *Harris v Goddard* (1983)

Facts: In very similar facts to *Re Draper's Conveyance*, a married couple were joint tenants at law and in equity of a matrimonial home. The marriage broke down and the wife petitioned for divorce. Under the Matrimonial Causes Act 1973, the wife sought 'such order as may be made by way of transfer of property and/or settlement in respect of the former matrimonial home . . . and otherwise as may be just'. Just three days before the court hearing, the husband was involved in a car crash and subsequently died.

Legal issue: Did, as the husband's executors argued, the divorce petition constitute an effective written notice of severance or had there been no severance and therefore survivorship operated to the advantage of the wife?

Judgment: The Court of Appeal held that the divorce petition failed to demonstrate an immediate intention to sever the joint tenancy. Slade LJ explained:

> I am unable to accept [the] submission that a notice in writing which shows no more than a desire to bring the existing interest to an end is a good notice. It must be a desire to sever which is intended to have the statutory consequence. Paragraph 3 of the prayer of the petition does no more than invite the Court to consider at some future time whether to exercise its jurisdiction under section 24 of the [1973 Act] and if it does, to do so in one or more of three different ways. Orders under section 24(1)(a) and (b) could bring co-ownership to an end by ways other than severance. It follows, in my judgment, that paragraph 3 of the prayer of the petition does not operate as a notice in writing to sever the joint tenancy in equity.

The joint tenancy had therefore not been severed and the wife was entitled to 100 per cent of the equitable ownership of the property under the doctrine of survivorship.

On what appear to be comparable facts, why did the court in *Re Draper's Conveyance* and *Harris* reach quite different results? The essential difference between the issuing summons in *Re Draper's* and the divorce petition in *Harris* was immediacy. Whilst in the former the summons coupled with the affidavit was accepted as giving rise to an immediate intention to sever, in the latter the petition lacked this quality.[24] Following *Harris* it is now clear that the commencement of legal proceedings or the swearing of an affidavit in those proceedings will suffice as a written notice of severance provided the necessary immediacy is present. It had been suggested in *Nielson-Jones v Fedden* (1975) that a summons could not constitute a notice of severance as initiating legal proceedings was not irrevocable. This suggestion was rejected by the Court of Appeal in *Harris* and confirmed by Sir John Pennycuick in *Burgess v Rawnsley* (1975) who noted that the fact that the claimant is not obliged to see through the proceedings is irrelevant as regards severance by notice.

When is a written notice of severance served?

Even if a written notice to sever demonstrating the required immediate intention to sever is found to exist, there is still a second and crucial requirement to be satisfied before severance is effected by written notice: service of that notice. Section 36(2) makes clear that a joint tenant wanting to sever must 'give' the written notice to 'the other joint tenants'. A written notice will only be effective to sever if it is served on *all* other existing joint tenants. Service to just a few or even service to a majority of joint tenants will not be enough. Service is also vital as it is the moment at which the joint tenancy is severed and therefore the moment from which the doctrine of survivorship no longer applies.

In the vast majority of cases, there will be only two co-owners and so service of a notice from one joint tenant to another is easily demonstrated. However, there may be several equitable joint tenants to whom the written notice must be given, and, in addition, difficult questions can arise where a notice is served and there is a death of a joint tenant or where a notice is posted and its delivery is intercepted or the notice is destroyed. Fortunately, Parliament has intervened in the form of s. 196 of the LPA 1925 to assist in resolving these issues. The effect of s. 196 of the LPA 1925 is that a written notice of severance is deemed to have been served when it is left at the joint tenants' last known address or place of business. Where delivery is made by way of registered post, a notice is served when it 'would in the ordinary course be delivered'. You should read the words of s. 196 very closely. The provision makes clear that a written notice does not actually have to be *received* by those joint tenants and equally does not have to be *read* by them to have been served but merely delivered.[25] A leading authority on service of a notice of severance is the rather tragic case of *Kinch v Bullard*.

---

[24] Initiating proceedings in the Court of Protection has also been found to constitute a written notice of severance for the purposes of s. 36(2): in *Quigley v Masterson* (2011) in Court of Protection proceedings brought by a joint tenant's daughter wishing to become her father's deputy, an application made by another joint tenant to be joined in the proceedings (and in which a 50–50 per cent split of the equity was conceded) amounted to a notice of severance.

[25] Of course, a notice of severance will not have been served if it is sent to the wrong address or wrong recipient: in *Quigley v Masterson* a notice of severance was sent to solicitors no longer instructed by the parties who had no authority to accept it.

KEY CASE *Kinch v Bullard* (1999)

Facts: Mr and Mrs Johnson were married and were co-owners of a matrimonial home as joint tenants at law and in equity. The marriage broke down and Mrs Johnson, who was terminally ill, petitioned for divorce. Mrs Johnson sent a written notice of severance by ordinary first-class post to Mr Johnson. The very next day, Mr Johnson suffered a heart attack and underwent a stay in hospital. Mr Johnson's notice of severance was delivered by the postman to Mr Johnson's residence but Mr Johnson had not seen it as he was in hospital at the time. On the basis that it looked like Mrs Johnson would now outlive her husband, she decided that she did not wish to sever the joint tenancy after all. She therefore intercepted the letter and destroyed it. Mr Johnson died a few weeks later in hospital followed several months later by the death of Mrs Johnson.

Legal issue: In an action brought by the executors of each party, the court was asked to determine whether severance had taken place or not. What was the position where a notice of severance had been sent, delivered, but destroyed before being read by its intended recipient? If severance had taken place, each party would enjoy a 50 per cent share in the proceeds of sale of the home. If not, survivorship would have operated on the death of Mr Johnson meaning Mrs Johnson's estate was set to enjoy ownership of the entire property.

Judgment: Neuberger J held that the written notice had been served or 'given' for the purposes of s. 196 of the LPA 1925 on delivery to Mr Johnson's residence. It was at this moment that severance had taken place and the subsequent destruction of the notice had no bearing on the issue of severance; the tenancy had already been severed. As severance had taken place, survivorship did not operate. The parties were each entitled to a 50 per cent share of the property. The position would only have been different, suggested Neuberger J, if before the letter had been delivered, Mrs Johnson had changed her mind and revoked the notice by communicating her change of heart to Mr Johnson.

Kinch is an important decision for confirming the clear rule that a written notice of severance is 'given' for the purpose of s. 196 when it is delivered to the joint tenant or tenants' last known address. Once delivery has taken place, destruction, removal, or other interception of the notice will be too late and will be futile to prevent severance, it having already taken place at the point of delivery, at the moment the letter is pushed through the letter box. In so far as a notice of severance can be withdrawn, effective withdrawal can only take place before the notice is delivered.[26]

In *Re 88 Berkeley Road* (1971), a decision similar to *Kinch*, two women were joint tenants in equity of a co-owned house in which they both lived. One month before Miss Eldridge was to be married, Miss Goodwin posted by recorded delivery to Miss Eldridge a notice of severance. When the letter was delivered, Miss Eldridge was not home and so Miss Goodwin signed for the letter on the former's behalf. Miss Goodwin subsequently died and the issue was whether the letter, having been signed for by its sender and never having been passed by Miss Goodwin to Miss Eldridge, had been effectively served. The court held that the notice had been served and severance had therefore taken place. Miss

---

[26] It is clear that a notice of severance that contains a mistake (e.g. land wrongly identified by solicitors drafting the notice) can be rectified by the court to reflect the true intentions of the parties if certain, strict, conditions are met, namely: (1) there is convincing proof of the intentions of those drawing up the notice; (2) there is an identified flaw in the notice such that it clearly did not give effect to the parties' intentions; (3) the specific intentions of the parties (joint tenants) are shown; (4) there is an issue capable of being contested (i.e. the result would be different in outcome the rectified and non-rectified notice): see *Lee v Lee* (2018).

Eldridge had sought to argue that whilst s. 36(2) of the LPA 1925 was concerned with the 'giving' of notice to sever, s. 196 was concerned with the 'serving' of notices. In essence, this was an attempt to argue that s. 196 did not apply to the 'giving' of written notice to sever under s. 36. Had this been accepted, it would have meant Miss Eldridge could argue that there had been no severance as the notice had not been 'given' to her. This argument was rejected by the court which found no grounds for distinguishing between the 'giving' of a the 'serving' of a notice. As a consequence, severance had taken place and Miss Goodwin was, at her death, a tenant in common and not a joint tenant.

5.5.2.2 Joint tenant operating on her own share

As Figure 5.5 sets out, under the *Hensman* catalogue severance can also take place through a unilateral act of a joint tenant operating on her own share.

You will doubtless have already thought: how can a joint tenant operate on her own 'share' when, under a joint tenancy, she has no entitlement to a 'share' in the first place? You would be entirely right. There is an obvious absence of logical consistency here. However, on reflection, we can say that what Page-Wood V-C was describing was a situation where a joint tenant carries out an act which demonstrates that she intends to treat her interest in the co-owned land as *constituting a share*. In other words, a joint tenant acts *as if she were* entitled to a share. This act will necessarily be inconsistent with the continued existence of a joint tenancy and severance will therefore have taken place. As Crown has argued,[27] any logical difficulties, or 'academic quibbling' as he describes them, can be overcome by accepting that the act itself is seen as creating the share rather than a joint tenant operating on a pre-existing share which of course she does not enjoy. For severance to take place under this head, there is no need to reach agreement with or obtain the consent of the other joint tenants. What, then, will and will not constitute 'acting on one's share'?

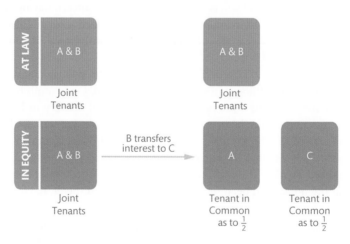

Figure 5.5 Scenario 1

---

[27] Crown, 'Severance of Joint Tenancy of Land by Partial Alienation', 478.

Joint tenant transfers her share to a third party

The most obvious example of operating on one's own share is to transfer the interest in the co-owned land to a third party. In technical speak this is termed an **alienation**. This transfer may be by way of sale or, alternatively, by way of gift. It is clear that under the equitable maxim 'equity treats as done that which ought to be done' that a specifically enforceable contract for the sale or transfer of a joint tenant's interest will amount to an act of severance: *Caldwell v Fellowes* (1870). Consider the following examples:

- Scenario 1: Anita and Ben are joint tenants of co-owned land at law and in equity. If Ben transfers his equitable interest to Cai, a third party, this will be an act of severance. As there were only ever two joint tenants in equity (Anita and Ben), the equitable joint tenancy is brought to an end when Ben severs. Anita and Cai are now tenants in common in equity, each enjoying a 50 per cent share in the property: Figure 5.5.

- Scenario 2: Dillon, Eva, and Freya are joint tenants of co-owned land at law and in equity. If Dillon transfers his equitable interest to Giovanni, a third party, Giovanni becomes a tenant in common in equity with a one-third share. Dillon, Eva, and Freya remain joint tenants as law (severance does not affect the position at law). Eva and Freya also remain joint tenants in equity as to the remaining two-thirds: Figure 5.6.

- Important to note is that, in both scenarios, the acts of severance take effect only in equity. Severance does not change the position of the parties at law.

Joint tenant transfers her share to another joint tenant

Where an equitable joint tenant transfers her interest in co-owned land to a fellow joint tenant, this will be an act of severance. This happens far more commonly than you might imagine. It is quite common for one joint tenant to wish to 'buy out' another. Where this takes place, the joint tenant purchasing the additional 'share' becomes a tenant in common in relation to that newly acquired share but remains a joint tenant as to her original interest. Okay, this sounds confusing but let's take another example to clarify how this works.

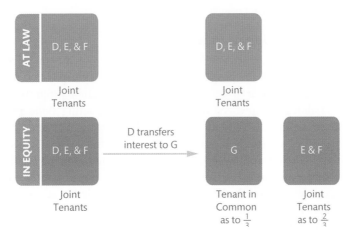

Figure 5.6 Scenario 2

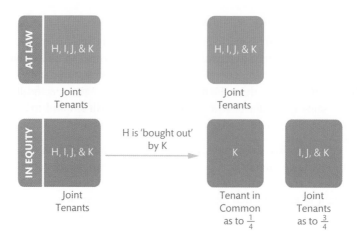

Figure 5.7 Joint tenant bought out by fellow joint tenant

Harry, Ingrid, Jo, and Krushi are joint tenants of co-owned land at law and in equity. If Harry sells his equitable interest to Krushi (i.e. Harry is 'bought out' by Krushi), Harry has severed his interest. Krushi becomes a tenant in common of a one-quarter share. Harry, Ingrid, Jo, and Krushi remain joint tenants at law. Krushi remains (along with Ingrid and Jo) a joint tenant in equity of the remaining three-quarters of the property. Krushi is thus simultaneously both a joint tenant in equity and a tenant in common in equity and enjoys a dual status: Figure 5.7.

Joint tenant mortgages her interest

The court in *Bedson* confirmed that a mortgage or charge of an equitable joint tenant's interest operates as an act of severance. Equally, equity will treat a specifically enforceable contract for a mortgage as an act of severance.

Fraudulent transfer or fraudulent mortgage

What is the position on severance where a joint tenant fraudulently purports to transfer or grant a mortgage of the *entire* property? The first thing to grasp is that no single legal co-owner alone can transfer or grant a mortgage over the whole property. This requires the agreement of all legal co-owners. If a sole joint tenant, acting alone, purports to do so, the disposition will not be valid as to bind the legal estate. Any entry that has been made in the register as a result of the fraud will be corrected at Land Registry. Under s. 63(1) of the LPA 1925, however, every conveyance is treated as being as effective as the grantor in question is able to effect. This means that the actions of a sole equitable joint tenant, though not binding on the legal estate, will be regarded as affecting her own interest. The actions of a sole joint tenant can, therefore, amount to severance of an equitable joint tenancy even where they have committed fraud. The leading authority on this point is *First National Security v Hegerty*.

KEY CASE *First National Security v Hegerty* (1965)

Facts: A married couple were co-owners of a property which was to become their retirement home. They were equitable joint tenants. The relationship broke down and the husband left the property. He subsequently forged his wife's signature on a legal charge over the property as security for a loan.

Legal issue: In view of the fraud, what was the effect of the husband's actions for his beneficial interest in the property? Had severance taken place or not?

Judgment: Bingham J noted (strictly obiter) that the actions of the husband did indeed constitute a disposition of the husband's own equitable share:

> [T]his disposition by the husband was a sufficient act of alienation to sever the beneficial joint tenancy and convert the husband and wife into tenants in common.

The disposition created an equitable charge over the husband's share of the beneficial ownership which could be enforced by the mortgage lender.

By way of final observation, you should note there will be no severance where all joint tenants band together to grant a legal mortgage or charge over the property. This is because their coming together impacts on the legal estate only and not on the position in equity: *C v S* (2008).

Commencing legal proceedings against other joint tenants

We discussed in section 5.5.2.1 that, in *Re Draper's Conveyance*, Plowman J accepted the serving of a summons accompanied by a sworn affidavit as sufficient to bring about severance of the wife's joint tenancy. Plowman J also noted that severance had also been effected under the first head of the *Hensman* catalogue—operating on one's own share. This leaves open the possibility that the commencement of legal proceedings by one joint tenant against other joint tenants may be enough to sever. A key issue to be resolved, however, is whether this would amount to a unilateral declaration of an intention to sever and whether this suffices as effective severance.

Unilateral declaration of intention to sever?

It is a key question for this first head of the *Hensman* catalogue whether a unilateral declaration by a joint tenant expressing an intention to sever suffices to effect severance. On a strict view, a unilateral declaration is insufficient as there is no *act* operating on one's own share as Page-Wood V-C explained. In this case, a far better route would be to pursue severance by written notice (which is a unilateral act) under s. 36(2). A more relaxed view seemed to be heralded in *Hawkesley v May* (1956) where Havers J noted:[28]

> [T]he first method indicated, namely an act of any one of the persons interested operating upon his own share, obviously includes a declaration of intention to sever by one party.

Walton J in *Nielson-Jones v Fedden* disagreed strongly, holding that there was 'no conceivable ground' for arguing that a unilateral declaration is sufficient to give rise to

---

[28] *Hawkesley v May*, 313.

effective severance under the *Hensman* catalogue. Indeed, it seems Walton J may be correct. A unilateral declaration of an intention to sever seems not to require any form of communication of this intention to other joint tenants. This could result in some sharp practice whereby joint tenants would be able to weigh up their options and argue that severance had or had not taken place whichever would produce the more favourable outcome. How could it be proved that a unilateral declaration had or had not been made? Evidentially, this would also pose significant problems. If an intention to sever exists, there is already statutory provision in s. 36(2) for how this intention is to be communicated. Permitting unilateral declarations of severance would seem to render s. 36(2) unnecessary. It would also make identifying how land was held in equity more difficult and, in addition to s. 36, it would render the other heads of the *Hensman* catalogue redundant. So far we have focused on voluntary acts amounting to 'operating on one's own share' but what about involuntary acts?

Severance by involuntary act—joint tenant's bankruptcy

Though not strictly an act of the joint tenant, becoming bankrupt serves to sever an equitable joint tenancy. This is, naturally, an involuntary form of alienation but nevertheless bankruptcy is treated as falling into this category of 'operating' on the joint tenant's share. There has been some debate as to the precise moment at which severance is regarded as having taken place. Is it the date on which an act of bankruptcy occurs? Is it the date on which the court makes a declaration of bankruptcy? Or, is it the date on which a trustee in bankruptcy[29] is appointed? The date at which severance operates matters. Imagine, for example, that a joint tenant dies during proceedings declaring her bankruptcy. Whether severance has taken place will determine if survivorship operates. If survivorship is operative, the deceased joint tenant's interest will survive to the remaining joint tenant(s) and escape the grip of any creditors.

The court in *Re Dennis* (1996) favoured the date of the act of bankruptcy rather than the later date of the declaration of bankruptcy by the court. The case of *Re Dennis* is, however, today largely of historical value only as in that decision the court was called upon to consider the old law of insolvency under the Bankruptcy Act 1914. Declarations of bankruptcy have, since 29 December 1986, been governed by the provisions of the Insolvency Act 1986. Although the issue has not been directly litigated, it seems that under ss. 278, 283, and 306 of the Insolvency Act 1986, severance takes place at the date the bankruptcy order is granted by the court: *Re Palmer* (1994). In summary it appears to be the position that bankruptcy will sever a joint tenancy and the date for severance will be the date at which the declaration of bankruptcy is made by the court.

5.5.2.3 Severance by mutual agreement

The precise dividing line between mutual agreement and the third head under the *Hensman* catalogue of mutual course of dealing can be difficult to grasp.[30] Mutual agreement falls short of an 'act' for the purposes of operating on one's own share and yet involves a more formalized 'agreement' than required for severance by mutual course of dealing.

---

[29] We consider the role of the trustee in bankruptcy in section 5.7.4.4.   [30] See section 5.7.4.4.

Mutual agreement therefore sits between the first and third heads under *Hensman*. Importantly, unlike severance by notice and operating on one's share, mutual agreement is *collective* in nature and not unilateral.

Severance by mutual agreement operates only where *all* equitable joint tenants agree to sever, so the essential requirement is therefore an agreement. The leading case here is *Burgess*.

KEY CASE *Burgess v Rawnsley* (1975)

Facts: Mr Honick and Mrs Rawnsley purchased a house in joint names in which Mr Honick lived. The conveyance declared that the parties held the property as joint tenants in equity. Mr Honick fully intended that he and Mrs Rawnsley be married but Mrs Rawnsley had other ideas. She had no desire to marry Mr Honick and intended to live in the upstairs flat while Mr Honick would live downstairs. When it became clear to both parties that they would not be married, an oral agreement was reached between them that Mrs Rawnsley would sell her interest in the property to Mr Honick for £750. Mr Honick's solicitor wrote to Mrs Rawnsley to confirm the agreement but, on reflection, she adjusted the price upwards to £1,000. Mr Honick took no further action. Matters did not progress and three years later, Mr Honick died.

Legal issue: Mr Honick's daughter, Mrs Burgess, acting as his administratrix, argued that severance had taken place, survivorship therefore did not operate on her father's death, and his estate was therefore entitled to 50 per cent of the proceeds of sale of the property. Had severance not taken place, Mr Honick's interest would have passed on his death to Mrs Rawnsley and Mr Honick's estate would have no interest in the proceeds of sale whatsoever.

Judgment: The county court made a clear finding of fact that Mr Honick and Mrs Rawnsley had reached an agreement for the sale of her interest for £750 and found for Mrs Burgess that severance had taken place. Mrs Rawnsley appealed. In the Court of Appeal, the court held that the oral agreement by which Mr Honick agreed to buy Mrs Rawnsley's interest had severed the beneficial joint tenancy even though, as a purely oral agreement, it was not specifically enforceable. Under s. 40 of the LPA 1925 (now replaced by s. 2 of the LP(MP)A 1989) a contract for the sale of an interest in land must be made in writing. For the purposes of severance, however, the absence of writing was immaterial. Counsel for Mrs Rawnsley had argued that an agreement had to be specifically enforceable to give rise to severance. The court rejected this. As Browne LJ explained:

> Mrs Burgess is not seeking to enforce by action the agreement by Mrs Rawnsley to sell her share to Mr Honick. She relies upon it as effecting the severance in equity of the joint tenancy . . . It seems to me that the point is that the agreement establishes that the parties no longer intend the tenancy to operate as a joint tenancy and that automatically effects a severance. I think the reference in Megarry & Wade to specifically enforceable contracts only applies where the suggestion is that the joint tenancy has been severed by an alienation by one joint tenant to a third party, and does not apply to severance by agreement between the joint tenants . . . The result is that I would uphold the county court judge's judgment on his second ground, namely, that the joint tenancy was severed by an agreement between Mrs Rawnsley and Mr Honick that she would sell her share to him for £750. In my view her subsequent repudiation of that agreement makes no difference.

Sir John Pennycuick added that:

> The significance of an agreement is not that it binds the parties; but that it serves as an indication of a common intention to sever, something which it was indisputably within their power to do.

Lord Denning MR accepted that severance had been effected by mutual agreement but added that severance could also be demonstrated on the facts by mutual course of dealing.

The effect of *Burgess* is that an informal, oral agreement will suffice to sever an equitable joint tenancy even if that agreement is later revoked. The agreement need not take the form of a specifically enforceable contract provided it demonstrates the parties' 'common intention to sever' (i.e. there must be a common intention to deal with the property in a manner inconsistent with the continued existence of the joint tenancy). Whilst no particular formalities are required and no particular words need be used, it is also clear that a written agreement can also operate to sever under this head: *Wallbank v Price* (2007).

Severance by mutual agreement can arise in a range of circumstances. In *Hunter v Babbage* (1994), an affidavit in support of a wife's application for ancillary relief in the course of divorce proceedings effected severance. The court even suggested that an informal agreement could, in an appropriate case, be inferred from all the circumstances. There is no requirement that the mutual agreement be acted upon or carried into action for severance to take place—severance occurs when the agreement is reached and not on its execution[31]—and the agreement reached must concern ownership of the property and not, for example, relate solely to use of the property or proceeds of any sale: *Nielson-Jones v Fedden*. In *Nielson-Jones*, an agreement reached in a written memorandum that the husband was able 'to use his entire discretion and free will' to decide whether to sell the former matrimonial home in order to purchase a smaller house in which to live was held not to have effected severance. Walton J held this agreement was concerned with the husband's use of the proceeds of sale and did not relate to his beneficial entitlement in them. The agreement must, therefore, go to the issue of ownership of co-owned land and how that land is to be held.

5.5.2.4 Severance by mutual course of dealing

Where a mutual agreement to sever cannot be established, severance may have taken place under the third head of the *Hensman* catalogue which serves as something of a last chance saloon. So, what constitutes a mutual course of dealing (sometimes also called 'mutual conduct')? We know from Page-Wood V-C's words in *Williams v Hensman* that it must be shown that all joint tenants have acted in a manner demonstrating that they regard themselves as entitled to specific shares in the co-owned land. As Blackett-Ord J explained in *Gore and Snell*:[32]

> A course of dealing is where . . . the parties have dealt with their interests in the property on the footing that they are interests in common and are not as joint.

As Gray and Gray explain, what is required is a consensus between the joint tenants, disclosed by a pattern of dealings with the co-owned property, which effectively excludes the future operation of survivorship. Note, this conduct must be mutual, collective, and any unilateral behaviour will not be enough to sever under this head. Let's briefly consider circumstances where severance by course of dealing might arise.

Ongoing or inconclusive negotiations

The greatest area of debate surrounding mutual course of dealing is the vexed issue of negotiations between joint tenants which are either ongoing or inconclusive. This was discussed as an alternative basis for severance in *Burgess* though the judges took quite

---

[31] As the facts of *Burgess* demonstrate.   [32] *Gore and Snell*, 462.

different stances. Lord Denning MR was prepared to accept that even if there was no firm agreement, the negotiations clearly evinced an intention to sever.[33] Sir John Pennycuick also accepted that severance could be inferred from negotiations but the facts of *Burgess* did not justify such an inference. The balance of decided case law suggests that it will prove challenging to mount a successful argument that inconclusive negotiations operate as mutual course of dealing. As if to make the point, the court in *McDowell v Hirschfield Lipson & Rumney and Smith* (1992) refused to accept that inconclusive negotiations between solicitors as to sale of a matrimonial home gave rise to severance by mutual course of dealing. The court stressed that the key difficulty with negotiations which are as yet incomplete is that severance is not the only possible or the inevitable outcome. Equally, in *Gore and Snell*, an argument that severance had taken place as a result of failed negotiations was rejected on the basis that there was no evidence the wife had intended to be treated as a tenant in common going forward. It seems that ongoing or incomplete negotiations will only give rise to severance where the agreement, *had it been reached*, would have operated to sever the joint tenancy: *Hunter v Babbage*.

Mutual wills

A joint tenant cannot, by unilateral act, sever her equitable joint tenancy merely by leaving her interest to heirs in a will. However, the making of mutual wills does suffice to sever on the basis of mutual course of dealing. Of course, severance here only operates where *all* joint tenants execute *mutual* wills: *In the Estate of Heys* (1914).[34]

Physical division of land?

Students routinely regard the physical division of co-owned land as an obvious example of severance—likely because it appears to physically represent a clear intention to dissect the land, to physically sever, if you will. However, beware! As the court noted in *Greenfield v Greenfield*, the physical division or conversion of co-owned land into separate parts with separate occupation is not necessarily inconsistent with the continued existence of an equitable joint tenancy.

KEY CASE *Greenfield v Greenfield* (1979)

Facts: In 1947, two brothers purchased a house as joint tenants at law and in equity. The two brothers along with their mother lived in the house. In 1962, the mother died. The two brothers were both married and so converted the house into two maisonettes. One brother lived with his wife in the upper half of the house and the other in the lower with his wife. No notice of severance was ever served and the evidence from the brothers was that neither considered the conversion to have impacted on their joint tenancy. In 1975, one of the brothers died and his wife sought to argue that she was entitled to a 50 per cent share in the property.

Legal issue: In order for the wife of the deceased brother to be entitled to a 50 per cent share in the property, severance of the brothers' equitable joint tenancy needed to have taken place. Had the

→

---

[33] *Burgess*, 440.

[34] In *Re Wilford's Estate* severance was effected when two sisters both agreed that they would each make wills leaving the property to the surviving sister and after her death to a named niece.

→

physical division and conversion into two distinct maisonettes effected severance by mutual course of dealing?

Judgment: Fox J held that the physical division, conversion, and separate occupation was not inconsistent with the continuation of the joint tenancy. The burden of proving that severance had taken place rested solely on the deceased brother's wife and she had failed to discharge this burden. As such, no severance had taken place and, on the brother's death, his interest passed to the surviving brother who became wholly entitled to the land under the doctrine of survivorship. As to when physical division will give rise to severance by mutual course of dealing, Fox J noted:

> The onus of establishing severance must be on the claimant. It seems to me that on the facts, the claimant comes nowhere near discharging that onus. Neither side made clear any intention of ending the joint tenancy. The defendant had no intention of ending it and never thought that he or [his brother] had ended it. The [surviving brother's] understanding was that [the deceased] was of exactly the same mind. Indeed, their mutual intention in 1962 was to continue the joint tenancy. And they so agreed. The mere existence of the separate maisonettes and of their separate occupation is not inconsistent with the continuation of the joint tenancy. The two can perfectly well exist together.

Following *Greenfield*, physical division of co-owned land will only amount to mutual course of dealing severing an equitable joint tenancy where it provides evidence of the parties' mutual, common intention that the joint tenancy should immediately come to an end and the parties thereafter be tenants in common.

5.5.2.5 Severance by operation of law: Forfeiture

Where one joint tenant is responsible for the unlawful killing of another, public policy through forfeiture will not permit that joint tenant to take a benefit from the death: s. 1 of the Forfeiture Act 1982. The unlawful killing is taken as severing the equitable joint tenancy and, in consequence, the doctrine of survivorship will not operate. Questions do, nevertheless, remain as to the scope of the forfeiture rule. It is quite clear that forfeiture will operate where one joint tenant murders another but what of manslaughter? Whilst there is some old authority that forfeiture will not apply to involuntary manslaughter,[35] the modern approach appears to be less definite and is that expounded in *Gray v Barr* (1971) that forfeiture will operate wherever a joint tenant is 'guilty of deliberate, intentional and unlawful violence or threats of violence'. Forfeiture will also apply even where there has been no formal, criminal conviction but the killing has satisfied the civil standard of proof.

Under s. 2(1) of the Forfeiture Act 1982, where, prima facie, the forfeiture rule is to apply, the court is given the power to offer relief by making an order 'modifying the effect' of the forfeiture rule taking into account the conduct of the offender, the deceased, and any other material circumstances.[36] Relief from forfeiture was granted in the cases of *Re K (deceased)* (1985) and *Dunbar v Plant* (1997). In *Re K (deceased)*, relief was granted where one joint tenant, the wife, had killed the only other joint tenant, her husband. In view of the unlawful

---

[35] *Tinline v White Cross Insurance Association Ltd* (1921).   [36] Section 2(2) of the Forfeiture Act 1982.

killing, prima facie the forfeiture rule applied. However, the court was prepared to grant relief from forfeiture on the basis that the wife had suffered prolonged and serious domestic violence at the hands of the husband and had only ever intended to threaten the husband with a gun rather than fire it. In *Dunbar* relief was granted in a case of a suicide pact resulting in just one joint tenant's death. In the tragic circumstances of the failed suicide pact, the forfeiture rule was set aside.

Drawing together the body of case law on the forfeiture rule, it is evident that the availability of relief from forfeiture rests firmly on the court's view of the culpability of the joint tenant who has committed homicide. By way of example, relief was refused in *Mack v Lockwood* (2009) where one joint tenant stabbed the other 54 times in a brutal attack and in *Chadwick v Collinson* (2014) relief was refused where the defendant, suffering from delusions, killed his partner and son. His illness reduced his culpability but he was still found to be aware of the nature of his actions and knew that what he was doing was wrong.

5.6 Termination of co-ownership

We have considered what co-ownership is, how it operates and how an equitable joint tenancy can be severed to create a tenancy in common. We turn to consider how co-ownership is brought to an end. Co-ownership is terminated in three principal ways.

5.6.1 Unity of co-owned land in one joint tenant

Co-ownership is brought to an end, under the doctrine of survivorship, where the land comes into the sole ownership of just one single joint tenant—the last standing in circumstances where the other joint tenants have died or where all other joint tenants have released their interest to one single joint tenant. Where this happens, the trust of land under which co-ownership operates is automatically terminated and the entire estate both at law and in equity passes to the last surviving joint tenant.

5.6.2 Purchase of the legal estate taking free of the trust of land

Co-ownership is also brought to an end when the legal estate held on trust is sold to a third party who takes free of the trust of land by complying with the requirements for overreaching. Where the proceeds of sale are paid to two or more trustees (ss. 2 and 27 of the LPA 1925), the purchaser will overreach any pre-existing equitable interests. Those co-owners' equitable interests will, however, be converted into the proceeds of sale.

5.6.3 Partition of co-owned land

Under the process of partition, it is possible for the trustees (the legal owners) and also by order of the court to bring co-ownership to an end. As the name suggests, the process of partition involves the physical division of co-owned land by the trustees and the transfer of each plot or portion of land into the sole ownership of the beneficiaries. This division of land destroys the unity of possession which is the minimum, essential ingredient for co-ownership. The law on partition is found in s. 7 of TOLATA 1996. Section 7 makes clear that the consent of beneficiaries is required before partition can take place and, in addition, there can only be partition of land where the beneficiaries are of full age, are absolutely entitled to the land and hold the co-owned land as tenants in common. This prevents trustees interfering with the operation of the doctrine of survivorship. Where beneficiaries refuse to consent to the partition, trustees can seek an order of the court that the land be partitioned.

5.7 The legislative framework

As we have seen, whenever there is co-ownership, there is a trust. This imposition of a trust is a fundamental tenet of the law of co-ownership. In this section, we consider the nature of the trust that is imposed and how it functions to provide rights to trustees (the legal owners) and beneficiaries (the equitable owners)—in other words, the legislative framework of the trust. Our discussion falls into five distinct areas:

- the nature and scope of the trust;
- the powers and duties of trustees;
- the rights of beneficiaries;
- the regime for resolving disputes involving co-owned land;
- disputes involving co-owners and creditors.

5.7.1 The nature and scope of the trust

Today, the trust imposed in every case of co-ownership is governed by the provisions of TOLATA 1996. However, co-ownership, of course, existed before the 1996 Act and then, as now, also operated behind a trust. Before the 1996 Act came into force, co-ownership existed under the machinery of the 'trust for sale'. TOLATA 1996 altered this position, replacing the trust for sale with the modern 'trust of land'. The Law Commission explained the nature of the old trust for sale and why reform was needed:[37]

> The defining feature of the trust for sale . . . is that the trustees are under a duty to sell the trust land. Implicit in this is the notion that this land should be held primarily as an investment asset rather than as a 'use' asset. This formulation may well have been suitable or convenient for the purposes which it was designed to serve. However, since the passing of the 1925 property legislation, social conditions have altered to such an extent that the invariable imposition of a duty to sell now seems wholly artificial. This is largely because the incidence of owner-occupation has . . . risen to such a level that most dwellings are now owner-occupied . . . the imposition of a duty to sell seems clearly inconsistent with the interests and intentions of the majority of those who acquire land as co-owners. In such cases the intention will rarely be that the land be held pending a sale; it is much more probable that it will be retained primarily for occupation.

The trust for sale therefore had as its primary focus that co-owned land was being held as an investment to be sold, at some later time, to realize that capital investment. A duty of

---

[37] Law Commission Report No. 181, *Transfer of Land: Trusts of Land* (1989), [3.1].

sale was therefore placed on the trustees and an eventual sale of co-owned land was inevitable. Any disputes as to co-owned land were therefore filtered through this sale-focus and the court would rarely deny an action seeking sale of the property. There were other consequences of the trust for sale:

- The effect of a trust for sale was that the interests of beneficiaries (recall: these are the equitable owners) were interests in the proceeds of sale of the co-owned land and not interests in the land per se.

- The courts began to develop a 'doctrine of collateral purpose' to side-step the artificiality of the trust for sale. Under this doctrine, where a subsisting 'collateral purpose' for the trust could be identified (i.e. collateral to the principal purpose of sale—for example, the provision a family home) and this collateral purpose was capable of fulfilment, the court in some cases was prepared to exercise its discretion to deny an action for sale.[38]

- The trust for sale was also said to be unintelligible to most non-lawyers and did not reflect the reality of their co-ownership arrangements.

By way of illustration of the second point, 'collateral purpose', in *Re Evers' Trust* (1980) a couple who had purchased a home subsequently split and the woman remained in the property with three children (two from a previous relationship). The court refused to order sale of the house as the property had been purchased to provide a home for the family children 'for the indefinite future' and this purpose endured and could be fulfilled. It was important to the court's reasoning that the man had alternative accommodation and therefore no immediate need to release capital from the house and also that the woman agreed to undertake responsibility for the mortgage and would not have been able to readily rehouse herself and the children.

The trust for sale came to be seen as out-of-step with changing social perceptions of home ownership and as an inappropriate mechanism for governing co-ownership of land. Reform came in the form of TOLATA 1996—legislation described by Harpum at the time as the most significant measure of property law reform since the legislation of 1925.

Under s. 1 of TOLATA, any trust consisting of land must take effect as a *trust of land* whether created expressly or impliedly by way of a resulting or constructive trust.[39] Any trust for sale in existence at the date of commencement of the 1996 Act[40] was converted into a trust of land.[41] The trust for sale has therefore largely been confined to history. That said, it is still possible to impose a positive duty of sale on trustees under a trust by way of an express term in a trust deed. Where an express duty to sell is imposed, the trust nevertheless remains subject to the provisions of TOLATA as discussed in this section.[42]

TOLATA therefore introduced new machinery for co-ownership and with it a new regime which we will now examine, beginning with the powers of trustees.

---

[38] See *Jones v Challenger* (1961), per Devlin LJ.

[39] We discuss resulting and constructive trusts in Chapter 6.

[40] 1 January 1997.   [41] Under s. 1(2)(b) of the TOLATA.

[42] By way of ibid., s. 4(1), irrespective of the terms of the trust, an implied power to postpone any sale is also given to the trustees which cannot be excluded.

5.7.2 The powers and duties of trustees

The powers enjoyed by trustees under a trust of land are laid down principally in s. 6 of TOLATA. Under s. 6(1), trustees have 'all the powers of an absolute owner'. This is a widening of the position under the old trust for sale and is a deliberate attempt to better reflect that many trustees are the co-owners of properties occupied as homes and will likely consider themselves to be owners of that land. The provision should be read closely, though, as it provides that trustees have the powers of an absolute owner 'for the purpose of exercising their functions as trustees'. What is the significance of this? Well, this means that trustees must act in accordance with the wider TOLATA regime. Trustees must act with regard to the rights of the beneficiaries,[43] must act in a manner which does not contravene any rule of law or equity,[44] and are subject to a duty of care when exercising their powers.[45] Importantly, endowed with the powers of an absolute owner, trustees are no longer subject to a duty to sell the land as was the case under the trust for sale. Under s. 6(3), trustees are given the power to acquire freehold and leasehold land either as an investment, for occupation by a beneficiary, or for any other reason in accordance with s. 8 of the Trustee Act 2000.

Section 6 does not, however, reflect the totality of the powers and duties of trustees. We have already seen in section 5.6 that trustees have the additional power to partition co-owned land. Under s. 13 of TOLATA, trustees can also exclude, restrict, or impose conditions on the right of beneficiaries to occupy co-owned land.[46] Under s. 9 of TOLATA, trustees can also, acting jointly, delegate any or all of their functions to any or all of the beneficiaries under the trust who are of full age and entitled to possession of the land. Despite the apparent breadth of trustees' powers, there are a series of important brakes on the operation of these powers:

- Under s. 8(1) of TOLATA, where a trust of land has been created expressly, any of the powers under ss. 6 and 7 of TOLATA can be expressly excluded or restricted.
- Under s. 8(2) of TOLATA, the disposition creating a trust of land can include a requirement that the consent of beneficiaries be obtained before the ss. 6 and 7 powers can be exercised.
- Finally, under s. 11 of TOLATA (discussed in section 5.7.3.1) trustees have a duty to consult beneficiaries when exercising any of their functions relating to land and, *so far as is practicable* and, so far as is consistent with the general interest of the trust, give effect to the beneficiaries' wishes.[47]

5.7.3 The rights of beneficiaries

Pre-TOLATA 1996, under the old trust for sale, the interests of beneficiaries were regarded as interests in the proceeds of sale of the co-owned land and not interests in the land itself. This is known as the equitable doctrine of conversion. Beneficiaries' interests were seen as 'converted' into the proceeds of sale even if the land had not yet been sold. The doctrine of

---

[43] Ibid., s. 6(5).   [44] Ibid., s. 6(6).   [45] Ibid., s. 6(9).

[46] We discuss this further in section 5.7.3.

[47] In the case of dispute, the wishes of the majority should be respected. This duty of consultation can be excluded by the terms of an expressly created trust: s. 11(2).

conversion is best seen as a reflection or effect of the duty of sale placed on trustees and the operation of the equitable maxim that 'equity sees as done that which ought to be done'. If a sale ought to be done, then equity would naturally treat beneficiaries through this prism of sale. Today, s. 3 of TOLATA has abolished the doctrine of conversion and beneficiaries are now regarded as enjoying interests in the land itself rather than enjoying only personal interests in the proceeds of sale. Section 3 puts the matter beyond doubt.[48] In addition, beneficiaries are endowed with two principal rights under a trust of land: first, the right to be consulted and, secondly, the right to occupy co-owned land.

5.7.3.1 Section 11 of TOLATA: The right to be consulted

Under s. 11, beneficiaries enjoy the right to be consulted by trustees exercising any function in relation to co-owned land. For many beneficiaries this is really a very important right. Imagine an equitable co-owner who is not also a legal owner. For this co-owner, the right to be consulted is their primary means of having their voice heard. There are, however, a number of qualifications to this right:

- The right applies only to beneficiaries of full age and those entitled to possession of the land.[49]
- Trustees only have to consult beneficiaries 'so far as is practicable'. Where beneficiaries are consulted, trustees must give effect to their wishes 'so far as is consistent with the general interest of the trust' and, in the event that the beneficiaries disagree, trustees can give effect to the wishes of the majority of beneficiaries determined by reference to the size of their equitable entitlement.[50]
- The duty to consult can be excluded or restricted by the terms of an express trust.[51]
- The duty to consult does not apply to all trusts existing at the time the 1996 Act came into force.[52]

5.7.3.2 Section 12 of TOLATA: The right to occupy

The right to occupy co-owned land is, by quite some way, the most meaningful right enjoyed by beneficiaries of co-owned land. In many co-ownership scenarios where the legal and equitable co-owners are the very same people—for example, a couple—it is quite obvious that the right to occupy that land is fundamental. Under the old trust for sale, however, the right to occupy land necessarily played second fiddle to the primacy of the doctrine of conversion and, as Martyn has documented,[53] considerable doubt remained as to the precise relationship between the trust for sale, the doctrine of conversion, and the right to occupy co-owned land. The position has been clarified by s. 12 of TOLATA[54] which places on a statutory footing the right of beneficiaries to occupy co-owned land.

[48] Even before the 1996 Act, the courts had already acknowledged the artificiality of the doctrine and, on occasion, refused to recognize it: *Williams & Glyn's Bank v Boland* (1981).

[49] Section 11(1)(a) of TOLATA 1996.   [50] Ibid., s. 11(1)(b).   [51] Ibid., s. 11(2).   [52] Ibid., s. 11(3).

[53] J. Martyn, 'Co-Owners and their Entitlement to Occupy their Land before and after the Trusts of Land and Appointment of Trustees Act 1996: Theoretical Doubts Are Replaced by Practical Difficulties' [1997] Conv 254.

[54] Recall also the right to occupy under the so-called 'home rights' under Family Law Act 1996, s. 30, which is discussed in Chapter 6.

As Hopkins has highlighted, however, the right to occupy under s. 12 will only arise where two requirements are satisfied:[55]

- Requirement 1: Under s. 12(1), it must be shown that the purpose of the trust was that the land was intended for occupation by the beneficiaries (s. 12(1)(a)) or, alternatively, the land is nevertheless being held so as to be available for occupation (s. 12(1)(b)). Demonstrating that the land was intended for occupation is done by reference to the express terms of the trust or by having regard to all the surrounding circumstances. Where the terms of the trust make it clear that the land is held purely as an investment or where there is an express duty on the trustees to sell the land, this may preclude occupation by the beneficiaries under s. 12.

- Requirement 2: Under s. 12(2), it must be shown that the land is 'suitable' for occupation by beneficiaries. This provision has caused some degree of uncertainty. Parker LJ explored the operation of the provision in *Chan Pui Chun v Leung Kam Ho* (2002):[56]

  > There is no statutory definition or guidance as to what is meant by 'unsuitable' in this context, and it would be rash indeed to attempt an exhaustive definition or explanation of its meaning. In the context of the present case it is, I think, enough to say that 'suitability' for this purpose must involve a consideration not only of the general nature and physical characteristics of the particular property but also a consideration of the personal characteristics, circumstances and requirements of the particular beneficiary. This much is, I think, clear from the fact that the statutory expression is not simply 'unsuitable for occupation' but 'unsuitable for occupation *by him*', that is to say by the particular beneficiary.

One common example that is often given is co-owned land consisting of a farm. Farm land, having regard to all the circumstances, would likely be 'unsuitable' for occupation by a non-farmer beneficiary. For a non-farmer beneficiary, no right to occupy would therefore arise under s. 12.

Once a right to occupy has arisen, the nature of this right is governed by the provisions of s. 13.[57] Under s. 13(1), where two or more beneficiaries are entitled to occupy co-owned land under s. 12, the trustees are permitted to exclude or restrict the right to occupy of any one or more beneficiaries but not all. There are five key aspects to the operation of s. 13:

1. In restricting the right to occupy under s. 13, trustees must neither unreasonably exclude any beneficiary's entitlement to occupy land nor exclude such entitlement to an unreasonable extent.[58]

2. In exercising the power to exclude or restrict under s. 13, trustees must have regard to the intentions of the person(s) who created the trust, the purpose behind the trust, as well as the circumstances and wishes of each beneficiary entitled to occupy the land.[59]

3. Trustees can impose 'reasonable conditions' on beneficiaries in relation to their occupation of land[60] and these conditions may include paying outgoings or expenses in respect of the land or assuming obligations in relation to activities taking place on the land.[61]

---

[55] N. Hopkins, 'The Trusts of Land and Appointment of Trustees Act 1996' (1996) 60 Conveyancer 411.
[56] *Chan Pui Chun v Leung Kam Ho*, [101].   [57] Section 12(3) of TOLATA 1996.   [58] Ibid., s. 13(2).
[59] Ibid., s. 13(4).   [60] Ibid., s. 13(3).   [61] Ibid., s. 13(5).

4. Where any beneficiary's right to occupy is excluded or restricted, conditions may be imposed on other beneficiaries including paying compensation to that excluded party.[62]

5. Finally, trustees' powers under s. 13 cannot be used to exclude from the land any person who is in occupation of the land nor can they be exercised in a manner likely to result in any such person ceasing to occupy the land.[63]

For a rather innovative application of ss. 12 and 13 of TOLATA, take a look at the fascinating case of *Rodway v Landy*.

KEY CASE *Rodway v Landy* (2001)

Facts: Two doctors, Dr Rodway and Dr Landy, entered into a business partnership. With the assistance of a mortgage, the two doctors purchased a property in joint names as joint tenants both at law and in equity. The existing building was demolished and a new purpose-built surgery constructed from which both doctors practised. After a dispute, their partnership came to an end. Dr Rodway sought orders of the court for the winding up of the partnership and sought to purchase the entire property. Dr Landy counterclaimed seeking either (1) an order under the provisions of TOLATA that the property be partitioned or alternatively (2) an order that the two doctors exercise their s. 13 powers to restrict the other's right to occupation so that each doctor was entitled only to occupy half of the property.

Legal issue: What was to be done with the property? Could the court order partition of the property under TOLATA 1996?

Judgment: The High Court held that the property could not be sold to Dr Rodway in light of complex rules governing sales of medical practices under the National Health Service Act 1977. Rather, the court ordered that the parties should exercise their powers as trustees under s. 13 TOLATA by dividing the property into two separate units and restricting Dr Landy's right to occupation to one single unit and Dr Rodway's right of occupation to the other. The cost of the works associated with the creation of two units should be shared equally by the parties. Dr Rodway appealed. The Court of Appeal dismissed Dr Rodway's appeal. The High Court had been entitled to make the order under s. 13 of TOLATA directing that the property should be divided into two units with each enjoying exclusive occupation of one unit.

As the rather unusual result in *Rodway* demonstrates, ss. 12 and 13 have proved to be somewhat controversial provisions and have attracted considerable attention from property law academics:

- Martyn has criticized ss. 12 and 13 for their failure to differentiate between different forms of entitlement to occupy land.[64] In particular, Martyn, draws attention to the practical problems that may result from failing to distinguish between rights arising as a result of being a co-owner, those arising as a result of trustees' discretion, and those based upon the purpose behind the trust.

- Barnsley has argued that the statutory right to occupation under s. 12 actually represents a more limited right than already existed under the common law.[65] The common

---

[62] Ibid., s. 13(6).   [63] Ibid., s. 13(7).

[64] J. Martyn, 'Co-Owners and their Entitlement to Occupy their Land Before and After the Trusts of Land and Appointment of Trustees Act 1996: Theoretical Doubts Are Replaced by Practical Difficulties' [1997] Conv 254.

[65] D. G. Barnsley, 'Co-Owners' Rights to Occupy Trust Land' (1998) 57(1) CLJ 123.

law right to occupation, argued Barnsley, is not subject to any of the statutory restrictions of s. 12 and s. 12 serves to erode the breadth of the common law position. For Barnsley, in an appropriate case, co-owners should still be able to rely on their common law right to enforce their occupation.

• Pascoe, in a broad analysis of the operation of ss. 12 and 13, concludes that the provisions governing occupation rights demonstrate 'a comprehensive lack of doctrinal cohesion' and betray a 'muddled legislative logic'.[66] Pascoe's criticism of the new statutory right is its lack of cohesiveness and its imperfect draftsmanship which, it is argued, stem from the 'doctrinal incongruities and disparate dogma' at the heart of the provisions:[67]

> Section 12 represents an amalgam and jumble of principles derived from the old law intermingled with explicitly new concepts of availability and suitability to constitute a qualified right, which may be the subject of great uncertainty and thus litigation due to the impreciseness of drafting of the section. The merits of such a hotchpotch of concepts challenges the sagacity and utility of instituting a new right which displays three conflicting characteristics: beneficiary autonomy, trustee authoritarianism and settlor interposition.

Sections 12 and 13 taken together might be seen as sending very mixed signals. On the one hand, there is a new, seemingly powerful statutory right to occupy. Yet, this right is itself conditional on demonstrating the purpose of the trust of land, the availability of the land for occupation, and the land's suitability for occupation. Power then shifts strongly in the trustees' favour under the provisions of s. 13. How far does this deeply qualified right to occupy, in practice, improve on the position of beneficiaries under the old trust for sale?

5.7.4 The regime for resolving disputes involving co-owned land

Co-ownership by its very nature involves a number of individuals each of whom may have quite different and, at times, conflicting views as to how the co-owned land should be dealt with or managed. Often many of these issues can be resolved by the trustees (the legal owners) exercising their powers and discretion but this may not always be possible. Quite understandably, where the beneficiaries and trustees are one and the same people, they are unlikely to be able to resolve the dispute between themselves. TOLATA 1996 therefore provides a mechanism for disputes over co-owned land to come before the court. Disputes can arise between co-owners or, in the event that a co-owner is in mortgage arrears, indebted, or insolvent, the dispute may involve a creditor. Most commonly encountered will be a dispute as to whether co-owned land should be sold with one party favouring sale (e.g. creditor or co-owner) and another co-owner strongly resisting. Section 14 of TOLATA provides the court with jurisdiction to hear disputes involving co-owned land. It is by way of an application under s. 14 that disputes find themselves before the court.

It is important to note that any person with an interest in land subject to a trust is able to make an application under s. 14.[68] The net is drawn more widely than you might first think. Obviously, a co-owner and trustees are covered but so is a registered mortgagee

---

[66] S. Pascoe, 'Right to Occupy under a Trust of Land: Muddled Legislative Logic' [2006] Conv 54.
[67] Ibid., 63.   [68] Section 14(1) of TOLATA 1996.

(e.g. a bank), a person entitled to a charging order over the property, a trustee in bankruptcy, or a receiver. The court's jurisdiction under this provision is far-reaching. Under s. 14(2), the court can make any such order relating to the trustees' exercise of their functions and, additionally, can declare the nature and extent of any party's interest in the land subject to a trust. The court can, for example, order trustees to behave in a specified way which would otherwise amount to a breach of trust or to not exercise their discretion in certain circumstances. The court cannot, however, order trustees to exercise a power which they do not have.[69] In most cases, the court will determine an application under s. 14 via a public hearing. As the recent case of *W v M (TOLATA Proceedings: Anonymity)* (2012) demonstrates, however, anonymity can be given to the parties if there is strong evidence that the publicity of the proceedings would be detrimental to the interests of any children or impact on any of the parties' Art. 8 rights.

Despite its broad scope, there are limits to s. 14. The court cannot, for example, appoint or remove trustees under this provision.[70] A recent, interesting case discussing the boundaries of s. 14 is *Bagum v Hafiz*.

KEY CASE *Bagum v Hafiz* (2015)

Facts: Mrs Bagum was the sole registered owner of a four-bedroom house in London in which she lived with her two eldest sons. The sons both made financial contributions to the purchase price of the house and to the subsequent mortgage instalments. The sons married and the property became over-crowded. One of the sons and his wife decided to leave the property. Before the departure, Mrs Bagum and both sons agreed to make a declaration of trust under which each was declared to be an equitable tenant in common with a one-third share in the property. Subsequently, a dispute arose as to the sale of the property and the matter came before the court under s. 14 of TOLATA. The judge concluded that she had no jurisdiction under s. 14 to make an order forcing one brother to sell his interest to the other. The court did, however, make an order directing the trustees to sell the property on terms that the brother seeking sale be given first opportunity to buy the property at a price determined by the court. If this was not successful, the property would be sold on the open market, at which point any party could bid to purchase the house.

Legal issue: In the Court of Appeal, the issue was whether the judge had jurisdiction to make the order she had made. If she did enjoy jurisdiction, was the making of this order a proper exercise of that jurisdiction under s. 14 of TOLATA?

Judgment: The Court of Appeal held that the judge was right to conclude that she did not enjoy jurisdiction to order that one beneficiary sell or transfer their interest to another beneficiary. This was not a function of the trustees and could not therefore be regulated by the court under s. 14. The court did however enjoy jurisdiction to direct trustees to sell trust property to particular beneficiaries without first obtaining the consent of the beneficiary to whom land was not being sold. The fact that, in effect, such an order procured the same result as a compulsory transfer did not mean it lay outside the scope of the trustees' powers. Whilst the form of order granted was certainly unusual, it represented a proper exercise of the judge's discretion under TOLATA. Clear and cogent reasons for the conclusions reached and underlying the order had been offered and the order was calculated to serve the divergent interests of all the beneficiaries.

---

[69] *Hopper v Hopper* (2008).

[70] Section 14(3) of TOLATA 1996. The court can, however, appoint and remove trustees under the Trustee Act 1925.

Once an application has been made to the court under s. 14, it falls to be resolved. The court determines these applications by reference to a list of factors laid down in s. 15 of TOLATA including:

- the intentions of those who created the trust
- the purpose for which the land subject to the trust is being held
- the welfare of any minor occupying or who might reasonably occupy the land as a home
- the interests of any secured creditor.

Section 15 puts on a statutory footing many of the factors the courts were already taking into account when resolving disputes in relation to trusts for sale under the old law.[71] For this reason, much of the old case law retains some value when considering applications under the new Act, though, for obvious reasons, should be treated with caution. We explore in section 5.7.4.2 how far s. 15 has changed the law in this area. Before that, let's consider how the s. 15 factors operate in disputes between co-owners.

5.7.4.1 Disputes between co-owners

In disputes between co-owners, the central issue is usually whether land subject to a trust should be sold or not. This can be especially hard-fought where the trustees and beneficiaries are the same people and the property was purchased as a family home and the relationship between the parties has broken down. As Gardner has observed,[72] the court is called upon to resolve a difficult tension founded on the stability and ties of those wishing to remain in the home versus the advantages of a clean break afforded by a sale, the desire to realize a capital investment, and quite simply to move on. As we explore the s. 15 factors which guide the court in these disputes, be warned: the court is still grappling with the precise interrelationship of the various subsections of s. 15.

Section 15(1)(a): The intentions of those who created the trust

Logically, only intentions which are identifiable or, at best, can be inferred from all the surrounding circumstances, can be taken into account by the court. These intentions may be express, provided in oral or written evidence by the parties, be provided in any express declaration creating the trust of land or otherwise capable of inference by the court. There is clearly some overlap between s. 15(1)(a) and (1)(b)—the intentions of the parties who created the trust (s15(1)(a)) will naturally bleed into the purpose for which the land subject to the trust is being held (s. 15(1)(b)). That said, there is a point of distinction. Section 15(1)(a) should be seen as directing the court to consider the intentions of the parties *at the time* or *before* the trust was created.[73] The pre-TOLATA case law is insightful here. In *Re Buchanan-Wollaston's Conveyance* (1939), a section of a sea-front promenade was conveyed to four individuals as joint tenants. It was made clear in a deed that the conveyance had been made to avoid a depreciation in the market value of the parties' adjacent properties. It also said that

---

[71] Such applications were brought under s. 30 of the LPA 1925.

[72] S. Gardner, 'Material Relief between Ex-Cohabitants 1: Liquidating Beneficial Interests Otherwise than by Sale' [2014] Conv 95.

[73] *White v White* (2001).

the land could only be dealt with unanimously or, at least, by way of majority vote. The court held that the purpose behind the trust was obvious and that no sale should be ordered that would work against the clear and unequivocal expression in the deed.

Section 15(1)(b): The purpose for which the land subject to the trust is held

Section 15(1)(b) directs the court to consider the purposes for which the land subject to the trust is held. The use of the present tense here is important in that it distinguishes this subsection from s. 15(1)(a). It was suggested in *Rodway*, per Peter Gibson, that s. 15(1)(b) should be interpreted as requiring an examination of the purpose(s) for which land *is held* on trust at the time the application under s. 14 falls to be determined by the court. This means that, taken together, s. 15(1)(a) and (1)(b) allow the court to take a broad view of both the initial purpose for which land was acquired and consider how, up to the date of the application, this purpose may have changed. Where, for example, a couple purchase land as a family home and this relationship fails, there may well be a considerable shift in how the property is being held from its initial purpose. Whether greater weight will be attached to the initial purpose or the new purpose for which the land is being held, the authorities are conflicting. *Grindal v Hooper* (1999) and *Rodway* suggest that it is the current purpose that wins out but *White v White* (2001) suggests the purpose can only change when the parties have reached agreement on this. In legislative terms, the 1996 Act is still very much in its infancy and we await further clarification. Again, looking to pre-TOLATA case law is helpful. A leading case on changing purpose is *Jones v Challenger*.

KEY CASE *Jones v Challenger* (1961)

Facts: In 1956, a husband and wife purchased a lease with ten years left to run as joint tenants both at law and in equity. The couple occupied the property subject to the lease as their matrimonial home. The marriage broke down and the pair were divorced in 1959. While the wife left the matrimonial home, the husband remained in possession of the property. The wife, who had remarried, wished to realize her share of the value inherent in the lease. She requested a sale of the lease but the husband refused. She applied to the court under s. 30 of the LPA 1925 (the predecessor to s. 14 of TOLATA) seeking sale of the property. The county court held that it had absolute discretion to do what was reasonable in all the circumstances and refused to order sale. The wife appealed.

Legal issue: In considering whether the county court was right to refuse sale, what weight should be attached to a change in the purpose for which the land subject to the trust is being held?

Judgment: The Court of Appeal allowed the appeal and ordered that the property be sold. Devlin LJ noted that the county court had applied the wrong test in focusing on the reasonableness or unreasonableness of whether the husband be entitled to remain in the home. Devlin stressed that the home had been purchased as a matrimonial home in which both spouses intended to live. However, when the marriage failed, 'this purpose was dissolved' and was no longer 'alive'. While the court enjoyed a discretion to delay sale for the husband to seek alternative accommodation, no delay was sought and so an order for sale was the proper exercise of the court's discretion. Sale was the only means by which both parties could derive equal benefit from the property and from their investment in it.

Although decided under the old trust for sale regime which inevitably placed great emphasis on sale and realization of investments, *Jones v Challenger* indicates that a key factor to be considered by the court is whether the initial purpose for which land was purchased is continuing or has come to an end. Where the initial purpose is continuing or 'alive', a court will be minded to refuse sale. Where that purpose has 'dissolved' or changed, a sale is more likely to be ordered. In *Rawlings v Rawlings* (1964), the court ordered a sale where the purpose of providing a matrimonial home had come to an end in circumstances where a couple had separated even though no divorce had been obtained. In *Jones v Jones* (1977), a father and son were joint tenants of a house which had been purchased in part to provide a home for the son for life. When the father died, the step-mother sought sale of the property. The court refused sale on the basis that the initial purpose of providing a home for the son endured. Don't forget: the purpose behind the trust is just one factor to be considered under s. 15. Other factors may be equally important including the right of a secured creditor to have its debt paid.

Section 15(1)(c): The welfare of associated minors

In *Rawlings*, Salmon LJ who had ordered a sale of co-owned land where the purpose of providing a matrimonial home had ceased, nevertheless, noted that:[74]

> If there were young children the position would be different. One of the purposes of the trust would no doubt have been to provide a home for them, and whilst that purpose still existed a sale would generally not be ordered. But when those children are grown up and the marriage is dead, the purposes of the trust have failed.

This pronouncement from Salmon LJ has proved to be a particularly important statement of the law both under the trust for sale and today under s. 15(1)(c) of TOLATA. Salmon LJ's approach was formally adopted in the case of *Williams v Williams*, a case decided under the old law.

KEY CASE *Williams v Williams* (1976)

Facts: A husband and wife were co-owners of a family home where they lived with their four children. The marriage broke down and the couple divorced. The wife remained in the house with the children and the husband moved out. When the oldest child was 12, the husband decided that he wished to realize his interest in the property and so he applied for an order for sale under s. 30 of the LPA 1925. In the county court, an order for sale was made. The wife appealed.

Legal issue: On an application for sale, what weight should the court attach to the welfare of minors living on the co-owned land?

Judgment: In the Court of Appeal, Lord Denning allowed the wife's appeal and refused to order sale of the property. Lord Denning noted that:

> When judges are dealing with the matrimonial home, they nowadays have great regard to the fact that the house if bought as a home in which the family is brought up. It is not treated as property to be sold nor as an investment to be realised for cash. The court, in executing the trust should regard the primary object as being to provide a home and not a sale. Steps should be taken to preserve it as a home for the remaining partner and children, but giving the outgoing partner such compensation, by way of a charge or being bought out, as is reasonable in the circumstances.

Unless it could be shown that alternative accommodation was available to the party wishing to remain in the home and at cheaper rate, no sale should be ordered.

---

[74] *Rawlings*, 419.

In subsequent case law, rather than order immediate sale, the court has been prepared to *postpone* an order for sale of the property rather than refuse a sale outright. In *Re Evers*, a non-married couple were co-owners of a property. They had one child and also lived with two children from the mother's previous relationship. The couple split and the father applied for an order for sale of the property. The court of first instance made an order for sale but postponed until the parties' child reached the age of 16. The Court of Appeal upheld the postponed sale on the basis that the purpose for which the property was acquired—to provide a family home—was ongoing, but gave the parties leave to reapply to the court if circumstances changed.

Today under s. 15(1)(c) of TOLATA, it seems that the age of the minor will be a particularly relevant factor with less weight attaching to their welfare the closer they are to reaching majority.[75] Before we turn to consider the last of the s. 15 factors—the interests of secured creditors—it is worth pausing to consider whether and how far, in disputes between co-owners, s. 15 of TOLATA has changed the law from that operating under the old trust for sale.

5.7.4.2 Has s. 15 of TOLATA changed the law?

In the case of *Re Mayo* (1943), Simonds J, considering the old law under the trust for sale, made clear that whilst the court could make any order it thought fit under s. 30 of the LPA 1925, the presumption would be in favour of sale. With the trust for sale giving way to the trust of land under TOLATA 1996, it is worth asking whether the law has shifted. In fact, the position under the trust for sale was not as clear-cut in favour of sale as might be first thought. Under s. 30, the court was given a broad discretion including the ability to refuse to order sale in an appropriate case. Out of this discretion came the doctrine of collateral or secondary purpose. Under this doctrine, where the court identified that the property had been acquired for a purpose beyond sale, for as long as that collateral purpose persisted sale should be refused.[76]

What is the position today under TOLATA? Well, in so far as s. 15(1)(a)–(c) requires the court to interrogate the intentions of the parties, the purpose behind the trust and the welfare of any relevant minors, it has been suggested that the doctrine of collateral purpose lives on. Indeed, in its Report No. 181, the Law Commission said that the court's discretion under TOLATA should be developed along the same lines as the pre-existing 'primary purpose doctrine' and that the new TOLATA regime should be read as putting 'on a statutory footing' much of the pre-TOLATA case law under trusts for sale.

The biggest change, today, from the old law is therefore the starting point. Under TOLATA, the starting point for resolution of disputes is a *neutral* one—neither biased in favour of sale nor biased against it. There has been a change in focus under which the court starts by locating the intentions of the parties and the purpose of the trust freed from the former presumption of sale. Beyond these rather abstract, theoretical statements, it can be difficult to assess the practical impact of this shift. This is in large part, as Hopkins has noted,[77] down to the dearth of case law under ss. 14 and 15 of TOLATA. For Dixon,

---

[75] *Bank of Ireland Home Mortgages Ltd v Bell* (2001).   [76] *Jones v Challenger.*

[77] N. Hopkins, 'Regulating Trusts of the Family Home: Private Law and Social Policy' (2009) 125 LQR 310.

however, there are signs of a novel 'highly flexible, circumstance-dependent approach' to disputes between co-owners under the recasting of the law in the 1996 Act:[78]

> The court clearly looks at the factors listed in section 15 as an aid to the exercise of its discretion, but is not prevented from considering other matters. There is no evidence to suggest that the default position of sale as pertained under section 30 Law of Property Act 1925 now carries any force . . . The intention of the parties still carries sway, as does the majority interest holding, but neither appear decisive . . . The parties stand level in law and it is the court's task to weigh the factors within section 15 and such additional factors as may be relevant. It is even possible for the court to change its mind, following a change in circumstances . . . Sale is now more easily refused or postponed . . .

The shift to a more flexible, fact-dependent, non-sale-biased approach under TOLATA also finds support in the decision of *Mortgage Corporation v Shaire* (2001) where Neuberger J expressed the view that 'section 15 has changed the law'. This decision which involves an application for sale brought by a mortgagee (mortgage lender) of a co-owner, will be considered in the following section, as we turn to consider how the court determines disputes over co-owned land between co-owners and their creditors.

5.7.4.3 Disputes involving creditors

In addition to disputes between co-owners, it is very common for an application to be made under s. 14 of TOLATA by a creditor of one or more of the equitable co-owners. Imagine a scenario where a co-owner's contribution to the purchase price of the co-owned land is financed by way of a mortgage loan. If the co-owner falls into arrears and defaults on mortgage payments, the mortgage lender (e.g. a bank) may, under s. 14, apply to the court for sale of the co-owned land to realize its debt. In considering applications under s. 14, s. 15(1)(d) provides that one factor to be taken into account by the court is 'the interests of any secured creditor of any beneficiary'. The interests of any secured creditors is, though, just one factor to be considered and must be weighed in the balance against the other factors in s. 15 as discussed. How has the court approached disputes where creditors are involved? We can usefully divide our discussion into three parts:

1. the approach of the court pre-TOLATA under s. 30 of the LPA 1925;

2. the approach of the court in *Shaire*;

3. the approach of the court post-*Shaire*.

The approach of the court pre-TOLATA under s. 30 of the LPA 1925

Pre-TOLATA, by and large the creditor's interests trumped those of beneficiaries and even their children except where there were exceptional circumstances. Invariably, the result was that a sale of co-owned land was ordered: *Lloyds Bank plc v Byrne and Byrne* (1991). In *Byrne*, a husband and wife were co-owners of a matrimonial home. The husband had secured against the property a debt of £25,000 relating to his company. The bank obtained

---

[78] M. Dixon, 'To Sell or Not to Sell: That Is the Question. The Irony of the Trust of Land and Appointment of Trustees Act 1996' (2011) 70 CLJ 579, 589.

a charging order against the property and when the debt was not paid sought, under s. 30 of the LPA 1925, an order for sale of the property. The Court of Appeal granted the order for sale. The court held that no distinction should be drawn between chargees such as the bank in the present case and the position taken as regards trustees in bankruptcy.[79] The upshot of this was that sale would be ordered in the absence of exceptional circumstances. In the later decision in *Abbey National plc v Moss* (1993), the court extended the principle in *Byrne* and held that the approach taken in bankruptcy cases should also be taken where a mortgagee (lender) sought sale of co-owned land, Hirst LJ noting that mortgage lenders were 'in an almost identical position' to Lloyds Bank in the case of *Byrne*.

With the enactment of TOLATA 1996 and with s. 15 citing the interests of creditors as just one of several factors to be considered by the court, how would the court exercise its discretion? This question was addressed directly in the case of *Shaire*.

The approach of the court in Mortgage Corporation v Shaire

The decision in *Shaire* does, very much, indicate a new approach to disputes involving co-owners and their creditors. In particular, it marks a significant departure from the old law under which, certainly, Mrs Shaire's case would have been decided differently, there being nothing exceptional about the circumstances of her case as Neuberger J, conceded. The law,

---

KEY CASE *Mortgage Corporation v Shaire* (2001)

Facts: A house was purchased as a family home in which Mr Fox, Mrs Shaire, and Mrs Shaire's son from a previous relationship were to live. Mr Fox and Mrs Shaire held the property in joint names. Without Mrs Shaire's knowledge, Mr Fox twice mortgaged the house by forging Mrs Shaire's signature. Mr Fox fell into arrears with the mortgage payments and subsequently died. One of the two mortgage lenders, Mortgage Corporation, made an application under s. 14 of TOLATA for possession and sale of the property.

Legal issue: As Neuberger J framed the issue, quite simply, ought the court to make an order for sale of the house? In particular, in defending the application, did Mrs Shaire need to point to 'exceptional circumstances' to succeed in resisting an order for sale?

Judgment: Neuberger J took time to consider the effect of the enactment of TOLATA 1996 and the extent to which the legislation had altered the law that existed pre-1996. Neuberger held that 'section 15 has changed the law'; the interests of creditors was just one of four factors to be considered by the court suggesting the interests of creditors were not alone decisive. It was no longer the case that the court would order sale in favour of a secured creditor unless exceptional circumstances were shown to exist. Neuberger J noted that:

> the court [under s. 15] has greater flexibility than heretofore, as to how it exercises its jurisdiction on an application for an order for sale.

Cases decided under s. 30 of the LPA should therefore be 'treated with caution' and whilst remaining a useful guide would not be determinative of the issue. Neuberger J went on to consider the s. 15 factors and how they applied on the particular facts of Mrs Shaire's case, holding:

→

---

[79] We discuss disputes where co-owners are bankrupt in section 5.7.4.4.

→

- Section 15(1)(a): The property had been purchased to provide a family home for Mr Fox, Mrs Shaire and her son.
- Section 15(1)(b): This was more problematic. For Mrs Shaire, the purpose of the property was primarily as a home but also as an asset.
- Section 15(1)(c): This did not apply as Mrs Shaire's son was an adult and earning a wage.
- Section 15(1)(d): The mortgage lender enjoyed a 25 per cent interest in the property which it was anxious to sell to realize as much of the money it was owed. The lender did not wish to be tied into a 25 per cent equity in a property producing no income and no certainty as to when its equity would be realized.
- Section 15(3): It was clear that Mrs Shaire held the majority share in equity: 75 per cent to the bank's 25 per cent.

Neuberger J noted that: 'to my mind, for Mrs Shaire to have to leave her home of nearly a quarter of a century would be a real and significant hardship, but not an enormous one'. Concluding, Neuberger J suggested a way forward: that the mortgage in favour of Mortgage Corporation would be converted into a loan of 25 per cent of the value of the property on which Mrs Shaire would pay 3 per cent above bank base rate. This compromise allowed the bank's debt to be paid and for Mrs Shaire to be entitled to the entire beneficial ownership of the property. If Mrs Shaire agreed to this arrangement, no order for sale would be made. If she did not, an order for sale would be made.

according to Neuberger J, had very much been changed by Parliament's intervention and he pinpointed eight factors which persuaded him to this view:

- Parliament would not have legislated if there was no intention to change the law.
- There is no hierarchy in the s. 15 factors.
- The was a shift from the trust for sale to trust of land under TOLATA.
- The TOLATA regime clearly envisages a different approach to bankruptcy and non-bankruptcy cases.
- Peter Gibson LJ had indicated that it was 'unfortunate' that some pre-1997 cases just missed being heard under the new TOLATA regime.
- The leading land law texts were of the view that pre-TOLATA cases were now of limited value only and likely would be decided differently under the new regime.
- The Law Commission's suggested in its Report No. 181 that the new regime 'rationalizes' the law.
- There was apparent dissatisfaction with the focus and harshness of the old law in disputes involving families.

Not everyone was welcoming of the new flexible, more sympathetic approach. Reflecting on the substance and effect of the decision in *Shaire*, Pascoe heavily criticized the result and Neuberger J's reasoning:[80]

> Neuberger J's approach is radical: it recognises more rights for beneficiaries and their children in relation to the land which is arguably a more accurate reflection of the ideals and purposes

---

[80] S. Pascoe, 'Section 15 of the Trusts of Land and Appointment of Trustees Act 1996: A Change in the Law?' [2000] Conv 315, 327–8.

behind modern home ownership. In his view, section 15 has done more than to codify judicial practice which had been working in the restrictive framework of the 1925 legislation. The new trust of land will therefore better reflect and protect the different expectations which have arisen with the change in our perception of the social role of land. Neuberger J's approach is not one of consolidation and rationalisation; rather he is wiping the slate clean and starting afresh with secured creditors the likely casualties of the new approach. It will be a welcome change in the law for spouses, partners and children living in the property, but an inexpedient, prejudicial and financially detrimental development if one is a secured creditor. Secured creditors must be asking whether the guidelines in section 15 were enacted with proper consideration and deliberation. It must be questionable whether section 15 has abdicated too much responsibility to the judiciary. Perhaps policy should have been formulated by Parliament, rather than relying on ad hoc developments in case law. This will inevitably have commercial and financial repercussions as creditors absorb the effects of the change. Only time will tell if judges are prepared to implement the consequences of Neuberger J's judgment and let a fresh wind blow away the remnants of the harshness for families of section 30 of the Law of Property Act 1925 when faced with applications by secured creditors.

Pascoe therefore questions whether Neuberger J went too far in his 'radical' interpretation of s. 15 and whether Parliament in legislating abdicated too much authority and discretion to the judiciary. Pascoe is adamant that the party to lose out, in view of Neuberger J's analysis, is the creditor. Is this necessarily true? In fact, when we look more closely at the reasoning and outcome in *Shaire*, was Neuberger not at pains to balance the interests of the lender against those of Mrs Shaire? As we will see in the next section, many of the concerns Pascoe raises as to the 'radical' nature of Neuberger J's reasoning and the anti-creditor sentiment have not materialized in the approach taken by the court in post-*Shaire* case law.

*The approach of the court post-*Shaire*: Has s. 15 of TOLATA really changed the law?*

In the case of *Bank of Ireland Home Mortgages Ltd v Bell*, decided after *Shaire*, the court endorsed Neuberger J's judgment; however, in the event, it engaged a far narrower interpretation of ss. 14 and 15. Let's take a look at the decision.

KEY CASE *Bank of Ireland Home Mortgages Ltd v Bell* (2001)

Facts: A property had been acquired to provide a family home for a husband, wife, and their son. The husband, without the wife's knowledge, mortgaged the property. The husband fell into arrears on the mortgage. The marriage broke down and the bank sought possession and sale of the property. At the time of the application for sale, the son was almost 18 years old.

Legal issue: Would the court order a sale of the property or, following *Shaire*, adopt a more beneficiary-friendly approach?

Judgment: At first instance, the court refused to order sale. The Court of Appeal overturned this and ordered sale of the property. Several factors were key to the court's decision:

- Mr and Mrs Bell were divorced at the time of the application and the Bell's son was just shy of 18 years old. As such, the initial purpose for which the property was purchased, to provide a family home, was not a material factor. The son's age could only be 'a very slight consideration'.

→

➔
- Evidence of Mrs Bell's ill-health at the time of the trial was not a factor that could prevent a sale and would, at best, result in a postponement.

- Whilst the 1996 Act had given the court scope for 'change in the court's practice' from that under the old law, 'a powerful consideration is and ought to be whether the creditor is receiving proper recompense for being kept out of its money.

- The debt owed was around £300,000 and increasing daily. No payment had been made to the bank in almost eight years.

In the final analysis, the court was persuaded to order sale of the property, emphasizing that:

> In the present case it is plain that by refusing the sale the judge has condemned the bank to go on waiting for its money with no prospect of recovery from Mr and Mrs Bell and with the debt increasing all the time, that debt already exceeding what could be realized on a sale. That seems to [the court] to be very unfair to the bank.

A very similar result was also reached in *C. Putnam & Sons v Taylor* (2009) where the court ordered sale of a co-owned property constituting a family home when a husband's debts had spiralled. The court made the order for a sale despite the purpose for which the property had been purchased continuing. The court noted that the wife had a sufficient share in the equity of the property to enable her to buy a smaller albeit less attractive property. Refusing sale would, said the court, be 'condemning the [creditor] to go on waiting for its money with no prospect of recovery from any other source and the debt increasing all the time'.[81] Is this justifiable? Was undue weight attached to the interests of the creditor over and above those of the wife?

In the same vein, in *Edwards v Edwards & Bank of Scotland* (2010), the sale of a co-owned family home was ordered where the wife had forged her husband's signature to mortgage the property, the marriage had come to an end, and the husband's share of the proceeds of sale were sufficient for him to purchase alternative accommodation. In a recent decision of the High Court, *Fred Perry Ltd v Genis* (2014), the interests of the creditor again prevailed in a case where the purpose of providing a family home continued, there were young children (aged 9 and 14) living in the property, and there was sufficient value in the property to cover the debt owed. The court noted the tension between the competing interests but said the authorities demonstrated that 'precedence was given to commercial interests and economic buoyancy rather than to the residential security of the family'.[82] An argument based on Art. 8 of the ECHR also failed. Sale was ordered but postponed for 12 months for arrangements to be made on alternative accommodation and for new schools to be found for the children.[83]

The decisions in *Bell*, *Putnam*, *Edwards v Edwards* and more recently in *Fred Perry Ltd* therefore swing the pendulum firmly in the favour of the creditor. How do you feel about this? In *Edwards v Lloyds TSB*, a different result was reached.

---

[81]　*Putnam*, [34].　　[82]　*Fred Perry Ltd*, [8].

[83]　The children attended specialist Jewish schools which were not accessible in every residential area.

KEY CASE *Edwards v Lloyds TSB* (2004)

Facts: Mr and Mrs Edwards co-owned a property in which they lived as their matrimonial home. Mr Edwards forged his wife's signature in order to secure a mortgage against the property. The marriage broke down and Mr Edwards disappeared and could not be located. Mrs Edwards remained living in the property with the children of the marriage. The bank brought an application for sale of the property.

Legal issue: Was the bank entitled to an order for sale in order to realize its security?

Judgment: Despite the bank receiving no interest payments against the mortgage, the judge found that to order an immediate sale would be 'unacceptably severe' to the wife and the children, Park J noting that, 'in part the purpose still survives, because the house is still the home for Mrs Edwards and the two children'. An order for sale was therefore postponed for five years until the youngest of Mrs Edwards' children reached 18 and, should the children then enter full-time education, with scope for further postponement.

Park J distinguished the facts of the present case from the near-identical factual nexus in *Bell* and in *Achampong* on two grounds:

- Doubt as to whether Mrs Edwards would be able to find alternative accommodation which was affordable and adequate to house her children, and

- There being sufficient value in the property to cover the debt (the creditor would therefore be able to realize its security at a later date).

How to characterize the approach of the court post-*Shaire*? The position is rather mixed.

As regards the purpose for which land was acquired, in *Bell* the court regarded the departure of Mr Bell as bringing that purpose (the provision of a family home) to an end. In contrast, in *Edwards v Lloyds TSB*, despite Mr Edwards' disappearance, the court considered a sale to be too harsh on the wife and children as the purpose for which the property was acquired still survived 'in part'. Probert has warned of the risks of the court adopting the narrow construction of 'purposes' as employed in *Bell*.[84] Probert argues that on this construction, the interests of creditors prevail and sale is an almost inevitable outcome.[85]

A second basis on which the apparently conflicting decisions of *Bell* and *Edwards v Lloyds TSB* can be distinguished concerns the respective positions of the creditors. In *Bell*, the debt was spiralling and there was, at the time of the application, insufficient value in the house to cover the debt. In these circumstances, the court had considerable sympathy for the plight of the creditor and sale was ordered. A similar result was reached in *Putnam*. By contrast, in *Edwards v Lloyds TSB*, there was sufficient equity in the property to cover the debt and therefore keeping the creditor waiting was not seen as unduly prejudicial. Sale could therefore be postponed.

In summary, the fear expressed by Pascoe that creditors would be the victims of the more flexible, liberalized approach taken by Neuberger J in *Shaire* was clearly somewhat premature. Rather, the pendulum has swung in the opposite direction and once again in favour of creditors. In cases such as *Bell*, *Putnam*, and *Edwards v Edwards*, it difficult to locate the apparent, more beneficiary-focused, more anti-creditor logic of the *Shaire* decision. Post-*Shaire*,

---

[84] R. Probert, 'Creditors and Section 15 of the Trusts of Land and Appointment of Trustees Act 1996: First Among Equals' [2002] Conv 61.

[85] Ibid., 66.

it appears that sale will only be refused where to do so would not prejudice the creditor. This will be demonstrated by showing that there is enough value in the property to satisfy the debt at a later time and therefore there is no risk to the creditor in waiting. Even then, this will likely lead to a postponement of sale rather than an outright refusal. A key statement on the current law is that of Master Price in *Fred Perry Ltd* who noted:[86]

> [T]he upshot [of decided case law] has been to give precedence to commercial interests rather than to the residential security of the family . . . whilst it may be argued that the precedence to such commercial interest fails to take adequate account of the public interest in maintaining a stable family unit, bearing in mind the attendant social costs of eviction and family breakup, this does seem to be the current state of the authorities in relation to sections 14 and 15 of the 1996 Act . . . the legislation goes nowhere near creating what are described as 'homestead rights' which would ring fence a family home from the claim of creditors . . .

Do Master Price's words merely summarize the present state of the law or messenger a broader return to a position closer to the old law presumption in favour of sale except where exceptional circumstances exist?

5.7.4.4 Disputes where a co-owner is bankrupt

Where a co-owner is bankrupt, an entirely different statutory regime applies to determination of disputes over co-owned land and the factors listed in s. 15 do not apply.[87] This distinct regime, under the Insolvency Act 1986 (IA 1986), only operates where co-owners are actually insolvent and not, as many students often misunderstand, when a co-owner is merely heavily indebted. You must distinguish between being officially bankrupt and a co-owner who finds herself under a mountain of debt but is not, at the date of the s. 14 TOLATA application, insolvent. See Figure 5.8.

When a co-owner becomes bankrupt, under s. 306 of the Insolvency Act 1986, her estate[88] is vested in a trustee in bankruptcy. It is then the job of the trustee in bankruptcy to realize the co-owner's property in order to cover, as far as possible, the debt owed to the co-owner's creditors.[89] Of course, where one co-owner becomes bankrupt and the other co-owners remain solvent, a fierce dispute may arise as to whether the co-owned property is to be sold. This is the context in which the trustee in bankruptcy will make use of s. 14 of TOLATA to bring an action for sale of the land. The trustee in bankruptcy is able to make a s. 14 application as a 'person who has an interest in property subject to a trust of land'.[90] Applications by a trustee in bankruptcy concerning co-owned land are governed by s. 335A of the IA 1986. As Figure 5.8 depicts, the timing of the application by the trustee in bankruptcy is key in determining how the court will resolve the dispute. Section 335A draws a distinction between those applications made less than 12 months after the vesting of the bankrupt's estate in the trustee in bankruptcy and those made more than 12 months after vesting.

---

[86] *Fred Perry Ltd*, [8]–[9].   [87] Section 15(4) of TOLATA 1996.

[88] Which includes any property to which she is beneficially entitled: s. 283 of the IA 1986.

[89] Ibid., s. 305(2). Under the so-named 'new start' scheme introduced by the Enterprise Act 2002, where a bankrupt has an interest in a family home, the trustee in bankruptcy has three years in which to realize that interest before it reverts back to the bankrupt: ibid., s. 283A.

[90] *Re Solomon (A Bankrupt)* (1967).

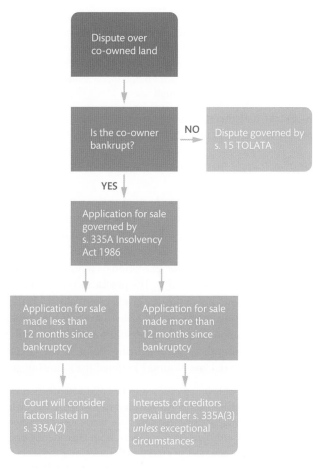

Figure 5.8 Disputes involving a bankrupt co-owner

Application for sale less than 12 months after vesting of bankrupt's estate in trustee in bankruptcy

If the application is made within 12 months of vesting, the court will resolve the dispute by reference to the factors listed in s. 335A(2). This means that the court must balance the competing interests of the bankrupt's creditors against the conduct of any spouse, civil partner, and former spouse or civil partner contributing to the bankruptcy; the needs of any spouse, civil partner, and former spouse or civil partner; the needs of any children; and all other circumstances other than the needs of the bankrupt. Importantly, these factors differ quite markedly from those listed in s. 15 of TOLATA. Most notably, the intentions of the parties and the purpose for which land was acquired and is being held are no longer relevant where a co-owner is bankrupt. Section 335A(2)(c) requires the court to consider all circumstances other than the needs of the bankrupt. As to what is understood as 'needs' for the purposes of s. 335A(2)(c), there is little authority. In *Everitt v Budhram* (2009) Henderson J noted:[91]

---

[91] *Everitt*, 181.

Curiously enough, there seems to be no authority . . . on the meaning of the word 'needs' in this subsection. However, I consider that counsel for the trustee is substantially correct . . . that the needs of the bankrupt in paragraph (c) should be broadly interpreted, just as the same word should be broadly interpreted in sub-paragraphs (b)(ii)(iii). Accordingly, the court must disregard not only the financial needs of the bankrupt but, also, relevantly for present purposes, the medical and psychological needs of the bankrupt.

The trial judge in *Everitt* had therefore been wrong to take the various chronic medical conditions suffered by the bankrupt and his wife into account.

Application for sale more than 12 months after vesting of bankrupt's estate in trustee in bankruptcy

If the application is made more than 12 months after vesting, s. 335A(3) operates far more harshly against the bankrupt. Under s. 335A(3), in these circumstances, the court will 'assume' that the interests of the bankrupt's creditors outweigh all other considerations unless exceptional circumstances exist. Where this 'assumption' applies, the court will order sale. If the bankrupt co-owner satisfies the court that exceptional circumstances exist, the court will then move to consider the factors in s. 335A(2). The practical consequence of s. 335(A)(3) is that, in many cases, a bankrupt and her family are given, essentially, a 12-month grace period in which to make necessary arrangements, prepare themselves for the point at which the interests of creditors become paramount, and on an application, the co-owned land will be sold.

What are exceptional circumstances? The starting point is the decision of *Re Citro* (1991), a case decided under the old law. Nourse LJ offered the following guidance:

> It is not uncommon for a wife with young children to be faced with eviction in circumstances where the realisation of her beneficial interest will not produce enough to buy a comparable home in the same neighbourhood, or indeed elsewhere; and, if she has to move elsewhere, there may be problems over schooling and so forth. Such circumstances, while engendering a natural sympathy in all who hear of them, cannot be described as exceptional. They are the melancholy consequences of debt and improvidence with which every civilised society has been familiar. It was only in *Re Holliday* that they helped the wife's voice to prevail; and then only, as I believe, because of one special feature of that case. One of the reasons for the decision given by Sir David Cairns was that it was highly unlikely that postponement of payment of the debts would cause any great hardship to any of the creditors, a matter of which Buckley L.J. no doubt took account as well.[92]

Exceptional really does mean exceptional. It requires something more than the 'melancholy consequences of debt' such as having to relocate or moving children to new schools. As Judge Moran QC noted in *Hosking v Michaelides* (2004), exceptional means 'out of the ordinary course, or unusual or special or uncommon'. The judgment of Sumption QC in *Re Bremner* (1999) offers the closest we have to a 'test' for exceptional circumstances:[93]

> The test is whether the problems which would result from an eviction are within the broad range of problems, necessarily distressing, which can be expected to arise from the process of bankruptcy and the resultant realisation of the bankrupt's assets, or whether they lie wholly outside that range.

According to *Re Bremner*, circumstances will therefore only be 'exceptional' where they lie 'wholly outside' the range of problems commonly associated with bankruptcy. Table 5.2 gathers together some of the key case law on the issue.

---

[92] *Re Citro*, 157.   [93] *Re Bremner*, 915.

Table 5.2 What amounts to 'exceptional circumstances'?

CIRCUMSTANCE	EXCEPTIONAL?	
The problem of finding a new home	✗	Re Citro (1991)
The problem of young children needing to move schools	✗	Re Citro (1991)
Bankrupt's son with special educational needs spending four days a week in the property	✗	Barca v Mears (2004)
Bankrupt with various chronic conditions related to stroke and diabetes	✓	Everitt v Budhram (2009)
Spouse of the bankrupt with paranoid schizophrenia	✓	Re Raval (1998)
Spouse of bankrupt with reduced life expectancy due to renal failure/arthritis	✓	Claughton v Charalambous (1999)
Bankrupt with terminal cancer with life expectancy of six months	✓	Re Bremner (1999)
Postponement of sale would significantly increase value of property due to insurance claim	✓	Foenander v Allan (2006)

Where the court accepts that exceptional circumstances exist, it moves to consider the factors in s. 335A(2) in deciding how to proceed. In most cases, the result will be a postponement of sale rather than an outright refusal. In *Re Bremner*, the court postponed sale until after the bankrupt's death. In *Everitt*, a modest 12-month postponement was felt appropriate. The length of the postponement is mostly determined by the degree of hardship the delay will cause to creditors. *Re Holliday* (1981), an unusual case and the only decision at the time of the judgment in *Re Citro* that had given rise to exceptional circumstances, warrants special mention. In *Re Holliday*, a husband became bankrupt and left the family home, leaving his wife and their children living in the property. The husband had himself petitioned for bankruptcy and not any creditor. The husband's debts were also relatively small. The trustee in bankruptcy sought sale of the property. The court considered all circumstances including that the husband had petitioned for bankruptcy himself, concluding that the wife's voice, who wished to remain living in the property with her children, should prevail. Sale was postponed for five years until the bankrupt's children reached 17. *Re Holliday* should be handled with care, however, in view of the string of modern cases demonstrating the strictness of the test for exceptionality which indicate, generally, nothing less than severe illness or disability will suffice to demonstrate exceptional circumstances. One rare case of exceptional circumstances which were finance-based is *Foenander v Allan* (2006). In *Foenander*, a property co-owned by two brothers had suffered severe subsidence. On an application by the trustee in bankruptcy for sale of the property, the court postponed sale as an outstanding insurance claim to repair the property would lead to an increase in the value of the property. An immediate sale would result in serious loss to the brothers and this outweighed any hardship the creditor would suffer waiting to receive its money.

The 'exceptional circumstances' test: Is it human rights compliant?

Where an application is made by a trustee in bankruptcy for sale of co-owned land and that application is made more than 12 months after the bankruptcy, there is, in effect, a presumption that the interests of creditors prevail, rebuttable only by evidence of exceptional circumstances. The court only enjoys a discretion on refusal or postponement of sale where exceptional circumstances can be proved. This raises the question whether the s. 335A presumption and the narrow construction adopted as 'exceptional circumstances' are human rights compliant. This was addressed directly in the case of *Barca v Mears* (2004). In *Barca*, it was argued that the presumption under s. 335A(3) infringed both Art. 8 and Art. 1 of Protocol 1 of the ECHR. Judge Nicholas Strauss QC noted that these rights were not absolute and interference by way of legislation was permitted so long as it pursued a legitimate aim and the interference was a proportionate means of achieving this end. Nicholas Strauss QC, nevertheless, raised certain objections. He noted that the 'almost universal rule' that s. 335A requires the court to adopt may, in some circumstances, result in an infringement of Convention rights. It was questionable whether, in particular, the narrow approach taken to 'exceptional circumstances' as adopted in *Re Citro* was human rights compliant. He added:[94]

> a shift in emphasis in the interpretation of the statute may be necessary to achieve compatibility with the Convention. There is nothing in the wording of section 335A, or the corresponding wording of sections 336 and 337, to require an interpretation which excludes from the ambit of 'exceptional circumstances' cases in which the consequences of the bankruptcy are of the usual kind, but exceptionally severe. Nor is there anything in the wording to require a court to say that a case may not be exceptional, if it is one of the rare cases in which, on the facts, relatively slight loss which the creditors will suffer as a result of the postponement of the sale would be outweighed by disruption, even if of the usual kind, which will be caused in the lives of the bankrupt and his family. Indeed, on one view, this is what the Court of Appeal decided in *Re Holliday*. Thus it may be that, on a reconsideration of the sections in the light of the Convention, they are to be regarded as recognising that, in the general run of cases, the creditors' interests will outweigh all other interests, but leaving it open to a court to find that, on a proper consideration of the facts of a particular case, it is one of the exceptional cases in which this proposition is not true. So interpreted, and without the possibly undue bias in favour of the creditors' property interests embodied in the pre-1998 case law, these sections would be compatible with the Convention.

Nicholas Strauss QC therefore argues that a wider interpretation is needed if s. 335A is to be human rights compliant. His discussion was, however, obiter and—as he himself described it—expressed only 'a tentative view'. That said, it is clear that he is railing against the apparent strictness of the 'exceptional circumstances' test and proposes a looser, more fact-sensitive approach to s. 335A(3). The question following *Barca* was whether these concerns and suggestions of a softer, broader approach to the question of 'exceptional circumstances' would be embraced. Did *Barca* open the door to more challenges to an application for sale founded on human rights grounds? Baker explores the case law following *Barca* and is rather pessimistic as to the current state of human rights jurisprudence in this area:[95]

---

[94] *Barca*, [41].

[95] A. J. Baker, 'The Judicial Approach to "Exceptional Circumstances" in Bankruptcy: The Impact of the Human Rights Act 1998' [2010] Conv 352, 366.

Certainly, express encouragement for the *Barca* objection is lacking. Even implicit support is hard to find. Instead, the case law evidences only a variety of alluring yet ultimately unpersuasive defences of the status quo, intended to keep the *Barca* objection at bay. Small wonder, then, that 'the human rights argument remains undeveloped' to date.

In fact, as Baker identifies, the judicial response post-*Barca* has been almost non-existent. Certainly, the tentative, wider interpretation advanced in *Barca* has not been picked up even implicitly. In no decided case has Nicholas Strauss QC's formulation led to a refusal or postponement of sale. Rather, subsequent case law has repeatedly concluded that s. 335A is entirely compatible with human rights' obligations. Indeed, in *Nicholls v Lan* (2007), Paul Moran QC noted:[96]

> For my part, I do not see that the statutory test [in s. 335A], leading to balancing exercise, is inconsistent with the qualified nature of the rights enshrined in Article 8 and in Article 1 of the First Protocol. Indeed, it might be contended that section 335A precisely captures what is required by Article 8 and Article 1 of the First Protocol.

5.8 Purchasers of co-owned land

Co-owned land, just like non-co-owned land, can be sold. When a purchaser acquires co-owned land, they want to know that they take that land free of any pre-existing equitable interests. The last thing a purchaser wants is to be bound by beneficial interests under a trust of land. So, how does the purchaser protect her position when purchasing co-owned land? Figure 5.9 sets out how purchasers are protected in unregistered and registered land.

5.8.1 Overreaching: The principal means of protection for purchasers

The principal means of protection for purchasers of co-owned land, whether that land be unregistered or registered, is provided by the doctrine of overreaching. As we saw in section 2.6, where the purchase price is paid to two or more trustees (or a trust corporation),

Figure 5.9 Protection for purchasers in unregistered and registered land

---

[96] *Nicholls v Lan*, [43]; in *Foyle v Turner* (2007), Judge Norris QC shared the view in *Lan* that Parliament had struck the balance between the bankrupt and his creditors and that no separate consideration of Art. 8 was required; see also *Ford v Alexander* (2012).

overreaching takes place: the beneficial interests in the land are detached and converted into an equivalent value in the purchase monies.[97] The doctrine applies in the same way to the sale of co-owned land. Where overreaching takes place, the effect is that the purchaser need not concern herself with the trust under which the co-owned land was held and acquires the land entirely free of those equitable interests. Where co-owned land is held by at least two trustees (legal joint tenants), overreaching is easily satisfied provided the purchaser deals with at least two of these legal owners.

What of those equitable interests under a trust of land that have not been overreached? In unregistered land, the enforceability of equitable interests that have not been overreached is governed by the doctrine of notice: see *Kingsnorth Finance Co. Ltd v Tizard* (1986), which we explored in section 3.4.5. In registered land, enforceability of these interests will be determined on the basis of Sch. 3, para. 2 of the LRA 2002 and whether the interest holder can satisfy the requirements for an overriding interest by establishing actual occupation: see section 2.7.4.2.

Over time, the doctrine of overreaching alone came to be seen as not providing enough protection for purchasers particularly where land was held under an implied trust as the purchaser was, perhaps, not even aware of the existence of any equitable owners let alone the need to deal with two or more trustees to guarantee overreaching. Parliament therefore legislated to offer greater protections for purchasers: for unregistered land this was under TOLATA and, for registered land, under the LRA 2002.

5.8.2 Unregistered land: Section 16 of TOLATA

In unregistered land, purchasers are provided with protection under s. 16 of TOLATA. The effect of this rather wordy and, in parts, obscurely drafted provision, is that a conveyance to a purchaser of co-owned, unregistered land will not be invalidated by any breach of trust committed by trustees provided the purchaser has no actual knowledge of that breach. Practically speaking, this means that if trustees convey co-owned land without having regard to the rights of the beneficiaries or without consulting with beneficiaries or without obtaining consent of the beneficiaries to a partition of the land, under s. 16(1) of TOLATA, the purchaser will not be affected by these breaches. There is, then, no duty on a purchaser to ensure the trustees have acted within their powers or, as we say, *intra vires*. Only where the purchaser actually knew of these breaches will the conveyance be invalidated.[98]

5.8.3 Registered land: Section 26 of the LRA 2002

Section 16 of TOLATA does not apply to registered land.[99] Protection for purchasers in registered land is provided by s. 26 of the LRA 2002. The effect of s. 26 is that no limitation on a person's right to exercise the powers of an owner, including the right of trustees to deal with registered land, will affect the purchaser of the registered estate unless that limitation has been protected by the entry of a restriction on the register. Put differently, any limitation on the powers of registered co-owners are intended to be contained in a restriction

[97] Sections 2(1)(ii) and 27 of the LPA 1925.
[98] For criticism of s. 16 of TOLATA 1996, see Pascoe, 'Right to Occupy under a Trust of Land: Muddled Legislative Logic', where he blasts the provision for being indeterminate in extent, ambiguous in nature, enigmatic in interpretation, and equivocal in purpose. See discussion of doctrine of notice in Chapter 3.
[99] Section 16(7) of TOLATA 1996.

entered on the register. Where any limitations have not been entered on the register, the purchaser will not be affected. An example will help you to grasp how s. 26 works.

Imagine that Arnold and Bree are co-owners of a property holding it on trust for Cali (an equitable owner) and that there is an express term of the trust that provides that Arnold and Bree cannot sell the land without first obtaining Cali's consent. This limitation should have been recorded on the register by entry of a restriction but imagine that this has not been done. Arnold and Bree subsequently sell the land to Darla (a third party purchaser) without Cali's consent and Darla is registered as the new proprietor of the land. Under s. 26 of the LRA 2002, Darla's title to the land cannot be challenged. No restriction was entered to reflect the limitation on Arnold and Bree's powers. Nor will it be relevant for the purposes of s. 26 of the LRA if Cali was in actual occupation of the land when sold. Cali may, however, be able to bring a personal action against Arnold and Bree for breach of trust. Darla may also be liable, again personally, for receiving trust property in breach of trust if she had knowledge of the breach.[100] Section 26 is therefore a vital protection to purchasers of registered land. In particular, note the breadth of the section. No provision is made for those in actual occupation who will lose out, as did Cali in our example.

5.9 Future directions

We have covered a lot of ground in this chapter from the nature of co-ownership, the imposition of a trust of land, to severance and to how disputes involving co-owned land are resolved. In this final section, we stop, gather our thoughts and reflect on potential areas for future development of the law.

5.9.1 Should the law of severance be reformed and if so, how?

Are the current five modes of severance satisfactory or should the law be reformed?

The Law Commission looked into reform of severance in its 1985 Working Paper *Trusts of Land*. Its proposals at the time were far-reaching. The Commission put forward two potential reforms: (1) that severance by written notice be the only mode of severing an equitable joint tenancy; and (2) that severance by will should be introduced. These reforms would have marked a fundamental rebalancing of the law of severance. Exciting stuff. Unfortunately, however, when the final report *Trusts of Land* was produced, there was no discussion of severance. It was said that severance would be dealt with in a later report. Sadly, that report never came and no follow-up work has been forthcoming. Would the Commission's proposals have been a positive move and should they be implemented? The Commission's proposals would have sounded the death knell for the *Hensman* catalogue of severance. We have seen the difficulties of interpretation of the three methods of severance under this catalogue, in particular, the overlap between the second and third methods. Limiting severance to written notice and by will would, quite plainly, have certainty and simplicity on its side. Tee subjected the Commission's reform proposals to scrutiny, observing:[101]

---

[100] You will cover 'knowing receipt' liability as part of your Trusts Law course.
[101] L. Tee, 'Severance Revisited' [1995] Conv 105, 110.

The abolition of severance by acting on one's share has a certain attraction in logic—there has always been an intellectual sleight of hand which allows the alienation both to transform and transfer the interest . . . The abolition of severance by mutual agreement or by mutual conduct would have fewer legal repercussions. It is arguable that severance on such grounds has been found so rarely by the courts over the last 50 years that the abolition of these methods would not in practice amount to a serious limitation, and would produce much needed certainty.

The Law Commission's second suggested reform, that severance could be effected by will, is a far more radical proposal which has serious implications especially for the scope of survivorship. The Law Commission cited two practical reasons for introducing this new mode of severance: (1) after marital breakdown, many spouses are anxious not to serve a written notice to avoid prejudicing negotiations and when settling arrangements involving children of the marriage; (2) in many cases, co-owners leave their 'share' by will to loved ones to inherit not realizing that their wishes can never be realized as severance has not taken place. These cases do not reach court because the law is clear on these points: survivorship operates. Tee explores two counter-arguments to the Commission's proposals, one grounded in fairness and the other in the practical consequences of construction:[102]

> [A] 'rogue' beneficial joint tenant could secretly sever by will and then enjoy the possibility of the right of survivorship without any risk to his estate. If he survived his co-tenant, he would take all, and if he pre-deceased, his chosen beneficiaries would inherit his share. Thus he could both 'have his cake and eat it'. His co-tenant, meanwhile, would not know of his severance by will, and would assume that the right of survivorship was going to operate. By the time she discovered her mistake, it would be too late . . . the other difficulty . . . is a practical one—the construction of the will . . . At present, it is sometimes uncertain whether inter vivos severance has taken place; the additional possibility of severance by will would no doubt result in still more uncertainty.

Reflecting on the Commission's proposals and Tee's cogent analysis of them, the question is essentially this: are the problems with the current law sufficiently serious to warrant such a radical reform? The reforms proposed operate in opposite directions. Limiting severance to written notice would circumscribe severance and give a greater role to survivorship. The introduction of severance by will would appear to entirely undermine the nature of the joint tenancy. The question of reform is therefore a fundamental one which, in truth, goes to a policy question (for Parliament) as to whether the equitable joint tenancy is desirable in twenty-first-century Britain. If you had the power, would you implement the Commission's reforms?

5.9.2 Should we abolish equitable joint tenancies?

We have seen in this chapter that severance can operate unfairly. Should we therefore abolish equitable joint tenancies? Should we accede to the equitable maxim that 'equity prefers a tenancy in common'? In other words, should it only be possible that co-owned land be held under a tenancy in common in equity? In many circumstances, tenancies in common are already presumed. The question of abolition really comes to life in the context of intimate co-owners whose relationships break down. This makes up the bulk of severance cases coming before the court and rests on the problem of the shifting intentions of the parties throughout the lifetime of their relationship. Smith notes the following:[103]

---

[102] Ibid., 112.   [103] R. Smith, *Plural Ownership* (Oxford: Oxford University Press, 2005), 88.

The main advantages of joint tenancies lie in fulfilling the wishes of co-owners when one dies during the relationship. Both joint tenancy and tenancy in common can cause inappropriate results once the relationship breaks down.

On relationship breakdown, the joint tenancy is unlikely to reflect the parties' intentions but, equally, a tenancy in common presents challenges. Under a tenancy in common, the burden is on former spouses to keep their will up-to-date which means accessing legal advice. The risk is that a will is not updated and thus property does not reach its intended beneficiary. For Smith, the arguments, on balance, support retention of the equitable joint tenancy because:[104]

> [A] joint tenancy is much more likely to produce the correct result [in relationship breakdown cases] because of the court's ability to find a suitable agreement or course of dealing to achieve severance, implying terms into wills is far more difficult . . .

Assuming we retain the equitable joint tenancy, this necessarily shifts the emphasis back onto a critique of our law of severance. On relationship breakdown, former spouses need decent legal advice to ensure that land law properly gives voice to their intentions.

5.9.3 Do the courts attach too much weight under ss. 14 and 15 of TOLATA to the interests of creditors?

Dixon has argued that:[105]

> The case law fails to recognise that in some types of case the parties to the dispute do not stand equal in terms of their property rights and that it is important to consider who, if anyone, has proprietary priority and how this has come about. Any diminution of proprietary priority through the ordering of sale—clearly contemplated as a possibility by section 14—should be recognised and explained.

Dixon distils the court's broad approach into four scenarios: (1) disputes between co-owners and no other party where the court 'fashions a solution that responds to the parties' particular circumstances'; (2) cases involving a non-priority mortgagee where the court tends towards ordering sale; (3) applicants seeking to enforce charging orders against co-owned land who are treated to the same generosity as non-priority mortgagees; and (4) disputes involving trustees in bankruptcy where legislation prioritizing sale (subject to exceptional circumstances) is 'executed faithfully [and] possibly slavishly' followed by the court.

Is Dixon's analysis right? If so, do you feel that the court leans too far in favour of sale? Is the court being sufficiently up-front in its reasoning?

5.9.4 'Exceptional circumstances' under s. 335A(3) of the IA 1986

One key area to watch for development in the law is the case law surrounding 'exceptional circumstances' under s. 335A(3) of the IA 1986. Might the court soften its approach to human rights arguments here and thereby install a more sympathetic, fulsome balancing act of the interests of creditors against the interests of bankrupt co-owners? Baker calls for greater engagement with human rights arguments but is not optimistic.[106] Why are these arguments not gaining more traction? In trying to get to grips with the court's reluctance in this area, Baker notes:[107]

---

[104] Ibid., 88–9.   [105] Dixon, 'To Sell or Not to Sell: That Is the Question', 604–5.
[106] Baker, 'The Judicial Approach to "Exceptional Circumstances" in Bankruptcy'.   [107] Ibid., 366.

A variety of reasons have been canvassed as to the preference of the law in this area for the interests of creditors over those of the family. Perhaps one of the principal things which the *Re Citro* jurisprudence has to recommend to it, however, is the *ex ante* certainty which it fosters for creditors. So whilst it was remarked that the majority view in *Re Citro*, would deter the exercise of judicial discretion, perhaps that was in some way the point . . . Instead, the balance struck accords neatly with Gray and Gray's credible perception that 'in the law of property, justice is never quite as important as order'. Certainty for both creditors and debtors is something that the law should seek to promote.

If we accept Baker's analysis, it becomes all too clear why human rights arguments are resisted in regard to s. 335A and how these arguments could be seen as a challenge—a threat—to the certainty and order of the law. The precise ambit of Art. 8 remains open to debate and, in this way, as Baker notes 'it might be thought that over-ready appeals to abstract entitlements based on social conscience would undermine transactional certainty'.[108] But is there really anything to fear from greater engagement with human rights arguments? Even under Nicholas Strauss QC's more liberal approach to exceptionality as discussed in *Barca*, it will remain a rare case where 'exceptional circumstances' arise. Equally, we must remember what is at stake. In most cases where the high hurdle of 'exceptional circumstances' is met, this leads only to a postponement of sale and not an outright refusal. Even where a case is shown to be exceptional, creditors need in the very worst-case scenario shoulder only a short delay in recovering their debt. The idea that human rights arguments inevitably lead to an anti-creditor outlook and the floodgates being flung open should also be questioned. Perhaps the time has come to think again about human rights in this context and in land law more broadly.[109]

Further reading

- A. J. Baker, 'The Judicial Approach to "Exceptional Circumstances" in Bankruptcy: The Impact of the Human Rights Act 1998' [2010] Conv 352.

- C. Bevan, 'The Search for Common Intention: The Status of an Executed, Express Declaration of Trust Post-*Stack* and *Jones*' (2019) 135(4) LQR 660.

- B. C. Crown, 'Severance of Joint Tenancy of Land by Partial Alienation' (2001) 117 LQR 477.

- M. Dixon, 'To Sell or Not to Sell: That Is the Question. The Irony of the Trust of Land and Appointment of Trustees Act 1996' (2011) 70 CLJ 579.

- S. Gardner, 'Material Relief between Ex-Cohabitants 1: Liquidating Beneficial Interests Otherwise than by Sale' [2014] Conv 95.

- S. Gardner, 'Understanding *Goodman v Gallant*' [2015] Conv 199.

- N. Hopkins, 'The Trusts of Land and Appointment of Trustees Act 1996' [1996] Conv 411.

- Law Commission Working Paper No. 94, *Trusts of Land* (1985).

- Law Commission Report No. 181, *Transfer of Land: Trusts of Land* (1989).

---

[108] Ibid., 367.

[109] We explore the interaction and interrelationship between land law and human rights in Chapter 14 and at pertinent moments throughout the book.

- J. Martyn, 'Co-Owners and their Entitlement to Occupy their Land Before and After the Trusts of Land and Appointment of Trustees Act 1996: Theoretical Doubts Are Replaced by Practical Difficulties' [1997] Conv 254.

- S. Nield, 'To Sever or Not to Sever: The Effect of a Mortgage by One Joint Tenant' [2001] Conv 462, at 473–4.

- S. Pascoe, 'Section 15 of the Trusts of Land and Appointment of Trustees Act 1996: A Change in the Law?' [2000] Conv 315.

- S. Pascoe, 'Right to Occupy under a Trust of Land: Muddled Legislative Logic' [2006] Conv 54.

- M. Pawlowski and J. Brown, 'Joint Purchasers and the Presumption of Joint Beneficial Ownership—A Matter of Informed Choice?' (2013) 27 Trusts Law International 3.

- R. Probert, 'Creditors and Section 15 of the Trusts of Land and Appointment of Trustees Act 1996: First Among Equals' [2002] Conv 61.

- R. Smith, *Plural Ownership* (Oxford: Oxford University Press, 2005), chapters 3–8 in particular.

- L. Tee, 'Severance Revisited' [1995] Conv 105.

 ## Online resources

Access the online resources at www.oup.com/uk/bevan2e/ to test yourself with self-test questions and scenario problems. You can also view additional supporting material relevant to the topics in this chapter, including:

- *Videos*
- *Audio podcasts*
- *Maps, diagrams, and flowcharts*
- *Interactive exercises*
- *Examples of real-life legal documentation*

Interests in the Family Home

6.1 Introduction

For many people, whether or not they enjoy an interest in the family home is absolutely fundamental to their sense of security, stability, and even their sense of self. However, as is often the case, a person may find themselves in a position where they are neither the registered legal owner of property nor do they enjoy an equitable interest under an express trust of land. How does this person acquire an interest in the family home? In this chapter, we examine how a person may acquire an interest in the family home through constructive and **resulting trusts**. For the avoidance of any doubt, in this chapter, we are concerned with non-married, non-civil partnered, cohabiting couples, or family members otherwise coming together to purchase property as a home. For married couples facing divorce or civil partners facing dissolution of their partnership, there are statutory frameworks under the Matrimonial Causes Act 1973[1] and the Civil Partnership Act 2004 which give the court jurisdiction to declare and adjust property interests.[2] For non-married, non-civil partnered, cohabiting couples, or family members who come together to purchase property as a home, no equivalent legislation exists. Where these parties have expressed their wishes as to how the purchased property is to be held in the form of an express declaration, this will, save in

---

[1] See ss. 23, 24, 24A, and 25 of the Matrimonial Causes Act 1973; ss. 1 and 11(1) of the Marriage (Same Sex Couples) Act 2013.

[2] See s. 66 and Sch. 5 of the Civil Partnership Act 2004.

exceptional cases, be conclusive of the position. However, where there is no express declaration,[3] determining the ownership interests in the family home in these non-formalized contexts is a question of property law and is governed by general property law principles: land law and trusts.

This question of the acquisition of interests in the home is a matter of crucial importance to the everyday lives of many of us and will likely touch us all at some stage. Beyond its clear practical relevance, the law surrounding interests in the family home has also seen some of the most energetic judicial exposition and academic commentary in the whole of land law. It is perhaps the closest thing to a 'sexy' area of land law that there is! Flanked by two of the most significant property law decisions in recent times—*Stack v Dowden* (2007) and *Jones v Kernott* (2011)—this area has certainly excited much debate as the courts have grappled, in the absence of parliamentary intervention, to determine an apparently simple yet vital question over the family home: who owns what? As you will discover, property law principles are seen to bend to accommodate the domestic context and in response to the particular challenges presented when parties not only share their home but share their lives. This chapter is introduced by asking two key questions: first, why does the family home really matter and, secondly, when will having an interest in the home be important?

6.1.1 Why 'home' matters

We all know that feeling after a long day at work or at university. It comes in various permutations, but can be summed up by this essential sentiment: 'I can't wait to get home.' Home is special. Home is, we are told, where the heart is. Every Englishman's home is his castle, and so on. Yet pinning down why 'home' matters is not as straightforward as you might think. It is a distinctly fuzzy notion. It is perhaps one of the most emotionally loaded, most subjective concepts in the whole of property law. We know that 'home' is clearly something more than house. It is more than the physical bricks and mortar that keep the structure standing. As Rapoport[4] conceives of it: 'home = house + x' with that 'x' representing the socio-cultural and psychological values that attach to 'home' beyond its mere physical foundations. As Fox[5] identifies, home is, as a result, a fluid concept which embraces several meanings, a series of 'cluster value types' as Fox describes it. Putting the jargon to one side, Fox argues that there are four central values that can be attributed to home: see Figure 6.1.

The challenge is determining how the law should respond and accommodate these values. Land law with its primary focus on providing certainty, clarity, and order in dealings with land faces a dilemma. What weight to attach to subjective notions of home? Should we treat 'home' differently from, say, other residential spaces? How far should how land is used determine the legal principles that govern it? These are precisely the questions with which the courts are beginning to grapple in determining interests in the family home. Most importantly, the flexibility of implied trusts (in particular the constructive trust), which today take centre-stage in questions of the acquisition of

---

[3] Alternatively, where the validity of the express declaration is called into question.

[4] J. Rapoport, 'A Critical Look at the Concept "Home"' in D. N. Benjamin (ed.), *The Home: Words, Interpretations, Meanings and Environments* (Aldershot: Avebury, 1995).

[5] L. Fox, 'The Meaning of Home: A Chimerical Concept or a Legal Challenge?' (2002) 24(9) Journal of Law and Society 580.

Figure 6.1 The four cluster value types to be attributed to 'home'

interests in the home, has given the courts the opportunity to take far greater account of the wider context in which people share land as their family home. Home, is, therefore a special type of property and one which raises distinct problems for law-makers and the judiciary. It calls on us to consider psychology, sociology, and perhaps even family law. For doctrinal land lawyers, 'home' therefore presents something of a headache but an issue that the courts simply cannot side-step. We will see in this chapter just how the courts have managed this difficult balancing act.

6.1.2 **When will having an interest in the home matter?**

So, the message is clear: 'home' matters but when, precisely, will having an interest in the home be important? Remember, that we only look to property law principles to determine interests in the family home when dealing with a non-married, non-civil partnered cohabiting couple or family members purchasing property and where there is no express declaration as to how the property is held. There are several circumstances in which it will be important to determine who enjoys an ownership interest in the family home. The Law Commission in its Report No. 278[6] identified four key examples:

- Where one party (typically in a cohabiting couple) leaves the family home usually after relationship breakdown: The question arises as to whether the party leaving has an interest in

---

[6] Law Commission Report No. 278, *Sharing Homes: A Discussion Paper* (2002).

the property. If so, can the property be sold so that they can get access to their share in the proceeds of sale?

- Where one party (typically in a cohabiting couple) sharing the family home has died: The question arises as to whether the deceased had an interest in the property. If so, what happens to that interest now?

- Where the family home is subject to a mortgage and the borrower has defaulted on mortgage payments: Here, when the mortgage lender seeks possession and sale of the property, the question arises whether those living in the home can assert an interest and prevent sale.

- Where a creditor is owed a debt not secured on the family home but nevertheless seeks sale of the home to satisfy the debt: The question arises as to whether any person can assert an interest in the property and resist sale.

As Baroness Hale noted in *Stack*, the need to resolve questions of ownership of the family home has taken on particular significance in recent decades:[7]

> The first development is, of course, the huge expansion in home ownership which has taken place since the Second World War and was given a further boost by the 'right to buy' legislation of the 1980s. Coupled with this has been continuing house price inflation, albeit with occasional interruptions such as occurred at the end of the 1980s. This has meant that it is almost always more advantageous for someone who has contributed to the acquisition of the home to claim a share in its ownership rather than the return of the money contributed, even with interest.

In the absence of a statutory scheme to determine property disputes involving cohabiting couples or family members purchasing property, it falls to property principles to determine the issue. As you will see in this chapter, this is achieved by looking to the intentions of the parties: how did the parties intend the property to be held? A person cannot, as the law currently stands in this jurisdiction, therefore acquire an interest on the basis of what the court considers to be a fair outcome.

As Dillon LJ explained in *Springette v Defoe* (1992), the court does not sit under a palm tree to exercise a general discretion to do what the man in the street on a general overview of the case must regard as fair.[8] Whilst not bending to 'palm tree justice', the courts in determining the acquisition of interests in the family home have had to respond, however, and adapt to the changing social backdrop against which such claims reach court. In particular, the courts have needed to accommodate the changing socio-economic make-up of the country and the increasing number of couples choosing to cohabit without formalizing their relationship through marriage or civil partnership. According to the Office of National Statistics Families and Households Statistics 2019, the cohabiting family continues to be the fastest growing family type in the UK, as it has been for several years, with some 3.5 million cohabiting family households. This amounts to 18.4 per cent of all families in the UK and represents an increase of over 25 per cent since 2008. As the data consistently exposes, many of the growing number of cohabiting couples still believe in the existence of 'common law marriage' under which, despite not being married or civil partnered, it is perceived that cohabitants are entitled to the same legal rights as their

---

[7] *Stack*, [41], per Baroness Hale.   [8] *Springette*, 557, per Dillon LJ.

counterparts in formalized relationships. There is no such thing as 'common law marriage' and they do not have these rights. When the rude awakening comes, these cohabiting couples are forced to fall back on property principles to argue they enjoy an interest in the family home.

The court has not sat idly by as the social make-up of Britain has shifted. One expression of this is seen in what Dewar[9] termed the 'familialization' of property law principles. As Dewar and Hayward[10] have explored, 'familialization' describes the phenomenon whereby the court, in the family home context, applies principles of land law or trusts law in a manner customized—adapted—to accommodate the specific needs of family members. The courts have been particularly active in this field of property law, perhaps more than any other, but this activism and 'familialization' must be viewed against a background of Parliament's refusal to intervene with legislation to provide a statutory system for determining property rights of cohabitants. In the vacuum left by Parliament's non-intervention, it means that the determination of interests in the family home is made by reference to established principles of resulting and constructive trusts as modified to offer a more fact-sensitive, context-appropriate, and 'familialized' system of rules. The result, according to the Law Commission in its Report No. 278, is a body of law which is:[11]

> unduly complex, arbitrary and uncertain in application . . . ill-suited to determining the property rights of those who, because of the informal nature of their relationship, may not have considered their respective entitlements.

The challenge in this chapter is therefore twofold: to expose the complexity and uncertainty in the area but, crucially, to provide a clear and structured approach to analysing how parties acquire interests in the family home. With this in mind, the chapter begins by exploring the role of trusts in the acquisition of interests in the home. We touch on express trusts before turning to implied trusts where our focus is on the '**common intention constructive trust**', which is now the central vehicle for acquiring rights in the domestic context. We consider proposals for reform of the law and close the chapter by considering how Parliament has intervened to also confer so-called 'home rights' to allow occupation of a family home in the absence of any proprietary interest.

 Visit the online resources to watch a video on modern land of trusts in the family home.

6.2 The role of trusts in the family home

In Chapter 5, we saw that concurrent co-ownership of land necessarily involves the imposition of a trust: the trust of land. Co-ownership of a family home, too, operates under a trust of land and the acquisition of interests in the home is therefore governed by trust principles. How does a person acquire rights in the family home under a trust? The first thing to note is that there is more than one 'type' of trust. As we saw in section 1.6.3, a trust

---

[9] J. Dewar, 'Land, Law and the Family Home' in S. Bright and J. Dewar, *Land Law: Themes and Perspectives* (Oxford: Oxford University Press, 1998) and (1998) 61 MLR 467.

[10] A. Hayward, 'Family Property and the Process of Familialisation of Property Law' (2012) 24(3) Child and Family Law Quarterly, 284.

[11] Law Commission Report No. 278, [1.1].

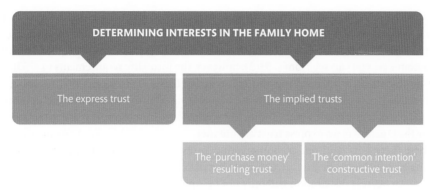

Figure 6.2 Determining interests in the family home

is an ingenious device which allows ownership of property to be divided between the 'legal' and 'equitable' ownership interests. The legal title to property is held by one or more people known as 'trustees'; the equitable title is held by those entitled to the benefit of the property known as 'beneficiaries'. The trustees are subject to a range of duties as well as enjoying powers (under TOLATA 1996)) over the land which they hold and manage for the benefit of the beneficiaries.[12] Trusts can be express—in other words, expressly created by the parties who declare a clear intention that the property is to be held on trust. Trusts can also be implied—a category which is subdivided into resulting and constructive trusts: Figure 6.2. Implied trusts, unlike express trusts, generally arise based on the presumed intentions of the parties. Let's first consider how a person may acquire an interest in the family home by way of express trust. We can deal with this briefly.

6.3 The express trust

An express trust is by quite some way the easiest method by which a person can acquire an interest in the family home. In practice, though, many interests in the home are not acquired this way. An express trust is a trust that arises from the explicit and expressed intentions of the parties. Parties can only make a valid declaration of an express trust over land if certain formality requirements are satisfied: s. 53(1)(b) and (2) of the LPA 1925:

(1) ...

   (b) a declaration of trust respecting any land or any interest therein must be manifested and proved by some writing signed by some person who is able to declare such trust or by his will;

(2) This section does not affect the creation or operation of resulting, implied or constructive trusts.

Imagine, for example, that Anish and Briony expressly declare that the family home is held on trust for them both as beneficiaries. If this declaration of trust is not 'manifested and

---

[12] We explored some of these in section 5.7.

proved by some writing' and signed, no valid express trust has been created. There can be no oral declaration of a trust over land. If, however, Anish and Briony declare their trust in writing, signed by the parties, a valid trust arises and both parties have an equitable interest in the home. As you can see from s. 53(2), however, the formality requirements in s. 53(1)(b) need not be satisfied for resulting and constructive trusts. This means that resulting and constructive trusts can be created without any writing whatsoever. As you can appreciate, these 'implied' trusts become very important where there is no express trust or the formalities for the creation of an express trust are not met.

Where there is a valid declaration creating an express trust, this is generally regarded as being conclusive, both that a trust exists but also how the property is held and in what shares.[13] An express declaration will only not be conclusive where the terms of the declaration can be shown to have been varied by subsequent agreement of the parties, are affected by proprietary estoppel,[14] or tainted by fraud or undue influence.

6.4 The implied trusts: The 'purchase money' resulting trust

A second route by which a person can acquire an interest in the home is by way of an implied trust. These are either 'purchase money' **resulting** trusts or 'common intention' constructive trusts. You will study resulting trusts in far greater detail as part of your Trusts Law course. The 'purchase money' resulting trust arises where one party makes a contribution to the purchase price of property but that contributor's name is not on the legal title. This category of resulting trust was identified by Eyre CB in *Dyer v Dyer* (1788):[15]

> [T]he trust of a legal estate . . . whether taken in the names of the purchasers jointly, or in the names of others without that of the purchaser; whether in one name or several; whether jointly or successive, results to the man who advances the purchase-money.

As Lord Reid clarified in *Pettitt v Pettitt* (1970), where a purchase money resulting trust arises, the party making the contribution to the purchase price gains an equitable interest in the property. As to quantifying the interest, or in other words, determining the size of the share, under a 'purchase money' resulting trust, the interest acquired is proportionate to the contribution made.[16] An illustration will help you grasp this: imagine Christy and Bilal both contribute towards the purchase of a property but the property is purchased in Christy's name only. Christy contributes £200,000 while Bilal contributes £100,000. There is a rebuttable presumption that Bilal did not intend to make a gift of the £100,000 without receiving an equitable interest in the property in return. Therefore, Christy is taken to hold the property on trust for herself and Bilal, both being equitable owners. This result is achieved by implying a purchase money resulting trust. Bilal enjoys an equitable entitlement in the property of one-third share, corresponding to the size of his contribution.

---

[13] *Goodman v Gallant* (1986); confirmed recently in *Pankhania v Chandegra* (2013).

[14] *Stack*, [49], per Baroness Hale; see also discussion in C. Bevan, 'The Search for Common Intention: The Status of an Executed, Express Declaration of Trust Post-*Stack* and *Jones*' (2019) 135(4) LQR 660.

[15] *Dyer*, 43.   [16] *Springette*.

Table 6.1 Contributions giving rise to presumption of resulting trust

NATURE OF CONTRIBUTION	AN EFFECTIVE CONTRIBUTION?	
Direct cash contribution or money raised by mortgage	YES	*Burns v Burns* (1984): direct, financial contributions suffice though no such contribution on the facts of this case
Contribution to deposit or legal, conveyancing expenses	YES	*Midland Bank v Cooke* (1995)
Discount or reduction in purchase price	YES	*Mumford v Ashe* (2000); *Springette v Defoe* (1992)
Payment of mortgage instalments	?	*Gissing v Gissing* (1971): mortgage payments should suffice—no resulting trust on the facts *Curley v Parkes* (2004): mortgage payments will not suffice—no resulting trust on the facts *Laskar v Laskar* (2008): mortgage payments did suffice (investment context)—resulting trust established on the facts
Household expenses	NO	*Burns v Burns* (1984)

6.4.1 What constitutes a contribution?

The purchase money resulting trust springs from a contribution made towards the purchase price of property. But, what suffices as a contribution for this purpose? We know that where one party contributes a sum of money directly to the purchase price, this amounts to a sufficient contribution: *Burns v Burns* (1984). But beyond this? See Table 6.1.

Mortgage repayments and household expenses have proved to be the most controversial. As to household expenses, it seems beyond doubt that household expenditure will not amount to a contribution for the purpose of establishing a resulting trust. This is perhaps unsurprising given that the resulting trust, by its essential nature, is concerned with and responds to financial contributions which are referable to the acquisition of proprietary interests. Household, domestic, or other living expenses are clearly not referable. Lord Diplock in *Gissing v Gissing* (1971) indicated, however, that mortgage payments should suffice as they are 'no less relevant' to the parties' common intention to share ownership than payment of a cash deposit.[17] Despite Lord Diplock's comments, the court in *Curley v Parkes* (2004) refused to accept that payments in the form of mortgage instalments could logically be regarded as part of the purchase price. Peter Gibson LJ concluded that these payments are sums paid to discharge the mortgage obligations and had nothing to do with the price paid to the vendor of the land. More recently in *Laskar v Laskar* (2008), the Court of Appeal was prepared to accept that mortgage instalments amounted to a contribution to the purchase price in a case where a mother and daughter had purchased a property as an investment rather than as a home. Further support is found in the minority judgment of Lord Neuberger dissenting in *Stack* who argued that mortgage instalments post-purchase should suffice as retrospective contributions to the purchase price. *Laskar* should be seen as reflecting the current if not finally settled position on the issue.

---

[17] *Gissing*, 906, per Lord Diplock.

6.4.2 **Rebutting the presumption of resulting trust**

The presumption of a 'purchase money' resulting trust is a *rebuttable* one. If evidence can be adduced to demonstrate that the contribution was made as a gift or on the basis of a loan,[18] the presumption will be rebutted and no resulting trust will arise. Where the presumption is rebutted, the party in whose name the property was purchased will be absolutely entitled to the land and the contributor has no interest in it at all. One way of demonstrating that the contribution was made by way of a gift is under what is known as the 'presumption of advancement'. Where the presumption operates, the contribution made is presumed to be a gift and that the contributor did not intend to acquire an interest in the property. The presumption springs from the relationship of the parties, has its provenance in the Victorian era, and derives from the moral obligations existing between certain individuals. Consequently, the categories in which this presumption arises are somewhat outmoded and, arguably, sexist. The presumption of advancement arises where there is a transfer:

- from a father to child: *Re Roberts* (1946); *Antoni v Antoni* (2007);
- from a husband to wife: *Pettitt* (1970);
- from a person *in loco parentis* to a child: *Hepworth v Hepworth* (1870).

Crucially, no presumption of gift arises where there is a transfer from a mother to her child, nor from a wife to husband or from cohabitee to cohabitee. The presumption of advancement is clearly biased against women and those in less formalized relationships. The Law Commission in its Report No. 278 even indicated this may infringe Art. 5 of Protocol 7 of the ECHR, which guarantees equal rights between spouses. The courts have attempted to modernize the presumption—suggesting it should be extended to transfers from mother to child (*Laskar*) and today its role is seriously diminished and of little meaningful significance. As Lord Neuberger explained in *Stack*, the presumption is mortally wounded and heavily weakened yet it clings on. Parliament has made provision for the abolition of the presumption[19] but this provision has not been brought into force and there must now be real doubt as to whether it ever will. The presumption cannot, therefore, be written off as an irrelevance. It will, though, be easily rebutted. The presumption is rebutted by evidence of the true intentions of the contributor—in other words, evidence that the party making the contribution did not intend a gift but instead intended to acquire an interest in the property.[20]

6.4.3 **Illegal purposes**

The court will not permit a person to rely on evidence of an illegal activity or illegal motives in order to rebut either the presumption of resulting trust or the presumption of advancement. Until recently, the leading case on illegal purpose was *Tinsley v Milligan*.[21] *Tinsley* provided for the 'reliance principle', which held that a person could not rely on

---

[18] *Re Sharpe (A Bankrupt)* (1980).   [19] Under s. 199 of the Equality Act 2010.
[20] *Warren v Gurney* (1944); *McGrath v Wallis* (1995).
[21] On which see P. S. Davies, 'The Illegality Defence: Turning Back the Clock' [2010] Conv 282; also *Gascoigne v Gascoigne* (1918) where a husband took a lease of land in his wife's name to defeat his creditors and prevent them from gaining possession of his property.

an illegal purpose or illegal motive to establish an equitable interest but any illegality was irrelevant if an interest could be established without needing to rely on it. The Supreme Court in *Patel v Mirza* (2016)[22] rejected the *Tinsley* approach as overly-technical and leading to arbitrary results. The majority held that whether a claim should be allowed was to be determined by considering three things: (1) why the alleged illegal conduct had been made illegal in the first place; (2) any public policy that might be affected by denying the claim; (3) the proportionality of denying the claim. Various factors would be relevant to this proportionality exercise including the seriousness of the conduct, its centrality to any contract or agreement, and whether there was a marked disparity in the parties' respective culpability. There was, however, no closed list of relevant factors to be considered. The minority, in dissenting, regarded this 'range of factors' test as potentially giving rise to wasteful, uncertain and unnecessary litigation. Today, *Patel* must therefore be applied and not *Tinsley*. Yet, despite this, the same result would, in any event, have been reached on the facts of *Tinsley*.

6.4.4 The relevance of the resulting trust today and mixed contexts

The precise scope, role, and importance of the purchase money resulting trust in the family home today was considered directly in the two headline decisions in this area: *Stack* and *Jones*. We examine these cases in detail in section 6.6 on joint legal ownership. Strong views were voiced. In short, the effect of *Stack* and *Jones* taken together is that, where property is purchased as a family home, the resulting trust no longer applies and, in its place, a constructive trust analysis takes centre stage. The court in both cases considered (Lord Neuberger dissenting in *Stack*) that the resulting trust was too narrow, too artificial, and too fixated on financial contributions to be the most appropriate vehicle for determining ownership of the family home. Domestic relationships, said the court, are complex, multifaceted and warranted a broader, more flexible approach than was provided by the resulting trust.[23] Baroness Hale in *Stack* noted that in law 'context is everything'[24] and identified:[25]

> [a] new pragmatism . . . apparent in the law of trusts. English courts have eventually conceded that the classical theory of resulting trusts, with its fixation on intentions presumed to have been formulated contemporaneously with the acquisition of title, has substantially broken down . . . the undoubted consequence is that the doctrine of resulting trust has conceded much of its field of application to the constructive trust, which is nowadays fast becoming the primary phenomenon in the area of implied trusts.

In a joint judgment, Lord Walker and Lady Hale in *Jones* explained that:[26]

> The time has come to make it clear, in line with *Stack v Dowden* . . . in the case of the purchase of a house or flat in joint names for joint occupation by a married or unmarried couple, where both

---

[22] On which see A. Grabiner, 'Illegality and Restitution Explained by the Supreme Court' (2017) 76(1) CLJ 18.

[23] See *Stack*, per Lord Hope, [3] that 'living together is an exercise in give and take, mutual co-operation and compromise . . . a more practical, down-to-earth . . . approach is called for'.

[24] Ibid., [69], per Baroness Hale.

[25] Ibid., [60], per Baroness Hale citing K. Gray and S. Gray, *Elements of Land Law* (2009), 864.

[26] *Jones* (2012), [24]–[25].

are responsible for any mortgage, there is no presumption of a resulting trust arising from their having contributed to the deposit (or indeed the rest of the purchase) in unequal shares.

As you can see, these remarks were confined to cases where cohabiting couples acquired a property as a family home and the property is purchased in their *joint names*. This leaves unresolved the question of the role of the resulting trust where property is placed in one party's name but the other has also contributed. That said, it is clear from the general tenor of the case law that the rigidity and artificiality of the resulting trust has given way to the more pragmatic, flexible constructive trust in family home cases. This arguably allows greater justice to be done to claimants who are statistically more likely to be women and, in turn, still (lamentably) the less economically powerful.[27]

So, when will a resulting trust analysis now be applied? It had seemingly been settled following *Stack*, *Jones* and *Laskar* that the starting presumptions as to the acquisition and quantification of interests in property under implied trusts were as follows: in the domestic or family home context, we would apply a common intention constructive trust analysis; in the commercial/investment context, we would apply a presumption of resulting trust analysis. However, things are not quite that straightforward. One particularly intriguing area has been so-called 'mixed contexts' (i.e. contexts which are part domestic, part commercial/investment). Here, which analysis should be applied: resulting or constructive trust? Well, it very much depends on the circumstances of the case and decisions of the court have gone both ways. So, in *Laskar*, where a mother and daughter purchased a property as a buy-to-let investment property, a resulting trust analysis was applied. By contrast, in *Adekunle v Ritchie* (2007), where a mother and son purchased a house as a family home, constructive trust principles were applied. Equally, in *Gallarotti v Sebastianelli* (2012), where two friends bought a flat together, again a constructive trust analysis was employed. These cases must now be read in light of the significant decision in *Marr v Collie* (2017) which indicates a growing role for the constructive trust in investment and mixed contexts. In this important judgment, the Privy Council has rather thrown the cat among the pigeons in suggesting that a constructive trust analysis should not be confined to the 'purely domestic setting' and could operate in investment contexts. *Marr* is an important decision and is worth reading in full.

KEY CASE *Marr v Collie* (2017)

Facts: Terry Marr and Bryant Collie had been in an intimate relationship for around 15 years and lived in the Bahamas. During the relationship, various properties had been purchased and registered in their joint names including at Harbour Island and South Westbridge. Mr Marr, a banker, had paid the purchase prices and fees for the properties and, when the relationship broke down in 2009, sought

→

---

[27] For feminist perspectives on the family home, see, amongst others: R. Auchmuty, 'Unfair Shares for Women: The Rhetoric of Equality and the Reality of Inequality' in H. Lim and A. Bottomley (eds.), *Feminist Perspectives on Land Law* (Abingdon: Routledge-Cavendish, 2007); A. Bottomley, 'From Mrs. Burns to Mrs. Oxley: Do Co-Habiting Women (Still) Need Marriage Law?' (2006) 14(2) Feminist Legal Studies 181; S. Wong, 'The Iniquity of Equity: A Home-Sharer's Tale' (2008) Singapore Journal of Legal Studies (December) 326; S. Wong, 'Shared Commitment, Interdependency and Property Relations: A Socio-Legal Project for Cohabitation' (2012) 24(1) Child and Family Law Quarterly 60.

a declaration that he was entitled to the full beneficial ownership of all of them. Mr Collie, a building contractor, argued that his role was as renovator of the properties and that the couple had always intended that the properties would be shared equally.

Legal Issue: What was each party's beneficial entitlement to the properties? Was Mr Marr the sole beneficial owner or, as Mr Collie argued, were they tenants in common in equal shares? What was the appropriate starting point in a case concerning a domestic relationship but one in which property had been purchased for commercial purposes?

Judgment: At first instance, the judge held that the *Stack* presumption of joint beneficial ownership under a constructive trust was confined to cases of purely domestic context (following *Laskar*). The properties in issue were purchased as investments and so a presumption of resulting trust arose which Mr Collie was not able to rebut. On appeal to the Bahamas Court of Appeal, the court held that Mr Collie's insistence that the properties were not investment properties was unsustainable in view of clear and repeated assertions by the parties. The court accepted that there was clear evidence that Mr Marr intended Mr Collie to enjoy an equal share of the Harbour Island purchases (not the South Westbridge property, however). Emphasis was placed on an email sent by Mr Marr to a bank admin clerk in which he discussed the joint purchase of property at Harbour Island and noted that this meant 'that we would [each] have a 50% interest'. On this basis, the presumption of resulting trust in favour of Mr Marr had been rebutted and the parties held the properties as tenants in common in equal shares. Mr Collie's appeal regarding a property at South Westbridge and a number of paintings failed.

Mr Marr appealed and before the Privy Council, argued: (1) the email regarding Harbour Island was inadmissible. It was a piece of evidence that had not appeared in the agreed court bundle and should therefore not be taken into account; (2) alternatively, the Bahamas Court of Appeal had placed too great a weight on the email and invested it with a significance it did not warrant; the email having been sent before acquisition of the property and, therefore, did not constitute direct evidence of Mr Marr's intentions; (3) additionally, the trial judge had been correct to apply the resulting trust presumption as the properties were purchased as investments and the Court of Appeal had wrongly interfered with findings of fact at first instance.

In the Privy Council, the panel comprised Lord Neuberger (who dissented in *Stack* and adjudicated in *Laskar*), Lady Hale (who delivered the leading judgment in *Stack* and jointly in *Jones*) Lords Wilson and Kerr (who dissented in *Jones*) and Lord Sumption. Lord Kerr, who gave the sole judgment of the court, allowing the appeal held:

1. Citing Australian authorities, 'it is the Board's views that to consign the reasoning in *Stack* to the purely domestic setting would be wrong'. There was no reason to doubt that Hale's presumption of equitable joint tenancy had 'possible applicability to property purchased by a couple in an enterprise reflecting their joint commercial as well as . . . personal, commitment'. Hale in *Stack* was clear the presumption was not intended to be confined solely to the domestic setting. Where a property was bought in the joint names of a couple, even as an investment, it did not follow necessarily that the 'resulting trust solution' had to be used to determine beneficial ownership. It was conceivable that a couple in a personal relationship might purchase an investment property conveyed in their joint names with the intention of sharing the beneficial ownership equally even if they had contributed in different shares to the purchase price.

2. A 'simplistic' approach might be that, 'if the property is purchased in joint names by parties in a domestic relationship the presumption of joint beneficial ownership applies but if bought in a wholly non-domestic situation it does not . . . [and] the resulting trust presumption obtains'. However, there is no clash of resulting trust/common intention constructive trust presumptions and no one triumphs over the other.

→

→

3. The parties' common intentions and context are key to determining whether joint equitable ownership should follow joint legal ownership or if a resulting trust analysis would be more appropriate; this was not undermined by the decision of *Laskar*: '[I]f it is the unambiguous mutual wish of the parties, contributing in unequal shares to the purchase of property, that the joint beneficial ownership should reflect their joint legal ownership, then effect should be given to that wish.' However, '[i]f, on the other hand, that is not their wish, or if they have not formed any intention as to beneficial ownership but had, for instance, accepted advice that the property be acquired in joint names, without considering or being aware of the possible consequences of that, the resulting trust solution may provide the answer'.

4. The Court of Appeal had failed to consider the finding of the instance judge that Mr Marr did not intend to share equally in equity and Mr Marr's claim that Mr Collie had agreed to make equal contribution to development of the properties. It was wrong to base its judgment on an email that Mr Marr was not permitted to challenge in the court.

5. The case was remitted to the Bahamas Supreme Court for a full consideration of the parties' respective common intentions concerning the investment properties.

As Sloan and George, exploring the case, have noted:[28]

> The impact of the Privy Council's decision in *Marr v Collie*, however, appears to be that ... the categorisation of a case as 'commercial/investment' will not necessarily preclude the operation of the Stack presumption [though] the converse may also be true and such an approach based on categorisation has been branded 'simplistic' ... the essential problem is that while both the resulting trust and the Stack presumption could be rebutted by evidence of some contrary common intention about their ownership, their very purpose is to provide a starting point where such evidence might be insufficiently clear. If both presumptions depend on an analysis of the parties' common intention before they arise in the first place, even after a case has been categorised, that function is lost ... It is also difficult to see how this contextual approach laid out in *Marr v Collie* might work in practice. Suppose that evidence is adduced that A and B did not wish their joint legal ownership of the property to be reflected as joint beneficial ownership. According to Lord Kerr, a resulting trust solution may provide the answer in these cases, but that could also constitute one of the factors to rebut the presumption of joint beneficial ownership under a constructive trust. That wish, in other words, does not of itself tell a court which trust path to take in the absence of a prior presumption about which framework is more appropriate to apply to the dispute between A and B.

What is the status of the *Marr* decision or, in other words, how seriously will the English courts take it? Several points can be made:

- On the one hand, *Marr* is a decision of the Privy Council and so is not binding precedent on English courts; English courts ought not follow a Privy Council decision if it is inconsistent with a decision under usual precedent rules.

- On the other hand, decisions of the Privy Council have been confirmed recently as being of 'great weight and persuasive value' by the Supreme Court recently in *Willers v Joyce (No. 2)* (2016).

---

[28] M. George and B. Sloan, 'Presuming Too Little about Resulting and Constructive Trusts? *Marr v Collie* [2017] UKPC 17' (2017) 4 Conv 303–12; see also A. Y. S. Georgiou, '*Marr v Collie*: The Ballooning of the Common Interest Constructive Trust' (2019) 82(1) MLR 145.

- Perhaps we should take the case of *Marr* as providing 'guidance' only as to how *Stack*, *Jones*, and *Laskar* operate?

- The Privy Council has the capacity to declare that an English case is wrong—but, in *Marr*, chose not to do this. Instead Lord Kerr argued the constructive trust analysis was never intended to be confined to the domestic context. Was this simply pragmatism and the court not wishing to contradict the English court? Certainly, academic opinion largely felt the distinct starting points in domestic and commercial cases was settled.

- The panel membership of the Privy Council in *Marr* is also significant; representing the leading judges (including dissentients) from *Stack* and *Jones*—seminal cases on interests in the family home. Surely, this adds weight to the judgment in *Marr*?

Imagine you are a judge in an English court, what would you do? Follow *Stack*, *Jones*, and *Laskar* as a matter of strict precedent or apply the reasoning of Lord Kerr in *Marr*? Has the Privy Council brought more confusion than clarity to an already vexed area of the law? If followed in English courts, will *Marr* lead to increased litigation as commercial parties fight over disputed common intentions rather than the more straightforward resulting trust analysis? Does *Marr*'s blurring of the lines between domestic/investment context add unnecessary complexity to the law?

What we can say is that whilst the resulting trust is not dead yet and will likely still play a role in pure commercial/investment scenarios, its application is diminishing. Instead, in contexts which are domestic and mixed domestic/commercial in nature, the constructive trust more and more takes centre stage and is increasingly regarded as the primary vehicle for determination of interests in property.[29]

6.5 The implied trusts: The 'common intention' constructive trust

The second implied trust to be considered is the constructive trust. The constructive trust is easily the most elastic and yet least well-defined category of trusts in English property law. As Lord Scott observed in *Yeoman's Row Management Ltd v Cobbe* (2008):[30]

> It is impossible to prescribe exhaustively the circumstances sufficient to create a constructive trust but it is possible to recognise particular factual circumstances that will do so and also to recognise other factual circumstances that will not.

The absence of a strict definition does, however, have its advantages and the constructive trust has evolved into a malleable device, particularly in the context of the family home. It was Edmund Davies LJ in *Carl Zeiss-Stiftung v Herbert Smith & Co. (No. 2)* (1969) who noted the constructive trust's potential as a vehicle for doing justice between the parties:[31]

> English law provides no clear and all-embracing definition of a constructive trust. Its boundaries have been left perhaps deliberately vague, so as not to restrict the court by technicalities in deciding what the justice of a particular case may demand.

---

[29] See also the decision in *Gallarotti v Sebastianelli* (2012) which seems to confine the role of the resulting trust still further: discussed in section 6.7.2.

[30] *Yeoman's Management Ltd v Cobbe*, 1769, per Lord Scott.

[31] *Carl Zeiss-Stiftung (No. 2)*, 300, per Edmund Davies LJ.

This is not the place for a discussion of all the circumstances in which the constructive trust operates. For us, we are concerned with what has become known as the 'common intention constructive trust'. Under the 'CICT', as it is often written shorthand, a claimant can establish an interest in the family home by demonstrating that she and the legal owner of property shared an express or implied 'common intention' that the claimant was to enjoy a proprietary interest and, further, that the claimant relied on that intention to her detriment. If a claimant succeeds in demonstrating this common intention plus detrimental reliance, a constructive trust arises under which the property is held on trust by the legal owner for that legal owner and the claimant in equity. Recall that under s. 53(2) of the LPA 1925 a constructive trust need not be in writing nor be evidenced in writing to operate. It was the decisions of *Stack* and *Jones* that really put the constructive trust front and centre of the determination of interests in the domestic, family home context. There is absolutely no substitute for reading these cases in full. In fact, every student coming to this topic really must do this.

Just as we did in our discussion of the resulting trust, in analysing the CICT we must again return to the distinction between two distinct 'stages' of our enquiry: namely (1) *acquisition* of an interest in the family home and (2) *quantification* of that interest. For a claimant to succeed, she must show that she actually has first acquired an interest under a CICT before the court will proceed to consider the quantification—the extent—of that interest (i.e. what size of share should she get): Figure 6.3. Each step must be considered and analysed quite separately.

6.5.1 The need to distinguish joint and sole ownership cases

In addition to considering the two separate stages of a claim to a CICT, following *Stack* and *Jones*, we are directed to distinguish between two types of case: *joint* legal ownership cases and *sole* legal ownership cases. A joint legal ownership case is one in which the legal title in

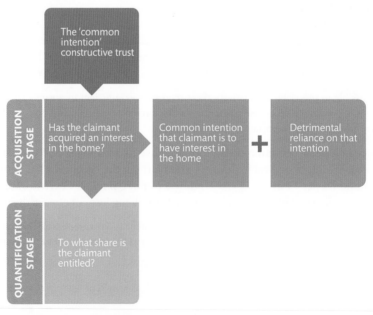

Figure 6.3 The acquisition and quantification stages

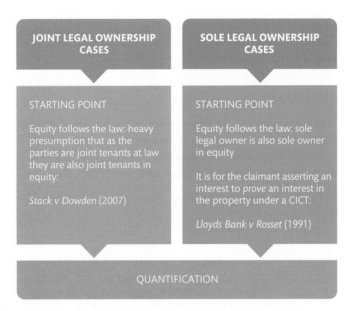

Figure 6.4 The differing 'starting points' in joint and sole legal ownership cases

the family home is conveyed into the names of the claimant and another person but there is no declaration as to extent of each party's share in equity. A sole legal ownership case is one where the legal title in the family home is conveyed to just one person (i.e. the claimant's name is not on the legal title). Why does this distinction matter? As Lord Walker and Lady Hale explained in *Jones*, the distinction matters because the 'starting point' for analysis of each scenario is quite different and therefore each must be kept separate. Attempts to argue that the starting point should be the same for both types of scenario have, for now at least, been resisted by the court.[32] The court in *Thompson v Hurst* (2014), for example, held that conflating joint and sole ownership cases was 'neither consistent with principle nor sound policy'.[33] We must therefore examine joint and sole cases quite discretely.

As Figure 6.4 depicts, the essential difference is that for joint ownership cases, the starting point is a rebuttable presumption that the parties hold as joint tenants in equity. By contrast, in sole ownership cases, the legal owner is regarded, prima facie, as the sole equitable owner. In sole cases, it is therefore for the claimant to *prove* that she has an interest in the property. The distinction between joint and sole cases is therefore centred on the differing evidential burdens shouldered by the parties.

6.6 Joint legal ownership cases

6.6.1 The acquisition stage: Establishing an interest

In a joint legal ownership case where legal title in the family home has been conveyed into joint names, the issue of acquisition of an interest is settled: each party already has an interest by reason of their holding the property jointly. This is because, as we found in

---

[32] We return to this issue in section 6.9.   [33] *Thompson v Hurst*, [20], per Etherton LJ.

Chapter 5,[34] co-ownership necessarily operates behind a trust. The conveyance into joint names relates to the extent of the interests in the home rather than to acquisition. We can therefore jump straight to the quantification stage.

6.6.2 **The quantification stage**

Where legal title is in joint names but the conveyance does not declare the extent of each party's respective share, quantification is determined according to the principles laid down by the House of Lords in *Stack* and clarified by the Supreme Court in *Jones*. Lord Walker and Lady Hale in *Jones* set out a summary of the relevant principles in joint ownership cases:[35]

> In summary, therefore, the following are the principles applicable in a case such as this, where a family home is bought in the joint names of a cohabiting couple who are both responsible for any mortgage, but without any express declaration of their beneficial interests.
>
> (1) The starting point is that equity follows the law and they are joint tenants both in law and in equity.
> (2) That presumption can be displaced by showing (a) that the parties had a different common intention at the time when they acquired the home, or (b) that they later formed the common intention that their respective shares would change.
> (3) Their common intention is to be deduced objectively from their conduct: 'the relevant intention of each party is the intention which was reasonably understood by the other party to be manifested by that party's words and conduct notwithstanding that he did not consciously formulate that intention in his own mind or even acted with some different intention which he did not communicate to the other party' (Lord Diplock in *Gissing v Gissing* [1971] AC 886, 906). Examples of the sort of evidence which might be relevant to drawing such inferences are given in *Stack v Dowden*, at para 69.
> (4) In those cases where it is clear either (a) that the parties did not intend joint tenancy at the outset, or (b) had changed their original intention, but it is not possible to ascertain by direct evidence or by inference what their actual intention was as to the shares in which they would own the property, 'the answer is that each is entitled to that share which the court considers fair having regard to the whole course of dealing between them in relation to the property': Chadwick LJ in *Oxley v Hiscock* [2005] Fam 211, para 69. In our judgment, 'the whole course of dealing . . . in relation to the property' should be given a broad meaning, enabling a similar range of factors to be taken into account as may be relevant to ascertaining the parties' actual intentions.
> (5) Each case will turn on its own facts. Financial contributions are relevant but there are many other factors which may enable the court to decide what shares were either intended (as in case (3)) or fair (as in case (4)).

There is a lot to take in here and so we need to unpack how all this hangs together. We need to consider a number of points:

- the starting point: a presumption of equitable joint tenancy;
- rebutting the presumption of equitable joint tenancy;

- the search for common intention;
- shifting or 'ambulatory' common intention.

6.6.2.1 Starting point: A presumption of equitable joint tenancy

In joint ownership cases, the starting point is a presumption of equality, of sharing, in equity. In other words, where there are two parties who are legal owners, each has an entitlement to a 50 per cent share in equity. If either party believes they are entitled to a greater share than 50 per cent, they bear the burden of demonstrating that the presumption of equality has been rebutted. The nature of the rebuttable presumption of equitable joint tenancy was explained in *Stack*.[36]

KEY CASE *Stack v Dowden* (2007)

Facts: Mr Stack and Ms Dowden lived together for almost 20 years as cohabitants and had four children. They purchased a home in their joint names with no express declaration as to the extent of their respective shares in equity. The family home was funded by the sale of their previous property (which had been held in Ms Dowden's sole name only), with Ms Dowden's savings and with the assistance of a mortgage loan in joint names. Both parties contributed towards the mortgage payments but Ms Dowden undertook the greater burden. For the length of their relationship, the parties kept their financial affairs entirely separate. Nine years after purchasing the family home, the relationship broke down and Mr Stack left the home. Mr Stack, subsequently, secured a declaration from the court that the home was held on trust for both parties in equal shares and an order for sale. Miss Dowden appealed claiming a greater share in the property than the 50 per cent declared, and, in the Court of Appeal, succeeded in establishing a 65 per cent share—35 per cent to Mr Stack. Mr Stack appealed to the House of Lords seeking reinstatement of the original declaration that each party was entitled to a 50 per cent share in the proceeds of sale.

Legal issue: What was the extent of each party's respective share in the property? Did a conveyance into joint names establish a presumption of equal shares in equity?

Judgment: In the House of Lords, the court unanimously agreed on the starting point in joint ownership cases (Lord Neuberger dissenting but on a different point). The court held that the starting point was a rebuttable presumption of equitable joint tenancy. The onus was then on the person seeking an unequal share in equity to show that the parties intended their beneficial interests to be other than equal. Context was everything and each case turned on its facts. The presumption of beneficial joint tenancy was however a heavy one that would only be rebutted in a 'very unusual' case. Baroness Hale explained:

> The burden will therefore be on the person seeking to show that the parties did intend their beneficial interests to be different from their legal interests, and in what way. This is not a task to be lightly embarked upon. In family disputes, strong feelings are aroused when couples split up. These often lead the parties, honestly but mistakenly, to reinterpret the past in self-exculpatory or vengeful terms. They also lead people to spend far more on the legal battle than is warranted

→

---

[36] On which generally see: N. Piska, 'Intention, Fairness and the Presumption of Resulting Trust after *Stack v Dowden*' (2008) 71(1) MLR 114; R. Probert, 'Equality in the Family Home? *Stack v Dowden* (2007)' (2007) 15 Feminist Legal Studies 341, 348.

➡

by the sums actually at stake. A full examination of the facts is likely to involve disproportion-ate costs. In joint names cases it is also unlikely to lead to a different result unless the facts are very unusual.

The onus lay firmly on Ms Dowden to show that there was a common intention to share other than equally in equity. On the facts, there were several factors on which she could rely. Key amongst them was the fact the parties had lived together for many years and yet had kept their finances rigidly sepa-rate. This indicated strongly that the parties did not intend their shares to be equal and warranted Ms Dowden receiving a greater share. This was, therefore, a 'very unusual case' that did justify rebuttal of the presumption of equitable joint tenancy. Ms Dowden was entitled to a 65 per cent share in the proceeds of sale as the Court of Appeal had declared.

6.6.2.2 Rebutting the presumption of equitable joint tenancy

The presumption of equitable joint tenancy can therefore be rebutted by showing (1) that the parties had a different common intention at the time when they acquired the home or (2) that they later formed a common intention that their respective shares would change.

In considering whether the presumption of equitable joint tenancy has been rebutted, Baroness Hale gave guidance in *Stack* as to the sort of factors that would be relevant. These have become known as the 'paragraph 69 factors'. As she explained:[37]

Many more factors than financial contributions may be relevant to divining the parties' true intentions. These include: any advice or discussions at the time of the transfer which cast light upon their intentions then; the reasons why the home was acquired in their joint names; the reasons why (if it be the case) the survivor was authorised to give a receipt for the capital moneys; the purpose for which the home was acquired; the nature of the parties' relationship; whether they had children for whom they both had responsibility to provide a home; how the purchase was financed, both initially and subsequently; how the parties arranged their finances, whether separately or together or a bit of both; how they discharged the outgoings on the property and their other household expenses . . . The parties' individual characters and personalities may also be a factor in deciding where their true intentions lay. In the cohabitation context, mercenary considerations may be more to the fore than they would be in marriage, but it should not be as-sumed that they always take pride of place over natural love and affection.

Whilst helpful, the paragraph 69 factors do not take us that far in deciphering precisely when the presumption will be rebutted except that 'many factors' beyond money are said to be rel-evant. Importantly, despite insistence that money is not determinative, it was organization of the parties' financial affairs in *Stack* that justified rebuttal of the presumption. Again money ruled the day in the case of *Fowler v Barron* (2008) though in this case the presumption was ultimately not rebutted as the parties' financial arrangements constituted nothing 'unusual' and were akin to 'one pool' from which household expenses were to be paid.[38] If the pre-sumption is rebutted, it falls to the court to determine the size of the share to which each party is entitled (i.e. to quantify the shares).

---

[37] *Stack*, [69].
[38] For a discussion of *Fowler* see A. Hayward, 'Family Values in the Home: *Fowler v Barron*' (2009) 21(2) CFLQ 242.

6.6.2.3 The search for common intention

Baroness Hale in *Stack* explained that the 'the search is to ascertain the parties' shared intentions, actual, inferred or imputed, with respect to the property in the light of their whole course of conduct in relation to it'.[39] As to the difference between inference and imputation, the court held that:[40]

> An inferred intention is one which is objectively deduced to be the subjective actual intention of the parties, in the light of their actions and statements. An imputed intention is one which is attributed to the parties, even though no such actual intention can be deduced from their actions and statements, and even though they had no such intention. Imputation involves concluding what the parties would have intended, whereas inference involves concluding what they did intend.

But *Stack* left questions unanswered, in particular, when a court is permitted to infer and when to impute an intention to the parties. The nature of the 'search' for common intention was clarified by the Supreme Court in *Jones* in which the court (unanimously) set down clear principles on when the court can impute an intention and when it cannot. In effect, the court drew a distinction between what we can term 'the sharing' and 'the shares' questions:

- The sharing question: When it comes to determining whether the presumption of equitable joint tenancy has been rebutted, the *actual* common intention of the parties is sought and, only where this is unknown or unclear, is the court permitted to *infer* a common intention based on the conduct of the parties. There can be no imputation at this acquisition stage. Often at the acquisition stage of jointly owned property, there is little to do! Easily more contested is the issue of quantification (i.e. who gets what share).

- The shares question: When it comes to determining the proportion or extent of the parties' respective shares, again the search is to ascertain the parties' common intention. The court begins by looking for an actual or inferred intention. If no actual or inferred intention can be found, the court is permitted to *impute* an intention to the parties. The test for imputation is that laid down by Chadwick LJ in *Oxley v Hiscock* (2004), namely that 'each is entitled to that share which the court considers fair having regard to the whole course of dealing between them in relation to the property'.[41]

In summary, whilst there can be no imputation of a common intention at the acquisition stage in addressing 'the sharing question', the court is permitted to impute at the quantification stage when considering the 'the shares question.' This distinction was recently confirmed in *Barnes v Phillips* (2015).[42]

Following *Stack* and *Jones*,[43] we waited to see how imputation would work in practice. Though the court is still very much feeling its way on this, a useful insight was provided in the case of *Aspden v Elvy* (2012). Having established an interest in the family home under

---

[39] *Stack*, [60].   [40] Ibid., [126], per Lord Neuberger.   [41] *Oxley*, [69].

[42] Note: HHJ Mostyn in the recent case of *Rothschild v De Souza* (2018) suggested that the court could impute an agreement as to beneficial ownership (i.e. at the acquisition stage). Respectfully, this must be challenged as being out of line with authority. Reaction to this judgment from the academic world has been swift, critical, and dismissive.

[43] Both of which involved inference of intention (though Lords Kerr and Wilson in Jones advanced arguments on the basis of imputation).

a constructive trust, the court moved to consider the extent of Mr Aspden's interest. The court could find no express agreement as to the proportion of the shares intended and so proceeded to impute a share of 25 per cent to Mr Aspden. This decision is useful in exposing some of the difficulties with imputation. First, it is unclear why the court jumped to imputation without first considering inferring a common intention as to shares. Secondly, as HHJ Behrens admitted in *Aspden* itself, imputation is necessarily 'somewhat arbitrary' and the 25 per cent figure was 'the best' he could do 'with the available material'. The arbitrariness of imputation is evident and clearly problematic. Once the court has concluded that no express agreement (or inferred agreement) as to shares can be found, reaching a figure as to the precise proportion of the share can be deeply subjective in the view of the particular judge deciding the case and not guided by any clear rule or principle. This does, however, permit justice to be done by reference to the particular facts of the case. We see this problem again in the case of *Graham-York v York* (2015).[44] In the Court of Appeal in *York*, the court stressed that, in imputing a share:[45]

> the court is not concerned with some form of redistributive justice. Thus it is irrelevant that it may be thought a 'fair' outcome for a woman who has endured years of abusive conduct by her partner to be allotted a substantial interest in his property on his death. The plight of Miss Graham-York attracts sympathy, but it does not enable the court to redistribute property interests in a manner which right-minded people might think amounts to appropriate compensation. Miss Graham-York is 'entitled to that share which the court considers fair having regard to the whole course of dealing between them *in relation to the property*'. It is these last words, which I have emphasised, which supply the confines of the enquiry as to fairness.

Gardner[46] has argued that without a guiding thesis as to the precise operation of imputation, the case law will lack the clarity needed to do consistent justice in future cases. Gardner therefore proposes a way forward, a novel approach to imputation, based on whether the relationship of the parties is 'materially communal' or 'non-materially communal':

> [T]he common intention imputed to parties having a materially communal relationship will give them equal shares in the house . . . while that imputed to parties not having such a relationship . . . will give them shares proportionate to their individual contributions to the acquisition of the house, though indirect contributions will count as much as direct ones. A 'materially communal' relationship is one in which C and D in practical terms pool all their material resources (including money, other assets, and labour), rather than keeping separate tallies. The presence of a joint bank account will strongly, almost conclusively, suggest a materially communal relationship, but its absence will not particularly prove the opposite. The parties' having, or not having, a sexual relationship will prove nothing either way; likewise even their having children together, though in this event it is probably commoner for their relationship to be materially communal. If they are married or civil partners, their relationship will necessarily be regarded as materially communal, regardless of the nature and scale of their contributions to the family economy . . . A non-materially communal relationship is one without this profile.

---

[44] A sole legal ownership case but nevertheless instructive as to the court's approach to imputation of a share and, in particular, how far fairness is a guiding force in the imputation exercise; on which generally see: S. Greer and N. Piska, 'Imputation, Fairness and the Family Home' [2015] Conv 512.

[45] *York*, [22], per Tomlinson LJ (emphasis added).

[46] S. Gardner, 'Family Property Today' (2008) 124 LQR 422, 431.

6.6.2.4 Shifting common intention: The 'ambulatory' trust

The courts have also recognized that the parties' common intentions can shift and change over time. This is called 'ambulatory' intent or an 'ambulatory trust'. Lord Walker and Lady Hale in *Jones* explained:[47]

> It [is] also accepted that the parties' common intentions might change over time, producing what Lord Hoffmann referred to in the course of argument as an '"ambulatory" constructive trust' . . . An example, given in para 70 [in *Stack*], was where one party had financed or constructed an extension or major improvement to the property, so that what they had now was different from what they had first acquired.

The case of *Jones*[48] itself provides an excellent example of this ambulatory trust and provides us with the opportunity to look more closely at what is a key decision in this area. Make sure you read it!

KEY CASE *Jones v Kernott* (2011)

Facts: Miss Jones and Mr Kernott purchased a property, 39 Badger Hall Avenue, in joint names in 1985 with the assistance of a mortgage. They lived together in the property and shared the household expenses for over eight years. In 1993, Mr Kernott moved out of the property but Miss Jones remained living there with their two children. She paid all the household expenses. Mr Kernott made no further payments towards the property. The parties agreed to cash in a life insurance policy and the proceeds were divided equally between them. This was done primarily to enable Mr Kernott to put down a deposit on a new home. This continued for over 14 years at which point the property was placed on the market to be sold. Mr Kernott brought proceedings seeking a declaration as to the equitable entitlements of each party in the property. A declaration was made in the county court that Miss Jones was entitled to a 90 per cent share and Mr Kernott a 10 per cent share. Mr Kernott appealed to the High Court. The High Court held that there had been a change in the intentions of the parties which could be inferred from the conduct of the parties. The trial judge's conclusion that the property be split 90–10 in Miss Jones' favour was appropriate. Miss Jones had contributed four times more than Mr Kernott and the larger part of the capital gain on the property had arisen after Mr Kernott's departure in 1993. Mr Kernott appealed to the Court of Appeal. The Court of Appeal allowed Mr Kernott's appeal holding, by a two to one majority, that the parties owned the property as tenants in common in equal shares in equity. Miss Jones appealed to the Supreme Court.

Legal issue: What was the extent of the parties' respective shares in 39 Badger Hall? Was there sufficient evidence to justify rebuttal of the presumption of equitable joint tenancy?

Judgment: Miss Jones' appeal was allowed in the Supreme Court and the 90–10 per cent split in miss Jones' favour as declared by the trial judge was reinstated. The Supreme Court confirmed that where property was purchased in joint names, there was a presumption of beneficial joint tenancy. This presumption could be rebutted by evidence of common intention to share other than equally. Any rebuttal of this presumption was, however, not to be lightly embarked upon as purchasing property jointly as a home indicated an emotional and economic commitment to a joint enterprise.

➡

---

[47] *Jones v Kernott* (2011), [14].

[48] On which see generally: B. Sloan, 'Keeping Up with the Jones Case: Establishing Constructive Trusts in "Sole Legal Owner" Scenarios' (2015) 35 LS 226; F. Garland, '*Jones v Kernott*' (2012) 34(4) Journal of Social Welfare & Family Law 479.

➡

In determining whether the presumption was rebutted the primary search was to ascertain the parties' common intention. Lord Walker and Lady Hale explained:

> We accept that the search is primarily to ascertain the parties' actual shared intentions, whether expressed or to be inferred from their conduct . . . where it is clear that the beneficial interests are to be shared, but it is impossible to divine a common intention as to the proportions in which they are to be shared . . . the court is driven to impute an intention to the parties which they may never have had.

In this case, there was no need for the court to impute an intention that the parties' beneficial interests would change as the trial judge had made a finding that the parties' intention did, in fact, change. This intention could be inferred from their conduct. At the outset when 39 Badger Hall was purchased, the common intention was to provide a home for Miss Jones, Mr Kernott, and their children. But their intentions changed. Around the time the life insurance policy was cashed in 'a new plan was formed' under which Mr Kernott would buy himself a new home. It was the 'logical inference' that his interest in Badger Hall Avenue was to crystallize at this time and Miss Jones would have the sole benefit of any capital gain in the property going forward. The result reached by the trial judge regarding the parties' respective shares was so close to that the Supreme Court would have imposed that it would be wrong to interfere with the trial judge's declaration which was reinstated.

A more recent example of ambulatory intent is found in the decision of *Barnes*;[49] a case which also involved the imputation of a common intention.[50]

KEY CASE *Barnes v Phillips* (2015)

Facts: Mr Barnes and Ms Phillips had been in a relationship since 1983 which had produced two children. In 1996, the couple purchased a property which was put into their joint names. Mr Barnes was self-employed and paid the mortgage as well as some of the bills. Ms Phillips worked full-time but had worked part-time when the children were young. During the relationship, Mr Barnes bought three investment properties all of which were registered in his name. In 2005, Mr Barnes was suffering with debt problems and the family home was remortgaged. Almost the entirety of the remortgage funds were exhausted paying off the existing mortgage and Mr Barnes' debts. In late 2005, the relationship broke down and Ms Phillips sought a declaration as to her interest under the property. The trial judge held that, at the time of the property's purchase, it was intended to provide a family home for the parties and their children. Subsequently, however, circumstances changed. In view of the remortgage and the fact the funds had been used to pay Mr Barnes' debts, the judge imputed an intention that the property was, at that time, held in shares of 75 per cent to Ms Phillips and 25 per cent to Mr Barnes. However, a further adjustment was needed in view of Ms Phillips's having taken financial responsibility for the children from 2008 onwards. The judge held that the property was held in shares of 85 per cent to 15 per cent in favour of Ms Phillips. Mr Barnes appealed.

Legal issue: Mr Barnes submitted that a judge could only impute a common intention as to shares if there had first been evidence that the presumption of equitable joint tenancy had been rebutted. This presumption could only be rebutted by evidence of an actual or inferred common intention

➡

---

[49] On which generally see: M. Pawlowski, 'Imputing Intention and the Family Home' (2016) 46(Feb) Family Law 189; A. Hayward, 'Common Intention Constructive Trusts and the Role of Imputation in Theory and Practice' [2016] Conv 227.

[50] See also the case of *Montalto v Popat* (2016).

→

to share other than equally. This step was missing from the trial judge's reasoning which seemingly jumped straight to imputation as to shares. Had it been open to the judge to impute an intention in these circumstances?

Judgment: The Court of Appeal held that the judge had been entirely correct in 'imputing' an intention to the parties. The judge had not confused 'inferring' with 'imputing'. The trial judge had used the word 'imputing' quite deliberately. The judgment was missing the first stage of the *Jones* process on whether there had been a common intention to share other than equally. Whilst the judge had not made explicit reference to any common intention to vary the shares, it was strongly arguable that the judge had nevertheless made this assessment albeit it was absent from his judgment. As a matter of principle, imputation was only possible at the second stage when determining the size of the respective shares and not when determining whether there had been a change in intention to share other than equally.

The weight of evidence supported an inference that the intentions of the parties had changed. The remortgage in 2005 operated to the sole benefit of Mr Barnes, to pay off his debts. After the remortgage, all monies remaining after paying off debts and the earlier mortgage went to Mr Barnes. The relationship ended soon after. It could be inferred from this that there was a common intention to vary their respective interests in the property. In addition, after 2008, Ms Phillips alone made mortgage payments. Mr Barnes would only have acted in this way and stopped making payments if there had been this change in intention.

Having inferred a common intention to vary their respective interests, it was appropriate for the judge to impute an intention to the parties as to their shares. The judge had reached an appropriate result in view of all the circumstances. It was also open to the court to take account of the payment and non-payment (as in this case) of child maintenance as part of the financial history of the case. This should only not be done where to take account of these matters would result in double liability. There was no double liability in this case.

Barnes therefore confirms that imputation of a common intention can only take place when determining the size of the parties' respective shares, but also demonstrates the apparent latitude given to the court in the imputation exercise. The Court of Appeal was prepared to overlook the trial judge's shortcomings in his analysis by assuming that the judge merely failed to include the first step of the *Jones* authority in his written judgment on the basis he must have considered this step albeit did not include it in his judgment. Did the Court of Appeal go too far in rescuing the trial judge's inadequate reasoning? For Hayward[51] this is a cause for concern:

The fact that HH Judge Madge shifted too readily towards imputing fair shares is controversial but perhaps not surprising. What is more concerning is the ease in which the Court of Appeal sought to minimise that oversight and revise the steps undertaken by the judge. Firstly, Lloyd Jones LJ stated that the first instance judge was 'well aware of the structure laid down in *Jones v Kernott*' as he had 'set it out in great detail in his judgment' . . . the Court of Appeal also concluded that HH Judge Madge:

---

[51] A. Hayward, 'Common Intention Constructive Trusts and the Role of Imputation in Theory and Practice' [2016] Conv 227, 247.

'. . . must have appreciated that there would be no point in discussing the shares in which the property is held following variation if no common intention to vary had been established.'

This reasoning is open to challenge. Of course a degree of deference should be given to the first instance judge who has seen and heard the litigants but here, and almost like an act of imputing intentions *to the judge* as opposed to the parties, additional steps in HH Judge Madge's analysis were simply assumed by the court. This approach is problematic on many levels but suggests that the judicial treatment of the distinction between inference and imputation, particularly in the lower courts, is not being rigorously policed.

Whatever our view of the trial judge's reasoning, the Court of Appeal in *Barnes* has affirmed the authority of *Jones* and reiterated the need to keep quite separate the acquisition and quantification stages.

6.7 Sole legal ownership cases

We have discussed joint ownership cases but what is the position where legal title is in one party's name only? Sole legal ownership cases are treated quite differently to joint legal ownership cases and different rules apply. The law on sole ownership cases was neatly summed by Lord Walker and Lady Hale in *Jones*:[52]

> [For] a family home which is put into the name of one party only . . . the starting point is different. The first issue is whether it was intended that the other party have any beneficial interest in the property at all. If he does, the second issue is what that interest is. There is no presumption of joint beneficial ownership. But their common intention has once again to be deduced objectively from their conduct.

The key differences between sole and joint ownership cases are therefore as follows:

1. In sole ownership cases, there is no presumption of equitable joint tenancy as exists for joint ownership cases.

2. In sole ownership cases, the starting point is different: where there is sole ownership at law there is a presumption of sole ownership in equity (as 'equity follows the law').

3. In sole ownership cases, it is for a claimant arguing that she enjoys an equitable interest in the home to prove she has acquired an interest.

Only where a claimant has demonstrated that she actually has an interest in the home, will the court then move to quantify that interest. Again, we need to consider the two stages of analysis: the acquisition and quantification stages.

6.7.1 The acquisition stage: Establishing an interest

As noted in the extract from *Jones*, in a sole legal ownership case, it is for the party claiming to have an interest to *prove* that they have acquired an interest. At the acquisition stage, proving an interest means demonstrating that there was a common intention to share

---

[52] *Jones*, [52].

the family home and the clamant relied on this common intention to her detriment. The leading authority on acquiring an interest in a sole ownership case is *Lloyds Bank v Rosset* which, despite coming in for quite some criticism from the court in *Stack* and *Jones* and from academics, has not been overruled and remains good law today. Let's take a closer look at the decision.

KEY CASE *Lloyds Bank v Rosset* (1989)

Facts: A husband and wife decided to purchase a derelict farmhouse to renovate in order to provide a family home for themselves and their two children. The property was purchased using money from the husband's family trust in Switzerland. The Swiss trustee insisted that the property be registered in the husband's sole name as this formed part of the trustee's duty under the terms of the trust to ensure trust money was used only to the advantage of the husband. The wife was fully aware of this arrangement. The vendors of the farmhouse permitted the husband and wife to enter the property with builders to carry out the renovation work before contracts were exchanged. The renovation was a joint endeavour and the wife herself carried out decoration work at the property on an almost daily basis as well as overseeing the building work. After contracts were exchanged but before sale of the property was completed, the husband, without the wife's knowledge, mortgaged the property. The sale was completed. The wife made no contribution to either the purchase price or the cost of renovations. Subsequently, the relationship between the parties broke down and the husband left the property. Mortgage payments were not made and the bank brought proceedings for possession and sale of the property. The wife resisted the claim from the bank on the basis that she enjoyed an equitable interest in the property under a constructive trust and her interest qualified as an overriding interest on the basis of her actual occupation (under the old law provision of s. 70(1)(g) of the Land Registration Act 1925).

Legal issue: Could the wife establish an equitable interest under a constructive trust which was binding on the bank?

Judgment: At first instance, the judge found that there had been a common intention between the husband and wife that the wife was to have an equitable interest in the property. This arose under a constructive trust. In carrying out the renovation work, she had relied on this common intention to her detriment. However, the wife had not been in actual occupation at the relevant time and so her interest did not bind the bank. The Court of Appeal, by a majority, allowed an appeal by the wife. In the House of Lords, the bank's appeal was allowed. The judge had erred in holding that there was sufficient evidence of a common intention that the wife should have an interest in the property. The judge had placed undue emphasis on the wife's renovation activities. The judge's finding of a constructive trust could not therefore be supported. In a leading judgment, adopted by all their other Lordships, Lord Bridge set out the two routes for the acquisition of an interest under a constructive trust in sole ownership cases: the first, being where there is evidence of an express bargain; the second, where an agreement can be inferred from direct contributions to the purchase price.

According to Lord Bridge in *Rosset*, an interest can be acquired in sole ownership cases in one of two situations which we can term 'Rosset 1' and 'Rosset 2': see Figure 6.5.

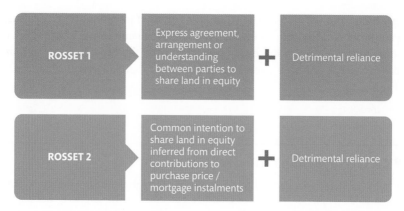

Figure 6.5 Acquiring an interest in the family home in sole ownership cases: Rosset 1 and 2

Before we get into the detail of each route, a few preliminary points should be borne in mind:

1. In sole ownership cases, as in joint cases, common intention is the central focus of acquisition of an interest in the family home. This common intention is demonstrated by words and conduct and can arise expressly under Rosset 1 or by inference under Rosset 2. Common intention cannot be imputed at the acquisition stage.

2. The common intention to share must exist between the claimant and legal owner of the home rather than a third party: *Smith v Bottomley* (2014). In *Smith*, Ms Smith claimed to have acquired an equitable interest in a barn. Her claim based on assurances made by her former cohabitee, Mr Bottomley, failed. The problem was that the barn had since become owned and controlled by Mr Bottomley's company which was a separate legal entity. There was no common intention to share in equity between Ms Smith and the company.

3. Whilst a common intention to share will commonly arise at the time of the purchase of the home, it may also arise subsequently: *James v Thomas* (2007).[53] It will, however, be harder to demonstrate this common intention after purchase as Sir John Chadwick explained:[54]

[I]n the absence of an express post-acquisition agreement, a court will be slow to infer from conduct alone that parties intended to vary existing beneficial interests established at the time of acquisition.

It is important to note the criticism that Lord Bridge's approach to acquisition in sole ownership cases has attracted. Fox O'Mahony,[55] amongst others, raises the concern that *Rosset* protects financial contributions and clearly expressed intentions and has:

---

[53] Affirmed in *Aspden*.   [54] *James*, [24].

[55] L. Fox O'Mahony, 'Property Outsiders and the Hidden Politics of Doctrinalism' (2014) 67 CLP 409, 430–1.

embedded a deeply conservative vision of property, in which claimants are judged for their conduct against normative expectations that favour acquisitive-individualism over family-communitarianism, self-interest over trust, and the 'tidy lives' of consent, private ordering, and capital investment over non-financial contributions and the messy realities of family life.

The argument can be made that the *Rosset* approach is unduly narrow permitting acquisition of an interest only where there is either an express agreement to share or payments made to the purchase price. This test has the great advantage of certainty (which should not be derided) but it also excludes, as Fox O'Mahony argues, a vast swathe of everyday and important aspects of family life which could demonstrate a common intention to share. In *Stack* itself, *Rosset* came under scrutiny, with Lord Walker (seemingly with the agreement of Baroness Hale) noting the 'trenchant criticism' the decision had received and arguing that, at least in her view, 'the law had moved on'. Lord Reid's judgment in *Gissing* though clearly preceding *Rosset* is also often cited as raising concerns that the acquisition of interests in the home should not depend on the precise time a contribution is made or on how a family organizes its finances:[56]

> Suppose . . . spouses have a joint bank account. In accordance with their arrangements [the wife] pays in enough money to meet the household bills and so there is enough to pay the purchase price instalments and their bills as well as their personal expenses. They never discuss whose money is to go to pay for the house and whose is to go to pay for other things. How can anyone tell whether she has made a direct or only an indirect contribution to paying for the house? It cannot surely depend on who signs which cheques. Is she to be deprived of a share if she says 'I can pay in enough to pay for the household bills', but given a share if she says, 'I can pay in £10 per week regularly'.

As a matter of precedent, however, *Rosset* remains binding and a Supreme Court decision dealing with sole ownership cases would be required to overrule it.

With these opening observations in mind, let us consider in more detail Lord Bridge's two routes to acquisition of an interest in sole ownership cases: Rosset 1 and Rosset 2.

6.7.1.1 Rosset 1: Express bargain constructive trust

An express bargain constructive trust will arise where there is evidence of an express agreement, arrangement, or understanding between the parties that the home is to be shared beneficially (i.e. shared in equity) and the claimant has relied on this agreement, arrangement, or understanding to her detriment.

Express bargain

According to Lord Bridge, an express bargain requires 'evidence of express discussions between the partners, however imperfectly remembered and however imprecise their terms may have been'.[57] In *Springette*, the Court of Appeal expanded on what was understood as an express bargain. According to *Springette*, for an express bargain to arise the parties' common intentions must have been 'communicated between them'.[58] An uncommunicated intention, said the court, was insufficient. In the family home context, there is surely an air of unreality here. Most personal or intimate relationships move to the beat of their

---

[56] *Gissing*, 896–7.   [57] *Rosset*, 132.   [58] *Springette*, 557.

own distinctive drum and parties are unlikely to sit down and 'communicate' their shared intentions in the way *Rosset* and *Springette* envisages. Lord Hodson recognized this in *Pettitt* noting as 'grotesque' the prospect of couples spending long winter evenings hammering out agreements over their property.[59]

The sense of pretence surrounding express bargains reaches its nadir with what have become known as the 'excuse' cases: *Eves v Eves* (1975), *Grant v Edwards* (1986), and *Hammond v Mitchell* (1992). In these cases, the court accepted that where one party had given an excuse as to why only one name appeared as legal owner on the title, this was enough to establish an express agreement to share in equity. This is striking because, it could be argued that the excuse is evidence of precisely the opposite conclusion—evidence of an absence of common intention to share. The judgments in these 'excuse' cases are unquestionably policy-based and grounded in the sympathy felt by the court for the party to whom the excuse was made. That is not to suggest sympathy was not deserved and indeed the defendants (all men) certainly behaved appallingly!

KEY CASE *Eves v Eves* (1975)

Facts: In 1968, Janet Eves, who was at the time under 21, began living with Stuart Eves and though not married took his name. In 1969, the couple had a daughter and they found a house which they intended to become their joint family home. The house was purchased in late summer of 1969 and placed in Stuart Eves' name only. Stuart told Janet that her name could not be on the title as she was under 21 and that, had she been older, the house would have been purchased in joint names. This was an excuse and not accurate in law. The property was run-down, very dirty, and dilapidated. Janet carried out much work on the property both in the house and in the garden. In particular, this involved wielding a 14lb sledgehammer to break large areas of concrete. A second child was born in 1970. In 1972, Stuart informed Janet that he was to marry another woman and later left the home. Subsequently, Janet made an application to the court seeking an equitable share in the house. At first instance, the court rejected her claim. Janet appealed.

Legal issue: Was there evidence of a common intention between Janet and Stuart to share the property in equity?

Judgment: Janet's appeal was successful. The court held that there had been an agreement to share the property in equity and Janet therefore enjoyed a 25 per cent interest in the property. The excuse given by Stuart was evidence that Janet had been led to believe that she was to have an interest in the home. She had relied on this in carrying out renovation, demolition, and other improvement works on the property.

KEY CASE *Grant v Edwards* (1986)

Facts: Linda Grant separated from her husband and set up home with George Edwards. In 1969, George purchased a house to provide a home for the couple, their child, and two children from Linda's marriage. The house was conveyed into George's name (and that of his brother) but not into Linda's name. George told Linda that her name was not included on the title as this might prejudice her divorce proceedings with her former husband. This was an excuse. George paid the deposit and

→

---

[59] *Pettitt*, 810.

> →
>
> mortgage instalments, Linda made substantial contributions to the household expenses. The couple split in 1980 and Linda claimed a beneficial interest in the property. The claim was dismissed at first instance. Linda appealed.
>
> Legal issue: Could Linda demonstrate a common intention to share the property in equity?
>
> Judgment: The Court of Appeal allowed the appeal. The court found that there was an agreement to share as evidenced by the excuse given by George for Linda's name not being on the title. This excuse raised an inference that Linda should have an interest in the house. Linda had acted in reliance on this agreement to her detriment in making substantial contributions to the household expenses. These contributions were far in excess of what would be expected as 'normal' contributions. Without these contributions, George would not have been able to maintain mortgage payments. Linda was awarded a 50 per cent share in the property.

These 'excuse' cases[60] demonstrate the inevitable artificiality in the approach taken by the court in the search for common intentions and they remain controversial however sympathetic one might be to the parties and the outcomes. One particularly strident and resonant voice here is Gardner[61] who blasts the reasoning of the court:

> If I give an excuse for rejecting an invitation to what I expect to be a dull party, it does not mean that I thereby agree to come: on the contrary, it means that I do not agree to come, but for one reason or another find it hard to say so outright. The fallacious quality of the reasoning in *Eves* v *Eves* and *Grant* v *Edwards* is thus clear. It is hard to think that the judges concerned really believed in it. One can only conclude that they too were engaged in the business of inventing agreements on women's behalf . . . All this is certainly no advertisement for the transparency of the law.

The Law Commission agreed with Gardner; acknowledging that in these cases there was no true 'common intention' or express bargain.[62] Do you agree? Note, however, not all the cases go the same way and in *Curran v Collins* (2015) the court rejected an argument by Ms Curran that she had an interest in properties purchased from the 1970s to 2010 but placed in the sole name of her partner, Mr Curran, based on apparent 'excuse'. Mr Curran had told her that the properties were in his sole name as to do otherwise would have prompted his mortgage lenders to insist that he take out a second life insurance and that this would incur unnecessary expense. Ms Curran's claim that this was an 'excuse' in line with *Eves* and *Grant* was rejected. Lewison LJ in the Court of Appeal distinguished the case on the basis that in *Eves* and *Grant* the properties were acquired as family homes and, secondly, there were positive assertions that but for the circumstances giving rise to the 'excuse' the claimant's names would have been on the title. Neither of these factors existed in Ms Curran's case. Equally, Ms Curran could not demonstrate the required detrimental reliance. As Lewison LJ explained:

> [I]t cannot be right that the giving of a reason why someone is not on the title deeds inevitably leads to the inference that it must have been agreed that they would have an interest in the property. If one who is not versed in the difference between legal and beneficial ownership asks to be

---

[60] See also *Hammond v Mitchell*, where an excuse not to include a partner on the legal title was made on the false grounds of tax arrangements and impending divorce proceedings.

[61] S. Gardner, 'Rethinking Family Property' (1993) 109 LQR 263, 265.

[62] Law Commission Report No. 278, [2.68].

on the deeds and is told 'No', the more usual inference would be that they would have understood that they were not to become owners or part owners of the property. I cannot see that the result is very different if the reason given is that it is too expensive. There are, however, two cases in which a specious excuse has been held to give rise to the inference of a constructive trust. However, these cases are fact-sensitive and need to be carefully examined.

Detrimental reliance

Establishing an express bargain to share in equity is not, of itself, enough. The claimant must, additionally, have acted to her detriment in reliance on that agreement, arrangement, or understanding. It is essential that the claimant acted to her detriment or significantly altered her position in reliance on the belief that she was to acquire a beneficial interest in the home (*Midland Bank Ltd v Dobson* (1986)). Detrimental reliance is assessed objectively but what counts as detriment? The leading authority on detriment is *Grant* itself. Nourse LJ, Mustill LJ, and Browne-Wilkinson V-C all took divergent approaches as to what was required in terms of detriment which demonstrates a measure of flexibility in this requirement. Let's take a look at how each judge framed this element:

- Nourse LJ explained that detriment required the court to look to whether the claimant has acted in a way that she could not reasonably be expected to do unless she was to have an interest.[63] The wielding of a 14lb sledgehammer in *Eves* was, as such, sufficiently detrimental.

- Mustill LJ's 'test' was founded on a contractual analysis which requires evidence of a quid pro quo between the claimant and the legal owner. The claimant must act in such a way as to 'complete' the bargain by way of conduct that is 'referable' to that bargain.[64]

- Browne-Wilkinson V-C adopted an altogether more flexible stance. For Browne-Wilkinson, once a common intention is evidenced 'any act done by her to her detriment relating to the joint lives of the parties'[65] can qualify as detriment and need not be directly referable to the property.

While three 'tests' of detriment emerged from *Grant*, subsequent case law has largely adopted the approach of Nourse LJ in looking for acts which would be unreasonable for the claimant to have undertaken but for the existence of a common intention to share in equity. Lawson[66] explains the logic behind Nourse LJ's test for detriment:

> Nourse L.J.'s test rests on the assumption that certain types of behaviour can reasonably be expected of people who believe that they have an interest in their home, but not of people who have no such belief. If the behaviour is of a type that can reasonably be expected of people acting purely out of love and affection or the desire to live in pleasant, comfortable surroundings, it will not normally be considered detrimental. It may be so regarded, however, if it was actually requested by the legal owner as the quid pro quo for the beneficial interest.

Table 6.2 considers what will and will not amount to acts of detriment.

---

[63] *Grant*, 648. [64] Ibid., 652. [65] Ibid., 656.
[66] A. Lawson, 'The Things We Do for Love: Detrimental Reliance in the Family Home' (1996) 16(2) LS 218, 219.

Table 6.2 What constitutes detriment?

ACTIVITY	SUFFICIENTLY DETRIMENTAL?	
Direct financial contribution to purchase price	YES	Financial contributions are perhaps the clearest example of a claimant's detriment (discussion in *Rosset* (1989)).
Indirect financial contributions to household expenses	YES	*Grant v Edwards* (1986)—substantial contributions to household expenses without which legal owner could not have met mortgage payments.
Substantial improvements to family home	YES	*Eves v Eves* (1975)—wielding of 14lb sledgehammer, extensive decoration, renovation of house and garden.
Minor improvements/redecoration of a purely 'ephemeral' nature	NO	*Pettitt v Pettitt* (1970)—Lord Reid noting that minor improvements which were 'ephemeral' or temporary in nature would not suffice: 'Redecoration will only last for a few years and it would be unreasonable that a spouse should obtain a permanent interest in the house in return for making improvements of this character.'
Acts of love and affection	NO	*Stack* (2007) per Baroness Hale—mere acts of love and affection will be insufficient detriment as they are a 'reasonable' part of intimate relationships.

For Lawson, the results arrived at in the case law are 'arbitrary and unrealistic' and Browne-Wilkinson's test should be adopted:[67]

> During the course of [intimate] relationships, the parties will inevitably change their positions in all sorts of ways and for all sorts of reasons . . . some of this arbitrariness cause by the operation of the detrimental reliance requirement . . . would be avoided if the approach advocated by Browne-Wilkinson V.C. in *Grant v Edwards* were adopted. He believed that acts which could easily be attributed to love and affection, such as setting up house together or having a baby, should be regarded as capable of amounting to detrimental reliance.

In addition to the requirement of detriment, those detrimental acts must also have been carried out *in reliance* on the common intention to share. Reliance requires a causal connection between the detrimental acts and the common intention to share. The leading case on reliance is the proprietary estoppel decision of *Wayling v Jones* (1993)[68] where Balcombe LJ laid down the test for reliance which applies equally to estoppel cases as it does to constructive trusts in the family home:[69]

(1) There must be a sufficient link between the promises relied upon and the conduct which constitutes the detriment . . .

(2) The promises relied upon do not have to be the sole inducement for the conduct: it is sufficient if they are *an* inducement—*Amalgamated Property Co. v. Texas Bank*.

---

[67] Lawson, 'The Things We Do for Love: Detrimental Reliance in the Family Home', 220.
[68] We explore this case in detail in section 8.3.4.   [69] *Wayling*, 173.

(3) Once it has been established that promises were made, and that there has been conduct by the claimant of such a nature that inducement may be inferred then the burden of proof shifts to the defendants to establish that he did not rely on the promises—*Greasley v. Cooke*; *Grant v. Edwards.*

Points (1) and (2) are self-explanatory. Point (3) requires some clarification. Although there has been no constructive trust case dealing directly with this issue, it seems that once detrimental acts have been proved and the necessary causal link between these acts and the common intention to share also demonstrated, the burden shifts to the defendant (the legal owner) to positively disprove reliance. A defendant can do this by showing that the claimant would have acted in the same way irrespective of the common intention to share equitable ownership in the property.

6.7.1.2 Rosset 2: Inferred bargain constructive trust

Where there is no express agreement, arrangement, or understanding that the parties are to share in equity, there may nevertheless be an inferred bargain to this effect. This is Rosset 2. Lord Bridge explained how this works:[70]

[D]irect contributions to the purchase price by the [party] who is not the legal owner, whether initially or by payment of mortgage instalments, will readily justify the inference necessary to the creation of a constructive trust. But, as I read the authorities, it is at least extremely doubtful whether anything less will do.

On a strict reading of Lord Bridge's judgment, an inferred bargain constructive trust will only therefore arise where the claimant has either:

1. contributed to the initial purchase price of the home, or
2. made mortgage payments post-purchase.

Once a direct financial contribution (to purchase price or mortgage instalments) has been proved, it must also be shown that the claimant relied on the common intention to their detriment. In a Rosset 2 scenario, this is easily satisfied. The conduct giving rise to the inference of a common intention to share will typically be taken as evidence of the claimant's detrimental reliance.

We close this section by reflecting on Lord Bridge's insistence in *Rosset* on a direct financial contribution. The effect of this is that indirect financial contributions and non-financial contributions falling outside these two categories will not give rise to an inferred common intention to share the family home in equity:

- Indirect financial contributions for example to the household expenses including paying utility bills and decorating are insufficient: *Burns.*
- Payments in relation to upkeep of the garden, furniture, and clothes for the family are insufficient: *Gissing.*
- Non-financial contributions to the household and other 'domestic' obligations such as looking after children are insufficient: *Burns.*
- Overseeing the renovation of the family home, organizing builders, and assisting with decoration is insufficient: *Rosset.*

---

[70] *Rosset*, 133.

We noted earlier in this section that the decision in *Rosset* has met with significant opposition from academics and in *Stack* yet has not been overruled. With its sharp focus on financial contributions, Rosset 2 is narrowly drawn. It is worth pausing to reflect on whether a more flexible approach should be adopted. Should, for example, indirect financial contributions be enough for an inferred bargain constructive trust under Rosset 2? The clear words of Lord Bridge that a direct financial contribution is needed and that he was 'doubtful whether anything less will do' mitigate against this and a Supreme Court judgment would be needed to overrule *Rosset*. That said, there is a body of support for adopting a more liberal approach:

- There is dicta from Lords Pearson and Diplock in *Gissing* that indirect financial contributions to the household expenses are sufficient where they are 'referable to the acquisition of the property'.[71]

- In the decision of *Le Foe v Le Foe* (2001) Nicholas Mostyn QC accepted that the wife's indirect financial contributions gave rise to a common intention to share beneficially as part of a 'family economy' thesis. According to this thesis, an indirect financial contribution necessarily frees up the legal owner to, for example, pay the mortgage instalments. *Le Foe* was, however, a first instance decision which has not been expressly followed since and which did not make references to case law which clearly affirmed the orthodoxy of *Rosset*.[72] This appears to render the *Le Foe* decision *per incuriam*.

- *Stack* and *Jones* may signal a move away from the narrow focus of *Rosset* towards a more holistic, broader, more flexible 'contextual' approach to the domestic, family home context. Though the issue of overruling *Rosset* was not a live one in *Stack*, Lord Walker 'respectfully doubted' *Rosset*, arguing that 'the law has moved on' and that a wider view of what is 'capable of counting as a contribution towards acquisition'[73] should be taken. Baroness Hale agreed adding that the hurdle may have been set 'rather too high'[74] in *Rosset*.

Serious doubt has therefore been cast on the strictness of the *Rosset* approach. Where does this leave the argument on a more flexible approach? Well, *Le Foe* has not been followed but also not overruled, but neither has *Rosset* been overruled. *Stack* is best seen as the judiciary sending a clear and unsubtle message to Parliament to legislate in this area and perhaps that, if Parliament is slow to act, the court will in an appropriate case in the future see fit to recast the law. Until then, the strictness of *Rosset* remains and should be applied in sole-ownership cases.

6.7.2 The quantification stage: What share?

Once a claimant has acquired an interest under Rosset 1 or Rosset 2, it comes to quantifying that interest: in other words, determining the share to which the claimant is entitled. The quantification stage is often far more controversial as, in many cases, there may be little dispute that the claimant actually enjoys an interest in the property but real disagreement

---

[71] See also judgment of Fox LJ in *Burns*.
[72] Including *Ivin v Blake* (1993) and *McFarlane v McFarlane* (1972).   [73] *Stack*, [34], per Lord Walker.
[74] Ibid. [63].

over what share. The court adopts the same approach to quantification in sole ownership cases as it does in joint ownership cases.[75] You will recall from section 6.6.2 Lord Walker and Lady Hale's summary of the law on quantification as laid down in *Jones*. In practice, this means:

1. The court will look for an express common intention as to size of each party's respective share. Where there is an express agreement, the court will give effect to it.

2. Where there is no evidence of express or actual common intention as to shares, the court will infer a common intention as to shares from the conduct and words of the parties judged objectively.

3. Only where there is no actual common intention and no possibility of inferring an intention will the court then proceed to impute an intention awarding a share as is considered 'fair having regard to the whole course of dealing between them in relation to the property'.[76] At the imputation stage, the court adopts a 'holistic' approach taking close account of all the circumstances of the case and whether the parties' intentions have changed over time.

A case which demonstrates the court's 'broad brush' approach to quantification is *Gallarotti v Sebastianelli*.[77]

KEY CASE *Gallarotti v Sebastianelli* (2012)

Facts: Two friends, Gallarotti and Sebastianelli bought a flat together. Sebastianelli paid £86,500 towards the purchase price; Gallarotti paid around £26,900. The flat was conveyed into Sebastianelli's name only. The purchase was also assisted by way of a mortgage. Sebastianelli paid the mortgage repayments. The parties' friendship came to an end and Gallarotti sought a declaration as to his interest in the flat. At first instance, the court found that Gallarotti and Sebastianelli had expressly agreed that would each have a 50 per cent share in the equity in the flat despite their unequal contributions but this had not been the subject of an express declaration. The court gave effect to the parties' express agreement and found a 50–50 split in equity. Sebastianelli who had made the greater contribution and paid the mortgage instalments appealed.

Legal issue: Had the court been right to conclude that the friends shared the property equally in equity?

Judgment: The Court of Appeal allowed the appeal, looked beyond the express agreement, and awarded Sebastianelli a 75 per cent share to reflect his greater contribution. The court held that:

1. On quantification, the court looked at the conduct of the parties throughout their entire relationship. Unlike a resulting trust analysis, under a constructive trust the court was not limited to examining financial contributions made at the time of the purchase. The constructive trust was far more flexible.

→

---

[75] *Jones*, [52].   [76] Ibid. [51].

[77] For another example, see the discussion of *York* in section 6.6.2.

2. Although the parties were friends and not husband and wife, the same principles on quantification applied.

3. The express agreement as to shares between the parties had to be examined closely. The agreement provided that each party have a 50 per cent share but also contained a rider that Gallarotti was to make larger contributions to the mortgage payments. There was little evidence that Gallarotti had made any contribution to the mortgage at all. It had, therefore, to be considered whether the agreement was still applicable at the end of the relationship.

4. In light of the events which unfolded, the agreement did not apply. The agreement anticipated that there would be only a slight 'imbalance' in contributions. This was not the reality. The agreement reflected that the parties intended the beneficial ownership of the flat to reflect their financial contributions.

5. The trial judge had erred in not taking account of how circumstances had changed and how the reality of contributions differed from the agreement. The court should have taken into account that Gallarotti had made no substantial contribution. The 50–50 agreement was clearly at an end.

The recorder's decision was set aside and shares in equity were split 75–25 in favour of Sebastianelli.

6.7.3 Constructive trusts and illegality

Where there is a claim to an interest in the family home founded on a common intention constructive trust, that claim will fail if the claimant needs to rely on an illegal purpose or illegal motive agreement: *Barrett v Barrett* (2008). In *Barrett*, Thomas Barrett owned a house but fell into arrears and became bankrupt. His brother, John, purchased the house from the trustee in bankruptcy. Thomas was subsequently discharged from bankruptcy. Some years later, John sold the property. Thomas sought a declaration that the property and proceeds of sale were held on trust for him on the basis that John had agreed to buy the property in order to prevent the trustee in bankruptcy repossessing it. The brothers had agreed that once John purchased the property, Thomas would pay for all expenses relating to the property including mortgage instalments. The court held that Thomas could not rely on this illegal purpose (intended to evade the bankruptcy rules) to establish a common intention constructive trust.

Where, however, a claimant can establish a constructive trust *without* having to rely on evidence of the illegal purpose, a claim may succeed: *O'Kelly v Davies* (2014). In *O'Kelly*, a couple had purchased a property conveyed into O'Kelly's sole name simply in order to commit a fraud so that O'Kelly could claim security benefits as a single mother. Davies had contributed significantly to the purchase of the property by cashing in an endowment policy, by paying mortgage instalments, and looking after the children. The court found that it was not necessary for Davies to rely on the fraudulent purpose in order to establish his claim to a constructive trust. The inference of a common intention constructive trust arose quite independently of the illegal purpose. Davies was entitled to a 50 per cent share in the property.

6.8 Trusts of the family home: Bringing it all together

We have now explored the role of express, resulting, and constructive trusts in determination of the ownership interests in the family home. This involves the apparently straightforward but crucial question: who owns what? Yet as the Law Commission have recognized:[78]

'Who owns what?' may be very simple to ask, but in a short time the enquirer will find themselves immersed in the off-putting, and sometimes obscure, terminology of the law of trusts . . .

Our challenge in studying this area of the law is not to be put off. Figure 6.6 provides a suggested structure for bringing together all the moving parts in your analysis of interests in the home.

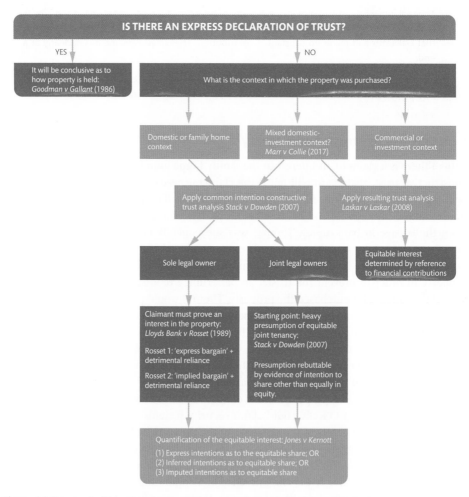

Figure 6.6 Bringing it all together: A suggested structure for analysing interests in the home

---

[78] Law Commission Report No. 278, [1.11].

6.9 A single regime for joint and sole cases?

Lord Walker's view in *Stack* was that 'the law has moved on' and the strict approach taken in *Rosset* as to the acquisition of interests in the home in sole ownership cases was doubted. The question for us in this section is whether there should be just one single regime for sole and joint ownership cases. In essence, what we mean by this is whether acquisition of an interest in sole ownership cases should be governed by the broad enquiry of Baroness Hale's para. 69 factors? As we have already seen, the rules on quantification are already the same for sole and joint cases so should we also collapse the distinction on acquisition? Gardner and Davidson[79] writing before the judgment in *Jones* made their preference clear:

> It is to be hoped, incidentally, that the Supreme Court will also make clear that constructive trusts of family homes are governed by a single regime, dispelling any impression that different rules apply to 'joint names' and 'single name' cases, and to the 'establishment' and the 'quantum' of the constructive trust.

Sadly, Gardner and Davidson were to be disappointed when the judgment in *Jones* was handed down. In *Jones*, Lord Walker and Lady Hale maintained the distinction between sole and joint cases, clarifying the 'different starting points' for each type of claim, adding that only at 'a high level of generality, there is of course a single regime: the law of trusts'.[80] In *Geary v Rankine* (2012) a decision that post-dates *Jones*, the court heard a claim to an equitable interest based on an inferred agreement following non-financial contributions.

KEY CASE *Geary v Rankine* (2012)

Facts: Mrs Geary and Mr Rankine were in a relationship from 1990 to 2009. In 1996, Mr Rankine purchased a guesthouse with his own money and in his sole name. At the time of the purchase, the couple neither intended to live in the property nor run the business themselves. A manager was installed to run the business. After problems with the manager, Mr Rankine began to take the lead in running the business. Mrs Geary became involved in assisting Mr Rankine in cleaning, cooking, doing the paperwork, and looking after the guests. Mrs Geary was not paid. The parties' relationship broke down and Mrs Geary claimed an interest in the guesthouse under a constructive trust. The trial judge rejected the claim holding that there was no common intention to share the property in equity whether at the time of the purchase or later when Mrs Geary began working at the guesthouse. Mrs Geary appealed.

Legal issue: Had the trial judge erred in law? Was there evidence of a common intention on the facts?

Judgment: Mrs Geary's appeal was dismissed. The Court of Appeal noted that the burden of establishing a constructive trust was on Mrs Geary. The relevant test was whether there was a common intention that Mrs Geary was to enjoy a beneficial interest in the property. The court held that the principles as laid down in *Jones* should be applied despite this being a sole name case. Common

→

---

[79] S. Gardner and K. Davidson, 'The Future of *Stack v Dowden*' (2011) 127 LQR 13, 15.
[80] *Jones*, [16].

> →
>
> intention was to be determined objectively from the parties' conduct. On Mrs Geary's evidence, the parties had a common intention to run the business together, however, per Lewison LJ:
>
> > it is an impermissible leap to reach a conclusion of a common intention that the property in which the business was run, and which was bought entirely with money provided by one of them, would belong to both of them.
>
> On the facts, there was no evidence of any common intention to share beneficial ownership of the property. There was no reason to conclude the trial judge had been wrong in reaching this conclusion.

Geary is a significant decision. It is significant because, in a sole legal ownership case, the Court of Appeal emphasized that it was the *Jones* principles that were to be applied and made no mention of the *Rosset* authority. As Lees,[81] discussing *Geary*, asserts with some confidence:

> *Geary v Rankine* provides the first post-*Kernott* consideration by a higher court of the applicability of the *Kernott* principles to sole name cases and confirms, as a number of first instance judges have already, that they are equally applicable to both the acquisition and quantification stages.

Lees is right that a series of first instance cases pre-*Jones* appeared to apply the *Stack* principles in sole ownership cases in place of *Rosset*.[82] Several decisions in the post-*Jones* era, have also taken this course.[83] With respect, however, Lees' argument of the conflation of sole and joint cases is overstated for two reasons. First, in several of these decisions, in particular in *Geary*, no discussion took place whatsoever of the role of *Rosset* and we should be cautious before jumping to confine the *Rosset* rules to obscurity for what may be oversights or less-than-complete judicial reasoning. Secondly, as Sloan[84] has noted, with the exception of *Aspden*, the results reached in these decisions—*Geary* and those at first instance—would have been precisely the same had the *Rosset* principles been applied. So, we may not yet be quite at the stage to embrace a single regime but certainly we do seem to be moving in that direction.

6.10 The common intention myth

The search for 'common intention' sits at the core of the operation of the common intention constructive trust. Following *Stack* and *Jones*, the role of common intention is even stronger with both 'the sharing question' and 'the shares question' determined by reference to the parties' common intentions. But is common intention the right basis, the right foundation on which to determine interests in the home? Academic opinion has long been divided on this question.

---

[81] E. Lees, '*Geary v Rankine*: Money Isn't Everything' [2012] Conv 412.
[82] See, for example, *Williamson v Sheikh* (2008); *Q v Q* (2009); *Hapeshi v Allnatt* (2010).
[83] See, for example, *CPS v Piper* (2011) and *Aspden*.
[84] Sloan, 'Keeping Up with the Jones Case: Establishing Constructive Trusts in "Sole Legal Owner" Scenarios'.

Glover and Todd[85] do not hold back in lambasting the search for common intention as a 'myth' and Dixon J, in the landmark Canadian Supreme Court case of *Pettkus v Becker* (1980), described common intention as a 'phantom'. The problem is one of artificiality, of judicial creativity, and of unpredictability. Matters were compounded by the clarification in *Jones* that the court is permitted, when considering the quantification of shares, to impute an intention to the parties which they never actually had. Further, the judges in *Jones* each appear to have quite differing views as to what 'imputation' involves. Lord Walker and Lady Hale, in the leading judgment, borrow from Chadwick LJ's observation in *Oxley* that imputation means: '[E]ach [party] is entitled to that share which the court considers fair having regard to the whole course of dealing between them in relation to the property.'[86] Lord Collins supported Lord Walker and Lady Hale's approach to imputation but added that: 'what is one person's inference will be another person's imputation'.[87] Lord Kerr, argued, 'it would be preferable to have a stark choice between deciding whether it is possible to deduce what their intention was and, where it is not, deciding what is fair, without elliptical references to what their intention might have—or should have—been'.[88] Lord Kerr therefore suggests equating imputation with a clear test of fairness. Finally, Lord Wilson asked: 'Where equity is driven to impute the common intention, how can it do so other than by search for the result which the court itself considers fair?'[89] Imputation, on any of the views expressed in the Supreme Court, has a clear connection with the notion of fairness yet the court persists in veiling its discussion of imputation in the language of common intention. Is the search for 'common intention' more legitimate than fairness? Is it more defensible? Perhaps common intention should be discarded altogether.

Gardner[90] discusses various alternative rationales for intervention in this area drawing on lessons from Canada, Australia, and New Zealand. Gardner argues that:

> [D]octrines which rely on the parties' thinking are in fact inappropriate to this area of the law, since by the nature of the relationships in question, the parties will deal with each other more by trust and collaboration than by organised thinking about their respective rights.

For Gardner, the search for common intention and 'parties' thinking' should be jettisoned as part of an acceptance that organization of the family home is governed by the parties' values of trust and collaboration. This leads Gardner to propose a relationship-based approach which centres on the fact of the relationship in order to bypass references to the parties' subjective 'thinking' and would allow the court to award remedies more freely. Barlow and Lind[91] have advanced an even more radical proposal under a 'modified community of property' approach. They explain how this might work in the following passage:

> The constructive trust in the family home should be abolished. Instead, legislation should dictate that a home which is owned or acquired by one party to an intimate, cohabiting relationship be beneficially owned in particular prescribed shares by both the parties. The nature and length of their relationship and the presence of children in that relationship will govern their respective

---

[85] N. Glover and P. Todd, 'The Myth of Common Intention' (1996) 16 LS 325.   [86] *Jones*, [32].
[87] Ibid., [65].   [88] Ibid.   [89] Ibid., [87].   [90] Gardner, 'Rethinking Family Property', 282.
[91] A. Barlow and C. Lind, 'A Matter of Trust: The Allocation of Rights in the Family Home' (1999) 19(4) LS 468, 488.

shares . . . a residuary discretion to reallocate beneficial entitlement to the home in exceptional circumstances, limited to proof of what we term 'manifest injustice', should be vested in the courts.

Neither Gardner nor Barlow and Lind's proposals have been adopted and the common intention constructive trust very much remains in place. In 2006, the Law Commission in its Report No. 278 cautioned against rejection of common intention as the basis for intervention in the family home finding that 'uncompromising rejection of intention, central to the scheme, was ultimately impossible to justify . . . to disregard intention altogether could have the result of prejudicing many of those who would have obtained a beneficial interest under the present law'.[92] Call it myth or phantom but unless and until Parliament intervenes with legislation to govern non-matrimonial disputes over the family home, the courts seem unlikely to depart from the current path of the common intention constructive trust.

6.11 Reform

Baroness Hale in *Stack* made the strong case for the family home to be treated differently from other forms of property and that the law should take account of changing social and economic circumstances. Parliament has, however, shown itself incapable or unwilling to intervene to legislate for a distinct statutory regime to govern disputes over the home between unmarried couples.[93] Legislation does exist, however, in Scotland.[94] With no prospect of movement from Parliament, the House of Lords in *Stack* and the Supreme Court in *Jones* saw it as their job to develop the law. Yet the court is not alone in seeking to reform and to rationalize the law. In fact, the Law Commission has, for over two decades, been looking at the question of property rights in the home.[95]

In 2002, the Law Commission published a Discussion Paper, *Sharing Homes*. This was unfortunately something of a non-starter which failed to produce any proposals, even provisional in nature, for meaningful reform.[96] Post-2002, the Commission narrowed and refocused its work on cohabitants (non-married or non-civil partnered) living as a couple in a shared household. The Commission published a Consultation Paper in 2006[97] and a final report proposing a statutory scheme for cohabitants on relationship breakdown in 2007.[98] The report recommended a new statutory scheme for cohabitants on separation.

---

[92] Law Commission Report No. 278, [3.76].

[93] Recall that a statutory scheme already governs the position of married couples on relationship breakdown under the Matrimonial Causes Act 1973.

[94] The Family Law (Scotland) Act 2006; Lady Hale in *Gow v Grant* (2012) called for similar legislation to be introduced in England and Wales.

[95] See judgment of Baroness Hale in *Stack*, [46], for a summary of the Commission's early work.

[96] Law Commission Report No. 278, [1.31(1)] noted that it was unable, at that time, to recommend a 'statutory scheme for the ascertainment and quantification of beneficial interests in the shared home which can operate fairly and evenly across the diversity of domestic circumstances'.

[97] Law Commission Consultation Paper No. 179 (2006), *Cohabitation: The Financial Consequences of Relationship Breakdown*.

[98] Law Commission Report No. 307 (2007), *Cohabitation: The Financial Consequences of Relationship Breakdown*.

The scheme would apply only to those cohabitants who either have a child together or have cohabited for a defined minimum duration (the suggested period is between two and five years).[99] Eligible cohabitants would only be entitled to remedies under the scheme where either the applicant would suffer economic disadvantage or the respondent would retain a benefit if no orders were made.[100] In order to respect the autonomy of cohabiting couples, the scheme could be excluded if the parties wished to make their own arrangements. If engaged, however, the scheme would allow the court to make orders for the transfer of property, lump sum payments, orders for sale, and pension sharing.[101] In providing a remedy, the court would be asked to have regard to a list of 'discretionary factors' including the welfare of any minors, the financial needs of the parties, the likely future financial positions of each party, and any relevant conduct.[102]

The statutory scheme proposed by the Commission is therefore far more flexible than the current property law principles governing interests in the home but many cohabitants, even if the scheme were to be introduced, would fall outside its purview. Where this happened, ownership of the family home would continue to be governed by property and trusts law: see Figure 6.7.

As to the status of the Law Commission's proposals, in 2011 the government made clear the proposals would not be implemented during that parliamentary term. Matters then went quiet. The 2014–15 parliamentary session saw the introduction of a private members'

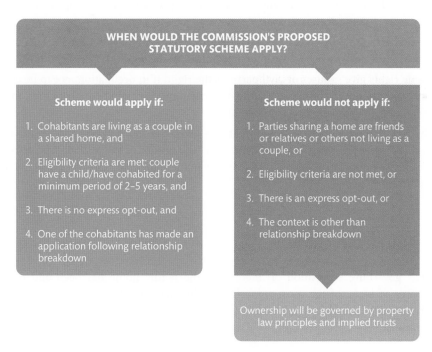

WHEN WOULD THE COMMISSION'S PROPOSED STATUTORY SCHEME APPLY?

Scheme would apply if:

1. Cohabitants are living as a couple in a shared home, and

2. Eligibility criteria are met: couple have a child/have cohabited for a minimum period of 2–5 years, and

3. There is no express opt-out, and

4. One of the cohabitants has made an application following relationship breakdown

Scheme would not apply if:

1. Parties sharing a home are friends or relatives or others not living as a couple, or

2. Eligibility criteria are not met, or

3. There is an express opt-out, or

4. The context is other than relationship breakdown

Ownership will be governed by property law principles and implied trusts

Figure 6.7 When would the Law Commission's proposed statutory scheme apply?

[99] Ibid., Part 3.   [100] Ibid., Part 4.   [101] Ibid., [4.40].   [102] Ibid., [4.38].

bill in order to implement the Commission's proposals, however, whilst the bill passed its second reading it progressed no further, largely due to the distraction of the General Election in May 2015. The Cohabitation Bill was reintroduced in the 2015–16 session and, again, whilst passing first reading in the Lords on 4 June 2015, it ran out of time. Lord Marks introduced a Cohabitation Rights Bill in House of Lords in the 2017–19 session to implement the Law Commission's 2007 reforms but this, equally, did not progress. The wait therefore goes on to see if the Commission's proposals will ever be implemented or are destined to languish on a dusty shelf.

6.12 'Home rights' under the Family Law Act 1996

A person enjoying a proprietary interest in the home (whether under an express, resulting, or constructive trust) is entitled under s. 12 of the TOLATA 1996 to occupy that home subject to the restrictions in s. 13. We considered these provisions in section 5.7.3.2. Beyond this, however, there are also certain, additional occupation 'home rights' that arise under the Family Law Act 1996.[103] For our purposes, the key provision is s. 30 of the 1996 Act and the following essential points should be noted:

- Section 30 confers rights on spouses or civil partners only and not on cohabitants.
- Home rights last only for the length of the marriage or civil partnership at which point they are automatically terminated.[104]
- Home rights are only enjoyed by spouses and civil partners who have no *legal* ownership of the home—in other words, do not appear on the legal title.[105]
- Home rights give spouses or civil partners the right, if in occupation, not to be evicted or excluded from the home and, if not in occupation, the right to apply to the court for permission to enter and occupy the home.[106]
- Though personal in nature, home rights are given the status of a charge on the estate with the same priority as equitable interests. The upshot of this is that, if protected by the entry of a notice on the register, statutory home rights can bind successors in title to the land.[107]

6.13 Future directions

The law governing acquisition of interests in the family home has been and remains the source of some of the most colourful developments in the whole of modern land law. What's more, the law is not standing still. This section considers areas for potential development.

---

[103] As amended by the Civil Partnership Act 2004.
[104] Sections 30(8) and 31(8) of the Family Law Act 1996.   [105] Ibid., s. 30(1).   [106] Ibid., s. 30(2).
[107] Ibid., s. 30(2), (3).

6.13.1 Should the legal principles on acquisition of interests in the family home be regarded as property law principles at all?

This is a key question which remains unanswered. How far are we seeing the 'familialization' of land law? Put differently, is the approach adopted by the court, in particular in *Stack* and *Jones*, evidence of family law principles creeping into and shaping property law?

These are deeply controversial questions not least because, in the property law vs family law binary debate, family law is portrayed rather pejoratively as the more context-led, discretionary, and fairness-based jurisdiction. In contrast, property law and particularly land law is portrayed as seeking to promote clarity, certainty, and clear rules in dealings with land. This binary position can of course be challenged: family law is not all about discretion and neither is all land law certain and clear-cut (take proprietary estoppel as an example, which we explore in Chapter 8). That said, the approach taken by the House of Lords in *Stack* means the question of the 'familialization' of land law remains a live one.

So, where is the evidence of family law operating here?

First, the largely indisputable fact that *a special regime* has been developed for property purchased as a family home: a regime which is not pure property law and one which draws on a wide range of family-centric, relationship-based factors to determine the parties' common intentions.

Secondly, there is the extensive discretionary jurisdiction that the court has carved out for itself in determining disputes over the family home. This is best epitomized by the availability of imputation as a tool for divining parties' common intention as to their respective shares—a common intention which, as we have seen, they never in fact held. In addition, the court's recourse to fairness on imputation seems far removed from the cold, hard-nosed, contribution-focus of the resulting trust which reflects a more traditional property law approach.

Thirdly, there is the general tenor of recent judgments, especially in *Stack* and *Jones*, as reflected in the dicta of Lord Walker that 'the law has moved on' and Baroness Hale's assertion in *Stack* that in law 'context is everything'. This might be construed as a challenge to the traditional property-law approach focused on rules from the status-focused principles said to typify family law. Whichever side one comes down on regarding the question of 'familialization', recent case law has certainly created a distinct body of rules that sits somewhat awkwardly within property law orthodoxy. As Dixon[108] argues:

> If we look for an explanation for the role and impact of [recent decided] cases within the jurisprudence of property law, we will not find it . . . It is something else: call it family law, call it an exercise of the court's equitable jurisdiction, but, maybe, do not call it property law.

Does it matter? Certainly, there is grumbling and some dissatisfaction from land lawyers in straining property principles to fit the family home context, but, in the absence of parliamentary intervention, perhaps the court had no choice. Hayward[109] has argued that we

---

[108] M. Dixon, 'Editorial' [2012] Conv 1, 2–3.
[109] A. Hayward, 'Finding a Home for Family Property: *Stack v Dowden* & *Jones v Kernott*' in N. Gravells (ed.), *Landmark Cases in Land Law* (Oxford: Hart, 2013), chapter 10.

should embrace this apparent 'familialization' of property law principles as an opportunity for 'modernization and dynamism' in land law. To fixate on the assault on land law ortho-doxy from the threat of an overly discretionary, contextualized family law would be to sty-mie development in the area. As Hayward argues:[110]

> While [*Stack* and *Jones*] have been criticised within the academic community for their engage-ment with 'context' and 'fairness', the more discretionary approach introduced may more sen-sitively engage with relationship dynamics . . . a beneficial by-product of this redevelopment is that it forces land lawyers to confront and reconsider the foundational tenets of the discipline . . . [this] should be welcomed, particularly if the modern application of land law is to reconcile its treatment of home ownership, possession and purchase with the realities of people's lived experi-ences . . . this process needs to take place within land law itself.

6.13.2 The future role of imputation in disputes over the family home

As things currently stand, a court is only permitted to impute a common intention to the parties at the quantification stage, but should this be relaxed to allow imputation at the earlier, acquisition stage? Lord Walker in *Jones* notably left this open saying sim-ply it would 'merit careful thought'. But a case can be made for collapsing the distinc-tion between acquisition and quantification and permitting imputation at both stages. Collapsing this distinction would mean that a court could impute a common intention to share the family home in equity ('the sharing question') either when displacing the presumption of beneficial joint tenancy in a joint case or when acquiring an interest in sole ownership cases as currently governed by *Rosset*. This argument was advanced by counsel for Ms Phillips in *Barnes* but was rejected as being out of line with decided authority.

Are there risks in accepting imputation at all stages of the enquiry? The key issue is that imputation involves the court ascribing a 'fair share' having considered the parties' whole course of dealing. To permit imputation at the acquisition stage would be to erode the 'common intention' focus of the common intention constructive trust and allow a court to use fairness to determine interests in the home. This would simplify the law but arguably give the court too great a discretion to declare rights in the home. We have already seen the difficulties with imputation and the suggestion that the court is fabri-cating party intention. To permit imputation at the acquisition stage would surely com-pound this and could result in a loss of certainty and predictability in outcome. How, for example, would lawyers advise their clients on the likelihood of a particular outcome? Gardner sees the courts as already applying a single test to determine disputes over the home—one which asks whether the parties agreed on their interests in the home and, if they did not, whether such an agreement should be imputed to bring about fairness.[111] This is not a view universally held and the matter does, as Lord Walker suggested, merit careful thought. We await further clarification on this from the Supreme Court.

---

[110] Ibid., 252.
[111] S. Gardner, 'Heresy—or Not?—in Family Property' [2015] Conv 332, 339.

6.13.3 Will (and should) the Law Commission's reform agenda ever come to fruition?

Finally, we return to this question regarding the Law Commission's reform agenda. The extensive reform work of the Commission in the early 2000s came to nothing and the 2007 proposals are only partial in nature in that they relate only to cohabitants. The result is that the proposed statutory scheme fails to capture many circumstances in which, even if the scheme is implemented, the current trust principles will still operate. That the scheme does not replace completely our current approach could be interpreted as a fatal weakness. The failure to launch of the Cohabitation Bills in the 2014–15 and 2015–16 parliamentary sessions, and another attempt by Lord Marks which got nowhere in the 2017–19 session, appears to signal that statutory reform has stalled and is certainly not especially pressing as a concern. Pearce and Barr[112] share this lack of optimism:

> The Law Commission [has] proposed a partial legislative solution, but this was neither comprehensive nor uncontroversial . . . there is little hope that this particular reform will ever now become law.

Further reading

- R. Auchmuty, 'Unfair Shares for Women: The Rhetoric of Equality and the Reality of Inequality' in H. Lim and A. Bottomley (eds.), *Feminist Perspectives on Land Law* (Abingdon: Routledge-Cavendish, 2007).

- R. Auchmuty, 'The Limits of Marriage Protection: in Defence of Property Law' (2016) 6(6) Oñati Socio-Legal Series.

- C. Bevan, 'The Search for Common Intention: The Status of an Executed, Express Declaration of Trust Post-*Stack* and *Jones*' (2019) 135(4) LQR 660.

- A. Bottomley, 'From Mrs. Burns to Mrs. Oxley: Do Co-Habiting Women (Still) Need Marriage Law?' (2006) 14(2) Feminist Legal Studies 181.

- J. Dewar, 'Land, Law and the Family Home' in S. Bright and J. Dewar, *Land Law: Themes and Perspectives* (Oxford: Oxford University Press, 1998) and (1998) 61 MLR 467.

- M. Dixon, 'Editor's Notebook: The Still Not Ended, Never-Ending Story' [2012] Conv 83.

- L. Fox, 'The Meaning of Home: A Chimerical Concept or a Legal Challenge?' (2002) 29(4) Journal of Law and Society 580.

- S. Gardner, 'Rethinking Family Property' (1993) 109 LQR 263.

- S. Gardner, 'Family Property Today' (2008) 124 LQR 422.

- S. Gardner, 'Heresy—or Not?—in Family Property' [2015] Conv 332.

- S. Gardner and K. Davidson, 'The Future of *Stack v Dowden*' (2011) 127 LQR 13.

- N. Glover and P. Todd, 'The Myth of Common Intention' (1996) 16 LS 325

- A. Hayward, 'Family Property and the Process of Familialisation of Property Law' (2012) 24(3) Child and Family Law Quarterly 284.

---

[112] R. Pearce and W. Barr, *Trusts and Equitable Obligations* (Oxford: Oxford University Press, 2014), 283.

- A. Hayward, 'Finding a Home for Family Property: *Stack v Dowden* & *Jones v Kernott*' in N. Gravells (ed.), *Landmark Cases in Land Law* (Oxford: Hart, 2013), chapter 10.

- A. Hayward, 'Common Intention Constructive Trusts and the Role of Imputation in Theory and Practice' [2016] Conv 227.

- Law Commission Report No. 278, *Sharing Homes: A Discussion Paper* (2002).

- Law Commission Report No. 307, *Cohabitation: The Financial Consequences of Relationship Breakdown* (2007).

- A. Lawson, 'The Things We Do for Love: Detrimental Reliance in the Family Home' (1996) 16(2) LS 218.

- E. Lees, '*Geary v Rankine*: Money Isn't Everything' [2012] Conv 412.

- M. Pawlowski, 'Imputing Intention and the Family Home' (2016) 46 (Feb) Family Law 189.

- N. Piska, 'Intention, Fairness and the Presumption of Resulting Trust after *Stack v Dowden*' (2008) 71(1) MLR 114.

- R. Probert, 'Equality in the Family Home? *Stack v Dowden* (2007)' (2007) 15 Feminist Legal Studies 341.

- J. Rapoport, 'A Critical Look at the Concept "Home"' in D. N. Benjamin (ed.), *The Home: Words, Interpretations, Meanings and Environments* (Aldershot: Avebury, 1995).

- U. Riniker, 'The Fiction of Common Intention and Detriment' [1998] Conv 202.

- B. Sloan, 'Keeping Up with the Jones Case: Establishing Constructive Trusts in "Sole Legal Owner" Scenarios' (2015) 35 LS 226.

- S. Wong, 'The Iniquity of Equity: A Home-Sharer's Tale' (2008) Singapore Journal of Legal Studies 326.

- S. Wong, 'Shared Commitment, Interdependency and Property Relations: A Socio-Legal Project for Cohabitation' (2012) 24(1) Child and Family Law Quarterly 60.

Online resources

Access the online resources at www.oup.com/uk/bevan2e/ to test yourself with self-test questions and scenario problems. You can also view additional supporting material relevant to the topics in this chapter, including:

- *Videos*
- *Audio podcasts*
- *Maps, diagrams, and flowcharts*
- *Interactive exercises*
- *Examples of real-life legal documentation*

7 Licences

7.1 Introduction

In Chapter 1, you were encouraged to approach the study of land law as a puzzle, a jigsaw of separate pieces combining to form a logical, coherent whole. This chapter considers where licences fit into this puzzle. You might be surprised to learn that on an almost daily basis you encounter licences over land though you may be entirely unaware of it. Consider, for example, a visit to the local pub, or when you go to watch a film or go shopping. Consider a postwoman delivering a parcel, or if you allow friends to use your garden for a New Year's Eve celebration. None of these activities involve ownership over land. When you cross the threshold into that pub or cinema, you do not in any sense own or 'possess' the land, nor do you have the right to exclude others from the land. Your rights are more limited, more precarious, more temporary. Equally, your rights do not fall within the scope of the law of easements which we consider in Chapter 10. It is here that licences spring into action. In this chapter, you will learn of the nature, status, and characteristics of licences, the different types of licences that exist, what makes them distinct from other interests in land law and how they can be brought to an end.

 Visit the online resources to watch a video on the differences between licences and leases.

7.2 Licences: Character and status

In Chapter 1, we explored the significance of the distinction between proprietary and personal rights. This distinction is crucial in this chapter also to help you understand how licences differ from other interests discussed in the remainder of the book—for example, leases and easements. Put simply, licences are fundamentally regarded as *personal* in nature rather than *proprietary*.

So, what precisely is a licence? You should already be familiar with licences. We require licences to drive, to watch television, and shop owners need licences to sell alcohol. You will see from these examples that licences provide authorization or give permission for an individual to do something that would otherwise be contrary to the principles of law. Licences in the context of land law function in a similar way. Licences in land arise when the owner of land grants to another person, who may or may not own any land himself, permission to use that land for a given purpose. A licence is therefore a permission to enter or do something on another's land. The person granting the licence is termed the 'licensor' and the party to whom the licence is granted the 'licensee'.

The licence is one of the most flexible interests in land law hence its description by Gray and Gray[1] as:

> a chameleonic device which performs many different kinds of function.

Licences are highly versatile and almost any permission to be physically present on land owned by another can amount to a licence. Licences can authorize both shorter as well as longer-term activities. A few examples will help you to get a better sense of the breadth of their application: see Figure 7.1.

You can see that licences can arise in a multitude of circumstances.[2] As you will discover, there is far more to licences than first meets the eye but that with flexibility comes

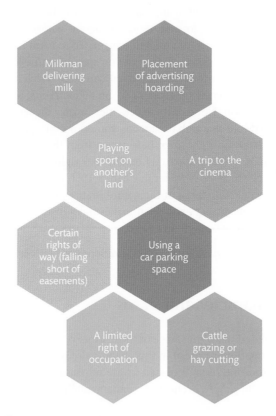

Figure 7.1 Examples of licences arising over land

[1] K. Gray and S. F. Gray, *Land Law*, 7th edn (Oxford: Oxford University Press, 2011), 539.
[2] See *Moody v Steggles* (1879); *Olympic Delivery Authority v Persons Unknown* (2012); *Zieleniewski v Scheyd* (2012).

a degree of precariousness. One important key is how to distinguish licences from other interests in land. This is not always easy to do as licences share similar characteristics with other interests in land—for example, leases and easements (e.g. a right of way). All three of these interests (i.e. licences, leases, and easements) involve one party making use to a varying degree of another's land. Sparkes[3] has noted that many cases found to involve licences could equally be analysed as scenarios involving leases or even freehold interests. On the same set of facts, there may be real debate as to how best to characterize the parties' relationship. Is it a lease? A licence? An easement? This difficulty is particularly apparent in so-called 'occupation licences' for example where a student rents out a room in halls of residence.

The classic statement of the nature and effect of licences is found in *Thomas* v *Sorrell* (1673) per Vaughan CJ who observed that a licence:[4]

> properly passeth no interest, nor alters or transfers property in anything, but only makes an action lawful, which without it had been unlawful.

Vaughan CJ therefore highlights a central feature of licences: that licences are traditionally regarded as *personal* permissions as opposed to being *proprietary* in nature. The significance of this is that licences are regarded as capable of binding the licensor and licensee only. Put another way, licences are interests that operate *over* land rather than being interests *in* land. Therefore according to the classic statement of licences, a licence can only be enforced against the party granting it and not against a purchaser or transferee of the licensor's land.

Let's take an example: imagine that Amil grants a licence to Brian permitting Brian to erect advertising signage on Amil's land. If Amil then sells or transfers his land to Carol, Brian will be unable to enforce the licence against Carol as the new landowner. We can see in this example that licences are not therefore proprietary rights capable of binding third parties. This was confirmed by the House of Lords in *National Provincial Bank v Ainsworth* (1965) by Lord Wilberforce who went on to set out the features necessary for a right to qualify as proprietary. Licences do not satisfy Lord Wilberforce's criteria and thus cannot qualify as proprietary rights. In particular, licences can be revoked by the party granting the licence (the licensor). Licences do not therefore enjoy the 'degree of permanence and stability' so fundamental to Lord Wilberforce's formulation of proprietary rights. This orthodox characterization of licences as having a purely *personal, non-proprietary* status has been subject to criticism and comment. This personal/proprietary question, which appeared settled and beyond question in *Thomas v Sorrell*, has provoked a heated debate amongst modern property lawyers in particular when considering so-called contractual licences which we explore in section 7.3.3. It is this debate which has led some to regard the law of licences as one of the most fluid areas of modern land law.

Beyond the classic statement of licences, a second essential feature that you need to grasp is that licences operate to render lawful that which might otherwise constitute a trespass on someone else's land. Recall our example of a postwoman delivering parcels.

---

[3] P. Sparkes, *A New Land Law* (Oxford: Hart, 2003), chapter 19.   [4] *Thomas v Sorrell* (1673), 351.

Without a licence permitting her to open your front gate and cross your path to deliver letters, her presence on your land would be actionable as a trespass.

Thirdly, there are generally no formal requirements for the creation of licences though note that certain types of licences (such as contractual licences) do require a degree of compliance with formality. Licences can be created orally or in writing, can be express or implied, and can be contained within deeds or as part of the conveyancing process. Licences may also arise where the formalities for creating proprietary interests fail to be satisfied. So, imagine that Darren wishes to create a legal easement (e.g. a right of way) over his land in Emma's favour. The creation of a legal easement requires a deed. If Darren fails to use a deed, a licence may nevertheless arise rescuing Emma from committing trespass when she crosses Darren's land. So, we can see the residuary role that licences can also play where attempts to create proprietary interests fail.

A final and important aspect is that the nature and extent of licences is determined by having regard to the specific terms of that licence. For as long as the licence remains operative (i.e. has not been revoked) the licensee has the right to be present on the land to the extent provided for by the terms of the licence. Only if the licensee exceeds this scope will they be open to an action for trespass.

7.3 Licences: Traditional categorization

The traditional method of categorizing licences is to group them into four distinct licence 'types': see Table 7.1. There is no good reason not to adopt this approach as it is helpful to our understanding. We will therefore consider each type in turn and in so doing we will focus on their nature, creation, their revocability (in other words, whether and how they are capable of being revoked), and, importantly, identify whether and in what circumstances each licence is capable of binding a third party.

Table 7.1 The four forms of licences

LICENCE TYPE	DESCRIPTION
Bare licences	A simple permission to enter or be present on another's land: *Robson v Hallett* (1967)
Licences coupled with an interest	A permission to enter another's land to remove something from that land: *James Jones v Earl of Tankerville* (1909)
Estoppel licences	A permission to enter or use land arising from the operation of proprietary estoppel: *Inwards v Baker* (1965)
Contractual licences	A permission to enter or use land resulting from an implied or express contract: *King v David Allen & Sons Billposting Ltd* (1916); *Ashburn Anstalt v Arnold* (1989)

7.3.1 Bare licences

A bare licence is a simple permission to enter another's land and is, in practice, extremely common: for example, an invitation given to a friend to enter your flat for a coffee may give rise to a bare licence. Bare licences are granted 'gratuitously'—in other words, without consideration passing from the licensee to the licensor—and do not arise from a contract between the parties. Bare licences are very limited in scope and can be created expressly, orally, or by implication. A bare licence may be implied—for example, where an individual enters another's land in circumstances where there is no protest or objection by the landowner.

Bare licences offer, however, weak protection to the licensee as they can be brought to an end or revoked *at any time* by the licensor on the giving of reasonable notice to the licensee: *Robson v Hallett* (1967). Where reasonable notice is given, the licensee must then leave the land within a reasonable period. So, what amounts to a 'reasonable period'? This very much depends on the nature and extent of the licence: just a few minutes may be reasonable for a police officer making enquiries on another's land whereas three months may be reasonable for a licensee occupying residential premises.

Where a bare licence exists, the effect is to save the licensee from committing trespass when entering or being present on the licensor's land. To really understand how the bare licence is to operate, the scope of the licence must be determined and this is done by a consideration of all the surrounding circumstances. As Scrutton LJ famously put it:[5]

> When you invite a person into your house to use the staircase, you do not invite him to slide down the bannister.

Simply stated, a bare licence does not constitute a proprietary interest in land. Yes, it is binding between the original parties to the licence but cannot bind a third party or anyone who acquires the licensor's land, and is seen, as a consequence, as offering little protection.

7.3.2 Licences coupled with an interest

In many cases, where an individual enjoys a proprietary interest over a parcel of land, whether that be a right to fish or to shoot game on another's land, they will require access to the land in order to exercise the right. Consider, for example, if you are given a right to fish in a neighbour's lake. In order for this right to be at all meaningful, you would require access to that neighbour's land. In these circumstances, a licence permitting access to that land will be implied (if no such licence has been expressly granted). We say that this licence is 'coupled' with the interest (in our example: the interest is the right to fish and take fish from the neighbour's lake). The case of *James Jones v Earl of Tankerville* (1909) in which a landowner contracted to sell timber growing on his land to a third party illustrates the 'licence coupled with an interest'. The court in *James Jones* found that the contract entered into by the parties necessarily conferred an implied licence to enter, cut, and carry away the timber.

We know that a licence can be coupled with a proprietary right (e.g. the right to take fish, timber, game, water: technically termed '*profits à prendre*') but can a licence be

---

[5] *The Carlgarth* (1927), [110].

coupled with a lesser non-proprietary right? In *Hurst v Picture Theatres Ltd* (1915) the Court of Appeal held that when Mr Hurst purchased a cinema ticket, he enjoyed a licence coupled with an interest. This meant that his removal from the theatre on the mistaken belief that he had not paid constituted an assault. This decision has proved controversial[6] because there was no proprietary interest on the facts with which a licence could be coupled. Mr Hurst had a personal contractual right only to watch the film. *Hurst* appears also to be contradicted by obiter comments of Megarry J in *Hounslow LBC v Twickenham Garden Developments Ltd* (1971) which supported the classic position that licences can only be coupled with proprietary rights. In Megarry's view, the court 'should hesitate very long' before accepting a licence coupled with a non-proprietary right.

What is clear is that the licence coupled with an interest is ancillary to but dependent upon the interest granted. This gives rise to three important consequences:

1. First, as to creation, it means that the licence is created or arises on the effective grant of the proprietary right—for example, when the right to take fish is itself granted.

2. Secondly, as to revocation, it means that the licence cannot be revoked as long as the interest with which it is combined endures. In practical terms, this means that if you enjoy a right to fish in a neighbour's lake for a six-month period, the implied licence coupled with this right to fish will also last for six months but no longer.

3. Thirdly, as to enforceability, given the licence is contingent upon the proprietary right, it takes on a proprietary character and is capable of binding whoever would be bound by that proprietary right.

As a final thought, it is worth pondering whether we actually need the concept of 'licence coupled with interest' at all or whether we could do away with it completely. Certainly, compared to other types of licence, there is little authority on these licences and, what's more, cases of licences coupled with interest could easily be analysed as other types of licences, most obviously as implied contractual licences. Let's take our fishing example to elaborate on this. Imagine, you are granted a right to fish in a neighbour's lake. If this right is conferred by way of a contract, access to the lake can easily be implied by way of an implied contractual licence. Even if there is no basis on which a contract can be implied, a bare licence to enter the land could also equally be identified. Perhaps the licence coupled with an interest should not even exist as a distinct concept.

7.3.3 Contractual licences

Now we turn to the contractual licence which, undoubtedly, has generated the most debate and commentary in the law of licences. Contractual licences are a clear example of the collision between contract law and land law principles and this means that big questions have been raised as to whether contractual licences are, amongst other things, able to bind third parties. What then makes a licence contractual? Well, what sets contractual licences apart from, say, a bare licence is that they are granted by the licensor in return for consideration

---

[6] *Winter Garden Theatre (London) Ltd v Millennium Productions Ltd* (1947) (Lord Greene MR) declined to follow this analysis. *Hurst* has not been followed in Australia or New Zealand.

passing from the licensee. In other words, there is a contract between the parties under which a licence is granted for the use of land for a given purpose. The distinction between a contractual and a bare licence is therefore that, in the former, a contractual obligation arises in favour of the grantee of the contractual licence (the person to whom the contractual licence is granted) whereas, in the latter, no contractual obligation arises.

Let's take an everyday example to unpack this. Imagine going to the cinema and purchasing a ticket to see a film. Purchasing of the ticket gives rise to a contract between you, as the customer, and the cinema. This contract contains a licence permitting you to enter the cinema where the screening of the film will take place. Therefore, we say that these circumstances give rise to a contractual licence. The cinema-goer is the licensee, the cinema the licensor. As you might envisage, contractual licences are exceptionally common and you will come across them all the time without realizing it! Other common examples include:

- paying for entry to car parks: *Ashby v Tolhurst* (1937)
- attending sporting events: *Wood v Leadbitter* (1845)
- university students staying in halls of residence
- guests staying in hotel and hostels.

Contractual licences are subject to the ordinary rules of the law of contract and this means that a contractual licence can only exist if a valid contract has itself been created. The requirements of (i) an intention to create legal relations, (ii) an offer, (iii) an acceptance, and (iv) capacity to contract must therefore be satisfied. You will recall from your study of the law of contract that contracts can be created either expressly or impliedly, in writing or orally. Perhaps as a reflection of this flexibility, the court has shown itself to be rather ingenious in finding an implied contractual licence even in the domestic/familial context: *Tanner v Tanner*.[7]

KEY CASE *Tanner v Tanner* (1975)

Facts: Mr Tanner, a married man, began a relationship with Ms Macdermott who subsequently gave birth to twins and changed her surname to 'Tanner' though the pair never married. In 1970, Mr Tanner purchased a house to provide a home for Ms Macdermott and the children. In the belief that she and the children would be able to live permanently in the new house or at least until the children had finished their schooling, Ms Macdermott surrendered her rent-controlled tenancy and began living in the new house. By 1973, Mr Tanner had divorced his wife, met another partner whom he had married and wished to eject Ms Macdermott from the property. Mr Tanner offered Ms Macdermott £4,000 to leave. Ms Macdermott refused the offer arguing that she had a right to remain in the house. Mr Tanner issued possession proceedings to remove Ms Macdermott.

Legal issue: Could Ms Macdermott be ejected from the house? What was the nature of her entitlement to occupy the property?

➡

---

[7] Do also be sure to refer to the discussion of interests in the family home in Chapter 6.

➡

Judgment: At first instance, Mr Tanner succeeded in his action. The court made a possession order and Ms Macdermott along with the children were housed in local authority accommodation. Ms Macdermott appealed. In the Court of Appeal, Ms Macdermott argued successfully that an implied contractual licence had arisen with the effect that she and the twins were entitled to remain in the property until the children had left school. Given that Ms Macdermott had already been rehoused by the local authority, no order reinstating her occupation of the house was sought. Instead, the Court of Appeal concluded that in ejecting Ms Macdermott and the children, Mr Tanner had breached the contractual licence and thereby caused loss. Ms Macdermott was awarded a 'just and equitable' sum in damages for this breach: £2,000. Lord Denning MR noted:

> It seems to me . . . that in all the circumstances, it is to be implied that [Ms Macdermott] had a licence—a contractual licence—to have accommodation in the house for herself and the children so long as they were of school age and the accommodation was reasonably required for her and the children. There was, it is true, no express contract to that effect, but the circumstances are such that the court should imply a contract by [Mr Tanner] . . . whereby they were entitled to have the use of the house as their home until the girls had finished school.

Lord Denning underlined the protections offered by a contractual licence:

> If therefore the lady had sought an injunction restraining [Mr Tanner] from determining the licence, it should have been granted.

The decision in *Tanner* serves to demonstrate the scope of the implied contractual licence as well as highlighting the creative reasoning of the court in circumstances where, arguably, the doctrinal basis of the contractual licence was simply strained to offer the 'deserving' Ms Macdermott a remedy. You might think that the contract that formed the basis of the contractual licence was simply invented in *Tanner*. You may agree with the result but does this not raise bigger questions as to whether the court should be implying contracts into domestic circumstances, essentially, in a bid to enforce what the court considers to be the man's familial duties and responsibilities? *Tanner* was followed in *Chandler v Kerley* (1978). In *Chandler*, after marital breakdown, Ms Kerley remained in the former matrimonial home and was joined by her new boyfriend, Mr Chandler, who later purchased the house. The relationship ended and Mr Chandler sought to evict Ms Kerley. The Court of Appeal found an implied contractual licence in favour of Ms Kerley, terminable on the giving of reasonable notice. The court considered 12 months to be a reasonable period in the circumstances, giving Ms Kerley a year in which to make alternative living arrangements for herself and her children.

Despite *Tanner* and *Chandler*, there must be serious doubt as to whether the same result would be reached if these cases were decided today.[8] Indeed, in *Southwell v Blackburn* (2014), on facts very similar to *Tanner*, the Court of Appeal accepted an argument based on proprietary estoppel (explored in Chapter 8) and it is suggested, today, this

---

[8] Particularly as, today, the court is able to make provision for the financial support of children under Sch. 1 of the Children Act 1989.

would be the preferable and likely more successful legal argument than one premised on implied contractual licence. In fact, in a decision of the court just six months after *Tanner*, the Court of Appeal refused to follow Lord Denning's approach and distinguished *Tanner* on the grounds that there was no basis on which the inference of a contractual licence could fairly be made: *Horrocks v Forray* (1976). The court found, on similar facts to *Tanner*, that the arrangements between the parties were purely informal; there was no intention to create legal relations and no evidence of consideration. Therefore no contract could arise. In distinguishing the facts, the court noted that, in *Tanner*, Ms Macdermott had given up her rent-controlled property as part of the 'bargain' under which Mr Tanner agreed she and the children could live in the property. No such consideration was present on the facts in *Horrocks*. The upshot is that it would be quite wrong to overstate the reach of *Tanner* and *Chandler*. The court will scrutinize very closely whether the elements of a valid, albeit implied contract, are present on the facts.

A final but vital observation regarding contractual licences must be made before we move on. As a licence is not an interest in land (a licence is not included within the list of interests that can exist as proprietary interests under s. 1 of the LPA 1925), the contract creating the contractual licence need not comply with the formality requirements of s. 2 of the Law of Property (Miscellaneous Provisions) Act 1989 (LP(MP)A 1989). Section 2 requires that contracts made for the sale of or involving interests in land must be made in writing. Writing is not therefore a requirement for contractual licences although, in many cases, writing will be present. Let's now turn to consider what rights a contractual licensee enjoys against the contractual licensor.

7.3.4 **Contractual licences: Rights of the licensee against the licensor**

As with any licence, the precise scope and extent of a contractual licence again is determined by reference to the terms of the contract entered into and, given that these licences are grounded in contract law, the licensor and the licensee can rely on the standard remedies for breach or anticipated breach of contract. A contractual licensee may, by way of example seek an injunction to prevent the licensor from revoking the licence before expiry of the contract,[9] or seek an order for specific performance to require the licensor to perform the contract,[10] or claim damages for loss.

7.3.5 **Contractual licences: Revocation**

An important issue is that of revocation of contractual licences. In other words, how and in what circumstances can contractual licences be brought to an end? Recall our cinema example: how far is the cinema entitled to eject a customer in the middle of a film screening, for example? In answering this question, a distinction must be drawn between the approach of the common law and the approach in equity: see Figure 7.2.

---

[9] *Winter Garden.*   [10] *Verrall v Great Yarmouth Borough Council* (1981).

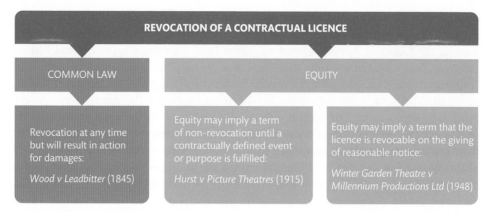

Figure 7.2 Revocation of contractual licences at common law and in equity

7.3.6 **Revocation at common law**

At common law, contractual licences are revocable *at any time* by the licensor. However, such revocation will entitle the licensee to bring an action for damages for breach of contract. The leading decision here is the nineteenth-century case of *Wood v Leadbitter*. In *Wood*, the claimant had purchased a ticket for a race meeting in Doncaster. He was asked to leave the event early and when he refused was removed by force. He argued this constituted an assault on the basis that he enjoyed a contractual licence which was irrevocable for the duration of the race meeting. Alderson B held that, given the claimant did not enjoy a licence coupled with an interest, the licence was revocable though an action in damages may be available for terminating the licence for no good reason. *Wood* stands as authority for the proposition that, at common law, a contractual licensor is entitled to revoke a contractual licence whenever he so chooses but, should he do so, he must be prepared to pay damages to the licensee if this amounts to a breach of contract.

7.3.7 **Revocation in equity**

Quite apart from the position at common law, equity has intervened and in certain circumstances, is prepared to imply a term into the contract to regulate or even prevent revocation in an appropriate case. The leading decision on equity's approach to revocation is *Winter Garden Theatre (London) Ltd v Millennium Productions Ltd*.

KEY CASE *Winter Garden Theatre (London) Ltd v Millennium Productions Ltd* (1947)

Facts: Millennium Productions granted a contractual licence to Winter Garden Theatre Ltd under which Winter Garden was allowed to make use of theatre premises to produce plays and concerts. The contract between the parties contained no term permitting Millennium Productions to revoke the licence and provided no fixed period for which the theatre could be used. Despite no breach

→

→

on the part of the Winter Garden, Millennium Productions gave the theatre company one month's notice to leave the theatre. Winter Garden brought legal proceedings seeking a declaration that the licence could not be revoked.

Legal issue: Was a contractual licensor entitled to revoke this licence at will in the absence of any breach of contract?

Judgment: In the Court of Appeal, Lord Greene MR held that the licence should not be seen as a separate entity from the contract itself and was, on this basis, subject to the standard contractual rules. There was no express power to revoke the licence and, consequently, it was irrevocable. In the House of Lords, it was held that on a true construction of the contract, the licence was revocable upon the giving of reasonable notice. The notice provided by Millennium Productions was therefore effective and valid. The court stressed that whether a contractual licence was revocable on the giving of notice was to be determined by construing the contract in all the circumstances of the case.

The House of Lords in *Winter Garden* confirmed that where there is no express term as to how the licence is to be terminated, the court will imply a term as is appropriate. Whether and how equity is prepared to intervene to regulate the revocation of a contractual licence is determined by construing the particular contract and its terms against the broader factual backdrop of the case. In summary, the position is therefore that some contractual licences will be revocable while others will not. Decisions of the court offer a crucial insight into the circumstances when a contractual licence will and will not be capable of revocation at the hands of equity:

- Contractual licences that are shorter in duration and clearly not intended to be perpetual but provide for no fixed duration or no term as to how the licence is to be determined will be revocable on the giving of reasonable notice: *Winter Garden*. As Viscount Simon noted in *Winter Garden*:[11]

  The implication of the arrangement . . . plainly is that the ticket entitled the purchaser to enter, and if he behaves himself, to remain on the premises until the end of the event which he has paid to see.

  Contractual licences are rarely intended to be perpetual or to last 'until the crack of doom' particularly in commercial contexts as explained in *Prudential Assurance Co. Ltd v London Residuary Body* (1992). Here the court is more likely to imply a term of revocation on the giving of reasonable notice. What is reasonable will, again, be determined by construing the contract as a whole.

- Contractual licences for a defined purpose or event, for example, the purchase of a ticket to watch a film will be irrevocable until that purpose or event has come to an end. Revocation before this time is unlawful and any forceful ejection will entitle the licensee to a claim for substantial damages for assault as in *Hurst v Picture Theatres*.

- A contractual licence may be interpreted so that it is to endure until the occurrence of a particular event or circumstance—for example, in *Tanner* where the court found an

---

[11] *Winter Garden*, 189.

implied contractual licence allowing Ms Macdermott to stay in the home until the children were of school-age. If this licence is breached or is not capable of performance, it can give rise to a remedy of damages as in *Tanner* itself.

- Contractual licences that have been acted upon by the licensee will be irrevocable for the duration of the term of the contract: *Hounslow*.[12] Megarry V-C in *Hounslow* noted:[13]

> All that I need say, in order to avoid possible misunderstanding, is that in light of the *Winter Garden* case I find it difficult to see how a contractual licensee can be treated as a trespasser so long as his contract entitles him to be on the land . . . Equity will not assist a man to break his contract.

In *Hounslow*, the landowner entered into a building contract with the defendants. Unhappy with the progress of the building work, the landowner applied to court to have the defendants removed from the land. Megarry J found a contractual licence and implied a term of non-revocation on the basis that the contract was for a specified task and for a defined period which was still running. The licence could not be revoked.

- Contractual licences that have not been acted upon and where the licensor has not yet entered the land *may* be irrevocable and enforceable by means of an order for specific performance: *Verrall v Great Yarmouth Borough Council* (1981). In *Verrall*, Great Yarmouth Borough Council entered a contractual licence under which the National Front was to hold a conference in a Council hall. After a change in political control, the Council sought to revoke the licence. Mr Verrall successfully brought legal proceedings seeking to force the Council to perform the contract. The Court of Appeal upheld the grant of an order for specific performance by the trial judge. Lord Denning noted:[14]

> Since the *Winter Garden* case, it is clear that once a man has entered under his contract of licence, he cannot be turned out . . . on principle it is the same if it happens before he enters. If he has a contractual right to enter, and the licensor refuses to let him come in, then he can come to the court and in a proper case get an order for specific performance to allow him to come in.

An order for specific performance will not be available in every case, however, as confirmed in *Thompson v Park* (1944). In *Thompson*, two schools were amalgamated under a contractual licence. The two head teachers subsequently fell out and one head, Mr Thompson, sought to revoke the licence. After leaving the school, the other head, Mr Park, later forcibly re-entered the school. Goddard LJ in the Court of Appeal held that whilst the revocation was a breach of contract, equity would not assist Mr Park as:[15]

> The court cannot specifically enforce an agreement between two people to live peaceably under the same roof.

- Contractual licences where the licensee has acted to her detriment in the belief that she will acquire certain rights over the licensor's land may be irrevocable under the doctrine of proprietary estoppel.[16] We discuss proprietary estoppel Chapter 8 but, for present

---

[12] In *Hounslow*, the court refused to grant a licensor an injunction which would have prevented the licensee from continuing to act upon a contractual licence for the completion of construction on the licensor's land.
[13] *Hounslow*, 248, 254–5.   [14] *Verrall*, 216.   [15] *Thompson*, 409.
[16] *Plimmer v Mayor etc. of Wellington* (1884).

purposes, it suffices to recognize that if an estoppel is raised in a licensee's favour, one way that the court can satisfy this claim is by holding that the contractual licence is irrevocable either for all time: *Plimmer v Major etc. of Wellington* (1884) or until the occurrence of particular events: *Inwards v Baker* (1965).[17]

If a court implies a term of non-revocation, it will directly or indirectly enforce the licence either by granting an injunction to the licensee (*Winter Garden*), refusing to grant an injunction (*Hounslow*) or by granting specific performance (*Verrall*). Note, however, that these are *equitable* remedies and are, on this basis, entirely at the discretion of the court. As we saw in *Thompson*, the court will not permit a result which is inequitable and will take account of all the circumstances when considering the most appropriate remedy.

7.3.8 Rights of the licensee against third parties

Up to this point, we have been concerned with the rights flowing between the person granted the licence, the licensee, and the person granting the licence, the licensor. In this section, we consider the relationship between the licensee and third parties. In principle, of course, a licence should not be capable of binding a third party as it is non-proprietary and is *personal* in nature only. The status of contractual licences has, however, always been somewhat more nuanced than this and warrants closer examination. We will first explore the position between the contractual licensee and a third party trespasser before turning to analyse the question of the enforceability of contractual licences against successors of the licensor—for example, those purchasing the licensor's land. It is this latter issue that has given rise to the most colourful legal developments in the law of licences.

7.3.9 Rights of the licensee against third party trespassers

The traditional conception of the licence provides that a licence is purely *personal* in nature, creates no interest in land, and therefore does not generate rights enforceable against third parties. As regards contractual licences, however, this view is far too simplistic and requires further thought. Imagine Fred grants to Gurdeep a contractual licence over Fred's land. In the event that Harry (a third party) trespasses onto Fred's land and thereby interferes with Gurdeep's licence, how far does Gurdeep have the right to bring a legal action against Harry to enforce his rights to exercise the licence? The starting point is dicta of Lord Upjohn in *National Provincial Bank v Ainsworth* where his Lordship explained, in the context of the family home, that a licensee may have the right to bring proceedings against a third party trespasser:[18]

> In this case in truth and in fact [the licensee] at all material times was in exclusive occupation of the home . . . has dominion over the house and . . . could clearly bring proceedings against trespassers.

---

[17] Where a licence was granted in favour of a claimant until such time as he no longer wished to exercise it.
[18] *National Provincial Bank v Ainsworth*, 1232.

A fascinating examination of this position was undertaken by the Court of Appeal in the decision of *Manchester Airport plc v Dutton* (2000). The court held that a licensee *is* entitled to instigate legal proceedings against a third party interfering with their rights under the licence even when the licensee is herself *not* in occupation of the land at the time. The decision may appear challenging but rewards a closer look.

KEY CASE *Manchester Airport plc v Dutton* (2000)

Facts: The National Trust owned a piece of woodland neighbouring the site of a proposed second runway at Manchester Airport. The airport needed to fell trees on the National Trust land in order for the second runway to be constructed and to prevent interference with flight paths. Environmental protesters opposed to the project occupied the woodland and built encampments, tree houses, and tunnels without the permission of the National Trust. The National Trust subsequently granted the airport a contractual licence to enter their land to undertake the necessary preparatory work. Before the airport or its authorized contractors could enter the land to begin the planned tree felling, Mr Dutton, an environmental protester, occupied the land in an attempt to disrupt the work.

Legal issue: Was the airport, as a contractual licensee and not in occupation or possession of the land, entitled to an order for possession against Mr Dutton, a trespasser on the licensor's land?

Judgment: The Court of Appeal held by a majority of 2:1 that the airport was entitled to an order for possession against the trespassers. Laws LJ noted:

> In my judgment, the true principle is that a licensee not in occupation may claim possession against a trespasser if that is a necessary remedy to vindicate and give effect to such rights of occupation as by contract with his licensor he enjoys. This is the same principle as allows a licensee who is in de facto possession to evict a trespasser. There is no respectable distinction, in law or logic, between the two situations. An estate owner may see an order whether he is in possession or not. So, in my judgment, may a licensee, of other things are equal. In both cases, the claimant's remedy is strictly limited to what is required to make good his legal right. The principle applies although the licensee had no right to exclude the licensor himself . . . the question must be, what is the reach of the right, and whether it is shown that the defendant's act violates its enjoyment.

Chadwick LJ (dissenting) disagreed:

> [The trial judge] did not make the distinction, essential in cases of this nature, between a claimant who is in possession and who seeks protection from those who interfere with that possession, and a claimant who has not gone into possession but who seeks to evict those who are already on the land. In the latter case (which is this case) the claimant must succeed by the strength of his title, not on the weakness (or lack) of any title in the defendant.

All three members of the court agreed that if a trespasser occupies land *after* a licensee has gone into possession, an action for possession could certainly be brought. It was on the position *before* a licensee goes into occupation where the court was split. The majority held that even before a licensee takes occupation of the licensor's land, an action for possession against a third party trespasser can be brought by a contractual licensee in its own right and there was no need to wait for the licensor to instigate proceedings. A licensee cannot, however, bring an action against a party enjoying a claim to possession equal or superior to its own.[19] The decision has ruffled some feathers and has been criticized by commentators

---

[19] See also *Mayor of London v Hall and Others* (2010); *Olympic Delivery Authority v Persons Unknown* (2012).

as appearing to award proprietary status to the contractual licence. The decision is therefore said to be inconsistent with the orthodoxy which asserts the non-proprietary nature of licences;[20] a point made powerfully by Chadwick LJ in a dissenting opinion. Swadling challenges the majority's assertion that there is no logical distinction between a licensee in and a licensee out of possession:[21]

> The reason why a licensee in possession can bring an action for possession is that he has a right of possession which is completely independent of the licence under which he occupies the land. The error into which, with respect Laws L.J. falls is in failing to notice that a contractual licensee in occupation of land has rights derived from two separate sources, some from the contract, some from the fact of possession. Those derived from the contract prevent the licensor from denying him possession of the land. But those rights, because of the doctrine of privity, and notwithstanding the recent reform of that doctrine, bind the licensor alone. It is the rights derived from the second source, from the fact of possession, which bind third parties.

Applying Swadling's analysis to the facts of *Dutton*, the airport should not be entitled to bring an action for possession against the trespasser as it has no rights deriving from its possession of the land. Instead, the airport should rely on its contractual relationship with the National Trust as landowner to force an action against Mr Dutton. Practically, this may not prove to be fruitful as the airport is at the whim of the landowner who may refuse to pursue legal proceedings.

There has, since *Dutton*, been obiter support for the controversial stance taken by the majority including from Lord Neuberger MR in *Mayor of London v Hall and Others* (2010) who noted:[22]

> There is obvious force in the point that the modern law relating to possession claims should not be shackled by arcane and archaic rules relating to ejectment, and, in particular, that it should develop and adapt to accommodate a claim by anyone entitled to use and control, effectively amounting to possession of the land in question.

Lord Neuberger therefore suggests that those who have a right to use and control of land even if they are not in possession of the land should be able to bring an action against a trespasser. Crucially, these comments are obiter and do not therefore reflect the current law. Interestingly, Lord Neuberger's comments have proved to be equally as controversial as those in *Dutton* itself.[23]

Where does *Dutton* leave us? Swadling would argue that *Dutton* represents an assault on the traditional characterization of licences as personal rights. Others, however, support the decision as affording greater protection to contractual licensees and as a broader move towards accepting that, in limited circumstances, contractual licences can and should be regarded as proprietary rights.[24] *Dutton* therefore provides us with a useful lens through which to consider the future direction of the law in this area.[25]

---

[20] See J. Hill, 'The Proprietary Character of Possession' in E. Cooke (ed.), *Modern Studies in Property Law*, Vol. 1 (Oxford: Hart, 2011); W. Swadling, 'Opening the Numerus Clausus' (2000) 116 LQR 354.

[21] Swadling, 'Opening the Numerus Clausus', 358. [22] *Mayor of London v Hall and Others*, 516.

[23] E. Lochery, 'Pushing the Boundaries of Dutton?' [2011] Conv 74.

[24] K. Gray and S. F. Gray, *Elements of Land Law*, 5th edn (Oxford: Oxford University Press, 2009), [10.5.13].

[25] For more see section 7.4.

7.3.10 Rights of the licensee against the licensor's successors

In this section, we explore the question of the enforceability of contractual licences when a licensor sells or transfers its land to a third party. How far is this third party bound by the contractual licence? In essence, this involves a fundamental question: to what extent can a contractual licence in these circumstances be regarded as constituting a proprietary right? This has proved to be one of the more controversial and vibrant areas of the law of licences.

Our discussion can usefully be divided into three parts: see Figure 7.3. Let's dive into each of these three stages in turn:

- the orthodox position
- the Denning era
- the return to orthodoxy.

7.3.11 The orthodox position

The traditional position is that a contractual licence is a purely personal interest and as a matter of contract law only those parties to the contract are bound by it. As there is no privity of contract between a licensee and a third party purchaser or successor of the licensor's land, the licensee is unable to enforce the licence against that third party. This orthodox statement derives from the House of Lords decision of *King v David Allen & Sons Billposting Ltd* (1916) as confirmed by the Court of Appeal in *Clore v Theatrical Properties Ltd* (1936). Lord Buckmaster LC in *King* explained that a contractual licence permitting David Allen & Sons, a billposting company, to mount posters on a cinema wall was not binding on a successor in title of the licensor, Mr King:[26]

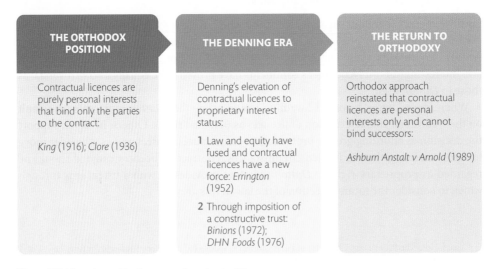

Figure 7.3 Three 'stages' in the status of contractual licences

---

[26] *King v David Allen & Sons Billposting Ltd*, 62.

[I]t seems to me that . . . [the licence] does not create any interest in land at all; it merely amounts to a promise on the part of [A] that he would allow the other party to the contract to use the wall for advertising purposes.

Whilst these decisions represent high authority, two important points deserve mention. First, neither case concerned a licensee who was in sole possession of the land which Maudsley[27] has argued may have shaped the judgments. Secondly, *King* and *Clore* were decided prior to *Winter Garden* and the approval of equity's intervention to render a contractual licence irrevocable. These two aspects may have changed the outcome in both decisions and should be borne in mind in assessing the strength of this traditional authority. Nevertheless, the authority of *King* clearly supports the orthodox position of the purely personal character of contractual licences. The House of Lords in *King* emphasized that contractual licences are not provided for in s. 1 of the LPA 1925, which lists those interests capable of being property interests in land. In addition, s. 4(1) of the LPA 1925 prohibits the creation of new interests in land:

> Interests in land validly created or arising after the commencement of this Act, which are not capable of subsisting as legal estates, shall take effect as equitable interests, and, save as otherwise expressly provided by statute, interests in land which under the Statute of Uses or otherwise could before the commencement of this Act have been created as legal interests, shall be capable of being created as equitable interests . . .

This provision leads Briggs[28] to argue that if contractual licences are ever to qualify as proprietary interests this would require evidence that they existed as interests in land prior to the enactment of the 1925 legislation. Briggs considers this 'impossible' in view of *King* and would require the courts to 'conjure out of existence' the prohibition on the recognition of new property rights under s. 4.

7.3.12 The Lord Denning era

In a series of decisions from the 1950s to the 1970s, Lord Denning set out to elevate the contractual licence to the status of a proprietary right capable of binding third parties. This began with the House of Lords decision in *Errington v Errington and Woods*; a decision which, it is fair to say, came as something of a surprise to property lawyers!

KEY CASE *Errington v Errington and Woods* (1952)

Facts: A father, Mr Errington, purchased a house in Newcastle with the assistance of a mortgage to provide a home for his son and daughter-in-law. Mr Errington paid £250 with the remainder of the purchase price covered by means of a mortgage loan. Mr Errington promised that if his son and daughter-in-law continued to pay the mortgage instalments, the pair could live there for as long as they wished and further that, on discharge of the mortgage, the house would be transferred into their names. Mr Errington died and left his entire estate to his widow. The son and daughter-in-law split

→

---

[27] R. H. Maudsley, 'Licences to Remain on Land (Other than a Wife's Licence)' [1956] Conv 281.
[28] A. Briggs, 'Contractual Licences: A Reply' [1983] Conv 285, 290.

> →
>
> and the son returned to live with his mother. The mother sought possession of the house from the daughter-in-law who had continued to reside there.
>
> Legal issue: Was the mother entitled to possession of the house or was there a basis on which the daughter-in-law might enjoy an entitlement to remain in the property?
>
> Judgment: At first instance, the court dismissed the mother's claim to possession. She appealed unsuccessfully to the Court of Appeal. In the Court of Appeal, Denning LJ (as he then was) found that the daughter-in-law held a contractual licence which was binding on the mother (a third party). Denning LJ noted:
>
>> [Mr Errington's] promise was a unilateral contract—a promise of the house in return for their act of paying the instalment. It could not be revoked by him once the couple entered on performance of the act ... if [son and daughter-in-law] continue to pay all the building society installment, [they] will be entitled to have the property transferred to them as soon as the mortgage is paid off.
>
> Denning LJ continued:
>
>> Law and equity have been fused for nearly 80 years, and since [*Winter Garden*] it has been clear that as a result of the fusion, a licensor will not be permitted to eject a licensee in breach of a contract to allow him to remain ... This fusion of equity means that contractual licences now have a force and validity of their own and cannot be revoked in breach of contract. Neither the licensor nor anyone who claims through him can disregard the contract ...
>
> The mother was not entitled to an order for possession and her appeal was dismissed.

Errington was a controversial decision and subjected to serious academic[29] as well as judicial[30] criticism. In particular, it is striking that no authority was provided by Denning for the elevation of the contractual licence to this proprietary status and little or no explanation offered to justify this beyond what is, you might think, a bold assertion that they simply *are* capable of binding successors. However we rationalize this, Denning's approach can be seen as stemming from his development of the so-called 'deserted wife's equity'[31] in the case of *Bendall v McWhirter* (1952).

It would, however, be wrong to suggest that was no academic or judicial support for the Denning approach in *Errington*. Watt,[32] for example, has written in defence of the decision and Fox LJ in *Ashburn Anstalt v Arnold* (1989) explained that the result reached in *Errington* could be justified albeit on different grounds:[33]

> It is not in doubt that the actual decision was correct. It could be justified on one of three grounds: (i) there was a contract to convey the house on completion of the payments giving rise to an equitable interest in the form of an estate contract which would be binding on widow ... who was not a purchaser for value. (ii) the daughter-in-law had changed her position in reliance upon a

---

[29] H. W. R. Wade, 'Licences and Third Parties' (1952) 68 LQR 337; A. D. Hargreaves, 'Licenced Possessors' (1953) 69 LQR 466; but compare G. C. Cheshire, 'A New Equitable Interest in Land' (1953) 16 MLR 1.

[30] *National Provincial Bank Ltd v Hastings Car Mart Ltd* (1964), per Russell LJ; *National Provincial Bank Ltd v Ainsworth*; *Re Solomon* (1967), per Goff J.

[31] This was a claim a deserted wife could assert meaning she had a proprietary right to remain resident in the matrimonial home, binding purchasers. This equity was rejected in *National Provincial Bank Ltd v Ainsworth*; *Re Solomon*.

[32] G. Watt, 'The Proprietary Effect of a Chattel Lease' [2003] Conv 61.   [33] *Ashburn*, 17.

representation binding on the widow [under an estoppel]. (iii) the payment and instalments by the son and daughter-in-law gave rise to direct proprietary interests by way of constructive trust, though it is true that, until *Gissing v Gissing*, the law relating to constructive trusts in this field was not much considered.

Despite Fox LJ's best efforts to justify the decision on alternative grounds, Denning had clearly relied squarely on the fusion of law and equity and, more specifically, the irrevocability of a contractual licence in equity under *Winter Garden*. It has been argued that Denning's reasoning reflects a misunderstanding of the fundamental character of property rights. McFarlane,[34] for example, argues that Denning fails to overcome the hurdles necessary to prove that a contractual right has become proprietary in nature. He explains:

> [Denning LJ] misunderstands the true effect of the availability of specific performance on the proprietary status of a right: it treats something which is at most a *necessary* condition of a right to use property's being proprietary as a sufficient condition of that consequence ... the mere fact that specific performance is available against [the contractual licensor] does not prove that [the contractual licensee's] right *must* be proprietary. The question of whether to confer proprietary status on a right involves considerations additional to those addressed when deciding that specific performance is available ... Most obviously, [the contractual licensee] must show why he should be protected as against a party who, unlike [the contractual licensor], has made no contractual promise to him ...

This criticism of Denning's reasoning was first recognized by Lord Wilberforce in *National Provincial Bank v Ainsworth* where he noted:[35]

> The fact that a contractual right can be specifically performed, or its breach prevented by injunction, does not mean that the right is any the less of a personal character or that a purchaser with notice is bound by it: what is relevant is the nature of the right, not the remedy which exists for its enforcement.

Lord Denning again attempted to revise the orthodox classification of contractual licences in the cases of *Binions v Evans* and *DHN Food Distributors Ltd v Tower Hamlets LBC* in holding that a contractual licence could bind third parties under the operation of a constructive trust.

KEY CASE *Binions v Evans* (1972)

Facts: The defendant, Mrs Evans was employed by the Tredegar Estate and lived rent-free with her husband in a cottage owned by the estate. The husband died and Mrs Evans was permitted to remain in the cottage 'as a tenant at will, rent free for the remainder of her life' on the proviso that she kept the cottage in repair and tended the garden. The cottage owners subsequently sold land which included the cottage to Mr and Mrs Binions 'subject to' Mrs Evans' interest in the cottage. This was reflected in a reduced purchase price paid by the Binions. The Binions issued legal proceedings seeking possession of the cottage and the removal of Mrs Evans from the land.

→

---

[34] B. McFarlane, 'Identifying Property Rights: A Reply to Mr Watt' [2003] Conv 473, 475.
[35] *National Provincial Bank v Ainsworth*, 1243.

→

Legal issue: Mrs Evans argued, first, that the agreement she had entered with the owners of the Tredegar Estate gave rise to a proprietary right that was binding on the Binions and, secondly, that the Binions had purchased the land 'subject to' her right and were, as a consequence, bound.

Judgment: The Court of Appeal all agreed that Mrs Evans could remain in the cottage but reached this result via quite different routes. The majority view (Megaw and Stephenson LJJ) was that the early agreement with the Tredegar Estate that she could live in the cottage gave rise to an equitable life interest in her favour which was capable of binding the Binions. On this basis, there was no need to endow contractual licences with proprietary character. Lord Denning MR, however, in the minority, held that Mrs Evans' contractual licence to make use of the cottage either constituted an equitable interest in the land capable of binding the Binions or, alternatively, a constructive trust arose in the circumstances as the Binions had purchased the land 'subject to' Mrs Evans' right. This was reflected in the reduced purchase price and it would be 'utterly inequitable' for the Binions to go back on this deal.

Lord Denning built upon his approach in *Binions* in *DHN*.

KEY CASE *DHN Food Distributors Ltd v Tower Hamlets LBC* (1976)

Facts: A fruit distributor, DHN, ran a business from land owned by Bronze Ltd under a contractual licence. Tower Hamlets London Borough Council enforced a compulsory purchase order of the land. The issue arose as to whether the Council owed compensation to the parties as a result of its compulsory purchase. Under statute, compensation was payable only where a party with an 'interest' (i.e. proprietary right) in the land had experienced a disruption to its business. The Council argued that Bronze Ltd was not conducting a trade from the land and, further, that DHN did not enjoy an 'interest' in the land—it being a licensee only.

Legal issue: Was DHN entitled to compensation for disruption to its business as a result of the compulsory purchase? If so, how could it be argued that the contractual licence under which DHN occupied the land amounted to an 'interest in land'?

Judgment: In the Lands Tribunal, the Council's argument that neither Bronze Ltd nor DHN were entitled to compensation succeeded. DHN appealed. In the Court of Appeal, DHN's appeal was allowed but, as in *Errington*, with the members of the court adopting different means of reaching the same result. Goff and Shaw LJJ held that due to the nature of the business relationship between Bronze Ltd and DHN, Bronze Ltd's right to the land was held on trust for the benefit of DHN. The result was that DHN enjoyed an equitable (proprietary) interest in the land and compensation was therefore payable.

Lord Denning MR took a different approach holding that the contractual licence between Bronze Ltd and DHN was irrevocable and, in those circumstances, in line with the authority of *Binions*, a constructive trust arose. Lord Denning explained:

> [the] contractual licence gives rise to a constructive trust, under which the legal owner is not allowed to turn out the licensee. So here. This irrevocable licence gave to DHN a sufficient interest in the land to qualify them for compensation for disturbance.

Lord Denning's analysis is highly contentious and, in truth, very difficult to justify. His approach involves an apparently unsubstantiated leap in reasoning from a finding of irrevocability of the contractual licence to the imposition of a constructive trust.

This automatic imposition of a constructive trust in these circumstances is neither faithful to the decision in *Binions*[36] nor to constructive trust principles more generally. The decision in *DHN* therefore represents the high watermark of the Denning era in his attempts to elevate the contractual licence to the status of a proprietary interest in land. Despite this, Browne-Wilkinson J reluctantly applied *DHN* in *Re Sharpe (A Bankrupt)* (1980) a case in which a contractual licence was held to be binding against a trustee in bankruptcy. The law was, however, ripe for a return to orthodoxy.

7.3.13 **The return to orthodoxy**

The case of *Ashburn* is credited with reinstating the orthodox position. Fox LJ delivering the judgment, engaged in a review of the authorities, and reaffirmed the traditional approach that a contractual licence was a purely personal interest and could not bind successors in title. Fox LJ reviewed all the key authorities on the status of contractual licences prior to *Errington* concluding that 'down to this point we do not think there is any serious doubt as to the law'. Fox LJ identified *Errington* as the only supporting authority for an argument for the proprietary status of contractual licences but rejected it as being inconsistent with the earlier authorities of *King* and *Clore*. Denning LJ's stance in *Errington* was noted as being:[37]

> not necessary for the decisions and *per incuriam* in the sense that it was made without reference to authorities which . . . would surely have persuaded the court to adopt a different ratio . . . there must be real doubts whether *Errington* . . . can be reconciled with the earlier decisions of the House of Lords. . .in our judgment the House of Lords cases . . . state the correct principle which we should follow.

Fox LJ rejected the *DHN* analysis in so far as it suggested that a contractual licence would be binding under a constructive trust imposed automatically where the licence was found to be irrevocable:[38]

> For the reasons which we have already noted, we prefer the line of authorities which determine that a contractual licence does not create a property interest. We do not think that the argument is assisted by the bare assertion that the interest arises under a constructive trust.

Importantly, Fox LJ's dicta in *Ashburn* were obiter only as, on the facts of the particular case, the court identified the existence of a lease rather than a licence and so was not called upon to determine the issue directly. On one view, this weakens the authority on the licences issue. Yet, the discussion engaged by Fox LJ was a fulsome and lengthy one and in line with the earlier judgments of the House of Lords.

Whilst obiter only, the Court of Appeal judgment in *Ashburn* is widely regarded as finally settling the matter of the status of contractual licences and has been endorsed in subsequent case law. In *Camden LBC v Shortlife Community Housing* (1993), Millett J stated that *Ashburn* had:[39]

---

[36] A case involving agreement 'subject to' the licensee's right and in circumstances that were said to be unconscionable. In *DHN*, neither of these positions was established.
[37] *Ashburn*, 22.   [38] Ibid., 24.   [39] *Camden LBC*, 341.

finally repudiated the heretical view that a contractual licence creates an interest in land capable of binding third parties.

The court's treatment of the Denning era and his attempts to elevate the status of the contractual licence may seem harsh but you should remember that the weight of authority was in support, even at the time of *Errington*, of the personal status of contractual licences. *Ashburn* is now widely regarded as good authority and represents settled law. Unless and until the matter reaches the Supreme Court, we can therefore safely proceed on the basis that contractual licences enjoy only a personal as opposed to a proprietary status.

7.3.14 Contractual licences: Outstanding arguments as to proprietary status

Whilst the personal status of contractual licences appears settled, a number of arguments can still be made that contractual licences should be regarded as interests in land. Three of these are explored here:

- The s. 116 LRA 2002 argument: There is an argument that s. 116 of the LRA 2002 allows contractual licences to bind third parties and therefore exude a proprietary character. Section 116 (discussed at greater length in section 7.3.17) confirms that a 'mere equity' (arising for example following a successful claim to proprietary estoppel) is capable of binding successors. It could, therefore, be argued that a contractual licence awarded as a remedy after a successful estoppel claim gives rise to a 'mere equity' capable of being enforced against third parties. It is, however, plain that this was not Parliament's intention[40] in enacting this provision and, in addition, this construction does not accord with the broader objective of the registration project to offer greater protections to third parties rather than impose greater burdens.

- The Art. 8 ECHR argument: A second argument is based on a licensee's right to respect for private and family life under Art. 8 of the ECHR. Imagine a scenario in which a licensee occupies a property as her 'home' under a contractual licence and that occupation is threatened by a third party acquiring title to the licensor's land. Would an Art. 8 argument permit the licence to be binding on that third party? The precise ambit and implications of human rights arguments in land law are explored fully in Chapter 14 but it suffices here to note some of the potential problems with this human rights' analysis. First, it will be a rare case where the third party in question is a public authority so as to engage Art. 8. Secondly, if a third party threatens to evict a licensee, a proportionality exercise will be conducted. Most likely, the availability of a contractual claim for damages by the licensee against the original licensor would offer sufficient protection for the licensee's Art. 8 rights and therefore prevent a successful Art. 8 claim. Finally, the message is loud and clear from Lord Neuberger in *Manchester City Council v Pinnock* (2010) that 'unencumbered property rights . . . are of real weight when it comes to proportionality'. It seems that in the vast majority of cases the personal rights of a licensee will yield to the proprietary right of any third party.

---

[40] Law Commission Report No. 271, *Land Registration for the Twenty-First Century* (2001), [5.32]–[5.32].

- The Maudsley exclusive possession argument: Maudsley[41] has argued that contractual licences under which the licensee enjoys **exclusive possession** of the licensor's land should be considered as giving rise to an equitable property right capable of binding third parties. Note: Maudsley was writing in the mid-1950s at a time when the accepted definition of a lease was far narrower in scope than is currently the case. In light of this, the force of Maudsley's argument is somewhat lost, as today, the grant of exclusive possession for a certain period will give rise to a lease and not a licence.[42] In view of this, there is no longer any real need to expand the status of contractual licences in modern land law to pick up the slack of a restrictive definition of a lease.

None of these arguments is ultimately convincing and so the current state of the law as established in *King* and *Clore* and reaffirmed in *Ashburn* remains firmly rooted in place.

7.3.15 Contractual licences and enforcement under a constructive trust

Whilst the Court of Appeal in *Ashburn* closed the door on the proprietary nature of contractual licences, nevertheless, it did identify one scenario in which a contractual licence would bind a third party—namely, where a court finds a constructive trust. So, how does this constructive trust work and when will it arise?

If a constructive trust is imposed on a third party acquiring the licensor's land, a contractual licence arising on the facts will be binding on that third party. This licence is not binding because the licence exhibits proprietary qualities but rather as a consequence of the constructive trust itself. Strictly speaking, we can say that the licence takes effect against the third party personally as opposed to being binding on the land. The constructive trust here is based on dicta of Denning in *Binions*. In *Ashburn*, Fox LJ considered an argument advanced by Counsel that in every case where land is sold 'subject to' a contractual licence (as in *Binions*), a constructive trust would automatically be imposed on the purchaser to give effect to that licence. Drawing on the case of *Lyus v Prowsa* (1982), Fox LJ rejected this argument:[43]

> The court will not impose a constructive trust unless it is satisfied that the conscience of the estate owner is affected. The mere fact that land is expressed to be conveyed 'subject to' a contract does not necessarily imply that the grantee is to be under an obligation, not otherwise existing, to give effect to the provisions of the contract.

There are therefore limits on when a constructive trust will be imposed on a third party acquiring the licensor's land. A constructive trust will only be imposed on a third party whose conscience is affected and will not be 'imposed in reliance on inferences from slender materials'.[44] A constructive trust will not arise automatically when land over which the licence is operating is transferred (for example, sold) to a third party and that transfer is said to be made 'subject to' the licence or licensee's rights. This is because 'subject to' clauses are relatively standard practice in land conveyancing and routinely included in contracts of sale: *Chaudhary v Yavuz* (2013).

---

[41] Maudsley, 'Licences to Remain on Land (Other than a Wife's Licence)'.
[42] *Street v Mountford* (1985) discussed at length in Chapter 9.
[43] *Ashburn*, at 25–6.   [44] Ibid., 26.

So, when will a third party's conscience be affected? Sir Christopher Slade in *Lloyd v Dugdale* (2001) explained:[45]

> The crucially important question is whether [the successor] has undertaken a new obligation, not otherwise existing, to give effect to the relevant incumbrance or prior interest. If but only if, he has undertaken such a new obligation will a constructive trust be imposed.

The most important phrase here is 'new obligation'. Payment of a reduced purchase price (as in *Binions*) may provide evidence of a new obligation. In *Chaudhary*, a term in a contract of sale that land was sold subject to incumbrances and prior interests 'discoverable by inspection of the property before the contract' was insufficient to demonstrate that the purchaser had undertaken a 'new obligation' to give effect to those rights. *Chaudhary* confirms that the court will be slow to impose a constructive trust. Lloyd LJ noted that *Lyus* was 'a very unusual case, and is not likely to be followed in more than a few others'. In summary, whilst a constructive trust analysis can result in a contractual licence being enforceable against a third party acquiring the licensor's land, it will not be easily established and will only arise where that third party's conscience is affected as a result of having undertaken a 'new obligation' to be bound by the contractual licence. Even then, the constructive trust will only operate to bind that particular third party and will not bind any further successors unless their conscience is also affected. It is in this way that we can say the constructive trust operates personally.

7.3.16 Contractual licensees and the Contracts (Rights of Third Parties) Act 1999

In certain circumstances, the Contracts (Rights of Third Parties) Act 1999 may provide a contractual licensee with a right against a third party (i.e. against someone who is not a party to the original licence).

Let's take an example to see how the 1999 Act works: imagine Arjan grants Beth a contractual licence over his land for two years. Arjan then decides to transfer his land to a third party, Cora. In the ordinary course, the contractual licence as a personal interest would not be binding on Cora. However, if at the time of the sale, Arjan extracts from Cora a promise that she will permit Beth to continue making use of the land within the terms of the original licence, the position is different. If the provisions of s. 1 of the Contracts (Rights of Third Parties) Act 1999 are satisfied, Beth will enjoy a right directly against Cora to enforce the licence. Under s. 1 of the 1999 Act, the promise made by Cora must be such that it 'purports to confer a benefit' on Beth. Additionally, the promise must be contractual in nature, in other words, it must comply with the provisions for a valid contract in s. 2 of the LP(MP)A 1989. If so, Beth will be able to enforce this benefit directly against Cora. This may sound all rather convoluted but, in practice, there are good reasons for Arjan, in our example, to insist that Cora make this contractual promise on the transfer of land. If Arjan were to transfer his land to Cora without this promise, he could find himself facing legal action from Beth for breach of contract. The 1999 Act is therefore a very useful statute for allowing the enforcement of personal contractual licences against third parties provided its provisions are satisfied.

---

[45] *Lloyd v Dugdale*, 182.

7.3.17 **Estoppel licences**

We now return to consider our final 'type' of licence: the estoppel licence. An estoppel licence is quite simply a licence which arises by means of the doctrine of proprietary estoppel. What sets apart estoppel licences from other licences is therefore the route by which they arise. A claim of proprietary estoppel is a claim to be entitled to an interest in land and requires a claimant to establish that assurances made have been relied on by the claimant to her detriment in circumstances in which it would be unconscionable for the maker of those assurances to go back on their assurances. We explore estoppel in the next chapter. For now, it suffices to appreciate that if a claim of proprietary estoppel is successful, the court will move to 'satisfy the equity' or, put another way, to award a remedy. The court has a range of remedies at its disposal. One option for the court is to grant the claimant a licence. This licence will be an estoppel licence. One example of a case where a licence was awarded as a result of a successful proprietary estoppel claim is *Inwards v Baker*. In *Inwards*, a son was encouraged to build a bungalow on land owned by his father. The Court of Appeal awarded the son an irrevocable licence to occupy the bungalow for as long as he wished.

In considering the scope of estoppel licences, key questions have been raised. How far, for example, and in what circumstances can an estoppel licence bind third parties? In addressing this question, we look to s. 116 of the LRA 2002 which, as we noted in section 7.3.14, provides that an 'equity by estoppel' is capable of binding successors from the time it arises subject to the rules of registration. Section 116 seems to have important implications for estoppel licences. According to this provision, from the moment the estoppel (often called an 'inchoate equity') arises but *before* the court makes an order as to remedy, that inchoate equity is *capable* of being registered and thereby binding third parties. This was the stated intention of the Law Commission in recommending the enactment of s. 116:[46]

> [P]roprietary estoppel is increasingly important as a mechanism for the informal creation of property rights. To put the matter beyond doubt, we recommend that the proprietary status of an equity arising by estoppel should be confirmed in relation to registered land.

The result is that the enforceability of estoppel licences is in apparent conflict with the confirmed personal status of contractual licences. McFarlane[47] explores this further:

> [T]he Law Commission's interpretation of [s. 116] re-awakens another such debate which might have been thought settled. As a result of section 116(a), a licence arising through proprietary estoppel would operate differently to a contractual licence: the former could bind [a third party], provided the land was transferred to him before a court order granting the . . . licence. It could be argued in such a case that it is not the licence itself which binds [a third party] but rather the independent 'equity' that arose as a result of the estoppel before the licence was awarded by the court. Yet why does no such 'equity' arise in the case of a contractual licence?

McFarlane therefore identifies an inconsistency of treatment between estoppel licences and contractual licences. McFarlane suggests that an inchoate equity should not bind third parties particularly in regard to those holding estoppel licences. Yet the Commission is crystal

---

[46] Law Commission Report No. 271, [5.30].

[47] B. McFarlane, 'Proprietary Estoppel and Third Parties after the Land Registration Act 2002' (2003) 62 CLJ 661, 690.

clear in its view and confirms in no uncertain terms that an inchoate equity is to be regarded as *capable* of binding successors subject to the relevant rules of registration. Hill[48] has noted the need for the development of precisely defined principles to avoid arbitrary results here:

> In order to avoid the charge of arbitrariness, at the same time maintaining that contractual licences are personal and estoppel licences are proprietary, the courts will have to evolve a theory which enables them clearly to distinguish estoppel interests from contractual licences. There is little to be said for a system of property law according to which the position of third parties depends on a dividing line which the position of third parties depends on a dividing line which the courts are unable to draw.

7.4 Future directions

In this chapter, we have explored the operation of the law of licences. Much of the law presented in this chapter is settled but there is one key area of ongoing debate: the precise status of licences. The debate continues as to the extent to which a licence (particularly a contractual licence) represents a proprietary interest in land. This involves a consideration of precisely what makes an interest in land *proprietary*. Lord Wilberforce in *National Provincial Bank Ltd v Ainsworth* said that an interest in land should be 'definable, identifiable by third parties, capable in its nature of assumption by third parties, and have some degree of permanence or stability'. How far do the various types of licence meet this definition? Certainly, issues remain unresolved in the law on contractual licences. How significant, for example, is the decision in *Dutton* in challenging the traditional view of the nature and status of licences? Does *Dutton* signal a greater willingness on the part of the court to embrace the proprietary nature of licences or does it reflect merely a judicial anomaly?

Further reading

- G. Battersby, 'Informally Created Interests' in S. Bright and J. Dewar (eds.), *Land Law: Themes and Perspectives* (Oxford: Oxford University Press, 1998).
- P. Birks, 'Equity in the Modern Law: An Exercise in Taxonomy' (1996) 26 University of Western Australia Law Review 1, 60.
- S. Bright, 'The Third Party's Conscience in Land Law' [2000] Conv 398.
- A. Goymour, 'Cobbling Together Claims Where a Contract Fails to Materialise' (2009) 68(1) CLJ 37.
- J. Hill, 'Leases, Licences and Third Parties' (1988) 51 MLR 226.
- W. Hohfield, 'Faulty Analysis in Easement and License Cases' (1917) Yale LJ 6.
- E. Lochery, 'Pushing the Boundaries of *Dutton*?' [2011] Conv 74.

---

[48] J. Hill (1988) 52 MLR 266. Hill considers the issue of consistency between contractual and estoppel licences after the decision in *Ashburn* suggesting any inconsistency may not be objectionable if arbitrary results are avoided and clear, defined principles identified.

- B. McFarlane, 'Identifying Property Rights: A Reply to Mr Watt' [2003] Conv 473.
- S. Moriarty, 'Licences and Land Law: Legal Principles and Public Bodies' (1984) 100 LQR 376.
- W. Swadling, 'Property' in A. Burrows (ed.), *English Private Law*, 3rd edn (Oxford: Oxford University Press, 2013).
- H. R. Wade, 'Licences and Third Parties' (1952) 68 LQR 337.

Online resources

Access the online resources at www.oup.com/uk/bevan2e/ to test yourself with self-test questions and scenario problems. You can also view additional supporting material relevant to the topics in this chapter, including:

- *Videos*
- *Audio podcasts*
- *Maps, diagrams, and flowcharts*
- *Interactive exercises*
- *Examples of real-life legal documentation*

Proprietary Estoppel

8.1 Introduction

In this chapter, you will be introduced to the doctrine of proprietary estoppel—a means by which a person may acquire a proprietary interest in another's land. The word 'estoppel' derives from old French and describes a situation where a person is prevented or, as we say, 'estopped' from denying the truth of a particular factual position or legal status. There are in fact many distinct forms of estoppel and you may have already come across promissory estoppel in the law of contract. It is, however, proprietary estoppel that is our focus in this chapter. If made out, a claim to proprietary estoppel allows for the informal creation and acquisition of rights in land rather than just being raised as a defence against legal actions (as is the case for example in promissory estoppel). It is this that sets proprietary estoppel apart and represents its major point of distinction from other estoppels. You come to proprietary estoppel at a time when the law has hit something of a fertile patch. With a bounty of case law, new decisions seemingly handed down almost monthly (and most involving farmland) and some even catching the attention of the mainstream media, proprietary estoppel is having its moment in the sun and remains one of the liveliest and most productive areas of land law today. What a great moment to study proprietary estoppel!

 Visit the online resources to watch a video on the future of proprietary estoppel.

8.2 Proprietary estoppel: Overview

The doctrine of proprietary estoppel is a form of equitable estoppel providing a means by which property rights are created. It can operate to give rights to someone who would otherwise have no rights in a piece of land at all. Moriarty describes the doctrine of proprietary estoppel as providing for:[1]

---

[1]   S. Moriarty, 'Licences and Land Law: Legal Principles and Public Policy' (1984) 100 LQR 376.

The informal creation of interests in land whenever a person has acted detrimentally in reliance upon an oral assurance [or representation] that he has such an interest.

The creation of interests in land normally requires a degree of *formality* such as the use of a deed, registered disposition, or specifically enforceable contract.[2] S. 2 of the LP(MP)A 1989 requires that contracts for the sale of land or disposition of any interest in land be made in writing, signed by or on behalf of the all the parties, and incorporating all the terms. (implied, resulting, and constructive trusts are excluded from these formalities requirements: s. 2(5) of the LP(MP)A 1989). Section 52 of the LPA 1925 (subject to the exception for short leases in s. 54(2)) requires that all conveyances of land or interests in land will be void unless made by deed.[3]

So, what of the interplay between proprietary estoppel and formality requirements? The doctrine of proprietary estoppel operates outside these formality requirements. A claim to an interest in land based on proprietary estoppel can be advanced where there is no deed or written contract at all. This is because proprietary estoppel, an equitable doctrine, springs from the conduct and importantly the *conscience* of the parties, usually as a result of a representation or assurance made by the landowner which is relied upon by the person claiming the right to her detriment. The doctrine therefore generates rights in land informally or in the absence of formalities.

Given proprietary estoppel operates outside the statutory formality requirements, there might be a concern that estoppel arguments are advanced to avoid the consequences of a failure of formality—for example, where a contract is invalid—and thereby to get round the statutory provisions. In *Yaxley v Gotts* (2000), the court said estoppel should not be used in this way to validate an otherwise unenforceable agreement. Lord Scott in *Yeoman's Row Management Ltd v Cobbe* (2008) took a stricter line, noting obiter:[4]

> [P]roprietary estoppel cannot be prayed in aid in order to render enforceable an agreement that statute has declared to be void. The proposition that an owner of land can be estopped from asserting that an agreement is void for want of compliance with the requirements of section 2 is, in my opinion, unacceptable. The assertion is no more than the statute provides. Equity can surely not contradict the statute.

Lord Neuberger in *Thorner v Major* (2009) explained, however, that, he did not consider 'that section 2 [of the LP(MP)A] has any impact on a claim such as the present, which is a straightforward estoppel claim without any contractual connection'.[5] Thus, Neuberger suggests that the formalities problem only bites if there is a 'contractual connection' in the arrangements between the parties. All this means is that the issue of the interplay between proprietary estoppel and formalities is not finally settled but, crucially, proprietary

---

[2] Of course, there are exceptions including short leases, easement by prescription to name but two.
[3] The requirements for deeds are found in s. 1 of the LP(MP)A 1989.
[4] *Yeoman's Row Management Ltd v Cobbe*, [29], per Lord Scott.
[5] *Thorner*, [99], per Lord Neuberger.

Figure 8.1 The two stages of a proprietary estoppel claim

estoppel operates in the absence of formality requirements and outside provisions such as s. 2 LP(MP)A and s. 52 of the LPA 1925.

So, how does proprietary estoppel work? Proprietary estoppel is the more ferocious property law manifestation of its contractual cousin, promissory estoppel, in that proprietary estoppel can be used both as a defence or shield when a landowner seeks to enforce his strict legal rights or as a sword in a claim seeking to establish rights over land.[6] Proprietary estoppel is therefore a powerful doctrine and, indeed, it has been suggested that the label 'estoppel' itself might be misleading in giving rise to an inaccurate perception that the doctrine operates only as a mere evidential device.[7] In short, proprietary estoppel is capable of creating rights in land arising from assurances, promises, or representations made as to an individual's rights. As Figure 8.1 depicts, there are two essential stages to mounting a successful claim for proprietary estoppel.

Let's consider each stage in turn.

8.3 Proprietary estoppel: Establishing an 'equity'

The first stage involves establishing an equity. Establishing an 'equity' is the process by which a claimant demonstrates that the requirements or conditions for an estoppel have been satisfied and that the claimant is entitled to call for a remedy. Before we move to examine the essential elements of estoppel in the modern law, we'll take a momentary historical detour to explore the evolution of the doctrine. This proves instructive in shining a light on the flexibility inherent in the law today.

8.3.1 The historical context

Proprietary estoppel has a lengthy pedigree in property law and reflects another example of equity's intervention in mitigating the harshness of the common law which is marked by its particularly unbending insistence on compliance with formalities for the creation of property rights. The doctrine of proprietary estoppel developed primarily in two nineteenth-century cases: *Ramsden v Dyson* (1866) and *Willmott v Barber* (1880). In this latter case, Fry J laid down five *probanda* (Latin for 'things needing to be proved') as prerequisites for a

---

[6] This shield/sword narrative describes the difference between mounting an estoppel argument as a defence (i.e. shield) to legal proceedings and, alternatively, mounting an estoppel argument as a positive tool (i.e. sword) to claim an interest in land.

[7] B. McFarlane, 'Understanding Equitable Estoppel: From Metaphors to Better Laws' (2013) 66 CLP 267.

successful claim of proprietary estoppel. These were strictly drawn and operated onerously, arguably stultifying the development and operation of the doctrine of proprietary estoppel,[8] requiring, amongst other things, that the claimant had made a mistake, money had been expended, and knowledge of that mistake. It was quite inevitable that with the passage of time and the shifting of social and economic conditions, the doctrine would cast off the shackles of Fry J's rigid *probanda*.

8.3.2 **The modern law**

In *Taylors Fashions Ltd v Liverpool Victoria Trustees Co. Ltd* (1982), Oliver J set down what is now regarded as the modern statement of the law, adopting a broader, more flexible approach to the requirements of the doctrine and identifying the four features necessary for a successful estoppel claim: Figure 8.2.

In two of the leading decisions on the operation of proprietary estoppel, *Gillett v Holt* (2001) and *Jennings v Rice* (2002), the court confirmed the view that the four features of estoppel should be regarded less as a rigid checklist to be followed in every case but instead as a series of interrelated factors to be considered 'in the round'.[9] This is an important recognition of the 'broad-brush', 'holistic' approach taken by the court to proprietary estoppel.[10] Of course, it is all well and good for the judiciary to signal the need for a broad-brush examination of the elements of a claim for proprietary estoppel but how should you, as a student getting to grips with the law, tackle this doctrine? For the sake of clarity, this chapter proceeds to consider in turn each of the four features of the modern law. Do keep in mind, however, that there is an obvious artificiality to this approach but one which is unavoidable in the interests of providing a clear elucidation of the principles. You should also heed the words of Gardner who has observed that:[11]

> There is no definition of proprietary estoppel that is both comprehensive and uncontroversial (and many attempts at one have been neither).

Let's now consider each of the four conditions for the modern law of proprietary estoppel: assurance, reliance, detriment, and unconscionability.

Figure 8.2 Proprietary estoppel: Features of the modern law

---

[8] Yet these requirements were applied as late as the 1970s: *Kammins Ballroom Co. v Zenith Instruments Ltd* (1971); *Crabb v Arun DC* (1976).

[9] Confirmed in *Ottey v Grundy* (2003).

[10] Expressly endorsed in *Thorner*; see also comments by Walker LJ in *Gillett*.

[11] S. Gardner, *An Introduction to Land Law* (Oxford: Hart, 2007), 101.

8.3.3 **The assurance**

The essence of the doctrine is that the claimant acted in the belief that she was entitled or would become entitled to an interest in land. Therefore, there must be an assurance or representation of an entitlement or that the landowner would desist from asserting his strict legal rights over its land. The assurance can be seen as bridging the gap between the behaviour of the landowner and the expectations of the claimant.

The assurance may be expressly made or communicated by the conduct of the landowner, viewed objectively. An express or active assurance will exist where a landowner, by words of conduct, leads the claimant to believe that she will enjoy an entitlement in the landowner's land. In *Pascoe v Turner* (1979),[12] a defendant's reassurance to his partner that a house they shared was hers along with all its contents constituted a valid assurance in support of her estoppel claim.

The assurance may be passive or communicated by the landowner's inaction—for example, where a landowner stands by and fails to disabuse a claimant of a mistaken expectation as to a present or future entitlement to an interest in that landowner's land. In *Cobden Investment Ltd v RWM Langport Ltd* (2008), the landowner stood by as the claimant carried out substantial building work in the knowledge that the claimant had an expectation of an interest in the land.

With what degree of clarity or certainty must the assurance have been made? In *Yeoman's Row Management Ltd v Cobbe*, Lord Scott suggested that the assurance needed to be 'clear and unambiguous'. This was later challenged in the House of Lords in *Thorner*[13] which held that it sufficed that the assurance be 'clear enough'.[14] *Thorner* is a decision that you should read in full.

KEY CASE *Thorner v Major* (2009)

Facts: David Thorner had worked for 30 years without remuneration on a farm owned by his father's cousin, Peter. David had an understanding and expectation that he would inherit the farm on Peter's death. No express representation had ever been made to this effect but there had been various hints and indirect remarks made by Peter over the years which David claimed had led him to believe that he was to inherit the farm. Peter died intestate and David claimed an interest in the land by way of proprietary estoppel.

Legal issue: What was the appropriate test for the character and quality of the representation or assurance needed to establish a successful proprietary estoppel claim?

Judgment: The judge at first instance found in David's favour holding that Peter had made an assurance that the farm would be inherited by David. The Court of Appeal reversed this decision, holding that there had been no clear and unequivocal intention on the part of Peter. There was no basis upon which Peter's statements could be interpreted as providing a definite assurance rather than a statement of present intention. On appeal, the House of Lords allowed David's appeal, holding that there

→

---

[12] See also *Griffiths v Williams* (1977): an assurance of a home for life.

[13] On which generally see: N. Piska, 'Hopes, Expectations and Revocable Promises in Proprietary Estoppel' (2009) 72(6) MLR 998; J. Mee, 'The Limits of Proprietary Estoppel: *Thorner v Major*' (2009) 21(3) CFLQ 367.

[14] The requirement for an assurance to be 'clear enough' has been affirmed recently by the Court of Appeal in *Liden v Burton* (2016), a case which offers a helpful summary of the law of proprietary estoppel more generally and, for that reason alone, well worth a read!

➞

was no uncertainty as to what had been promised to David and that the assurance needed only to be 'clear enough' (per Lord Walker). Explaining this further, Lord Rodger said:

> What matters, however, is that what Peter said should have been clear enough for David, whom he was addressing and who had years of experience in interpreting what he said and did, to form a reasonable view that Peter was giving him an assurance that he was to inherit the farm and that he could rely on it.

Here, the assurances made by Peter were, objectively assessed, construed as a binding commitment in David's favour as opposed to a statement of present, revocable intent. The court declared that Peter's representatives were to hold the farm and its stock on trust for David.

Lord Walker therefore identified, in the following terms, the test of certainty for assurances:[15]

> [T]o establish a proprietary estoppel the relevant assurance must be clear enough. What amounts to sufficient clarity, in a case of this sort, is highly dependent on context.

An assurance need not be 'clear and unequivocal' and the court will have regard to the entire context including potential events taking place after the assurance was made. As Lord Hoffmann in *Thorner* observed:[16]

> Past events provide context and background for the interpretation of subsequent events and subsequent events throw retrospective light upon the meaning of past events. The owl of Minerva spreads its wings only with the falling of dusk.

The recent case of *Habberfield v Habberfield* (2019) helpfully confirmed the elements of an estoppel claim, that an assurance must be 'clear enough' but also demonstrated that even where a series of assurances of future ownership may appear somewhat ambiguous, the court will be prepared, in the particular context of the case, to patch together assurances and, taken as a whole, to find rather disparate assurances as sufficiently clear for the purposes of an estoppel claim. In *Habberfield*, a daughter had worked on the family farm from the 1980s until her father's death in 2014 and relied on various assurances that she understood as meaning she would inherit the farm including comments such as 'they are your cows'; that all her hard work would pay off 'one day'; and that she could not take time off if she 'wanted the farm'. Equally, in *Thompson v Thompson* (2018), although the court could not pinpoint a specific occasion on which promises had been made to a son, Gilbert, to inherit the family farm, the court was satisfied looking over the whole history of events going back years that there was a long-standing and widely understood promise within the family that the son would inherit the farm after his life-long dedication to the business.

The assurance need not demonstrate the same certainty as would be required for a binding contract (*Walton v Walton* (1994)) but it must relate to some identified property

---

[15] *Thorner*, at 794.

[16] Ibid., 780; the use of Hegel's metaphor here is to signify that, in some cases, the truth is only knowable after the event has taken place. Hegel used this imagery to argue that we only gain wisdom through hindsight: see Hegel's *Philosophy of Right*, trans. T. Knox (Oxford: Clarendon, 1967).

of the landowner or property which that landowner is about to own.[17] In most cases this will be unproblematic but consider *Layton v Martin* (1986) in which no effective assurance was found as a man's promise to provide 'financial security' for a woman did not relate to identifiable assets. Whilst the assurance must concern identifiable property, it is plain that there is no need for the assurance to be made as to a specific property right—for example, there is no need for statements such as: 'I promise you freehold ownership of my house.' This was confirmed in *Thorner* itself where despite Peter having made no assurance as to a specific property right, David's claim was upheld. In *Re Basham* (1986) an assurance that the claimant would become entitled to the entirety of the deceased's estate was sufficient identification of the relevant property for the claim to succeed. We see this again in the recent Court of Appeal decision in *Southwell v Blackburn* (2014). In this case, Mr Blackburn assured Miss Southwell that 'she would always have a home and be secure in this one'. Whilst the discussions between the parties were not specific as to ownership of the home, they nevertheless gave rise to a valid assurance for the purposes of Miss Southwell's estoppel claim. In summary, the assurance must relate to some identifiable land though need not constitute a recognized property right. The courts draw a distinction between domestic and commercial contexts; being far more flexible and insisting on less clarity in the domestic sphere than in business. We see this point made in *Ely v Robson* (2016) but perhaps most evidently in *Arif v Anwar* (2015) where, in a familial context, an assurance of 'some sort of interest to be sorted out later' was held to be sufficiently clear.

Despite a degree of flexibility, ill-defined assurances or representations will not otherwise be enough as noted in *Orgee v Orgee* (1997) where it was held there was a need for an assurance as to an entitlement of 'sufficiently concrete character'— the claim to an agricultural lease by estoppel failed as the claimant had no clear expectation as to the terms of that lease. Assurances which are overly vague in nature—for example, assurances that a lover 'did not need to worry her pretty little head about money'[18]—are therefore insufficiently defined. The cases of *Smyth-Tyrrell v Bowden* (2018) and *Dobson v Griffey* (2018) are timely reminders that a claimant must actually be able to point to some form of assurance. In these cases, the court could find no such assurances and thus the claims to estoppel failed. In *Dobson*, Ms Dobson claimed an interest in her former partner's farm, having left her job to work there full time and extensively renovating the land. The judge held that her 'expectation [of an interest] did not spring from any assurance or other conduct of the defendant' even though Mr Griffey had been aware of Ms Dobson's expectation.

One particularly difficult area is that of pre-contractual negotiations—that is, for example, negotiations for the sale of land which never culminate in the form of a valid contract. Pre-contractual negotiations are problematic as their nature is inherently informal and prone to change. In *Attorney-General of Hong Kong v Humphreys Estate (Queen's Gardens) Ltd* (1987) the Privy Council rejected a claim for proprietary estoppel based on an agreement for the purchase of land which was in principle 'subject to contract' and from which the vendor ultimately withdrew. The court held that no assurance of an entitlement

---

[17] In Australia and the US, there is no equivalent requirement that an assurance must relate to an interest in land: *Waltons Stores v Maher* (1988); Restatement (Second) of Contracts, s. 90.   [18] *Lizzimore v Downing* (2003).

existed on which an estoppel could be based as the purchaser was aware, at all times, that the vendor retained the right to withdraw from the agreement. This is further illustrated by the case of *Yeoman's Row Management Ltd v Cobbe*.

KEY CASE *Yeoman's Row Management Ltd v Cobbe* (2008)

Facts: Yeoman's Ltd orally agreed to sell a block of flats to Mr Cobbe for £12 million if Mr Cobbe received planning permission to redevelop the flats and subsequently completed the works at his own expense. The parties orally undertook that the precise terms of their agreement would be set down in a legally enforceable contract at some later time. This never took place. Mr Cobbe, however, spent over £100,000 of his own money in line with the oral agreement. Realizing that the sale to Mr Cobbe at a price of £12 million reflected a substantial undervalue, Yeoman's Ltd resiled from the oral agreement. Mr Cobbe issued proceedings claiming an interest in the property.

Legal issue: Would Mr Cobbe's claim for proprietary estoppel succeed in this pre-contractual, commercial context?

Judgment: Reversing the Court of Appeal's judgment on the issue of proprietary estoppel, the House of Lords held that Mr Cobbe had no basis for his claim. The court held unanimously that no estoppel could arise where both parties were fully aware that the agreement reached was pre-contractual, binding only as a 'gentleman's agreement', and that further legal steps needed to be taken to formalize a contract. The only expectation generated in Mr Cobbe's mind, Lord Scott said, was 'the wrong sort of expectation' namely an expectation of further negotiations. Mr Cobbe was, however, awarded an *in personam* (personal) remedy to reflect the expenses he had incurred.

It appears following *Cobbe* that in a *commercial* context, pre-contractual negotiations will rarely provide the basis for a successful estoppel claim. As Lord Walker explained 'hopes by themselves are not enough' and 'reliance on honour alone will not give rise to an estoppel'. The decision in *Cobbe* can therefore be seen as curtailing the utility of proprietary estoppel in this particular business context. *Cobbe* creates a distinction between commercial and domestic contexts with the latter adopting a more flexible, permissive approach.[19] The commercial/domestic distinction appears to proceed on the basis that in the commercial context, particularly where there are pre-contractual negotiations, the parties are likely to understand assurances or representations as signalling an expectation of further negotiation and not as giving rise to an expectation that the representee will acquire a particular interest in land.[20]

Must an assurance be irrevocable? Put another way, can a claimant rely on an assurance which he knows or knew might be withdrawn? In *Taylor v Dickens* (1998) an elderly lady assured her gardener that she would leave him her entire estate upon her death. The lady changed her mind and amended her will without informing her gardener. The court refused a claim of proprietary estoppel on the basis that the lady had not raised any

---

[19] This distinction was discussed by Lord Neuberger in *Thorner* who contrasted the arm's length commercial context in *Cobbe* with the familial, personal circumstances of *Thorner*.

[20] See Lord Neuberger, 'The Stuffing of Minerva's Owl? Taxonomy and Taxidermy in Equity' (2009) 68(3) CLJ 537 who argued that this was 'probably all to the good' as the business world requires certainty and not the uncertainty proprietary estoppel imports.

expectation that she would not change her mind. The decision has, however, been sub-jected to heavy criticism[21] and was disapproved in the key decision of *Gillett*:

KEY CASE *Gillett v Holt* (2001)

Facts: Mr Holt, an affluent farmer, made a series of wills leaving the bulk of his estate to Mr Gillett, a farmhand who had worked on the farm for low pay for over 40 years. Mr Gillett's parents had wanted their son to pursue further education but Mr Gillett had left school at 15 to work on Mr Holt's farm. Mr Holt took a shine to Mr Gillett, trained him up in the farming business, and promised to Mr Gillett that 'all this will be yours'—in other words, that the business would pass to Mr Gillett on Mr Holt's death. This was reflected in a number of wills drawn up by Mr Holt which named Mr Gillett as benefi-ciary. Mr Gillett accepted these assurances and worked on the farm for long hours; not seeking other employment or educational opportunities. The relationship between the parties broke down and Mr Holt sacked Mr Gillett and changed his will excluding Mr Gillett entirely. Mr Gillett brought a claim for proprietary estoppel based on the earlier assurances made to him.

Legal issue: How far is the revocability of an assurance relevant in a claim for estoppel concerning a promise of testamentary gift (i.e. one made in a will)?

Judgment: Mr Gillett's claim failed at first instance, the judge holding that as Mr Holt's wills were always subject to the possibility of being changed there had been no irrevocable promise on which Mr Gillett could rely. Mr Gillett appealed. The Court of Appeal held, per Robert Walker LJ, that the revocability of an assurance was irrelevant as the assurance was 'more than a mere statement of pres-ent (revocable) intention' and was 'tantamount to a promise'. Mr Gillett's claim succeeded. He was awarded the freehold of the farmhouse, 42 hectares of land and a sum of £100,000 to compensate him for being excluded from the rest of the farming business.

The court in *Gillett* therefore confirmed that a claim for estoppel will succeed where an assurance is made which was intended to be relied upon, was so relied upon, and consti-tutes more than a mere statement of present intention. This will be the case even where the assurance is not expressly stated to be irrevocable. Sir Robert Walker LJ explained that estoppel could not be subdivided into 'watertight compartments'. In essence, the point is that the quality of the assurance made may influence the issue of reliance and, in turn, the reliance and detriment may equally be entwined.[22] We turn next to consider reliance.

8.3.4 **The reliance**

The claimant must have acted in reliance on the assurance/representation. Reliance is the element which links the detriment suffered with the assurance of the landowner. This re-liance aspect is very closely connected with the third requirement—detriment—and some commentators even conflate the two by referring to 'detrimental reliance'. Reliance

---

[21] M. P. Thomson [1998] Conv 220; W. Swadling, 'Restitutionary Claims: A Comparative Analysis' [1998] RLR 220.

[22] For one example of an assurance held to be conditional and thus the estoppel claim failed, see *Uglow v Uglow* (2004).

concerns the inducement of the claimant in response to the assurance made whereas detriment connotes some degree of unconscionable disadvantage which arises as a result of that reliance. In respect of reliance, several points can be made:

1. Reliance involves demonstrating that the claimant was induced to act differently because of the assurance made. In *Thorner*, the House of Lords noted that reliance on the assurance must be 'reasonable'. In other words, it must be shown that it was objectively reasonable for the claimant to rely on the assurance even if the landowner did not intend or expect the claimant so to rely. This point is helpfully explained in the case of *James v James* (2018). In this case, Sam, gave evidence that comments from his father, Charles, had raised an expectation that Sam would one day inherit the farm on which the son had worked. Rejecting the claim, however, the court could find no evidence of assurances whether by words or conduct that would have raised such an expectation. At its highest, Sam could point to comments from his father that he 'would be farming [the land] one day'. The court held that a reasonable person, objectively judged, would not have misinterpreted the father's words in the way the son had and that Sam had (unreasonably) persuaded himself that he was being promised something when he was not.

2. In many cases, it may be difficult to prove reliance particularly in the domestic/familial context given the nature of the relationship between the parties. To this end, the case of *Greasley v Cooke* (1980) establishes a 'presumption of reliance' whereby the claimant/representee (person to whom the representation or assurance was made) will be presumed to have relied on an assurance or representation made if the following conditions are met:

   - a clear assurance/representation has been made, and
   - the assurance/representation was intended to influence the mind of the claimant, and
   - the assurance/representation would have influenced the mind of a reasonable person.

   If satisfied, a presumption is raised that any detriment suffered is deemed to have been incurred in reliance on the assurance made by the landowner. The burden of proof then shifts to the defendant to show that no causal link exists. Although not overruled, we should perhaps approach the *Greasley* presumption with some caution. The Court of Appeal has said it does not apply to other forms of estoppel and it has been rejected in Australia in relation to proprietary estoppel where the court was clear that it is firmly for a claimant to prove all the elements of a claim. So, be aware of the *Greasley* presumption but perhaps explore whether reliance could, in spite of *Greasley*, be expressly proved by the claimant.

3. Beyond *Greasley*, the court adopts a flexible and light-touch approach to reliance in many cases. Generally, only where there is evidence that the detriment would have been incurred irrespective of the assurance, will a finding of no reliance be made. We see evidence of this more relaxed approach in the case of *Wayling v Jones* where the Court of Appeal held that only a 'sufficient link' between the assurance made and the detriment suffered by the claimant was required.

> ## KEY CASE *Wayling v Jones* (1993)
>
> Facts: Mr Wayling and Mr Jones were in a same-sex relationship which had begun in 1967. Over many years, Mr Wayling worked in several of Mr Jones' businesses and received only 'pocket money' remuneration for his services. No regular wage was paid. Mr Jones provided in his will that Mr Wayling was to receive the Glen-y-Mor Hotel. This particular hotel was later sold and a new hotel, the Royal, purchased but Mr Jones' will was not amended. In 1987, Mr Jones died and his will made no other provision for Mr Wayling. Mr Wayling claimed that he was entitled to ownership of the Royal Hotel under the doctrine of proprietary estoppel on the basis that a series of assurances had been made to him that he was to be the owner of the Glen-y-Mor hotel and, later, that he would be the owner of the Royal.
>
> Legal issue: The central issue concerned the question of reliance. Could Mr Wayling demonstrate that he had relied upon the assurances made?
>
> Judgment: At first instance, the judge found against Mr Wayling on the basis of evidence provided during the trial. Mr Wayling, when asked, had responded that he would have stayed with Mr Jones even if there had been no promise to ownership of the hotels. Largely on this evidence, Mr Wayling's claim to proprietary estoppel failed for want of reliance. Mr Wayling appealed. The Court of Appeal allowed Mr Wayling's appeal. Balcombe LJ noted that:
>
> > [Mr Wayling's] helping run the . . . Glen-y-Mor Hotel and managing the Royal Hotel for what was at best little more than pocket money . . . was conduct from which his reliance . . . could be inferred.
>
> The Court of Appeal was satisfied that promises had been made, that it could be inferred that those promises were an inducement, and finally that the defendants (Mr Jones' executors) could not prove that Mr Wayling had not relied upon those promises. Mr Wayling was entitled to a sum of £72,386.65 plus interest to be paid from Mr Jones' estate, a sum equivalent to the proceeds of sale of the Royal Hotel.[23]

Wayling can, however, be criticized as being overly benevolent to the claimant and policy-led as Mr Wayling had not acted in reliance on the assurances made. The promises made were not the reason Mr Wayling stayed with Mr Jones. The court seemingly found Mr Wayling to be deserving of a remedy. As Cooke explains:[24]

> When we say that someone acted in reliance upon a promise we generally mean that he would not have so acted *but for* the making of the promise. We cannot say that of *Wayling* . . . the treatment of reliance in *Wayling* is thus unusually generous. Despite the obvious justice of the result, the means of reaching it was inconsistent with earlier estoppel cases.

The recent case of *Dobson v Griffey* (2018) demonstrates a stricter approach particularly where the parties are in or have been in an intimate relationship. The court in *Dobson*, as well as not being able to locate any effective assurances, could find no real reliance. The court held that Ms Dobson had undertaken work on the farm and significant renovation of the land in order to make a family home with Mr Griffey and not in the expectation of receiving any rights in

---

[23] Today Mr Wayling would have been able to bring a claim under the Inheritance (Provision for Family and Dependants) Act 1975 as a dependant of the deceased. This power was not available to the court as regards same-sex partners at the time *Wayling* was decided.

[24] E. Cooke, 'Reliance and Estoppel' (1995) 111 LQR 389, 391.

the land. *Dobson* therefore demonstrates the extra hurdle that claimants must overcome if it appears that their behaviour might be ascribed to or explained as evidence of commitment to a relationship.

The assurance need not be the sole inducement, however, for a claimant's change of position. A claim will not fail simply because there are mixed motives for the claimant's behaviour. In *Campbell v Griffin* (2001), Mr Campbell, a lodger, devoted considerable time to looking after the two frail landowners, Mr and Mrs Ascough, who had assured him routinely that, on their deaths, he had a home for life. The Court of Appeal held that just because Mr Campbell admitted helping the Ascoughs out of friendship and common humanity, he had also gone beyond friendship and was able to demonstrate reliance.[25] Too strict a test of reliance would prevent the giving of honest witness testimony in court. In *Stillwell v Simpson* (1983), by contrast, a tenant who had carried out repairs on a house failed to establish reliance on the basis that the works were completed principally for his own benefit and not in reliance on assurances by his landlady who had represented to him that he would become the freehold owner of the property.

8.3.5 The detriment

Equity does not respond to the mere fact of an assurance relied upon by a claimant.[26] A claimant must also establish that, were the landowner to assert its strict legal rights, the claimant would suffer detriment as a result of relying on that landowner's assurance. Technically the 'test' for detriment is this: given the claimant's reliance on the assurances made by the landowner, the claimant would suffer detriment if she had no claim for proprietary estoppel. On nature of detriment, Robert Walker LJ in *Gillett* noted that:[27]

> [Detriment] is not a narrow or technical concept. The detriment need not consist of the expenditure of money or other quantifiable financial detriment, so long as it is something substantial. The requirement must be approached as part of a broad enquiry as to whether repudiation of an assurance is or is not unconscionable in all the circumstances.

Detriment must be substantial, is to be assessed at the moment when the landowner seeks to resile from the assurance made, and must be suffered by the party to whom that assurance was communicated.[28] So, what amounts to detriment? The categories are not closed,[29] and Table 8.1 offers a flavour of the types of conduct which have been recognized by the court as sufficient to establish detriment.

The recent case of *James v James* (2018) is a useful example of how the court assesses detriment. We considered the facts of the case briefly in section 8.3.4 on reliance. *James* was an unusual case as a son had, in fact, been properly paid for his work on the farm; had been bought cars as 'bonuses' for his work; had occupied a property rent-free; had been made a partner in the family business; and had received some land, cash, and a stake in a haulage business. Equally, the son, Sam, had never contemplated leaving the farm to work elsewhere. Sam could not therefore demonstrate any detriment.

---

[25] His claim had failed at first instance on the basis that he could not show reliance.

[26] 'Equity will not assist a volunteer' (i.e. equity will not enforce a promise made to someone who has done nothing in return for it).

[27] *Gillett*, 232.   [28] As clarified in *Lloyd v Dugdale* (2001).

[29] As confirmed by the Court of Appeal in *Watts v Storey* (1984).

Table 8.1 Examples of detriment recognized by the court

DETRIMENT	CASE LAW
Improvement of the landowner's land by the claimant	• *Dillwyn v Llewellyn* (1862): construction of a house • *Inwards v Baker* (1965): construction of a bungalow • *Pascoe v Turner* (1979): improvements, repairs, and redecoration of property
Other financial disadvantage suffered by the claimant	• *Crabb v Arun DC* (1976): selling part of one's own land without reserving a right of way • *Wayling v Jones* (1993): helping out in businesses for pocket money only • *Lloyd v Dugdale* (2001): failing to seek alternative commercial premises to buy • *Gillett v Holt* (2001): forgoing alternative employment opportunities and deprivation of the opportunity to better oneself • *Porntip Stallion v Albert Stallion Holdings (Great Britain) Ltd* (2009): failing to seek ancillary relief on divorce • *Southwell v Blackburn* (2014): giving up of a rent-controlled tenancy, having spent considerable money on that property • *Davies v Davies* (2016): working on a parent's farm at low wage, forgoing higher wages and giving up other employment • *Gee v Gee* (2018): working for minimum wage when claimant's qualifications could have garnered higher wages; unpaid overtime; not taking opportunities to set up own farming business • *Habberfield v Habberfield* (2019): working at low wage, long hours with few permitted holidays
Non-financial, personal disadvantage suffered by the claimant	• *Jennings v Rice* (2002): Giving up spare time at evenings and weekends to care for landowner and undertake gardening • *Gee v Gee* (2018): impact of working on claimant's family life; putting up with employer (father's) 'difficult behaviour' • *Campbell v Griffin* (2001): general care-taking, cleaning, gardening, shopping, and cooking • *Greasley v Cooke* (1980): staying on as an unpaid housekeeper

A claimant can succeed in their claim, however, even if there is evidence that they have received some benefit from their actions in reliance.[30] In *Gillett*, Mr Gillett succeeded in his estoppel claim despite the fact he had received the benefits of living with his wife on the farm in 'The Beeches' farmhouse.[31] As the Privy Council case of *Henry v Henry* (2010) clarifies, in assessing detriment, the crucial question is whether the benefits received outweigh the detriment that the claimant would suffer if the person making the assurances were to be allowed to go back on those assurances. Benefits received must therefore be balanced against prejudice or detriment suffered. In *Henry*, the Privy Council allowed Calixtus's claim to a 50 per cent share of rural land on a mountain side on the basis of proprietary estoppel and assurances made by his grandmother that he would inherit a share in the land if he cultivated it and cared for her. Yes, Calixtus had benefited from rent-free

---

[30] Consider the cases of *Bradbury v Taylor* (2012) and *Suggitt v Suggitt* (2012). We reflect on these in the 'Future Directions' section in section 8.7.

[31] The degree of benefit received may prove crucial, however, when the court turns to consider 'satisfying' the equity and to the selection of a remedy: see *Sledmore v Dalby* (1996)

accommodation and living off the produce of the land but this had to be balanced against his giving up of opportunities to better his life and his feeding and caring for his grandmother. The benefits received did not outweigh the detriment suffered.[32]

On a different point, as the case of *Pascoe* demonstrates, in extreme cases, the conduct relied upon as constituting detriment may even be quite minimal. Here the detriment consisted of just £230 decoration and repair costs to a quasi-matrimonial home over a two-year period.

8.3.6 Unconscionability

In *Taylors Fashions*, Oliver J clearly envisaged unconscionability as sitting at the very heart of a claim for proprietary estoppel. Recall Sir Robert Walker LJ's assertion:[33]

> The fundamental principle that equity is concerned to prevent unconscionable conduct permeates all the elements of the doctrine ... The requirement must be approached as part of a broad inquiry as to whether repudiation of an assurance is or is not unconscionable in all the circumstances.

Carnwath J elaborated on this in *Gillett* when he stated that:[34]

> [I]t is the promisor's knowledge of the detriment being suffered in reliance on his promise which makes it 'unconscionable' for him to go back on it.

Unconscionability is, therefore, not strictly a separate requirement but reflects an overarching component of the other features of an estoppel claim, running as a thread through—or as an umbrella over—the other elements of an estoppel claim. A successful claim will only stand in equity if there is an assurance, relied upon to the claimant's detriment, and *as a result* it would be unconscionable for the landowner to assert his strict legal rights. As Lord Neuberger colourfully notes, unconscionability alone is no basis for the award of a remedy:[35]

> [E]quity is not a sort of moral US fifth cavalry riding to the rescue every time a claimant is left worse off than he anticipated as a result of the defendants behaving badly, and the common law affords him no remedy.

Lord Walker in *Cobbe* regarded unconscionability as 'unifying and confirming' the other elements of an estoppel claim, noting that if the other elements appear to be present but the result does not 'shock the conscience of the court', a claim will fail. Sadly, there is no particular consensus either academically or judicially as to the precise status of the unconscionability requirement. Hopkins has argued that what emerges from decided case law is a focus on unconscionability as connecting the other elements in a proprietary estoppel claim.[36] In this way, unconscionability may, for example, provide a court with the latitude to reject a claim where—despite proof of assurance, reliance, and detriment—a change in circumstances makes the award of a remedy inequitable.[37] Others take a different approach. Dixon has argued that unconscionability must be given a distinct legal meaning:[38]

---

[32] In *Gee v Gee* (2018) the court considered the 'difficult behaviour' of the claimant's father (who was the claimant's employer on the family farm) as forming part of the benefit–detriment balancing act.

[33] *Gillett*, 232.   [34] Ibid.   [35] Lord Neuberger, 'The Stuffing of Minerva's Owl?', 540.

[36] N. Hopkins, 'Proprietary Estoppel: A Functional Analysis' (2010) 4 Journal of Equity 201.

[37] For example, if the landowner has subsequently sold its land for a laudable or charitable purpose.

[38] M. Dixon, 'Proprietary Estoppel and Formalities in Land Law and the Land Registration Act 2002: A Theory of Unconscionability' in E. Cooke (ed.), *Modern Studies in Property Law*, Vol. 2 (Oxford: Hart, 2003).

All judges are agreed that unconscionability is vital, but few seem willing to share their under-standing of the concept . . . If it is to true that unconscionability is now to be regarded as no more than a function of assurance, reliance and detriment, this author submits that the approach is flawed and unprincipled . . . *Taylors Fashions* suggests that assurance, reliance and detriment are necessary but not sufficient . . . [the court must also] be satisfied that it would be unconscionable to allow the party making the assurance to go back on it.

Dixon notes how the doctrine of proprietary estoppel undermines the general position that formalities are required for the creation of interests in land. It is the requirement for 'un-conscionability' that justifies estoppel's informal creation of rights in circumstances where formalities are not met. These broader theoretical questions are academically fascinating but how does the court, in practice, determine unconscionability?

8.3.6.1 The detriment/benefit balancing act

In assessing unconscionability, the court balances the alleged detriment suffered against any likely benefits accrued to the claimant—we saw this in *Henry v Henry*. Only where the detriment suffered by the claimant outweighs any benefits enjoyed, will the claim for es-toppel succeed. In *Sledmore v Dalby* (1996), Mr Dalby and his wife moved into a property owned by his parents-in-law. Mr Dalby was led to believe the house would be transferred to him and his wife. However, on the father-in-law's death, this was not done. Despite this, Mr Dalby continued to live in the property rent-free although only for a few nights each week. For the remainder of the week, he lived with his new partner. The Court of Appeal emphasized the need to counterbalance the detriment suffered by Mr Dalby (in this case repair work to the property) with the advantages he had received in living there rent-free for 18 years. Ultimately, the court held that Mr Dalby was not entitled to any remedy at all as the benefits he had enjoyed outweighed any detriment incurred. As Hobhouse LJ noted, it could not 'be properly said that there was anything unconscionable' in the circumstances of this case. The decision of *Southwell*[39] provides a further and more contemporary exam-ple of the balancing-act approach to unconscionability.

KEY CASE *Southwell v Blackburn* (2014)

Facts: Mr Southwell met Miss Blackburn in 2000. Miss Blackburn was of limited means and was, at the time, living in a rent-controlled property under a secure tenancy. She had spent £15,000 on both fur-nishing and fitting out the property. The couple set up home together in 2002 in a house purchased in the sole name of Mr Southwell from his capital savings and with the assistance of a mortgage in Mr Southwell's name. The couple separated in 2012 and Miss Blackburn claimed an interest in the property on the basis of proprietary estoppel. She claimed that Mr Southwell had assured her that she would always have a home and promised her secure rights of occupation. She argued that without these assurances she would not have given up her secure tenancy to share a property with Mr Southwell.

→

---

[39] See A. Hayward, 'Cohabitants, Detriment and the Potential of Proprietary Estoppel' (2015) 27(3) CFLQ 303.

→

Legal issue: Could Miss Blackburn establish that she had relied on the assurances made to her detriment such that it would be unconscionable for Mr Southwell to assert his legal rights?

Judgment: At first instance, the judge concluded that without the assurances made, Miss Blackburn would not have given up the security she enjoyed under her previous tenancy and this constituted detriment incurred on her part. The judge calculated the loss suffered by Miss Blackburn in the sum of £28,500. Mr Southwell appealed arguing that the judge had been wrong in that: (1) the assurances made were not sufficiently specific to engage the doctrine of proprietary estoppel, and (2) any detriment suffered by Miss Blackburn was outweighed by the benefits accruing during the course of their relationship.

The Court of Appeal dismissed the appeal. A broad approach should be taken to the question of unconscionability and the judge had made no error of law in assessing detriment. Detriment was to be assessed over the course of the parties' relationship and this involved a balancing act between the benefits of the relationship and the losses Miss Blackburn had suffered. The judge had rightly identified Miss Blackburn's detrimental reliance as her abandonment of a secure home and her investment of what little money she did have in the shared home in which she held no legal title. It was this detrimental reliance that gave rise to the unconscionability in this case.

Tomlinson LJ noted:

> Running through the evaluation of all of the elements is the requirement of unconscionability, such that the identification of promise or assurance, reliance and detriment might not of itself be sufficient to give rise to the equity . . . It is the detrimental reliance which makes the promise irrevocable and leads to the conclusion, at the end of a broad enquiry, that repudiation of the assurance is unconscionable.

The relationship between detriment and unconscionability is therefore a close one—as we saw in the previous section in the case of *Henry v Henry*.

8.3.6.2 The conduct of the landowner

The court will look also to the conduct of the landowner, the party who made the assurance or representation. In *Gee v Gee* (2018), the landowner's 'difficult behaviour' was taken into account. The landowner must have behaved in such a manner that it would be unconscionable for him to assert his strict legal rights. The courts will consider whether the landowner's conduct is objectively unconscionable irrespective of his own particular state of mind. A claim for proprietary estoppel can therefore succeed even where the landowner did not know of its own rights or of the true position.[40] Equally, a claim may succeed even where the landowner does not know of the claimant's reliance on the assurance. In *Joyce v Epsom & Ewell BC* (2012), it did not matter therefore that the defendant was not actually aware of the claimant's erection of a garage on a strip of land. The claimant's proprietary estoppel claim succeeded. In the recent Court of Appeal decision of *Hoyl Group Ltd v Cromer Town Council* (2015), it was established that it suffices for proprietary estoppel if the claimant acts in a manner consistent with having the right promised (with the knowledge of the representor) (a right of way in this case) even if the landowner who made the assurance does not have actual knowledge of any acts in reliance.

---

[40] *Taylors Fashions.*

8.3.6.3 The conduct of the claimant

Finally, if the claimant has conducted herself in a manner which is itself unconscionable, it is patent that her claim for proprietary estoppel will fail even if the other elements of assurance, detriment, and reliance are made out. This is because equity insists that she 'who comes to equity must do so with clean hands'. In *Murphy v Rayner* (2011), the claimant failed to establish her estoppel claim as a result of her own dishonest conduct in stealing documents and procuring money from a man for whom she acted as carer.

As you can see, the 'requirement' for unconscionability remains broadly drawn and lacks precise definition. This is somewhat problematic as Mee notes:[41]

> Despite much reverential talk on the part of legal commentators and judges about equitable flexibility and the prevention of unconscionability, it is not in the public interest for the legal system to tolerate an indulgent and confused proprietary estoppel jurisdiction. It is to be hoped that the trend represented by [recent case law] will not continue and that the courts will begin to take a more restrained and analytical approach.

8.4 Proprietary estoppel: Satisfying the 'equity'

Once a claimant has successfully *established* the features of an estoppel claim—assurance, reliance, detriment and unconscionability—the claimant is entitled to an 'estoppel equity'. This equity is not a remedy in itself but rather acts to prevent the landowner from asserting their strict legal rights and, in so doing, defeat the expectation of entitlement raised by the assurance. This 'equity' arises from the moment the claimant relies on the assurances made.[42] As Scarman LJ famously noted in *Crabb v Arun DC* (1976), 'the court will consider the extent of the equity and decide how best to satisfy it'. It is for the court to determine how best to satisfy this equity or, put differently, what interest to award the claimant. There are two aspects for us to explore here:

- How does the court determine what is an appropriate satisfaction of the equity?
- What spectrum of remedies is available to the court?

8.4.1 How does the court determine the appropriate satisfaction of the 'equity'?

In determining an appropriate satisfaction of the 'equity', the expectation of entitlement generated by the landowner's assurance is the maximum that he can be awarded[43] and the claimant should never receive more than was assured.[44] Scarman LJ in *Crabb* stated the central aim of the court was to identify 'the minimum equity to do justice' to the claimant.

For some time, there was a lack of clear principle as to whether, in satisfying the equity, the court should determine an appropriate remedy according to an expectation-based or reliance-based approach. On the former approach, the claimant would be awarded what they were promised/expected to receive and, on the latter, the claimant would receive a

---

[41] J. Mee, 'Proprietary Estoppel and Inheritance: Enough Is Enough?' [2013] Conv 280, 297.
[42] *Crabb.*   [43] *Dodsworth v Dodsworth* (1973).   [44] *Orgee.*

remedy to reflect the extent of their detrimental reliance. The current approach of the court is a pragmatic amalgamation of the two approaches which might be described as a proportionality-based approach. The leading authority is *Jennings* which must be read closely to fully grasp its significance.

KEY CASE *Jennings v Rice* (2002)

Facts: Mr Jennings provided services to Mrs Royle, a widow for over 25 years, primarily as her gardener but subsequently as her principal carer when she became older and frail. This included working at times without pay and sleeping on her sofa as she did not wish to be alone. Mrs Royle had made a series of ambiguous, indirect assurances that Mr Jennings would inherit her house upon her death. She told him that 'he would be alright' and that 'this will all be yours one day'. In 1997, Mrs Royle died without having made a will. Mr Jennings brought a claim, amongst other things, for proprietary estoppel arguing that he had a right to the house.

Legal issue: The court held that Mr Jennings had established his claim to an estoppel 'equity' but what was the appropriate remedy to satisfy this equity?

Judgment: Robert Walker LJ stressed that the court did not have an unfettered discretion and must adopt 'a principled approach' as opposed to reaching a result which was just according to an individual judge's notion of fairness. The claimant's expectation was the starting point but, 'the equity arises not from the claimant's expectations alone, but from the combination of expectations, detrimental reliance, and the unconscionableness of allowing the [landowner] to go back on the assurance'.

Robert Walker LJ drew a distinction between what will be called 'bargain' and 'non-bargain' cases. Bargain cases are those where there is a clear bargain between the parties, just short of a contract, and with little uncertainty as to the expectations raised by the landowner's assurances. In these cases, the court's starting point should be awarding a remedy to meet those expectations most likely by awarding the specific property promised to the claimant. Non-bargain cases are those where the claimant's expectations are far less fixed, the assurances made were vague and there is no discernible expectation of a specific property right. Thus, where expectations are uncertain, 'extravagant, or out of all proportion to the detriment which the claimant has suffered, the court can and should recognize that the claimant's equity should be satisfied in another (and generally more limited) way'.

In determining an appropriate remedy (and particularly in non-bargain cases), the court should consider a range of factors including but not limited to:

- any misconduct of the claimant
- any oppressive conduct by the defendant
- the need for a clean-break between the parties
- changes to the landowner or representatives' assets or circumstances
- the effect of taxation
- any other claims on the landowner's assets or estate.

The Court of Appeal upheld the trial judge's award to Mr Jennings of £200,000 compensation. This was less than the expectation that Mrs Royle's assurances had raised in Mr Jennings' mind. This more limited remedy was justified on the basis that he had not been aware of the extent of Mrs Royle's wealth, the value of her estate was out of proportion to the services he had provided, and the house was unsuitable for him to occupy alone. Aldous LJ confirmed that in seeking to satisfy the equity:

> the task of the court is to do justice. The most essential requirement is that there must be proportionality between the expectation and the detriment.

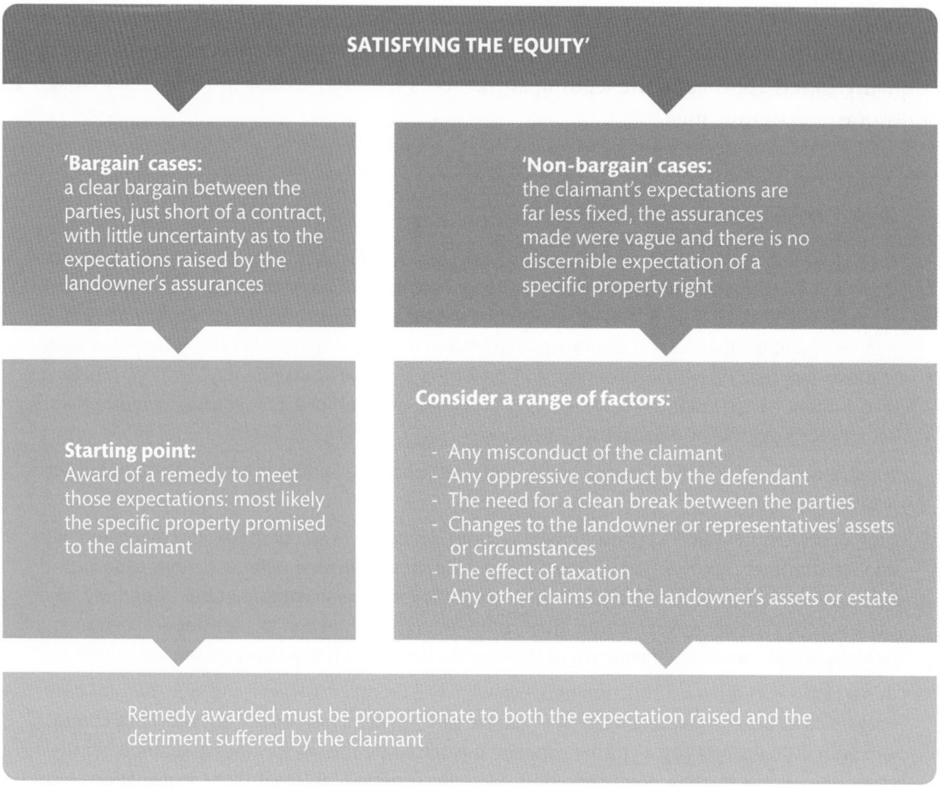

SATISFYING THE 'EQUITY'

'Bargain' cases:
a clear bargain between the parties, just short of a contract, with little uncertainty as to the expectations raised by the landowner's assurances

'Non-bargain' cases:
the claimant's expectations are far less fixed, the assurances made were vague and there is no discernible expectation of a specific property right

Starting point:
Award of a remedy to meet those expectations: most likely the specific property promised to the claimant

Consider a range of factors:
- Any misconduct of the claimant
- Any oppressive conduct by the defendant
- The need for a clean break between the parties
- Changes to the landowner or representatives' assets or circumstances
- The effect of taxation
- Any other claims on the landowner's assets or estate

Remedy awarded must be proportionate to both the expectation raised and the detriment suffered by the claimant

Figure 8.3 Satisfying the 'equity' and proportionality under *Jennings v Rice*

Figure 8.3 will help you to visualize how the court, according to Robert Walker LJ in *Jennings*, is to determine the appropriate remedy when 'satisfying the equity'.

The *Jennings* approach has since been confirmed and discussed in a series of cases including *Henry v Henry*, *Davies v Davies* (2016), and *Moore v Moore* (2018). The Privy Council in *Henry*, in affirming *Jennings*, held that just because a proprietary estoppel claim is made out does not automatically mean that the full expectation should be awarded as a remedy. This had been the approach taken by the court below and was roundly rejected, the Privy Council saying this 'betrays a fundamental misconception as to the doctrine of proprietary estoppel ... Proportionality lies at the heart of the doctrine ... and permeates its every application.' This does rather beg the question: what does 'proportionality' actually entail? Further clarity was offered by Lewison LJ in the Court of Appeal in a case dubbed 'the Cowshed Cinderella case' by the media: *Davies v Davies*.

KEY CASE *Davies v Davies* (2016)

Facts: Mr and Mrs Davies owned and ran a farm in Wales. They wanted the farm business to remain within the family after they had died but their daughter, Eirian, was the only one of their children who had any concern for the farm. Eirian lived and worked on the farm for many years for low pay. A series of assurances were made to Eirian, starting in 1985 with an assurance that she would inherit the farm.

→

→

This promise had been made on the proviso that she work on the land but, after a disagreement, Eirian left the farm in 1989. She returned in 1991 and recommenced work for which she was paid. Mr and Mrs Davies assured Eirian that she could join the partnership that managed the business but Mr and Mrs Davies never signed the relevant paperwork. In light of this, Eirian left the farm again but subsequently returned to live in the farmhouse with an assurance in 2007 that she could live there for the rest of her life. In 2008, Eirian gave up a paid job off the farm to concentrate on her work there and in 2009 was shown a draft will which recorded that on her parents' death she would receive the farmland, the buildings, and a share in the company. In 2010, Eirian was shown another will under which she was set to receive nothing. The relationship between Mr and Mrs Davies reached a new low in 2012 and Eirian finally left the farm for good. The farm, the land and the business were together valued at approximately £3 million.

Legal Issue: Could Eirian succeed in her claim to proprietary estoppel and, if so, what would be the appropriate remedy to satisfy the equity? Eirian's parents offered to settle the estoppel claim by paying Eirian £350,000 which they argued comprised: (1) £180,000 to pay off Eirian's mortgage and thus ensuring she had secure accommodation for life elsewhere other than on the farm; (2) £22,000 to reflect profits that Eirian would have received had she been a partner in the business from 1998; (3) £120,000 to reflect a 50 per cent share of the profits made by the business from 2008 to 2012; (3) £28,000 to reflect underpayment of wages to Eirian for her work on the farm. Eirian rejected this offer and argued she was entitled to have the farm and the business transferred to her.

Judgment: At first instance, the judge accepted Eirian's estoppel claim was made out. The issue was how to satisfy the equity. Given that Mr and Mrs Davies were still alive, transfer of the farm and business to Eirian was held not to be appropriate. Instead, Mr and Mrs Davies were ordered to pay Eirian a lump sum of £1.3 million which amounted to around one-third of the net value of the farm and business. On appeal, Mr and Mrs Davies argued that this lump sum award was significantly too high in that it amounted to £65,000 per year after tax for every year that Eirian had worked on the farm. After a lengthy judgment, Lewison LJ reduced the sum awarded to £500,000 but in so doing made some important observations on how to approach the remedial stage of an estoppel action. Lewison LJ laid down the applicable principles as follows:

(1) The essence of the doctrine of proprietary estoppel is to do what is necessary to avoid an unconscionable result.

(2) In deciding how to satisfy any equity the court must weigh the detriment suffered by the claimant in reliance on the defendant's assurances against any countervailing benefits she enjoyed in consequence of that reliance.

(3) Proportionality lies at the heart of the doctrine of proprietary estoppel and permeates its every application. In particular there must be a proportionality between the remedy and the detriment which is its purpose to avoid. This does not mean that the court should abandon expectations and seek only to compensate detrimental reliance, but if the expectation is disproportionate to the detriment, the court should satisfy the equity in a more limited way.

(4) In deciding how to satisfy the equity the court has to exercise a broad judgmental discretion. However, the discretion is not unfettered. It must be exercised on a principled basis, and does not entail what HHJ Weekes QC memorably called a 'portable palm tree'.

Lewison LJ continued:

there is a lively controversy about the essential aim of the exercise of this broad judgmental discretion. One line of authority takes the view that the essential aim of the discretion is to give effect to the claimant's expectation unless it would be disproportionate to do so. The other takes the view that essential aim of the discretion is to ensure that the claimant's reliance interest is protected, so that she is compensated for such detriment as she has suffered.

→

> →
>
> The two approaches, in their starkest form, are fundamentally different. Others argue that the outcome will reflect both the expectation and the reliance interest and that it will normally be somewhere between the two . . . Fortunately, I do not think that we are required to resolve this controversy on this appeal.
>
> As to how the figure of £500,000 was reached, Lewison LJ explained that the first instance judge had erred:
>
> - In applying too broad brush an approach to the facts;
>
> - In not explaining which of the various 'expectations' arising on the facts he was vindicating with the lump sum awarded of £1.3 million;
>
> - In not recognizing the series of different and 'sometimes mutually incompatible' expectations some of which were repudiated and others superseded by later expectations;
>
> - In not analysing closely Mr and Mrs Davies's offer of £350,000, which covered much of Eirian's expectations;
>
> - In not explaining how the jump was made from the offer of £350,000 to the eventual lump sum of £1.3 million (the judge must have ascribed a value of around £1 million to the non-financial aspects of detrimental reliance by Eirian);
>
> - In failing to closely analyse Eirian's detriment (the judge had, for example, failed to recognize that what Eirian had apparently given up she could now take up, i.e. she had not positioned her entire life on the assurances made, and on this basis, any award for detriment should be modest).
>
> In summary, the court should only increase Mr and Mrs Davies's offer by £150,000 in view of the fact of the shifting assurances and the relatively modest detriment suffered.

While Lewison LJ's judgment is helpful as an example of how the proportionality exercise is undertaken, in failing to articulate or express a clear view on which of the three 'essential aims' is being ultimately being pursued (i.e. expectation-based, reliance-based; proportionality between the two), the judgment leaves us wanting. Lewison hinted his preference for the reliance-based approach which he described as being favoured by some academics and in his view 'logical' yet proportionality was also discussed. Certainly, it seems from the final award made that Eirian's modest detriment played a key role in the reduction of the lump sum to £500,000.

Ultimately, it remains unsettled which of the three approaches or interpretations of the proportionality exercise is to be favoured. Each approach has its proponents and its detractors. Mee has argued, as a matter of logic, the *Jennings* approach based on proportionality is problematic in that it seeks to award a remedy that is proportional to two distinct values, both the expectation and detriment.[45] For Mee, having the expectation interest as a starting point (and only reducing the award if it would be disproportionate) leads to an 'absurdity' where a claimant will be in a stronger position if she can show that the expectation induced in her was sufficiently low as to not count as disproportionate to the detriment suffered.

Others have argued that a better interpretation of the proportionality exercise is one that responds to the reasonable reliance of a claimant on assurances made. This reliance-based

---

[45] J. Mee, 'Proprietary Estoppel, Promises and Mistaken Belief' in S. Bright (ed.), *Modern Studies in Property Law*, Vol. 6 (Oxford: Hart, 2011).

approach founded on awarding the extent of a claimant's detrimental reliance is preferred by Robertson:[46]

> [T]he proportionality principle can be justified on the basis that both reliance loss and expectation loss are necessary to an estoppel claim. Where the lesser interest has been met, the equity is satisfied because an essential element of the claim has been removed. In those rare cases in which the expectation interest is less valuable, it will provide a cap on the claim. Almost invariably, however, the reliance interest is the smaller. That is why the minimum equity principle requires the courts to go no further in granting relief than is necessary to prevent reliance loss.

Lewison LJ in *Davies* was attracted by this interpretation noting that: 'there is much to be said for the [reliance-based] approach. Since the essence of proprietary estoppel is the combination of expectation and detriment, if either is absent, the claim must fail. If, therefore, the detriment can be fairly quantified and a claimant receives full compensation for that detriment, that compensation ought, in principle, to remove the foundation of the claim.' This reliance-based approach whilst being less predictable than simply awarding the expectation interest does have the benefit of being easily explained (the award reflects the detriment suffered as assessed by the court) and appears consistent with the outcomes in cases such as *Jennings* and *Davies*.

A third interpretation which delivers a remedy reflecting both the expectation and the reliance interests is favoured by Gardner, who proposes a new approach under which the court would seek to award a remedy to redress unconscionability based on the claimant's expectation *and* reliance interests:[47]

> [The] judge should be told to seek the outcome that . . . best redresses the unconscionability . . . To redress the unconscionability, the outcome must therefore reflect *both* the claimant's expectation and reliance, *and* the degree to which these can be ascribed to the defendant.

However, problems in particular of how this approach would work in practice have been raised, for example, by Mee who explains:[48]

> There must be some principled way of determining the extent to which the expectation impacts upon the remedy. However, no such principled mechanism is available. One must ask, how as a matter of logic, the remedy can be made proportional to two different values, the expectation and the detriment?

As things stand, the *Jennings* approach centred on a proportionality exercise remains good law: see Figure 8.3. For the latest on the proportionality approach, we look to the Court of Appeal decision in *Habberfield v Habberfield* (2019) in which Lewison LJ returned to the question of how to satisfy the equity in a successful estoppel claim. The trial judge had satisfied the equity by ordering that Lucy Habberfield be paid a lump sum of £1.2m after she had spent 30 years working on the family dairy farm; relying on assurances from her late father that she would take over the dairy business and inherit the farm

---

[46] A. Robertson, 'The Reliance Basis of Proprietary Estoppel Remedies' [2008] Conv 295, 303; see also S. Bright and B. McFarlane, 'Proprietary Estoppel and Property Rights' (2005) 64(2) CLJ 449, 454.

[47] S. Gardner, 'The Remedial Discretion in Proprietary Estoppel—Again' (2006) 122 LQR 492.

[48] Mee, 'Proprietary Estoppel, Promises and Mistaken Belief', 406.

when both her parents were deceased. The appeal centred on the appropriateness of the remedy ordered. Lucy Habberfield's mother, Jane, appealed the first instance decision arguing that Lucy's earlier refusal to join the partnership running the business should defeat her estoppel claim; that the award was disproportionate to the detriment suffered; and that a lump sum was inappropriate so long as the mother remained alive. The Court of Appeal dismissed the appeal. Lucy's refusal of the partnership offer did not defeat her estoppel claim as she had expected control of the business in view of the assurances made and accepting the partnership would not have met this expectation. The lump sum ordered was both appropriate and proportionate to the detriment suffered. Lewison LJ reiterated that expectation alone was not determinative of the relief to be granted. The question was, having identified the expectation, if the award was out of all proportion to the detriment. Approving the approach as advocated in *Jennings* and *Davies*, Lewison LJ emphasized that where the assurances and reliance were clearly defined, the court would likely vindicate the claimant's expectations. The trial judge had been justified in regarding the claimant's defined expectations as an important factor. In order to raise the money to cover the lump sum, the farm would need to be sold and, yes, this would deprive Jane of her home. However, Jane had sufficient resources to rehouse herself and Lucy, at 51, required an immediate award so that, at last, she could begin her own farming business. The benefits of the clean-break in the context of familial relationship breakdown were again underlined.

Although questions remain the approach outlined in *Jennings*, clarified in *Davies* and affirmed in *Habberfield* represents the current law. It is unlikely, however, that these judgments represent the final word on the issue . . . so, watch this space!

8.4.2 What spectrum of remedies is available to the court?

Having considered the mechanics of the court's approach to satisfying the equity, the final stage is to consider the remedies available to the court. The court has a wide variety of remedial options at its disposal from the award of an interest in land to a personal interest, occupational rights, and even to monetary compensation, whichever is deemed most appropriate: see Figure 8.4.

In *Pascoe* and *Dillwyn v Llewellyn* (1862), the court awarded the claimant the fee simple in the land. In *Yaxley*, a 99-year lease, rent-free, of a ground-floor house was deemed the appropriate remedy. In other cases, the court has awarded an easement (e.g. a right of way) to satisfy the equity.[49] Alternatively, the court may determine that no proprietary interest in land should be awarded and, in its place, order a personal remedy such as a licence for life as in *Matharu v Matharu* (1994). Equally, the court may determine that no interest over land at all should be provided to the claimant. Here, the court may award compensation in lieu of a proprietary remedy as in *Wayling*, *Jennings*, and *Habberfield*. More recently, in *Guest v Guest* (2019), a son's estoppel claim relating to family farmland succeeded in circumstances where the farm owners, his mother and father, were—unusually for an estoppel claim—still alive. So acrimonious was the relationship between the son and his parents

---

[49] *Crabb*; *E. R. Ives Investment Ltd v High* (1967); *Sommer v Sweet* (2005).

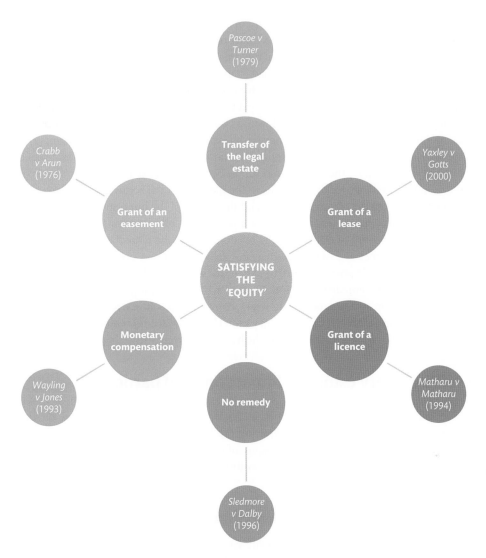

Figure 8.4 Remedial choices available to the court

that the court ordered that the only appropriate remedy was to satisfy the equity by order-ing that the son receive a lump sum payment to reflect a 50 per cent share of the market value of the farm business and 40 per cent of the freehold land and buildings comprising the farm. This would allow for a clean-break between the parties.

In *Moore v Moore*, the Court of Appeal was called upon to consider how to satisfy the equity in a case concerning a farm where the party making the assurances, a father, was still alive but lacked mental capacity. The son, Stephen, argued that his father, Roger Moore (no relation to the famous actor!) had made assurances that he would inherit his father's share of the farm. The judge at first instance allowed Stephen's estoppel claim and ordered that the father's interest be transferred to the son on the proviso that Stephen allow his parents to continue to live in the farmhouse, pay them a weekly allowance, and pay outgoings and reasonable care expenses. On appeal, the Court of Appeal expressed concern that the trial judge had overlooked the practicalities of the order granted, in particular, the crucial factor that the relationship between the parties had irreparably broken down and a clean-break was needed. The order made forced the parties to be financially dependent on one another. The case would be remitted to the High Court for a further hearing. The Court of Appeal offered guidance on the nature of the order that would be appropriate: (1) in view of the father's incapacity, his share in the land and partnership assets should be transferred to the son; (2) the son was to provide the mother with a lump sum, raised within a matter of months, to enable her to rehouse herself; (3) the son was to continue being responsible for the father's care costs and to continue making weekly payments to the mother; (4) the son was to bear any tax liabilities arising from the transfer of assets and the raising of the lump sum. *Moore* serves as a reminder of the complexities of the factual matrices that often exist in estoppel claims, of the need to take account of difficult family relationships, of the remedial flexibility inherent in proprietary estoppel, and of the advantages of delivering a clean-break. Where these challenges are ignored or down-played, orders may prove impracticable and open to appeal.

The spectrum of remedies therefore reflects a hierarchy, ranging from the award of freehold ownership of the land to monetary compensation. In extreme cases, of which *Sledmore* is but one example, the court may even elect to award no remedy at all if the detriment suffered has been extinguished by the benefits enjoyed by the claimant.[50]

8.5 Proprietary estoppel: Impact on third parties

Where a claim to proprietary estoppel succeeds, what is the impact of this on third parties—for example, third parties acquiring the land in relation to which the estoppel claim was made? In order to gain a real sense of the effect of proprietary estoppel on third parties, it is useful to consider briefly the position prior to the LRA 2002 before turning to examine the current law.

8.5.1 Prior to the Land Registration Act 2002

An estoppel equity, also called an 'inchoate equity', is generated in favour of a claimant from the moment the claimant relies on assurances made by the landowner to her detriment. We have seen that this equity is then 'satisfied' by the award of a remedy by the court. Proprietary estoppel therefore involves essentially a two-step process. Prior to the enactment of the LRA 2002, this created a fascinating question: what was the effect of this 'inchoate' estoppel equity on third parties *before* the court orders a remedy. Put another way, was this estoppel equity a proprietary interest capable of binding third parties? There were two schools of thought.

The first school argued that an estoppel equity, not yet satisfied by the award of a remedy by the court, was not proprietary as it did not fall within the traditional categories of interests recognized as being proprietary. Adherents of this view[51] argued an estoppel

---

[50] See also *Appleby v Cowley* (1982); *Clarke v Swaby* (2007).
[51] T. Bailey [1983] Conv 36; D. Hayton [1990] Conv 370; D. Hayton, 'Developing the Law of Trusts for the Twenty-First Century' (1990) 106 LQR 87.

equity could therefore not bind third parties and cited case law authority in support of this position.[52] On this view, the estoppel equity was merely a first step in the process towards the creation of rights in land by the court at the remedial stage. Thus, once the court awarded a remedy—say, an easement—it was that proprietary right which was capable of binding third parties and not the estoppel equity itself. The advantage of this analysis was that it empowered the court. It would be for the court to determine whether a proprietary or a personal right should be awarded as a remedy and therefore whether the result generated would bind a third party. Aside from a handful of decisions, however, there was little judicial support for this analysis.

The second school of thought argued that an estoppel equity, not yet satisfied by the award of a remedy by the court, was proprietary in nature and thus capable of binding third parties. It is fair to say that this reflected the more favoured interpretation by academics in England.[53] In essence, under this analysis, irrespective of the remedy ultimately awarded by the court, the estoppel equity itself had proprietary status meaning it was capable of binding a purchaser of the landowner's land.[54] In particular, in *Birmingham Midshires Mortgage Services Ltd v Sabherwal* (2000) the court suggested (albeit only by intimation) that an estoppel equity might constitute an overriding interest under the then provisions of s. 70(1)(g) of the LRA 1925, a clear expression of its proprietary status. Some doubt remained, however, as it was possible to explain all of these decisions along different, alternative lines which did not require a conclusion on the proprietary status or otherwise of an estoppel equity.

8.5.2 The current law

Fortunately, s. 116 of the Land Registration Act 2002 puts beyond all doubt the current status of an 'inchoate' estoppel equity in registered land. Section 116 confirms that an estoppel equity is, from the time the equity arises, proprietary in nature and, crucially, whether this equity will bind a third party depends on the priority rules for registered land. The binding nature of an estoppel equity therefore rests on the application of the priority rules of registered conveyancing: whether a notice has been entered to protect the estoppel or whether there is an overriding interest founded on actual occupation.[55] Recommending the enactment of s. 116, the Law Commission had explained that:[56]

> To put the matter beyond doubt, we recommend that the proprietary status of an equity arising by estoppel should be confirmed in relation to registered land. It could therefore be protected by the entry of a notice in the register, or where the claimant was in actual occupation of the land in relation to which he or she claimed an equity, as an overriding interest.

---

[52] *Jones (AE) v Jones (FW)* (1977); *Pennine Raceway v Kirklees Council* (1983).

[53] G. Battersby, 'Contractual Licences as Proprietary Interests in Land' [1991] Conv 36; S. Baughen, 'Estoppels over Land and Third Parties: An Open Question?' (1994) 14 LS 147; G. Battersby, 'Informal Transactions in Land, Estoppel and Registration' (1995) 58 MLR 637.

[54] Cases such as *E. R. Ives Investments v High*, *Inwards*, and *Re Sharpe* were cited as authority for this position.

[55] We discussed these in Chapter 3.

[56] Law Commission Report No. 271, *Land Registration for the Twenty-First Century: A Conveyancing Revolution*, [5.30].

McFarlane has explored three distinct 'interpretations' that could be afforded to the operation of s. 116 of the LRA 2002.[57] The first, as supported by the Law Commission, is that the 'inchoate equity' has proprietary status from the moment it arises. A second interpretation is that no rights at all arise until a court order has been made. The third is a 'new model'. In arguing for this 'new model', McFarlane finds the first two interpretations wanting. McFarlane does concede however that his 'new model' reflects a strained interpretation of the provision and is inconsistent with the clear direction of the Law Commission's proposals. Under this 'new model', the reference to 'equity by estoppel' in s. 116 should be given a narrow reading as embracing only a recognized proprietary right arising through estoppel. The effect is that only interests that are proprietary in nature will be capable of binding successors from the moment they arise under s. 116. Whilst this may be tautologous, McFarlane argues that if the provision is to operate 'for the avoidance of doubt' then its effect should not be as wide-ranging as the interpretation of the Law Commission allows.

McFarlane's discussion of s. 116 is stimulating but does not, with respect, alter the obvious intention of the Law Commission and the welter of case law which supported the view that an inchoate equity does have proprietary status. With this in mind, let's consider the *practical* application of s. 116 of the LRA. We will do this by examining three separate scenarios:

- Scenario 1: Anita makes assurances to Ben that Ben is to have an interest in her farm which Ben relies upon to his detriment. This gives rise to an estoppel equity in Ben's favour. Imagine that Anita then sells the farm to Cai. Under s. 116 of the LRA 2002, the estoppel in Ben's favour is capable of binding Cai from the moment it arises. In order that this estoppel equity is binding on Cai, Ben must have entered a notice on the Charges Register or, alternatively, argue for an overriding interest founded upon his actual occupation. If not, Cai will take the farm free of the estoppel equity.

- Scenario 2: Anita makes assurances to Ben that Ben is to have an interest in her farm which Ben relies upon to his detriment. Ben brings an action in court under the doctrine of proprietary estoppel and the court 'satisfies the equity' by ordering that the farm be transferred to Ben. This conveyance will be registered and Ben will be protected. Imagine, however, that Anita sells the farm to Cai after the court order was made but before the order is implemented. Here, Ben will be able to rely on the capacity for his estoppel equity to bind, under s. 116 of the LRA, and will be able to argue an overriding interest binding on Cai.

- Scenario 3: Anita makes assurances to Ben that Ben is to have an interest in her farm which Ben relies upon to his detriment. Ben brings an action in court under the doctrine of proprietary estoppel and the court 'satisfies the equity' by awarding a *personal* remedy such as a licence or monetary compensation. Imagine that, subsequently, Anita sells the farm to Cai. The remedy awarded to Ben is personal only and Cai will not be bound by it. Can Ben, however, assert that under s. 116 of the LRA 2002 his inchoate estoppel equity nevertheless binds Cai? This has proved to be something of a vexed issue.

---

[57] McFarlane, 'Proprietary Estoppel and Third Parties after the Land Registration Act 2002', 690.

On one view, once the court has satisfied the equity, the estoppel equity ceases to exist and Ben will be unable to rely on s. 116 in asserting that Cai is bound. This appears to be the most appropriate reading of the provision. The criticism of this approach would be that it has the potential to render worthless a personal remedy ordered by the court. Consider this: if Ben is granted a personal licence, this licence is all too easily defeated when Anita sells the land to Cai. This neatly optimizes the fragility of personal versus proprietary interests in land. We await judicial adjudication on this point.

We have focused so far on registered land. What of unregistered land? In unregistered land s. 116 of the LRA 2002 does not apply. In our discussion of the position pre-2002, we found that the weight of academic opinion favoured the proprietary nature of estoppel equities and their potential to bind third parties. The effect is that, in unregistered land, whether an estoppel equity is binding on a third party is determined by the 'doctrine of notice'.[58]

8.6 Proprietary estoppel and constructive trusts: Doctrines compared

Having examined proprietary estoppel in this chapter and constructive trusts in Chapter 6, it is worth pausing to consider how far the two principles overlap. At a fundamental level, we can see that the two serve a similar function in that they both create interests in land *informally* and are both devices developed by the court of equity. Both estoppel and constructive trusts arise in circumstances where a claimant has acted to their detriment on a belief encouraged by the owner of land that the claimant is to have some right in that land. What's more, the subjective motivations, conscience, and conduct of the parties is key to the operation of both doctrines. Nevertheless, as things currently stand, the two are regarded as quite distinct. By way of illustration and to prove the point, in *Southwell* the court rejected Miss Blackburn's claim for a constructive trust but nevertheless upheld her claim for proprietary estoppel. The Court of Appeal could locate no express common intention to share ownership of the house on which a constructive trust could be found yet did identify assurances sufficient for proprietary estoppel. As the court noted, 'the two are not inconsistent'. For now, at least, the distinction between the operation of the two concepts remains real. Table 8.2 helps to identify some potential differences between the two concepts.

Warning! Proceed with caution as these ostensible 'differences' are susceptible to serious challenge and are offered as food for thought—duly chewed over here—rather than as incontrovertible fact.

It is said that a constructive trust analysis is more suited to a domestic context concerning a matrimonial or quasi-matrimonial home than proprietary estoppel. Certainly, the leading authorities in constructive trusts do occupy this domain and in *Stack v Dowden* (2007), the majority view of the court was of the particular suitability of the trust device in

---

[58] *E. R. Ives Investments v High* was accepted as authority in *Lloyds Bank plc v Carrick* (1996) and *Birmingham Midshires Mortgage Services Ltd v Sabherwal*. There are, however, decisions going the other way—*Re Sharpe*; *United Bank of Kuwait v Sahib* (1997)—which suggest that express notice or an affected conscience is required; see section 3.4.3.

Table 8.2 Proprietary estoppel and constructive trusts compared

PROPRIETARY ESTOPPEL	CONSTRUCTIVE TRUST
Applied in a range of contexts which can include the domestic	Applies chiefly in the matrimonial or quasi-matrimonial context
Founded on 'assurances,' 'promises,' 'expectations'	Founded on 'common intention' of the parties
Can be interpreted as operating unilaterally	Can be interpreted as operating bilaterally or mutually
Flexibility as to requirements	Less flexibility as to requirements
Broad spectrum of remedies open to the court to vindicate the claim	Remedy limited to award of a share of the equitable ownership of the property
No specific statutory exemptions from formality requirements	Specific statutory exemptions from formality requirements e.g. s. 53(2) of the LPA 1925

the domestic context. Proprietary estoppel appears to be far less constrained and operates in a broader range of circumstances. Interestingly, however, there is a growing tendency for claimants to plead both causes of action in the same case.[59]

Both proprietary estoppel and constructive trusts are based on representation, reliance, and detriment though this may be where the similarities in the essential requirements of the concepts end. In a constructive trust claim, the court looks for a 'common intention' to share ownership in equity. We might characterize this 'common intention' as a meeting of the minds and in this sense bilateral or mutual in nature. In contrast, proprietary estoppel is more unilateral, arising from one party's self-directed assurance to the other. Beware, however, of the attraction of this apparently simple and logical analysis for it may not entirely withstand scrutiny. Indeed, might we interpret a case such as *Gillett* or *Southwell* as giving rise to a mutual understanding or meeting of the minds? It may be similarly artificial to analyse cases such as *Stack* or *Jones v Kernott* as involving expressions of common intentions as to ownership. Additionally, it was thought easier to prove 'detriment' for the purposes of an estoppel claim than in an action based on constructive trust. However, the apparent stricter detriment requirement in constructive trust cases appears to be relaxing in light of the decisions of *Stack* and *Jones*.

There is much debate as to the flexibility of the doctrine of proprietary estoppel versus the relatively less flexible constructive trust. It is clear that the remedial position in an estoppel claim does support this view as the court has an entire spectrum of remedial choices open to it. This is not so for constructive trusts where the imposition of the trust itself serves as the remedy, securing the priority of the claimant's position against the defendant. A party succeeding in establishing a constructive trust over a family home, for example,

---

[59] *Oxley v Hiscock* (2004); *Southwell.*

will be awarded an equitable interest or share in the land which reflects what was intended between the parties according to their common intention. In an estoppel claim, it is for the court, in its wide discretion, to determine the remedy having regard to the expectations raised, the principle of proportionality, doing the 'minimum' to achieve justice in the case. Beyond this, an assessment of the differences of estoppel and constructive trusts based on flexibility may prove fruitless. It has been said that it is more challenging to prove a constructive trust claim than one founded on estoppel. Whilst there is little evidence for this, some would argue that given the outcome of a trust claim results in a proprietary interest in every case the court may approach these claims with greater scrutiny. Yet similarities also exist: both concepts are equitable and are therefore at the absolute discretion of the court. Equally, both can generate proprietary interests capable of binding third parties.[60]

Statutory provisions expressly exempt the constructive trust from specific formality requirements such as s. 53(2) of the LPA 1925 for dealings with land. Proprietary estoppel does not enjoy these explicit exemptions. The clear statutory exemptions perhaps provide a degree of legitimization for the constructive trust which is not present for proprietary estoppel. Might it be said, that this recognition of the exemptions for constructive trusts may place the trust device on a firmer footing than its estoppel counterpart? In contrast, the doctrine of proprietary estoppel must grapple more directly and explicitly with ill-defined notions of unconscionability.

How distinct do you think the two concepts really are?

8.7 Future directions

In this chapter, we have explored the doctrine of proprietary estoppel. As we have seen, there has been a wealth of recent case law on proprietary estoppel. Whilst these decisions do not change the foundational principles underlying the doctrine; they are helpful in clarifying how the court approaches estoppel claims and in identifying the areas requiring clarification. While there is certainly room for further development and greater precision, particularly in relation to the appropriate rationale for the proportionality exercise at the remedial stage, the four central principles of proprietary estoppel are sufficiently delimited (assurance, reliance, detriment, unconscionability). We can anticipate further case law in the coming years. In considering the future directions of the law in this area, two issue are especially ripe for further reflection.

8.7.1 How far should courts mitigate against unpredictability when adjudicating estoppel decisions?

The modern incarnation of the doctrine is often presented as 'flexible' and, as we have explored in this chapter, its operation is highly discretionary. Indeed, the shift to the modern law in *Taylors Fashions* represented a liberalization of the requirements of

---

[60] Though not inevitably in estoppel claims where a personal remedy or no remedy may be deemed appropriate: see section 8.4.2.

estoppel. Flexibility, however, comes at a cost—namely, unpredictability and the risk of greater litigation. How far should courts mitigate against this unpredictability? Mee has recently argued against the apparent generosity of the courts in estoppel claims, contending that the courts appear to be going too far in remedying the equity in estoppel claims:[61]

> Proprietary estoppel is a very powerful and a very unpredictable doctrine . . . the unpredictability of proprietary estoppel generates a great deal of additional . . . litigation. In terms of the related issue of generosity to claimants, part of the problem may be that all the fun in equity lies in providing remedies for claimants where 'the rigours of strict law' will not allow it. The rhetoric of centuries encourages judges to 'temper the harsh wind to the shorn lamb'. From the point of view of some judges (although other judges might have a different preference), it could seem more fulfilling to dispense discretionary justice to the parties before the court than to feel obliged to apply, in a more mechanical way, the strict rules of property law and succession law. However, there is a cost in terms of the certainty of the law, certainty that would benefit members of the public who would, as a result, never come into contact with the judges administering equity. Despite much reverential talk on the part of legal commentators and judges about equitable flexibility and the prevention of unconscionability, it is not in the public interest for the legal system to tolerate an indulgent and confused proprietary estoppel jurisdiction. It is to be hoped that the [more generous] trend . . . will not continue and that the courts will begin to take a more restrained and analytical approach.

Do you agree with Mee? What might the implications be in the event that courts adopt this more restrained approach at the remedial stage of an estoppel claim?

On the issue of flexibility in proprietary estoppel, consider the cases of *Bradbury v Taylor* (2012) and *Suggitt v Suggitt* (2012). In both cases (worth perusing!) arguably the court offered a remedy exceeding the detriment suffered and apparently overlooking significant advantages gained by the claimants. In *Bradbury*, the claimants lived rent-free in a very large home in Cornwall whilst retaining rental income from a property they owned in Sheffield. The court awarded the claimants the full freehold despite only equivocal assurances of ownership and the clear benefits they enjoyed. In *Suggitt*, a father left a farm to his daughter with a power for her to transfer the land to the son (her brother) if he showed himself capable of managing the land. The son claimed to be entitled to the freehold by way of proprietary estoppel. He relied on rather unsubstantiated and ambiguous work he claimed to have conducted on the farm as evidence of his detriment. Certainly, his detriment was not substantial yet the court awarded the son the full freehold. The daughter appealed arguing that the remedy was disproportionate to the detriment suffered. The Court of Appeal disagreed holding that, under *Jennings*, the question was whether the remedy was 'out of all proportion' and here it was not. Do you agree with *Bradbury* and *Suggitt*? Should a lesser remedy have been awarded? Was *Jennings* applied faithfully and appropriately and, where next for the proportionality exercise, in view of the decision in *Davies*?

---

[61] Mee, 'Proprietary Estoppel and Inheritance: Enough Is Enough?', 296–7.

8.7.2 The possibility and desirability of the assimilation of estoppel and constructive trust analyses

There is debate around this issue. In section 8.6 we considered some of the similarities and differences between the two concepts. Do we need both or could a single hybrid doctrine occupy the same ground and serve the functions currently governed by estoppel and constructive trusts? One important issue remains unresolved, however, and that is the interplay between proprietary estoppel and s. 2 of the LP(MP)A 1989 which provides for the formality requirements necessary for a contract for sale of land. Constructive trusts are exempted[62] from the operation of the provision but what about proprietary estoppel? There is no similar exemption for estoppel raising the potential to frustrate the statute's purpose 'if an estoppel would have the effect of enforcing a void contract and subverting Parliament's purpose'.[63] Recall that Lord Scott in *Cobbe* was firm in his view that:[64]

> The proposition that an owner of land can be estopped from asserting that an agreement is void for want of compliance with the requirements of section 2 is, in my opinion, unacceptable. The assertion is no more than the statute provides.

Lord Neuberger in *Thorner* appeared far more relaxed as to estoppel and s. 2:[65]

> I do not consider that section 2 has any impact on a claim such as the present, which is a straightforward estoppel claim without any contractual connection. It was no doubt for that reason that the respondent, rightly in my view, eschewed any argument based on section 2.

The point has not been directly argued and therefore not fully considered by the court. At present, however, it seems that Neuberger's view is the most likely to be followed.[66] Do you agree with this position? Adopting a more limited view of estoppel and s. 2 could severely restrict the ambit of the doctrine. Does this more expansive approach make it more likely or less that estoppel and constructive trusts could one day assimilate?

Further reading

- P. Birks, 'Equity in the Modern Law: An Exercise in Taxonomy' (1996) 26 University of Western Australia Law Review 1, 60.

- S. Bright and B. McFarlane, 'Proprietary Estoppel and Property Rights' (2005) 64(2) CLJ 449.

- M. Dixon, 'Confining and Defining Proprietary Estoppel: The Role of Unconscionability' (2010) 30 LS 408.

- S. Gardner, 'The Remedial Discretion in Proprietary Estoppel—Again' (2006) 122 LQR 492.

- A. Goymour, 'Cobbling Together Claims Where a Contract Fails to Materialise' (2009) 68(1) CLJ 37.

---

[62] LP(MP)A 1989, s. 2(5). [63] Robert Walker LJ in *Yaxley*.
[64] *Yeoman's Row Management Ltd v Cobbe*, 1769. [65] *Thorner*, 804.
[66] See comments of Bean J in *Whittaker v Kinnear* (2011).

- K. Hawkins, *The Uses of Discretion* (Oxford: Clarendon, 1992).
- A. Hayward, 'Cohabitants, Detriment and the Potential of Proprietary Estoppel' (2015) 27(3) CFLQ 303.
- N. Hopkins, 'Proprietary Estoppel: A Functional Analysis' (2010) 4 Journal of Equity 201.
- B. McFarlane, 'Proprietary Estoppel and Third Parties after the Land Registration Act 2002' (2003) 62 CLJ 661.
- B. McFarlane, 'Understanding Equitable Estoppel: From Metaphors to Better Laws' (2013) 66 CLP 267.
- B. McFarlane, Sir Philip Sales, 'Promises, Detriment, and Liability: Lessons from Proprietary Estoppel' (2015) 131 LQR 610.
- J. Mee, 'Proprietary Estoppel, Promises and Mistaken Belief' in S. Bright (ed.), *Modern Studies in Property Law*, Vol. 6 (Oxford: Hart, 2011).
- J. Mee, 'Proprietary Estoppel and Inheritance: Enough Is Enough?' [2013] Conv 280.
- M. Pawlowski, 'Satisfying the Equity in Estoppel' (2002) 118 LQR 519.
- A. Robertson, 'The Reliance Basis of Proprietary Estoppel Remedies' [2008] Conv 295.
- R. Smith, 'How Proprietary Is Proprietary Estoppel?' in F. D. Rose (ed.), *Consensus Ad Idem: Essays on Contract in Honour of Günter Treitel* (London: Sweet & Maxwell, 1996), chapter 11.
- M. Thompson, 'The Flexibility of Estoppel' [2003] Conv 225.
- R. Wells, 'The Element of Detriment in Proprietary Estoppel' [2001] Conv 13.

 ## Online resources

Access the online resources at www.oup.com/uk/bevan2e/ to test yourself with self-test questions and scenario problems. You can also view additional supporting material relevant to the topics in this chapter, including:

- *Videos*
- *Audio podcasts*
- *Maps, diagrams, and flowcharts*
- *Interactive exercises*
- *Examples of real-life legal documentation*

9 Leases

9.1 Introduction

The concept of a lease is well-known. It describes that commonly encountered scenario when a landowner permits another person to use their land for a period of time usually in return for the payment of rent. For most of us when we think of a lease, the classic residential lease comes to mind. Many of you reading this will have already entered a lease and will be tenants right now. A lease is often our very first encounter with land law, though when we sign those tenancy agreements, we may not see it quite in these terms! In Chapter 7 we encountered the licence in its many forms (a permission to be on or do something on another's land). In particular, we noted that licences are *personal* in nature. The key distinguishing feature of a lease from the licence is its ability to bind third parties as a *proprietary* right. It is this proprietary status that gives the lease its potency. Before jumping in to examine the particular legal facets of the lease, we begin this chapter by reflecting on the importance and place of leases in modern land law.

9.1.1 Why leases matter

Of all the topics encountered in the land law course, it is often the lease which is most directly relevant to you as students of the subject: it being the legal relationship under which the majority of students occupy or share their student digs. For many, the lease is the most formalized legal arrangement entered into after leaving home. In fact, the significance of the lease extends far beyond a shared student house. Leases are crucially important across a diverse array of practical contexts. Why? Well, leases allow land to be enjoyed and exploited for a range of purposes without the capital cost associated with owning the land. Leases are of significant social and economic importance not least for those renting properties as homes where the lease allows access, for a monthly or weekly rent, to a safe, stable base from which to live contented and productive lives. These residential leases can range from very long leases which may last 999 years to the shorter, more common weekly, monthly, or yearly leases with which you are likely most familiar. In 2019, well over a third of homes in the UK were subject to this form of short, residential lease.[1] Residential leases may be granted by private individuals termed 'private landlords' but may equally be granted by 'public landlords' such as local authorities.

On first coming to the subject, it is quite understandable to think only of residential leases but leases, in fact, extend deep into the commercial world too. Picture your local high street: those shops, cafes, gyms, and bars that you frequent and those offices where friends perhaps work. Many if not the majority of these properties will be held by businesses under a lease. Even many farms are operated under a lease. Leases therefore embrace a multiplicity of contexts from the residential to the commercial to the agricultural. Whether a lease is residential, commercial, or agricultural gives rise to quite distinct consequences as to how the lease operates. These issues are largely beyond the scope of this book but it is useful to briefly consider how the context in which a lease arises impacts on how the lease functions. A student renting a room operates quite differently from a lease over a pub or a shopping outlet. Two key observations can be made:

1. As to duration: Residential leases tend to be shorter than their commercial counterparts. Whilst the average residential lease lasts one year, the average commercial lease is around five years in duration. This makes logical sense as the student renting a room has quite a different and more short-term perspective and needs than the business owner who is wanting to establish a profitable and lasting commercial enterprise.

2. As to the statutory protections governing the landlord–tenant relationship: In particular, if we focus on the key issue of obligations to repair leased property, we see that in residential leases, the landlord will typically be responsible for maintaining and repairing the property. In commercial leases, it is the tenant who is usually bears the responsibility for meeting the cost of repairs. In this way, the residential tenant is afforded far greater protection under statute than commercial tenants. There are many reasons for this but chief among them is the obvious motivation that residential leases tend to be granted to those establishing a 'home', a shelter which may also be the location for bringing up children. Residential tenants are also presumed not to enjoy the same bargaining power as landlords. Residential tenants are, therefore, regarded as being in greater need of protection under the law. This protection is provided, for example, to residential tenants under the Landlord and Tenant Act 1985 (LTA 1985) which implies certain repairing obligations into short leases. There are also strict controls over the circumstances in which a residential tenant can be evicted by her landlord.

For many who cannot afford to own land, entering a lease is either the most practical or advantageous option. A major attraction of the leasehold arrangement is that it involves a more limited relationship to land. In other words, it involves a shorter commitment to a piece of land. Take a small business owner who is in the early stages of developing their business. A short commercial lease allows this novice entrepreneur to occupy a small commercial space for a short period rather than tying them down to the longer-term commitment involved with owning land. A second key attraction to leasing property is cost. Acquiring the freehold can be extremely expensive and can involve administrative and

---

[1] *UK Housing Review*, 2019.

conveyancing fees which do not apply in leasehold arrangements. If you are low on funds, opting for a lease rather than buying a property outright may be your only option. The lease is therefore a highly valuable and flexible device which can bend to suit a wide range of diverse contexts, perspectives, and needs—both social and financial.

There is, however, more to the study of the law of leases than merely cataloguing the circumstances in which they arise. A lease is one of the two legal estates listed in s. 1 of the LPA 1925 (the other being freehold). Recall: an 'estate' describes enjoyment of land in time: a freehold denotes enjoyment of land for an indeterminate period (the closest thing we have to outright 'ownership' of land) whereas a lease denotes enjoyment of land for a specified period. Clearly, the longer the lease, the closer it is, in effect, to freehold ownership.

Yet, a lease is not just a contract or even an estate; it is also a *relationship*. As the Law Commission noted in its Report No. 174, the purpose of a lease is to create 'temporary property ownership'.[2] At the heart of the leasehold arrangement therefore sits a fascinating relationship: that of landlord and tenant. This relationship presents something of a conceptual puzzle, however, because whilst it is the landlord who (in most cases) remains the ultimate owner of the leased land, the party leasing the land, the tenant, is regarded during the lifetime of the lease as a 'temporary owner'. This can cause friction and this rubbing up of powerful landlords against tenants can be seen in the law's attempt to balance the remedies available to both landlords and tenants in the event of breach of the terms of the lease. As we move through this chapter, try to keep in your mind the potential power struggle that exists at the heart of the landlord–tenant relationship. How well does the law do in seeking to address or perhaps redress the power imbalance that exists between the parties to a lease?

We begin by looking at the nature and essential characteristics of a lease before considering how leases are created (at law and in equity), and how they are brought to an end.

 Visit the online resources to watch a video on recent developments in the law of leases.

9.2 The nature of leases

The multiplicity of circumstances in which the lease is found is mirrored in the diversity of terminology used to describe the landlord–tenant relationship. A lease may be termed 'leasehold estate', 'term of years', or a 'tenancy'. Equally, the parties to a lease are variously described as 'landlord' and 'tenant' or 'lessor' and 'lessee'. The terminology employed usually depends on the context: in the residential context, the term 'tenancy' is preferred, whereas 'term of years' is more frequently found in the commercial world. It is important not to become too bogged down in terminology. Instead, you need to be able to grasp the fundamental nature and characteristics of leases, which are as follows:

1. In many instances, the freehold owner of a parcel of land may not wish to occupy or use her land. Leasehold ownership permits a freehold owner to grant to another person a right to occupy and use that freeholder's land. The lease therefore provides a freehold owner with a means of exploiting the economic value inherent in her land by granting a lease to another (usually at a rent—see section 9.3.3).

---

[2] Law Commission Report No. 174 (1988), [3.26].

2. The lease allows two or more individuals to take a simultaneous benefit from the same parcel of land. The freehold owner or landlord remains the legal owner and receives the rent and any profits from the land. The tenant also benefits from the enjoyment, possession, and occupation of the land. The landlord retains his ownership but, vitally, subject to the rights of the tenant.

3. The lease or 'leasehold estate' is one of the two estates listed in s. 1 of the LPA 1925 as capable of subsisting at law and in equity. Leases can, as a result, be either legal or equitable. This is largely determined by the extent to which formality requirements for the creation of a lease are satisfied.[3]

4. It is possible for a second lease to be 'carved out' from the original lease (we call this original lease the '**headlease**') creating a new lease called a '**sublease**' or 'subtenancy'. This new sublease must, naturally, be shorter in duration than the headlease and permits even more people to benefit from the land. Imagine Amil is the freeholder owner and grants a lease over residential premises to Ben for a term of 99 years. Ben then grants a sublease over the same premises to Carol for 12 months. In this scenario, Carol will pay rent to Ben who will, in turn, pay rent to Amil. Carol will enjoy physical occupation of the land. This is further evidence of the flexibility and versatility of the leasehold estate. Theoretically, Carol could even carve out a further sublease in favour of other individuals.

5. The landlord, the tenant, and any subtenants all enjoy a proprietary right in the land.[4] The landlord is said to own the '**reversion** expectant upon the determination of the lease'. This simply means that the landlord has the right to possession of the leased property when the lease comes to an end. The landlord and tenant's proprietary rights can be assigned or sold to third parties. If the landlord sells his reversion, the third party 'assignee' becomes the new landlord. If a tenant sells his lease, that third party 'assignee' becomes the new tenant. Similarly, the assignees can themselves go ahead and assign their interests to further parties and so on.

6. Leases contain covenants which are promises made between landlord and tenant either to do or not to do particular things in relation to the land. These 'promises' can be express, implied into the leases by statute (such as by s. 11 of the LTA 1985), or implied into the lease by customary, common use. These 'leasehold covenants' are discussed in detail in Chapter 12.

So, we have examined the fundamental nature of the lease but what makes a lease a lease? In other words, what are the essential elements of a lease?

9.3 The essential elements of leases

Whilst there is a statutory definition of the 'term of years' in s. 205(1) (xvii) of the LPA 1925, the classic statement of the essential characteristics of a lease is that of Lord Templeman in *Street v Mountford* (1985) when he noted:[5]

---

[3] We explore what determines whether a lease is legal or equitable in section 9.5.

[4] Subject to the discussion that follows in section 9.4.6 as to *Bruton v London & Quadrant Housing Trust* (2000).

[5] *Street*, 818.

[T]o constitute a tenancy the occupier must be granted exclusive possession for a fixed or periodic term certain in consideration of a premium or periodic payments.

Regarded as the starting point for a consideration of the modern law of leases, *Street* provides us with the three essential elements of a lease:

- the grant of exclusive possession
- for a certain term
- at a rent.[6]

Importantly, whilst describing the central elements of a lease, these attributes can also be used as a tool for determining the dividing line between a lease and a licence. In particular, as we will discover in section 9.3.1, a lease can only exist where there is exclusive possession. If an occupier enjoys no exclusive possession, no lease can arise but a licence may be found to exist. This matters because, as we saw in Chapter 7, licences are purely personal interests and leases are proprietary. The lease/licence distinction was once an extremely significant and key battleground. Which side of the dividing line one found oneself would determine the extent and potency of your rights. Tenants under a lease were given far greater protection—for example, under the Rent Acts, a guaranteed fair rent. Today, the lease/licence distinction is of far less significance than it once was (though remains important in the commercial sector). We will return to reflect on the significance of the distinction in section 9.3.1.2. For now, each of the three essential ingredients of a lease as set out in *Street* will be unpacked.

9.3.1 First essential element: Exclusive possession

Exclusive possession is the beating heart of the lease and without it no lease can exist. It is also the key distinguishing feature in the lease/licence divide. If a lease does not exist because of a lack of exclusive possession, a licence may nevertheless be found.[7] Whether exclusive possession is present on a given set of facts is the central determinant of whether the legal arrangement constitutes a lease or a licence.[8] So, what does 'exclusive possession' look like? One simple way of grasping the concept is to see exclusive possession as the characteristic which gives the tenant the right to exclude others, including the landlord, from the land.

Let's take an example: imagine that you own a house and you grant a friend a right to occupy your house. If your friend has a legal *right* to exclude you as landowner and any other person (except police and emergency services), that friend has exclusive possession. If, however, you retain a right to share occupation of the house with your friend or, alternatively, to let other people join your friend in occupation, there will be no exclusive possession. It is vital you distinguish the *right* to exclude from the *ability* to exclude. You may be *able* to exclude someone physically but only where you have the legal *right* to do so will exclusive possession exist. As we can see, the central thrust of exclusive possession is the right of the tenant to exclude all persons from the leased premises during the term of the lease.

---

[6] Rent is not strictly required for a lease to arise, however, see section 9.3.3.

[7] On which, see Chapter 7.

[8] For more on this lease/licence distinction and its significance, see section 9.3.1.2.

That is not quite the end of the matter. We need also to isolate and distinguish exclusive *possession* from exclusive *occupation*.[9] Both are subtly distinct but share a close connection. Exclusive possession, as we have said, is the right to exclude others from the land. Exclusive occupation describes a situation where a person occupies land on her own without others. Exclusive possession confers a legal entitlement and is the mark of a lease whereas exclusive occupation reflects a purely factual notion (living in premises without others). Exclusive occupation alone is insufficient for a lease to exist but may provide evidence of the existence of exclusive possession. It has been argued that the presence of exclusive occupation can gives rise to a presumption that exclusive possession is conferred. This presumption is, of course, rebuttable in all the circumstances of the case. As you can imagine, the courts have grappled with what amounts to exclusive possession. A series of principles can be distilled from decided cases:

1. Whether exclusive possession exists is determined by reference to all the facts of the case, the wider surrounding circumstances, the course of dealing between the parties, the particular nature of the land occupied, and the manner of occupation: *Street*.

2. Exclusive possession confers something akin to 'territorial control' on the occupier in that the tenant is able to keep out from the land strangers and even the landlord (subject to any rights reserved to the landlord under the specific terms of the lease). In this way, as Lord Templeman asserts, a tenant with exclusive possession has the control rights commonly associated with ownership and:[10]

   > is able to exercise the rights of an owner of land, which is in the real sense his land albeit temporarily and subject to certain restrictions.

3. The central task of the court is to ascertain the true construction of the agreement, the true bargain between the parties. This involves looking beyond the label given to an agreement to determine the nature and quality of the occupation as well as what the landlord knew of the reality of the arrangement. As Lord Templeman made clear in *Street*, the parties 'cannot turn a tenancy into a licence merely by calling it one'.

KEY CASE *Street v Mountford* (1985)

Facts: Mr Street entered into an agreement under which Mrs Mountford would have exclusive possession of two rooms in a property Mr Street owned. The agreement was described, on its face, as a 'licence agreement' and the agreement contained a specific clause which declared, in no uncertain terms, that the parties did not intend to create a lease. The agreement contained the following clause: 'I understand and accept that a licence in the above form does not and is not intended to give me a tenancy protected under the Rent Acts.' Mrs Mountford applied for the registration of a fair rent under the Rent Acts (which apply only to leases and not to licences). Mr Street brought an action in court, seeking a declaration that Mrs Mountford was a licensee and not a tenant.

→

---

[9] A point made by the Court of Appeal in *Watts v Stewart* (2017) which is discussed in section 9.3.1.1.
[10] *Street*, 816.

> →
>
> **Legal issue:** Was Mrs Mountford occupying the two rooms as a tenant or as a licensee and how far was the 'licence agreement' determinative of her legal relationship to the land?
>
> **Judgment:** The House of Lords unanimously reversed the decision of the Court of Appeal which had found Mrs Mountford to be a licensee. Lord Templeman, delivering the judgment of the court, noted that where accommodation was granted for a certain term with exclusive possession, the legal consequence of this was the granting of a lease notwithstanding the use of the words 'licence' or 'licence agreement'. Mrs Mountford was therefore a tenant of the two rooms. In determining the lease/licence divide, the court will consider all the surrounding circumstances of the case, the nature of the land, and the manner of occupation in order to ascertain the 'true construction' of the agreement. In so doing, it is the substance of the rights created that will be determinative. The label used by the parties to describe their relationship will be a material consideration but will not be decisive.

9.3.1.1 Exclusive possession: Some common scenarios

There are a number of common scenarios in which the issue of exclusive possession routinely arises. As you can see from Table 9.1, what has developed is a body of decided case law which now offers vital guidance on how the court will approach the issue of exclusive possession in these contexts.

Let's look at each scenario in Table 9.1 in a little more detail.

Lodgers

A lodger is someone who shares the occupation of premises with the owner of the land or receives services (often called 'attendances'), such as cleaning/laundry, from the landlord. Lodgers do not enjoy the exclusive possession required to give rise to the status of tenant. Lodgers are regarded as licensees of the property in which they live. This was made clear by Lord Templeman in *Street* where he noted that:[11]

> [T]he occupier is a lodger if the landlord provides attendance or services which require the landlord or his servants to exercise unrestricted access to and use of the premises. A lodger is entitled to live in the premises but cannot call the place his own.

If the lodger is unable to prevent access to the land by the landowner, then she cannot be said to enjoy exclusive possession and she is not a tenant. The landowner is, in theory, quite entitled to enter at will the lodger's designated bedroom or work areas and this is wholly inconsistent with the existence of a tenancy.

The provision of services

Where the landowner has arranged or agreed that regular services ('attendances') be provided to the occupier this will prevent a finding of exclusive possession and preclude the existence of a lease: *Markou v De Silvaesa*. Services may include cleaning of the occupier's room, daily meals, or change of linens and laundry.

---

[11] Ibid., 817–18.

Table 9.1 Exclusive possession: Some common scenarios

SCENARIO	CASE LAW
Lodgers	• *Street v Mountford* (1985): a lodger is someone sharing occupation of premises with the owner of the land or receives services. A lodger does not enjoy exclusive possession and is therefore not a tenant.
Provision of services	• *Markou v De Silvaesa* (1986): where the landowner has arranged or agreed that regular services ('attendances') be provided to the occupier, this will prevent a finding of exclusive possession and thus prevent the finding of a lease.
Hotels, hostels, almshouses and care homes	• *Appah v Parncliffe Investments Ltd* (1964); *Westminster City Council v Clarke* (1992): hotel occupants will be licensees not tenants due to an absence of exclusive possession. • *Abbeyfield Society v Woods* (1968): a long-term care home resident was deemed to be a licensee as a result of the receipt of services such as regular meals, heating, and electricity. • *Watts v Stewart* (2016): residents of almshouses are licensees and not tenants.
Retention of keys	• *Aslan v Murphy* (1990): the retention of keys by the landlord will not automatically prevent an agreement being construed as a lease.
Shared occupation	• *AG Securities v Vaughan* (1990); *Antoniades v Villiers* (1990): whether shared occupation gives rise to separate licence agreements or a joint tenancy is to be determined by a close examination of the facts of each individual case.
Shams and pretences	• *Street v Mountford* (1985): the court will 'be astute to detect and frustrate sham devices and artificial transactions whose only object is to disguise the grant of a tenancy' (per Lord Templeman). • *Aslan v Murphy* (1990): where the terms of an agreement are 'wholly unrealistic and . . . clearly pretences', the court will strike down these clauses to ascertain the true bargain between the parties.
'Property guardians'	• *Camelot Property Management Ltd v Roynon* (2017); *Camelot Guardian Management Ltd v Khoo* (2018): whether a property guardian occupying shared land under a 'licence' or 'occupation agreement' is a licensee or a tenant depends on a close reading of the terms of the agreement and on a realistic assessment of issues such as access, services provided, and repairing obligations.

It is irrelevant that an occupier of land has, on a number of occasions, refused to accept services provided by the landowner. Here, an occupier will still be regarded in law as a lodger. This was made plain in the case of *Marchant v Charters* (1977). Equally, students occupying university halls of residence usually do so as lodgers and not as tenants in view of the cleaning and other services offered.

KEY CASE *Markou v De Silvaesa* (1986)

Facts: Several people occupied individual, furnished rooms in a house owned by Mr De Silvaesa under agreements which were all described, on their face, as 'licences'. Under the agreements, the 'licensor' retained keys to the rooms as well as the absolute right to enter the rooms at any time and require the occupiers to vacate the premises. The licensor agreed to provide services including cleaning, rubbish collection, and the laundering of bed linens.

Legal issue: Were the occupiers lodgers or tenants?

Judgment: Given the broad right to access the premises for the provision of services and further rights reserved to the landowner, it could not be said that the occupiers enjoyed exclusive possession over the premises. Per Gibson LJ held:

> The agreement does require the landlord to provide attendance and services which require the landlord and his servants to exercise unrestricted access to and use of the room. Possession and control of the room are reserved by clause 2 of the agreement to the landlord for the purposes of discharging the obligation to provide attendance and services and that shows, in my judgment, that exclusive possession was not given.

The court will consider all the circumstances. The mere fact that the landowner can access the premises does not, of itself, conclusively exclude the possibility of the finding of a lease. However, where the landowner is permitted near-unrestricted access to enter the premises for the provision of services, this will preclude the finding of a lease. In such cases, occupiers will be lodgers (licensees) and not tenants.

Hotel, hostel, almshouse, and care home residents

What about those residing long-term in hotels, hostels, almshouses, or homes for the elderly? It is now settled that it is the nature and quality of the occupation and not the duration of the stay which determines the legal status of the arrangement. Therefore, a long-term hotel occupant for whom daily housekeeping was provided was a licensee due to the absence of exclusive possession in *Appah v Parncliffe Investments Ltd* (1964). Equally, in *Abbeyfield Society v Woods* (1968) an octogenarian was deemed a licensee and not a tenant entitled to the Rent Act protections from eviction when living in a care home which provided a range of services from the provision of regular meals to heating and electricity. It appears that accommodation within a hostel will also be under a licence rather than a tenancy in circumstances where there are restrictions placed on the nature of the occupation. In *Westminster City Council v Clarke* (1992) a homeless man occupying one of several, single rooms in a London homelessness hostel was held not to enjoy exclusive possession and was a licensee. Particularly important to this decision was a night-time curfew and the right reserved to the Council to move individuals to alternative accommodation without notice. In *Watts v Stewart* (2016), the Court of Appeal was called upon to consider the status of residents of almshouses (accommodation provided by charities for the poor).[12] Ms Watts had been allocated housing in an almshouse by a charity which gave poor, single women over 50 somewhere to live. After 11 years of occupation, the charity wanted to remove Ms Watts from the property due to her antisocial behaviour. She resisted, arguing she was a tenant and therefore had protections against eviction. The court held that Ms

---

[12] There are approximately 35,000 almshouse residents and an estimated 1,700 almshouses in the UK.

Watts and almshouse residents more broadly were not tenants but licensees and therefore could be readily removed from the property. The court focused in particular on the terms of the letter by which Ms Watts had been appointed the almshouse accommodation. On a close reading of this letter, the court held that it did not grant exclusive possession to her as: (1) the letter expressly provided that Ms Watts was not to be a tenant and was not to have any legal interest in the almshouse; (2) the charity reserved the right to require residents to vacate the property and move temporarily or permanently to another almshouse; (3) visitors were not allowed to stay overnight except with permission of the charity; (4) residents were not permitted to vacate the premises for more than 28 days a year without the consent of the charity; (5) residents needed to inform the charity if they were to be away for more than one week at any time; and (6) the resident's appointment to almshouse accommodation could be set aside by the charity for good cause. The charity also reserved for itself a right of reasonable access for inspection, repairs, and redecoration. The Court of Appeal held that Ms Watts, and almshouse residents more generally, were licensees, stressing that if charities could not house residents under revocable licences then they would not be able to meet their charitable objective of helping those in greatest financial need.

The retention of keys by the landowner

You may think that retention of a key to the premises by the landowner would necessarily be inconsistent with exclusive possession and the finding of a lease. How can an occupier enjoy territorial control and a right to exclude all others from the land if the landlord can enter the premises at any time? The retention of keys by the landlord will not, however, automatically prevent an agreement being construed as a lease. In *Aslan v Murphy* (1990), an agreement described as a 'licence' was held to constitute a lease even though the landlord had kept a key to the property. The Court of Appeal emphasized that what matters was the purpose for which the keys were retained. It was entirely consistent with the finding of a lease that a landlord might wish to retain keys in the event of an emergency (such as burst pipes), for the purposes of gas and electricity meter readings, or in order to carry out repairs. None of these grounds for retaining a key to the premises would, said Lord Donaldson MR, be indicative of a licence in law rather than a lease. *Aslan* serves as a timely reminder of the need for a fact-sensitive analysis of the question of exclusive possession.

Shared occupation

Where more than one person occupies the same premises, this may give rise to individual licences. However, such an arrangement does not inevitably preclude a finding of exclusive possession. Indeed, shared occupation may give rise to a joint tenancy provided that the four unities of time, possession, interest, and title are present.[13] Imagine that you and a group of fellow land law students band together to rent a property close to the university. You may each hold separate, individual licences in the land or perhaps, separate lease agreements, or, alternatively, you may collectively enjoy exclusive possession over the premises and therefore be joint tenants. It is fair to say that identifying precisely when a joint tenancy will arise has presented a challenge for the courts.

---

[13] Recall that we explored the four unities in the context of co-ownership in section 5.2.

In *AG Securities v Vaughan* (1990) four occupiers had each entered separate 'licence agreements' with the owner of a four-bedroom property. Each agreement had been granted at a different time, on different terms and each reflected a different 'licence fee'. In the event that an occupier left the premises, the agreements entitled the landowner to replace them with another occupier so that the premises would be kept at capacity. The House of Lords held that, in the circumstances, these agreements were accurately described as licences. The fact the landowner could replace individual occupiers with others meant that to deem the arrangement a joint tenancy would be to do violence to the parties' intentions.

AG Securities can be contrasted with the decision in *Antoniades v Villiers*, where a joint tenancy was found.

KEY CASE *Antoniades v Villiers* (1990)

Facts: A cohabiting couple occupied an attic flat consisting of a single bedroom with one bed. The landowner had insisted that the couple both sign separate agreements described as 'licences' on the basis that they were each to pay 50 per cent of the rental price. The agreements both contained clauses reserving to the landowner the right to occupy the flat or to nominate additional occupiers. There was a living space with a small sofa which may have made this, theoretically, possible. At the time of legal proceedings, the landowner had neither himself occupied the flat nor nominated any additional occupiers.

Legal issue: When the landowner later brought proceedings for possession of the premises, the court was called upon to determine the nature of the couple's occupation: as licensees or as joint tenants.

Judgment: It was held that the two separate 'licence' agreements signed by the couple were 'interdependent' and should be read together as a single agreement. The right reserved to the landowner to occupy the premises himself or to nominate additional occupier was a pretence designed to destroy the 'four unities' and to avoid the statutory protections of the Rent Acts afforded to tenants but not licensees. The terms of the agreements signed by the couple did not reflect the true intention of the parties as to occupation of the flat. The reality of the situation was that there had been an intention for the couple to enjoy exclusive possession for a term at a rent. Accordingly, this was a joint tenancy. The couple had applied jointly to occupy the flat and they jointly enjoyed exclusive occupation of the premises giving rise to a joint tenancy. The four unities of: possession, interest, title and time were present.

Shams

As we discussed in the introduction to this chapter, statutory protections are afforded to tenants under a lease which are not available to licensees. For this reason, attempts may be made (usually but not solely by landowners[14]) to evade the operation of these protections. Generally, this will be done by the landowner to deny the grant of exclusive possession to occupiers of their land. These shams or pretences may include impractical, purposeless, or meritless clauses (never intended to be implemented) inserted into agreements which may be expressly described as 'licences' in a bid to avoid the advantages that a tenancy brings to occupiers. Fortunately, the court is alive to the prevalence of sham devices and, through a full assessment of the surrounding circumstances of a

---

[14] A tenant may argue she is a licensee to avoid the payment of rent.

case, has shown itself more than willing to disregard pretences and to strike out sham clauses to determine the true substance of an agreement. As Lord Templeman noted in *Street*, the court should 'be astute to detect and frustrate sham devices and artificial transactions whose only object is to disguise the grant of a tenancy'.

It is important to appreciate that in the private rented sector where supply of good-quality and affordable rental properties is low and demand for properties is high, there is a risk that individuals agree to unreasonable terms in order to secure much-needed accommodation. In *Aslan*, this point was made by Lord Donaldson MR when noting that:[15]

> [T]here is enormous pressure on the homeless to agree to any label which will facilitate the obtaining of accommodation . . . Quite apart from labelling, parties may succumb to the temptation to agree to pretend to have particular rights and duties which are not in fact any part of the true bargain. *Prima facie* the parties must be taken to mean what they say, but given the pressures on both parties to pretend, albeit for different reasons, the courts would be acting unrealistically if they did not keep a weather eye open for pretences. This identification and exposure of such pretences does not necessarily lead to the conclusion that their agreement is a sham, but only to the conclusion that the terms of the true bargain are not wholly the same as that of the bargain appearing on the face of the agreement.

Lord Donaldson MR raises an important point which is that the court is not concerned to defeat the entire agreement where one aspect appears to reflect a sham but instead the task is to ascertain the 'true' rather than the 'apparent' bargain between the parties. It is this true bargain which determines the question of whether a lease or a licence exists. Equally, as the case of *Markou* aptly demonstrates, merely because an agreement is found by a court to constitute a sham does not mean the occupier will ultimately benefit. In *Markou*, occupiers of furnished rooms entered 'licence agreements' which contained clauses prohibiting use of the premises between the hours of 10.30 a.m. and noon every day and permitted Mr De Silvaesa to remove furniture from the flats. The court held that while these clauses may be construed as shams this did not mean that the agreement reflected a lease. In spite of the pretence, the occupiers remained licensees on the basis of an absence of exclusive possession due to the services provided by the landowner. The court reached an altogether different result in *Aslan* which concerned a very similar clause restricting use of a basement room.

KEY CASE *Aslan v Murphy* (1990)

Facts: Mr Murphy occupied a tiny room (4 feet by 12 feet) in a basement owned by Mr Aslan under a 'licence agreement'. The agreement expressly provided that Mr Murphy did not enjoy exclusive possession of the premises, that Mr Aslan retained a key to the property, and reversed the right to permit others to use the basement room. The agreement also provided for the payment by Mr Murphy of a 'licence fee' and prohibited the use of the premises between 10.30 a.m. and noon. Mr Aslan was to provide services

→

---

[15] *Aslan*, 770.

> including housekeeping, rubbish collection, and laundering of bed linens. In fact, nobody aside from Mr Murphy was permitted to occupy the basement room and no services were provided.
>
> Legal issue: Was this 'licence agreement' a sham which, in reality, gave rise to a tenancy rather than a licence?
>
> Judgment: The provisions in the agreement that there was no exclusive possession, providing for additional occupier to make use of the basement room and the provision of services and restricting Mr Murphy's access did indeed represent a pretence designed for the single purpose of defeating the application of the Rent Acts. The retention of keys by Mr Aslan did not automatically negative a finding of exclusive possession and references to a 'licence agreement' did not accurately represent the true bargain between the parties. This was a lease. Where the terms of an agreement are 'wholly unrealistic and . . . clearly pretences' the court will strike down these clauses to ascertain the true bargain between the parties.

The judgment in *Aslan* lends further support to the authority of *Street* that the labels agreed the parties are not of themselves conclusive. The court did stress, however, that 'prima facie parties must be taken to mean what they say'. It would therefore be wrong to disregard labels too quickly out of hand. By way of a cautionary note, there is dicta in *National Car Parks Ltd v Trinity Development Co. (Banbury) Ltd* (2001) that due weight should attach to the label selected by the parties particularly where they enjoy equal bargaining power and have received professional advice prior to entering the agreement.

'Property guardians'

A property guardian is a vacant property occupier—that is, someone who enters an agreement usually with a property management firm to occupy empty premises at a rent below the market value, sharing the land often with several other individuals. The idea of property guardianship, which is becoming increasingly popular (especially in expensive rental areas), is that by having people in these properties (which may be left empty awaiting development or resale) offers a degree of security for the landowner's asset but also helps prevent squatting and vandalism. The vast majority of property guardians enter this form of shared occupation under agreements either described as licence or 'occupation' agreements drafted to avoid the protections of a tenancy. The court in two cases, *Camelot Property Management Ltd v Roynon* (2017) and *Camelot Guardian Management Ltd v Khoo* (2018), made it clear that whether a property guardian occupies land as a licensee or a tenant is highly fact-specific and depends on a close reading of the terms of the agreement and on a realistic assessment of issues such as access, the provision of services, and repairing obligations. In *Roynon* (2017), Mr Roynon occupied two rooms of a vacant care home as a property guardian under what was called a 'licence agreement'. The agreement did not provide for exclusive possession and contained restrictions including that no more than two guests at one time were allowed in the rooms and no overnight visitors. Under its terms, room allocation was determined between the housing management company and the guardian. However, the reality on the ground was quite different. On arrival at the property, Mr Roynon was able to choose his own rooms and was given keys to the rooms to which no other occupier subsequently had access. The agreement did not give the management company an express right to access the property and, while it did contain a clause permitting a right of inspection at any time without notice, on the evidence, inspection had routinely taken place monthly, on the giving of 24 hours' notice and amounted to little more than a viewing of the rooms from the doorway only. There was no staff on the premises and no services such as laundry or cleaning were provided. The court found that Mr Roynon enjoyed exclusive possession and was a tenant and not a licensee. Restrictions such as maximum guests and monthly inspections with notice were entirely compatible with the finding of a lease. Interestingly, had the management firm stuck more faithfully to the terms of its agreement with Mr Roynon (especially around inspections without notice and room allocation), the court would likely have found this arrangement gave rise to a licence. In contrast in *Khoo* (2018), the High Court held that Mr Khoo, a property guardian occupying office space under a 'licence agreement' was indeed a licensee and not a tenant. Focusing on the issue of exclusive possession, the court held that Mr Khoo along with his fellow property guardians were all entitled to occupy the property 'as a whole' and he did not therefore enjoy exclusive possession of any particular room. The court rejected Mr Khoo's secondary argument that the 'licence agreement' was a sham, finding that the parties both knew the basis of the agreement entered. It was, said the court, essential to the very nature and purpose guardianship scheme that the landowner be able to regain possession at short notice—hence the licence arrangement. As a licensee, Mr Khoo could be evicted on the giving of one month's notice. The cases of *Roynon* and *Khoo* serve as another warning to landowners (and occupiers) to make sure the terms of any agreement are clear, watertight, and understood by all parties when drawn up.

Where there is exclusive possession but no lease arises

So far we have been concerned with identifying exclusive possession as the prerequisite to the finding of a lease. In this section, we adopt a different focus. Here, we consider those exceptional circumstances where despite an occupier enjoying exclusive possession, no lease exists. Lord Templeman explained this in *Street*:[16]

> [S]ometimes it may appear from the surrounding circumstances that there was no intention to create legal relationships. Sometimes it may appear from the surrounding circumstances that the right to exclusive possession is referable to a legal relationship other than a tenancy.

Lord Templeman's dicta in *Street* builds upon a lengthy discussion in *Facchini v Bryson* (1952) by Denning LJ. These two decisions taken together reveal a series of exceptional circumstances, of legal relationships in which, while exclusive possession is granted, the finding of a lease is negatived due to the absence of an intention to create legal relations. These can be summarized as follows:

- where there is a 'service occupier'—a person occupying property as a consequence of his or her employment: such as a school teacher occupying a school: *Smith v Seghill Overseers* (1875); *Norris v Checksfield* (1991)

---

[16] *Street*, 826–7.

- where there is occupation based on a family relationship or family connections: *Cobb v Lane* (1952)

- where occupation is granted on the basis of friendship: *Booker v Palmer* (1942); *Heslop v Burns* (1974) *Rhodes v Dalby* (1971)

- where occupation is granted on the basis of charity or generosity: *Gray v Taylor* (1998)

- where an individual is allowed into occupation of premises over which there exists an enforceable contract for sale: *Bretherton v Paton* (1986).

9.3.1.2 The significance of the lease/licence distinction

The presence or absence of exclusive possession remains the key determinant of whether a lease or a licence exists. Where exclusive possession is present, a lease may arise but where no exclusive possession exists, a licence only is possible. So, just how significant is the lease/licence distinction? In practice, the lease/licence distinction is only of limited, marginal importance. This is because today a private landlord can grant what is known as an 'assured shorthold tenancy' (AST) in full confidence that it carries with it no duty on the landlord to guarantee the tenant a fair rent and, vitally, the lease can be terminated without much trouble at the end of the agreed lease term. Historically, this was not the case and only leases regulated by the Rent Act 1977 gave tenants a right to a fair market rent. For this reason, the lease/licence distinction was a source of many hotly contested court proceedings. In *Street* and *Antoniades*, for example, the parties were actively fighting for lease status to gain the protection of the 1977 Act. The lease/licence distinction does, however, remain significant in modern land law in the following ways:

- By far the most important advantage of being a tenant (as we explored in section 9.2), is that a lease is *proprietary* and can therefore bind (i.e. is enforceable against) a third party, whereas a licence, which is *personal* in nature only, cannot. There is a further consequence of this: a tenant can assign (i.e. transfer) her interest in the leased land to another person if the terms of the lease allow this.

- Those occupying land as tenants do still enjoy greater statutory protection than is afforded to licensees (even if not as significant as it once was). Tenants under short residential leases have a right to enforce a repairing obligation against their landlords which is implied into leases of less than seven years under ss. 11 and 13 of the LTA 1985. Licensees enjoy no such right.[17] It is easy to overlook but, as a tenant, being able to insist on repairs is a really very important right that licensees cannot access.

- Tenants (depending on their particular nature and the circumstance) are afforded a measure of protection from eviction under housing legislation which licensees do not enjoy. In contrast, licensees can potentially be evicted at will or, in the case of a contractual licence, after a term of notice provided for in the terms of the contract.

- Tenants can bring an action for trespass (even against the landlord) and may sue in nuisance in circumstances when this course would not be open to a licensee (unless in exceptional circumstances).[18]

---

[17] Section 11 can be excluded or otherwise restricted by the express terms of the lease agreement.
[18] *Hunter v Canary Wharf* (1997).

- The lease/licence distinction remains crucial in the commercial context where business tenancies attract protection under the LTA 1954. This means that following expiry of the lease, the tenant has a right to remain occupying the premises, to request renewal of the lease on the same terms, and to compensation if the renewal is refused. This is available only to business tenants and not commercial licensees.

In these ways (albeit more limited than was historically the case) and particularly in the commercial context, the lease/licence distinction still carries real weight.

9.3.2 Second essential element: 'For a certain term'

The second essential ingredient for a valid lease as established by Lord Templeman in *Street* is certainty of term. In essence, this means that a lease must grant exclusive possession over land for a defined, limited, certain period of time. In the absence of this certainty of term, the grant of a lease will fail. This requirement has a lengthy history with Lush LJ in *Marshall v Berridge* (1881) noting that:[19]

> [T]here must be a certain beginning and a certain ending, otherwise it is not a perfect lease.

Whilst the requirement for certainty of term is therefore long-established, it is not without its detractors. The requirement recently came under sustained and cogent criticism by the Supreme Court in *Berrisford v Mexfield* (2011) and, according to Lord Neuberger, there was 'no apparent practical justification' for it. This case will be discussed in greater detail in section 9.3.2.3. Yet despite protests, the requirement for certainty of term survived the judicial assault of *Berrisford* and remains a key element of a lease, and so we must examine precisely what it involves.

9.3.2.1 What is meant by 'certainty of term'?

The rule can be simply stated. There are, in effect, two key aspects to certainty of term:

- certainty of commencement of the lease; and
- certainty of maximum duration of the lease.

This means that the lease must commence at a certain, defined time and, at commencement, it must be possible to identify precisely the maximum duration of the lease.

9.3.2.2 Certainty of commencement

This first aspect is mostly self-explanatory and straightforward. In the vast number of cases, this requirement is easily satisfied. It must be possible to say that the purported lease commences on a particular date. If no defined and certain date for commencement of the lease is provided, no valid lease will exist. In *Harvey v Pratt* (1965) a purported lease failed for want of certainty of term where there was a clearly written agreement between the parties for the lease of a garage but no detail as to when the lease was to begin. The

---

[19] *Marshall v Berridge*, 245.

requirement is perhaps a little more flexible than it may first appear. So, a lease which purports to commence on the happening of an apparently uncertain event will not be invalidated for uncertainty of term *if*, at the time the lease is sought to enforced, that event has in fact taken place. Consider *Swift v Macbean* (1942) where an agreement for the grant of a lease in 1939 stated to run from the occurrence of hostilities between Britain and Germany was found to be valid as hostilities (an uncertain event) had indeed erupted and the lessees had taken possession of the property.[20]

9.3.2.3 Certainty of maximum duration

This second aspect of the certainty of term requirement has proved more controversial than the first. In considering the development of this second facet of the certainty requirement, four phases can be identified:

- the traditional common law approach: *Say v Smith* (1563)
- the orthodoxy reimagined: *Ashburn Anstalt v Arnold* (1989)
- tradition reinstated: *Prudential Assurance Co. Ltd v London Residuary Body* (1992)
- orthodoxy challenged but affirmed: *Berrisford.*

The traditional common law approach: Say v Smith

As early as 1563 in *Say v Smith,* the common law recognized that for a lease to arise, there was a need for certainty of duration. In *Say,* a perpetual series of ten-year leases failed for an absence of certainty of duration. Regarded as establishing the traditional approach to certainty, the court noted that:[21]

> [E]very contract sufficient to make a lease for years ought to have certainty in three limitations, viz. in the commencement of the term, in the continuance of it and in the end of it: so that all ought to be known at the commencement of the lease, and words in a lease which don't make this appear are but babble . . . And these three are in effect but one matter, shewing the certainty of the time for which the lessee shall have a land, and if any of these fail, it is not a good lease for then there wants certainty.

The essential proposition of the traditional approach was that for a lease to be valid it must be possible to define both its commencement date and its maximum duration. Put differently, it must be possible to define the start date and the time at which the lease will come to an end. As to duration, in most instances, the parties to a lease will set out clearly at the outset when a lease is to terminate, for example, after 12 months, 3 years, or 99 years. The requirement will therefore be readily met. The requirement for certainty of maximum duration guarantees that leases do not endure indefinitely, which would plainly be inconsistent with the fee simple estate out of which the leasehold is carved.

More difficult is where the length of a lease is demarcated by the occurrence of an event rather than by reference to a time-period. One example is *Lace v Chantler.*

---

[20] For a further example see *Brilliant v Michaels* (1945).   [21] *Say v Smith,* 415.

> **KEY CASE** *Lace v Chantler* (1944)
>
> Facts: A tenant of a house granted a sublease over the property to the defendant purportedly 'for the duration of the war' by which was meant the lease was to last for the length of the Second World War.
>
> Legal issue: Was 'the duration of the war' sufficiently certain as to the maximum duration of the lease for an effective lease to have been granted?
>
> Judgment: The Court of Appeal held that the requirement for certainty of duration was not satisfied. Lord Greene MR noted that:
>
> > A term created by a leasehold tenancy agreement must be expressed either with certainty and specifically or by reference to something which can, at the time when the lease takes effect, be looked to as a certain ascertainment of what the term is meant to be. In the present case, when this tenancy agreement took effect, the term was completely uncertain. It was impossible to say how long the tenancy would last.

The Court of Appeal in *Lace* refused to follow the earlier authority of *Great Northern Railway Co. v Arnold* (1916) in which a lease purportedly for the duration of the First World War was interpreted as a lease for 999 years terminable at the end of the war and therefore valid. *Arnold* demonstrated how shrewd drafting of leasehold agreements can escape the apparent harshness of the certainty rule. The effect of the *Lace* decision was catastrophic for many wartime leases which were, consequently, rendered void. In response, Parliament legislated in the form of the War-Time Leases Act 1944 to remedy this unfairness, allowing war-time leases to be regarded as sufficiently certain during a period of upheaval for the country.

The orthodoxy reimagined: Ashburn

In *Ashburn*, a decision we have already encountered in relation to the law of licences, the Court of Appeal attempted to reimagine the traditional approach to certainty of maximum duration. As you will recall, in *Ashburn*, Mr Arnold occupied commercial premises with a view to running a retail outlet. The premises were part of a larger commercial complex which was to be redeveloped by the landowner. Arnold was allowed to remain in occupation rent-free unless and until three months' notice was given. Crucially for present purposes, no maximum duration was specified and, at least theoretically, Mr Arnold's occupation could have continued indefinitely. Fox LJ found the agreement to be a lease and, on the question of certainty of duration, distinguished *Lace* and the traditional approach by asserting that the question was not whether maximum duration was fixed but whether the lease would be terminated upon a sufficiently certain event. Fox LJ, applying this reinterpretation of the certainty rule, held that the giving of three months' notice amounted to a sufficiently certain event. As Fox LJ explained:[22]

> [T]he arrangement could be brought to an end by both parties in circumstances which are free from uncertainty in the sense that there would be no doubt whether the determining event had occurred.

---

[22] *Ashburn*, 12.

The approach in *Ashburn* represented a significant and radical liberalization of and departure from the traditional *Say* and *Lace* certainty rule and one which, ultimately, would not survive a close examination by the House of Lords.

Tradition reinstated: Prudential Assurance

In one of the leading decisions in the law of leases, the House of Lords in *Prudential Assurance* decisively rejected the reinterpretation of the certainty of duration test advanced by Fox LJ in *Ashburn* and restored to prominence the traditional approach.

KEY CASE *Prudential Assurance Co. Ltd v London Residuary Body* (1992)

Facts: In 1930, under a sale and lease-back arrangement, London County Council leased a strip of land fronting a highway to Mr Nathan for a rent of £30 per annum. As part of the agreement, the lease was to 'continue until . . . the land is required by the Council' for the purposes of highway widening. There was evidence that the agreement between the parties was only ever intended to be short-term in nature. Mr Nathan constructed a temporary single-storey building on the strip of land. In the event, the highway widening programme did not materialize and Mr Nathan continued to occupy the land for over 60 years. Prudential Assurance and London Residuary Body were the successors of Mr Nathan and London County Council respectively. London Residuary Body had no powers to widen the highway and, moreover, the market rent for the land had soared to around £10,000 per annum despite Prudential paying the agreed £30 annual rent under the original agreement.

Legal issue: Had the original agreement, in fact, created a valid lease and was the requirement for certainty of maximum duration satisfied?

Judgment: The House of Lords held that no valid expressly-granted lease existed on the facts as there was no certainty of maximum duration. *Ashburn* had been wrongly decided in rendering it 'unnecessary for a lease to be of a certain duration'. It was a strict requirement that all leases were of certain duration. The purported lease, being for an uncertain period, was therefore void. The court was, however, prepared to *imply* a yearly lease on the facts given that Prudential was in possession of the land and had continued to pay the yearly rent as per the original agreement. This entitled the landowners to serve a notice to quit on Prudential and bring the tenancy to an end.

Addressing directly Fox LJ's reinterpretation of the certainty requirement in *Ashburn*, Lord Templeman noted that 'a term must either be certain or uncertain. It cannot be partly certain because the tenant can determine it at any time and partly uncertain because the landlord cannot determine it for an uncertain period.'

In an important judgment, Lord Browne-Wilkinson (who agreed with Lord Templeman on the result but 'with no satisfaction') offered his own scathing critique of the certainty of term requirement. Lord Browne-Wilkinson noted that the 'bizarre outcome' ran contrary to the intentions of the parties and argued that:

> no one has produced any satisfactory rationale for the genesis of that [certainty] rule. No one has been able to point to any useful purpose that it serves at the present day . . . but for this house to depart from a rule relating to land law which has been established for many centuries might upset long established titles.

In the *Prudential Assurance* case, the orthodoxy of the certainty of duration require-ment was therefore reinstated though with the House of Lords expressing some degree of reluctance in doing so. It seemed that the matter was settled that, to be valid, a lease must be of certain maximum duration ascertainable from the outset and that any fur-ther reconsideration would be at the hands of the Law Commission only. Yet in 2011, the certainty requirement once again fell to be examined by the country's highest court, the Supreme Court.

Orthodoxy challenged but affirmed: Berrisford

In *Berrisford*, the Supreme Court engaged in a sustained assault upon the certainty require-ment though, ultimately, confirmed its continued application.

KEY CASE *Berrisford v Mexfield* (2011)

Facts: Ms Berrisford owned and occupied a house. She encountered financial difficulties and entered an 'occupancy agreement' with Mexfield under which the Housing Co-Operative would buy her property and lease it back to her at a rent. The agreement contained terms such that, provided Ms Berrisford continued to meet rental payments, Mexfield would only have limited rights to seek pos-session of the premises. Despite no breach of the terms of the agreement by Ms Berrisford, Mexfield sought possession arguing that the 'occupancy agreement' constituted an implied periodic monthly tenancy and Ms Berrisford was only entitled to minimal statutory protections from eviction including four weeks' notice to quit the tenancy.

Legal issue: Was the 'occupancy agreement' a valid lease in law? If so, what was the nature of that lease and was Mexfield entitled to serve just four weeks' notice to evict Ms Berrisford from the premises?

Judgment: The Supreme Court held that the 'occupancy agreement' gave Ms Berrisford a right to exclusive possession but for an uncertain term, determinable on limited grounds. It was a long-established principle that there could be no lease where there was an uncertain term. The principles laid down in *Lace* and *Prudential Assurance* were good law and should be followed. Nevertheless, the court expressed its frustration at the *Prudential Assurance* authority, holding that its practical effects were unsatisfactory and, in certain aspects, without justification. Lady Hale argued that the '[certainty] rules have an Alice in Wonderland quality which makes it un-surprising that distinguished judges have sometimes had difficulty with them'. Lord Neuberger argued that:

> the law is not in a satisfactory state. There is no apparent practical justification for holding that an agreement for a term of uncertain duration cannot give rise to a tenancy, or that a fetter of uncertain duration on the right to serve a notice to quit is invalid. There is therefore much to be said for changing the law, and overruling what may be called the certainty requirement, which was affirmed in the *Prudential* case, on the ground that, in so far as it had any practical justifica-tion, that justification has long since gone, and, in so far as it is based on principle, the principle is not fundamental enough for the Supreme Court to be bound by it.

Whilst, for Lord Neuberger, there was much to merit changing the law, the court refused to jettison a rule which had been regarded as fundamental for 'many centuries', received support from the 1925 legislation, may have a detrimental effect on established titles, and had been confirmed by the House of Lords in *Prudential Assurance* some 20 years earlier.

→

→

Crucially, the Supreme Court found a means by which Ms Berrisford could, despite the uncertain term, remain in the property and free from the threat of eviction. The court held that the purpose of entering into the arrangement had been to provide Ms Berrisford with a home and that her right of occupation was not intended to be precarious in nature. This was construed by the court as a right in Ms Berrisford's favour to occupy the premises for her life, determinable only on the limited grounds set out in the agreement. This analysis was founded on ancient common law principles. These principles created a tenancy for life which, under s. 149(6) of the LPA 1925, was automatically converted into a lease for 90 years determinable on Ms Berrisford's death or according to the terms expressly agreed between the parties. In short, Ms Berrisford could not be evicted by Mexfield.

Lord Neuberger also noted another avenue of argument open to Ms Berrisford; namely that the 'occupancy agreement' be construed as a contractual licence determinable according to the terms of the contract.

The Supreme Court in *Berrisford* therefore heavily criticized yet affirmed the traditional approach to certainty of term as applied in *Lace* and in the *Prudential Assurance* case. Yet, the court achieved a just result vis-à-vis Ms Berrisford in spite of the 'unsatisfactory' practical effects of the traditional certainty approach by reaching for ancient common law principles and the provisions of the 1925 Act. In assessing the potential scope of these tactics employed by the Supreme Court for future decisions, it is important to note that s. 149 of the 1925 Act can only apply to leases granted to individuals and could not have been argued in the *Prudential Assurance* case or other scenarios involving a purported lease to a company. The reasoning of the court in *Berrisford* can be explained as follows:

- The agreement between the parties granted Ms Berrisford exclusive possession for an uncertain term.
- An ancient common law principle converted Ms Berrisford's right into exclusive possession for her life, determinable on the terms of the agreement.
- Section 149(6) of the LPA 1925 automatically converted Ms Berrisford's right into a lease for 90 years, determinable on her death and/or on the terms of the agreement.
- Ms Berrisford could not be evicted by Mexfield upon the giving of four weeks' notice.

What, then, does *Berrisford* signal for the future of the certainty rule?

In confirming the continued application of the traditional, orthodox approach to the requirement for certainty of maximum duration, the Supreme Court has strongly rejected the *Ashburn* reinterpretation. To this extent, the decision provides a degree of welcome clarity and assists lawyers in advising their clients in the drafting of leasehold agreements. However, confirmation of the orthodox approach does little to silence its opponents; nor does it sweep aside the reasoned critique of the unsatisfactory and 'impractical' certainty rules. Strong grounds remain for arguing in favour of a wholesale reappraisal of the certainty rule. As Bridge has argued, provided the parties to a lease know where they stand, what purpose does the certainty rule actually serve?[23] Bridge argues that:

[23] S. Bridge, 'Periodic Tenancies and the Problem of Certainty of Term' [2010] Conv 492, 497.

If the parties . . . know where they stand, in the sense that the contract between them is suffi-ciently certain, then that should be enough. If a landlord, in [the *Berrisford*] case, a fully mutual housing association, decides that its tenants should be entitled to remain in possession unless and until they fall into arrears with their rent or break other provisions contained in the tenancy agreement, it is difficult to see what policy objectives are being furthered in denying the tenant the rights that the agreement seeks to create.

Berrisford is a timely reminder of the flexibility of legal analysis. Essentially, the reasoning of the Supreme Court reflected a legal 'workaround' to circumvent the harshness of the certainty rule. In the same vein, Lord Templeman in *Prudential Assurance*, commented that it had long been straightforward for parties with competent legal advisers to avoid the strictness of the certain term requirement through shrewd legal drafting. So, for example, while the grant of a lease 'until the highway is required to be widened' fails for uncertainty; in contrast, a lease 'for 999 years or until the highway is required to be widened' will be valid.

Berrisford also begs a further question: given the highest court in the country was unable to locate a convincing and meaningful doctrinal rationale for the certainty of term require-ment, should the rule not have been abolished altogether? Whilst this may come down to a technical argument in that neither party actively sought abolition in legal argument before the Supreme Court, it is rather unsettling when both the House of Lords in *Prudential As-surance* and the Supreme Court in *Berrisford* engage in loud and hefty criticism of the rule and yet confirm its survival.

Berrisford was revisited in *Southward Housing Co-Operative Ltd v Walker* (2016). In *Southward*, tenants of a mutual housing association had what were described as 'weekly tenancies'. Clause 7(3) of the agreements provided that the association would serve no-tice to quit before commencing possession proceedings. The tenants fell into significant arrears; the landlord served notice to quit and began possession proceedings. The ten-ants argued (1) relying on *Berrisford*, that the tenancy was for an uncertain term and under s. 149(6) of the LPA 1925 was to be treated as a 90-year tenancy; or (2) hous-ing legislation should be read compatibly with Arts. 8 and 14 of the ECHR to provide the tenants with security of tenure preventing eviction. The High Court rejected both arguments and upheld the validity of the association's notices to quit. The court held that the tenancies granted by Southward were neither periodic nor fixed term tenan-cies and, theoretically, could have been construed as tenancies for life converted into 90-year leases. However, the court focused on the parties' *intentions* and found that there was no intention to create tenancies for life unlike in *Berrisford*. The *Berrisford* s. 149(6) argument did not therefore apply. Instead, the claimants occupied the properties not as tenants at all but under contractual licences which could lawfully be terminated by the landlord on giving notice to quit. The human rights' arguments failed as to treat the agreements as granting secure tenancies was to 'trespass impermissibly into matters re-served to Parliament'. The landlord was equally not a public authority within s. 6 of the Human Rights Act 1998.

Southward therefore distinguishes *Berrisford* on the facts but does nothing to cast doubt on *Berrisford* itself. Instead, it clarifies *Berrisford* in so far as it tells us that parties' inten-tions sit front-and-centre in any analysis where an argument of tenancy for life converted into a 90-year lease is raised. A *Berrisford* argument of a lifetime tenancy was advanced in *Gilpin v Legg* (2017) in relation to occupiers of a number of beach huts at Portland Bill in Dorset but rejected by the court on the basis that the evidence indicated that the agreements were intended to run year-to-year and not for the occupiers' lifetimes. HHJ Matthews went on (obiter) to express 'respectful doubt' at the reasoning of the court in *Berrisford* even if the result was justified (albeit on a contractual analysis) arguing that authority suggested that s. 149(6) should not be taken as converting a periodic term of years not determinable by one side into a lease for life. The debate continues.

9.3.2.4 Statutory provisions that 'cure' uncertain terms

Where there appears to be an uncertain term, there are a series of statutory provisions that have the effect of curing this uncertainty:

1. As we encountered in *Berrisford*, under s. 149(6) of the LPA 1925, a lease granted for the period of a person's life takes effect as a valid 90-year lease determinable on the death of that person or under the terms of the agreement.[24]

2. Again under s. 149(6) of the LPA 1925, a lease granted to a person until marriage also takes effect as a 90-year lease determinable upon the occurrence of the marriage.

3. Under s. 145 and Sch. 15, para. 1 of the LPA 1925, a lease which is perpetually renewable takes effect as a lease for 2,000 years determinable only by the lessee.[25] Clearly a lease granted for a term of 2,000 years is, for all intents and purposes, akin to the grant of the freehold in land.

9.3.3 Third essential element: 'At a rent'?

We have now explored the first two of the three essential elements of a valid lease as provided by Lord Templeman in *Street*: (1) exclusive possession, (2) for a certain term. The third and final characteristic of a valid lease to be considered is the payment of rent. The key question here is really how far rent is an *essential* (i.e. necessary) requirement for a valid lease to exist?

A key motivation for a landowner to lease her property is the realization of profits and to generate an income. Rent is the consideration paid by the tenant in return for the lease and the rights that it confers. Rent usually takes the form of a financial payment but might also consist of the provision of benefits or services in kind in the landowner's favour. *Bostock v Bryant* (1990) confirms that in order to be regarded as rent, any financial sum must be of certain definition. Here the payment of shifting utility bills was not, therefore, to be regarded as rent. Equally, rent may be tokenistic and minimally remunerative, - sometimes termed a 'peppercorn rent'. One notorious example is Temple Island in the River Thames in Oxfordshire which is leased to the Henley Regatta on the delivery of an egg each year. Similarly, there is nothing to prevent the yearly supply of a crate of champagne or bags of sugar as constituting rent.

---

[24] Section 149(6) only applies where the lease was granted 'at a rent or in consideration of a fine'.

[25] See *Re Greenwood's Agreement* (1950); *Re Hopkins Lease* (1972).

9.3.3.1 Is the payment of rent a strict requirement of a lease?

In Lord Templeman's classic definition of the lease in *Street*, rent is included and repeatedly referenced suggesting that the payment of rent is indeed an essential characteristic of a lease. However, on closer examination, we discover that rent is not strictly necessary for the creation of a valid lease. First, under s. 205(1)(xxvii) of the LPA 1925 the 'term of years' is said to include 'a term of years . . . whether or not at a rent'. In addition, the Court of Appeal in *Ashburn*[26] confirmed that a valid lease can arise where there is the grant of exclusive possession for a certain term in the absence of any provision for the payment of a rent. As Fox LJ noted:[27]

> [W]e are unable to read Lord Templeman's speech [in *Street*] . . . as laying down a principle of 'no rent, no lease'.

This aspect of the *Ashburn* decision remains good law and has been subsequently confirmed in *Prudential Assurance* and other cases.[28] Where does this leave Templeman's classic statement in *Street*? You will recall that the facts of *Street* concerned the applicability of the statutory protections provided to tenants under the Rent Acts. As part of the statutory regime, only leases for which a rent is paid benefit from the legislative safeguards. In light of this, it is perhaps unsurprising that weight was therefore attached to the requirement of a rent in that case.

Our discussion here does not mean, however, that the payment of rent or lack thereof is irrelevant. While not a strict prerequisite for the finding of a valid lease, the presence or absence of a rent is nevertheless useful as an analytical tool: see Figure 9.1.

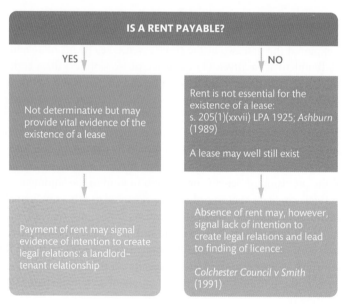

Figure 9.1 The evidential value of the payment or non-payment of rent

---

[26] Not overturned on this point.   [27] *Ashburn*, 9.

[28] See *Birrell v Carey* (1989); *Canadian Imperial Bank of Commerce v Bello* (1992).

More specifically, the payment of a rent (which, in practice, will arise in the vast majority of cases) may provide evidence of an intention to create legal relations. As seen in *Street*, the court is prepared to look beyond labels such as 'occupation fee' or 'licence fee' to identify the payment of a rent. Equally, the absence of an express or implied term as to the payment of rent may be vital evidence of a lack of intention to create a landlord–tenant relationship.

9.4 Types of leases

Having explored the nature and characteristics of a lease, we turn now to consider the different 'types' of leases that exist. It is important from the outset that you appreciate the differences between these varieties of lease before we move, in the next section, to examine how leases are created at law and in equity. For our purposes, there are six types of leases to explore:

- fixed term leases
- periodic tenancies
- tenancies at will
- tenancies at sufferance
- tenancies by estoppel
- the '*Bruton* tenancy'.

9.4.1 Fixed term leases

A fixed term lease is precisely as the name suggests: a lease which runs for a fixed period of time, that period having been made clear in the terms of the lease. This might be for one month, one year, or 99 years. Evidently, the longer the fixed term, the more the lease takes the appearance of the grant of the freehold estate. Fixed term leases are regularly for very long fixed terms under which an initial lump sum or 'premium' is paid followed by a nominal rent. In contrast to periodic tenancies,[29] fixed term leases can only be created expressly.

9.4.2 Periodic tenancies

A **periodic tenancy** is a lease that continues from period to period. These periods are routinely one week, one month, or one year. An essential feature of the periodic tenancy is that as each period comes to an end, a new period begins automatically and therefore the lease continues until it is terminated. As you will discover in section 9.6, periodic tenancies are brought to an end by the giving of notice to quit the tenancy; the length of that notice period is determined by the reference period of the periodic tenancy. This can cause problems for the tenant whose tenancy can be brought to an end relatively easily on the giving of notice.

---

[29] We explore periodic tenancies in section 9.4.2.

Periodic tenancies, unlike fixed term leases, can be created expressly or by implication. When a periodic tenancy is created expressly, the terms of the lease will most likely provide for the reference period. Where no reference period is made clear, the period is taken to be the period by which the rent is calculated and not the frequency with which rent is paid. By way of example, a lease with a rent of £1,000 per week to be paid annually will create a weekly periodic tenancy and not a yearly tenancy: *EON Motors Ltd v Secretary of State for the Environment* (1981).

An implied periodic tenancy will arise where a freehold owner allows another to enjoy exclusive possession over their land, the occupier pays rent, and that rent is accepted by the freehold owner: *Javad v Mohammed Aqil*. The reference period for this implied periodic tenancy will be the period by which the rent is calculated. The leading decision here is *Javad* which clarified that an implied periodic tenancy will not be found where the wider context and factual nexus of the individual case does not support this conclusion.

KEY CASE *Javad v Mohammed Aqil* (1991)

Facts: Mr Javad and Mr Aqil were in the process of negotiating a ten-year lease over business premises and both parties believed an agreement would be reached. During the negotiations, Mr Aqil was permitted to take possession of the property and in return £2,500 was paid, expressed to be 'rent for three months in advance'. Negotiations subsequently broke down and Mr Javad sought possession of the premises. Mr Aqil refused to surrender possession of the premises on the basis that an implied periodic tenancy had arisen and, as such, he benefited from protection from eviction under relevant landlord and tenant legislation.

Legal issue: Was Mr Aqil a tenant under an implied periodic tenancy as a result of his taking possession and paying Mr Javad a rent?

Judgment: Upholding the decision of the trial judge, the Court of Appeal rejected Mr Aqil's assertion that an implied periodic tenancy had been created, instead finding that Mr Aqil was a tenant at will only. In view of this, Mr Javad was entitled to recover possession of the business premises. According to Nicholls LJ, a lease springs from the consensus reached between two parties. The extent and nature of the parties' rights is determined by reference to all the surrounding circumstances and the intentions of the parties. Although the payment of a rent accepted by the landowner may be an indicator of an implied periodic tenancy, it is but one indicator. In the instant case, the court found that the parties had not intended for there to be anything more than a tenancy at will while the negotiations proceeded. Allowing possession to a person during a period of negotiations is a classic example of a tenancy at will.

Nicholls LJ added that:

> when and so long as such parties are in the throes of negotiating larger terms, caution must be exercised before inferring or imputing to the parties an intention to give the occupant more than a very limited interest . . . otherwise the court would be in danger of inferring or imputing from conduct, such as payment of rent and the carrying out of repairs . . . an intention to grant an . . . interest, such as a periodic tenancy, which the parties never had in contemplation at all . . . Because of the widespread intervention of statute in the landlord–tenant area, a typical case [of implied periodic tenancy] invariably involves more than the simple facts of possession and an unexplained payment of rent.

We explore tenancies at will in section 9.4.3. In *Hutchison v B & DF Ltd* (2008), Peter Smith J drew a distinction between those cases, such as *Javad*, where the parties remain in the process of negotiating terms of a proposed lease and those cases where the parties have concluded negotiations for the grant of a lease but dispute remains as to specifically what terms had been agreed between them. According to Peter Smith J, no periodic tenancy arises in the former category but a periodic tenancy will be implied in the latter. The position was clarified in *Barclays Wealth Trustees v Erimus Housing* (2014), where Patten LJ noted:[30]

> When a party holds over after the end of the term of a lease he does so, without more, as a tenant on sufferance until his possession is consented to by the landlord. With such consent he becomes at the very least a tenant at will and his continued payment of the rent is not inconsistent with his remaining a tenant at will even though the rent reserved by the former lease was an annual rent. The payment of rent gives rise to no presumption of a periodic tenancy. Rather, the parties' contractual intentions fall to be determined by looking objectively at all relevant circumstances. The most obvious and most significant circumstance in the present case, as in *Javad v Aqil*, was the fact that the parties were in negotiation for the grant of a new formal lease. In these circumstances, as in any other subject to contract negotiations, the obvious and almost overwhelming inference will be that the parties did not intend to enter into any intermediate contractual arrangement inconsistent with remaining parties to ongoing negotiations. In the landlord and tenant context that will in most cases lead to the conclusion that the occupier remained a tenant at will pending the execution of the new lease. The inference is likely to be even stronger when any periodic tenancy would carry with it statutory protection . . .

9.4.3 Tenancies at will

A tenancy at will exists where a person occupies land with exclusive possession and the consent of the landowner but where either party is able to determine (i.e. terminate) the lease at any time: *Errington v Errington and Woods* (1952). Tenancies at will can be created expressly though will more commonly arise by implication during a period of negotiation as a more formalized relationship is being agreed (*Heslop*). Of course, no tenancy at will or of any kind exists where it is clear from the surrounding circumstances that there was no intention to create legal relations. Some examples of when a tenancy at will may arise should assist you here:

- where a would-be tenant is permitted to take possession of land during negotiations: *Javad*; *James v Evans* (2000), or
- where an existing lease expires or comes to an end and the tenant remains in possession of the land with the consent of the landlord: *Banjo v Brent LBC* (2005).

It is possible for a tenancy at will to metamorphose into an implied periodic tenancy but, importantly, there is no presumption to this effect and all the surrounding circumstances will be considered including a close focus on the intentions of the parties to the arrangement.

---

[30] At 93.

9.4.4 **Tenancies at sufferance**

A tenancy at sufferance exists where a tenant remains in possession of land after the expiry of a lease *without* the consent or disapproval of the landlord: *Wheeler v Mercer* (1957).
Should the landlord subsequently consents to the tenant's possession, a tenancy at will
arises. Where the landlord objects to the tenant's possession, the tenant will become a trespasser and, following the decision in *Oliver Ashworth Ltd v Ballard* (2000), can be ordered
to pay the landlord twice the rental value of the land for the period of possession after the
expiry of the pre-existing lease term.

9.4.5 **Tenancies by estoppel**

A tenancy by estoppel arises where the party purported to have granted a lease holds
neither the legal fee simple nor a superior leasehold estate from which to carve out the
purported lease. If a would-be tenant makes out the elements of an estoppel claim, the
grantor will be estopped from denying that a lease exists – this is an estoppel lease. As
between the parties to the purported lease and their successors, a tenancy by estoppel behaves entirely like a full legal tenancy: *Webb v Austin* (1844). Vitally, should the
landlord later acquire the legal fee simple or a superior leasehold estate, this acquisition will 'feed the estoppel' so that the purported lease becomes a fully effective, ordinary legal tenancy: *First National Bank plc v Thompson* (1996). According to Millett
LJ in *Thompson*, a tenancy by estoppel can only arise in circumstances where the purported landowner does not hold the freehold at the time of the purported grant. Some
dispute arose as to whether under a tenancy by estoppel it is the estoppel which gives
rise to the tenancy or vice versa. Lord Hoffmann in *Bruton v London and Quadrant
Housing Trust* (2000) appears to put the matter beyond doubt in explaining that:[31]

> It is not the estoppel which creates the tenancy, but the tenancy which creates the estoppel. The
> estoppel arises when one or other of the parties wants to deny one of the ordinary incidents or
> obligations of the tenancy on the ground that the landlord had no legal estate. The basis of the
> estoppel is that having entered into an agreement which constitutes a lease or tenancy, he cannot
> repudiate that incident or obligation.

9.4.6 **The *Bruton* tenancy**

The Latin maxim *nemo dat quod non habet* ('no one gives that which he does not have')
is traditionally taken to mean that a lease cannot be granted unless the grantor (the
party granting the lease) herself holds an estate in land from which to carve out the
lease. This orthodox position has long endured in this jurisdiction. The decision of
the House of Lords in *Bruton*, however, significantly disrupted this orthodox stance
and has given rise to a new breed of lease that is sometimes referred to as the *Bruton*
tenancy.

---

[31] *Bruton*, 416.

> **KEY CASE** *Bruton v London and Quadrant Housing Trust* (2000)
>
> **Facts:** London and Quadrant Housing Trust (LQHT) was a charitable trust that provided accommodation on a short-term basis to the homeless. LQHT offered this temporary housing in a block of flats, Oval House, in Brixton which was owned by Lambeth London Borough Council. In 1986, Lambeth had granted a licence to LQHT in order for the trust to provide this housing service to the homeless. Lambeth had no statutory power to grant a lease to LQHT. Mr Bruton occupied one of the flats. The flat had fallen into a state of disrepair. Mr Bruton claimed that the agreement with LQHT under which he occupied the flat (which was described as a 'licence') was in fact a lease rather than a licence. He did so as repair obligations under s. 11 of the LTA 1985 apply only to tenants under a lease and not to licensees.
>
> **Legal issue:** Was Mr Bruton occupying the flat as a tenant or as a licensee? Mr Bruton would only be entitled to have his flat repaired by LQHT if he was a tenant. LQHT argued strongly that, given they did not hold a legal estate in the property and as they were only licensees of the property themselves, they had no freehold or superior leasehold from which to grant Mr Bruton a tenancy.
>
> **Judgment:** The House of Lords reversed the decision of the Court of Appeal which had found Mr Bruton to be a licensee. Lord Hoffmann, delivering the leading judgment, held that the agreement between LQHT and Mr Bruton satisfied the essential characteristics of a lease (i.e. conferred exclusive possession for a certain term at a rent). Therefore, the agreement gave rise to a lease in Mr Bruton's favour even though LQHT itself had no proprietary interest in the land. As a consequence, LQHT were subject to the implied repair obligations.
>
> Per Lord Hobhouse added:
>
>> The case of Mr Bruton depends upon his establishing that his agreement with the Housing Trust has the legal effect of creating a relationship of tenant and landlord between them. That is all. It does not depend upon his establishing a proprietary title good against all the world or against the Council. It is not necessary for him to show that the Council had conveyed a legal estate to the Housing Trust.
>
> The court said it was the agreement between the Mr Bruton and LQHT which generated the lease and it was not concerned with whether or not the grantor of the lease held a legal estate. The lease arising in Mr Bruton's favour was, however, binding against LQHT only and not, said the court, against the freehold owner of the land, Lambeth London Borough Council.

9.4.6.1 *Bruton*: Making sense of the decision

Bruton has been described as one of most important decisions in modern land law since the turn of the century[32] and has been subject to significant discussion and, it must be said, criticism too.[33] How are we to make sense of a case in which a lease springs from a grantor who holds no legal estate? How can a lease be created where there is no 'proprietary base'?

---

[32] A. Baker, '*Bruton*, Licences in Possession and a Fiction of Title' [2014] Conv 495.

[33] As if to make the point see amongst others: D. Rook, 'Whether a Licence Agreement Is a Lease: The Irrelevance of the Grantor's Lack of Title' [1999] Conv 517; S. Bright, 'Leases, Exclusive Possession and Estates' (2000) 116 LQR 7; M. Dixon, 'The Non-Proprietary Lease: The Rise of the Feudal Phoenix' (2000) 59 CLJ 25; P. Routley, 'Tenancies and Estoppels: After *Bruton v London & Quadrant Housing Trust*' (2000) 63 MLR 424; M. Pawlowski, 'Occupational Rights in Leasehold Law: Time for Rationalisation' [2002] Conv 550; J. Hinojosa, 'On Property, Leases, Licences, Horses and Carts: Revisiting *Bruton v London & Quadrant Housing Trust*' [2005] Conv 114; M. Pawlowski, 'The *Bruton* Tenancy—Clarity or More Confusion' [2005] Conv 262; M. Lower, 'The *Bruton* Tenancy' [2010] Conv 38.

It is important to be aware that the decision in *Bruton* could have wide-ranging consequences for our understanding of the nature and creation of leases, challenging our traditional understanding of the lease/licence distinction.[34] The decision might be taken to signify (as Lord Hoffmann himself noted), that a lease is not always to be regarded as a proprietary right. This is surely controversial. Put another way and, as Bright has argued,[35] the decision in *Bruton* appears to create a new category of lease, the 'non-estate' lease which sits in addition to our traditional understanding of the 'normal' proprietary lease. It is this which has led Pawlowski to describe the *Bruton* tenancy as contractual in nature, 'non-proprietary', or as an '*in personam*' lease.[36] Certainly, we know that the *Bruton* tenancy is enforceable only as between the parties to the lease and not against the freehold owner or other third parties: confirmed in *Kay v Lambeth LBC* (2006).

So, should we say that *Bruton* was wrongly decided? Generally, we should resist the urge to race to conclude too hastily that a case is wrongly decided merely because its outcome conflicts with our traditional understanding of pre-existing legal principles. That said, if we accept *Street* as underscoring that the fundamental nature of the lease is its proprietary status, we could conclude that *Bruton* is inconsistent with this authority and therefore open to challenge. An argument could be mounted that Mr Bruton enjoyed exclusive occupation of the flat but not exclusive possession as required for the creation of a lease or, perhaps, that the outcome was policy-driven so that Mr Bruton would receive the repairs to the flat that were so urgently and deservedly needed. Whilst we might feel sympathy for Mr Bruton, had his flat not required repair would the result on the determination of his relationship to LQHT been different? Should the principles of land law be distorted to achieve a results-orientated outcome?

Bruton has been applied in two further decisions of the court: *Kay v Lambeth LBC* (2006) and *Islington LBC v Green* (2005). In both cases, the *Bruton* tenancies that arose were held to be capable only of binding parties to the agreements. In other words, *Kay* and *Green* confirm the contractual, non-estate, 'non-proprietary' nature of the *Bruton* tenancy with its inability to bind the freehold owner or other third parties.

Routley has argued that the result in *Bruton* might have been reached by reference to established principles of tenancy by estoppel rather than via the concept of the non-estate, 'non-proprietary' lease.[37] Essentially, Routley argues that a fair result was reached in *Bruton* but according to the wrong principles. For Routley, the mischief which the House of Lords was attempting to avoid was that LQHT might escape their repair obligations to Mr Bruton after having granted to him exclusive possession over the flat. For Routley, in view of this, LQHT could be estopped from denying Mr Bruton had a lease on the basis of an estoppel tenancy. Whilst persuasive, Routley readily acknowledges that his reasoning is plainly not consistent with the approach taken by the House of Lords.

McFarlane and Simpson argue that the decision in *Bruton* can be rationalized as reflecting an exercise in purposive statutory interpretation. They contend that:[38]

---

[34] For the argument that *Bruton*, in fact, clarifies the lease/licence distinction, see Hinojosa, 'On Property, Leases, Licences, Horses and Carts: Revisiting *Bruton v London & Quadrant Housing Trust*'.

[35] Bright, 'Leases, Exclusive Possession and Estates'.

[36] Pawlowski, 'Occupational Rights in Leasehold Law: Time for Rationalisation'.

[37] Routley, 'Tenancies and Estoppels: After *Bruton v London & Quadrant Housing Trust*'.

[38] B. McFarlane and E. Simpson, 'Tackling Avoidance' in J. Getzler (ed.), *Rationalizing Property, Equity and Trusts: Essays for Edward Burn* (Oxford: Oxford University Press, 2002), 175.

> [I]t may be possible to justify the decision in *Bruton* by arguing that 'lease' and 'tenancy' when used in the Landlord and Tenant Act 1985, include an occupier under an agreement which fails to confer a legal right to exclusive because of the grantor's lack of title . . . the purpose of the legislation is to regulate the relationship between grantor and occupier and the lack of title of the grantor . . . should not deny the occupier the protection of the Act.

McFarlane and Simpson's 'statutory interpretation' justification for the *Bruton* tenancy is attractive for its simplicity but, as the authors themselves concede, it fails to accord with Lord Templeman's traditional, orthodox definition of a lease in *Street*. Plainly, McFarlane and Simpson's approach requires a benevolent and liberal reading of the statutory language but where is the evidence that this is what Parliament intended? Given all of this, perhaps *Bruton* is more convincingly viewed as a case very much confined to its particular facts.

9.5 The creation of leases

In the previous sections, we identified both the fundamental nature and the essential characteristics of the lease as well as the different 'types' of leases that exist. What has not been examined is how a lease is created. Principally, the matter of the creation of leases turns on the formality requirements that must be satisfied to give rise to an effective lease and on issues of registration. As you will discover, these formality requirements are prescribed by statute and are concerned less with the substantive content of leases (terms of the lease) and more with the required form that leases must take. The formality requirements act chiefly as a gateway to enforcement of the lease by the courts and exist to ensure formal legal relationships concerning land are created with certainty and clarity. The formality requirements also serve another vital role. The observance or otherwise of these formality requirements will also be determinative of whether the lease created is a *legal lease* or an *equitable lease*. As this section explores, whether a lease takes effect at law or in equity can have significant ramifications—for example, for the registration position under the LRA 2002 and for the effect on third parties.

9.5.1 The creation of legal leases

As we have noted throughout this book, the creation of legal rights almost invariably involves compliance with strict formality requirements. The creation of a legal lease is no different and depends on satisfying rules provided by statute. The particular formality requirements that must be satisfied are determined, in large part, by the duration of the lease:

1. Leases of three years or less: Here, provided the tenant is granted an immediate right to possession of the land (*Long v Tower Hamlets LBC* (1998)) without requiring payment of an initial sum (a premium) and the lease is granted 'at best rent' (taken to mean market value: *Fitzkriston LLP v Panayi* (2008)), a legal lease of three years or less can be created orally, by written contract, or by deed: ss. 52(2)(d) and 54(2) of the LPA 1925.[39] This category of 'short leases' will cover most residential leases and 'periodic tenancies' as discussed in section 9.4.2.

---

[39] Short leases of three years or less must be created by deed in order to take effect at law if the conditions of s. 54(2) are not satisfied (i.e. if a premium is paid, if there is no right to immediate possession, or the lease is not granted at best rent).

2. Leases of more than three years: In order to be legal, a lease of more than three years must be made by deed under s. 52(1) of the LPA 1925. A deed is akin to a very formal contract and, under s. 1 of the LP(MP)A 1989, a document only takes effect as a deed if: (i) it makes clear, on its face, it is intended to be a deed and (ii) it is signed and witnessed.

3. In registered land, leases of over seven years: Where a lease of more than seven years is granted out of a freehold which is a registered title, under s. 27(2) of the LRA 2002, the lease must be substantively registered as a title at Land Registry. Recall our discussion in Chapter 2 that 'substantively registered' means that the lease will be registered with its own title number and be registered in its own right. Under s. 27(1) of the LRA 2002, if the lease is not registered, it cannot take effect at law and will give rise to an equitable lease only.[40]

4. In unregistered land, leases of over seven years: Where a lease of more than seven years is granted out of a freehold which is an unregistered title, under s. 4(1) of the LRA 2002, the lease must be substantively registered as a title at Land Registry. The grant of this lease is a trigger for first registration. Under s. 7 of the LRA 2002, if the lease is not registered, it will take effect as an equitable lease only.

9.5.2 Legal leases: The effect on third parties

Having explored how legal leases are created, we turn to consider the effect of legal leases on third parties acquiring the land over which the lease exists. It is important to identify whether we are dealing with *registered* or *unregistered* land as very different rules apply in each context.

9.5.2.1 The effect of legal leases on third parties in registered land

In registered land, the effect of legal leases on third parties is determined by the provisions of the LRA 2002.

1. Legal leases of three years or less: These leases *cannot* be the subject of a notice entered on the Charges Register (s. 33(b) of the LRA 2002) but, as they are for a period of seven years or less, under Schs. 1 and 3 of the LRA 2002, they constitute overriding interests. As a result, short legal leases will bind third party purchasers of the land over which they operate under ss. 28 and 29 of the LRA 2002.

2. Legal leases of more than three years but not exceeding seven years: These leases can be voluntarily entered on the register, and their priority guaranteed, by way of entry of a notice on the Charges Register. However, even if this is not done, given that these leases are for a period of seven years or less, they will, again, constitute overriding interests under Schs. 1 and 3 of the LRA 2002. As a result, these legal leases will bind third party purchasers of the land over which they operate under ss. 28 and 29 of the LRA 2002.

---

[40] Under s. 27(2) of the LRA 2002 certain other shorter leases also require substantive registration including certain Housing Act 1985 leases and leases for which possession is postponed for more than three years from grant of the lease.

3. Legal leases of more than seven years: These leases will have been substantively registered in their own right under s. 27(2) of the LRA 2002 and will therefore bind third parties. If these leases have not been substantively registered and they take effect as equitable leases only, the rules governing equitable leases will apply (see section 9.5.3).

9.5.2.2 The effect of legal leases on third parties in unregistered land

Where a legal lease is granted over an unregistered freehold and where compulsory first registration is not triggered under the LRA 2002, the principles of unregistered conveyancing which we examined in Chapter 3 will determine the effect of the lease on third parties acquiring the land over which the lease exists. Where compulsory first registration is triggered, the registered land regime (as just outlined) will apply. Dealings in unregistered land are becoming increasingly rare in particular in the light of the breadth of the triggers for first registration which include, among other common scenarios, a transfer of a qualifying estate.

9.5.3 The creation of equitable leases

Equitable leases can arise in a number of contexts including through operation of the doctrine of proprietary estoppel. By far the most common, however, is where the parties to an agreement attempt to grant a legal lease but the necessary formality requirements (just explored in section 9.5.1) are not satisfied. Here the circumstances of this defective legal lease may nevertheless give rise to an equitable lease: *Parker v Taswell* (1858).[41] The most common scenario is where parties purport to create a legal lease of more than three years in duration but fail to make use of a deed in the granting of that lease as required under s. 52 of the LPA 1925. Provided there is a specifically enforceable contract between the parties for the grant of a lease, equity will regard this contract as constituting an equitable lease: *Walsh v Lonsdale* (1882). Equity, which historically has always looked to the substance and not the form of an agreement, is prepared to intervene to 'treat as done that which ought to be done'. Therefore, the equitable lease that arises will be on precisely the same terms as the purported but failed, defective legal lease: *Rochester Poster Services Ltd v Dartford BC* (1991). As Stamp LJ elaborated in *Warmington v Miller* (1973):[42]

> [T]he equitable interests . . . arise because the intended lessee has an equitable right to specific performance of the agreement. In such a situation that which is agree to be done ought to be done is treated as having been done and carrying with it the attendant rights.

As you can see, equity's intervention is activated by the availability of specific performance of the agreement between the parties.[43] The leading judgment on equitable leases is *Walsh*.

---

[41] In *Parker v Taswell* an agreement purporting to grant a legal lease was defective as no deed was used. Equity would, however, recognize the failed legal lease as a contract for a lease, operating from the date the contract was entered and on the same terms as the purported legal lease.

[42] *Warmington*, 887.

[43] No equitable interest arose in *Warmington* due to the unavailability of specific performance.

> ### KEY CASE *Walsh v Lonsdale* (1882)
>
> Facts: Lonsdale agreed in 1879 to grant to Walsh a seven-year lease over a cotton mill in return for the payment of a rent of 30 shillings per annum for each loom that Walsh ran. The agreement contained a clause permitting the rent to be payable one year in advance on request by Lonsdale. No deed was executed as required to create a legal lease of this duration. Walsh took possession of the mill and ran 560 looms. Lonsdale demanded that Walsh pay a year's rent in advance in accordance with the clause in their agreement. Lonsdale was not paid and Walsh fell into arrears. Lonsdale entered the property and seized goods to recover the sums due under the remedy of 'distress'.
>
> Legal issue: In the absence of a deed, what was the nature of the relationship between the parties? Did the agreement give rise to an implied periodic tenancy and, therefore, with rent payable in arrears, had Lonsdale lawfully exercised the remedy of 'distress'?
>
> Judgment: The Court of Appeal, per Lord Jessel MR, held that an equitable lease arose on the facts on the same terms as the agreement reached between the parties. The effect was that Londsdale was rightfully entitled to request rent be paid one year in advance. Lonsdale's exercise of the remedy of distress was, therefore, also lawful and Walsh's claim for damages for unlawful distress was rejected. Lord Jessel MR identified a key feature in the operation of equity here, namely that:
>
>> it being a case in which both parties admit that relief is capable of being given by specific performance. That being so, he cannot complain of the exercise by the landlord of the same rights as the landlord would have had if a lease had been granted.
>
> Lord Jessel MR underscored the primacy of the equitable lease. According to the court, following the Judicature Acts which provided that, in cases of conflict, equity prevails over the common law, the parties enjoyed an equitable lease rather than a legal periodic tenancy as Walsh had sought to argue: 'there is only one Court and the equity rules prevail in it. The tenant holds under an agreement for a lease'.

Following *Walsh*, *Warmington*, and more recent decisions of the court including *Rochester Poster Services Ltd*,[44] two conditions must be met before an equitable lease will arise:

- Condition 1: there is a valid contract for the grant of a lease complying with s. 2 of the LP(MP)A 1989; and
- Condition 2: the remedy of specific performance is available.

Where *both* conditions are met, an equitable lease arises on the same terms as the purported but defective legal lease: *Walsh*.

9.5.3.1 Condition 1: A valid contract for a lease exists

An equitable lease can only arise where there is a valid contract for the grant of a lease. From 27 September 1989,[45] this means that the provisions of the LP(MP)A 1989 must be satisfied. Under s. 2 of the 1989 Act, the contract granting a lease must:

---

[44] A case concerning the purported grant of a 12-year lease without a formally executed deed where an equitable lease arose entitled Rochester Poster Services Ltd to compensation when the land in question was compulsorily purchased.

[45] Before 1989 s. 40 of the LPA 1925 permitted the enforcement of oral contracts so long as the doctrine of part performance was operative: see *Mason v Clarke* (1955).

1. be made in writing; and

2. incorporate all the terms expressly agreed by the parties; and

3. be signed by both parties.

Provided s. 2 of the 1989 Act is satisfied, it does not matter that the document appears somewhat informal, does not refer to itself as a 'contract', or does not have the appearance of a traditional contract.

9.5.3.2 Condition 2: The remedy of specific performance is available

In addition to a valid contract, the remedy of specific performance must also be available if an equitable lease is to arise. Specific performance is an equitable remedy by which parties are compelled to perform a contract and is available only at the discretion of the court and not as of right.[46] Specific performance is only available where:

1. valuable consideration has been given for the contract; and

2. the award of damages would be an inadequate remedy; and

3. the parties have not behaved unconscionably or otherwise inequitably.

As we have already seen, where both essential conditions are satisfied, the court will regard the contract for the grant of a lease as giving rise to an equitable lease on the same terms as the defective legal lease. It is quite possible that on the same set of facts, a finding of an equitable lease or, alternatively, an implied periodic tenancy could be made. Recall that, where either construction is possible, it is the equitable lease that will prevail: *Walsh*. Finally, whilst many equitable leases come into existence according to the *Walsh* principles discussed in this section, equitable leases can arise in different ways. It is possible, for example, for an equitable lease to arise expressly or via the operation of the doctrine of proprietary estoppel where the court establishes an equity and 'satisfies' that equity by the award of an equitable lease.[47]

9.5.4 Equitable leases: The effect on third parties

Just as with legal leases, in considering the effect of equitable leases on third parties, we again draw a distinction between the principles applicable in *registered* and *unregistered land*.

9.5.4.1 The effect of equitable leases on third parties in registered land

As to the status of equitable interests in registered land, two points should be noted:

1. It is possible to enter a notice on the Charges Register against the land over which the lease is granted. We might call this a first route of protection. If a notice is entered, it is likely to be an Agreed Notice given the written agreement that will necessarily exist between the parties (in a *Walsh* scenario). Under ss. 28 and 29 of the LRA 2002, an equitable lease protected by way of a notice will bind third party purchasers of the land.

---

[46] Specific performance may be unavailable where there has been an apparent breach of any covenant in the agreement (*Coatsworth v Johnson* (1886)) or an order for specific performance would lead either party into breach of another contract with a third party: *Warmington v Miller* (1973).

[47] Revisit Chapter 8 on proprietary estoppel and the pertinent principles here.

2. Secondly and notwithstanding the entry of a notice, in many cases, an equitable lease will bind third parties as an overriding interest under Sch. 3, para. 2 of the LRA 2002. We might call this a second route of protection. Under para. 2, the equitable tenant may be in actual occupation of the land over which the lease operates. This second route of protection is significant, will be available to most equitable tenants, and requires the equitable tenant to do little more than be physically present on the land. This removes much of the urgency to enter a notice (under the first route of protection) to guarantee enforceability against third parties. The requirements of Sch. 3, para. 2 on actual occupation must, of course, be satisfied.[48]

9.5.4.2 The effect of equitable leases on third parties in unregistered land

In unregistered land, equitable leases which arise as a result of an enforceable contract are registrable as Class C(iv) land charges as estate contracts under the LCA 1972. This registration will be against the name of the landowner and if registered will bind third parties. In contrast to the position in registered land, no protection is conferred by means of occupation alone. Where the lease is not registered under the LCA 1972, it will be void as against a purchaser.[49] Where the third party is not a purchaser, however, for example, the recipient of a gift, the equitable lease will be binding despite non-registration.

9.5.5 Legal and equitable leases compared

Having now explored both the nature and creation of legal and equitable leases, it is worth gathering together the key differences between the two. Table 9.2 sets out the key distinctions between legal and equitable leases.

Table 9.2 Distinguishing legal and equitable leases

LEGAL LEASES	EQUITABLE LEASES
Leases must generally satisfy strict formality requirements in order to be effective at law with the exception of short or implied tenancies.	Leases arise more informally in equity: under *Walsh v Lonsdale* (1882) or via proprietary estoppel.
Certain, longer, legal leases require substantive registration to be effective at law.	Many equitable leases depend on the availability of the remedy of specific performance of an enforceable contract.
Legal leases are considered to be less vulnerable upon sale of freehold or leasehold land and therefore more desirable.	Equitable leases are considered more vulnerable upon sale of freehold or leasehold land and therefore less desirable.
In registered land, shorter legal leases of 7 years or less are overriding interests.	In registered land, equitable leases require entry of a notice to be protected unless the tenant is in actual occupation.
Section 62 of the LPA 1925—which can operate so as to create easements upon a conveyance by deed of a legal estate (freehold or leasehold)—applies to legal leases.	Section 62 of the LPA 1925 does not apply to equitable leases and cannot be relied upon by equitable lessees to create easements upon a conveyance.

---

[48] On which section 2.7.   [49] Under ss. 2 and 4 of the LCA 1972.

9.6 The termination of leases

As Figure 9.2 demonstrates, a lease can be brought to an end in a number of different ways. When a lease does come to an end, the tenant no longer enjoys any estate in the land and the freehold owner is entitled to immediate possession of the land. Should the tenant remain on the land, he may be committing a trespass and the freeholder can seek a court order for the now ex-tenant's removal.[50] Each method of termination will now be examined.

9.6.1 Expiry of contractual term

By far the simplest method of termination of a lease involves expiry of a contractual term in a fixed lease. So, imagine a tenant is granted a three-year lease; that lease will automatically terminate at the end of that specified three-year period. There are, however, a few caveats to this position. First, many residential leases, on expiry of the specified term, are converted by statute into periodic tenancies.[51] Secondly, for commercial tenancies, under s. 26 of the LTA 1954 (where the statute has not been expressly excluded), a business tenant has a right to request a renewal of their commercial tenancy. Note that this request for renewal can be refused by the landlord in certain, defined circumstances.[52]

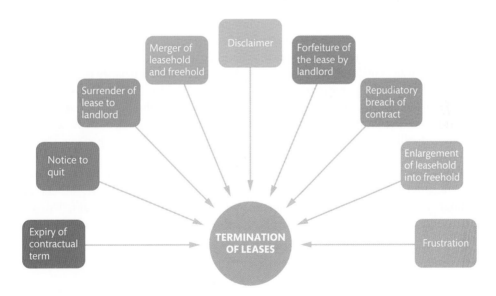

Figure 9.2 Methods of termination of leases

---

[50] As to the requirement for a court order, see s. 3 of the Protection from Eviction Act 1977.
[51] For example, under the Rent Act 1977 and Housing Acts 1985 and 1988.
[52] On which see ss. 25, 26, and 30 of the LTA 1954.

9.6.2 **Notice to quit**

A lease may provide either party in the landlord–tenant relationship with the right to terminate the lease before the end of a fixed contractual period by the giving of notice. When considering how the giving of notice operates, it is useful to draw a distinction between fixed leases, periodic tenancies, and tenancies at will.

9.6.2.1 Notice and fixed term leases

In a fixed term lease, the giving of notice to terminate a lease is only possible if the agreement expressly contains a clause permitting this. That said, these clauses (often referred to as 'break clauses') are relatively commonplace, particularly in long leases.[53] Vitally, however, where the lease is held by joint tenants and the agreement expressly provides for a 'break clause', all joint tenants must agree to the giving of notice and thereby activate the break clause if it is to be effective in terminating the lease.[54] Subject to the particular terms of the lease, notice need not take any particular form provided, of course, the intention and purpose of the notice is clear. As Lord Hoffmann explained in *Mannai Investment Co. Ltd v Eagle Star Life Assurance Co. Ltd* (1997), a notice will suffice provided it is 'quite clear to a reasonable tenant [or landlord] reading it' and that he would not be misled by it.[55]

9.6.2.2 Notice and periodic tenancies

The giving of notice is the essence of a periodic tenancy which, by its nature, operates from period to period until terminated (sometimes called 'determination') by notice.[56] Subject to any express term in the tenancy agreement, a periodic tenancy is terminated by the giving of notice equivalent in duration to one period. A monthly periodic tenancy is, for example, determinable upon the giving of one month's notice. A key exception to this position is the yearly periodic tenancy which is terminable by giving six months' notice (*Prudential Assurance*). Additionally, Parliament has legislated to offer a minimum floor of protection to tenants of dwelling-houses for which a period of at least four weeks' notice to quit must be provided.[57]

Where there is a joint periodic tenancy (i.e. a periodic tenancy held by two or more joint tenants) notice to quit need only be given by one joint tenant regardless and without consideration of the intentions or wishes of any other joint tenant. This was discussed at length in the Court of Appeal case of *Hammersmith and Fulham LBC v Monk.*

---

[53] See *Industrial Properties Ltd v Associated Electrical Industries Ltd* (1977).
[54] See *Crawley v Ure* (1996) and *Hounslow LBC v Pilling* (1993).
[55] In *Mannai*, a notice was held to be effective even though an incorrect date had been included in the notice.
[56] As explained in *Javad* and *Prudential Assurance*.
[57] Section 5(1)(b) of the Protection from Eviction Act 1977.

KEY CASE *Hammersmith and Fulham LBC v Monk* (1992)

Facts: Mr and Mrs Monk were joint tenants of a council flat determinable upon the giving of four weeks' notice to quit. Mr and Mrs Monk quarrelled and Mrs Monk moved out of the accommodation. After discussions with the local council, it was agreed that Mrs Monk would be rehoused but only if she terminated the joint tenancy. Mrs Monk subsequently gave the required four weeks' notice to quit but entirely without the knowledge of Mr Monk.

Legal Issue: Was the giving of notice to quit a joint periodic tenancy effective to terminate the lease when provided by a single joint tenant?

Judgment: In the House of Lords, it was held that the giving of notice by one joint tenant is effective to determine a joint periodic tenancy. The court reasoned that it was effective as any joint tenancy requires the consent of all tenants if it is to continue. Per Lord Bridge:

> in any ordinary agreement for an initial term which is to continue for successive terms unless determined by notice, the obvious inference is that the agreement is intended to continue beyond the initial term only if and so long as all parties to the agreement are willing that it should do so . . . the application of ordinary contractual principles leads me to expect that a periodic tenancy granted to two or more joint tenants must be terminable at common law by an appropriate notice to quite given by any one of them whether or not the others are prepared to concur.

Concern had been expressed that the *Monk* approach to the giving of notice for joint periodic tenancies may not be human rights' compliant under the ECHR in denying the non-concurring joint tenant's Art. 8 right to a private and family life. However, in *Sims v Dacorum Borough Council* (2014), the Court of Appeal dismissed this, holding that the *Monk* ruling was fully ECHR-compatible. Article 8 was engaged in possession proceedings but not engaged as regards the giving of notice which is a rule of substantive property and contract law. The ability of one joint tenant to bring the lease to an end was an inherent part of joint tenants' rights which arose from the outset of the tenancy. In fact, the result achieved in *Monk* does not prove to be as controversial as it might first appear. This is because when one joint tenant gives notice to quit a joint tenancy, the remaining joint tenants are able to continue occupying the property and, provided rent is paid and accepted by the landlord, a new periodic tenancy will arise in the tenants' favour: *Burton v Camden LBC* (1997).

9.6.2.3 Notice and tenancies at will

A tenancy at will can be brought to an end by either party at any time. Equally, should either party conduct him or herself in a manner inconsistent with the continuation of the tenancy, the tenancy will automatically terminate. Thereafter, the tenant is provided with a reasonable period to vacate the property (enough to leave the property and no more) before her presence is taken to constitute trespass.

9.6.3 Surrender of the lease to the landlord

Surrender involves the return of the lease to the landlord. Given that a leasehold estate is granted or carved out of the freehold estate, the process of surrender necessarily brings the tenancy to an end. A lease may be surrendered expressly or impliedly by operation of law and requires a clear intention that the lease is to be terminated: *Charville Estates Ltd v Unipart* (1997). Express surrender of a lease constitutes a conveyance of an interest in land and therefore must be effected by deed under s. 52(1) of the LPA 1925. Implied surrender by operation of law need satisfy no formality requirements and is exempt from s. 52(1) of the LPA 1925. A classic example of implied surrender is where a tenant gives up possession of the land and returns to the landlord any keys to the premises: *E. S. Schwarb & Co. Ltd v McCarthy* (1976). This constitutes implied surrender and will terminate the lease. Where a sublease exists, surrender by the headlessee to the headlessor will not affect the sublease in that, in this scenario, any subtenants now hold their tenancy directly from the landlord: *Mellor v Watkins* (1874).

9.6.4 Merger of leasehold and freehold

Where the tenant acquires the landlord's freehold interest in the land, this 'merger' of the leasehold and the reversionary estate necessarily brings the lease to an end.

9.6.5 Termination by disclaimer

Every lease contains an implied covenant that the tenant will not deny the landlord's superior title. Should this implied covenant be breached, the tenant is said to 'disclaim' the landlord's title entitling the landlord to forfeit the lease: *Wisbech St Mary Parish Council v Lilley* (1956). This mode of termination of a lease has been said by the Court of Appeal to constitute 'a largely outdated medieval procedure' and one that, if it still applies today, does so only where the tenant's disclaimer is such as to represent a repudiation of the lease, accepted by the landlord: *Eastaugh v Crisp* (2007).

9.6.6 Forfeiture of the lease by the landlord

As you will discover in Chapter 12, where a tenant is in breach of covenants (promises) contained within the tenancy agreement (called 'leasehold covenants') the landlord may be entitled to forfeiture of the lease. Where there is a successful forfeiture, this has the effect of bringing the lease to an end.

9.6.7 Repudiatory breach of contract

As you may already know from contract law, where a party to a contract breaches a fundamental condition of that agreement, this entitles the other party to treat the breach as a repudiation of the contract and sue for damages. For some time, this remedy was regarded as inapplicable to the law of leases; however, the High Court has held that the remedy of repudiation should apply to leases on the ground that leases ought not be treated differently from other contracts.[58] Forfeiture is not available to tenants so a tenant's ability to rely on a

---

[58] *Total Oil Great Britain Ltd v Thompson Garages* (1972); *Hussein v Mehlman* (1992).

landlord's repudiatory breach is an important weapon in their armoury—for example, where a landlord refuses to comply with fundamental leasehold covenants in the tenancy agreement.

9.6.8 Enlargement of leasehold into freehold

Under s. 153 of the LPA 1925, tenants of long leases of more than 300 years where there are at least 200 years remaining to run, have the right to 'enlarge' their leasehold interests into freehold interests. This naturally brings the lease to end.

9.6.9 Frustration

In the case of *National Carriers Ltd v Panalpina (Northern) Ltd* (1981), the House of Lords, by bare majority, held that the doctrine of frustration of contract applies to the law of leases. The result is that if, after the lease has been granted, there is a fundamental change in circumstances which renders the lease impossible to perform or alters the rights and obligations of the parties, the whole lease will be discharged. Note: 'frustration events' are very rare and not often accepted by the court as terminating a lease.[59]

9.7 Future directions

In this chapter, we have explored the nature, essential characteristics, creation, and termination of leases. The law of leases has seen a flurry of recent activity from both Government and the Law Commission. There are a number of developments in the law surrounding leasehold land of which it would be useful for you to be aware; three warrant mention. Whilst these do not alter the fundamental legal principles underlying the law of leases, they go to wider leasehold environment and give a flavour of the importance of leases in real people's live. First, from 1 June 2019, under the Tenant Fees Act 2019,[60] most letting fees have been banned and caps introduced on tenancy deposits in the private rented sector in England. Applying to new or renewed tenancy agreements signed after 1 June, the aim of the legislation is to reduce the steep costs that people face at the outset of their tenancies and on renewal. The ambition (a laudable one) is that tenants will be able to see more easily precisely what a property will cost them to rent without any hidden fees which have all too-often been lurking in the shadows, unadvertised yet payable when the tenancy agreement has been drawn up. With the private rental sector growing in scale and importance year on year, these measures are welcome, if not sufficient, to meet the barriers and challenges the rental sector presents; in particular as to affordability and demand.[61] Secondly, in July 2017, the Government launched a consultation, *Tackling Unfair Practices*

---

[59] As was the case in *Panalpina* itself where the closure of an access road by a local authority was deemed to be an interruption to tenants of a warehouse but insufficient to constitute the requisite 'gravity of a frustration event'.

[60] For a helpful guide to the new law, see Landlords Guild guide, *Understanding the Tenant Fees Act 2019*; available online at: https://www.landlordsguild.com/understanding-the-tenant-fees-act-2019/.

[61] In 2019 the Government launched a consultation on reform of the 'rogue landlord database' in a bid to allow greater access to the database to help individuals make more informed choices before entering leasehold agreements and to encourage better behaviour from landlords generally.

in the Leasehold Market prompted in particular by unfair and unreasonable abuses of lease-hold land as perhaps most visibly and publicly demonstrated by the issues encountered in selling leasehold homes and onerous ground rents. In December 2017, the Government issued its response including a commitment to introducing new legislation to prohibit new residential long leases from being granted on houses whether new build or existing free-hold, restricting ground rents in new leasehold homes to a peppercorn, and measures to support existing leaseholders to make extending a lease easier, faster, fairer, and cheaper. Thirdly, and aligned to the work around leasehold land initiated by the Government, the Law Commission in 2018 launched its consultation designed to breathe new life into com-monhold ownership of flats, *Reinvigorating Commonhold: The Alternative to Leasehold Ownership*. Commonhold was first introduced under the Commonhold and Leasehold Act 2002 as a new model for flat ownership (similar to condominium in North America). In a commonhold arrangement, flat owners own the freehold of their flats and communally own the freehold of the common parts through a commonhold association which is re-sponsible for the management of the development paid for by the flat owners. A common-hold community statement, binding on all flat owners within the commonhold governs the relationship between flat owners. It is therefore an alternative to leasehold in which there is no landlord and no ground rent; instead flat owners own their property outright and enjoy a stake in how the wider building is run and managed. Uptake of commonhold has, how-ever, been woeful with reports of just 20 commonhold developments built in England and Wales in total since the 2002 legislation came into force. The Law Commission is therefore proposing reforms to remove barriers to commonhold's update and kickstart a new wave of enthusiasm for commonhold. Preliminary recommendations from the Commission in-clude allowing a commonhold development to include residential and commercial units, making it easier to convert leasehold into commonhold, and means of increasing mortgage lenders' confidence in financing commonhold.

Beyond these policy developments, whilst the essential ingredients of leases appear largely settled, there are areas overdue for reform and issues which reward further thought. There are a number of issues to watch out for as the law of leases evolves according to con-temporary property law impulses.

First, a key debate continues to rage as to how, in view of the controversial decision in *Bruton*, we should categorize and conceptualize the 'lease'. Is a lease essentially a contrac-tual right or a proprietary right? Millett LJ in *Ingram v IRC* (1997) stated strongly that 'there is no doubt that a lease is property. It is a legal estate in land.' But, how far can the de-cision in *Bruton* can be squared with this purely proprietary view of leases. For McFarlane, this tension between the two different views of the lease is an illusion; it is entirely possible for a right to be simultaneously contractual and proprietary in nature.[62] This is because the classification of a right as proprietary derives from the 'content question' (i.e. does it bind the world?) and as contractual from the 'acquisition question' (i.e. how was the agree-ment formed?). Taking this view, a lease is a proprietary right that, in most cases, arises through contract. For McFarlane, on this approach, there is no difficulty in seeing the lease as being both contractual and proprietary in nature. Despite this apparent rationalization,

---

[62] B. McFarlane, *The Structure of Property Law* (Oxford: Hart, 2008), 697.

the *Bruton* tenancy continues to pose big questions as to the 'contractualization' of the lease and to the diminishing distinction between the lease and the licence.

A second but related issue is how far the decisions in *Bruton* and *Berrisford*, in as much as they might be construed as examples of flexible judicial reasoning, are indicative of the direction the wind is blowing in the law of leases? Whilst the Supreme Court in *Berrisford*, for example, acknowledged and affirmed the orthodoxy as to the requirement for certainty of term, the court was prepared to pursue an analysis under s. 149(6) of the LPA 1925 despite this not having been raised in argument by counsel in the case. How far does this approach signal the beginning of the end for the requirement of certainty of term? Williams thinks not and argues that 'the rule does have a plausible doctrinal underpinning' and continues to serve a useful purpose although perhaps less so today than was the case in its historical heyday.[63] Bridge has argued, however, that:[64]

> If the parties . . . know where they stand, in the sense that the contract between them is sufficiently certain, then that should be enough. If a landlord, in [the *Berrisford*] case, a fully mutual housing association, decides that its tenants should be entitled to remain in possession unless and until they fall into arrears with their rent or break other provisions contained in the tenancy agreement, it is difficult to see what policy objectives are being furthered in denying the tenant the rights that the agreement seeks to create.

If we follow Bridge's reasoning, the certainty of term rule described as 'bizarre' and 'ancient and technical'[65] could be dispensed with, leaving exclusive possession as the only remaining *essential* feature of a lease. Would this be desirable? This brings into sharp focus an issue which was considered in the Introduction to this chapter, namely the *relationship* that sits at the core of the leasehold arrangement. We noted that a lease is a contract, an estate in land, and importantly also a *relationship* between landlord and tenant. If the sole essential attribute of the lease were to become exclusive possession, would this provide further evidence that it is the landlord–tenant *relationship* and associated status it brings that is more important than the form the lease takes?

Bridge has written that there is greater political, academic, and judicial consensus as to the fundamental elements that make up the law of leases than has ever before existed.[66] For Bridge, this consensus signals the need for a reform agenda focused on achieving greater clarification and simplification in the law. A broader question is surely as to how Parliament will balance protection of tenants in a growing private rented sector with the need not to stifle landlordism with over-regulation.[67] The Tenant Fees Act 2019, rogue landlord database, and the Homes (Fitness for Human Habitation) Act 2018 (discussed in Chapter 12) are perhaps three examples of attempts to reset the landlord–tenant relationship. Yet, there is a more fundamental aspect to Bridge's assertion.

---

[63] I. Williams, 'Explaining the Certainty of Term Requirement in Leases: Nothing Lasts Forever' (2015) 74(3) CLJ 592.

[64] Bridge, 'Periodic Tenancies and the Problem of Certainty of Term', 497.

[65] *Prudential Assurance*, [396], per Lord Browne-Wilkinson.

[66] S. Bridge, 'Leases: Contract, Property and Status' in L. Tee (ed.), *Land Law: Debates, Issues, Policy* (Cullompton: Willan, 2002), chapter 4.

[67] See D. Cowan, L. Fox O'Mahony, and N. Cobb, *Great Debates in Property Law* (Basingstoke: Palgrave, 2012), Chapters 3 and 4.

The suggestion is that the law of leases is, in many senses, stable. But is this right? In section 9.3 we set out the three 'essential elements' of lease. However, as we found in the discussion of these elements that followed, there is far more complexity and uncertainty in the law than Lord Templeman's dicta in *Street* indicates. A few examples serve to illustrate the point:

- Exclusive possession, which has been described in this chapter as the 'beating heart' of the lease turns out not to be so 'exclusive' after all when we consider that a landlord is entitled, subject to the terms of the tenancy agreement, to enter the leased premises. In other words, the notion of a tenant's territorial control, her ability to exclude all others from the leased property including the landlord, is heavily qualified. As we discovered in section 9.3.1.1, in certain situations, even where exclusive possession is found to exist, a lease may nevertheless not arise. This provides further evidence that exclusive possession cannot be regarded as the absolute, determinative factor for the existence of a lease as is so often peddled in academic circles and in decisions of the court.

- The assertion in *Street* that the payment of rent is a requirement for the creation of a valid lease is heavily undermined. As we discovered, there is nothing 'essential' about the requirement for rent in the creation of a valid lease. Whilst the presence of payment of rent may be a strong indicator of a lease, it is not a necessary ingredient for a lease to exist.

- We saw how the court is prepared to intervene directly into the parties' own characterization of their legal arrangement, to look beyond 'labels', to blast apart shams and pretences, and to seek the 'true' bargain between the parties: *Street*; *Aslan*. Gardner has noted the use of 'caricatured relationships in the construction' of this 'true' bargain between the parties.[68] For example, for occupiers in a romantic relationship, their agreements on occupation are treated by the court as 'interdependent' and any attempt by a landowner to separate these agreements is deemed a 'pretence'. In contrast, where occupiers are merely flatmates, agreements are regarded as 'independent' and any separation of agreements is treated as genuine: *AG Securities*. The result is that the court is seeking to determine the 'true' bargain between landowner and occupier based upon the caricatured nature of the parties' relationships. If correct, this must be an entirely crude and unreliable measure. Relationships, whether between lovers or friends surely contain both interdependent and independent facets. As Gardner concludes:

  > What emerges is that the 'substance and reality' of a transaction, on which the pretence doctrine depends, is a fragile—because ultimately impressionistic—concept.

Gardner argues that a judicial 'project' is at play here whereby the courts intervene on a case-by-case basis to ensure that certain social situations are covered by statutory protections appertaining to tenants that would not be available to licensees. All the court must do is decide whether 'on the ground' and according to stereotypes of interpersonal relationships whether the particular circumstances 'ought' to be covered by legal protections or not. The court's power to look beyond 'labels' endows the court with considerable discretion to disregard the negotiated position of the parties. Is this unacceptable

---

[68] S. Gardner, *Introduction to Land Law* (London: Bloomsbury, 2015), 245.

judicial intervention? This once again highlights the multifaceted nature of the lease—at once, a contract, an estate, a relationship.

By way of a final observation, we will now reflect upon the Law Commission's work in 2006 *Renting Homes*, which it described as 'one of the largest consultation exercises ever undertaken'. The project considered and recommended wide-ranging reforms to the law concerning statutory protection for short-term residential tenants. The Commission's work began with three central aims of simplification, comprehensibility, and flexibility and in its final report recommended two key reforms including the creation a single social housing tenure (there are currently several distinct tenures) and, more importantly for our present purposes, a new focus on 'consumer protection'. As part of this new consumer protection focus, the Commission recommended that the availability of statutory protections would no longer 'depend on technical issues of whether or not there is a tenancy as opposed to a licence'. The effect of the reforms, as far as concerned access to statutory protection, would have been to collapse the lease/licence distinction. The Commission explained its thinking in the following terms:[69]

> We regard the contract between the landlord and the occupier and central to the operation of our scheme. We see no reason why any distinction should be drawn between a contract which comprises a lease and a contract which comprises a licence. This distinction is essential where the proprietary consequences of the contract are concerned, and should remain so, but it should not affect the statutory regulation of the contract as between the contracting parties themselves.

The Commission's work was well-received by academics and practising lawyers alike but the proposals, sadly, never made it onto the statute books in England (though were implemented in Wales). Had the proposals been adopted, they would have had a considerable impact on the law of leases. First, far less weight would attach to the 'status' of a lease given that the lease/licence distinction would be of little practical importance, at least for the purpose of statutory protections. Secondly, the reforms would have freed the courts from further delimitation and navigation of the lease/licence dividing line. Implementation of the proposals is off the table but how far would the proposals have improved the law? Do you agree that there is a strong case for a reform agenda that attaches less weight to the lease/licence distinction?

Further reading

- S. Bridge, 'Former Tenants, Future Liabilities and the Privity of Contract Principle: The Landlord and Tenant (Covenants) Act 1995' (1996) 55 CLJ 313.
- S. Bridge, 'Leases, Contract, Property and Status' in L. Tee (ed.), *Land Law: Issues, Debates, Policy* (Cullompton: Willan, 2002).
- S. Bridge, 'Periodic Tenancies and the Problem of Certainty of Term' [2010] Conv 492.
- S. Bright, 'Beyond Sham and into Pretence' (1991) 11 OJLS 138.
- S. Bright, 'Uncertainty in Leases—Is it a Vice?' (1993) 13 LS 38.
- S. Bright, 'Avoiding Tenancy Legislation: Sham and Contracting Out Revisited' (2002) 61(1) CLJ 146.

---

[69] Law Commission Report No. 297, *Renting Homes* (2006), Part 1.

- M. Davey, 'Privity of Contract and Leases—Reform at Last' (1996) 59 MLR 78.
- P. Harrison and C. Bernard, 'Implications of the Mexfield Ruling for Housing Co-Operatives' (2015) 19(4) L&TR 148.
- J. Hill, 'Intention and the Creation of Proprietary Rights: Are Leases Different?' (1996) 16 LS 200.
- Law Commission Report No. 297, *Renting Homes* (2006).
- Law Commission Report No. 303, *Termination of Tenancies for Tenant Default* (2006).
- M. Lower, 'The Bruton Tenancy' [2010] Conv 38.
- M. Pawlowski, 'The Bruton Tenancy: Clarity or More Confusion?' [2005] Conv 262.
- N. Roberts, 'The Bruton Tenancy: A Matter of Relativity' [2012] Conv 87.
- I. Williams, 'The Certainty of Term Requirement in Leases: Nothing Lasts Forever' (2015) 74(3) CLJ 592.

Online resources

Access the online resources at www.oup.com/uk/bevan2e/ to test yourself with self-test questions and scenario problems. You can also view additional supporting material relevant to the topics in this chapter, including:

- *Videos*
- *Audio podcasts*
- *Maps, diagrams, and flowcharts*
- *Interactive exercises*
- *Examples of real-life legal documentation*

10 Easements and Profits

10.1 Introduction

Much of our focus in this book so far has been on rights which entitle people to *possess* land. We have seen this, for example, in our discussion of freehold and leasehold estates. As students coming to land law, concepts of ownership and possession of land are naturally at the forefront of your minds as the clearest expression of what it means to enjoy rights in land. But there is far more happening on land and far more value in land than possession of it alone. In this chapter, we consider two rights in land that fall short of an entitlement to possession, rights which fall short of freehold or leasehold estates. As you will see, these lesser, *non-possessory* rights—of which easements and *profits à prendre* are but two—are a vital way in which even more of the value in land can be unlocked.

To really make the point, it helps to draw a comparison between an easement, a licence, and a lease. We saw in Chapter 9 that a lease arises in circumstances where there is exclusive possession of another's land, for a certain duration, usually in return for the payment of rent. A lease gives rise to an extensive entitlement over the landlord's land and brings with it territorial control and the ability to exclude all others from that land (including the landlord). It is in this way that we regard the tenant as enjoying 'temporary ownership'. A licence is a purely personal permission to do something on another's land. In sharp contrast is the status of an easement. Take the classic example of an easement: a right of way over another's land. Yes, the lease, the licence, and the easement all involve the grant of rights over someone else's land; however, whilst the lease carries with it a right to possession of that other's land, an easement most certainly does not. Indeed, by definition, for an easement to be an easement at all it must not grant a right to possession of that other's land. We can see that easements are therefore less powerful than leases and grant a far less extensive entitlement than the freehold or leasehold estates, but are more powerful than purely personal licences.

Easements (and profits) are, nonetheless, significant rights. Picture, for example, a parcel of land which is entirely landlocked with no route in and out. An easement (e.g. a right of way) will provide access to that land and will considerably increase the utility, amenity and, crucially, the financial value of the land. This neatly encapsulates the power and reach of easements and also explains why the law is prepared to *imply* easements in certain circumstances in order to ensure land is alienable and capable of being exploited to its maximum protection.

So, what exactly is an easement? An easement is a right of one landowner to enjoy limited use of another's neighbouring land. In this chapter, our primary focus is easements but we will also briefly consider profits or '*profits à prendre*' in section 10.8. A profit is right to remove something from another's land—for example, wood, turf, or animals. Easements are ancient, though in their present form only recognizable in the last hundred years or so. It was as agricultural land became organized, bounded, and enclosed that easements took on a growing role.[1] As Britain embraced the industrial revolutions, larger towns and cities emerged meaning that exploiting land to its maximum potential became a priority. Since this time, easements have taken on a mounting significance guaranteeing the full utility and enjoyment of land. Today, for example, many everyday activities are underpinned by easements: see Figure 10.1.

Figure 10.1 Some common examples of modern easement

---

[1] See S. Gardner and E. MacKenzie, *Introduction to Land Law* (Oxford: Hart, 2012), 286–7.

Figure 10.2 A hierarchy of rights in and over land

As Figure 10.1 demonstrates, easements provide for rights of way, rights to light, the right to install and maintain a water supply, rights to drainage, and rights for the supply of electricity. Many everyday activities simply could not take place without easements and, according to Land Registry,[2] over 65 per cent of registered freehold titles and 24 per cent of leasehold titles are subject, in some degree, to easements.

Where does the law of easements and profits sit within the wider puzzle that is modern land law? First, these lesser, non-possessory rights offer further evidence of the uniqueness of land and its ability to support a whole gamut of different rights and interests reflecting the many uses and purposes to which land can be put. Secondly, recognizing these rights helps us to appreciate an emerging hierarchy of interests in and over land which we first encountered in Chapter 1: see Figure 10.2.

At the top tier of our hierarchy is freehold ownership which carries with it the greatest, most extensive entitlement over land—the closest thing we have to a concept of 'outright ownership'. This is followed at the second tier by the leasehold estate—the only other estate that is capable of existing at law and one which (as we have just explored in Chapter 9) endows the tenant with an extensive entitlement to both possess and exclude others from the landlord's land. At the third tier comes a series, a clutch of less extensive rights. This group comprises easements, profits, and covenants.[3] We focus on easements and profits in this chapter. Freehold covenants will be explored in Chapter 11. Licences, as we explored in Chapter 7, give rise to personal rights only, occupy a final and fourth tier and represent some of the least potent rights over land. This depiction of a hierarchy of rights should help you better visualize and grasp how the multitude of rights and interests that can exist over land interrelate and operate. Yet that is not the end of the story. It says little of how you are to differentiate practically between these rights.

10.1.1 Distinguishing easements from other rights in land

In many instances, distinguishing easements from other rights in land will not present any difficulty at all. For example, it is obvious that a postman walking up your path to deliver your post has only a very transitory, implied permission (licence) to do so. The postman

---

[2] Law Commission Consultation Paper No. 186, *Easements, Covenants and Profits a Prendre* (2008), Appendix A.

[3] This group of rights is sometimes described as constituting 'servitudes'.

enjoys no rights of possession or of any permanence over the land and is clearly not the freehold owner. The real question comes in distinguishing easements from other more similar rights in and over land. Table 10.1 sets out some of the differences between these rights which might, at first, appear similar in nature but which you need to be able to distinguish. Do not worry too much about freehold covenants at this stage as we will discuss these in depth in Chapter 11.

Table 10.1 Easements distinguished from leases, licences, covenants, and profits

Distinguished from leases	• A lease is a possessory right. An easement is non-possessory in nature (i.e. does not involve a right of possessory control). • A lease is akin to 'temporary ownership' of another's land and is a recognized legal estate. An easement is an interest in land and not an estate. • A right which is incompatible with the true landowner's right to possession cannot exist as an easement.
Distinguished from licences	• Both easements and licences relate to the use of another's land but the categories of user recognized as easements are far narrower and more strictly defined than those recognized as licences. By contrast, licences provide for permission to use another's land in an almost unlimited range of circumstances. • A licence may carry with it a degree of exclusive occupation of land. Such exclusive occupation would likely prove fatal to the finding of an easement. • There are greater formality requirements for the creation of an easement than for licences which can arise far more informally. • An easement cannot exist **'in gross'** which means it must be tied to ownership of land rather than being granted in favour of individuals personally. By contrast, you do not need to own any land to benefit from a licence. • Easements are proprietary interests capable of binding third parties. Licences, according to orthodoxy, are merely personal rights and cannot bind successors.
Distinguished from restrictive covenants	• Restrictive covenants are promises (made in a deed) not to do something on land for the benefit of other land. Easements and covenants are closely related. Some would argue restrictive covenants are simply negative easements. Yet, there are differences. • The categories of easements are more limited and strictly defined than those of restrictive covenants. • Easements are enforceable both at law and in equity. Only the burden of restrictive covenants is enforceable and then only in equity, not at law. • Easements can be acquired by long user (we call this 'prescription'). Covenants cannot be so acquired.
Distinguished from profits	• Both easements and profits are non-possessory rights. However, an easement does not extend to the taking or extracting of something from another's land as for a *profit à prendre*. A profit, for example, provides for the right to remove wood or fish from another's land. • Unlike easements, profits can exist 'in gross' which means they do not need to be fixed to any land but can exist in favour of individuals.

The place of easements in modern land law is secure but many fascinating questions remain, stemming largely from the fact that there is no single, incontrovertible definition of the elements that make up an easement. In breaking down the complexity of the law in this area, several key issues must be addressed in order to fully understand how easements work. This chapter therefore begins by considering the nature and essential characteristics of easements before exploring easements are created and their scope; the effect of easements on third parties; and how they are brought to an end. We then briefly consider the position of profits.

 Visit the online resources to watch a video of the Supreme Court judgment in *Regency Villas*.

10.2 The nature of easements

We have said that an easement is a limited right enjoyed by one landowner over the land of another. Central to the law of easements is therefore the need for there to be two plots of land. These are called the **dominant** and **servient tenements**. One persistent challenge for the student of land law is getting to grips with the terminology of the subject which, in many cases, finds its origins in medieval times! The law of easements is no different. It is important that you appreciate at the outset of this chapter the distinction between the dominant and servient tenements, as set out in Table 10.2.

Easements concern the benefit and burden of rights attaching to *land* and not to *individuals*. Easements are proprietary interests in land as opposed to merely personal rights (such as licences).[4] Easements are, therefore, capable of binding third parties such as purchasers of the dominant and servient tenements subject to the rules governing registered and unregistered land. This means that the benefit of an easement is capable of passing on the transfer of the dominant land and the burden of an easement can also run on transfer of the servient land.

As we will explore later in this chapter, easements can be created expressly or arise by implication, can be legal or equitable, and can be positive or negative in nature. A positive easement, for example, may involve a right of the dominant landowner to use a pathway that crosses the servient landowner's property. A negative easement, in contrast,

Table 10.2 The distinction between dominant and servient tenements

Dominant tenement	The land to which the right is attached (i.e. the land which benefits from the easement).
Servient tenement	The land over which the right is exercised (i.e. the land that is burdened by the easement).

---

[4] Though note that where a claim to an easement fails, a licence may nevertheless exist.

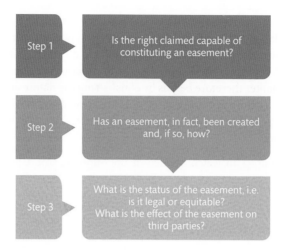

Figure 10.3 Framework for how to approach analysis of an easements scenario

essentially provides the dominant landowner with the right to receive something (such as air or light) from the servient land without obstruction. We say this easement is 'negative' as the dominant landowner is not permitted to do anything affirmative or positive over the servient land.

How should you tackle the study of the law of easements? Figure 10.3 provides a framework for how to approach analysis of an easements scenario.

In studying easements, the vital first step is to determine whether a right arising is *capable* of constituting an easement: we do this by exploring the essential characteristics of easements. It is only if a right is capable of amounting to an easement that we can continue with our analysis to examine its nature and effect.

10.3 The essential elements of easements

In determining which rights are capable of being easements, the law must strike a fine balance. On the one hand, if the scope of the law of easements is drawn too broadly, the use and enjoyment of the servient burdened land may be seriously threatened. On the other hand, if drawn too narrowly, the utility and value of dominant land may be undermined. The law must therefore walk a difficult line between accommodating the dominant land while ensuring that the servient land is not excessively burdened. This is particularly important in view of changing economic and social conditions and the increasing uses to which land is being put. The courts have met this challenge by establishing a series of requirements which govern whether a purported right is *capable* of constituting an easement. There are four requirements. They were laid down by the Court of Appeal in the seminal decision of *Re Ellenborough Park* (1956) and are taken as reflecting the essential characteristics of easements.

> **KEY CASE** *Re Ellenborough Park* (1956)
>
> Facts: Ellenborough Park in Weston-Super-Mare consisted of a series of houses adjoining a park. The owners of the houses exercised rights over the land and made use of the amenity. During the Second World War, the park was requisitioned by the War Office giving rise to a dispute as to how State compensation should be distributed. A central issue was whether the landowners surrounding the park had proprietary rights over the park or mere personal rights in the form of licences.
>
> Legal issue: Did the house owners surrounding Ellenborough Park enjoy an easement over the park?
>
> Judgment: The Court of Appeal held that the owners enjoyed a right to use the park which constituted an easement. The right satisfied all the essential requirements of an easement and, consequently, compensation was shared between them.
>
> Evershed MR noted:
>
> > For the purposes of the argument before us Mr Cross and Mr Goff were content to adopt, as correct, the four characteristics formulated in Dr Cheshire's Modern Real Property 7th ed pp 456 et seq. They are (1) there must be a dominant tenement and a servient tenement; (2) an easement must 'accommodate' the dominant land; (3) dominant and servient owners must be different persons; and (4) a right over land cannot amount to an easement, unless it is capable of forming the subject matter of a grant.

There are therefore four essential characteristics which can be used as analytical tools to determine whether a right is capable of being an easement. The flowchart in Figure 10.4 sets out a structure for considering these elements. Again, recall these essential characteristics do nothing more than tell us that a subsisting right is *capable* of being an easement. It must then be considered whether an easement, in fact, exists and what is its scope. As we will discover in section 10.4, this involves an assessment of how the easement was created, whether appropriate formalities were satisfied and whether the easement takes effect at law or in equity. Before we get to that, let's consider each of the *Re Ellenborough Park* elements in turn.

10.3.1 There must be a dominant and servient tenement

There are two aspects to this requirement:

1. There must be two parcels of land: a **dominant** and a **servient tenement**.
2. The dominant and servient tenements must be identifiable at the time of the creation of the purported easement.

10.3.1.1 There must be two parcels of land: a dominant and a servient tenement

At a basic level, this requirement is self-explanatory. There must be two pieces of land: a dominant and a servient tenement. This requirement is a central tenet of the law of easements. In *Alfred F. Beckett Ltd v Lyons* (1967), Winn LJ explained that it was an 'essential element of any easement' that the right was linked to two parcels of land—its benefit attaching to the dominant tenement and its burden to the servient tenement. As we have already seen, easements by their very nature involve the enjoyment of a right of one

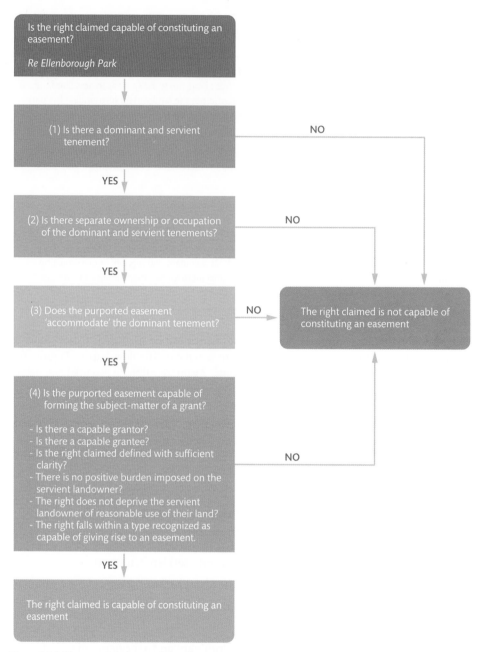

Figure 10.4 The essential characteristics of an easement

landowner over another's land. This requirement is therefore unsurprising. We say, therefore, that easements cannot exist 'in gross' (confirmed in *Hawkins v Rutter* (1892))—in other words, an easement cannot exist where there is only servient land.[5] By contrast, a profit can exist in gross as we will explore in section 10.8.

---

[5] Note that easements are permitted 'in gross' in certain other jurisdictions—for example, in the United States.

The rule against easements in gross has not been without its critics. In particular, in the 1980s, Sturley argued strongly that English law should recognize the validity of easements in gross and that the requirement for both a dominant and servient tenement was 'without authority or justification'.[6] The Law Commission considered Sturley's viewpoint in a 2008 Consultation Paper but recommended that no change to the law be made.[7]

10.3.1.2 The dominant and servient tenements must be identifiable at the time of the creation of the purported easement

Related to the requirement for distinct dominant and servient tenements is that, at the time the purported easement is created, the dominant and servient tenements must be *identifiable*. This was confirmed in *London & Blenheim Estates Ltd v Ladbroke Retail Parks Ltd* (1994). In this case a claim of an easement for the parking of vehicles failed because, at the relevant time, the land alleged to represent the dominant tenement was not sufficiently identified. Peter Gibson LJ explained:[8]

> If one asks why the law should require that there should be a [defined] dominant tenement . . . the answer would appear to lied in the policy against encumbering land with burdens of an uncertain extent . . . A right intended as an easement and attached to a servient tenement before the dominant tenement is identified would in my view be an incident of a novel kind.

Both the requirement for dominant and servient land and, further, that they be sufficiently defined and identifiable at the time of the creation of the alleged easement can be seen as a wider recognition that certainty and the need not to burden servient land are of prime importance in the law of easements.

10.3.2 There must be separate ownership or occupation of the dominant and servient land

The court in *Roe v Siddons* (1889) confirmed that it is impossible for an easement to exist over your own land. Therefore, there is a requirement that the dominant and servient land be in separate ownership or occupation. Where the dominant and servient land fall into the same ownership, any pre-existing easement will be extinguished. Where the dominant and servient land is owned by two different people but, subsequently both plots fall into common occupation,[9] under the authority of *Canham v Fisk* (1831), any easement is suspended for as long as that period of common occupation endures.

10.3.3 The purported easement must 'accommodate' the dominant land

An easement must 'accommodate' the dominant land. Here we happen upon pretty obscure terminology. Fortunately, the essence of this requirement can be understood quite easily. This requirement means that the right must *benefit* the dominant land per se and not merely provide personal advantage to the dominant landowner. Parallels can clearly be

---

[6] M. F. Sturley, 'Easements in Gross' (1980) 96 LQR 557.
[7] Law Commission Consultation Paper No. 186, [3.16].   [8] *London & Blenheim Estates*, 37.

[9] Imagine, for example, where the servient landowner enters a lease of the dominant land.

drawn with the concept of 'touching and concerning' which we will encounter in the law of freehold and leasehold covenants in Chapters 11 and 12. We can say that an easement will 'accommodate' (i.e. benefit) the dominant land where it increases the value of the land and contributes to the quality or mode of user of that land. Each case is very much, however, decided on its own facts. Where the right confers no benefit at all, there can be no possibility of an easement arising. In *Kennerley v Beech* (2012), it was held that no easement arose permitting the right of way along a footpath in circumstances where the footpath led nowhere (i.e. it was a dead-end). Similarly, the right to cross another's land to park a car in a garage that does not exist would also fail.

Evershed MR in *Re Ellenborough Park* explained this requirement in the following terms:[10]

> A right enjoyed by one over the land of another does not possess the status of an easement unless it accommodated and serves the dominant tenement, and is reasonably necessary for the better enjoyment of that tenement, for if it has no connexion therewith, although it confers an advantage upon the owner and renders his ownership of the land more valuable, it is not an easement at all, but a mere contractual right personal to and enforceable between the two contracting parties.

A series of further observations can be made on this 'accommodation' requirement which might be termed the '*Ellenborough Park* glosses'.

10.3.3.1 Gloss 1: Normal enjoyment

'Accommodation' requires more than a straightforward increase in the economic value of the dominant land though this will be a factor to be taken into account. What is required is that the right is connected to the 'normal enjoyment of the land', as Evershed MR in *Re Ellenborough Park* explained:[11]

> The right did, in some degree, enhance the value of the property, and this consideration cannot be dismissed as wholly irrelevant. It is, of course, a point to be noted; but . . . it is in no way decisive of the problem; it is not sufficient to show that the right increased the value of the property conveyed unless it is also shown that it was connected with the normal enjoyment of that property.

The effect of this 'normal enjoyment gloss' is that mere increase in value is not enough. It must also be shown that the right is connected to the normal (usual) use to which the dominant land is put (e.g. farming, residential, etc.).

10.3.3.2 Gloss 2: Proximity

There must be sufficient proximity and a geographical 'nexus' between the dominant and servient land before it can be said that the right 'accommodates' that dominant land: *Bailey v Stephens* (1862). The dominant and servient tenements must therefore be nearby to one another though need not share a boundary nor be adjacent. A degree of distance will not prove fatal[12] but, as Byles J noted in *Bailey*, a right of way over land in Kent **appurtenant** to land in Northumberland will be impossible.

---

[10] *Re Ellenborough Park*, 170.   [11] Ibid., 173.

[12] In *Re Ellenborough Park* itself, the fact that some houses were further from and not adjacent to the park was held not to negative the finding of an easement.

10.3.3.3 Gloss 3: More than personal advantage

The right must do more than merely confer a personal advantage on the dominant land-owner: *Hill v Tupper* (1863). In *Hill*, a canal owner granted a lease to the claimant of adjoining land. Under the lease, the claimant was granted a 'sole and exclusive' right to put pleasure boats on the canal. The defendant was landlord of a pub situated on land which was also adjacent to the canal and he too put boats onto the canal impacting on the claimant's trade. The claimant argued that this constituted an interference with his easement. The court found that the claimant enjoyed a licence to put boats on the canal and not an easement. As a purely personal right, the licence was not enforceable against the defendant. The right conferred on the claimant a personal advantage only as it was not sufficiently annexed to the land and was 'unconnected with the use and enjoyment of the land'. Pollock CB explained that the claimant would have benefited from the right even if he had held no estate in the land at all. The claimant's right to put boats on the canal was therefore in the nature of a personal advantage. For a right to constitute an easement, it must confer a benefit on the *land* and not the *person*. Citing the decision in *Ackroyd v Smith* (1850), Pollock CB held that it was not possible to create easements in respect of 'rights unconnected with the use and enjoyment of land'. There was no connection between and no accommodation of the right and the dominant land. It could not therefore constitute an easement.

There may be an important policy argument also at play in *Hill*. It is likely that the court was minded to find against the existence of an easement in order to prevent the law being invoked as a means of protecting the claimant's commercial advantage. Had the right amounted to an enforceable easement, the claimant would, in effect, have secured for himself a monopoly in the pleasure boat trade on the canal. It seems fair to conclude that the court was keen to avoid this result. *Hill* therefore offers further evidence of the court's desire to keep the law of easements within strict parameters.

10.3.3.4 Gloss 4: 'Mere recreation . . . amusement', and sporting rights as easements?

The traditional view was that rights conferring benefits of recreation and leisure pursuits would rarely (if ever) give rise to easements. This was because easements were regarded as existing in order that the value and quality of land be increased and not to aid in delivering greater social amenity. Evershed MR in *Re Ellenborough Park* noted:[13]

> a proposition stated in Theobald's *The Law of Land*, 2nd ed. (1929), at p. 263, where it is said that an easement 'must be a right of utility and benefit and not one of mere recreation and amusement.'

In *Mounsey v Ismay* (1865), for example, a right to hold an annual horse race on land belonging to another was not capable of giving rise to an easement as it was not a 'right of utility'. However, a softening of the position against recognition of recreational easements was already present in the decision in *Re Ellenborough Park*.[14] For Evershed MR the use of a garden in *Re Ellenborough Park* was to be regarded as giving rise to utility and benefit in

---

[13] Ibid., 178.

[14] The court refused to accept an argument advanced on recreation but stopped short of rejecting outright the traditional rule against rights of leisure and amusement.

the same way as crossing a field to reach a railway station. In support of recognizing recreational and sporting easements, Gray and Gray suggest that:[15]

> The judicial animus against recreational easements has undoubtedly receded in recent times. It may be an index of a more hedonistic (or even more health conscious) age that it no longer seems appropriate to acknowledge the easement character of certain recreational facilities annexed to dominant land. This is particularly the case where the claim of easements refers to a defined area over which a right of recreational enjoyment has been given not to the public but to a limited number of lot holders.

Helpfully, in *Regency Villas Title Ltd v Diamond Resorts (Europe) Ltd* (2018),[16] the Supreme Court was given the chance, for the first time in England, to address head-on the question of whether rights of sport and recreation could amount to easements, a question which was answered with a resounding yes. *Regency Villas* is easily one of the most important land law decisions in recent times and you should certainly read the judgment (especially the Supreme Court decision which you can watch online).

KEY CASE *Regency Villas Title Ltd v Diamond Resorts (Europe) Ltd* (2018)

Facts: The dispute centred on the use of purely recreational facilities by owners of timeshare properties at Broome Park, a country estate in Kent, comprising a mansion house and surrounding land. The facilities were wide-ranging from swimming pools to squash courts, an 18-hole golf course, putting and croquet lawn, as well as indoor facilities including a billiard and TV room, restaurant, bar, gym, and sauna. A transfer in 1981 had granted to owners of timeshare properties on the land the right to use the leisure facilities at the Park. Over time, the facilities fell into disrepair and, for example, an outdoor pool was filled in with concrete.

Legal Issue: Could the timeshare owners secure a declaration that their sporting and recreational rights amounted to valid easements that would be binding on the Park owners? If so, were the timeshare owners entitled to an injunction to prevent interference with use of the facilities and damages?

Judgment: HHJ Purle QC in the High Court found without difficulty that the recreational rights readily 'accommodated' the land just as the pleasure ground had 'accommodated' the land in *Re Ellenborough Park* and that the rights increased enjoyment of the land. As a major attraction to owning the timeshare properties, the rights could not be described as 'mere rights of recreation'. The rights were expressed in terms that were neither too wide nor vague; the Park owners could not be described as having been deprived of possession of their land by the exercise of these rights (there was no 'ouster') and while no case in England had explored whether rights of this broad recreational character could amount to easements, there was no impediment to recognizing these rights as easements. The Park owners appealed arguing that (1) the rights could not amount to easements in view of the significant cost implications in maintaining them; (2) the rights granted could not extend to facilities not even contemplated at the time of the 1981 transfer; (3) the rights could not be easements as there was no positive duty on the Park owners to maintain them; and, crucially, (4) the High Court had failed to unpack the bundle of rights to assess them one-by-one.

→

---

[15] K. Gray and S. F. Gray, *Elements of Land Law*, 5th edn (Oxford: Oxford University Press, 2009), [5.1.39].

[16] For a discussion of this significant Supreme Court judgment see C. Bevan, 'Opening Pandora's box? Recreation Pure and Simple: Easements in the Supreme Court' [2019] Conv 55; as to the decision of the Court of Appeal in *Regency Villas*, see N. Pratt, 'A Proprietary Right to Recreate' [2017] Conv 312; J. Bray, 'More than just a walk in the park: a new view on recreational easements' [2017] Conv 418.

→

The Court of Appeal held that the absence of a positive maintenance obligation did not preclude the finding of an easement and nor would an easement lapse if facilities were not maintained. The court found there to have been 'no element of futurity in the words' of the 1981 transfer, meaning that the rights would only extend to new or improved facilities if they amounted to a substitution of an existing facility or a facility moved from one location to another and could be said to fall within the terms of the original grant. The Court of Appeal agreed with the Park owners that the High Court should have considered each facility separately and 'unpacked' each in turn. Undertaking this exercise, the court held that the timeshare owners enjoyed a number of easements but had no rights, for example, in a new indoor swimming pool in the mansion as it fell outside the terms of the original grant. The Park owners appealed to the Supreme Court seeking dismissal of all claims arguing that the 1981 transfer granted no enduring rights in the nature of easements. By way of cross-appeal, the timeshare owners sought restoration of the High Court judge's order to its full extent including regarding the new indoor pool.

In the Supreme Court, by a majority of 4:1 (Lord Carnwath dissenting), the court dismissed the appeal and allowed the cross-appeal. Lord Briggs, delivering the main judgment (with whom Lady Hale and Lords Kerr and Sumption agreed) began by drawing three conclusions on what he called the 'true construction' of the 1981 transfer: (1) it was abundantly plain that the parties intended to confer property rights in the nature of an easement rather than a purely personal right; (2) the 1982 transfer should be construed as the grant of 'a single comprehensive right to use a complex of facilities' including facilities in use in 1981 but also later replacement facilities and those put into operation during the lifetime of the timeshare development; (3) there was no provision requiring the timeshare owners to make any contribution to the costs of operating, maintaining, or replacing the facilities and no term was to be implied.

Turning to the 'main controversy' of the case, Lord Briggs explored whether rights of recreation and sport could be said to accommodate the dominant tenement as required under *Re Ellenborough Park*. Lord Briggs held it was 'plain beyond a doubt' that the rights to use the recreational facilities were 'of service, utility and benefit' to the timeshare land as the communal pleasure garden had been in *Re Ellenborough*. An argument based on *Hill v Tupper* that the rights were so extensive that they could not be said to be 'ancillary' to the timeshare properties and therefore could not be easements was also rejected. Lord Briggs argued this was a misreading of *Hill* and that, provided the rights were of utility and benefit to the dominant tenant, easements could arise even if the recreational rights were more than ancillary. Nor did the 'ouster principle' (which Lord Briggs heavily criticized in any event) operate on these facts. Nothing in the 1981 transfer impinged on the Park owners' rights of management and control of their own land. The 1981 transfer contained no positive duty on the Park owners to maintain the facilities and this satisfied the condition that easements require nothing more than 'mere passivity' on the part of the servient owner. All the essential characteristics of easements were present and while this case was 'breaking new ground', a single, composite easement covering all the recreational facilities was recognized even though it concerned rights that were of sport and recreation 'pure and simple'. The order of the High Court was restored in full (including rights over the new swimming pool) and the timeshare owners were entitled to monetary compensation for the payments they had made under protest for use of the facilities in and after 2012.

In an important dissenting opinion (certainly worth reading), Lord Carnwath, who would have allowed the appeal by the Park owners, emphasized that the rights claimed could not be achieved without the active participation of the Park owners as to maintenance and management. There was nothing in principle, nor the 70 authorities cited in argument covering over 350 years of jurisprudence, which came near to supporting the submission that a right of this kind could take effect as an easement. What was being claimed, argued Lord Carnwath, was not a simple property right but 'a wholly new form of property right' akin to a permanent membership of a country club.

What is the significance of the decision in *Regency Villas*? First, on any view, the court's decision is highly significant for its recognition, for the first time in this jurisdiction, that purely recreational and sporting rights can amount to valid easements, expanding dramatically the approach of Evershed MR in *Re Ellenborough Park* that use of a pleasure garden could give rise to an easement. Secondly, the decision is important for the acceptance by the majority that the law should move with the times and recognize increasing social awareness of the value and importance of sporting activity. Might the court's approach in *Regency Villas* signal a greater willingness going forward to recognize rights arising in other novel scenarios? How far can *Regency Villas* go? Will it be taken up by the courts and applied outside the timeshare context? Set against the court's historical reluctance to create new species of easements, does *Regency Villas* messenger a shift towards a more flexible and enthusiastic judicial activism in land law? Finally, we might reflect on the limits and potential scope of the decision going forward. In my recent Conveyancer article, I explore the significance of *Regency Villas*, questioning if the decision of the majority constitutes an opening of Pandora's Box. My article argues:[17]

> The wide-reaching nature of the majority's approach may be alarming to some who will interpret the Supreme Court as endorsing an erosion of some of the traditional constraints that existed formerly on the creation of easements. As Lord Carnwath noted in dissent, 'our view of the merits should not allow us to distort the correct understanding of a well-established legal concept' . . . The context in which the case was decided is crucial here. In *Re Ellenborough Park*, the easement arose in an exclusively residential context. *Regency Villas*, by contrast, sees an easement of purely recreational rights arise vitally in a context which is mixed in nature: both residential (timeshare development) but also commercial (the wider leisure complex development). This is important for it broadens enormously the potential scope of the *Regency Villas* decision and takes it some way from the narrow, communal 'pleasure ground' easement of a park garden as seen in *Re Ellenborough Park* . . . Yet the decision extends the scope of easements seemingly even further in its discussion of ouster and positive obligations owed by servient land owners . . . The majority held there was 'nothing inherently incompatible' with the recognition of rights over land where the parties share an expectation that the servient land owner will undertake management, maintenance and repair of any structures, fittings or even chattels thereon. There was no difficulty, said the court, so long as there was no legal obligation of that kind owed to the dominant owner. This is a significant judicial sleight of hand, for, as the Park owners argued, the positive obligations of maintenance placed on them was potentially vast . . . According to the majority's reasoning, it appears the court has abolished or at least engaged in a dramatic re-framing of the classic statement that rights imposing positive obligations cannot amount to easements.

However one assesses *Regency Villas*, it is a crucial moment for our land law. In short, the effect is that, subject to satisfaction of the *Re Ellenborough Park* characteristics, rights of mere or pure recreation can amount to easements in England thus confining to history the old law objections to recognizing rights of mere amusement and recreation as easements.

Moving beyond rights of recreation, rights which bring a commercial or business advantage should be considered. These can constitute easements provided there is a sufficient connection between the right and the dominant land: *Moody v Steggles* (1879). After *Hill*, there was a view that rights conferring commercial advantage could never be considered

---

[17] See generally C. Bevan, 'Opening Pandora's Box? Recreation Pure and Simple: Easements in the Supreme Court' [2019] Conv 55.

easements. This stance must be revisited and is discredited in light of the decision in *Moody*. In *Moody*, a right of owners of a pub to fix advertising signboards to the wall of an adjacent house was held to constitute an easement as the right conferred a benefit on the land and not on individuals. Fry J explained:[18]

> It is said that the easement in question relates, not to the tenement, but to the business of the occupant of the tenement, and that therefore I cannot tie the easement to the house. It appears to me that that argument is of too refined a nature to prevail, and for this reason, that the house can only be used by an occupant, and that the occupant only uses the house for the business which he pursues, and therefore in some manner (direct or indirect) an easement is more or less connected with the mode in which the occupant of the house uses it.

In *P. & S. Platt v Crouch* (2003), a right to moor boats on the shoreline was regarded as capable of 'accommodating' the dominant land as it benefited the hotel situated on that land. Moreover, in *London & Blenheim Estates*, a right to park vehicles on land adjoining a supermarket and to walk across with shopping trolleys was held to be capable of constituting an easement. Clearly, rights which confer a commercial advantage can be seen as 'accommodating' the dominant land but only where the right is connected with *that land* in the sense of depending on the land for the benefit to exist rather than being connected to an individual. The court plainly enjoys a degree of discretion in how this requirement is satisfied. This could potentially be seen as affording a latitude to the court to refuse 'easement status' in a particular case on distinctly policy or fairness grounds.

10.3.4 The purported easement must be 'capable of forming the subject matter of a grant'

On its face, this fourth requirement is deceptively straightforward: a right can give rise to an easement only if it is capable of being expressly granted by deed. This is what is meant by the phrase 'subject matter of a grant'. This requires a grantor and a grantee who have the capacity and the relevant title from which to create the easement. In fact, this fourth essential characteristic of an easement has proved to be quite contentious and has been described as 'obscure and unhelpful'[19] and its rationale unclear. *Re Ellenborough Park* offers little assistance in understanding this requirement and there is no guidance on how the court ought to proceed. It is clear that the continued existence of this fourth requirement gives the court a significant freedom to exercise absolute discretion as to whether an easement will arise on a given set of facts. This fourth prerequisite appears to engage a series of issues which reach beyond its initial proposition and which we will discuss. Six aspects of this requirement can be identified:

1. There must be a capable grantor.
2. There must be a capable grantee.
3. The right claimed must be sufficiently certain.
4. The right must not impose a positive burden on the servient owner.

---

[18] *Moody*, 266.   [19] M. McClean, 'The Nature of an Easement' (1966) 5 West LR 32, 61.

5. The right must, generally, fall within a type recognized as capable of giving rise to an easement.

6. The right must not amount to possession of the servient land.

10.3.4.1 There must be a capable grantor

There must be someone who has legal capacity and an estate from which the grant of an easement can arise. This means someone in possession of an estate which is to become the servient tenement.

10.3.4.2 There must be a capable grantee

There must be someone to whom an easement can be granted. This means an individual in possession of an estate which is to become the dominant tenement.

10.3.4.3 The right claimed must be sufficiently certain

This requirement is not confined to easements, of course, and applies equally to all propri-etary rights and indeed to all legal rights and obligations. The justification is self-evident. It is important that the dominant landowner is able to ascertain the scope of the right and also that the servient landowner is aware of the obligations burdening their land. It is vital that there is sufficient certainty, clarity, and definition of the right conferred. This is particularly important because easements enjoy proprietary status and can bind third parties. There is, as Gray and Gray note, therefore a 'heightened emphasis on rigorous definitional clarity'.[20] The more 'vague and wide'[21] the right, the less likely it will be that an easement is generated. By way of example, there is no general right to a view: *William Aldred's Case* (1610) or a general right to privacy; *Browne v Flower* (1911). There is no right to uninterrupted light but there may be a right to light flowing through a particular window: *Easton v Isted* (1903).

10.3.4.4 The right must not impose a positive burden on the servient owner

An easement must not require the servient landowner to do any positive act but merely to permit the dominant landowner to enjoy the right conferred without obstruction. The servient owner cannot be required to undertake positive obligations such as repair or main-taining drain pipes or road surfaces: *Duke of Westminster v Guild* (1985). As regards ease-ments of water, this means that the servient landowner can only be expected not to interfere with the supply rather than being subject of a positive obligation to ensure that supply: *Schwann v Cotton* (1916); *Rance v Elvin* (1985).[22] In *Rance*, the claimant argued he enjoyed a right over the defendant's land whereby the defendant was obliged to supply water. The defendant argued (and succeeded at first instance) this could not be an easement as it in-volved a positive obligation. The claimant's appeal was, however, allowed. The court held

---

[20] Gray and Gray, *Elements of Land Law*, [5.1.41].   [21] Evershed MR in *Re Ellenborough Park*.
[22] The same is true of the supply of electricity: *Duffy v Lamb* (1998).

that (1) the claimant enjoyed a right to uninterrupted water that came via the pipes from the defendant's land—this was a negative obligation (i.e. obligation on defendant not to obstruct the water) and could amount to an easement; (2) as to the claimant's alleged right to the supply of water, this could not amount to an easement but the court found an implied contract under which the claimant would pay the defendant for any water consumed. *Rance* demonstrates a workaround to the 'no positive burden rule'. There are other examples of case law exceptions, in particular concerning the right to have the servient land fenced or to keep a wall in repair. In *Crow v Wood* (1971) and *Jones v Price* (1965) easements were recognized despite positive obligations on the servient owner. Equally, in *Regency Villas* (which we discussed in 10.3.3.4), the Supreme Court held that the fact the Park owners would be responsible for the maintenance of recreational facilities did not preclude the finding of an easement as to exercise of recreational rights over those facilities by timeshare owners. Why? Well, the court argued that an easement could be recognized here because there had been no positive, legal obligation undertaken by the Park owners to take positive action under the conveyance. Is this a convincing argument or a judicial sleight of hand? Does *Regency Villas* signal the slow death of the 'no positive burdens rule' or another judicial exception? In any event, as things stand, the rule against positive burdens on the servient owner remains intact (if undermined by the court in *Regency Villas*).

By way of brief diversion, on the issue of whether a positive obligation to maintain a fence exits as an easement, this question has been somewhat thrust back into the limelight by the recent case of *Churston Golf Club Ltd v Haddock* (2019). *Churston* concerned a golf club that was the tenant of land which neighboured a farm leased by Mr Haddock. In a conveyance in 1972 the former owners of the golf club had sold the land to the local authority. Clause 2 of the conveyance provided that the local authority and all those deriving title under it covenanted to maintain and 'forever hereafter keep in good repair' a fence along stipulated boundaries with the neighbouring land. Mr Haddock wished to have the fence maintained and issued proceedings against the local authority and the golf club. He argued that his farming business had been impacted by the poor maintenance of the fencing and sought damages of up to £200,000. At first instance, the judge found that clause 2 did not merely create a covenant to fence the land but a fencing easement which burdened the golf club. The High Court agreed that an expressly granted fencing easement had been created. In the Court of Appeal, two issues were argued: (1) did clause 2 create a fencing easement or was it simply a positive covenant to fence; (2) was it even possible to create a fencing easement by express grant? Allowing the appeal, Patten LJ confirmed there was no justification for construing clause 2 as anything other than a positive covenant to fence which was incapable of binding successors in title without a chain of indemnity covenants. The 1972 conveyance had been drafted professionally and the words should be given their clear and conventional meaning. It was a covenant and not an easement. Given no easement arose, Patten LJ refused (rather frustratingly) to rule on whether a fencing easement could be created by express grant. Instead, the court noted the decision in *Crow* (where a grant of a fencing easement was found), holding that 'fencing easements have a long history but an uncertain legal basis'. Any decision on the issue, however, should be confined to a case where it was essential to the outcome. Patten LJ repeated the 'no positive obligations' rule for easements and indicated his view that obligations to fence do not sit comfortably within the essential characteristics of easements. Therefore, while not settling the problem of whether positive fencing easements should exist and can be expressly granted, the Court of Appeal nevertheless suggests that fencing obligations can readily (and more faithfully) arise as positive covenants and, further, emphasizes the importance of professional drafting of conveyances if parties are to avoid being fenced in (if you pardon the pun!).

Another case in which an easement was found to exist despite positive obligations on the servient landowner is *Liverpool City Council v Irwin* which shows us that positive obligations will not be fatal to the finding of an easement, in all the circumstances of the case:

KEY CASE *Liverpool City Council v Irwin* (1977)

Facts: Liverpool City Council were the owners of a block of flats. The defendant occupied one of the Council's flats as a tenant. The communal areas of the block had fallen into significant disrepair including the lifts, staircases, and rubbish chutes. The tenants enjoyed easements over these communal areas. A rent strike was organized and implemented by the tenants in response to the Council's refusal to repair. The Council sought to evict the defendant for non-payment of rent. The defendant counterclaimed for breach of an obligation to repair. Importantly, the tenancy agreement made no mention of any obligations on the Council to repair the flats.

Legal issue: Could the Council be subject to repair obligations in the absence of an express term in the tenancy agreement?

Judgment: The House of Lords held that, in the very particular circumstances of this case, the easements gave rise to an obligation on the part of the Council to maintain the common parts of the building to a reasonable standard.

Lord Wilberforce addressed directly the principle that easements cannot impose positive obligations:

> I accept, of course, the argument that a mere grant of an easement does not carry with it any obligation on the part of the servient owner to maintain the subject matter. The dominant owner must spend the necessary money, for example, in repairing a driveway leading to his house. And the same principles may apply where a landlord lets an upper floor with access by a staircase; responsibility for maintenance may well rest on the tenant. But there is a difference between that case and the case where there is an *essential means of access*, retained in the landlord's occupation, to units in a building of multi-occupation, for unless the obligation to maintain is, in a defined manner, placed upon the tenants, individually or collectively, the nature of the contract, and the circumstances, require that it be placed on the landlord.

Outside these case law exceptions, the rule still remains that where there is a right which imposes a positive burden on the servient landowner this will prevent the finding of an easement.

10.3.4.5 The right must, generally, fall within a type recognized as capable of giving rise to an easement

Whilst the categories of easements are not closed (*Jones v Price*) and the existing classes 'must alter and expand with changes that take place in the circumstances of mankind' (Lord St Leonard in *Dyce v Lady James Hay* (1852)), there is nevertheless a degree of reluctance from the courts to recognize new forms of easement—*Regency Villas* is a major exception here, of course. As a general rule, however, a right is likely to be accepted as giving rise to an easement only if it falls within a pre-existing class that has already been recognized as generating a valid easement. If a new form of easement is claimed, it appears that it must be argued as being in line with a previously recognized class if it is to be accepted. The court has shown itself particularly disinclined to recognize negative easements: *Phipps v Pears* (1965).[23]

10.3.4.6 The right must not amount to possession of the servient land

Easements by their very nature involve a limited right over the servient land. Where a right provides the dominant landowner with a significant measure of control or possession of the servient land, an easement will not arise. In *Re Ellenborough Park*, Evershed MR explained the principle by noting that an easement must, 'not amount to rights of occupation or . . . substantially deprive the owners of proprietorship or legal possession'. Whilst easy to state, determining what constitutes too great a measure of possession can be far less straightforward. As the Law Commission has noted:[24]

> [A]n easement is an interest in land, not an estate. If what the dominant owner can do on the servient land actually amounts to an ownership right . . . then it cannot be an easement. That much is clear. What is more difficult is to delineate precisely the point at which the dominant owner's rights can be said to be 'too much' to be merely an interest in land.

Clearly where the effect of a right is to exclude the servient owner, there will be little difficulty concluding that no easement is generated. The real challenge comes in those cases where the right falls short of this. On one level, every easement to some extent interferes with the servient landowner's enjoyment of their land and this only renders the tasks of drawing that dividing line more difficult. Decided case law offers some guidance here, though it can, at times, be tough to discern a single, coherent judicial approach. Chiefly, the battleground for this issue (often described as 'the ouster principle') has been cases concerning rights of storage and car parking.

In *Wright v Macadam* (1949) the right acquired by a tenant on renewal of a lease to store coal in a shed was capable of constituting an easement. In *Grigsby v Melville* (1972), however, a right of storage in a cellar beneath the servient land, accessible only through the dominant tenement, was not capable of constituting an easement as it amounted essentially to exclusive possession of the servient land. In *Copeland v Greenhalf*, the court was concerned with a purported easement of parking.

KEY CASE *Copeland v Greenhalf* (1952)

Facts: A wheelwright claimed to have acquired an easement by long user to park vehicles pending repair on a strip of land adjoining that of the claimant. The wheelwright had made use of the strip of land for over 50 years and on a regular basis.

Legal issue: Did the right constitute an easement or consist of too exclusive a use of the adjoining land?

         →

---

[23] In this case, a claim against the owner of a house that had been demolished for a right to be protected from the effects of weather failed.

[24] Law Commission Report No. 327, *Easements, Covenants and Profits à Prendre* (2011), [3.191].

➡

Judgment: Per Upjohn J, the right claimed was not capable of existing as an easement on the grounds that:

> the right claimed goes wholly outside any normal idea of an easement, that is, the right of the occupier or the occupier of a dominant tenement over a servient tenement. This claim . . . really amounts to a claim to joint user of the strip of land . . . he can leave as many or as few lorries there as he likes for as long as he likes, he may enter on it by himself, his servants and agents to do repair thereon. In my judgment, this is not a claim which can be established as an easement. It is virtually a claim to possession of the servient tenement, if necessary to the exclusion of the owner, or, at any rate, to a joint user. No authority has been cited to me which would justify the conclusion that a right of this wide and undefined nature can be the proper subject matter of an easement.

Upjohn J went on to suggest that a claim for adverse possession may have proved successful.

We could minimize the significance of the *Copeland* authority as being relevant only to easements of long user (so-called easements by prescription). Hill-Smith has, however, argued cogently that this argument is unsustainable and *Copeland* remains good authority in its broader sense.[25] In *Hair v Gillman* (2000), however, the right to park a car anywhere on a 'forecourt capable of taking two or three cars' did constitute an easement. The question, it seems, is very much one of degree.

Regarding the appropriate 'test' under the 'ouster principle', there are two leading authorities with each advancing a different stance and distinct take on the matter. First, the Court of Appeal in *Batchelor v Marlow* and, secondly, the Scottish House of Lords decision in *Moncrieff v Jamieson* (2007).

KEY CASE *Batchelor v Marlow* (2003)

Facts: Mr and Mrs Marlow, who ran a garage business, claimed an easement by prescription (long user) to park six cars on adjoining land owned by Mr Batchelor between the hours of 8.30 a.m. and 6.00 p.m. from Monday to Friday each week.

Legal issue: Was the right to park capable of forming an easement? Did the right fall foul of the 'ouster' principle?

Judgment: At first instance, the court held the right to park was capable of giving rise to an easement on the basis that the right was limited in time and was not, therefore, operating to the exclusion of Mr Batchelor. The Court of Appeal reversed the decision at first instance and applied the 'reasonable use' test as laid down by Paul Baker QC in *London & Blenheim Estates* according to which:

> The essential question is one of degree. If the right granted in relation to the area over which it is to be exercisable is such that it would leave the servient owner without any reasonable use of his land, whether for parking or anything else, it could not be an easement though it might be some larger or different grant.

➡

---

[25] A. Hill-Smith, 'Rights of Parking and the Ouster Principle after *Batchelor v Marlow*' [2007] Conv 223.

> →
>
> Relying on the *London & Blenheim Estates* 'reasonable use' test, the Court of Appeal held that the right enjoyed by Mr and Mrs Marlow was incapable of constituting an easement as it deprived Mr Batchelor of any reasonable use of his property.
>
> Tuckey LJ elaborated on this by adding:
>
> > If one askes the simple question: 'Would the appellant have any reasonable use of the land for parking? The answer, I think must be 'No'. He has no use at all during the whole of the time that parking space is likely to be needed. But if one asks the question whether the appellant has any reasonable use of the land for any other purpose, the answer is even clearer. His right to use his land is curtailed altogether for intermittent periods throughout the week. Such a restriction would, I think, make his ownership of the land illusory.
>
> That Mr Batchelor could sell his land if he wished or use the land for parking at times other than those issued to Mr and Mrs Marlow, did not mean Mr Batchelor enjoyed 'reasonable use' of his land.

The decision in *Batchelor* appeared to cement the 'reasonable use' test but Lord Scott in the House of Lords in the Scottish case of *Moncrieff v Jamieson* engaged in an assault on and roundly rejected the *London Blenheim Estates/Batchelor* approach:[26]

> If an easement can be created by grant it can be acquired by prescription and I can think of no reason why, if an area of land can accommodate nine cars, the owner of the land should not grant an easement to park nine cars on the land. The servient owner would remain the owner of the land and in possession and control of it . . . How could it be said that the law would recognise an easement allowing the dominant owner to park five cars or six or seven or eight but not nine? I would, for my part, reject the test that asks whether the servient owner is left with any reasonable use of his land, and substitute it for a test which asks whether the servient owner retains possession and, subject to the reasonable exercise of the right in question, control of the servient land.

Lord Neuberger admitted to seeing 'considerable force' in Lord Scott's views and acknowledged that if Lord Scott's test was accepted as the appropriate one, *Batchelor* must be wrongly decided. It was, however, not necessary for the House of Lords to decide the point in order to dispose of the appeal before it and therefore the *Batchelor* authority remained untouched. Comparing the two approaches, we can see that the *Batchelor* 'reasonable use' test operates more strictly against those claiming a right as an easement than the Lord Scott 'possession and control' test which leans more favourably towards a claimant.

As to which test ought to be applied as a matter of strict precedent, the court in *Virdi v Chana* (2008) and in *Kettel v Bloomfold Ltd* (2012) concluded that it was bound by the Court of Appeal in *Batchelor*. Nevertheless, in spite of accepting the 'reasonable use' test as the applicable principle, the court in both cases found, in any event, that the right claimed did not deprive the servient landowner of reasonable use of their land. The recent case law indicates a move away from a stricter application of the test towards a far more lenient, claimant focus. Thus, in *Virdi*, a right to park a car in a single space was capable of constituting an easement notwithstanding that the servient owner could clearly not park in it while it was being used by the dominant landowner. The court held that the servient owner

---

[26] *Moncrieff v Jamieson*, [47].

retained reasonable use of the land as it was able to select the surface material from which the car parking space was constructed and, in addition, was able to choose the planting arrangements around the space.

In *Kettel*, the court again noted that a right to parking did not deprive the servient owner of reasonable use of the land as that owner retained the right to use the space beneath the car parking space for pipelines and the airspace above the space could be utilized as well as the car parking space itself when not being used by the dominant landowner. *Virdi* and *Kettel* are significant decisions in that they indicate the willingness and, perhaps, the inventiveness of the court to circumvent the strictness of the *Batchelor* 'reasonable use' test.[27] These cases provide a further example of the inherent flexibility in this fourth 'capable of grant' requirement from *Re Ellenborough Park*.

The so-called 'ouster principle' has unsurprisingly attracted comment from the Law Commission as well as the academic community. Luther,[28] for example, has argued that the courts should be less concerned with what the servient landowner cannot do on their own land but rather with the positive attributes of the right claimed which 'must be easier [for the court] than to assess its negative impact' on the servient landowner. The Law Commission in its 2011 Report into the law of easements, covenants, and profits has recommended the abolition of the 'ouster principle' and that the decision in *Batchelor* be reversed by statute. In the view of the Commission:[29]

> It is hard to see that the principle is particularly useful. Easements will not, of course, normally deprive the servient owner of any reasonable use of the servient land, but if the parties wish to make such an arrangement (without conferring exclusive possession) it is hard to see why they should not do so.

Finally, in an interesting article, Xu argues that in effect the courts have already abolished the ouster principle in relation to car parking but that its retention can serve a purpose in affording the courts discretion in non-parking cases:[30]

> The ouster principle is highly useful and flexible tool in the hand of the court, allowing some intensive-use easements while denying others. Of course, uncertainty is unavoidable with any flexible test . . . in the realm of car parking, the ouster principle should be abolished, either in substance or formally . . . in recognition of the social demand and commercial reality. On the other hand, the wholesale abolition of the principle in all contexts seems unnecessary, excessive and potentially damaging to too much of the established property law.

10.3.5 The extent of the grant of an easement: The rule in *Harris v Flower*

In the previous sections, we have explored the essential characteristics of easements without which a right cannot amount to an easement. In this section we explore what we might call 'the extent of grant' question: Figure 10.5.

---

[27] There are evident echoes of this more generous approach in *Wright* where the court may have felt sympathy towards the tenant of an unscrupulous landlord.

[28] P. Luther, 'Easements and Exclusive Possession' (1996) 16 LS 51, 62.

[29] Law Commission Report No. 327, [3.207].

[30] L. Xu, 'Easement of Car Parking: The Ouster Principle Is Out but the Problems May Aggravate' [2012] Conv 291, 301.

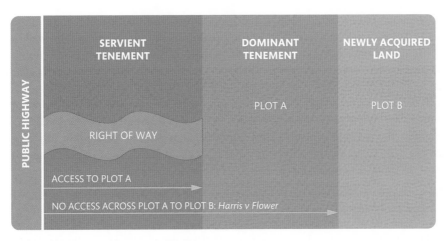

Figure 10.5 The rule in *Harris v Flower* (1904)

In Figure 10.5, a dominant landowner (owner of Plot A), who enjoys a right of way over the servient land in order to access her plot, later acquires additional land adjacent to the dominant land (Plot B). A simple but important question emerges: is the dominant landowner able to exercise the easement for the benefit of that newly acquired land, Plot B? This is where the 'rule in *Harris v Flower*' comes in.

Under the rule in *Harris v Flower*, the dominant landowner is *not* able to exercise the easement for the benefit of the additional land and, if it is so exercised, may very well commit a trespass to the servient land. Romer LJ in *Harris v Flower* explained that:[31]

> [I]f a right of way be granted for the enjoyment of Close A, the grantee because he owns or acquires Close B cannot use the way in substance for passing over the Close A to Close B . . .

Harris v Flower makes plain that a dominant landowner acquiring additional land is not permitted to exercise a right of way in favour of the newly acquired land by walking across the servient land and onto the new plot. In *Das v Linden Mews* (2002), the rule in *Harris v Flower* was considered in a slightly different scenario. In *Das*, several mews houses in London enjoyed access along a privately owned street. Two of the homeowners acquired parcels of land at either end of the street for the purpose of parking their cars. The servient landowner (i.e. the owner of the street) succeeded in arguing that, under the *Harris v Flower* rule, the servient land could not be used in order to reach the newly acquired land to park cars. Importantly, the rationale for the *Harris v Flower* rule is not excessive user or 'ouster' (as discussed in section 10.3.4.6) but rather that the new exercise of the easement falls outside the terms of the original grant of the easement.

Where it can be established that the use of the right for the additional land falls *within* the terms of the original grant and is 'merely ancillary' to the use of the dominant land, the rule in *Harris v Flower* will not operate. This ancillary use principle has been examined in a series of decisions which are not always easy to reconcile.

---

[31] *Harris v Flower*, 132.

In *National Trust v White* (1987), the High Court held that use of a right of way in order to access a car park located outside the dominant land by the public wishing to visit the dominant land was regarded as ancillary to the enjoyment of the dominant land. This use fell within the terms of the grant and therefore outside the *Harris v Flower* rule.

In *Peacock v Custins* (2002), Peacock accessed a parcel of land 'the red land' via a right of way over Custin's property 'the yellow strip'. Peacock had acquired another parcel of land adjacent to 'the red land', 'the blue land', and wished to exercise the right of way (once or twice per year) to access this additional land. This claim failed. The Court of Appeal considered the broader rationale for the *Harris v Flower* rule noting:[32]

> The authorities indicate that the burden on the owner of the servient tenement is not to be increased without his consent. But burden in this context does not refer to the number of journeys or the weight of vehicles. Any use of the way is, in contemplation of law, a burden and one must ask whether the grantor agreed to the grantee making use of the way for that purpose.
>
> . . . [T]he grantor did not authorize the use of the way for the purpose of cultivating the blue land. This cannot sensibly be described as ancillary to the cultivation of the red land.

In *Macepark (Whittleberry) Ltd v Sargeant (No. 2)* (2003) the High Court sought to rationalize the conflicting authorities on the operation of the ancillary use principle. A hotel enjoyed a right of way across adjacent land. The hotel sought to argue that its guests should be able to make use of the right of way and then follow a route through a piece of woodland close by to access directly the Silverstone racecourse. The claim failed as the use of the right of way would offer a commercial benefit to the hotel but also the owners of the woodland (who could charge for the shortcut to the racecourse) and Silverstone itself. Gabriel Moss QC concluded that the *Harris v Flower* and ancillary use principles operated as follows:

- Use of an easement exercised over additional, non-dominant land will fall within the scope of the original grant and be ancillary if the use is not 'in substance' for the benefit of that additional land.
- Not 'in substance' for the benefit of that additional land means either that:
  (i) there is no benefit provided to that additional, non-dominant land, or
  (ii) the extent of the use of the easement for the benefit of the additional, non-dominant land is 'insubstantial' so that, in essence, the use remains for the benefit of the dominant land.
- 'Benefit' includes use of the easement to make a profit from the additional, non-dominant land or extracting other 'commercial value'.

In the case of *Gore v Naheed* (2017), the Court of Appeal revisited the controversial 'rule in *Harris v Flower*'. The court did not recast the law but the case is useful as a further example of how the 'extent of grant' question is resolved in a distinct factual nexus; namely, a case involving access to a garage:

---

[32] *Peacock v Custins*, 1824.

> ### KEY CASE *Gore v Naheed* (2017)
>
> **Facts:** Mr Gore owned a property, the Granary, and the Naheeds owned the neighbouring land from which they ran a business. By virtue of a 1921 conveyance, the Granary benefited from a right of way over the driveway of the neighbouring land for the purposes of loading and unloading and 'for all purposes connected with the use and occupation' of the land. Mr Gore used the driveway, however, additionally to access a garage that he also owned and which was adjacent to the Granary. Vehicles delivering goods to the Naheeds' premises often blocked the driveway.
>
> **Legal Issue:** Was Mr Gore's access to his garage within the scope of the original 1921 grant of the easement so that he was entitled to an injunction to prevent the vehicular obstruction?
>
> **Judgment:** At first instance, it was held that the rights granted under the 1921 conveyance included a right of way over the driveway for the purposes of accessing and parking in the garage. The injunction was granted in Mr Gore's favour with conditions that the Naheeds could park vehicles on the driveway for a maximum of 20 minutes for unloading goods. Mr Gore also received damages. The Naheeds appealed arguing that, under the rule in *Harris v Flower*, use of the driveway for parking in the garage fell outside the scope of the original grant of the easement and that, in any event, only allowing the Naheeds a maximum of 20 minutes to unload goods was unreasonable and should be set at two hours. Patten LJ delivering the sole judgment held:
>
> 1. The judge had been entitled to find that access to the garage was ancillary to use of the Granary (the dominant land). Parking in the garage was not to be regarded as use of the garage in its own right independent of the dominant land. The use therefore fell within the terms of the original grant which was wide enough to include access to the garage for parking in connection with the residential use of the Granary.
>
> 2. There were no grounds on which to interfere with the judge's selection of 20 minutes as the maximum duration for the Naheeds' delivery vehicles to obstruct the driveway as per the injunction granted. Neither side had disputed this duration at the time of the judgment.
>
> Patten LJ did note, however, that the outcome would have been different and access to the garage would not have fallen within the scope of the original grant, 'if the garage were let to or used by a third party separately from the occupation of the Granary.' This serves as a reminder that the original grant should be read very closely as its construction will be central to the court's judgment on the issue of extent of grant.

In *Parker v Roberts* (2019), again the court urged a close reading and careful construction of the original conveyance granting the easement. Mr Roberts had planning permission to build a house on a plot which had been created by carving off part of the garden of his present home, No. 40. So that he could access the new house, he needed to use a private road over which he already enjoyed a right of way. The road was owned by his neighbours, the Parkers, who also used the road to access their home. The right of way had been expressly granted in a conveyance in 1968 to Mr Roberts' predecessor, 'for all purposes connected with the present and every future use of the land hereby transferred.' The Parkers argued that the use of the right of way to access this new plot fell outside the terms of the original grant as it could not be considered part of the 'land hereby transferred' under the 1968 conveyance. Mr Roberts argued that a common sense reading of the conveyance led to the conclusion that the new plot would be covered by the terms of the grant. The trial judge held that Mr Roberts could use the easement to access the new plot. The Parkers were successful in their appeal to the Court of Appeal. Having construed the 1968 convey-ance closely and criticizing the opaque drafting of it, the court concluded that the 1968 conveyance intended to grant the right of way to No.40 only. Once the new plot was hived off from No. 40, any ancillary use evaporated. The right of way granted under the 1968 con-veyance did not benefit the new plot and Mr Roberts' construction project was therefore scuppered. Equally, there was no basis on which an easement could be implied either by necessity or common intention. Only in exceptional circumstances would the court imply an easement that would contradict the terms of an expressly-negotiated conveyance.

The *Harris v Flower* rule has been heavily criticized—for example, by Paton and Sea-bourne, who assert that its application 'produces some odd doctrinal consequences' and introduces 'guilt by intention' whereby a lawful exercise of an easement becomes unlawful where the dominant landowner *intends* to exercise the right to access an additional parcel of land.[33] Paton and Seabourne recommend modifying and relaxing the rule in *Harris v Flower* by drawing on the principle of excessive user:[34]

> As a controlling principle, excessive user is clearly related to the law of nuisance, in which the courts are more accustomed to balancing the competing activities, rights and convenience of neighbours . . . a court considering a claim of excessive user can have regard to the likely duration and nature of the proposed user, and the likelihood and severity of any actual or threatened damage, and can impose temporary or permanent conditions/restrictions on any relief granted . . . So long as the proposed additional activity bears some connection to the original dominant tenement, and does not generate excessive user or damage, the servient owner is protected.

So far in this chapter, we have concerned ourselves with the nature and essential qualities or characteristics which signal that a right is *capable* of constituting an easement. Recall, in Figure 10.3, we saw that satisfaction of these essential characteristics is just the first step in our analysis. We must now move to consider whether an easement has, *in fact*, been cre-ated, the particular modes of creation of easements, and the consequences of this for third parties.

10.4 The creation of easements

10.4.1 Overview

Easements can be created in a variety of different ways. They can be expressly or impliedly granted or reserved and they can be presumed from long user (we call this 'prescription'). In addition, they may arise through operation of the doctrine of proprietary estoppel[35] or by statute. The particular method by which the easement is created is important. It is important because it determines whether the easement is *legal* or *equitable* in nature. We discuss the implications of the legal/equitable distinction for easements in section 10.5. Wrapping your head around these different methods for the creation of easements can be one of the more challenging aspects in the law of easements, but Figure 10.6, which sets out

---

[33] E. W. Paton and G. C. Seabourne, 'Can't Get There from Here? Permissible Use of Easements after *Das*' [2003] Conv 127.   [34] Ibid., 134.   [35] We explored estoppel in Chapter 8.

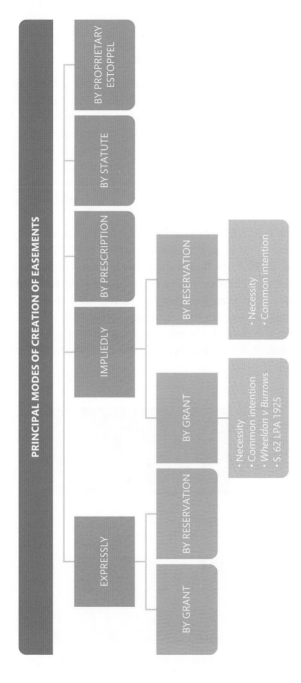

Figure 10.6 Modes of creation of easements

the principal ways easements are created, will help you to get to grips with this. It may take a few return visits before the material settles with you. We just noted that easements can be 'granted' and can be 'reserved'. Let's begin by considering what we mean by these terms as it is important that you understand the difference between the two.

10.4.2 Grant and reservation of an easement

The essence of the distinction between an easement by grant and an easement by reservation turns on the person in whose favour the easement is created. Let's unpack this a little further. Imagine a scenario in which Anita owns a large plot of land. Anita decides to subdivide the land into two plots: Plot 1 and Plot 2. She intends to remain the owner of Plot 1 but wants to sell Plot 2 to Bertie. On the sale of Plot 2 to Bertie, Anita may *grant* to Bertie, as part of the conveyance, an easement—for example, a right of way over her land. We say this easement has been 'effected by grant' or, simply, that the easement was *granted* to Bertie. The key here is that it is Bertie who takes the benefit of the easement: see Figure 10.7.

Now, let's change the facts a little to take a slightly different scenario. Here, Anita owns two plots of land (Plots 1 and 2) and intends to dispose of Plot 2 by selling it to Bertie. Whilst Anita wants to sell Plot 2 to Bertie, she wants to retain for herself the ability to access Plot 1 by walking across Plot 2 even after Bertie becomes the freehold owner of Plot 2. To achieve this, upon the conveyance of Plot 2 to Bertie, Anita *reserves* a right of way for the benefit of herself and Plot 1 which she retains: see Figure 10.8.

With the terminology explained, we need to examine in greater detail the principal methods by which easements are created, starting with expressly created easements.

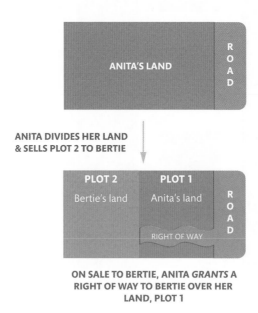

Figure 10.7 Grant of an easement

Figure 10.8 Reservation of an easement

10.4.3 **Expressly created easements**

By far the most straightforward and most frequently encountered mode of creation of easements is express grant or express reservation.

10.4.3.1 **Express grant**

This is where express and appropriate words are used in a deed to create an easement. Recall that s. 52 of the LPA 1925 requires that all conveyances of land or interests in land must be made by deed. An express grant of an easement will usually be incorporated into deeds of transfer (i.e. the creation of the easement forms part of the formal documentation conveying or transferring a freehold estate to a purchaser, for example). It need not be a transfer of the freehold, however, and easements routinely arise expressly where a lease is granted to a tenant. A classic example of express grant can be seen operating in the house-building trade. Imagine a property developer building a housing estate. When each plot of land is sold to a purchaser, the developer will expressly grant easements of drainage, electricity, gas, and rights of way to all those purchasing property. This will be by express grant contained within the deeds transferring the freehold. There is no set or special form of words required for creation by express grant (*Russell v Watts* (1885)) but clarity of drafting is important if disputes further down the line are to be avoided on the precise scope and extent of the easements granted.

10.4.3.2 **Express reservation**

Again, express reservation of an easement involves the use of express and appropriate words in a deed; usually forming part of the conveyance or transfer of land: s. 52 of the LPA 1925. As with express grant, no special form of words is required and clauses such as 'this transfer is subject to a right of way' will suffice to expressly reserve an easement for the benefit of the retained land: *Pitt v Buxton* (1970). As we will discover in section 10.5, the status and degree of formality of the document in which the easement is granted or reserved (i.e. whether it is a valid deed or a mere contract) will determine whether the easement is legal in nature or equitable only.

10.4.4 Impliedly created easements

Easements can also be created in a situation where there are no express words, where there is no express grant, nor any express reservation in a deed of conveyance or transfer of land. Indeed, there may be circumstances where in spite of the absence of express words, the court is prepared to imply the creation of an easement. This may arise where a plot of land is being conveyed to a purchaser or where a larger plot is subdivided and part of the land is being conveyed. Alternatively, an easement may also be impliedly created where a lease is granted out of freehold estate or where an existing tenant purchases the freehold from her landlord. This implication of an easement arises either by implied grant or by implied reservation. It is important to note that the easement is implied *into a document*. This means that if the conditions for implication are met, the easement will be implied into a deed of conveyance, for example, on the transfer of land. The status of the easement created (legal or equitable) will be determined by the nature of the document into which it is implied: if implied into a deed or legal conveyance, the easement is legal; if implied into a contract or equitable conveyance, the easement will be equitable. Generally, however, implied easements are recognized as constituting legal easements.

As Figure 10.6 demonstrates, implied easements arise either by implied grant or implied reservation. Within this, there are four principal routes by which implied easements are created:

1. by necessity;
2. by common intention;
3. under the rule in *Wheeldon v Burrows*;
4. by operation of s. 62 of the LPA 1925.

As you will discover, there is a certain measure of overlap between these methods and, for this reason, the Law Commission has been particularly critical of this area of the law, emphasizing the 'complex matrix ... of rules' which have developed 'in piecemeal and uncoordinated fashion'.[36] Before proceeding to examine each implication route, it is worth pausing to consider the rationale for the implication of easements. Hopkins[37] has argued that the underlying logic of these modes of implication[38] derives from the principle of non-derogation from grant. Bowen LJ explained the principle of non-derogation in *Birmingham, Dudley and District Banking Co. v Ross* (1887) as follows:[39]

---

[36] Law Commission Consultation Paper No. 186, [4.109] and [4.99].
[37] N. Hopkins, *The Informal Acquisition of Rights in Land* (London: Sweet & Maxwell, 2000), 205.
[38] In particular, as to the first three listed methods of implication.
[39] *Birmingham, Dudley and District Banking Co. v Ross*, 313.

A grantor having given a thing with one hand, is not to take away the means of enjoying it with the other.

In essence, where a landowner transfers land to another (the transferee) and that land is to be put to a particular purpose, the transferor should not be permitted to use their land to defeat the transferee's purpose. Whilst the principle of non-derogation provides one justification for implication, there are others: most notably that all four methods of implication of easements can be said to respond to the intentions of the parties in varying degrees. As we proceed, see how far you agree with this intention-based approach. Alternatively, could it be said that easements are implied on policy grounds in order that the utility and value of the land in question is not stymied?[40] In fact, as we will explore later in this chapter, the Law Commission advocates that *utility* be the central focus of proposals for reform to implied easements.[41]

10.4.4.1 Implied easements of necessity

An easement can be impliedly granted and, in rare cases, impliedly reserved where an easement is necessary for the land in question to be capable of use. The classic example is of land which, without the implication of an easement, would be landlocked and would therefore be inaccessible. In this case, a right of way may be implied into, for example, a conveyance transferring the relevant land. It is clear from the case law that necessity will not, however, be lightly inferred and certainly an easement will not be implied simply to ensure that access to a parcel of land is made more convenient. Stirling J in *Union Lighterage Co. v London Graving Dock Co.* (1902) underscored the exceptional nature of implication by necessity:[42]

> [A]n easement of necessity . . . means an easement without which the property retained cannot be used at all, and not merely necessary to the reasonable enjoyment of the property.

As Stirling J indicates, implication flows from necessity and not from want of convenience. Where, for example, a means of access to land does exist (however inconvenient or undesirable), an easement of necessity will not be implied: *Manjang v Drammeh* (1991). In *Manjang*, the court refused to imply an easement of necessity (a right of way) as the claimant was able to access its land via boat along a river. In *Re MRA Engineering* (1988), the court refused to imply an easement to permit vehicular access to land where land could be reached on foot. As confirmed in the recent decision of *Walby v Walby* (2012), the test of necessity is a stringent one as to what is strictly necessary for the essential use of the land. An easement will only be implied where, without it, the land could not be used at all. One example of an apparently more lenient application of the test is *Sweet v Sommer*.

---

[40] Easements of necessity offer the clearest example of the tension between the parties' intentions and public policy considerations.

[41] This is also under serious discussion in Australia: F. Burns, 'Easement and Servitudes Created by Implied Grant, Implied Reservation or Prescription and Title-by-Registration Systems' in M. Dixon (ed.), *Modern Studies in Property Law*, Vol. 5 (Oxford: Hart, 2009).

[42] *Union Lighterage*, 573.

KEY CASE *Sweet v Sommer* (2004)

Facts: The Sweets owned land known as Forge Meadow which neighboured that of the defendants, the Sommers. The only means of vehicular access to the land was by crossing land owned by the Sommers known as Old Forge Yard. In 1988, both parcel of land had been owned by Mr Lovering who later transferred Old Forge Yard to himself and his wife. Due to an error in the transfer, no right of way was reserved to Mr and Mrs Lovering. Later in 1988, Mr Lovering sold Forge Meadow to Mr and Mrs Martin who ultimately sold the land to the Sweets. In the same year, the Sommers also purchased Old Forge Yard from the Loverings. The Sweets purchased an additional field adjacent to the Old Forge Yard believing that this gave them a right of way over the Sommer's land. Due to a series of conveyancing errors, the Sweets did not enjoy an effective, legal easement permitting access by vehicle to their land via Old Forge Yard.

Legal issue: Could the Sweets bypass the conveyancing errors by arguing that an easement of necessity was implied into the 1988 transfer to Mr and Mrs Lovering? The Sweets argued that their land was essentially landlocked (though there was access by foot) without an implied easement. Alternatively, could the Sweets rely on the doctrine of proprietary estoppel to bind the Sommers?

Judgment: There was evidence before the court that, theoretically, vehicular access to the Sweets' land was available but would require the demolition of a workshop on other land that all the parties to the original transfer had agreed should remain standing. The High Court held that an easement (right of way) was impliedly reserved at the time of the original transfer. It was obvious from the nature of the house and the circumstances of the grant that vehicular access was regarded as being necessary. The house was not capable of meaningful use without it. In addition, the Sweets were entitled to assert their right of way under the doctrine of proprietary estoppel. The Court of Appeal confirmed the High Court judgment though relied more heavily on the proprietary estoppel aspect.

Sweet is an important decision in several respects. First, it appears to provide an example of a more liberal approach to what constitutes 'necessity'. It seems that a right of way can be impliedly reserved even in circumstances where the land in question is not entirely inaccessible. Secondly, the decision appears to hold significance for the question of vehicular access in particular. In view of modern society's dependency on cars, the court has shown itself prepared to accept that land inaccessible to vehicles is not capable of meaningful use, even where other routes of access (by foot in *Sweet* itself) are theoretically possible. Finally, *Sweet* is one of only a small number of examples of implied *reservation* of an easement by necessity. *Sweet* can also be explained as a case of implication of an easement of common intention; the parties sharing an understanding of the purpose to which the land was to be put and vehicular accessary being necessary to realize this purpose (see section 10.4.4.2 on easements of common intention).

Regarding the rationale for implication, the Court of Appeal in *Adealon International Corp. Pty Ltd v Merton LBC* (2007) accepted that easements of necessity arise from the intention of the parties rather than on public policy grounds. This view is supported by dicta from Brightman LJ in the earlier case of *Nickerson v Barraclough* (1981).[43] There are certain consequences which flow from this. First, the focus on the parties' intentions means that an easement of necessity will not arise from adverse possession or from a case of compulsory

---

[43] In this case, an easement by necessity was implied where without this right of way over a bridge, the claimant's land was effectively landlocked.

purchase. Secondly, if there is evidence of a contrary intention then this must be weighed as part of the court's assessment and will surely prevent the implication of an easement by necessity. Certain commentators have argued against intention as the rationale of implication and advocate public policy as the more appropriate test. Bradbrook, for example, contends that the courts have leaned in favour of intention as the basis for implication merely 'due to the jurist tenancy . . . to treat all legal transactions as if they were based on contracts' and that accepting public policy as the basis of implication would liberalize the application of the law in this area making it more flexible and responsive.[44] Do you agree?

10.4.4.2 Implied easements of common intention

Easements can also be implied into a transfer conveyance, for example, to give effect to the common intention of the parties. Lord Parker in *Pwllbach Colliery Co. Ltd v Woodman* (1915)[45] identified two circumstances when an easement might be implied to give effect to comment intention:[46]

> The first is where the implication arises because the right in question is necessary for the enjoyment of some other right expressly granted . . . [secondly] the law will readily imply the grant or reservation of such easements as may be necessary to give effect to the common intention of the parties . . . with reference to the manner or purposes in and for which the land granted or some land retained by the grantor is to be used . . . But it is essential for this purpose that the parties should intend that the subject matter of the grant or the land retained should be used in some definite and particular manner.

In *Pwllbach*, the court held that an easement of common intention will therefore be implied where (1) it is necessary for the enjoyment of a right that has been expressly granted; or (2) where it is necessary for the dominant landowner to make use of the land for a definite and particular purpose where the land was sold for that stated purpose.

An example of the first instance was given in *Pwllbach* itself. Lord Parker noted that, where a right to draw water from a spring was expressly granted, an easement of common intention (right of way) might be implied to allow the grantee of the right to access the land to draw that water. A good example of the second instance is the decision in *Wong v Beaumont Property Trust Ltd* (1965).[47] In *Wong*, a lease was taken out in respect of a basement for the purposes of running a Chinese restaurant. The terms of the lease confirmed the land would be used for this purpose and required that Mr Wong eliminate all odours, comply with health and safety legislations, and otherwise not commit a nuisance. Mr Wong requested that the landlord replace the existing ventilation pipe with a larger and more efficient flue. The landlord refused. The court was prepared to imply an easement under which

---

[44] A. J. Bradbrook, 'Access to Landlocked Land: A Comparative Study of Legal Solutions' (1983–85) 10 Syd LR 39.

[45] The claimant butcher brought a nuisance claim against his neighbour, the Pwllbach Colliery, for dust emitted as a result of their mining operation produced by screening apparatus. The question arose as to whether Pwllbach enjoyed an implied easement to defeat the nuisance claim. No easement arose neither by necessity (the screening was not strictly necessary for the mining to take place) nor by common intention (there was no mutual intention that screening take place).   [46] *Pwllbach*, 646.

[47] You should note that the case was, strictly speaking, decided on the basis of necessity but is perhaps better understood on common intention grounds.

Mr Wong was permitted to erect a ventilation duct in order that he comply with the terms of the lease. Applying a common intention analysis, we can say that the purpose to which the land was to be put was defined and particularized (a restaurant) at the time the lease was granted and the ventilation duct was necessary for this defined purpose to be carried out.

In *Stafford v Lee*, Nourse LJ again examined closely what is required for a claim to an implied easement of common intention.

KEY CASE *Stafford v Lee* (1993)

Facts: In 1955 by deed of gift, an area of woodland was conveyed by Mr Lee's predecessor in title to Mr Stafford's predecessor in title. While the deed described the land as fronting a private roadway, it contained no express grant of a right of way by which to access the land. Mr Stafford, who later acquired the land, wished to build a house on the woodland and claimed that an easement permitting vehicular and pedestrian access should be implied into the 1955 deed on the basis of common intention.

Legal issue: Mr Stafford argued that the parties to the 1955 conveyance shared a common intention that a house would be built on the woodland and that an easement should therefore be implied. Mr Lee conceded that a right to use the roadway had passed under the 1955 deed but argued that its use was limited to purposes necessary for the enjoyment of the land as a woodland (as the land was being used in 1955) and not for house-building.

Judgment: Nourse LJ identified the two 'hurdles' that needed to be overcome before an easement of common intention could be implied:

> He must establish a common intention as to some definite and particular user. Then he must show that the easements he claims are necessary to give effect to it.

Nourse LJ noted that all the circumstances surrounding the conveyance had to be taken into account and that the question was not how the land was to be enjoyed in 1955 at the date of transfer but whether the parties to the deed had intended that the land be used for a definite and particular purpose. Importantly, the existence of this common intention was to be determined 'on the balance of probabilities'. Certainty was not required. A plan of the land in question which had been annexed to the deed was relied upon by the court to establish the parties' common intentions as to the envisaged use of the land. Relying on the plan (which depicted a plot adjoining two other plots on which dwellings had been constructed) and, on the balance of probabilities, the court found that the parties could only have intended that the land be used for the construction of another dwelling. No other intention could reasonably be imputed to them. The easement claimed by Mr Stafford was therefore necessary to give effect to that common intention and would be implied into the 1955 transfer.

Post-*Stafford*, we can summarize the law as follows. An easement by common intention will be implied where, *on the balance of probabilities* and *considering all circumstances* of the case:

- there is evidence of a common intention between the parties that the land was to be put to some definite and particular use or purpose, and

- an easement is necessary to give effect to that stated use or purpose.

A helpful example of how these *Stafford v Lee* criteria are applied is *Donovan v Rana* (2014). At auction, an owner of land (Mrs Donovan) sold an adjoining plot for the purposes of residential development. The transfer granted an express right of way over part of the seller's retained land (known as 'the blue land') 'for all purposes connected with the use and enjoyment of the property but not for any other purpose'. Mr and Mrs Rana were the successor in title to the original purchasers and built a house on the land. Without Mrs Donovan's permission, the Ranas allowed workmen to dig up the blue land to install and connect utilities to the mains service. Mrs Donovan claimed damages as a result of the works. The judge at first instance dismissed the damages claim holding that it was the common intention of the parties to the original transfer that it would be used to build a house in a residential area and that this property would require modern facilities connected to the mains service. In the Court of Appeal, Vos LJ who gave the leading judgment, held than an easement by common intention could be implied. Following the approach laid down in *Pwllbach* and *Stafford* as: (1) the parties to the original transfer must be taken to have intended that the building of a dwelling-house on the plot would have included connection to mains utility services across the blue land (an obvious route of access); and (2) the implied easement was necessary to achieve the parties intended purpose of building a dwelling. The implied easement of common intention therefore allowed the Ranas as successors of the original transferee to install and maintain connections to the utility mains services.

There is evidently overlap between implied easements of necessity and those implied to give effect to the common intentions of the parties: the case of *Sweet* can be explained on either basis. Perhaps unhelpfully, it will not have escaped your notice that the word 'necessary' is used repeatedly in the case law surrounding implied easements. What is clear, however, is that implication of an easement into a transfer on the grounds of common intention enjoys a far greater scope than does implication strictly of necessity. Lawson has examined the overlap between necessity and common intention and argues that easements by common intention under the *Pwllbach* authority should in fact be seen as easements by necessity:[48]

> The distinction between easements of necessity and the *Pwllbach* intended easements is frequently clouded by a judicial tenancy to refer to both as easements of necessity. It may be that, in any event, it is a distinction without a difference . . . it is arguable that, as the courts are not prepared to imply a common intention to use the land in a specific way, they will be able to find such an intention whenever landlocked plot is conveyed—thus eclipsing the traditional easements of necessity. The view that the easement of necessity, at least in relation to implied grant, has been subsumed within the *Pwllbach* intended easement is very attractive. Both are driven by the policy that land should not become sterile but be used to its full potential.

10.4.4.3 Implied easements under the rule in *Wheeldon v Burrows*

The rule in *Wheeldon v Burrows* (1879) can prove challenging to grasp when first introduced to it. Do not let this put you off. The rule operates in circumstances where an individual is selling or leasing part of their own land. If the conditions for the rule to operate are met, an easement will be implied into the conveyance and the purchaser or tenant will enjoy a right benefiting the land. The newly purchased/leased parcel of land becomes the dominant tenement and the land retained by the seller/landlord becomes the servient

---

[48] A. Lawson, 'Easements' in L. Tee (ed.), *Land Law: Issues, Debates, Policy* (Devon: Willan, 2002), 85.

tenement. Importantly, the rule in *Wheeldon v Burrows* operates only to *grant* easements. There can be no implied reservation under *Wheeldon*, as confirmed in *Peckham v Ellison* (1998). So, what is the rule?

Under the rule in *Wheeldon v Burrows*, when an individual conveys their own land to another (by way of sale or lease), there will be implied into that conveyance the grant of all **quasi-easements** exercised by the seller/landlord prior to the transfer. What is a quasi-easement? Quasi-easements are rights that would be easements but for the fact that the land in question is in common ownership. It is illogical to talk of enjoying an easement over land of which you are the freehold owner. Therefore, we call these rights quasi-easements. Essentially, we can say that the effect of the rule in *Wheeldon v Burrows* is that upon conveyance of land, quasi-easements enjoyed prior to the conveyance mature into

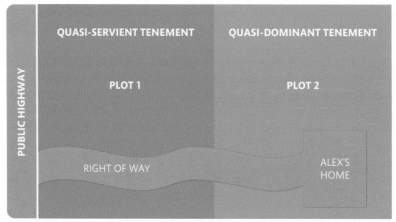

Stage 1: Alex exercises quasi-easement over his own land

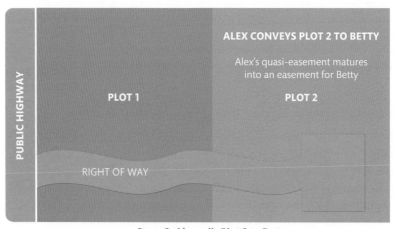

Stage 2: Alex sells Plot 2 to Betty

Figure 10.9 The rule in *Wheeldon v Burrows*

fully effective, fully fledged easements. The operation of the rule is best clarified by considering an example: Figure 10.9.

Alex owns two plots of land. Plot 1 is a field which adjoins the highway. Plot 2 consists of a house in which Alex lives. Alex crosses Plot 1 every day to gain access to his home. This right is 'in the nature of an easement' except that Alex is the owner of both Plot 1 and 2. We therefore call this a 'quasi-easement'. Alex cannot enjoy an easement over his own land. Alex subsequently decides to sell Plot 2 to Betty. On the transfer to Betty, under the *Wheeldon v Burrows* rule, the quasi-easement matures into a fully operative easement benefiting Plot 2 (the dominant tenement) and burdening Plot 1 (the servient land). The easement has been implied into the deed of conveyance transferring the land to Betty. Betty now enjoys a proprietary right and is able to exercise and enforce a right of way across Plot 1 to access her land without obstruction or interference from Alex.

As you might expect, there are limits placed on the rule in *Wheeldon v Burrows*. This is unsurprising given that the rule operates to impose proprietary burdens. The rule will, therefore, only operate where certain conditions are met. These conditions were laid down by Thesiger LJ in the case of *Wheeldon v Burrows* itself:[49]

> [I]n the case of a grant you may imply a grant of such continuous and apparent easements or, in other words, all those easements as are necessary to the reasonable enjoyment of the property conveyed, and have in fact been enjoyed during the unity of ownership, but that, with the exception . . . [that] you cannot imply a similar reservation in favour of the grantor of land.

Thesiger's LJ's language is less than clear and could certainly be phrased more lucidly. Nevertheless, the essential ingredients for the rule can be distilled into three conditions:

1. The transferor (seller/lessor or her agents) was using the quasi-easement for the benefit of the land at the time of the transfer.

2. The quasi-easement was 'continuous and apparent'.

3. In addition to the second condition, or in the alternative, the quasi-easement was reasonably necessary for the enjoyment of the land.

These conditions require some further elaboration.

The first requirement that the quasi-easement was in use at the time of the transfer is mostly self-explanatory and straightforward. It springs from the principle of non-derogation from grant: *Sovmots Investments Ltd v Secretary of State for the Environment* (1979) and acts as a brake to prevent the implication of easements that were either never used or were not for the benefit of the land. Where the quasi-easement was not in use at the time of transfer, the rule in *Wheeldon v Burrows* simply cannot apply: *Alford v Hannaford* (2011).

The second and third elements of the *Wheeldon v Burrows* rule have proved to be more contentious. This has stemmed from an ongoing debate as to whether the second and third aspects should be read as cumulative, alternative, or synonymous. Must the quasi-easement have been continuous, apparent, *and* be reasonably necessary for the enjoyment

---

[49] *Wheeldon v Burrows*, 58–9.

of the land for the rule to operate? Or, alternatively, will the rule in *Wheeldon v Burrows* apply where either element is satisfied? The case law is inconclusive on this question:

- Thesiger LJ in *Wheeldon v Burrows* itself appeared, unhelpfully, to leave open all potential interpretations.

- The case of *Millman v Ellis* (1996) lends support to the view that both elements must be satisfied as the elements are discussed at length as discrete and cumulative requirements.

- Peter Gibson LJ in *Wheeler v J. J. Saunders* (1996) was quite clear that the two elements were to be understood as synonymous based on Thesiger's use of the phrase 'or, in other words' when formulating the *Wheeldon v Burrows* rule:[50]

  > There have been some doubts as to whether the requirement that the easement should be continuous and apparent is an alternative to the requirement that the easement be necessary for the reasonable enjoyment of the property granted: see *Megarry & Wade, The Law of Real Property*, 5th ed. (1984), pp. 862–863. But to my mind it is tolerably clear from Thesiger L.J.'s introduction of the test of necessity by the words 'or, in other words' that he was treating the first requirement as synonymous with the second.

- Most recently in *Wood v Waddington* (2015), the Court of Appeal left the matter open by underlining the important role played by the requirement for 'reasonable necessity' but by concluding that whether the quasi-easement must also, additionally, be 'continuous and apparent' was 'less clear'. After *Wood* it seems, on balance, that the current weight of judicial opinion is leaning towards placing greater emphasis on the final element of Thesiger's test and far less emphasis on the continuous and apparent requirement.

Academic commentators are also divided on the matter. Douglas suggests both elements of the test offer different forms of evidence from which a court can attempt to ascertain the unexpressed intention of the transferor.[51] This suggests the elements should be understood as operating in the alternative and courts enjoy a discretion as to which of the two elements is applied on the particular facts of the case before them. Douglas explains:[52]

> [I]f an easement is 'reasonably necessary' then a reasonable grantee may have understood the grantor to have intended to grant the relevant easement so as to prevent the transaction producing a useless outcome; if there was a quasi-easement which was obvious on inspection (i.e. it was continuous and apparent) then this could create a reasonable expectation on the part of the grantee of its continuance after the grant.

Harpum, by contrast, argues effectively that each limb serves a distinct purpose and should therefore be seen as cumulative: one relates to 'discoverability' and the other derives from the principle of non-derogation.[53]

In view of the unresolved debate, as students of the subject, it is perhaps wise and best practice to proceed with caution and consider *all* three conditions for the operation of the rule. You should fully acknowledge, however, the continuing uncertainty that surrounds the

---

[50] *Wheeler*, 31.   [51] S. Douglas, 'Reforming Implied Easements' (2015) 131 LQR 251.   [52] Ibid., 256.
[53] C. Harpum, 'Easements and Centre Point: Old Problems Resolved in a Novel Setting' [1977] Conv 415, 422.

relationship between the three elements of Thesiger's test. Pragmatically, of course, in many cases, where the quasi-easement is found to be 'continuous and apparent', this will inevitably mean the right is also 'reasonably necessary' for the enjoyment of the land.

What are we to understand by the phrase 'continuous and apparent'? Let's consider each aspect separately. 'Continuous' derives from the French Civil Code[54] and is to be understood as requiring an *obvious and permanent* alteration to the land as opposed to repeated, continual use of a right. In other words, we can take the word 'continuous' as connoting that the quasi-easement is available for exercise if and when it is needed.

Perhaps more important is the second aspect: the requirement that the right be 'apparent'. For a right to be considered 'apparent' it must be discoverable on a reasonably careful inspection of the land: *Pyer v Carter* (1857). This will be satisfied, in most cases, by evidence of a visible, physical, non-transitory feature on the land such as a pathway or other road surface[55] which provides a tangible sign or marker of a right of way or right of access. In *Millman*, for example, this element was satisfied by evidence of visible signs of tarmac. The case of *Ward v Kirkland* offers a useful example of a case where a quasi-easement was considered not sufficiently 'apparent' for the rule in *Wheeldon v Burrows* to operate.

KEY CASE *Ward v Kirkland* (1967)

Facts: The Ward family owned a cottage on land adjoining farmland owned by the Kirklands. Some years previously, the two plots of land had been in common ownership. The walls of the cottage were positioned in such a way that they could only be maintained by entering the Kirklands' land. The Ward family (and their predecessors) had regularly entered the farmland in order to maintain the walls without objection.

Legal issue: Was the right exercised by the Ward family and their predecessors 'continuous and apparent' for the purposes of the rule in *Wheeldon v Burrows*?

Judgment: Ungoed-Thomas J noted that the words 'continuous' and 'apparent' should be read and understood together. On the facts, the right in question was certainly 'continuous' in that it had been used whenever the need arose. The issue was of discoverability of the right and the requirement that it be 'apparent.' Ungoed-Thomas J held that:

> the words 'continuous and apparent' seem to be directed to there being on the servient tenement a feature which would be seen on inspection and which is neither transitory nor intermittent, for example, drains, paths, as contrasted with the bowsprits of ships overhanging a piece of land.

Applying this to the present facts, the court held that there was no apparent, discoverable 'feature' on the servient land and, consequently, there was not a continuous and apparent easement within the requirements of *Wheeldon v Burrows*.

The third requirement that the right be 'reasonably necessary' for the enjoyment of the land should not be read as importing a strict test of necessity: *Millman*. Despite this

---

[54] A. W. B. Simpson, '*Wheeldon v Burrows* and the Code Civile' (1967) 83 LQR 240; *Suffield v Brown* (1864), per Lord Westbury.

[55] *Borman v Griffith* (1930) where there were visible signs of a roadway and the grant of an easement was therefore implied.

clarification, the precise scope of this requirement has not always proved easy to identify. In *Wheeler*, the claimants owned a farmhouse which had previously been in common ownership with the neighbouring property owned by the defendants. There were two routes of access to the farmhouse, one of which meant crossing the defendant's land. The court held that, in view of the availability of a passage to the farmhouse that did not involve crossing the defendant's land, a second route of access was not to be treated as 'reasonably necessary' for the enjoyment of the land. *Wheeler* can be contrasted with *Borman v Griffith* (1930) where a second route of access was found to be 'reasonably necessary' as it offered a significant additional advantage over the other available access point. This right of way claimed permitted a poultry trader to make use of heavy goods vehicles all year round which the other route could not support.

Three final points must be noted:

- Operation of the rule in *Wheeldon v Burrows* can be excluded by an express term in the conveyance: *Borman*. Indeed, it is now common conveyancing practice for this kind of exclusion to be included in any dealings where the rule may potentially apply. It is important, however, that clear and unambiguous wording is used if such an exclusion is to prove effective in preventing application of the *Wheeldon v Burrows* rule: *Millman*.

- As with all other modes of creation of easements discussed in this chapter, only rights capable of constituting easements by satisfying the essential characteristics identified in *Re Ellenborough Park* can be subject to the rule in *Wheeldon v Burrows*.

- Finally, whether the easement implied into the transfer or conveyance will be legal or equitable in nature is determined by the document into which it is implied. If there is a transfer (sale or lease) by means of a deed, the resulting implied easement will be legal. If the document is an enforceable written contract for a sale or a lease (i.e. not by deed), the easement will be equitable only: *Borman*. We will explore this further in section 10.5.

Figure 10.10 pulls all of these points together and depicts diagrammatically how the rule in *Wheeldon v Burrows* can be analysed.

Crucially, in view of the recent and important decision of the Court of Appeal in *Wood*, the need to resort to the rule in *Wheeldon v Burrows* appears to have been significantly curtailed. *Wood* is considered in detail in section 10.4.4.4.

10.4.4.4 Implied easements by operation of s. 62 of the LPA 1925

An easement may also be impliedly created under s. 62 of the LPA 1925. Section 62 operates in circumstances where a landowner sells or leases part of her land to another person. As you will discover, there are important similarities between the function of s. 62 and the rule in *Wheeldon v Burrows* but, despite this, the two methods of implied easement creation are (for now at least) distinct and should be seen as separate. Nourse LJ, for example, in *Platt* acknowledged the undeniable similarities but drew attention to the 'more extensive . . . effect in section 62 Law of Property Act 1925'.

How does s. 62 of the LPA 1925 operate? Let's first examine the terms of the provision itself:

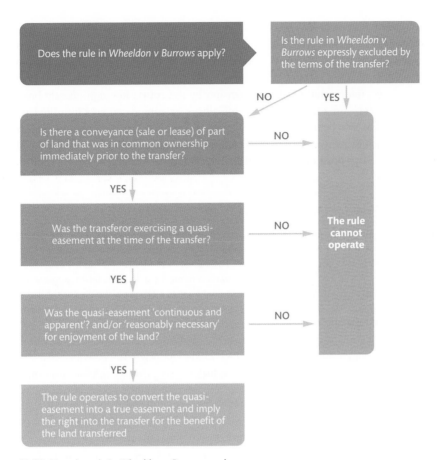

Figure 10.10 How the rule in *Wheeldon v Burrows* works

(1) A conveyance of land shall be deemed to include and shall by virtue of this Act operate to convey, with the land, all buildings, erections, fixtures, commons, hedges, ditches, fences, ways, waters, water-courses, liberties, privileges, *easements*, rights, and advantages whatsoever, appertaining or reputed to appertain to the land, or any part thereof, or, at the time of conveyance, demised, occupied, or enjoyed with, or reputed or known as part or parcel of or appurtenant to the land or any part thereof. [Emphasis added.]

It may not be immediately apparent how it is that this provision gives rise to the implied grant of easements. The provision was enacted chiefly as a word-saving measure under which 'general word clauses' would be implied into conveyances of land. The logic behind these clauses is that, on a conveyance (sale of land or grant of a lease), all rights attaching to the land conveyed would pass without the need to provide for this expressly for each and every right or interest.

Simply stated, the effect of s. 62 is that where there is a conveyance of land, the conveyance carries with it automatically all rights and benefits that are attached to the land conveyed. Any pre-existing easements benefiting the conveyed land will therefore automatically pass: *Graham v Philcox* (1984). Section 62 does not, however, operate to create an implied reservation: *Kent v Kavanagh* (2006). So far so straightforward. The impact of s. 62 is however far broader than this. We know that the provision does not only automatically pass pre-existing easements upon a conveyance but actually creates new easements. How does it do this? In essence, interpretation of the provision by the courts has significantly broadened its power and scope. In addition to implying all pre-existing easements into the legal conveyance, s. 62 has also been interpreted so as to elevate, convert, or transform pre-existing lesser rights such as mere permissions (licences) exercised over the land into fully effective legal easements. This position was established in *Wright*.[56]

KEY CASE *Wright v Macadam* (1949)

Facts: Mrs Wright was a weekly tenant of two rooms located on the top floor of a house owned by Mr Macadam. Mrs Wright, with Mr Macadam's permission, used part of a shed in the garden for storage of her coal. In 1943, Mr Macadam granted a new tenancy to Mrs Wright and her daughter over the two rooms plus an additional room. There was no reference in the new tenancy agreement to use of the garden shed. Mrs Wright, nevertheless, continued to make use of the shed as she had done previously. Subsequently, a dispute arose between the parties and Mr Macadam demanded that Mrs Wright pay for use of the shed.

Legal issue: Could Mrs Wright assert an easement to use the shed for storage of her coal by relying on the word-saving provisions of s. 62 of the LPA 1925 when the new tenancy was granted in 1943?

Judgment: Prior to the grant of the new tenancy in 1943, Mrs Wright enjoyed a licence to use the coal shed. The grant of that new tenancy constituted a conveyance for the purposes of s. 62 and under this provision, Mrs Wright's licence was taken as having been converted into a full, proprietary, legal easement. Jenkins LJ made several important observations regarding the operation of s. 62:

- The right to use the coal shed was a right capable of existing as an easement.
- There was no evidence that the parties intended the right of storage to be temporary in duration.
- The parties had not expressed an intention in the 1943 tenancy agreement that the operation of s. 62 be excluded.

Citing from the decision in *Lewis v Meredith* (1913), Jenkins LJ held:

> a 'right' permissive at the date of the grant may become a legal right upon the grant by the force of the general words in [s. 62 of the LPA 1925].

Wright concerned the operation of s. 62 on the grant of a new tenancy to Mrs Wright but s. 62 also operates to convert pre-existing licences into fully effective easements in circumstances where an existing tenant purchases the freehold from her landlord. This was what took place in the case of *International Tea Stores Co. v Hobbs* (1903). Let's explore this a little further by considering an example: Figure 10.11.

Alex is the freehold owner of two plots of adjoining land. At stage 1, Alex occupies Plot 1 as his home. He grants a lease over Plot 2 to Betty. Through Alex's goodwill, during the lifetime of the lease, Alex has allowed Betty vehicular access to her house on Plot 2 across Plot 1. This right of access is in the nature of a licence and could be revoked by Alex at any

---

[56] An early decision recognizing this transformative effect is *International Tea Stores Co. v Hobbs* (1903).

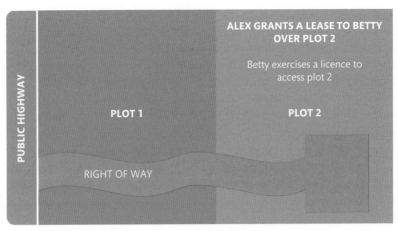

Stage 1: Alex grants a lease to Betty over Plot 2

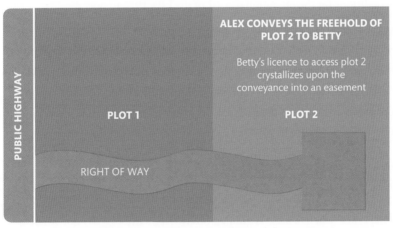

Stage 2: Alex conveys the freehold of Plot 2 to Betty

Figure 10.11 The operation of s. 62 of the LPA 1925

time. At stage 2, Alex decides to sell the freehold of Plot 2 to Betty. On the conveyance to Betty of Plot 2, under s. 62 of the LPA 1925, the pre-existing, precarious, and purely personal licence which Betty exercised is converted into a fully operative, fully fledged easement for the benefit of Plot 2. This easement (right of way) is implied into the legal conveyance of the freehold to Betty. Betty therefore now enjoys a legal proprietary right and is able to exercise and enforce a right of way across Plot 1 to access her land without obstruction or interference from Alex.

This transformative role of s. 62 has proved controversial, has been strongly criticized, and its abolition has even been recommended by the Law Commission.[57] Tee offers a

---

[57] Law Commission Report No. 327, [3.64]. Incidentally, abolition of the metamorphosis effect of s. 62 has been the preferred reform for the Law Commission since 1971.

cogent analysis of the 'metamorphosis from personal to property right' that we see operating under s. 62 and has also heavily disapproved the approach of the court in *Wright*.[58] By contrast, Douglas offers something of a defence of the so-called 'uplift' effect under this provision.[59] For Douglas, it is entirely reasonable that a word-saving provision has the effect of incorporating into conveyances both formal proprietary rights as well as informally created, mere personal permissions. Douglas does, however, concede that the impetus for reform is strong in circumstances where transferors and transferees of land are unaware of the implications of the section. For Douglas:[60]

> The uplift is a consequence of an entirely reasonable interpretation of the words of the section . . . When parties are aware of the operation of s. 62 . . . then the 'uplift' can be said to be an intended consequence. Conversely, when parties are unaware of the section, it is not possible to say that any resulting easement is an intended outcome. This conclusion is significant as it demonstrates the potential of s. 62 to impose an uncovenanted burden upon the grantor of land. In this respect, therefore, the Law Commission's criticism of the s. 62 uplift is justified, and it is a legitimate target of statutory reform.

How do you feel about this 'uplift' effect? As with the rule in *Wheeldon v Burrows*, there are certain conditions for the operation of s. 62 of the LPA 1925 to operate:

- There must be a legal conveyance of land.
- Only rights capable of constituting easements will be converted into easements.
- Only rights exercised at the time of the conveyance will be converted into easements.
- Section 62 must not have been expressly or impliedly excluded.
- Where there is no prior diversity of occupation or ownership, exercise of the right claimed to be an easement must have been 'continuous and apparent'.

There must be a legal 'conveyance of land'

This means there must be a grant or transfer of a legal estate or legal mortgage by deed: s. 205(1)(ii) of the LPA 1925. Most commonly this will take the form of a sale or a lease. There is no 'conveyance' where a lease is granted orally (*Rye v Rye* (1962)) nor where an equitable easement is created or any other equitable interest by enforceable written contract: *Borman*.

Only rights capable of constituting easements (Re Ellenborough Park) will be converted into legal easements under s. 62

In *Wright*, Mrs Wright's licence did have the characteristics of an easement and so could be transformed upon the conveyance into a full legal easement. A mere permission which does not possess the essential characteristics of an easement will not be converted. As Lord Denning explained in *Phipps v Pears*:[61]

> A fine view, or an expanse open to the winds may be an advantage to a house, but it would not pass under section 62. Whereas a right to use a coal shed or to go along a passage would pass

---

[58] L. Tee, 'Metamorphosis and Section 62 of the Law of Property Act 1925' [1998] Conv 115, 115.
[59] S. Douglas, 'How to Reform Section 62 of the Law of Property Act 1925' [2015] Conv 13.
[60] Ibid., 19.   [61] *Phipps v Pears*, 84.

under section 62. The reason being that these last are rights known to the law, whereas the others are not. A right to protection from the weather is not a right known to the law. It does not therefore pass under section 62.

Importantly, even where the right in question is 'known to the law' and capable of constituting an easement, it may not pass under s. 62 where it is expressed to be personally for the benefit of an individual or where it is temporary or precarious in nature: *Green v Ashco Horticulturist Ltd* (1966). Therefore, in *Goldberg v Edwards* (1950), while a right of access through a house did pass under s. 62, further rights (including the right to install advertising signage, a bell, and letterbox) were held to be mere personal favours and not falling within the purview of s. 62.[62]

Only those rights exercised at the date of the conveyance can be converted into legal easements

As Megarry V-C explained in *Penn v Wilkins* (1974):[63]

> Section 62 was apt for conveying existing rights, but did not resurrect mere memories of past rights.

The burden rests on the party claiming their right has been transformed into a full legal easement to adduce evidence that the right was in use prior to the conveyance. If the claimant is unable to prove this use, the claim will fail and so too will a claim in which the right was exercised *after* the conveyance took place: *Campbell v Banks* (2011).

Section 62 will not operate where the provision has been expressly or impliedly excluded

Section 62 will not apply if expressly excluded by the parties within the terms of the conveyance (s. 62(4)) or has been impliedly excluded having regard to all the circumstances of the case: *Hair v Gillman*. As to what will constitute 'express' exclusion, it is clear after *Wood* that very clear evidence indeed is required.[64] Reference to specific easements which were to be granted upon conveyance was insufficient to exclude the wider operation of s. 62: *Wood*.

Where there is no prior diversity of occupation or ownership, exercise of the right claimed to be an easement must have been 'continuous and apparent'

It had long been regarded as a strict requirement that there had to be prior diversity of occupation or ownership. What this meant, practically, was that before the conveyance took place, the relevant plots of land should have been occupied or owned by different people. The requirement for prior diversity of occupation has proved to be rather controversial. The requirement was laid down in the classic case of *Long v Gowlett* (1923) and approved

---

[62] Gardner and MacKenzie—in *An Introduction to Land Law*, 298—criticize this distinction between legal rights and personal favours as evidencing a 'degree of carelessness' in analysis as to whether rights are capable of constituting easements.

[63] In *Penn* the passage of sewage over land, that had ceased years prior to the conveyance, could not be converted into an easement under s. 62.

[64] Whilst implied exclusion is possible it is prudent that parties wishing to so exclude the operation of s. 62 do so by explicit reference in the conveyance. Most dealings with land conducted by professional conveyancers will ensure express exclusion is beyond doubt. Implied exclusion was, however, confirmed in *Platt*.

by the minority in the House of Lords' decision in *Sovmots*, where Lord Wilberforce explained the rationale:[65]

> The reason is that when land is under one ownership one cannot speak in any intelligible sense of rights, privileges, or easement being exercised over one part for the benefit of another. Whatever the owner does, he does as owner and, until a separation occurs, of ownership or at least of occupation, the condition for the existence of the rights etc., does not exist.

Other decisions of the court have taken a different stance. Whether prior diversity was an absolute requirement was therefore left unhelpfully unresolved in *Campbell v Banks* and the decision in *Platt* injected further confusion into the area. In *Platt*, there had been no prior diversity of occupation over the relevant plots. Nevertheless, the claimant was able to establish easements of rights of way, mooring and signage. Peter Gibson LJ in the Court of Appeal held that:[66]

> [T]he rights were continuous and apparent, and so it matters not that prior to the sale . . . there was no prior diversity of occupation of the dominant and servient [tenements].

The case of *Alford* offered additional support for the *Platt* interpretation and the issue came before the Court of Appeal most recently in the decision of *Wood*.[67] *Wood* approved the controversial approach taken in *Platt*, confirming that prior diversity of occupation/ ownership is not a strict requirement under s. 62 but, where it was not demonstrated, the right claimed to be an easement must be shown to have been 'continuous and apparent'.

KEY CASE *Wood v Waddington* (2015)

Facts: In 1998, a plot of land was sold in two parts: Plot 1 and Plot 2. The Sharmans acquired Plot 1 and the respondent, Mr Waddington, acquired Plot 2. The conveyance to Mrs Sharman was 'subject to and with the benefit of all liberties privileges and advantages of a continuous nature now used or enjoyed by or over the property'. There were several tracks and two bridleways crossing Mr Waddington's land, Plot 2. In 2009, the appellants (the Woods) purchased Plot 1 from the Sharmans and carried out extensive work on the land to create a livery stables business. The Woods and their clients regularly crossed over Plot 2 to gain access to the stables. In 2012, Mr Waddington erected a gate on his land preventing this access. The Woods issued legal proceedings claiming the benefit of easements of way over Plot 2.

Legal issue: Were the Woods entitled to the benefit of easements of way on any of the alternative grounds pleaded? The Woods argued that easements of way arose: (1) by express grant; (2) under s. 62 of the LPA 1925; (3) under the rule in *Wheeldon v Burrows*; (4) by common intention of the parties.

Judgment: In the High Court, Morgan J held that:

1. On the facts of the case, there had been no express grant of easements of way.

2. Under s. 62 of the LPA 1925 there was no strict rule that required prior diversity of occupation and a right of way could pass under s. 62 without diversity of occupation provided always that the

→

---

[65] *Sovmots*, 169.   [66] *Platt*, [42].

[67] See E. Lees, '*Wood v Waddington*: Section 62 and Apparently Continuous Easements' [2015] Conv 423.

→ right was 'continuous and apparent'. The court followed the decision in *Platt* and in *Alford* to this effect.

3. On the facts of the case, none of the rights claimed satisfied the *Wheeldon v Burrows* rule as they were not 'reasonably necessary for the enjoyment' of the land conveyed.

4. Equally, there was no evidence that the land was to be used for a definite and particular purchase for the implication of an easement by common intention.

The Woods appealed this decision to the Court of Appeal on two bases, namely that the judge had erred in holding there had been no express grant of easements and moreover in holding that the rights claimed were not 'continuous and apparent' for the purposes of section 62. The Court of Appeal held that:

1. The judge had not erred in holding that no express grant of easements arose in this case.

2. The judge was right that there was no requirement for prior diversity of occupation for the operation of s. 62 of the LPA 1925. All that was required was that the easement was 'continuous and apparent in the sense developed for the purposes of the rule in *Wheeldon v Burrows*'. The court thus confirmed that the phrase 'continuous and apparent' is identical to that in *Wheeldon v Burrows*.

On the facts of the present case, and reversing the High Court on this point, there were visible signs of a track on the ground and evidence of vehicular use such that easements of way were 'continuous and apparent'. The Woods were therefore entitled to the benefit of easements of way over Mr Waddington's land, Plot 2.

The effect of *Platt* as affirmed by the court in *Wood* is very significant indeed. Many had hoped that the scope of s. 62 would be constrained by the Court of Appeal and that the requirement for prior diversity of occupation would be reasserted. This did not happen and the position is unlikely to change without a reappraisal of the law by the Supreme Court. The practical consequence of *Wood* is that, provided there is a legal conveyance and no contrary intention is expressed excluding the application of s. 62, claimants will no longer need to resort to the alternative route of implication of an easement under the rule in *Wheeldon v Burrows* and can rely on s. 62 which is, undoubtedly, a simpler and more straightforward route to implication of an easement: see Figure 10.12. In this way, the decision in *Wood* may be welcomed. After *Platt*, *Alford*, and *Wood*, it seems the assimilation of s. 62 and *Wheeldon v Burrows* is almost complete. Differences do, however, still remain and in section 10.4.4.5 we will explore the central similarities and outstanding differences between these two methods of implication of easements.

10.4.4.5 The rule in *Wheeldon v Burrows* and s. 62 of the LPA 1925 compared

The rule in *Wheeldon v Burrows* and s. 62 of the LPA 1925 can arise in very similar factual scenarios and in many cases including *Wood*, claimants will plead both in the alternative. Both *Wheeldon v Burrows* and s. 62 can be seen as founded upon the principle of non-derogation from grant. Whilst there may, however, be judicial moves towards assimilation (*Platt* and *Wood*) and there may be good grounds for this development, we are not quite there yet. While there is increasingly very little that distinguishes the two principles,

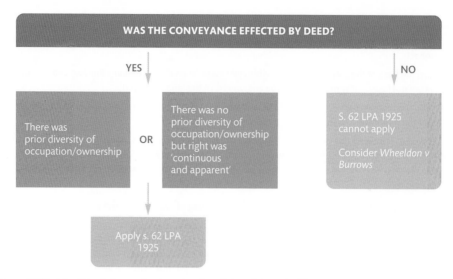

Figure 10.12 After *Wood*, the application of s. 62 and the rule in *Wheeldon v Burrows*

a key distinction that does remain is the nature of the rights that can be implied under s. 62 which remains broader in its application than those under *Wheeldon v Burrows*. Some of the key similarities and differences are brought together in Table 10.3.

10.4.4.6 Implied reservation

The courts have shown far more reluctance to imply an easement by reservation than has been the case for the implication of an easement by grant. As was explained in *Neil v Duke of Devonshire* (1882), this is because whilst deeds are construed in favour of the grantee, grantors are fully expected to act in their own interests. The general principle on implied reservation was affirmed in no uncertain terms by Thesiger LJ in *Wheeldon v Burrows*:[68]

> If the grantor intends to reserve any right over the tenement granted, it is his duty to reserve it expressly in that grant.

Despite adopting this strict stance, Thesiger LJ acknowledged that the reservation of easements will be implied in two limited circumstances:

1. Implied reservation of an easement of necessity: It is possible for reservation of an easement of necessity to be implied in circumstances where the dominant land would otherwise be landlocked. The same principles apply as discussed in section 10.4.4.1 in relation to implied grant of an easement of necessity.

2. Implied reservation of an easement of common intention: The court in *Pwllbach* confirmed that where the parties shared a common intention that the land sold be used for a definite and particular purpose, the reservation (as well as grant) of an easement could be implied. Given the general reluctance towards implied reservations, it is perhaps

---

[68] *Wheeldon v Burrows*, 49.

Table 10.3 *Wheeldon v Burrows* and s. 62 of the LPA 1925 compared

THE RULE IN *WHEELDON V BURROWS*	SECTION 62 OF THE LPA 1925
Operates upon a pre-existing quasi-easement	Operates upon a pre-existing legal right: proprietary or non-proprietary (e.g. a licence)
Operates where the land was in single ownership prior to transfer	Operates where either: (1) there was prior diversity of occupation/ownership; or (2) there was no prior diversity of occupation but the right was 'continuous and apparent' (*Wood v Waddington* (2015))
Operates to create *legal* as well as *equitable* easements (i.e. can be used to imply easements into legal conveyances as well as equitable transfers)	Operates to imply and to create *legal* easements only—applies only to legal conveyances
Operates only where the right is 'continuous and apparent' and/or 'reasonably necessary' for the enjoyment of the land	Where there is prior diversity of occupation, operates automatically upon a conveyance of land
Operates only as to rights capable of constituting easements under the *Re Ellenborough Park* (1956) principles	Also only operates as to rights capable of constituting easements under the *Re Ellenborough Park* (1956) principles
The rule can be excluded by express words or by implication	Section 62 can also be excluded by express words or by implication
Operates only by means of implied grant and not by implied reservation	Also only operates by means of implied grant and not by implied reservation

unsurprising that the court has generally required a greater degree of certainty in demonstrating this common intention than expected for implied grant of an easement of common intention. By way of example, Lord Evershed MR in *Re Webb's Lease* (1951) explained that in a case of implied reservation the grantor must be capable:[69]

at least to prove affirmatively that such a reservation was clearly intended by him and his grantee at the time of the grant.

No reservation of an easement was implied in *Re Webb's Lease* and the argument again failed in *Walby* where: the court underlined the general principle that clear and positive evidence of an intention to reserve an easement was required. This is a heavy burden to discharge. It is clear then that whilst reservation of an easement can be implied on the grounds of necessity or common intention, the court will be slow to depart from the general proposition of Thesiger LJ in *Wheeldon v Burrows* that if a grantor wishes to reserve an easement, he should do so expressly. The Law Commission's recommendations for reform of this area propose that the rules on implication of easements should not distinguish between implied grant or implied reservation.[70]

---

[69] *Re Webb's Lease.*   [70] Law Commission Report No. 327, [3.30].

10.4.5 **Easements presumed by prescription**

Prescription is a process by which exercise of a right over land for many years (referred to as 'long user') can generate an easement. Easements by prescription arise, therefore, as a direct result of the repeated use of the right over time. The precise length of time required for an easement to be generated is governed by the particular legal 'method' selected for establishing an easement by prescription. There are three such 'methods', and they are examined in section 10.4.5.2. An easement can only be generated by prescription if the right exercised is capable of constituting an easement under the authority of *Re Ellenborough Park* and all easements created in this way by prescription will be legal in character. Before considering the requirements for prescription, it is worth asking why the law recognizes prescription as a means by which easements can be created. The rationale for the law of prescription was explained by Lord Hoffmann in *R v Oxfordshire CC ex parte Sunningwell Parish Council* (2000) who noted:[71]

> [A]ny legal system must have rules of prescription which prevent the disturbance of long-established de facto enjoyment of land.

The rules of prescription are built, essentially, upon a legal fiction. According to this fiction, where there is evidence of 'long user' of a right over what becomes the servient land, the law is prepared to presume the grant of an easement. Of course, no such grant has, in fact, taken place. This is the fiction. By proceeding on the basis of this presumption of grant,[72] the exercise of the right or 'user' is not seen as adverse to the servient landowner's title. The servient owner is taken to have acquiesced in the exercise of the right.

The 'presumption of grant' rationale for the prescription rules has been the subject of sustained criticism primarily from academic commentators but also from the courts. In *Angus v Dalton* (1877), the traditional justification of prescription was said to rest upon a 'revolting fiction'. McMahon J in *Walsh v Sligo CC* (2010) issued a plea that the fiction be dropped to 'embrace and acknowledge the real position in law' and not 'become a slave to historical fiction'. Goymour argues that the traditional basis 'offends common sense and is inconsistent with the technical requirements for prescription'.[73] In particular, Goymour notes that the fallacy of presumed grant is inconsistent with a general condition for the operation of prescription (discussed in section 10.4.5.1) that the exercise of the right or 'user' must be without the servient landowner's permission. This necessarily introduces an element of adversity which appears wholly out of step with the presumed grant thesis.

10.4.5.1 Requirements for prescription

There are certain general conditions for a claim to prescription which must be satisfied irrespective of which of the three 'methods' for prescription is adopted. This section considers these general conditions:

---

[71] *R v Oxfordshire CC ex parte Sunningwell Parish Council*, 349.

[72] Indeed, easements generated by prescription are often referred to as 'by presumed grant' for this reason.

[73] A. Goymour, 'Rights in Property and the Effluxion of Time' in E. Cooke (ed.), *Modern Studies in Property Law*, Vol. 4 (Oxford: Hart, 2007), 182.

- User must be by a freehold owner against another freehold owner.
- User must be 'as of right'.
- User must be lawful.
- User must be continuous.
- User must be in the nature of an easement.

The language here can, at first, seem inaccessible and requires some clarification. Recall that in this context, references to 'user' simply mean the continued exercise of a right over land.

User must be by a freehold owner against another freehold owner

An easement by prescription can only be generated where a right has been exercised by one fee simple owner over another fee simple owner's land: *Simmons v Dobson* (1991); *Kilgour v Gaddes* (1904). As a result, an easement by prescription cannot be generated in favour of a tenant over a landlord's neighbouring land nor can an easement by prescription be generated over an equitable estate.[74] Problems may arise where an easement by prescription is claimed over servient land which is leased to tenants: *Llewellyn v Lorey* (2011). The court in *Llewellyn* held that a vital element in the acquisition of a right of way by prescription was that the fee simple owner of the land both knew, or was taken to have known, of the user, and was in a position to prevent it if she so wished.

User must be 'as of right'

There are several elements to the requirement that the right exercised must be 'as of right'. The position has been summed up succinctly by Riddall and Trevelyan:[75]

> For the user to be 'as of right', it must be nec vi, without force; nec clam, without secrecy; and nec precarious, without permission . . . user 'as of right' means that the user must be in the same fashion as if there was a legal right to use the way.

An easement by prescription will only be generated where the owner of the purported dominant land acted peaceably and 'without force' in the exercise of the right. Where there is evidence of force, no easement will be presumed to have been granted by prescription. 'Force' can be seen as encompassing two meanings: first, where there is physical action such as breaking a lock to exercise a right and, secondly, where the right continues to be exploited after opposition to its exercise by a servient landowner: *Eaton v Swansea Waterworks Co.* (1851); *Dalton v Angus* (1881). No easement by prescription will be generated from long user unless the right is exercised openly (i.e. 'without secrecy'). This flows from the nature of the presumed grant which connotes a measure of acquiescence by the servient landowner. Where the right is exercised in a secretive or hidden manner, there can be no acquisition of an easement by prescription. As Romer LJ explained in *Union Lighterage*, the long user must be:[76]

---

[74] This requirement has been heavily criticized in Hong Kong where all land is leasehold: *China Field Ltd v Appeal Tribunal (Buildings) (No. 2)* (2009).

[75] J. Riddall and J. Trevelyan, *Rights of Way: A Guide to Law and Practice*, 4th edn (London: Ramblers' Assoc., 2007).

[76] *Union Lighterage*, 571.

[O]f such a character that an ordinary owner of land, diligent in the protection of his interests, would have, or must be taken to have, a reasonable opportunity of becoming aware.

In *Union Lighterage*, no easement arose by prescription in circumstances where a dock had been affixed to a wharf for 20 years using underground rods invisible to the servient landowner. Equally, no easement by prescription was generated in favour of the alleged dominant landowner in *Liverpool Corp. v H. Coghill and Son Ltd* (1918) where waste product had been released into a sewer at irregular intervals during the night for over 20 years. As for 'user without permission', the servient landowner must not *acquiesce* in the right exercised by the dominant landowner. Where *permission* is given to that dominant landowner for the exercise of a right over the servient, this will prove fatal to the claim for an easement by prescription: *Odey v Barber* (2007).[77] In *Hill v Rosser* (1997), the claim to an easement by prescription failed where the servient landowner had granted a licence for the user to the dominant landowner. The granting of the licence was regarded as the giving of consent or permission for the user. Permission need not be mutual in the sense that it can be unilaterally granted by the servient landowner. It need not have been solicited by the dominant landowner (*Odey*). An easement by prescription can be claimed where user of land is in excess or beyond the scope of the permission granted or continued after the expiry of permission. The dominant landowner's belief that permission has been granted when it, in fact, has not, will not defeat a claim to prescription nor will permission that has lapsed if the user is continuing: *London Tara Hotel Ltd v Kensington Close Hotel Ltd* (2011). In *London Tara Hotel*, permission in the form of a licence had been granted to the owners of the hotel for the use of a service road. The permission did not extend to the use of the road by coaches and provided for payment of an annual fee. The hotel was conveyed to several new owners. The road was used for 20 years and no annual fee was ever paid. The Court of Appeal held that the permission had been personal to the original owners and the non-payment of the annual fee was evidence of the absence of permission for the user. The claim to an easement by prescription succeeded.

User must be lawful

An easement will only be generated by prescription if it can be lawfully granted and where the user is not illegal in nature. Easements must not exist to fulfil an illegal purpose and servient landowners will not be presumed to have granted such easements. The leading case on illegal user is *Bakewell Management Ltd v Brandwood* which demonstrates that the law may be more flexible than the strict requirement for lawfulness might first suggest.

The effect of the *Bakewell* decision is that substantive unlawfulness and criminality will be a bar to a claim for prescription but where the right claimed as an easement is capable of being lawfully granted and any illegal conduct thereby rendered lawful by the servient landowner, a claim in prescription may be available.

---

[77] See R. Meager, 'Prescription and User "As of Right": Ripe for Wholesale Reform?' in S. Bright (ed.), *Modern Studies in Property Law*, Vol. 6 (Oxford: Hart, 2011), 254.

KEY CASE *Bakewell Management Ltd v Brandwood* (2004)

Facts: Bakewell was the owner of a house adjoining a large 140-acre common. There was no direct route of access to the house from a nearby public road but a track across the common had been used regularly for well over 20 years. The owner of the common had not given permission for this user. Under s. 193(4) of the LPA 1925, it was an offence to drive on common land without lawful authority.

Legal issue: Was Bakewell entitled to an easement by prescription permitting vehicular access across the common? The owner of the common argued that the use of the track had been a trespass and, crucially, a criminal offence preventing an easement arising.

Judgment: The Court of Appeal found that no easement could be generated by prescription to permit conduct which was itself prohibited by statute under the authority of *Hanning v Top Deck Travel Group Ltd* (1993). Bakewell appealed. The House of Lords, allowed Bakewell's appeal, overruled *Hanning* and reversed the decision of the Court of Appeal holding that it was in the very nature of prescription that the use of the right in question constituted a trespass and was therefore unlawful until sanctioned by the operation of prescription. Lord Scott noted:

> A statutory prohibition forbidding some particular use of land that is expressed in terms that allows the landowner to authorise the prohibited use and exempts from criminality use of the land with that authority is an unusual type of prohibition. It allows a clear distinction to be drawn between cases where a grant by the landowner of the right to use the land in the prohibited way would be a lawful grant that would remove the criminality of the user and cases where a grant by the landowner of the right to use the land in the prohibited way would be an unlawful grant and incapable of vesting any right in the grantee.

The House of Lords therefore held that where conduct constitutes an offence merely for lack of 'lawful authority' from the landowner, an easement can be generated by prescription. Where, in contrast, conduct is substantively criminal and a landowner could not lawfully grant the right, prescription remains unavailable. Driving across common land is a right that could be lawfully authorized and lawfully granted, therefore an easement by prescription was capable of being generated in Bakewell's favour.

User must be continuous

There must have been regular user in order for an easement by prescription to be generated. While the right need not have been exercised ceaselessly, long periods of unexplained non-use will be fatal to a claim for prescription. Continuous user is a question of fact for the court.

User must be in the nature of an easement

No easement can be generated by prescription unless the user by the alleged dominant landowner is in the nature of a right capable of constituting an easement according to the essential characteristics laid down in *Re Ellenborough Park*. The fundamental basis for the operation of prescription is that of presumed grant. Plainly, an easement cannot be presumed to have been granted by prescription unless it would have been capable of express grant.

10.4.5.2 Methods for establishing an easement by prescription

Where a right has been exercised according to the general principles identified in the previous section, we turn to consider under which of the three 'methods' prescription operates. As noted in the introduction to this section, there are three methods for establishing an easement by prescription. They are:

1. at common law;
2. by lost modern grant;
3. under the Prescription Act 1832.

A claimant wishing to launch a claim for an easement by prescription can elect between the three methods, though, practically, in many cases claimants plead more than one method in the alternative: *Bakewell*. The key distinction between each of the methods is not the character of the user but the length of time for which a right must have been exercised to succeed in a claim for prescription. The various methods have been described as 'anomalous and undesirable',[78] replete with 'messy overlaps',[79] and the Law Commission has proposed replacement with a single route based on long user of 20 years.[80] Let's consider these methods in turn.

Prescription at common law

At common law, an easement by prescription could be generated if it was shown that a right had been exercised over land dating back to before 'legal memory' or 'time immemorial' which was decreed under the Statute of Westminster 1275 to be AD 1189, the date of accession to the throne of Richard I. Proving that a right had been exercised since this early time was clearly a high hurdle to overcome and so it was recognized that long user of 20 years would give rise to a presumption that a right has been exercised since before AD 1189: *Bryant v Foot* (1867). The presumption was, however, rebuttable by adducing evidence to show that the right had not in fact been exercised before AD 1189 or that the land had been in common ownership at some time since AD 1189 both of which, in many cases, proved relatively easy to do. Today, as a consequence of the idiosyncrasies in the common law route, this method of prescription is rarely relied upon by claimants.

Prescription by lost modern grant

In response to the peculiarities and pitfalls of the common law approach, a further method of prescription was developed. This is the doctrine of 'lost modern grant'. Under this doctrine, where there is evidence of long user of 20 years' duration, the law assumes that a fictitious express grant of the right was made after AD 1189 and that this grant has since been lost: *Dalton v Angus* (1881). Importantly, unlike the position at common law just discussed, this fiction cannot be rebutted so that provided a claimant can prove that a right has been exercised for 20 years, a legal easement will be generated. This remains the position even in circumstances where it can be shown as a matter of fact that no express grant was made:

---

[78] *Tehidy Minerals Ltd v Norman* (1971), per Buckley LJ.
[79] Goymour, 'Rights in Property and the Effluxion of Time', 185.
[80] Law Commission Report No. 327, [3.123].

Tehidy Minerals Ltd v Norman (1971). Even where there has been an interruption in the exercise of a right, an easement may be generated on the basis of 'lost modern grant' provided that a long user of 20 years can be demonstrated before that interruption began: *Mills v Silver* (1991). One accepted (though arguably questionable[81]) exception is where there is evidence that the servient landowner would have lacked the necessary capacity to make the grant (*Oakley v Boston* (1976)), was a minor, or was not the owner of the servient land at the relevant time.

The doctrine of 'lost modern grant' remains a highly significant route for the acquisition of an easement by prescription. Under this rule, simply demonstrating continuous use for 20 years will, in most cases, suffice to generate an easement by prescription. A recent example serves to illustrate the doctrine in operation: *Orme v Lyons*.

KEY CASE *Orme v Lyons* (2012)

Facts: The Ormes and the Lyons were neighbours. A dispute arose as to whether the Lyons were permitted vehicular access over a track which passed through land owned by the Ormes. There was evidence that the Lyons had used the track between 1971 and 1989 approximately 12 times per year. From 1989 and the later 1990s, the track had been used but far less frequently and only when an alternative access route was blocked.

Legal issue: The Lyons claimed an easement had been generated in their favour by prescription under the doctrine of 'lost modern grant'. The central issue was whether the Lyons could demonstrate sufficiently 'continuous use' for a 20-year period.

Judgment: According to the deputy adjudicator who first heard the case and subsequently by the High Court who approved his decision, the Lyons had indeed shown sufficient use of the track over their period of ownership so that an easement of access had been acquired in their favour by 'lost modern grant'. Of particular relevance was that there were visible ruts in the track and it being hard for the Ormes to have taken any other view except that the Lyons had been using the passage to access their land.

Prescription under the Prescription Act 1832

A final method for establishing an easement by prescription lies in statute under the Prescription Act 1832. Regrettably, the 1832 legislation has been described as 'one of the worst drafted Acts on the Statute Book',[82] with the result that 'lost modern grant' remains the most commonly used method of acquisition of an easement by prescription. Although one of the central aims in legislating for the 1832 Act was to support the existing common law principles and to facilitate claims to an easement by prescription, the statute arguably does not achieve this. Nevertheless, we must consider how the statute operates. The legislation essentially consists of two separate regimes under which easements of light are treated separately from all other easements.

---

[81] Given the doctrine rests on an absolute fiction, one wonders why so much import is then attached to the particular attributes of the fictitious grantor.

[82] Law Reform Committee, *Fourteenth Report: Acquisition of Easements and Profits by Prescription* (Cmnd 3100, 1966), 40.

Prior to the 1832 Act, easements of light proved particularly difficult to establish by prescription. Under s. 3 of the 1832 Act, 20 years' uninterrupted use of a right of light is 'deemed absolute and indefeasible' unless there is written consent or agreement for that use. Therefore, under s. 3, a continuous use of a right to light will generate an easement by prescription even if there would have been some defect under the common law principles (for example, evidence the right could not have been exercised in AD 1189). As to whether there is 'written consent' for the use, *Salvage Wharf Ltd v G. & S. Brough Ltd* (2009) confirms that this is largely a question of construction of any agreement existing between the parties. In *Salvage*, an agreement concerning existing rights was held not to amount to written consent for the purposes of s. 3 of the 1832 Act. By contrast, in *CGIS City Plaza Shares 1 Ltd v Britel Fund Trustees Ltd* (2012), the High Court construed a term in a conveyance permitting a servient landowner to build on its land as constituting written consent under s. 3 of the 1832 Act thereby barring the acquisition of an easement of light.

For all easements other than relating to light, s. 2 of the 1832 Act operates so that an easement by prescription will be generated where:

- there is use of the right for 20 years, and
- the use is uninterrupted, and
- the use immediately precedes the legal action or suit.

Evidence that the use only began after AD 1189 will not defeat the claim under s. 2 but a claim is barred where there was agreement or consent for exercise of the right. Section 2 of the 1832 Act provides for a further, alternative means of establishing an easement by prescription. Here, an easement will be generated where there is evidence of 40 years' uninterrupted use. In these circumstances, the right is 'deemed absolute and indefeasible' and will generate an easement even if there was consent or agreement concerning the exercise of that right unless this consent was committed to writing: *Gardner v Hodgson's Kingston Brewery Co. Ltd* (1903). As with 20 years' statutory prescription, an easement will only be acquired on the bringing of legal proceedings and the 40-year period of user must immediately precede this action. The principal difference between the 20- and 40-year routes is that for the latter, if satisfied, the right is deemed absolute and indefeasible.

One fundamental and final point must be grasped which underscores the continued utility of the doctrine of 'lost modern grant' as compared to statutory prescription under the Prescription Act 1832. The 1832 Act requires that the period of continuous user, whether that be 20 or 40 years, *immediately precedes* legal action or suit. There is no similar limitation placed upon the doctrine of 'lost modern grant'. As a result, where long user of 20 years can be demonstrated but arising some considerable time in the past, lost modern grant will generate an easement in circumstances where statutory prescription will not.

10.4.6 Easements created by statute

Easements can also be created by statute. Local authorities, private enterprises, and even individuals can be granted easements under statutory provision—for example, under the enfranchisement provisions of the Land Registration Act 1967 and by the exercise of compulsory purchase powers under the Local Government (Miscellaneous Provisions) Act 1976. In addition, utility companies supplying gas, water, and electricity are endowed with easements in order that they are able to enter onto private property for the purposes of installation of supply pipes.[83] Easements created by statute are legal in nature. There is also a wider raft of legislation which provides landowners with access to neighbouring land for the purpose of carrying out necessary works—for example, under the Access to Neighbouring Land Act 1992 and the Party Wall etc. Act 1996.

10.4.7 **Easements created by proprietary estoppel**

In Chapter 8 you were introduced to the doctrine of proprietary estoppel under which proprietary rights in land are created in the absence of formality requirements. We saw that the doctrine operates in circumstances where a claimant has reasonably relied to her detriment upon a representation or assurance made as to her present or future rights in property such that it would be unconscionable for the party making that representation or assurance to deny those rights. Where a claimant succeeds in establishing an 'estoppel equity' under the doctrine, the court then moves to determine the appropriate remedy in 'satisfying the equity'. One way that the court may decide to satisfy the equity is by granting an easement in the claimant's favour. Examples of this can be seen in the cases of *Ward*, *E. R. Ives Investment v High* (1967), and *Crabb v Arun* (1976). In *Ward*, for example, the court held that an easement had been created by estoppel in favour of the owner of a cottage who had been given permission by the owners of neighbouring farmland to lay drainage across the yard. The court found that the farmland owners had given permission for the drainage to be installed for an indefinite period and the claimant had incurred expense in reliance on these assurances. Easements by estoppel also arose in *Sweet*; *Chaudhary v Yavuz* (2013) and in the decision of *Joyce v Epsom & Ewell Borough Council* (2012). Despite proprietary estoppel being an equitable doctrine, the court has a wide discretion when selecting the appropriate remedy and can just as easily grant a legal easement as an equitable one.

In the next section, we turn to the third and final step in our suggested analysis of easements: see Figure 10.3. Let's just recap on this. At Step 1, we ask whether the right in question was capable of constituting an easement according to the requirements laid down in *Re Ellenborough Park*. At Step 2, we ask whether an easement has, in fact, been created and how by exploring the methods of creation of easements. Our final step, Step 3, calls for a consideration of whether the easement created is *legal* or *equitable* in nature and its effect on third parties. Let's explore this final step now.

10.5 The effect of easements on third parties: The legal/equitable distinction

As with many other proprietary interests in land, easements can be either legal or equitable[84] and this is determined by the manner in which the easement is created and the extent to which formality requirements are satisfied. Whether an easement is legal or

---

[83] See J. F. Garner [1956] Conv 208.   [84] Section 1 of the LPA 1925.

equitable, as in other areas in land law, carries real significance when evaluating the ability of easements to bind third parties. So, when will an easement be legal and when will it be equitable?

10.5.1 When will an easement be legal?

There are four prerequisites or conditions which must be satisfied if an easement is to be *legal* in nature. These conditions are cumulative. The upshot of this is that if *any* of the four requirements is not met, the easement cannot operate as a legal easement and will, at best, be equitable. Let's examine the requirements:

1. An easement can only be legal if it is 'carved out of a larger estate or interest' which is itself legal: *Willies-Williams v National Trust* (1993). This means that an easement must be created out of a legal fee simple or a legal leasehold if it is to operate at law. If an easement is created from an equitable estate, it cannot be legal and can only ever be equitable.

2. An easement can only be legal if it is granted for a period equivalent to a fee simple absolute in possession or for a term of years absolute.[85] The practical effect of this is that an easement can only be legal if it is, in some way, time-limited. An easement which purports to be created in perpetuity or for some indeterminate period, for example, an easement 'for A's life' can only ever be equitable.

3. An easement can only be legal if it is created according to one of the methods for creation set out in Figure 10.6, in other words, by grant or reservation (whether express or implied), by prescription, by statute, or by estoppel. We have already seen that express easements created by deed will be legal as will those implied into a legal conveyance or transfer of land. We found also that easements presumed by prescription through long user are legal in character as are those arising under statute.

4. Finally, for the purposes of registered land, an expressly granted easement (whether by grant or reservation) is a registrable disposition, which under s. 27(2)(d) of the LRA 2002, is required to be completed by registration if it is to operate at law.[86]

10.5.2 When will an easement be equitable?

As we have just seen, in order for an easement to take effect at law, it must satisfy certain prerequisites or conditions. Where these are not met, an easement may nevertheless take effect *in equity*. Equitable easements arise, therefore, in many cases (though not exclusively) from a failure of legal formalities or as a result of a defective or failed attempt to create a legal easement. Equitable easements will arise in the following circumstances:

1. where there is a failure to meet *any* of the four prerequisites in section 10.5.1 as to legal status; or

2. where there is a specifically enforceable written contract for the creation of an easement: s. 2 of the LP(MP)A 1989: *Walsh v Lonsdale*.

---

[85] Ibid., s. 1(2)(a); Sch. 2 paras. 6(3), 7(1)(a) of the LRA 2002.   [86] Section 27 and Sch. 2 of the LRA 2002.

An easement will therefore be equitable in nature if it is carved out of an equitable estate, if it is not granted for a period equivalent to a fee simple absolute in possession or leasehold; if there is a failure to comply with the formality requirements for the principal modes of creation; or, finally, if the registration requirements for an easement to operate at law are not satisfied.

Equity being more flexible than the common law looks to substance and not form. Therefore, equity regards as done that which ought to be done. In this way under the rule in *Walsh v Lonsdale*,[87] an equitable easement will arise where the parties have sought to expressly grant or reserve a *legal* easement over land but have failed to comply with the relevant legal formalities. Imagine, for example, that Amanda wishes to grant to Burt a legal easement comprising a right of way. This will need to be created by deed: s. 52 of the LPA 1925. If the deed is defective in some way, no legal easement can be created. However, provided there is a contract for an easement between Amanda and Burt which the court regards as specifically enforceable, an equitable easement will have been created. This is the *Walsh v Lonsdale* principle operating in the law of easements. What form must the contract take to create an equitable easement? An equitable easement will only be created where:

- under s. 2 of the LP(MP)A 1989, there is a valid contract for an easement which is in writing, incorporates all the terms and is signed by both parties, and
- equity would regard the contract as specifically enforceable.

A final point to appreciate here is that only a *written* contract for the creation of an easement will give rise to an equitable easement under this principle. An oral contract will not be enough. Where there is an oral contract for an easement, this may, nevertheless, be interpreted by the court as giving rise to a licence.

10.5.3 Easements and third parties

An easement is a proprietary right. This means that easements are capable of binding and being enforceable as against and between successors of the original tenements. The ability to bind third parties acquiring the affected land is clearly of real significance. If the original parties to an easement convey their land to successors, those successors will want to know where they stand. They will be eager to know if they can enforce or prevent exercise of the easement. This is a question of the enforceability of easements.

Whether an easement is enforceable between successors is a question of whether the benefit (the right to sue to enforce an easement) and the burden (the ability to be sued on the easement) have passed to those successors: see Figure 10.13.

In Figure 10.13, an easement has been created to the benefit of A's land and burdens B's land. There has, subsequently, been a transfer of both the dominant land and the servient land to C and D who are successors of each respective tenement. If C as successor of the dominant land wishes to enforce the easement against D, two things must be shown:

1. that the benefit of the easement has passed to C, and
2. that the burden of the easement has passed to D.

---

[87] We explored *Walsh* in section 9.5.3.

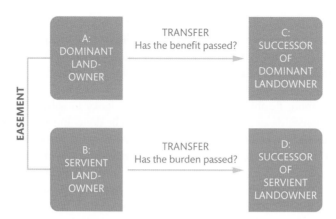

Figure 10.13 Effect of easements on successors

As regards the passing of the benefit, this is extremely straightforward. A legal easement in registered land must be completed by registration under s. 27 of the LRA 2002 in order to operate at law. By registering the easement, the benefit of the easement is entered in the Property Register of the dominant land.[88] When this land is conveyed, the benefit passes automatically to the successor of the dominant land. For equitable easements, the benefit passes automatically under s. 62 of the LPA 1925 as the benefit of any easements existing over land is deemed to be included within any conveyance of the benefited land unless there is evidence of express contrary intention. This is important as it means that in almost every case where land benefiting from an easement is transferred to a third party, the transferee ('C' in this example) will be able to demonstrate that the benefit has passed.

Once the benefit has been shown to pass, it must next be demonstrated that the burden of the easement has also passed. For us, this is the real question of enforceability of easements given that, in almost every case, passing of the benefit is automatic. So, in our example in Figure 10.13, it must be shown that the burden of the easement has passed to D as successor of the servient land. Just as in many other areas of land law explored in this book, the rules on the passing of the burden differ according to two key issues:

1. whether the land in question is unregistered or registered land, and

2. whether the easement is legal or equitable in nature.

So, what are the applicable rules?

10.5.3.1 Easements over unregistered land

Where an easement exists over unregistered land and there is a transfer of that land, the rules governing first registration under the LRA 2002 will spring into action. On first registration, the registrar must examine title to the land and enter a notice on the register in respect of any interests affecting that estate.[89] In addition, under Sch. 1, para. 3, legal

---

[88] Land Registration Rules 2003, r. 5(b)(ii).

easements constitute overriding interests for the purposes of first registration. It is useful, however, to briefly consider how easements are protected in unregistered land generally. We need to consider separately the position of legal and equitable easements.

Legal easements in unregistered land

Legal rights in unregistered land 'bind the whole world'. As a result, a third party acquiring the servient land will be automatically bound by the burden of a legal easement. Practically, this means that the third party must allow the dominant landowner to exercise the easement without obstruction or interference.

Equitable easements in unregistered land

Most equitable easements require protection if they are to bind third parties. In unregistered land, an equitable easement must be registered as a Class D(iii) land charge[90] if it is to bind a purchaser of a legal estate in the servient land for money or money's worth. If the equitable easement is not registered, the easement will be void against a purchaser for money or money's worth under s. 4(6) of the LCA 1972. An equitable easement that is not registered will still bind non-purchasers including those squatting on the land or inheriting under a will: *Midland Bank v Green* (1981). Equitable easements arising via the doctrine of proprietary estoppel have been held to be incapable of registration as Class D(iii) land charges and enforceability will be governed by the doctrine of notice: *E. R. Ives Investment v High*. Recall: according to the doctrine of notice, an equitable easement will bind all except a bona fide purchaser for value of a legal estate without notice of the easement: *Pilcher v Rawlins* (1872).[91]

10.5.3.2 Easements over registered land

As we have seen, in registered land, the benefit of an easement will pass automatically to a successor of the dominant tenement either following registration under s. 27 of the LRA 2002 or via operation of s. 62 of the LPA 1925. The decisive issue governing the enforceability of easements vis-à-vis successors is once more the passing of the burden of the easement. Again, we need to consider separately the position of legal and equitable easements.

Legal easements created pre-LRA 2002

Legal easements created before the coming into force of the LRA 2002 amounted to overriding interests under s. 70(1)(a) of the LRA 1925. Under the LRA 2002, the overriding status of these earlier-created rights is preserved by Sch. 12, para. 9. These easements will therefore continue to be binding, on a transfer of the servient land, as overriding interests.[92]

---

[89] Ibid., r. 35.　　　[90] Section 2(5)(iii) of the LCA 1972.

[91] We explored the doctrine of notice in section 3.4.5.

[92] We noted that Sch. 1, para. 3 of the LRA 2002 affords overriding status to legal easements in existence at the time of first registration.

Legal easements expressly created after the coming into force of the LRA 2002

As we noted in section 10.5.1, legal easements expressly granted or reserved after the coming into force of the LRA 2002 constitute registrable dispositions under s. 27 of the 2002 Act and must therefore comply with 'registration requirements' and be completed by registration in order to operate at law.[93] This means that the benefit of the easement must be entered in the Property Register of the dominant title and the burden of the easement must be entered by notice in the Charges Register of the servient estate.[94] The legal status of the easement and its ability to bind third parties is not therefore generated until the easement has been registered. Where registration has taken place, the burden of the easement will bind a successor of the servient land. Where there is a failure of registration, the easement can only be equitable in nature. If the easement operates in equity only, its enforceability will be determined by the rules on equitable easements in registered land discussed later in this section.

Legal easements impliedly created (whether by grant or reservation) after the coming into force of the LRA 2002

There is no requirement under the LRA 2002 that implied legal easements[95] must be registered in order to secure legal status as is required for express legal easements. The effect of this is that protection for impliedly created easements and their enforceability against successors of the servient land[96] is determined by the availability of overriding status. Schedule 3, para. 3 of the LRA 2002 is the relevant provision here. Schedule 3, para. 2, which provides for actual occupation, has been held not to apply to easements: *Chaudhary*. Schedule 3, para. 3 is notoriously labyrinthine in its wording and requires some clarification so bear with it. The provision reads as follows:

(1) A legal easement or *profit à prendre*, except for an easement, or a *profit à prendre* which is not registered under Part 1 of the Commons Act 2006, which at the time of the disposition—

    (a) is not within the actual knowledge of the person to whom the disposition is made, and

    (b) would not have been obvious on a reasonably careful inspection of the land over which the easement or profit is exercisable.

(2) The exception in sub-paragraph (1) does not apply if the person entitled to the easement or profit proves that it has been exercised in the period of one year ending with the day of the disposition.

In summary, under Sch. 3, para. 3, an impliedly created easement will constitute an interest which, whilst unregistered, nevertheless overrides a registered disposition (i.e. will be an overriding interest) if:

1. it is registered under the Commons Act 2006; or

2. the third party acquiring the servient land knew of the existence of the easement; or

---

[93] Ibid., s. 27 and Sch. 2, para 2   [94] Ibid., s. 38 and Sch. 2 para. 7(2)(a); LRR 2003, r. 9(a).

[95] Including easements by prescription, necessity, common intention and those arising under s. 62 of the LPA 1925 and the rule in *Wheeldon v Burrows* (1879).

[96] Such easement will bind non-purchasers of the servient land under ss. 28 and 29 of the LRA 2002.

3. the existence of the easement would have been obvious on a reasonably careful inspection of the land; or

4. the easement has been exercised during the year immediately leading up to the date of the disposition.

The complex language of Sch. 3, para. 3 is an attempt to strike a balance between affording protection to implied easements which retain some utility (i.e. those which are in use and have been used within the previous year) and those which a purchaser knew about or would have been obvious. While the provision is worded rather negatively, it is likely than the vast majority of implied easements will qualify as overriding interests under para. 3. Only those legal easements not exercised within the last year, those not obvious, and those of whose existence the purchaser was not aware, will slip outside the paragraph's protective net.

Equitable easements created pre-LRA 2002

Equitable easements created prior to the coming into force of the LRA 2002 enjoyed overriding status under s. 70(1)(a) of the LRA 1925.[97] Equitable easements created after the enactment of the 2002 Act no longer enjoy this protection. That said, equitable easements enjoying overriding status prior to the 2002 Act retain this protection under Sch. 12, para. 10.[98]

Equitable easements created over registered land after the coming into force of the LRA 2002

Equitable easements created over registered land after the enactment of the LRA 2002 *do not* qualify for overriding status under Sch. 3, para. 3, it being a central goal of the registration project that, as far as possible, interest holders be required and encouraged to protect their interests by registering them. Schedule 3, para. 2 will also not apply: *Chaudhary*. In order for equitable easements to bind purchasers of the servient land, a notice[99] must be entered on the Charges Register of the title of the servient land. If no notice is entered, an equitable easement will be unenforceable against any purchaser of the servient land but will remain binding on non-purchasers such as recipients of gifts or those receiving land under a will.[100] It is vital to recognize that under s. 28 of the LRA 2002 all non-purchasers of registered land will take that land encumbered by all pre-existing legal and equitable easements irrespective of whether they appear to qualify for overriding status or have been registered.

Returning one last time to our example in Figure 10.13, we can say that whether C can enforce the easement against D therefore depends on whether the land in question is registered or unregistered and, additionally, whether the easement is legal or equitable.

---

[97] See also *Celsteel v Alton* (1985); *Thatcher v Douglas* (1996).

[98] As to equitable easements at the time of first registration, if such easements were registered as Class D(iii) land charges prior to the trigger for registration, they will remain binding on purchasers of the servient land as the Registrar examines the title under Land Registration Rules 2003, r. 35.

[99] Either an agreed notice or a unilateral notice.

[100] Sections 28 and 29 of the LRA 2002.

The principles on the enforceability of easements may at first seem complicated but, in truth, it is merely another instance where the fundamental distinctions of unregistered/registered land and law/equity again rule the day. Do take time to read and reread this section until the principles sink in and do practise some questions to test how far you grasp the material.

10.6 Remedies for interference with an easement

What happens when there is an interference with the exercise of an easement or, to put it differently, what can you do if you are prevented from fully exercising your easement? Now, you need to be aware that this is a separate question from issues of 'excessive user' (discussed later in section 10.7) and matters going to the 'extent of grant' (as discussed in section 10.3.5). With interference we are concerned with a situation where the exercise of the easement is limited, curbed, or hampered in some way. This is quite distinct from issues around intensification in the use of an easement or questions of how far the grant of an easement extends. Only where there is an *actionable* interference will a dominant owner be able to seek a remedy. If actionable, available remedies will be a claim for an injunction to prevent the interference or an action for damages for loss caused. So, when will an interference be actionable?

The leading case is *B&Q plc v Liverpool and Lancashire Properties Ltd* (2001) which confirms that an interference is actionable if two conditions are met:

1. there is a substantial interference with the reasonable enjoyment of the easement; and
2. it is reasonable for the easement holder to insist on exercise of the entire easement.

In *B&Q plc*, B&Q leased a retail unit (Unit 1) and, under that lease, enjoyed an easement (right of way) over a service yard which it used for deliveries to its store. The freehold owner and landlord of the retail park, Liverpool and Lancashire Properties Ltd (L&L), wanted to construct an extension to Unit 2 which, B&Q argued, would prevent exercise of its easement by blocking its delivery vehicles. Blackburne J adopted the 'test' for interference as laid down by Scott J in *Celsteel Ltd v Alton House Ltd* (1985), that there are 'two criteria relevant to the question whether a particular interference with a right of way is actionable: the interference will be actionable if it is substantial. And it will not be substantial if it does not interfere with the reasonable use of the right of way.' Blackburne J concluded that three propositions could be distilled from the case law:

1. The test for an actionable interference was not whether what was left after the interference was taken into account was 'reasonable' but whether the dominant landowner's insistence on continuing to use the full extent of the easement for which it had contracted was reasonable.
2. It is not open to a servient landowner to deprive an easement holder of its preferred modus operandi and then argue that someone else would prefer to do things differently, unless the preference is unreasonable or perverse.

3. If the easement holder has contracted for the 'relative luxury' of an ample right, he should not be deprived of that right in the absence of an explicit reservation merely because it is a relative luxury and the reduced, non-ample right would be all that was reasonably required.

As you can see, this test weighs heavily in the favour of the easement holder on a broad and subjective assessment of what is reasonable in the circumstances. Applying the test, Blackburne J held that the new extension was an actionable interference with B&Q's right of way. B&Q therefore succeeded in their claim.

Some other case law examples will help you grasp when an interference will be actionable:

- *Saint v Jenner* (1973): Installation of speed bumps on a lane over which rights of way existed was not of itself an actionable interference; however, it became actionable when the bumps fell into disrepair: damages were awarded.

- *Celsteel Ltd v Alton House Holdings Ltd* (1985): Planned construction of a car wash on a driveway over which rights of way existed for garage tenants to reach their lock-ups was an actionable interference even though access would have still been possible if more difficult (reduced by 50 per cent). This was an actionable interference as it would prevent one garage tenant from reversing into his garage: injunction granted.

- *Emmett v Sisson* (2014): Dominant landowners enjoyed a right to access their property along the whole length of a land boundary and so the building by servient landowners of a 2-metre high wall along the boundary constituted an actionable interference even though an access point was to be left in the wall. It was reasonable to expect access along the whole length of the right of way—this was neither unreasonable nor perverse.

- *Page v Convoy Investments Ltd* (2015): When an easement of access was granted, a pair of wooden and unusable gates existed on the land but were permanently open. Servient landowners subsequently installed electric gates at the entrance to the driveway operated by fob or digital code. This amounted to a substantial interference and the dominant landowner was entitled to require the electronic gates be kept open. The parties were urged to arrive at workable agreement to ensure security.

- *Kingsgate Development Projects Ltd v Jordan* (2017): A series of gates had been installed on a track over which a right of way existed. Dominant landowners argued the gates amounted to substantial interference. Gate 1 was left unlocked and easily opened by the push of a button (no interference); Gate 3 was again left unlocked and merely separated farmland from domestic property (no interference); Gate 2 represented the third gate in less than 100 metres and did amount to a substantial interference: injunction granted requiring the removal of this gate.

10.7 The termination of easements

There are limited means by which easements can be 'extinguished'; chiefly, just five:

- unification of tenements;
- release or abandonment;
- obsolescence;

- estoppel;
- excessive user.

In particular, note that there is no express statutory machinery that allows parties to apply to court for the termination of an easement.[101] We explore each mode of extinguishment of easements here.

10.7.1 Unification of tenements

We have already seen that it is an essential feature of an easement that the dominant and servient tenements are in separate ownership or occupation. Should the dominant and servient tenements become unified and there is common ownership and occupation, any easement will be extinguished. Unification of tenements is by some way the most common method by which an easement is terminated.

10.7.2 Release or abandonment

An easement will be extinguished where the dominant landowner releases the servient land from the burden of the easement. Release can be express (by deed) or more controversially by implication where the court finds that the dominant landowner has 'abandoned' the easement as proved by conduct.[102] Merely failing to make use of an easement will not, of itself, necessarily constitute abandonment or implied release: *Benn v Hardinge* (1993); *Swan v Sinclair* (1924). Buckley LJ in *Tehidy* explained what was required for implied release or abandonment of an easement:[103]

> Abandonment of an easement or profit can only, we think, be treated as having taken place where the person entitled to it has demonstrated a fixed intention never at any time thereafter to assert the right himself or to attempt to transmit it to anyone else.

This is a stringent test and, as decided cases demonstrate, the court is reluctant to accept that an easement has been released or been abandoned impliedly.[104] There are instances where a claim of implied release or abandonment has proved successful, however. An example is *Swan*, where an easement of access had not been used for over 38 years and there was strong evidence of acquiescence on the part of the dominant landowner which made exercise of the right evermore impossible. In a rather drastic example of abandonment, in *Moore v Rawson* (1824),[105] an easement was extinguished in a case of a right to light through a window when the building was entirely demolished and replaced with a stable without any windows at all. It seems that, in the absence of an express, fixed intention to abandon, implied release will require some degree of physical alteration to the dominant land.

---

[101] The Law Commission (Report No. 327) has recommended that a statutory procedure for extinguishing easements is introduced to allow for the termination at the discretion of the Lands Chambers of the Upper Tribunal of easements that are either obsolete or no longer of practical benefit.

[102] See K. Shorrock, 'Non-User of Easements' (1998) 4 Nott LJ 26.   [103] *Tehidy*, 553.

[104] See ibid.; *Benn v Hardinge*; *Williams v Sandy Lane (Chester) Ltd* (2006)) where claims of abandonment failed.

[105] See also *Ecclesiastical Commissioners for England v Kino* (1880).

10.7.3 Obsolescence?

The Court of Appeal in *Huckvale v Aegean Hotels Ltd* (1989) accepted the possibility that an easement might be extinguished by frustration if the easement were to be obsolete due to a change in circumstances. Slade LJ noted:[106]

> I would ... be prepared to accept in principle that ... circumstances might have so drastically changed since the date of the original grant of an easement (for example by supervening illegality) that it would offend common sense and reality foe the court to hold that an easement still subsisted ... the court should be slow to hold that an easement has been extinguished by frustration, unless the evidence shows clearly that because of change in circumstances since the date of the original grant there is no practical possibility of its ever again benefiting the dominant tenement in the manner contemplated by that grant.

In the event, in *Huckvale*, the court found that the easement (a right of way) had not been rendered obsolete[107] as there remained the possibility that the right may, at some point in the future, benefit the dominant land. In *Jones v Cleanthi* (2007), an easement in a lease was not extinguished even when a wall had been constructed (in order to comply with statutory obligations) which had the effect of preventing the easement from being exercised. The easement had not been extinguished said the Court of Appeal as there was a real and practical possibility that at some time during the remainder of the term granted by the lease there would no longer be any statutory impediment to the exercise of the right and the easement might once again become exercisable. *Jones* is further evidence that the court is largely unwilling to accept the extinguishment of an easement except in the rather extreme circumstances we encountered in *Moore*.

10.7.4 Estoppel?

It may be possible for an easement to be extinguished a result of the doctrine of proprietary estoppel. A case illustrating extinguishment by estoppel is *Lester v Woodgate* (2010). In *Lester*, a dominant landowner enjoyed a right of way over a footpath on adjoining servient land. The servient landowner extended a parking area on a hillside with the result that the right of way could no longer be exercised. The dominant landowner failed to object to the physical obstruction to the exercise of the right of way until several years later when he wished to build a house on his land and make use of the easement. The Court of Appeal held that the dominant landowner had acquiesced in the obstruction on which the servient landowner had relied to his detriment and that it would be unconscionable for the dominant landowner to insist on his strict legal right to make use of the right of way. An argument of estoppel by acquiescence employed in this 'defensive' manner therefore appears to afford another means by which an easement can be terminated.

McFarlane has argued in favour of the estoppel analysis employed in *Lester*:[108]

> In general, a party with a property right does not have the power to simply give up that right: if he wishes to dispose of the right, he needs to transfer it to another ... [the dominant owner]

---

[106] *Huckvale*, 174.   [107] The right of way had not been registered and had become effectively unenforceable.
[108] B. McFarlane, *The Structure of Property Law* (Oxford: Hart, 2008), 873.

can of course release an easement but only if a deed is used. Cases of so-called informal aban-donment are hence better seen as example of . . . defensive estoppel or . . . [the servient owner] relying on proprietary estoppel to show that [the dominant owner] is under a duty to release his easement.

10.7.5 Excessive user

Where the dominant landowner exceeds the scope of the easement granted, the servient owner will be entitled to bring an action for nuisance for excessive user. Remedies avail-able will include the grant of an injunction to stop the excessive user; an award of damages for any loss suffered; and, exceptionally, the complete extinguishment of the easement. In determining whether the exercise of an easement exceeds its scope, the court will first con-strue the terms of the grant. This is unproblematic if the easement was created by express grant. In a case of implied grant, the court will look to all the circumstances of the case at the time of the grant: *British Railways Board v Glass* (1965). The case law establishes that a simple increase in the use of a right does not amount to excessive user. What is required is a radical change in the character of the user of the dominant land resulting in a substantial increase in the burden on the servient landowner: *McAdams Homes Ltd v Robinson*.

KEY CASE *McAdams Homes Ltd v Robinson* (2005)

Facts: On a plot of land stood a derelict bakery. Drainage for the bakery was provided via pipes connected to the cottage which ran underneath the house and into the public sewerage system. The owners of the bakery gained planning permission to build two houses on the land and sold the plot to the McAdams. The McAdams intended that both houses would make use of the drainage pipes previously enjoyed by the bakery. During the construction of the houses, Robinson blocked the drainage pipe, concerned that during periods of high rainfall, backflow of sewage would threaten to engulf Robinson's garden. As a result, the McAdams were forced to install new drainage and brought proceedings to claim for the cost of the newly installed drainage system.

Legal issue: It was accepted by both parties that the 1982 conveyance of the bakery had included, by implication under the rule in *Wheeldon v Burrows*, an easement of drainage in favour of the purchaser of the land. On appeal, the issue was whether the easement of drainage could be exercised for the benefit of the two newly built houses on the site of the former bakery. In particular, this involved de-termining whether an easement granted by implication on the conveyance of land which had been used for a specified purpose (e.g. a bakery) can be enjoyed in circumstances of change of user of that land (e.g. change to residential housing).

Judgment: At first instance, a jointly instructed expert had estimated the flow of water which would have emanated from a bakery and compared this to the likely flow from two residential properties. Armed with this information, the trial judge held that there had been a radical change in the charac-ter of the land and that, based on the expert evidence of the increased flow of water, this change in character resulted in a substantial increase in the burden on the servient landowner. The McAdams' claim to the costs of the newly constructed drainage failed.

The Court of Appeal approved the reasoning of the trial judge underlining that when considering the issue of excessive user, two questions must be addressed:

→

> ➡
> 1. First, would the user of the dominant land represent a 'radical change in the character' or 'change in identity' of the site? This change would be more than a mere change or intensification of user.
> 2. Secondly, would the change in character lead to a 'substantial increase' in the burden on the servient land?
>
> The McAdams' user was excessive and represented a change from a purely industrial to a purely residential user of the land. This provided evidence of the substantial increase in the burden on the servient land.

In *Jelbert v Davies* (1968), another decision on excessive user, an easement was granted to the owner of a farm allowing access under a right of way over servient land 'at all times and for all purposes'. At the time of the grant, the right of way was exercised for the purposes of agriculture. Subsequently, the dominant landowner decided to redevelop his farm into a site for caravans with a capacity of 200 vehicles. The matter came before the court as to whether this represented excessive user. The Court of Appeal held the intended user would be excessive and would be an unreasonable interference with the rights of the servient landowner. In the circumstances, the court ordered that Jelbert was entitled to exercise the right of way using caravans but not in a manner that would cause a substantial interference with the rights of the servient landowner or cause a nuisance. Perhaps unhelpfully, the court refused to express a view on how many caravans would constitute an interference.

After *Jelbert* and *McAdams*, what will constitute a 'radical change in character' of the user of the dominant land is very much a matter of degree to be determined in all the circumstances of the particular case. In *Stanning v Baldwin* (2019), a former coach house was to be redeveloped into a number of houses and the issue was whether the change of user of the dominant land was 'excessive'. The court rejected this argument holding that, yes, the change of user amounted to an intensification in user, from six houses using a track for vehicular access (before the redevelopment) to nine houses using the track (post-development of the land) but this was not 'excessive' under *McAdams*.

10.8 *Profits à prendre*

We will cover profits only very briefly. Profits, or '*profits à prendre*' to give their full title, are commonly examined in connection with easements. This is because profits, like easements, involve the rights of one individual over another's land and constitute proprietary interests.

10.8.1 **What is a profit?**

A profit involves a right to take something from another's land. It involves more than a mere limited right over another's land but rather entails a right to appropriate some part of the natural product of that land (i.e. to remove something from another's land). By way of example, the right to enter neighbouring land to fish: *Barton v The Church Commissioner for England* (2008) or to shoot game will constitute a profit as will a right to gather firewood or to graze cattle: *Robertson v Hartropp* (1889). As you will appreciate from these examples, profits can be financially extremely valuable.[109]

The grantee of a profit automatically enjoys a licence permitting lawful access to the servient land for the purposes of severing or appropriating the subject of the profit (i.e. permission to access the land to exercise the profit). The scope and extent of a profit, just as for easements, is determined by reference to all the terms of the grant of the right.

10.8.2 **The rules governing profits**

These rules are, in many ways, the same as those that we have explored on easements. There are, however, certain important differences. One key distinction is that while for an easement to exist there must be both a dominant and a servient tenement, a profit can exist over servient land in circumstances where the grantee of the profit does not own a dominant tenement. Profits, unlike easements, can therefore exist *in gross*: *Lord Chesterfield v Harris* (1908). This is a vital distinguishing feature of profits setting them apart from easements. Where a profit is attached to land, however, it must accommodate the dominant tenement: *Bailey*.

10.8.3 **Types of profits**

Where only one individual enjoys the right to take something from the other's land, the profit is said to be 'sole' or 'several'. Where the profit is shared between a number of individuals (which may also include the servient owner), it is described as being 'in common'.

10.8.4 **The creation of profits**

Subject to a few exceptions, the rules regarding creation of profits mirror those of easements as discussed in this chapter: express grant, reservation, implied grant, and prescription. Given that the rules for creation of profits and easements are very similar, we will not discuss them at length but rather we focus on the differences that exist:

- Profits can be expressly granted or reserved but will only operate at law if the relevant formality requirements are satisfied. This means that a deed must be used: *Wood v Leadbitter* (1845) and, as it constitutes a registrable disposition under s. 27 of the LRA 2002, it must be completed by registration.

- Profits can be impliedly created under s. 62 of the LPA 1925 but, importantly, the rule in *Wheeldon v Burrows* does not apply. Why is this? Quite simply, the rule in *Wheeldon v Burrows* cannot operate as profits are not 'continuous and apparent' and therefore a key constituent or condition of the rule cannot be satisfied.

---

[109] This is reflected in s. 3 of the LRA 2002, which permits profits which are legal in nature to be registered with their own title.

- Lastly, a profit can be created by prescription through long user. You should note, however, that the relevant statutory periods for prescription under the Prescription Act 1832 are longer for profits: there must be 30 years' use where there was no permission granted; 60 years' use is required where oral permission was granted. Beware: the Prescription Act does not apply to profits in gross. Interestingly, the Law Commission in its 2011 Report, *Making Land Work: Easements, Covenants and Profits à Prendre*, has recommended that profits should not be capable of acquisition by prescription.

10.8.5 The extinguishment of profits

The same methods of termination apply for the extinguishment of profits as those discussed for the termination of easements: see section 10.7. Most commonly, profits will be extinguished where the interest holder expressly or impliedly grants a release from the right or where there is unity of ownership (i.e. where the interest holder acquires the servient land). A period of non-use appears to be insufficient to terminate a profit. There is, as yet, no statutory scheme for the discharge or modification of either easements or profits which have fallen into disuse. However, alteration of the dominant land with the result that the profit can no longer operate will terminate the profit.

10.9 Proposed reform of easements and profits

The Law Commission Report No. 327, *Making Land Law Work: Easements, Covenants and Profits*, was published in 2011 and whilst the bulk of report concerned the law of freehold covenants (which we explore in Chapter 11), it did contain some interesting and level-headed proposals for reform of the law of easements. The report also offered an marvellously accessible précis of the current law which is, of itself, very useful to you as students of the subject. For this reason alone, the report is well worth a read—or, at least, key sections of it! The principal recommendations for reform contained within the Commission's report are these:

1. the statutory abolition of the 'ouster principle';
2. that s. 62 of the LPA 1925 should no longer be permitted to operate to transform mere licences into full easements;
3. the introduction of a single method for the implication of easements which draws no distinction between the grant and reservation of easements; implication of easements would, instead, be founded on 'utility' on the basis of what is 'necessary for the reasonable use of the land';[110]
4. the introduction of a single, statutory mode of prescription to replace all the current methods of prescription;
5. the clarification of the means by which easements can be extinguished including a rebuttable presumption of abandonment after 20 years of non-use;

---

[110] See Douglas in 'Reforming Implied Easements', where he rejects the logic of the Law Commission's proposals on implied easements as being unnecessary and unhelpful.

6. the reversal (by statute) of the decision in *Wall v Collins* (2007) where the court held that an easement benefiting a lease survived the termination of the leasehold estate by merger with the freehold (this has proved to be a deeply controversial decision);

7. the abolition of profits by implication or by prescription.

You may think these proposals are radical but, in truth, they reflect no more than a tidying-up, a rationalization, and a clarification of some of the more inconsistent aspects of the law of easements and profits. There is no wholesale reform proposed and no change in the essential characteristics of easements. The Law Commission's recommendations have met mostly with a positive response but are, as yet, still awaiting implementation by Parliament.

10.10 Future directions

The law of easements and profits has been described by Lawson in the following terms:[111]

> Though easements have been part of English and Welsh property law for many centuries, a considerable amount of controversy surrounds many aspects of their existence and operation ... these controversies and confusion make the subject both frustrating and fascinating.

Having explored the essential characteristics, creation, and scope of easements (and profits) in this chapter, we turn here to ponder areas for future development. Remember that we should also keep a close and watchful eye on the fall-out from the significant decision of the Supreme Court in *Regency Villas*.

10.10.1 The implication of easements

This has always been one of the most controversial areas of the law of easements whether it be by necessity, common intention, under s. 62 of the LPA 1925, or under the principle in *Wheeldon v Burrows*. This issue has very recently again reared its head in light of the important decision in *Wood* which could be interpreted as condemning the rule in *Wheeldon v Burrows* to near extinction (at least in practice). This begs the question whether we may be moving towards a complete assimilation or, more accurately, an absorption of *Wheeldon v Burrows* into the operation of s. 62 of the LPA 1925. As the court expands its interpretation of s. 62, might this be the next step for the law on implication of easements? Is it a desirable one? Certainly, this move is entirely at odds with the recommendations of the Law Commission that proposes an overhaul of the modes of implication of easements and favours a more restrictive interpretation of s. 62. We pick up the Commission's proposals next.

10.10.2 The Law Commission's proposals

Property lawyers have long called for the Commission to turn its attention to a consideration of the merits (or otherwise) of reforming the law of easements. In 2002, Gaunt and Morgan wrote:[112]

---

[111] Lawson, 'Easements', 96.

[112] J. Gaunt and P. Morgan, *Gale on Easements*, 17th edn (London: Sweet & Maxwell, 2002), vi.

The Law Commission has ducked the law of easements more than once. We understand it may now be girding its loins for the task of cleansing this particular Augean stable.

As we explored in this chapter, the Law Commission published its final report in 2011 which proposed wide-ranging reforms to the law of easements focused on simplifying and streamlining the law and ironing out inconsistencies. Looking forward, we might reflect onwhether these reforms will suffer the same fate as earlier work by the Commission around easements which has been abandoned. In broad measure, the reforms proposed appear sensible and deliverable but that does not mean they will be implemented. How might the reforms reframe and reshape the law in this area? In particular, how might the new statutory test for the implication of easements change the law?

The reform proposals in the 2011 report have not met with universal support. Douglas, for example, has argued against the need for adoption of the reforms proposed and questions the need for reform in this area:[113]

> The law currently provides a single intention-based test for implication. This test . . . is a simple and coherent one and its reputation for complexity is undeserved. Further . . . the statutory test being proposed by the Law Commission would not be an improvement upon the current law. By introducing a test that is difficult to justify, and which draws an arbitrary distinction between express and implied easements, the Law Commission's proposal may actually serve to confuse the law of implication.

Is there not an argument that the conclusions Douglas reaches would serve to entrench and sustain inconsistency and obscurity in the law? How far do you share Douglas' view that the current law on implication of easements is 'simple and coherent'? Is the transformative effect of s. 62 of the LPA 1925 either simple or coherent? What of the uncertainty surrounding the test of 'necessity' for implication by necessity and the overlap between *Wheeldon v Burrows* and s. 62? Would it not be far simpler and more coherent to recognize the implication of easements where a right is 'necessary for the reasonable enjoyment of the land' as the Law Commission proposed?

10.10.3 Developments as to easements of car parking

Though perhaps not the liveliest concern of modern property law, Xu calls for special attention to the development of bespoke principles on easements of car parking.[114] In fact, this may not be as odd a suggestion as it first appears. Xu explains:[115]

> There are inherent difficulties in allowing an easement as extensive and interfering as car parking to exist over land, which may partly explain why it took so long for such rights to be accepted as easements in the first place. However, now that they are, or will be, accepted one way or another, the court should adopt a much bolder approach and take the lead in developing clear and useful principles to deal with practical difficulties.

---

[113] Douglas, 'Reforming Implied Easements', 274.

[114] Xu, 'Easement of Car Parking: The Ouster Principle Is Out but the Problems May Aggravate'.

[115] Ibid., 305.

For Xu, this means that the Law Commission's recommendation for abolition of the 'ouster principle' may be premature:[116]

> In eradicating one problem, which may be on its way out in any case, the [Commission's] proposal would create many more serious problems in areas where presently there is none. If enacted, it will create great uncertainty in established principles and case law far beyond the issue of car parking that it was specifically targeting . . . It is simply problematic in the context of car parking. But the ouster principle continues to serve many essential and irreplaceable functions elsewhere and the baby certainly should not be thrown out with bath water. If there is to be statutory intervention on this point at all, it should be clearly restricted in scope to the parking of motor vehicles. It may even be feasible to take no legislative action at this stage and allow the common law to grow out of the shadow of *Batchelor*.

In view of the decisions in *Virdi* and *Kettel* which suggest a greater willingness of the court to adopt a flexible approach to the *Batchelor* test of 'reasonable use', we must watch this space to see how the 'ouster principle' develops if the Law Commission's reforming, abolitionist vision is not realized. Might *Virdi* and *Kettel* signal the beginning of the end for the 'ouster principle' rendering Parliament's intervention unnecessary?

10.10.4 Should easements be allowed to exist 'in gross'?

As things stand, an easement can only exist where there is both a dominant and a servient tenement. No easement can exist where there is only servient land. Sturley, writing in the 1980s, argued quite robustly that easements in gross should be recognized. Sturley began by identifying the two traditional arguments mounted against the recognition of easements in gross:[117]

> The first, which may be labelled the 'surcharge argument' holds that an easement in gross, not being limited to the needs of the dominant tenement is likely to burden the servient tenement with excessive use. The second and somewhat more convincing, which may be labelled the 'clogs on title argument' holds that an easement in gross is likely to be an unjustified incumbrance on the title of the servient tenement . . .

Sturley gave several examples of rights which he argued would make for potentially very useful easements in gross. This list included:

* the right to land a helicopter on another's land;
* the right to maintain telephone, power, or cable television lines over another's land;
* the right to maintain advertising signs on another's land.

Although the Law Commission has set its mind against permitting easements in gross, it conceded that the objections to easements in gross were 'not insurmountable'.[118] So, should the rule against easements in gross be abolished? Sturley argued that the rule against easements in gross:[119]

> exists on the weakest of authority for reasons that are no longer compelling. The judicial statements cited for the proposition are either unreasoned dicta or essentially irrelevant.

---

[116] Ibid.   [117] Sturley, 'Easements in Gross', 562.
[118] Law Commission Consultation Paper No. 186, [3.13].   [119] Sturley, 'Easements in Gross', 567.

For Sturley, both arguments advanced in support of the rule had been exaggerated and over-emphasized. In particular, he contended that any concerns of excessive burden of servient land and 'clogging' title could be remedied. First, the terms of the grant could be used to limit the scope of any easement in gross thus preventing any undue burden of the servient land. On the second argument, Sturley contended that the anxiety here was essentially a concern that easements in gross would not be capable of discovery and would render the land unmarketable. This, he argued, could be easily countered by requiring that easements in gross must be registered against the servient land in order for the easement to operate at law. Alternatively, easements in gross could be registered with their own substantive title.

Support for the recognition of easements in gross is also found from outside this jurisdiction. In the United States, for example, easements in gross are already recognized, prove largely unproblematic, and their use is widespread. In particular, as regards service utilities, rights to telephone lines, gas pipes, and electricity cables regularly exist in gross. In England, we currently provide for these rights under specific statutory exceptions to the 'no easement in gross' rule. Statute therefore provides for special powers under which utilities companies can enter private land to install services. The requirement for a dominant tenement is statutorily abrogated. Similar exceptions operate in Scotland and Australia. What objections remain? For the Law Commission, the principal grounds for maintaining the 'no easements in gross' rule can be summed up as follows:

- The law should be slow to create new interests which have the capacity to burden land potentially in perpetuity.
- Many of the rights that might become easements in gross currently exist as contractual licences. Permitting easements in gross would endow these personal rights with proprietary status.
- Finally, the very existence of the statutory exceptions to the rule addresses one of the key arguments against its abolition.

Where does this leave the debate? Well, according to the Law Commission, the majority of those who responded to its consultation in 2008 (one question of which was whether easements in gross should be permitted), felt that a change in the law in this area was neither necessary nor desirable. Unless and until there is a groundswell of opinion pressing for recognition of easements in gross, it seems the issue has, for the foreseeable future at least, been put on ice.

Further reading

- C. Bevan, 'Opening Pandora's Box? Recreation Pure and Simple: Easements in the Supreme Court' [2019] Conv 55.
- J. Bray, 'More than Just a Walk in the Park: A New View on Recreational Easements' [2017] Conv 418.
- F. Burns, 'Prescriptive Easements in England and Legal Climate Change' [2007] Conv 133.
- E. Cooke, 'Re Ellenborough Park (1955) A Mere Recreation and Amusement' in N. Gravells (ed.), Landmark Cases in Land Law (Oxford: Hart Publishing, 2013), chapter 3.

- D. Cowan, L. Fox O'Mahony, and N. Cobb, 'Third Party Interests in the Use and Control of Land' in *Great Debates in Property Law* (Basingstoke: Palgrave Macmillan, 2012), chapter 7.

- S. Douglas, 'How to Reform Section 62 of the Law of Property Act 1925' [2015] Conv 13.

- S. Douglas, 'Reforming Implied Easements' (2015) 115 LQR 251.

- A. Goymour, 'Rights in Property and the Effluxion of Time' in E. Cooke (ed.), *Modern Studies in Property Law*, Vol. 4 (Oxford: Hart Publishing, 2007), chapter 8.

- M. Haley and L. McMurty, 'Identifying an Easement: Exclusive Use, De Facto Control and Judicial Constraints' (2007) 58 NILQ 490.

- A. Hill-Smith, 'Rights of Parking and the Ouster Principle after *Batchelor v Marlow*' [2007] Conv 223.

- A. Lawson, 'Easements' in L. Tee (ed.), *Land Law: Issues, Debates, Policy* (Devon: Willan, 2002).

- P. Luther, 'Easements and Exclusive Possession' (1996) 16 LS 51.

- R. Meager, 'Prescription and User "As of Right": Ripe for Wholesale Reform?' in S. Bright (ed.), *Modern Studies in Property Law*, Vol. 6 (Oxford: Hart, 2011), chapter 12.

- N. Pratt, 'A Proprietary Right to Recreate' [2017] Conv 312.

- Special Edition on Easements [2012] Conv 1–65.

- M. F. Sturley, 'Easements in Gross' (1980) 96 LQR 557.

- L. Tee, 'Metamorphoses and Section 62 of the Law of Property Act 1925' [1998] Conv 115.

- L. Xu, 'Easement of Car Parking: The Ouster Principle Is Out but the Problems May Aggravate' [2012] Conv 291.

Online resources

Access the online resources at www.oup.com/uk/bevan2e/ to test yourself with self-test questions and scenario problems. You can also view additional supporting material relevant to the topics in this chapter, including:

- *Videos*
- *Audio podcasts*
- *Maps, diagrams, and flowcharts*
- *Interactive exercises*
- *Examples of real-life legal documentation*

11 Freehold Covenants

11.1 Introduction

A covenant is a promise made in a deed. We first encountered the covenant briefly in the context of leases in Chapter 9. In this chapter, we consider covenants in freehold land—also known as 'freehold covenants'. As the name suggests, these are promises made between freehold owners of land. Let's take an example: imagine that Anna owns a plot of land which adjoins another parcel of land belonging to Ben. Anna may covenant (i.e. promise) to ensure the frontage of her house is painted annually to maintain the amenity of the area. Ben may also covenant not to run a commercial business on his property. These promises are freehold covenants. As you can see from this example, freehold covenants can be positive—where one party promises to positively, actively, do something—for example, to plant trees, to pay a contribution to the maintenance of a road, or to paint frontage as with Anna in our example. Alternatively, freehold covenants can also be negative or 'restrictive' in nature—where one party promises not to do something on their land—for example, not to erect any structures on their land higher than two storeys, or not to run a business as with Ben in our example.

Freehold covenants are another example of rights which affect the enjoyment of adjoining or neighbouring land. Some of the terminology that will be used in this chapter, we will meet again—for example, the language of 'benefit' and 'burden' will make another appearance in the next chapter when we discuss leasehold covenants. Importantly, freehold covenants are contracts and therefore are necessarily binding between the original parties to the deed but may, if certain conditions are met, also be enforceable by and against successors of these parties. This means that freehold covenants, like their leasehold counterparts, are interests which enjoy a proprietary character and can, therefore be extremely powerful rights in land. This enforceability question forms a central focus of our discussion in this chapter. Just think about it: if you purchase of a parcel of land, you would want to know if you could be compelled to paint a façade or contribute to maintenance costs, or be prevented from extending an existing property or from running a business, would you not?

11.1.1 Why covenants matter

Whilst freehold covenants are now firmly established as part of the land law catalogue of proprietary rights, this was not always the case. The change came in the industrial revolution with the major shift from agriculture to commerce. Soon, vast swathes of people made the move from rural areas into the cities to find work. In turn, this made urban land an extremely valuable and sought-after commodity. Management of this urban land became increasingly important to landowners as the burgeoning middle classes wanted to develop spheres of more attractive housing away from the slums of the day. The properties of the middle classes boasted beautiful terraces, gardens, and spaces to socialize and they wanted to keep them this way.[1] How could these areas be maintained and protected?

In the mid to late nineteenth century, it was equity that offered a solution when the Court of Chancery developed the restrictive covenant, a novel proprietary interest in land capable of binding third parties. The restrictive covenant offered a means of protection for the much-vaunted high standard of living of the middle classes by ensuring, if conditions were met, that promises to secure and maintain the value and amenity of land were binding on successors in title. In essence, the Court of Chancery had devised (through the law of covenants) what might be seen as an early forerunner to modern planning law, allowing controls to be placed on the user of land. The result of equity's intervention was the transformation of the principles surrounding the law of covenants with the result that covenants became proprietary rights with the capacity to bind third parties.

If we fast-forward to today, there is now a whole plethora of different State-initiated measures restricting the use of land including health and safety, building regulations, and extensive planning laws. Yet the arrival of building regulations and planning laws did not stymie the continued role for covenants. This is because freehold covenants allowed and continue to allow for a broader, far more particularized, and bespoke control over land than planning law could ever impose. Perhaps unsurprisingly, according to the Law Commission, today around 79 per cent of freehold land is the subject of at least one freehold covenant.[2] Freehold covenants therefore occupy a central place within modern land law. This chapter aims to provide a clear exposition of the key principles as well as to engage some of the wider thematic debates surrounding covenants including the long-standing calls for reform to the area which, spearheaded by the Law Commission, have been growing in strength since the 1980s.[3] This chapter begins with a consideration of the nature and essential characteristics of freehold covenants before turning to examine 'the

---

[1]   See S. Gardner and E. MacKenzie, *Introduction to Land Law* (Oxford: Hart, 2012), 390.

[2]   Law Commission Consultation Paper No. 186 (2008).

[3]   We consider the Law Commission's latest work on reform of the law of covenants, Report No. 327, *Making Land Work: Easements, Covenants and Profits à Prendre*' (2011) in sections 11.9 and 11.10.

enforceability question'—namely, in what circumstances covenants can bind original parties to the covenant and successors i.e. third parties acquiring land subject to covenants.

 Visit the online resources to watch a video walkthrough of answering a covenant problem question.

11.2 The nature of freehold covenants

In order to fully understand the principles governing freehold covenants, we must first lay the groundwork by examining the nature of covenants and by demystifying some of the terminology in the area.

You have already been introduced to the basic idea of a freehold covenant: a promise between freehold owners made in a deed either to do something or not to do something on their own land for the benefit of neighbouring land. We call the party making the promise 'the **covenantor**' and the person to whom the promise is made 'the **covenantee**'. The covenantor is the party subject to the burden of the promise; the covenantee enjoys the benefit of that promise. This terminology should be familiar to you from your study of contract law. Let's unpack a little further the essential nature of freehold covenants:

- Freehold covenants must be created by deed. Three consequences flow from this. First, the formality requirements for the creation of deeds must be satisfied: s. 1 of the LP(MP)A 1989. Secondly, the use of a deed removes the need for any contractual consideration on the promise. Thirdly, the covenant will, as a matter of contract law, be automatically enforceable between the original parties to the covenant under the doctrine of privity of contract.

- Freehold covenants can be either positive or negative ('restrictive') in nature. Positive covenants will, by their nature, involve some form of positive action such as expenditure. In contrast, under a negative, 'restrictive' covenant, the covenantor promises to refrain from doing something on her own land to the benefit of the covenantee's land (e.g. not to build residential properties on the land).

- Under s. 1 of the LPA 1925, freehold covenants are equitable, proprietary interests that exist over land. It is this proprietary status that endows covenants with the *potential* to be enforceable between successors in title of the original parties (i.e. those coming into possession or ownership of the land which was originally subject to the covenant, e.g. purchasers of the original covenantor and covenantee's land).

- How is enforceability of a covenant determined? Well, it is here that you encounter what is sometimes called the 'duality principle'. Covenants by their very nature involve both a benefit and a burden (hence the reference to 'duality'). Enforceability of covenants where there are successors to the original parties is determined by considering whether the benefit and burden of the covenant have passed (or, as we say, have 'run') with the land so that the covenant is binding. The simple point to grasp is this: in every case where a person is seeking to enforce a freehold covenant, it needs to be shown (1) that the benefit of the covenant has run to the claimant; and (2) that the burden of the covenant has run to the defendant. As you will discover in sections 11.4 to 11.6, a body of principles has developed governing when the benefit and burden will run with the land. For now, however, the essential rule remains—and you must not forget this—that before a freehold covenant can be enforced, it must be shown, quite separately, that the benefit has passed to the claimant (under the relevant rules) and that the burden has passed to the defendant (under the relevant rules). If this 'duality' is not demonstrated, the covenant cannot be enforced.

Let's look at three scenarios to hopefully bring this to life. We begin with the most straightforward situation where there is a parcel of land subject to a freehold covenant and that land is still held by the original parties to the covenant: Figure 11.1. Here, Anna covenants with Ben not to carry on a trade or business on her own land, Plot 1. This is a negative or restrictive covenant because Anna has promised not to do something on her land. Anna is the covenantor (shouldering the burden of the covenant) and Ben is the covenantee (enjoying the benefit of the covenant). We call Plot 1 the servient land (the burdened land) and Plot 2 the dominant land (the benefited land). Ben, enjoying the benefit of the covenant, will be able to sue Anna in contract either if the negative covenant is breached or if Ben anticipates that Anna will breach the covenant. Ben may also be entitled to an order for specific performance, an injunction, or damages. Anna and Ben are the original parties to the covenant and, so long as the land is not transferred to successors, there is no need to consider whether the benefit and burden have passed. They can rely on the doctrine of privity of contract.

Let's consider a second scenario in which the original covenantor's land is sold to a new owner: Figure 11.2. Here, Anna sells her land (Plot 1) to Carol. Carol is Anna's successor. Carol is not an original party to the covenant but is a successor of the original covenantor's land. Ben cannot sue Carol for breach of covenant under the normal contractual principles as there is no privity of contract between them. Instead, if Ben wishes to sue Carol, he must demonstrate 'duality'—namely, that (1) he has the benefit of the covenant; and (2) that the burden of the covenant has passed to Carol as a successor of the burdened land. As Ben is an original party to the covenant (i.e. he has not transferred his land to a successor), he enjoys the benefit of the covenant. Only if it can be shown, additionally, that the burden has passed to Carol, however, can Ben enforce the covenant.

Finally, we consider a third scenario in which both the original covenantor and original covenantee's land is sold to new owners: Figure 11.3. Here, Anna and Ben both sell their land to successors, Carol and Daljit respectively. Neither Carol nor Daljit are original parties to the covenant. Carol is a successor to the original covenantor's land; Daljit is a successor to the original covenantee's land. Imagine that Daljit wants to enforce the covenant

Figure 11.1 Where there is an original covenantor and original covenantee

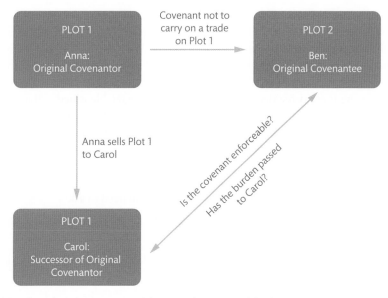

Figure 11.2 Where there is a successor of the original covenantor's land

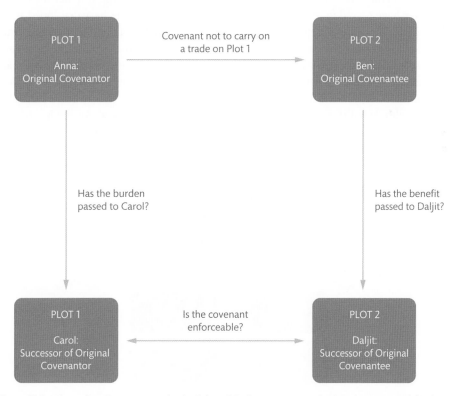

Figure 11.3 Where there is a successor both of the original covenantor and original covenantee's land

against Carol. The enforceability of the covenant between these new owners, Carol and Daljit, will depend again on the 'duality principle'—namely: (1) whether Daljit as the claimant can show that the benefit of the covenant has passed to him; and (2) that the burden of the covenant has passed to Carol as the defendant. Only where the burden and the benefit can be shown to have passed will the covenant be enforceable.

In considering these three distinct scenarios what we have identified is that, where the original parties to covenants remain in possession as freehold owners of their respective land, covenants are enforceable very straightforwardly between themselves under privity of contract (we explore this further in section 11.3). However, where there are successors in title to the original parties to the covenant, it is the 'duality principle' (passing of the benefit and burden) that will determine enforceability.

To emphasize the point, under the duality principle, you need to ask:

1. Has the benefit of the covenant passed to the would-be claimant so that she can enforce the covenant?
2. Has the burden of the covenant passed to the intended defendant so that the defendant is bound by the covenant?

There is one final consideration to bear in mind as to the nature of freehold covenants here: law and equity. Yes, that familiar distinction between law and equity is again relevant in this chapter. You have just been introduced to the 'duality principle' of benefit and burden. Well, when it comes to considering the relevant rules for determining whether the benefit and burden have passed to the claimant and defendant, distinct rules have developed at law and in equity. There are therefore 'legal rules' for passing the benefit and burden and 'equitable rules' for passing the benefit and burden. Ultimately, whether we use the legal rules or equitable rules, if the rules allow for the passing of the benefit and burden, the covenant will be enforceable (though there may be a differences concerning remedy as we explore in section 11.4). As you will see, in some respects the legal rules are more limited than the equitable rules. What this means is that when it comes to thinking about the law of covenants, we can therefore identify what might be called 'the four dimensions' of covenants—namely: law and equity, benefit, and burden: see Figure 11.4.

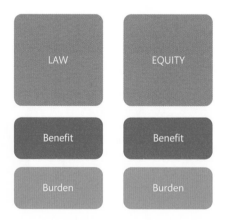

Figure 11.4 The 'four dimensions' of covenants: (i) law, (ii) equity, (iii) benefit, and (iv) burden

In this section, we have introduced the nature of freehold covenants and the importance of the 'duality principle' of benefit and burden in determining the enforceability of freehold covenants as well as the role of law and equity. In the next section, we examine in a little more depth the enforceability of covenants between the original parties to the covenant before turning to explore the legal and equitable rules for the passing of benefit and burden.

11.3 Enforcing freehold covenants: Original parties

As we have seen, between the original parties to a covenant, there exists 'privity of contract' and therefore, any covenants will be enforceable as a simple matter of contract law: see Figure 11.1. This applies equally to both positive and negative restrictive covenants. Generally, the position between original parties is therefore really quite straightforward. There are, however, certain issues that require further thought.

11.3.1 Who is an original party? The definition of 'original parties'

It may sound obvious, but defining who constitutes an 'original party' is vital to determining who is to benefit and who is burdened by the terms of a covenant. In many cases, this will be an easy question: those expressly named in the deed that created the covenant will be the original parties. As we saw in Figure 11.1, Anna (who owns Plot 1) covenants with Ben (who owns Plot 2) not to carry on a trade on Plot 1. Anna and Ben are the original parties to the covenant. In addition, any person explicitly named as a covenantee in the deed will also be able to enforce the covenant even if that person is not strictly a party to it. Section 56 of the LPA 1925 extends still further the category of original covenantees (but not covenantors to which the provision does not apply). Section 56 provides:

> A person may take an immediate or other interest in land or other property, of the benefit of any condition, right of entry, covenant or agreement over or respecting land or other property, although he may not be named as a party to the conveyance or other instrument.

Section 56 of the LPA 1925[4] therefore allows a person to be considered a 'party' to the covenant despite not being expressly named in the deed so long as the covenant contains a general description of covenantees and that person falls within this given description.[5] How does this work, in practice? Imagine that Anna covenants with Ben and 'all the owners of adjoining plots of land' not to carry on a trade. In this situation, all those adjoining landowners will, under s. 56 of the LPA 1925, be regarded as original covenantees to the covenant and, on this basis, will be able to enforce the covenant even though they are not explicitly named in the deed. Section 56 must not be drawn too broadly, though, as to do so would be in effect to abolish the doctrine of privity of contract. The court has sought to clarify the true scope of s. 56. In *White v Bijou Mansions* (1937), the court confirmed that the provision operates to allow particular, defined and identifiable individuals to be treated

---

[4] Which is not to be taken as signalling the end of privity of contract, despite suggestions of this by Lord Denning MR in *Smith and Snipes Hall Farm Ltd v River Douglas Catchment Board* (1949).

[5] *Churchill v Temple* (2010).

as parties to the covenant where there is evidence that they were intended to benefit from the covenant and not to bestow benefits on scores of people through vague and widely drafted clauses. The court seemingly went further in *Amsprop Trading Ltd v Harris Distribution* in noting that it is not enough that an individual is merely intended to benefit; that individual must be intended as being part of the covenant in the sense that the covenant was made with that person and not simply for them. As *Amsprop* demonstrates, whether s. 56 is engaged rests squarely on the attention to detail and precision of those drafting the deed creating the covenant.[6]

KEY CASE *Amsprop Trading Ltd v Harris Distribution* (1997)

Facts: Harris was the subtenant of a property and covenanted with the tenant to repair the premises and to allow the head-landlord, Amsprop's predecessor in title, or their agents to enter the property to assess the repairs and, where these had been improperly carried out, to recover the cost of rectifying them. There was no privity of contract between Amsprop and Harris and so Amsprop could not directly recover the costs of the repairs. Amsprop brought proceedings against Harris, contending that mention in the covenant of 'the superior landlords' allowed Amsprop to enforce the covenant under s. 56(1) of the LPA 1925.

Legal issue: Did s. 56 of the LPA 1925 operate to afford Amsprop the right to enforce the covenant?

Judgment: The High Court dismissed Amsprop's claim. According to the court, someone could only take advantage of s. 56 where the covenant had been made for his benefit and it was intended that that person be treated as a party to the covenant. As the court identified, drawing on Megarry and Wade: 'The true aim of s. 56 seems to be not to allow a third party to sue on a contract merely because it is for his benefit; the contract must purport to be made with him.'

Amsprop, therefore, followed a line of case law, including *Beswick v Beswick* (1968), which adopted a narrower reading of s. 56. The result is that, under s. 56, there is no need for those benefiting under a covenant to be named expressly in the deed; it will suffice if they are instead referred to by some general, generic description by class—for example, 'the owners of Plot 1'. They must, however, be identifiable and in existence at the date the covenant was created, and it must be shown that the covenant was intended to be made with them and not just for their benefit.

11.3.2 Enforcement by a third party against the original covenantor

Another way a covenant can be enforced by a party not expressly named in the covenant is under the Contracts (Rights of Third Parties) Act 1999, which modifies the traditional privity of contract rule. Under s. 1(1) of the 1999 Act, a third party who is not party to a contract may enforce 'in his own right' a term of the contract if the contract provides expressly that he is so able or, alternatively, if the contract purports to confer a benefit on

---

[6] See also *Kelsey v Dodd* (1881) and *White v Bijou Mansions Ltd* which establish s. 56 only operates in favour of an individual who could, in fact, have been a party to the covenant at the time it was granted.

him. This provision is excluded, however, where 'if on a proper construction of the contract it appears that the parties did not intend the term to be enforceable by the third party'.[7] By s. 1(3) of the Act:

> The third party must be expressly identified in the contract by name, as a member of a class or as answering a particular description but need not be in existence when the contract is entered into.

As you can see, the provisions of s. 1 of the 1999 Act are far broader in scope than s. 56 of the LPA 1925 discussed in section 11.3.1 primarily because s. 56 only operates if an individual is in existence and falls within the description in the covenant *at the time of the grant*. The 1999 Act therefore makes a significant contribution to the passing of the benefit of covenants to third parties and is a very handy added level of protection for would-be original covenantees.[8]

11.3.3 The position where the original covenantor has parted with her land

Where the original covenantor has parted with her land, she nevertheless still remains liable on all covenants under general contract law principles. This means that she can be sued for any breach. In practice, however, where there is a breach of covenant, the wronged party is more likely to want to bring an action against the offending party who has actually committed that breach rather than the original covenantor who is no longer in possession of the land. This is because the wronged party wants to secure performance of the covenant or to seek an injunction to prevent further breach rather than receive a mere award of damages from the original covenantor. Where would this really get you? It certainly will not affect performance of the covenant. Of course, if the party in breach is penniless or cannot be found, an action against the original covenantor still holds some attraction and value, albeit limited.

11.3.4 The position where the original covenantee has parted with her land

Where the original covenantee has parted with her land, she is still able to enforce the covenant against any person subject to the burden of that covenant. If, however, damages are awarded for breach, the award will be nominal only as the original covenantee is very unlikely to have suffered any real loss.[9] Equally, the court may refuse to order an injunction or specific performance as the original covenantee no longer enjoys possession of the land and again will have suffered only minimal loss.[10]

11.4 Enforcing freehold covenants: The role of law and equity and remedies

The distinction between law and equity has reared its head repeatedly throughout this book and, as we have seen, exerts a considerable influence on the means of enforcement of interests in land law. As we touched on briefly in section 11.2, when it comes to

---

[7] Contracts (Rights of Third Parties) Act 1999, s. 1(2).
[8] The 1999 Act only applies to contracts entered into after 11 May 2000.
[9] *Formby v Barker* (1903).   [10] *Chambers v Randall* (1923).

enforcement of covenants, there are two distinct bodies of rules for the passing of benefit and burden (as required under the 'duality principle'): *the legal rules* and *the equitable rules*. These rules provide different 'methods' or 'routes', for demonstrating that the benefit and burden of freehold covenants have passed to successors in a claim on the covenant. We examine these legal and equitable rules in detail in sections 11.5 and 11.6 and, as you will discover, in certain important respects the equitable rules are far more flexible than those at law. Note, however, there is no difference in terms of whether a covenant is enforceable, if it is the legal rules or equitable rules that are used—no set of rules is more favourable, in this sense, than the other, though generally, as you will see, the equitable rules are more permissive (i.e. allowing for enforceability of more covenants than the more limited legal rules).

According to the court in *Miles v Easter* (1933), there can be no mixing of the rules of law and equity. This means that, for example, where a claimant relies on the equitable rules to demonstrate that the burden has passed, the equitable rules must also be used to demonstrate the benefit of the covenant has passed. There was, unhelpfully, earlier authority which took entirely the opposite view[11] and suggested that there was no rule against the mixing of the rules. Although the mixing 'issue' has not yet been finally resolved, for the sake of analytical simplicity and symmetry, it is perhaps best to proceed on the basis of the *Miles* authority and avoid mixing. But before we get to exploring the legal and equitable rules, it is worth pausing to consider the remedies available to the court where there has been a successful claim to enforce a covenant. Imagine that there has been a breach of covenant, the claimant has brought proceedings and has proved her case against the guilty party in breach. How will the court remedy the situation?

Strictly speaking, the remedial stage is one area where it does matter if it is the legal or equitable rules that are applied. According to orthodoxy, claims brought to enforce the covenant applying the legal rules give rise to a claim for damages for breach of covenant whereas a wider range of more flexible, discretionary[12] remedies is available in a claim brought under the equitable rules. That said, whether it is the legal rules which are engaged or those of equity to demonstrate the passing of the benefit and burden is today of less and less importance. This is because, since the fusion of the courts of law and equity, there is a growing recognition that the same menu of remedies is open to the court whether the clam is brought at law or in equity.[13] So, what remedies are available? The court is likely to select one of the following principal remedies:

- An injunction to prevent the breach: This is the most common remedy. It is equitable is nature, entirely at the discretion of the court, and will be refused in cases of unreasonable delay (known as 'laches').

- An order for specific performance: This is available only in the case of positive covenants.

- An award of damages in lieu of an injunction: This remedy will be used sparingly and only where an injunction would be inappropriate—for example, where it would be oppressive or overly burdensome. In *Wrotham Park Estate v Parkside Homes* (1974), a case where a

---

[11] *Rogers v Hosegood* (1900).

[12] Remember that no equitable remedy is available as of right but at the absolute discretion of the court.

[13] *Gafford v Graham* (1998).

covenant not to develop land without prior approval was breached, the court refused to grant an injunction as to do so would involve demolition of houses already built. This breach could theoretically be undone but the houses now existed and it would be 'an unpardonable waste of much needed houses' to direct they be pulled down. Damages in lieu were awarded to the value of 5 per cent of the profits made by the party in breach.

11.5 Enforcing freehold covenants: The legal rules

As was made clear in section 11.2, in considering the enforceability of freehold covenants, you should begin your analysis by considering the 'duality principle': whether the benefit of the covenant has passed to the would-be claimant and whether the burden has passed to the intended defendant. The passing of benefit and burden should therefore be explored quite separately. In this section, we explore the legal rules for the passing of benefit and burden of freehold covenants. Before we embark on this, however, a key preliminary point needs to be made: namely, that because the legal rules are more limited than the equitable rules and because we are told that the rules should not be 'mixed', the result is that the equitable rules tend to be applied more often than the legal rules to show the passing of the benefit and the burden.[14] Nevertheless, the legal rules are still important and we consider how they operate here.

11.5.1 Passing of the benefit at law

What are the principles governing the passing of the benefit of positive and negative covenants at law? At law, the benefit of a covenant will pass or 'run' with the land if five conditions are satisfied, as confirmed recently by Norris J in *Bryant Homes Southern Ltd v Stein Management* (2016): see Figure 11.5. Let's consider each condition in turn.

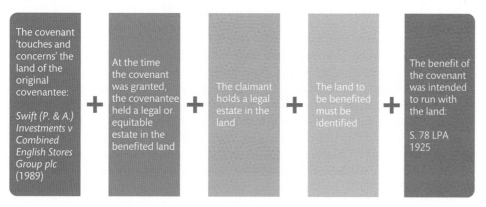

The covenant 'touches and concerns' the land of the original covenantee:

Swift (P. & A.) Investments v Combined English Stores Group plc (1989)

+

At the time the covenant was granted, the covenantee held a legal or equitable estate in the benefited land

+

The claimant holds a legal estate in the land

+

The land to be benefited must be identified

+

The benefit of the covenant was intended to run with the land:

S. 78 LPA 1925

Figure 11.5 Passing the benefit of a covenant at law

---

[14] See *Miles*; *Gafford v Graham*.

11.5.1.1 The covenant 'touches and concerns' the land of the original covenantee

Rogers v Hosegood (1900) established the first condition that the covenant must 'touch and concern' the original covenantee's land. In essence, 'touching and concerning' means that the covenant must be related to the mode of user, the quality of *land*, and not be purely *personal* to the parties to the covenant. The test has been formulated in different ways:

- Tucker LJ in *Smith & Snipes Hall Farm v River Douglas Catchment Board* (1949) adopted a 'value of land' formulation. According to this construction, a covenant will 'touch and concern' the land if:[15]

  > it . . . either affects the land as regards mode of occupation, or must be such as per se, and not merely from collateral sources, affects the value of the land.

- Lord Oliver in *Swift (P. & A.) Investments v Combined English Stores Group plc* (1989) adopted a three-stage test. According to this construction, a covenant will 'touch and concern' the land if:[16]

  (1) The covenant benefits only the [landowner] for the time being, and if separated from the [land] ceases to be of benefit to the covenantee;

  (2) The covenant affects the nature, quality, mode of user or value of the land . . .

  (3) The covenant is not expressed to be personal . . .

Lord Oliver's formulation has since been approved by the court including in *Sugarman v Porter* (2006).

11.5.1.2 At the time the covenant was granted, the covenantee held a legal estate in the benefited land

This condition is entirely self-explanatory and, in the vast majority of cases, very easily determined on the facts of the particular case.

11.5.1.3 The claimant must hold a legal estate in the land

The claimant must hold a legal estate in the land but it need not be the same legal estate as the original covenantee. This means that while the original covenantee may have held the freehold, the claimant may hold a legal lease, for example, as happened in *Smith & Snipes Hall Farm*. In these circumstances, the requirement is satisfied as both the original covenantee and the claimant can be said to hold legal estates. Recall there are only two legal estates recognized today: freehold and leasehold. In addition, s. 78(1) of the LPA 1925 deems 'the owners and occupiers for the time being' to constitute successors in title for the purpose of enforcing restrictive (but not positive) covenants. It therefore appears that any occupier or squatter will be able to enforce the benefit of a restrictive covenant under this provision.[17]

---

[15] *Smith & Snipes Hall Farm*, 506.   [16] *Swift (P. & A.) Investments*, 636.

[17] Section 78(1) provides, '"successors in title" shall be deemed to include the owners and occupiers for the time being of the land of the covenantee intended to be benefited'.

11.5.1.4 The land to be benefited must be identified

Again, entirely self-explanatory; it is crucial that the land that is to benefit from the covenant is identified. Note, however, that this can be done with the aid of extrinsic evidence.

11.5.1.5 The benefit of the covenant was intended to run with the land

The benefit of the covenant must be shown to have been intended to run with the benefited land. To express this another way, we can say that the benefit of the covenant must have been 'annexed' to the benefited land. Annexation means that the benefit of a covenant is fixed, glued to the land for all time, and thereafter passes automatically on a conveyance of that land. Annexation can take place in three principal ways (though, today, by far the most straightforward and commonplace is statutory annexation):

* express annexation;
* implied annexation;
* statutory annexation under s. 78 of the LPA 1925.

These three methods of annexation have been described by Kenny as giving rise to 'one of the richest areas of fantasy in printed English'.[18] As Kenny identifies, after developing a body of rules of 'unnecessary difficulty', the courts have 'for twenty years been striving to relax their own rules'. Kenny explains the consequences of this:[19]

> There may be said to be two opposing rules: the 'conveyancer's view', if it may be so called, advocates compulsory formality; and the 'judicial view' which at present indicates away from formality, and which at all times is concerned to temper the injustice which compulsory formalities entails.

As we will discover, this tension plays out in the extent to which and in what circumstances an intention to 'annex' the benefit of a covenant is discernible and how far annexation extends. Let's consider each of the three methods of annexation.

Express annexation of the benefit

Express annexation, as the name would suggest, involves the use of express words in the deed of covenant which make plain that the covenant is granted for the benefit of a particular parcel of land or that the covenant is intended to benefit successors of the covenantee. Ultimately, whether the benefit has been expressly annexed is a matter of construction of the terms of the deed in the eyes of the court[20] but it is clear that the land in question must be identified in the deed for express annexation to have taken place. The nature of express annexation can be appreciated by contrasting the two decisions of *Rogers* and *Renals v Cowlishaw* (1878):

* In *Rogers*, the benefit of a covenant restricting the building of more than one house on a plot of land was found to be expressly annexed. A term in the deed of covenant stated that the covenant was 'to endure to the benefit of the [mortgagees], their heirs, and assigns'. This clause was evidence of an intention that the benefit of the covenant was to run with the land.

---

[18] J. Kenny, 'Conveyancer's Notebook' [2006] Conv 1, 2.   [19] Ibid.
[20] *Chambers v Randall* (1923).

- By contrast, in *Renals*, a covenant expressed to be granted for 'the vendors, their heirs, executors, administrators and assigns' did not give rise to express annexation of the benefit to the land as the word 'assigns' was not enough to link the benefit of the covenant to successors of the land.

It is apparent from *Rogers* and *Renals* that for express annexation to have taken place, there must be a clear reference to the land to be benefited. Particular difficulties have arisen in the context of very large areas of land and where there has been a subdivision of the covenantee's land. Here the key issue has been determining the land to which the benefit of the covenant is annexed. In *Re Ballard's Conveyance* (1937), the benefit of a covenant restricting building works was purported to have been annexed to an estate extending to 1,700 acres. The court held that the land was so large that it was impossible to prove that the entire estate was to benefit from the covenant. The annexation was therefore ineffective. Whilst the covenant was purported to annex the benefit to the whole estate, the covenant did not 'touch and concern' the whole land. The court was also not prepared to sever the covenant so that the benefit could pass to that annexed part.

In *Marquess of Zetland v Driver* (1939), however, a slightly different issue arose. Here, the court upheld a claim that the benefit of a covenant had passed with the land where the deed expressed that the covenant was to be annexed to 'each and every part of the estate'. This meant that the successor in title of the covenantee who had purchased just part of the original benefited land was able to enforce the covenant. After *Driver* it was assumed that the terms of a deed of covenant needed to be precisely drafted to avoid the outcome seen in *Re Ballard's Conveyance*. The requirement for this exact drafting was doubted, however, by Brightman LJ in *Federated Homes Ltd v Mill Lodge Properties Ltd* (1980):[21]

> I would have thought, if a covenant is, on a proper construction of a document, annexed to the land, prima facie it is annexed to every part thereof, unless the contrary clearly appears.

Brightman LJ's approach has since been followed in the High Court in *Small v Oliver & Saunders* (2006) and appears to reflect a more liberal approach to annexation and a shift away from the stance taken by the court in *Re Ballard's Conveyance* and *Driver*.

Implied annexation of the benefit

Under the authority of *Marten v Flight Refuelling Ltd* (1962), the court may be prepared to imply from all the surrounding circumstances that the benefit of a covenant has been annexed to the land. In *Marten*, the benefit of a covenant providing that land would only be used for the purposes of agriculture and expressed to be made with the covenantee and 'its successors in title' was found to have been impliedly annexed to the whole estate which extended to 7,500 acres. Despite *Marten*, implied annexation is extremely rare and, given the availability of express and statutory annexation, today plays very little role.

---

[21] *Federated Homes Ltd*, 606.

Statutory annexation of the benefit under s. 78 of the LPA 1925

The problems associated with proving express and implied annexation have been bypassed by s. 78 of the LPA 1925 which provides for the automatic annexation of covenants granted on or after 1 January 1926. Statutory annexation is therefore the most important method of annexation today. Section 78 provides:

(1) A covenant relating to any land of the covenantee shall be deemed to be made with the covenantee and his successors in title and the persons deriving title under him or them, and shall have effect as if such successors and other persons were expressed.

For the purposes of this subsection in connection with covenants restrictive of the user of land 'successors in title' shall be deemed to include the owners and occupiers for the time being of the land of the covenantee intended to be benefited.

The effect of s. 78 is that covenants relating to land are deemed or assumed to be made not only with the original covenantee but with her successors in title—thereby indicating that the benefit of the covenant was intended to run with the land. The operation of s. 78 was considered at length in *Federated Homes*.

KEY CASE *Federated Homes Ltd v Mill Lodge Properties Ltd* (1980)

Facts: Mill Lodge Ltd was a land developer and purchased part of a larger development site from the site owner. Mill Lodge entered a covenant with the site owner that no more than 300 homes would be built on the land it had purchased. This was to maintain the value of the other adjoining plots. Federated Homes subsequently purchased the rest of the development land in two separate transactions: the red and the green land on a plan produced for the court. Upon learning of Mill Lodge's intention to build 32 additional houses on the land, Federated Homes brought legal proceedings against Mill Lodge seeking an injunction to prevent the anticipated breach of the covenant not to build more than 300 homes.

Legal issue: Had the benefit of the covenant been annexed to the land so that Federated Homes was able to enforce it?

Judgment: At first instance, the judge found that there had been no express annexation of the benefit over the red land on the plan but the benefit had passed in relation to the green land (under a chain of express assignments of the benefit). Mill Lodge appealed.

In the Court of Appeal, Mill Lodge's appeal was dismissed. The language of the conveyance evidenced an intention to expressly annex the benefit of the covenant but, in any event, under s. 78 of the LPA 1925, the benefit of the covenant was statutorily annexed to the land. Accordingly, the benefit of the covenant had passed with the conveyance of the land and Federated Homes was therefore entitled to enforce the covenant as to both the green and the red land.

Brightman LJ rejected the 'narrowest' reading of s. 78 which had been advanced by counsel for Mill Lodge that the provision was intended as a 'statutory shorthand' or short-cut for those drafting conveyances. This view, said Brightman LJ, flew in the face of the very wording of the section. Brightman LJ explained:

If, as the language of section 78 implies, a covenant relating to land which is restrictive of the user thereof is enforceable at the suit of (1) a successor in title of the covenantee, (2) a person deriving title under the covenantee or under his successors in title, and (3) the owner or occupier of the land intended to be benefited by the covenant, it must, in my view, follow that the covenant runs with the land, because ex hypothesi every successor in title to the land, every

→

> derivative proprietor of the land and every other owner and occupier has a right by statute to the covenant. In other words, if the condition precedent of section 78 is satisfied—that is to say, there exists a covenant which touches and concerns the land of the covenantee—that covenant runs with the land for the benefit of his successors in title, persons deriving title under him or them and other owners and occupiers.
>
> Simply put, where there is a covenant 'relating to land' (i.e. touches and concerns the covenantee's land), s. 78(1) of the LPA 1925 does not merely provide a shorthand in the drafting of a conveyance but rather has the effect of annexing the benefit of the covenant to the covenantee's land.

The decision of the Court of Appeal in *Federated Homes* was a highly controversial one,[22] not least for those who argue its interpretation rejects what Newsome called 'the conveyancer's view'.[23] Three key arguments have been advanced which call into question the interpretation of s. 78 employed by the Court of Appeal:

1. First, Parliament only ever intended s. 78 to be a word-saving provision. There is no reference at all within the provision to 'annexation'. On this view, *Federated Homes* goes too far and reaches a result contrary to Parliament's legislative intention. Newsome argues precisely this point: that annexation is a matter of intention and that this intention must be found from more than just statutorily implied language.[24]

2. Secondly, the *Federated Homes* construction of s. 78 is inconsistent with its sister provision, s. 79 of the LPA 1925. While s. 79 may give rise to a statutory presumption of annexation of the *burden* of a covenant, it does not give rise to *automatic* annexation.[25] On this basis, it is argued neither should s. 78. Snape, however, engages in a close linguistic analysis of the two provisions and concludes that ss. 78 and 79 are distinct in one central respect:[26]

   > The crucial difference between the two sections is that, whilst s. 78 deems the covenant to be made 'with the covenantee and his successors in title and the person deriving title under him or them', s. 79 . . . deems the covenant to be made 'on behalf of [the covenantor] and his successors in title and the persons deriving title under him or them'. Whatever the precise scope of the word 'deemed' in each section, this difference in wording makes it clear that the benefit is, in principle, to pass to the covenantee's successors etc. quite easily, whilst s. 79 is intended, in the absence of contrary intention, to ensure that the burden remains firmly with the original covenantor.

3. By way of a final argument, unlike the s. 79, which provides for the possibility of contrary intention to negate its operation, s. 78 does not contain this caveat. To hold as the court did in *Federated Homes* that s. 78 provides for the automatic annexation of the benefit of covenants without consideration of the wider circumstances is therefore problematic. The *Federated Homes* construction appears to annex the benefit of covenants without any examination of the intentions of the parties.

---

[22] G. H. Newsome, 'Universal Annexation' (1981) 97 LQR 32; (1982) 98 LQR 202; J. Snape, 'The Benefit and Burden of Covenants: Now Where Are We?' (1994) 3 Nott LJ 68.   [23] Newsome, 'Universal Annexation'.
[24] Ibid.   [25] *Re Royal Victoria Pavilion, Ramsgate* (1961); *Rhone v Stephens* (1994).
[26] Snape, 'The Benefit and Burden of Covenants: Now Where Are We?', 71.

Controversial, yes, but the interpretation of s. 78 in *Federated Homes* has been subsequently scrutinized and endorsed by the court in the important case of *Roake v Chadha*. In so doing, however, the High Court in *Roake* recognized an important limitation on the operation of s. 78:

KEY CASE *Roake v Chadha* (1984)

Facts: A parcel of land was laid out in separate plots and sold to various purchasers in standard term conveyances. As part of the standard term conveyances, covenants were created under which no more than one dwelling-house was to be built on the plots sold. The covenants contained the following clause:

> And the purchaser to the intent and so as to bind (so far as practicable) the land hereby transferred . . . hereby covenants with the vendor but so that this covenant shall not enure for the benefit of any owner or subsequent purchaser of any part of the . . . estate unless the benefit of this covenant shall be expressly assigned . . .

The effect of the clause was that the benefit of a covenant should not run with the land except where there was an express **assignment** of the benefit. The defendants, the Chadhas, purchased one of the plots of land and wished to build two houses on the plot. The claimants, the Roakes, owned another of the plots and there had been no express assignment of the benefit of the covenants. The Roakes issued legal proceedings seeking a declaration of their entitlement to the benefit of the covenants and an injunction to prevent the anticipated breach of covenant by the Chadhas.

Legal issue: In the absence of any express assignment of the benefit of the covenants to the Roakes, did s. 78 of the LPA 1925 operate to annex the benefit?

Judgment: Judge Paul Baker QC held that although s. 78 did not require any express terms for the benefit of a covenant to be annexed to the land, its operation did have to take into account the terms of the covenant in each individual case. Where, as in the instant case, the terms of the covenant provided that the benefit could not pass except by express assignment, it was clear that the benefit of the covenant was not annexed to the land. Judge Paul Baker QC rejected the assertion by counsel for the Chadhas that s. 78 of the LPA 1925 operated in a mandatory fashion:

> where a covenant is deemed to be made with successors in title as section 78 requires, one still has to construe the covenant as a whole to see whether the benefit of the covenant is annexed . . . one has to consider the covenant as a whole to determine its true effect. When one does that, then it seems to me that the answer is plain and in my judgment the benefit was not annexed.

Roake therefore establishes a potential brake on the operation of s. 78 in that the provision can be excluded if, considering all the circumstances of the case, its operation is *contrary to the intentions* of the parties. In *Margerison v Bates* (2008), a conveyance which made reference to the vendor in places and to 'vendor and successors in title' in others was said to have been deliberately drafted so as to prevent the benefit of the covenant running with the land and thereby avoid s. 78's application. This was affirmed and another limitation added by the Court of Appeal in *Crest Nicholson Residential (South) Ltd v McAllister*.

> **KEY CASE** *Crest Nicholson Residential (South) Ltd v McAllister* (2004)
>
> Facts: Land was sold to two brothers operating as a company for the purposes of building develop-ment. The company sold off some of the land in plots to separate buyers under conveyances which contained covenants that restricted the user and further development of the land. Some of the cov-enants contained words of express annexation, others did not. Crest, the owner of several of the plots of land, proposed to develop its land and Mrs McAllister, a resident of another of the plots, was strongly opposed. She argued that the planned construction of new houses by Crest was in breach of the terms of the covenants and that she was entitled to the benefit of those covenants either as a result of express annexation or under s. 78 of the LPA 1925.
>
> Legal issue: Had annexation of the benefit taken place either expressly or statutorily under s. 78?
>
> Judgment: The Court of Appeal rejected Mrs McAllister's claim to enforce the covenant under either express annexation or s. 78 and confirmed the *Roake* authority that evidence of contrary intention can exclude the operation of s. 78. Crucially, in this case there was nothing in the original conveyance that enabled the court to identify what land, if any, was intended to be benefited by the covenants. The covenants were therefore not enforceable. As to what is required in terms of identification of the ben-efited land for the purposes of s. 78, Chadwick LJ noted that the land benefited must be identifiable:
>
>> from a description, plan or other reference in the conveyance itself, but aided, if necessary, by external evidence to identify the land so described, depicted or otherwise referred to.

Crest therefore confirms *Roake* but also sets down a further limitation on the operation of s. 78 of the LPA 1925 in that the land benefited must be specifically identified or, at the very least, capable of identification by reference to external evidence. It must be remembered that the identification of land benefited by a covenant is not always a straightforward busi-ness. As Howell has noted, identifying land, for example, after many years has elapsed or where the land has subsequently been divided up can prove problematic:[27]

> The problem is that actually identifying the land on the ground which is to be benefited may be impossible and raise all the difficulties of enquiry which Chadwick L.J. deplored. Simply stating as in *Rogers v Hosegood* that the land to be benefited 'is nearby' and is all the land owned by X is surely no identification at all.

The effect of the *Federated Homes* decision and subsequent case law can be condensed into four qualifications or requirements for the operation of s. 78:

1. The covenant must have been granted on or after 1 January 1926: *J. Sainsbury plc v Enfield LBC* (1989).

2. The covenant must 'touch and concern' the covenantee's land: *Federated Homes*.

3. There must be no contrary intention excluding operation of the provision: *Roake*; *Crest*.

4. The land to be benefited must be identified or be capable of identification: *Crest*.

Remember: given the scope of s. 78, recourse to express and implied annexation of the ben-efit of a covenant is increasingly rare and generally only relevant if and when s. 78 is found not to operate.

---

[27] J. Howell, 'The Annexation of the Benefit of Covenants to Land' [2004] Conv 507, 513.

It is helpful to pause momentarily to summarize the position. At law, the benefit of freehold covenants will run with the land provided the five requirements identified in section 11.5.1 and Figure 11.5 are satisfied. That is not the end of the story, of course, because we need to demonstrate, additionally, that the burden of that covenant has also passed to the intended defendant.

11.5.2 Passing of the burden at law

At law, quite simply, the burden of any covenant (whether positive or negative) *cannot* run with the land: *Austerberry v Corporation of Oldham*. This means that, at law, it is impossible for a claimant to enforce a covenant directly against a successor of the original covenantor.[28]

KEY CASE *Austerberry v Corporation of Oldham* (1885)

Facts: A landowner conveyed by deed a parcel of his land to trustees who, in return, covenanted to make use of the land as a road, to maintain it, and keep the land at all times in repair. Subsequently, the same landowner sold a parcel of adjoining land to Austerberry and the trustees sold the road to the Corporation of Oldham.

Legal issue: Was Austerberry, as a successor in title of the original covenantee, able to enforce the covenant against Oldham, the successors in title of the original covenantor? In other words, had the benefit of the covenant passed to Austerberry and the burden of the covenant passed to Oldham?

Judgment: The Court of Appeal held that, in the circumstances, the benefit of the covenant had not passed to Austerberry as the covenant was held not to have touched and concerned the land. Additionally, however, the burden of the covenant had also not passed to Oldham. The covenant was not therefore enforceable between the parties. Lindley LJ explained:

> I am not prepared to say that any covenant which imposes a burden upon land does run with the land, unless the covenant does, upon its true construction, amount to either a grant of an easement, or a rent-charge, or some other estate or interest in land . . . I am not aware of any other case which either shews, or appears to shew, that a burden such as this can be annexed to land by a mere contract . . . in the absence of authority it appears to me that we shall be perfectly warranted in saying that the burden of this covenant does not run with the land.

The *Austerberry* 'rule' was confirmed by the House of Lords in *Rhone v Stephens* (1994) where Lord Templeman explained:[29]

> [Y]our lordships were invited to overrule the decision of the Court of Appeal in the Austerberry case. To do so would destroy the distinction between land and equity . . . it is plain from the articles, reports and papers to which we were referred that judicial legislation to overrule the Austerberry case would create a number of difficulties, anomalies and uncertainties and affect the rights and liability of people who have for over 100 years bought and sold land in the knowledge, imparted at an elementary stage to every student of the law of real property, that positive covenants, affecting freehold land are not directly enforceable except against the original covenantor.

---

[28] As confirmed in *Rhone*.   [29] *Rhone*, 321.

The position at law is therefore settled: the burden of covenants (positive or negative) will not pass to successors. This is an ancient rule and there is no current prospect of it being overturned. That is not to say that the rule is justified nor that it is accepted with any particular relish. The *Austerberry* rule was, for example, only very reluctantly affirmed in the Court of Appeal decision of *Thamesmead Town Ltd v Allotey* (2000) on the basis that any change in the law would require the involvement of Parliament. The court in *Allotey* expressed criticism of the rule and noted the widespread calls for reform.[30] As Gravells has argued:[31]

> [F]ew would dissent from the view that in appropriate circumstances positive covenants should be capable of enforcement against successors in title to the original covenantor, that enforcement should be through direct means rather than through indirect means, which are artificial and frequently unreliable; and that the continued absence of such direct means is inconvenient and potentially unjust. Since the House of Lords has now clearly ruled out a judicial solution, it is for Parliament to provide a legislative solution.

However, the enduring vigour of the *Austerberry* principle does not mean that there are no avenues open to avoiding its consequences. First, an action by the original covenantee against the original covenantor if there is a breach of covenant remains available.[32] Secondly, as Gravells highlights, there are certain *indirect* means by which covenants have been held to be enforceable which circumvent the *Austerberry* rule. We discuss these indirect methods in the next section. Beyond this as you will discover in section 11.6, equity allows for the passing of the burden of covenants in certain defined circumstances.

11.5.3 Indirect methods for the enforcement of positive freehold covenants

There are five indirect methods by which positive covenants may be enforceable and which, therefore, can serve as a workaround to the rule against the passing of the burden of covenants at law:

- the doctrine of benefit and burden;
- a chain of indemnity covenants;
- the long lease: s. 153 of the LPA 1925;
- estate rentcharges and rights of re-entry.

Always keep in mind that these devices have been developed as a reaction to the restrictive legal principles on the passing of the burden. In many instances, these indirect methods of enforcement prove, as a result, to be less than satisfactory and the Law Commission has, for example, recommended that the burden of positive covenants should be capable of running directly with the land. We discuss proposals for reform in section 11.9.

---

[30] Including the Report of the Committee, chaired by Lord Wilberforce on Positive Covenants Affecting Land (Cmnd 2719, 1965), and the Law Commission's 1984 Report: *Transfer of Land, The Law of Positive and Restrictive Covenants*, Law Com. No. 127.

[31] N. Gravells, 'Enforcement of Positive Covenants Affecting Freehold Land' (1994) 110 LQR 346.

[32] On which see section 11.3 as to the limitations of this.

11.5.3.1 The doctrine of benefit and burden

The first indirect method to consider is the doctrine of benefit and burden.[33] This principle springs from a long-standing equitable maxim that 'he who takes the benefit of a right must bear the burden'. The principle therefore responds to the mutuality or reciprocity of benefits and burdens. The doctrine can be summed up as follows: where a covenant confers benefits as well as burdens on a covenantor, any successor in title to that covenantor will not be permitted to take advantage of the benefits without also being subject to the burdens: *Halsall v Brizell*.

KEY CASE *Halsall v Brizell* (1957)

Facts: Several purchasers of houses on a building estate in Liverpool were granted the right to use roads, the promenade, the sea wall, and the drainage system of the estate subject to covenanting to contribute to the cost of repairs and maintenance of these facilities. Brizell, who was a successor in title to one of the original purchasers of a plot of land on the estate, objected to the means by which his contribution was calculated.

Legal issue: Was Brizell obliged to pay the contribution? Could Brizell escape liability on the basis that the burden of a positive covenant could not run with the land and so he could not be bound to pay?

Judgment: The High Court held that though the burden of a positive covenant could not run with the land so as to be enforceable against successors, successors such as Brizell were not entitled to enjoy the benefit of rights (such as the right to use the roads, sea wall, promenade) and at the same time escape the burdens also imposed. Upjohn J explained:

> it is ancient law that a man cannot take benefit under a deed without subscribing to the obligations thereunder. If authority is required for that proposition, I need but refer to one sentence during the argument in *Elliston v. Reacher*, where Lord Cozens-Hardy M.R. observed: 'It is laid down in Co. Litt. 230b, that a man who takes the benefit of a deed is bound by a condition contained in it, though he does not execute it.' If the defendants did not desire to take the benefit of this deed, for the reasons I have given, they could not be under any liability to pay the obligations thereunder. But, of course, they do desire to take the benefit of this deed. They have no right to use the sewers which are vested in the claimants, and I cannot see that they have any right, apart from the deed, to use the roads of the park which lead to their particular house, No. 22, Salisbury Road. The defendants cannot rely on any way of necessity or on any right by prescription, for the simple reason that when the house was originally sold in 1931 to their predecessor in title he took the house on the terms of the deed of 1851 which contractually bound him to contribute a proper proportion of the expenses of maintaining the roads and sewers, and so forth, as a condition of being entitled to make use of those roads and sewers. Therefore, it seems to me that the defendants here cannot, if they desire to use this house, as they do, take advantage of the trusts concerning the user of the roads contained in the deed and the other benefits created by it without undertaking the obligations thereunder. Upon that principle it seems to me that they are bound by this deed, if they desire to take its benefits.

---

[33] See C. Bevan, 'The Doctrine of Benefit and Burden: Reforming the Law of Covenants and the Numerus Clausus "Problem"' (2018) 77(1) CLJ 72; C. Davis, 'The Principle of Benefit and Burden' (1998) 57 CLJ 522.

There has been a degree of uncertainty as to the precise ambit of the doctrine of benefit and burden. Thus, in *Tito v Wadell (No. 2)* (1977), Megarry V-C sought to identify what he called the 'pure doctrine of benefit and burden', which was broader than that recognized in *Halsall* in that it appeared to hold that any party deriving a benefit from a conveyance must accept the burdens imposed in that same conveyance. This would constitute a significant blunting of the *Austerberry* principle which provides that the burden of covenants cannot pass at law. The House of Lords in *Rhone* rejected Megarry V-C's 'pure doctrine of benefit and burden', with Lord Templeman explaining:[34]

> I am not prepared to recognise the 'pure principle' that any party deriving any benefit from a conveyance must accept any burden in the same conveyance . . . it does not follow that *any* condition can be rendered enforceable by attaching it to a right nor does it follow that every burden imposed by a conveyance may be enforced by depriving the covenantor's successor in title of every benefit which he enjoyed thereunder. The condition must be relevant to the exercise of the right. In *Halsall v Brizell* there were reciprocal benefits and burdens enjoyed by the users of the roads and sewers . . . in *Halsall v Brizell* could, at least in theory, choose between enjoying the right and paying his proportion of the cost or alternatively giving up the right and saving his money.

The principle therefore did not apply on the facts of *Rhone* as the owners of Watford house, whose roof extended over an adjoining cottage, could neither in theory nor in practice refuse to repair the roof and so be deprived of the benefit of mutual rights of support. The effect of the decision in *Rhone* was to affirm *Halsall* but also to acknowledge that there needed to be limitations on the operation of the principle of benefit and burden. In *Allotey*, the Court of Appeal considered what those limitations should be.

KEY CASE *Thamesmead Town Ltd v Allotey* (2000)

Facts: London County Council built a large residential estate, Thamesmead, and in July 1987 all the land at Thamesmead vested in the claimant, Thamesmead Town Ltd. In 1988, the Boormans, tenants on the estate, purchased the freehold reversion of their house under the Conservative government's 'Right to Buy' scheme. As part of the conveyance, the Boormans covenanted that they and their successors in title would contribute to the maintenance and repair of all roads, footpaths, and landscaped and communal areas. The conveyance granted the Boormans the right to make use of the roads, paths, and drainage owned by the claimant, Thamesmead Town Ltd. Nowhere in the conveyance were the Boormans granted a right to use the landscaped or communal areas of the estate. In 1992, the Boormans sold their house to Mr Allotey, who subsequently queried the service charge that he was asked to pay by Thamesmead Town Ltd. Thamesmead issued proceedings against Mr Allotey, seeking to recover sums owing.

Legal issue: Was Mr Allotey bound by the covenant contained in the original conveyance to the Boormans concerning the contribution to maintenance of the estate, or might he escape liability under the principle of benefit and burden?

Judgment: At first instance, applying the principles established in *Rhone* which affirmed *Halsall*, the court held that a successor in title to a covenantor is not permitted to take the benefit of a right without undertaking the burdens dependent upon it. Applying the principle of benefit and burden, Mr Allotey was therefore required to pay the service charge but, crucially, not those sums relating to the landscaped and communal areas. Thamesmead Town Ltd appealed seeking the full service charge.

→

---

[34] *Rhone*, 322.

→

In the Court of Appeal, Thamesmead's appeal was dismissed. The court identified the requirements for the operation of the principle of benefit and burden as being: (1) the discharge of the burden had to be relevant to the exercise of the rights that enabled the benefit to be obtained; (2) the successors in title had to have an opportunity to choose whether to take the benefit or, having taken it, to renounce it, even if only in theory, and thereby to escape the burden. It was not enough for the principle to operate that the taking of an incidental benefit enabled the enforcement of a burden.

Peter Gibson LJ explained that in *Rhone* the mutual obligations of support were unrelated to and independent of the covenant to maintain the roof and so the doctrine did not operate. Mr Allotey had no right under the conveyance to him to make use of the landscaped and communal areas. The principle of benefit and burden did not therefore extend to these areas and Mr Allotey could not be asked to pay the contributions to the landscaped and communal areas.

The court in *Thamesmead* therefore demonstrated that the amount of any contribution under a maintenance covenant could be apportioned according to the nature and extent of the reciprocal benefits and burdens in question.

Sir Andrew Morritt C in the later decision of *Davies v Jones* (2010) provided a helpful précis of the law in this area, noting the three core requirements necessary for the doctrine of benefit and burden to apply: that the benefit and burden must be conferred in or by the same transaction; that enjoyment of the benefit must be relevant to the imposition of the burden in the sense that the former must be conditional on or reciprocal to the latter; and that the person on whom the burden is alleged to have been imposed had the opportunity of rejecting or disclaiming the benefit, not merely the right to receive the benefit.

The first requirement will be satisfied in most cases by construing the deed of conveyance and any associated documents. The second requirement, that the benefit be 'relevant to the imposition of the burden', has been held to be 'a matter of substance rather than form'[35] and is again determined by construing the words of the conveyance. The effect of this is that the benefit does not need to be *expressed* in the deed as being conditional upon the burden provided there is a clear and obvious link between the two. Determining the extent to which the benefit and burden are related and linked is clearly a challenging exercise and there is no denying that this is an area which would merit further judicial clarification. We do, however, have a series of decided cases to guide us here: from *Rhone* to the more recent judgments in *Wilkinson v Kerdene* (2013) and *Elwood v Goodman* (2014)—all of which are worth a read. As to the third requirement for the operation of the doctrine of benefit and burden, that the party on whom the burden is imposed must have or have had the opportunity or choice to reject the benefit, in most cases this will come down to a theoretical opportunity to renounce the benefit rather than an actual, real possibility of doing so. Clearly, where a claimant has no choice (even theoretically) in exercising the right or whether to disclaim a benefit conferred, the claim to enforce the burden of a positive covenant will fail: *Halsall*.

---

[35] Patten LJ in *Elwood v Goodman* (2014).

Bringing together all the authorities in this area we can distil five requirements for the doctrine of benefit and burden:

1. a transaction that confers a benefit and imposes a burden;
2. that the benefit conferred is real and substantial (*Rhone*);
3. that no other right to the benefit exists;
4. that the benefit was taken voluntarily and there is at least a theoretical opportunity to reject it and thereby avoid the associated burden;
5. that there is a link between the benefit and burden so that they are conditional, reciprocal, or relevant to one another.

11.5.3.2 A chain of indemnity covenants

It is possible for the burden of positive covenants to be enforced by way of an unbroken chain of indemnity covenants: see Figure 11.6. This is our second indirect method. In practice, it is quite common for conveyancers of land to establish a chain of personal covenants between all successors of the covenantor's land. The idea is to guarantee that contractual liability passes from the original covenantor to the first successor then on to the next successor and so forth until we reach the current owner of the burdened land. The effect is as follows: if the current owner of the burdened land breaches a covenant, the covenantee will be entitled to sue the original covenantor for breach. As a result of the chain of indemnity covenants, that original covenantor is able to sue his direct successor under the indemnity covenant, who can, in turn, sue their direct successor until, finally, the party in breach is reached. The burden of a positive covenant can thereby be indirectly enforced.

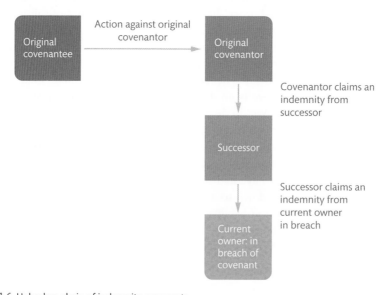

Figure 11.6 Unbroken chain of indemnity covenants

There are, however, two significant drawbacks to this method. First, the covenantee is limited to an action for damages. There can be no claim for an injunction under a chain of indemnity covenants. Secondly, this method only operates to fix the party in breach with liability if the chain of indemnity covenants remains unbroken. The precarious chain can be easily broken where one or more of the successors in title of the covenantor vanishes, dies, or becomes insolvent.

11.5.3.3 The long lease: Section 153 of the LPA 1925

Clever conveyancers have seized on an opportunity that is presented by long leases as a third method of enforcing the burden of positive covenants. So, it is possible to create a long lease which contains positive leasehold covenants and then have that lease 'enlarged' from a leasehold estate into a freehold estate under the provisions of s. 153 of the LPA 1925. Section 153 operates in such a way that the positive covenants that originally formed part of the lease now bind the freehold land and its successors.[36]

11.5.3.4 Estate rentcharges and rights of re-entry

An estate **rentcharge** is a legal interest which obliges an owner of burdened land to make a periodic payment. An estate rentcharge may be enforced by exercising a right of re-entry which is annexed to the rentcharge.[37] It is therefore possible to enforce the burden of a positive covenant by a combination of an estate rentcharge with an annexed right of re-entry. This is a question of careful drafting. If drafted prudently, failure to comply with a positive covenant could result in the exercise of the right of re-entry to forfeit the estate. The court does, however, retain jurisdiction to grant relief from forfeiture here. As the Law Commission has recognized, this use of rentcharges and rights of re-entry represents a workable yet clumsy and cumbersome method for the enforcement of positive covenants.[38]

11.6 Enforcing freehold covenants: The equitable rules

We have considered the legal rules for the passing of benefit and burden and found them to be somewhat limited (particularly in relation to the burden). In this section, we now turn to consider the principles by which the benefit and burden will run with the land in equity which, as you will discover, are more flexible. We begin by considering how the burden of covenants passes in equity. We start our discussion with the burden (rather than the benefit) because as we have already found with the legal rules, it is the passing of the burden which proves to be the most difficult.

---

[36] See s. 153 of the LPA 1925 and s 8(3) of the Leasehold Reform Act 1967.
[37] S. Bright, 'Estate Rentcharges and the Enforcement of Positive Obligations' [1988] Conv 99.
[38] Law Commission Report No. 327, [5.25].

11.6.1 **Passing of the burden in equity**

Equity has intervened, in its characteristic manner, to mitigate the harshness of the common law. The result is that it is possible in equity for the burden of certain covenants to pass on the transfer of land to successors of the original covenantor. Equity permits the passing of the burden of restrictive covenants[39] to successors in title of the original covenantor, but only where a series of conditions are met. Equity does not permit the passing of the burden of positive covenants. The result is that, the only *direct* means of passing the burden of any covenant will be in equity. The equitable principles and the conditions that must be met derive largely from the case of *Tulk v Moxhay*.[40]

KEY CASE *Tulk v Moxhay* (1848)

Facts: In 1808, Tulk sold a plot of land in Leicester Square to Elms who, by means of a covenant within the conveyance, promised to keep the Garden Square 'uncovered with any buildings, in neat and ornamental order' in order to preserve the land for leisure activities. The plot of land was subsequently sold to various successors, culminating with Moxhay. Moxhay had been aware of the covenant at the time of the conveyance to him but refused to comply with its terms and made plans to build on the land. Tulk brought proceedings seeking an injunction to prevent an anticipated breach of the covenant.

Legal issue: Was Tulk entitled to an injunction on the basis that Moxhay as a successor in title of the original covenantor was bound to comply with the covenant?

Judgment: Moxhay was bound to comply with the covenant and, consequently, Tulk was entitled to the injunction sought. The court relied heavily on Moxhay's knowledge and notice of the covenant when purchasing the land, which, said Lord Cottenham, gave rise to a new right in favour of Tulk that the covenant must be observed.

The decision of *Tulk*[41] was subsequently rationalized and refined through decisions of the court in the late nineteenth century.[42] The precise requirements for the operation of the *Tulk* doctrine have now been honed into five defined conditions: see Figure 11.7. Where these five conditions are satisfied, the burden of a restrictive covenant will run with the land so that a successor of the original covenantor will be bound to comply with its terms. Let's consider each condition in turn.

11.6.1.1 **The covenant must be restrictive in character**

The court in the decisions that followed *Tulk* made clear that equity would only permit the burden of *negative* covenants to run. As we have seen, a negative covenant amounts to a promise not to do something on land and in this way acts as a constraint on the servient

---

[39] But not positive covenants.

[40] *Tulk* itself built on the decision of *Whatman v Gibson* (1839) and *Mann v Stephens* (1846).

[41] On which generally, see B. McFarlane, '*Tulk v Moxhay* (1848)' in C. Mitchell and P. Mitchell (eds.), *Landmark Cases in Equity* (Oxford: Hart, 2012), 203.

[42] *Morland v Cook* (1868); *Haywood v Brunswick Permanent Benefit Building Society* (1881); *London CC v Allen* (1914).

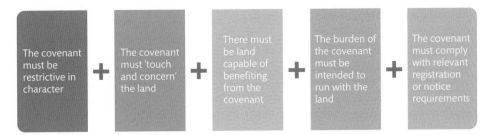

Figure 11.7 The *Tulk v Moxhay* conditions

landowner. In contrast, a positive covenant is often said to require the covenantor to put hands in her pockets to reach for the wallet to fund repairs, maintenance, or some similar affirmative action.[43] But beware: what at first appears to be positive in character may, on closer inspection, in fact be negative. For example, a covenant permitting use of the land 'for any and all residential purposes' might initially appear to constitute a positive covenant. However, on closer inspection, it is in fact a restrictive covenant forbidding non-residential purposes.

The precise nature of a covenant is determined by construing the words used and the broader terms of the conveyance. In *Crest*, a covenant was granted upon conveyance of various plots of land which provided that the land was not to be used for 'any purpose other than those of or in connection with a private dwelling house'. A dispute arose as to whether this covenant prevented the building of more than one single house or whether it was intended to prevent non-residential construction generally. Neuberger J engaged in a close interpretation of the terms of the covenant, holding that, according to the strict wording of the covenant, only one dwelling-house could be built:[44]

> As a matter of ordinary language, the indefinite article 'a' tends to carry with it the concept of a singularity as opposed to a plurality. Restriction to use as a 'private dwelling house' appears to me, at least in the absence of contextual or factual contra-indications, to mean restriction to a single dwelling house.

Neuberger J clearly envisaged circumstances where the broader context and factual nexus will be relevant in assisting the court in the interpretative exercise in construing the true nature of covenants.

What, then, is the rationale for allowing the burden of restrictive covenants to pass in equity but not those of a positive character? Two points should be noted here:

1. As regards restrictive covenants, the most the covenantor is required to do is nothing (i.e. passively not to act). In this way, the covenantor is not given the capacity to *actively* breach the covenant. Under a positive covenant, however, there is a very real additional burden or obligation to act placed upon the servient landowner. Equity is therefore prepared to allow enforcement of restrictive covenants which are, by their nature, less burdensome than positive covenants.

---

[43] *Haywood v Brunswick Permanent Benefit Building Society.*   [44] *Crest*, [15].

2. Secondly, as Lord Templeman explained in *Rhone*:[45]

> Restrictive covenants deprive an owner of a right which he could otherwise exercise. Equity cannot compel an owner to comply with a positive covenant entered into by his predecessors in title without flatly contradicting the common law rule that a person cannot be made liable upon a contract unless he was a party to it. Enforcement of a positive covenant lies in contract; a positive covenant compels an owner to exercise her rights. Enforcement of a negative covenant lies in property; a negative covenant deprives the owner of a right over property.

The decision in *Rhone* is a leading decision in this area and one in which the House of Lords was invited by counsel but refused to abolish the *Austerberry* rule.

KEY CASE *Rhone v Stephens* (1994)

Facts: A property known as 'Watford House' was divided into two dwellings consisting of a house and a cottage. As a result of the division of the land, a bedroom of the cottage sat under the roof of the larger house. The cottage was subsequently sold and, as part of the conveyance, the owner of the house covenanted with the purchaser of the cottage that the roof would be kept in good repair. Over time, the roof fell into a state of disrepair and the cottage owner, Rhone, brought legal proceedings against Stephens, the new owner of the house.

Legal issue: Could the covenant benefiting Rhone be enforced against the new owner, of the house, Stephens, a successor in title of the original covenantor?

Judgment: At first instance, the court found in favour of Rhone. The court held that Stephens, as the owner of the house, was liable for the repair of the roof under the covenant. Stephens appealed the decision and, in the Court of Appeal, succeeded in overturning the first instance decision on the basis of the established *Austerberry* rule that, in relation to positive covenants, successors in title of the servient land could not be bound.

Rhone appealed to the House of Lords in 1994. The appeal was dismissed. The Court of Appeal had been right to apply the *Austerberry* rule. The House of Lords confirmed that while equity would prevent or punish the breach of a restrictive covenant, it would not compel compliance with a positive covenant. The court acknowledged the criticisms of the *Austerberry* rule and the recommendations from academics and the Law Commission on reform. Noting the difficulties and uncertainties that overruling *Austerberry* would create, their lordships refused this invitation from counsel. Parliamentary intervention would be the only means by which reform would come to this area of the law. The House of Lords also rejected a second ground advanced by Rhone under the doctrine of 'benefit and burden'. This ground failed on the basis that the covenant to repair the roof was an independent provision and was not therefore part of a necessary relationship of reciprocal benefits and burdens.

11.6.1.2 The covenant must 'touch and concern' the land

It is perhaps self-explanatory that equity is only prepared to permit enforcement of a covenant if it can be shown that the promise 'touches and concerns' land. We discussed the test for 'touching and concerning' in section 11.5.1.1. Be sure to revisit this.

11.6.1.3 There must be land capable of benefiting from the covenant

There are three aspects to this requirement:

1. The covenant must have been granted to benefit some land: *London and South Western Railway v Gomm* (1882).

---

[45] *Rhone*, 318.

2. At the time when the covenant was granted, the covenantee must have been the owner of the land or had an interest in the land to be benefited: *London CC v Allen* (1914). In *Allen*, Mr Allen entered into a covenant with the London County Council under which he covenanted not to build on land at the end of a proposed road. Mr Allen sold the land to his wife who subsequently began construction. The Council failed in their attempt to enforce the covenant against Mrs Allen as the Council did not own any land benefiting from the promise at the time the covenant was granted. There is, however, no requirement that the covenantee be a freehold owner of land to be benefited. A restrictive covenant can, for example, be enforced against mortgagees.[46]

3. The land benefiting, the 'dominant tenement', must be capable of identification with reasonable certainty. The court may be prepared, however, to look beyond the conveyance to the wider, surrounding circumstances in identifying the land.[47]

11.6.1.4 The burden of the covenant must be intended to run with the land

The penultimate condition is that the burden of the covenant must be intended to run with the land of the covenantor. In other words, there must be evidence that successors of the covenantor's land were intended to bear the burden of the covenant. This might be proved by express words in the deed of covenant. Fortunately, however, there is no need for express words in view of the enactment of s. 79 of the LPA 1925 which provides:

> A covenant relating to any land of the covenantor . . . shall, unless a contrary intention is expressed, be deemed to be made by the covenantor on behalf of himself, his successors in title and the persons deriving title under him.

The effect of s. 79 is that, unless contrary evidence exists, the burden of a negative covenant is deemed to have been intended to run with the land. Section 79 therefore provides a statutory presumption of an intention that the burden of covenants 'relating to any land' will run. Contrary evidence was accepted in the rare case of *Re Royal Victoria Pavilion, Ramsgate* (1961) and need not consist of an explicit exclusion of the operation of s. 79 in the conveyance itself. In *Morrells of Oxford Ltd v Oxford United Football Club Ltd* (2001), s. 79 was held not to operate based on an assessment of all the facts of the case. The court held that to impose s. 79 would be to read words into the covenant which were clearly not intended by the parties. It was apparent from other covenants within the conveyance that successors were to be bound. As such, the absence of similar words in the particular clause in question showed a contrary intention (i.e. that s. 79 should not apply in relation to that clause). For those wishing to exclude the operation of s. 79, it seems that the most prudent approach is to include express words of exclusion in the deed of covenant but the court will take a broad view of the wider conveyance or deed of covenant.

[46] *Regent Oil Co. Ltd v J. A. Gregory (Hatch End) Ltd* (1966); equally, Parliament has now legislated to the effect that many public bodies such as local authorities are able to enforce restrictive covenants even where they own no land benefited at the time the covenant is granted. One example is the Housing Act 1985, s. 609.

[47] *Marten*.

11.6.1.5 The covenant must comply with relevant registration or notice requirements

The final condition to be met if the burden of a restrictive covenant is to run in equity concerns the relevant registration requirements or notice requirements. Recall that in *Tulk* it was Moxhay's knowledge of the covenant at the time of purchase that proved central to the court's conclusion that it was enforceable. Today, the burden of a restrictive covenant will only pass to a successor of the covenantor if the relevant rules of registration or notice requirements have been satisfied. We need to draw a distinction between the position in registered and in unregistered land.

In registered land

In registered land, the relevant rules are those contained within the LRA 2002. Under s. 29 of the LRA, if a successor in title of the covenantor is a purchaser of a registered title for valuable consideration and that disposition is duly registered, the burden of the covenant will only be enforceable if a notice has been entered.[48] Where no notice has been entered, the covenant will lose priority to that registered disposition.[49] There are, however, instances where the covenant will retain priority under s. 28 of the LRA 2002 whether or not a notice has been entered (i.e. if s. 29 does not apply): (i) where the successor in title is not a purchaser of the covenantor's land for valuable consideration (e.g. a devisee under a will, an adverse possessor or someone who receives the land by way of gift), and (ii) where the successor in title of the covenantor's land is a purchaser of an *equitable* estate in that land only.[50]

In unregistered land

In unregistered land, the relevant rules are those contained within the LCA 1972 for covenants created on or after 1 January 1926 and the doctrine of notice for those created pre-1926.

For covenants created on or after 1 January 1926 to be enforceable, the covenant must have been registered as a Class D(ii) land charge[51] against the name of the original covenantor. If the covenant has not been registered, it will be void and unenforceable against a purchaser of the legal estate for money or money's worth.[52] There are, however, three instances where the covenant will be enforceable despite the failure to register under the LCA 1972: (i) against a non-purchaser;[53] (ii) where the requirement for 'money or money's worth' is not satisfied; or (iii) against a purchaser of an equitable estate.

For covenants created before 1 January 1926, the doctrine of notice determines the enforceability of the covenant.[54]

In practice, given that any transfer of an estate in land for valuable consideration is a triggering event for first registration, the rules on first registration will most likely apply to many cases involving unregistered land. On first registration, the *new* registered proprietor takes the land subject to any interest protected by means of an entry in the register. The registrar is required to enter a notice in the register of any interest which, from

---

[48] Section 29(2) of the LRA 2002.   [49] Ibid., s. 29(1).
[50] For example, where the successor is an equitable lessee.
[52] Under ibid., s. 4(6).   [51] Under s. 2(5) of the LCA 1972.
[53] For example, a devisee under a will, adverse possessor or someone receiving the land by way of gift.
[54] We explored the doctrine of notice in Chapter 3.

examination of the title, appears to affect the registered estate.[55] If, before the triggering event, the covenant had been registered as a Class D(ii) land charge, the registrar will enter a notice against the burdened title. In these circumstances, the purchaser of the burdened land will therefore be bound by the covenant.

11.6.2 Passing the benefit in equity

If it can be shown that the burden of a covenant passes in equity, you will then need to demonstrate that the benefit of the covenant has also passed in equity. Whilst the rules for passing of the benefit *in equity* share similarities with those for the passing of the benefit *at law*, there are subtle differences, so you must stay alert! In order to demonstrate that the benefit of a covenant has passed *in equity*, two conditions must be satisfied. See Figure 11.8.

11.6.2.1 The covenant 'touches and concerns' the land of the original covenantee

This requirement operates in precisely the same way as for the passing of the benefit at law. The tests for 'touching and concerning' in *Smith & Snipes Hall Farm* and *Swift (P. & A.) Investments* are again relevant. Be sure to revisit these in section 11.5.1.1.

11.6.2.2 The benefit of the covenant was intended to run with the land

As with passing the benefit at law, for the benefit of a covenant to run in equity, it must be established that the benefit was intended to run with the land. This can be demonstrated in a number of ways. In equity, there are four:

- express or implied annexation;
- statutory annexation under s. 78 of the LPA 1925;
- express or implied assignment;
- under a 'scheme of development' or 'building scheme'.

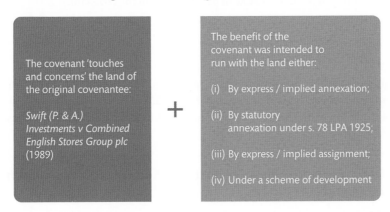

The covenant 'touches and concerns' the land of the original covenantee:

Swift (P. & A.) Investments v Combined English Stores Group plc (1989)

+

The benefit of the covenant was intended to run with the land either:

(i) By express / implied annexation;

(ii) By statutory annexation under s. 78 LPA 1925;

(iii) By express / implied assignment;

(iv) Under a scheme of development

Figure 11.8 Passing the benefit of a covenant in equity

---

[55] Land Registration Rules 2003, r. 35(1).

Certain (but not all) of these methods will now be familiar to you following our discussion in section 11.5.

Express or implied annexation

In the same way as at law, the benefit of a covenant can be annexed expressly or implied in equity. We considered these modes of annexation in section 11.5.1 and need not repeat them here.

Statutory annexation under s. 78 of the LPA 1925

Again, as at law, annexation of the benefit in equity is most easily demonstrated through operation of statute. Again, you should familiarize yourself with the full discussion of statutory annexation at section 11.5.1.

Express or implied assignment

Whilst the ease of statutory annexation under s. 78 has made assignment practically far less significant, that is not to say assignment is irrelevant especially express assignment. Indeed, for many conveyancers, assignment remains a preferred method for passing the benefit of a covenant for the certainty it can bring. So, what is assignment?

Just as the benefit of a contract can be 'assigned' or transferred to another person, the same is true of the benefit of a covenant. Assignment can be express where clear words of assignment are used or can be implied from a consideration of all the circumstances of the case. Assignment is distinct from annexation in that it takes places on the transfer of the benefited land to the successor, as opposed to annexation which fixes the benefit *to the land* at the date of the grant of the covenant, for all time. This means that a claimant arguing that the benefit of a covenant has passed to her by assignment must show that, on the transfer of the original covenantee's land to her, the transfer documents contained an effective assignment. Romer LJ in *Miles* identified the three requirements for an effective assignment of the benefit in equity:

1. The land conveyed must be capable of benefiting from the covenant.

2. The land to be benefited must be 'ascertainable' or 'certain'.

3. The assignment must take place at the same time as the transfer of the land so that it forms part of the transaction.

The requirements for assignment were examined by Upjohn J in *Newton-Abbot Co-Operative Society Ltd v Williamson and Treadgold Ltd*, a case which demonstrates the degree of flexibility with which the court is prepared to apply the principles of assignment in equity.

KEY CASE *Newton-Abbot Co-Operative Society Ltd v Williamson and Treadgold Ltd* (1952)

Facts: Mrs Bessie Marsdon owned land known as Devonia. She ran an ironmongery business on this land. She sold a parcel of land opposite the business to purchasers who covenanted that they would not use the purchased land to run a business in competition with the ironmongers. The covenant

→

→

made reference to 'Mrs Marsden of Devonia' but did not refer specifically to the land which was to benefit from the covenant. Mrs Marsdon died and Devonia passed to her son under her will. The executors of the will failed to expressly assign the benefit of the covenant to the son. The son subsequently leased the land to the claimants, Newton-Abbot Co-Operative Society, and the conveyance included an express assignment of the benefit of the covenant. The defendants, Williamson and Treadgold Ltd, successors in title of the original covenantor, began trading as ironmongers. The claimants brought legal proceedings to enforce the covenant.

Legal issue: Were the claimants entitled to enforce the covenant against the defendants, particularly given that the precise land to benefit from the covenant had not been specifically identified and the executors had failed to expressly assign the benefit of the covenant to the son?

Judgment: The High Court held that the benefit of the covenant had not been annexed to the land due to the failure to properly identify the dominant land. However, the court found that, upon Bessie's death, the executors held the benefit of the covenant on bare trust for the son. The effect of this was that the son was entitled to the benefit of the covenant and, moreover, capable of expressly assigning it to a successor. The absence of an express assignment by the executors did not therefore defeat the son's entitlement. The son's express assignment of the benefit to the successor of the covenantee's land had been effective to pass the benefit of the covenant to the claimants.

In addition, the court rejected that the benefit of the covenant had been expressed to be for Bessie personally and found that the benefited land was sufficiently identifiable as it was 'ascertainable' from the wider circumstances surrounding the grant of the covenant.

The effect of a valid assignment of the benefit is that the assignee is able to enforce the covenant against any person subject to the burden of the covenant, for as long as the assignee owns the benefited land. If, however, the benefited land is subsequently sold, the benefit of the covenant will only pass to the new owner by way of assignment if it is again assigned at the time of this subsequent conveyance. If there is no assignment at this time, quite simply the benefit will not run with the land. In this way, assignment is a far more precarious method of passing the benefit of a covenant than annexation, which, as we have seen, fixes or cements the benefit to the land itself for all time.

Attempts have been made to argue that the effect of an express assignment of the benefit is to affix the benefit to the land for all time under a 'delayed annexation' of the benefit with the result that further assignments are not necessary in order to pass the benefit to subsequent successors.[56] This argument has been considered but largely rejected.[57] In *Stilwell v Blackman* (1968), Ungoed-Thomas J addressed the 'delayed annexation' thesis head-on:[58]

> There is no reason either in contract or in the relevant principles of equity why an express assignment of the benefit of a covenant with the passing of land should automatically operate exclusively as an annexation of the covenant to the land.

[56] See discussion in *Renals*; *Rogers v Hosegood*; T. Bailey (1938) 6 CLJ 339; W. Wade (1957) CLJ 146; P. V. Baker (1968) 84 LQR 22; D. Hayton (1971) 87 LQR 539.

[57] See *Re Pinewood Estates* (1958), per Wynn-Parry J, who held that, on sale and resale of land, an unbroken chain of assignments was required; also *Federated Homes* at first instance. There is also no implied assignment under s. 62 of the LPA 1925: *Kumar v Dunning* (1989) indicating that restrictive covenants fall outside the scope of the provision.

[58] *Stilwell*, 526.

The position is therefore clear: where benefited land passes through the hands of a series of purchasers, an unbroken chain of assignments is required if the current owner is to be entitled to enforce the covenant. Despite the apparent vulnerability of assignment, however, as we saw in *Newton-Abbot*, the court may nevertheless find ways around a failure of assignment.

Under a 'scheme of development' or 'building scheme'

A final means by which the benefit of a covenant can pass in equity is under a 'scheme of development' also called a 'building scheme'. The scheme of development is an equitable device which developed as early as the 1830s in the Court of Chancery offering special recognition to the importance of the mutual enforcement of covenants in a development context.

The concept of a 'scheme of development' can be quite difficult to grasp in the abstract but an example will help you to understand how it works: imagine that ConstructCo is the owner of a large parcel of land. It divides the land into three plots and sells each separately to different owners. The developer wants the owners of each of the plots to be subject to restrictive covenants on the user of the land (for example, that the land can be used for residential purposes only). Crucially, the developer wants the covenants to be enforceable by each owner against all the other owners to ensure the integrity of the development. Where a scheme of development is found to exist, this is precisely the result achieved: see Figure 11.9.

Where land is found to be subject to a scheme of development, all the current owners of land within that scheme are entitled to sue on the covenants, irrespective of when the covenants were originally granted and irrespective of when each individual owner acquired their plot. The scheme of development or 'building scheme' therefore allows the benefit

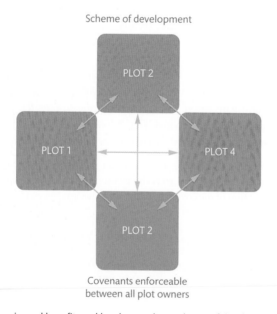

Figure 11.9 Mutually reciprocal benefits and burdens under a scheme of development

of covenants entered into by subsequent purchasers of land to be enforced over land previously sold. This resulting mutual enforceability of covenants gives rise to what Cozens-Hardy MR in *Reid v Bickerstaff* (1909) called 'a local law'. Naturally, there are certain constraints on when a scheme of development will arise. These requirements have been laid down and refined by decisions of the court.

The conditions required for a scheme of development to arise can be split into two distinct stages:

- the traditional requirements laid down in *Elliston v Reacher* (1908);
- the contemporary requirements of the modern law, which reveal a far more relaxed and flexible approach.

The traditional requirements for a scheme of development were far more rigid than is the case today. The traditional position was established in the case of *Elliston*. In the 50 years that followed, there were only a handful of reported cases where the conditions were satisfied. The landscape was ripe for a relaxation in the law which was to come in the 1960s and 1970s not that this meant proving the existence of a scheme was easy:

KEY CASE *Lund v Taylor* (1976)

Facts: An estate owner divided a portion of its land into 24 plots, leaving a considerable area unplotted. Each plot was subsequently sold and the conveyances, which were mostly identical, contained restrictive covenants to the effect that the purchasers were not permitted to build blocks of flats on the purchased land. Lund and Taylor both purchased separate plots. Taylor wished to build flats on his land. Lund sought an injunction arguing that Taylor's intended construction constituted an anticipated breach of the restrictive covenant. Lund argued that the original estate owner had established a scheme of development which generated a 'local law'.

Legal issue: Had a scheme of development been established with the result that Lund was entitled to an injunction to prevent Taylor's anticipated breach of covenant?

Judgment: At first instance, Lund succeeded and an injunction was ordered to prevent Taylor building the block of flats. Taylor appealed. In the Court of Appeal, Taylor's appeal was allowed. Whilst there was evidence that the original estate owner had drawn up architect's plans for the proposed development, it had not been demonstrated that any of the purchasers had sight of these plans. The purchasers had not been informed of any intention that there be mutually enforceable covenants between the plot owners. In summary, the purchasers had not been made aware that a defined area of land was intended to be sold off as plots. Stamp LJ noted:

> In the instant case there is no evidence that the Estate Plan was brought to the attention of any of the purchasers . . . there is no evidence that any proposing purchaser of a plot was told that the vendor was proposing to exact similar covenant, or indeed any covenants, from the purchasers of other plots.

KEY CASE *Re Dolphin's Conveyance* (1970)

Facts: Mr Dolphin owned the 'Selly Hill Estate' located in Birmingham. On his death, the majority of the estate was sold off. There were nine conveyances in total with the first four being administered by Mr Dolphin's sisters and the remaining five conveyances by his nephew. Eight of the nine conveyances

➡

> took identical form and contained restrictive covenants on the nature of the dwellings that could be built on the plots sold. One of the purchasers, Birmingham Corporation, planned to develop their plot in a manner inconsistent with the terms of the covenant.
>
> Legal issue: Was the Birmingham Corporation entitled to a declaration from the court that it was no longer subject to the obligations under the covenants or did they remain bound?
>
> Judgment: The High Court held that a scheme of development had been established despite there being no common vendor and the estate not having been laid out in plots prior to the subsequent sale of the land as required under the traditional *Elliston* authority. The court held that, taking into account all the circumstances of the case, the covenants had been imposed for the mutual benefit of the vendors and the purchasers of the estate. There was a discernible intention that the covenants should be enforceable by each owner against all others.

Re Dolphin's Conveyance therefore demonstrated a move towards a more relaxed approach to schemes of development.[59] However, although the requirements have been relaxed, the law governing schemes of development remains, admittedly, quite anachronistic. As Megarry J put it in *Brunner v Greenslade* (1971):[60]

> Equity readily gives effect to the common intention notwithstanding any technical [theoretical] difficulties involved. It may be, indeed, that this is one of those branches of equity which work best when explained least.

Today, the leading and latest key authority which lays down the requirements for and operation of a scheme of development is *Birdlip v Hunter* (2016)—the first major case on schemes of development to reach the Court of Appeal in over 20 years and one which appears to suggest a new narrowing or tightening of the circumstances in which a scheme will be found. Clarifying the law in this area, Lewison noted six key characteristics of schemes of development:

1. It applies to a defined area.
2. Owners of properties within that area have purchased their properties from a common owner.
3. Each of the properties is burdened by covenants which were intended to be mutually enforceable between the different owners.
4. The limits of that defined area are known to each of the purchasers.
5. The common owner is himself bound by the scheme, which crystallizes on the occasion of the first sale of a plot within the defined area, with the consequence that he is not entitled to dispose of plots within that area otherwise than on the terms of the scheme.
6. The effect of the scheme will bind future purchasers of land falling within the area, potentially forever.

Birdlip purchased a plot of land on which it wished to build two further houses and secured planning permission to do so. The Hunters, owners of neighbouring land objected.

---

[59] Recently confirmed in the High Court decision in *Birdlip Ltd v Hunter* (2015).   [60] *Brunner*, 1006.

Birdlip's land was subject to a covenant not to build more houses on it. Birdlip's predecessors acquired the land as a result of two conveyances in 1909 and 1910. Both the Hunters' and Birdlip's land had been part of a single plot purchased in 1910. The Hunters sought to enforce the restrictive covenant but could not demonstrate that the covenant had been annexed or assigned to the land. They therefore argued there was a scheme of development. This succeeded in the High Court but was overturned by the Court of Appeal which held that the evidence fell far short of proving the existence of such a scheme. Lewison LJ focused primarily on the express terms of the conveyances themselves. The documentation available did not clearly show defined plots to be sold; the covenants were said to be given for the benefit of a larger area of land than that alleged to now be part of the scheme; the conveyances contained no express statement of mutual enforceability; some of the covenants were positive and therefore not enforceable in any event and other covenants required the vendor's consent for building work which pointed against there being a mutual scheme. It was essential to a scheme of development that all buyers knew of the scheme's extent. On the available plans and documents, a buyer of one plot would have had no idea which other land would have been included within the scheme. Lewison LJ identified the two overarching prerequisites as being: (1) identification of the land to which the scheme relates; and (2) a clear intention and acceptance by all the purchasers of plots that they are to be subject to mutual and reciprocal covenants. These conditions were not satisfied and so no scheme could exist. Birdlip was not bound by the restrictive covenant.

What do we take away from the case of *Birdlip*? First, the court confirms that the starting point is to focus on the terms of any conveyances, transactional documents, and plans. Secondly, the court will be slow to find a scheme on extrinsic evidence alone, not wanting to burden land based on vague, imprecise evidence or speculative inferences. Thirdly, the court has clarified the characteristics of the scheme of development in the modern law. Fourthly, in so doing, the court has indicated its readiness to analyse forensically the evidence on which the scheme is said to exist. Finally, *Birdlip* shows that clearly identified land and strong evidence of intention by all purchasers to be bound by mutual and reciprocal covenants will be required before a scheme of development will be found.

11.7 Summary of the principles for the passing of benefit and burden

We have covered quite some ground so let's pause for a moment to summarize the position and reflect on the passing of benefit and burden at law and in equity: see Table 11.1. What we have discovered is that, whilst the benefit of positive and negative covenants is able to pass at law and in equity, only the burden of restrictive covenants can pass and, in any event, only in equity and not at law. At law, the burden of neither positive nor negative covenants can pass. The consequence of this is that many claims to enforce freehold covenants will seek to rely on the equitable rules. It is not possible for the burden of a positive covenant to be enforced directly either at law or in equity. However, not content with the inconvenience of this position, conveyancers (who can be an inventive lot!) set about devising, therefore, a series of indirect methods by which the burden of positive covenants can run with the land. We explored these indirect methods in section 11.5.3.

Table 11.1 Summary of the rules for the passing of benefit and burden at law and in equity

	DOES THE BENEFIT OF THE COVENANT RUN?	DOES THE BURDEN OF THE COVENANT RUN?
AT LAW	Yes: for positive and negative covenants	No: *Austerberry* (1885); *Rhone* (1994)
IN EQUITY	Yes: for positive and negative covenants	Yes: but only the burden of negative covenants

11.8 Discharge and modification of freehold covenants

What if a parcel of land is subject to a restrictive covenant and an interested party wishes to bring that covenant to an end? Can they do so? Well, under s. 84(1) of the LPA 1925, the Lands Chamber of the Upper Tribunal has the power 'wholly or partially to discharge or modify any . . . restriction' affecting an interest in freehold land. An application for discharge or modification can be made by 'any person interested'.[61] Note that s. 84(1) does not apply to positive covenants. As Sutton has identified, in most cases, applications are made to the Lands Chamber for the modification of restrictive covenants with the aim of allowing greater residential development of land.[62]

The grounds on which the Lands Chamber is permitted to discharge or modify a restrictive covenant are strictly drawn and are contained in s. 84(1) of the LPA 1925. The grounds for discharge or modification of a covenant can be condensed into four categories:

- Obsolescence under s. 84(1)(a): A restrictive covenant can be discharged or modified where the restriction has become 'obsolete' due to 'changes in the character' of the property or neighbourhood. Obsolescence is determined by considering how far the original purpose of the restriction can still be achieved.[63]

- Impediment of reasonable user under s. 84(1)(aa): A restrictive covenant can be discharged if the continued existence of the restriction 'would impede some reasonable user of the land for public or private purposes'. Under s. 84(1A) and (1B), the Upper Tribunal must: (i) be satisfied either that the covenant no longer provides any practical benefit of substantial value or advantage to the dominant owner,[64] or (ii) be satisfied that the covenant is contrary to the public interest.[65] The Tribunal must also be satisfied that money will be adequate compensation for those suffering loss as a result of discharge or modification.[66]

- Those benefiting from the restrictive covenant agree to discharge or modification under s. 84(1)(b): A restrictive covenant can be discharged or modified if those entitled to benefit from the covenant are of age, are legally competent, and agree either expressly or impliedly to discharge or modification.[67]

---

[61] Section 84(7) of the LPA 1925.   [62] T. Sutton, 'On the Brink of Land Obligations Again' [2013] Conv 17.

[63] *Re Truman Hanbury Buxton & Co. Ltd's Application* (1956); *Re Quaffers Ltd* (1988).

[64] *Stannard v Issa* (1987); *Re Kennet Properties Ltd Application* (1996); *Sheppard v Turner* (2006).

[65] *Re Collins' Application* (1974); *Re Azfar's Application* (2002).

[66] *Re University of Westminster* (1998); *Duffield v Gandy* (2008).

[67] *Re Fettishaw's Application (No. 2)* (1973); *Re Memvale's Securities Ltd's Application* (1974).

- Those benefiting from the restrictive covenant will suffer no injury under s. 84(1)(c): A restrictive covenant can be discharged or modified where this 'will not injure the persons entitled to the benefit of the restriction'.[68]

The jurisdiction afforded to the Lands Chamber is a recognition that 'restrictive covenants cannot be regarded as absolute and inviolable for all time'.[69] Discharge and modification of restrictive covenants under these provisions therefore should be seen as offering a means by which the amenity and utility of land can be maintained as opposed to being encumbered in perpetuity by useless or obsolete restrictions.

11.9 Reform of freehold covenants

We have now explored the nature of freehold covenants and the rules governing their enforceability, both between the original parties and between successors, but what of reform?

The Law Commission's 2011 Report No. 327, *Making Land Work: Easements, Covenants and Profits à Prendre* reflects the most up-to-date reform proposals in this area and the agenda put forward was pretty radical.[70] The Commission's proposals[71] would see the creation of a new legal interest in land, 'the land obligation', which would replace covenants with rights enjoying a true and unquestionably proprietary status as opposed to the current position which Wade has described as 'a peculiar species of personal contract'.[72] Land obligations could be positive or negative, would need to be created by deed, and the issue of enforceability would be determined by questions of registration. In addition, the original parties to the land obligations would cease to be liable for breaches occurring after they had parted with the land.[73]

The reforms proposed were clearly bold and would serve to eradicate many of the overly technical and convoluted rules that govern the enforceability of freehold covenants. What's more, the proposals had the advantage of simplicity: positive and negative promises, if registered, would be enforceable by and against successors in title. Met with wide-ranging approval, the recommendations sadly have yet to be taken up by Parliament and this now looks unlikely. Not everyone approved of the proposals, however. O'Connor, for example, argued there is no need for the creation of a new proprietary interest as the current methods for the enforcement of positive obligations are generally satisfactory and abolition of the *Austerberry* principle carried significant risks:[74]

> The 'easy option' of opening the door to positive covenants may turn out to be the hard option in the long run. One person's onerous obligation is another person's valuable property right, the barriers to ex post relief are formidable. In an era of human rights, the need to provide compensation

---

[68] *McMorris v Brown* (1991).   [69] *Jaggard v Sawyer* (1995), per Lord Bingham, [43].

[70] The Law Commission has also recommended the introduction of 'conservation covenants' for the first time in the law of England and Wales. A conservation covenant is a voluntary agreement between a landowner and a responsible body (charity, public authority/local government) to do or not do something on land for a conservation purpose and could survive changes in land ownership: see Law Commission Report No. 349, *Conservation Covenants* (2014).

[71] See Law Commission Report No. 327, [5.69]–[5.70].

[72] W. Wade, 'Covenants: A Broad and Reasonable View' (1972) 31 CLJ 157, 170.

[73] Law Commission Report No. 327, [5.82].

[74] P. O'Connor, 'Careful What You Wish For: Positive Freehold Covenants' [2011] Conv 191, 206.

for extinguishment of property rights will significantly limit the ability of future legislators to protect purchasers and to relieve against onerous covenants. This may explain the reluctance of legislators in many jurisdictions to act upon recommendation to abolish the *Austerberry* rule.

11.10 Future directions

Despite enduring criticism of the law of freehold covenants, there has been little movement towards reform. Lawyers seem resigned to the law's flaws. Yet, as we saw in section 11.9, in 2011 the Commission recommended a dramatic overhaul of the law. It is therefore this reform agenda which will occupy our thoughts as we consider the future direction of the law.

The first element to consider is whether the introduction of a new interest in land, 'the land obligation', is really necessary. McFarlane has cautioned against the creation of new proprietary interests in land.[75] In particular, the reform, if implemented, will see the enforceability of positive obligations and a reversal of the *Austerberry* rule. As O'Connor identifies, there has been growing dissatisfaction with the *Austerberry* rule, with legislation allowing positive covenants to run with land introduced in Northern Ireland, the Northern Territory, New Zealand, and Ireland. Scotland has had positive covenants or 'real burdens' since 1840. In England, there have been serious calls for reform since a Law Commission report in 1984. O'Connor notes:[76]

> By the 1980s, the *Austerberry* rule was under frequent challenge from authors of legal textbooks and articles, and from law reformers. The general tenor of the criticisms is that the distinction between covenants imposing land use restrictions and covenants that impose positive obligations is mere formalism, reflects no important functional difference, lacks any sound policy foundation and causes practical inconvenience.

The law is also said to be inconsistent in that it permits the running of positive burdens in leasehold covenants but not freehold. For O'Connor, the *Austerberry* debate must be seen as part of a 'conflict zone' of competing interests: the interests of today's owners to be free to contract as they wish vs the interests of later owners to avoid the 'over-encumbering' of property. Mahoney has framed the issue by asking:[77]

> Why should the owners of today be empowered to exert 'dead hand control' over land, constraining the choices of future generations whose needs and circumstances may be very different?

Lord Templeman in *Rhone* offered a rationale for the continued force of *Austerberry*, arguing (admittedly with some degree of circularity):[78]

> [E]nforcement of a positive covenant lies in contract; a positive covenant compels an owner to exercise his rights. Enforcement of a negative covenant lies in equity; a negative covenant deprives the owner of a right over property.

There are also practical concerns in allowing the burden of positive covenants to run with land. First, research carried out by the Scottish Law Commission in 2000 found that a

---

[75] B. McFarlane, 'The Numerus Clausus Principle and Covenants Relating to Land' in S. Bright (ed.), *Modern Studies in Property Law*, Vol. 6 (Oxford: Hart, 2011), chapter 15.

[76] O'Connor, 'Careful What You Wish For: Positive Freehold Covenants', 193.

[77] J. Mahoney, 'Perpetual Restrictions on Land and the Problem of the Future' (2002) 88 Va L Rev 739, 768–9.

[78] *Rhone*, 318.

majority of purchasers of land surveyed had little or no understanding of what a positive burden was or of its significance. The Commission concluded that purchasers were buying without knowledge or any choice in relation to the nature of the land they were acquiring. Secondly, the high cost of discharging or modifying covenants may offer a further justification for the continued existence of the *Austerberry* rule. For O'Connor, the rule is therefore both defensible and coherent:[79]

> The refusal of courts to allow positive obligations to run as freehold covenants is doctrinally coherent and based on sound policy. It accords with the general resistance of both civil and common law systems to allowing land titles to be encumbered with enduring positive obligations enforceable by other landowners as a property right. The widely recognised distinction in property law between land use restrictions and positive obligations is not neither formalistic nor incoherent. As explained by Lord Templeman in *Rhone*, restrictive covenants subtract specified use rights from the landowner's original endowment, while positive obligations add a burden to landownership which was never part of the landowner's endowment. Like other limiting rules in the law of covenants, the *Austerberry* rule serves to balance competing interests: 'freedom of contract' versus 'freedom from transaction' or inter-generational equity.

The Law Commission has clearly taken the opposite view to O'Connor in recommending an end to the *Austerberry* rule. So, how far has the Commission sought to meet head-on the concerns expressed by opponents to reform such as O'Connor? The Law Commission has provided three potential brakes on the impact of their proposals:

- A land obligation (whether positive or negative) will only be capable of running with the land if it 'touches and concerns' the benefited land.
- A land obligation will only run with the land if it complies with registration requirements.
- The Upper Tribunal will enjoy a power under the s. 84 of the LPA 1925 to discharge or modify these new land obligations.

Taken together, how far do these measures provide enough of a counterweight to concerns of the over-burdening of future owners' land? The answer to this question depends on your faith and adherence to the system of land registration. It is hard to see how the 'touch and concern' brake will offer comfort to future owners and, in addition, the s. 84 jurisdiction is tightly drawn and costly to access. The great advantage of the registration requirement is, of course, that at the very least it will deliver discoverability and visibility of the interest to potential purchasers of the land. Consider the practical perspective: the land obligation would require registration in order to be enforceable. The effect of this would be that any potential purchaser of burdened land would have ample warning of the burden and could use this as a basis for negotiation of a lower purchase price or payment of lower rent and could exploit the opportunity to consider taking out insurance. For Sutton:[80]

> The safeguards suggested by the Law Commission, and in particular the proposals to extend the jurisdiction of the Lands Chamber . . . have the potential to provide a strong framework for counterbalancing the extra demands the new legal proprietary right encompassing both positive and negative obligations will bring.

Do you agree?

---

[79] O'Connor, 'Careful What You Wish For: Positive Freehold Covenants', 205.
[80] Sutton, 'On the Brink of Land Obligations Again', 29.

Further reading

- C. Bevan, 'The Doctrine of Benefit and Burden: Reforming the Law of Covenants and the Numerus Clausus "Problem"' (2018) 77(1) CLJ 72.

- D. Cowan, L. Fox O'Mahony, and N. Cobb, *Great Debates in Land Law* (Basingstoke: Palgrave, 2016), chapter 7.

- C. Davis, 'The Principle of Benefit and Burden' (1998) 57(3) CLJ 522.

- S. Gardner, 'The Proprietary Effect of Contractual Obligations under *Tulk v Moxhay* and *De Mattos v Gibson*' (1982) 98 LQR 279.

- N. Gravells, 'Enforcement of Positive Covenants Affecting Freehold Land' (1994) 110 LQR 346.

- N. Gravells, '*Federated Homes Ltd v Mill Lodge Properties Ltd* (1979) Annexation and Intention' in N. Gravells (ed.), *Landmark Cases in Property Law* (Oxford: Hart, 2013), chapter 5.

- J. Howell, 'The Annexation of the Benefit of Covenants to Land' [2004] Conv 507, 513.

- B. McFarlane, 'The Numerus Clausus Principle and Covenants Relating to Land' in S. Bright (ed.), *Modern Studies in Property Law*, Vol. 6 (Oxford: Hart, 2011), chapter 15.

- B. McFarlane, '*Tulk v Moxhay* (1848)' in C. Mitchell and P. Mitchell (eds.), *Landmark Cases in Equity* (Oxford: Hart, 2012), at 203.

- G. Newsome, 'Universal Annexation?' (1981) 97 LQR 32.

- P. O'Connor, 'Careful What You Wish For: Positive Freehold Covenants' [2011] Conv 191.

- J. Snape, 'The Benefit and burden of Covenants: Now Where Are We?' (1994) 68 Nott LJ 68.

- T. Sutton, 'On the Brink of Land Obligations Again' [2013] Conv 17.

- H. W. R. Wade, 'Covenants: A Broad and Reasonable View' (1972) 31 CLJ 157.

 ## Online resources

Access the online resources at www.oup.com/uk/bevan2e/ to test yourself with self-test questions and scenario problems. You can also view additional supporting material relevant to the topics in this chapter, including:

- *Videos*

- *Audio podcasts*

- *Maps, diagrams, and flowcharts*

- *Interactive exercises*

- *Examples of real-life legal documentation*

Leasehold Covenants

12.1 Introduction

In Chapter 9, we identified the essential characteristics of leases, how they are created, and how they are terminated. But what of the content of leases? Leasehold covenants provide this content. We first encountered covenants in Chapter 11 but of the freehold variety. In this chapter, we consider covenants made between landlords and tenants in the leasehold context. Leasehold covenants are found in the tenancy agreement and, as with any legal document, the precise nature of these covenants falls to be construed according to the intentions of the parties in all the circumstances, the purpose, and context in which the lease arises: *Linpac Mouldings Ltd v Aviva* (2010). Leasehold covenants govern the landlord–tenant relationship and will usually be expressly agreed by the parties in the leasehold agreement. A tenant's covenants will include promises to pay rent, not use the property for a business or other specified purpose, not to assign or sell the lease to others and covenants governing a tenant's responsibilities for repair and maintenance. A landlord's covenants will include a promise of quiet possession and details of repairing and insurance obligations. Many covenants are also implied into tenancy agreements whether by common law or statute. Looking at some examples of covenants routinely implied into leases will help you better grasp the nature of leasehold covenants and the sort of subject matter they govern: see Figure 12.1. An important and new development in this area has been made by the Homes (Fitness for Human Habitation) Act 2018 (H(FHH)A 2018)[1] which introduces a new s. 9A into the LTA 1985 which implies into residential leases of less than 7 years' duration created on or after 20 March 2019 an implied covenant owed by the landlord that (i) the dwelling is fit for human habitation at the time the lease is granted; and (ii) that the dwelling will remain fit for human habitation during the term of the lease. It might come as a surprise to some that it took until 2019 (when the new law come into force) for such a term to be implied. In fact, a term of human habitation was provided for under the 1985

---

[1] On which see C. Bevan, 'Improving Housing Conditions in the Private and Social Rented Sectors: The Homes (Fitness for Human Habitation) Act 2018—Fit for Habitation but Fit for Purpose?' (2019) 82(5) MLR 897.

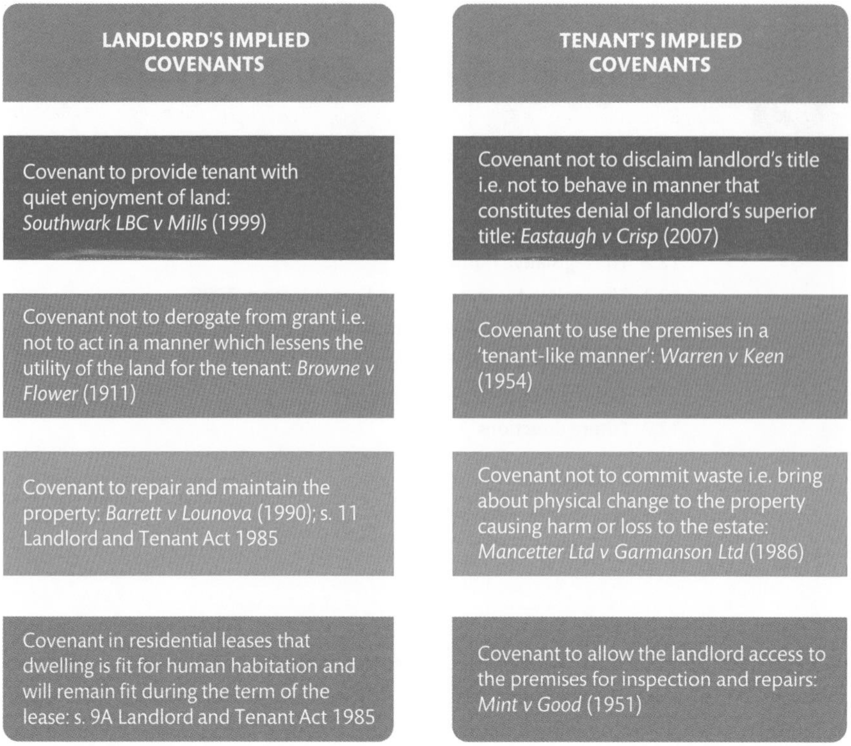

LANDLORD'S IMPLIED COVENANTS	TENANT'S IMPLIED COVENANTS
Covenant to provide tenant with quiet enjoyment of land: *Southwark LBC v Mills* (1999)	Covenant not to disclaim landlord's title i.e. not to behave in manner that constitutes denial of landlord's superior title: *Eastaugh v Crisp* (2007)
Covenant not to derogate from grant i.e. not to act in a manner which lessens the utility of the land for the tenant: *Browne v Flower* (1911)	Covenant to use the premises in a 'tenant-like manner': *Warren v Keen* (1954)
Covenant to repair and maintain the property: *Barrett v Lounova* (1990); s. 11 Landlord and Tenant Act 1985	Covenant not to commit waste i.e. bring about physical change to the property causing harm or loss to the estate: *Mancetter Ltd v Garmanson Ltd* (1986)
Covenant in residential leases that dwelling is fit for human habitation and will remain fit during the term of the lease: s. 9A Landlord and Tenant Act 1985	Covenant to allow the landlord access to the premises for inspection and repairs: *Mint v Good* (1951)

Figure 12.1 Examples of commonly implied leasehold covenants

Act but, due to a very circumscribed ambit, had fallen into disuse and was inapplicable in almost every conceivable tenancy agreement.

12.1.1 Clarifying leasehold terminology: Assignment, privity of contract, and privity of estate

The specific rules concerning the enforceability of leasehold covenants will be examined closely in the next section. Before we get to that, it is worth pausing to consider some of the terminology and key concepts arising in the law of leasehold covenants. This terminology can sometimes seem impenetrable and overwhelming but be assured, it will become familiar with time. We have already encountered the basic terminology of the landlord–tenant relationship, and, in Chapter 9, discussed the potential for the landlord's reversion and the tenant's leasehold interest to pass to third parties. When these interests pass, we say that the landlord's reversion and tenant's lease is 'assigned' to a successor. '**Assignment**' means that an interest has been either sold or transferred to a third party who is then described variously as the 'purchaser of the reversion' and 'purchaser of the lease' or 'landlord's assignee' or 'tenant's assignee'.

Two further concepts warrant mention, namely 'liability based on privity of contract' and 'liability based on privity of estate'. In order to make sense of these concepts, we must first recall that a lease is both proprietary and contractual in nature and in this way exhibits a dual character. So, between the original landlord and original tenant, there exists a contract but also a proprietary interest taking the form of the leasehold estate. Liability on the covenants can therefore be either contract-based (founded upon the contractual relationship between parties) or be estate-based (founded upon the leasehold relationship). When we add assignment of the landlord's reversion and tenant's leasehold interest into the picture, a more complex nexus emerges: see Figure 12.2. Simply put, when parties enjoy a contractual relationship, there is said to be 'privity of contract'—we saw this operating in Chapter 11 on freehold covenants. When parties enjoy a leasehold relationship, there is said to be 'privity of estate'.

We need to unpack Figure 12.2 a little further. As between the original landlord and original tenant, there is privity of contract and, for the duration of that original lease, this privity of contract endures even if the parties assign their interests. Privity of estate will exist between those parties in whom the leasehold and reversion are vested. This may vary during the lifetime of the original lease. Should the original tenant assign her leasehold interest, the tenant's assignee will have privity of estate with whomsoever is holding the freehold reversion at that time (the original landlord or the landlord's assignee). The original tenant will no longer enjoy privity of estate with the original landlord. Equally, should the

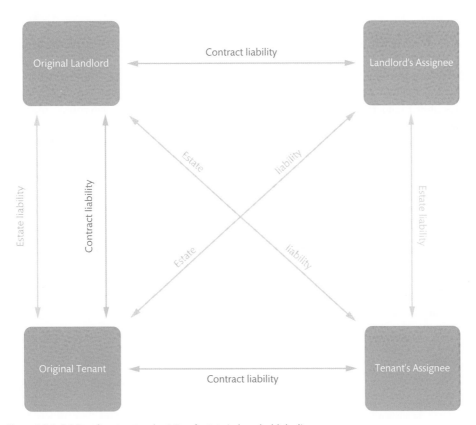

Figure 12.2 Privity of contract and privity of estate in leasehold dealings

original landlord assignee the reversion, the landlord's assignee will have privity of estate with the original tenant.

The concepts of privity of contract and estate have a long pedigree and sit at the heart of the principles governing enforcement of leasehold covenants. Nourse LJ in *City of London Corp. v Fell* (1994) explained the interrelationship of the two concepts in the following terms:[2]

> [L]andlord and tenant stand together in one or other of two distinct legal relationships. In the first it is said that there is privity of contract between them, in the second privity of estate.

Where there exists privity of estate, positive and negative leasehold covenants are enforceable by as well as against the parties to the leasehold estate. As to the nature of privity of estate, Nourse LJ in *Fell* explained its substance:[3]

> [T]he contractual obligations which touch and concern the land having become imprinted on the estate, the tenancy is capable of existence as a species of property independently of the contract.

Having outlined some of the fundamental concepts, we now turn to examine the particular rules going to enforcement of leasehold covenants.

 Visit the online resources to watch a video on forfeiture: ending leases and reform.

12.2 The legislative framework

The rules governing the enforceability of leasehold covenants vary according to when the lease was granted. Leases created before 1996 are treated quite differently to those created on or after 1 January 1996. As we will explore in section 12.3, the pre-1996 rules came to be seen as producing perverse results and, following extensive work by the Law Commission,[4] far-reaching reforms were proposed which ultimately found voice in the Landlord and Tenant (Covenants) Act 1995 (LTCA 1995). The principles determining enforceability of leasehold covenants whether pre- or post-1 January 1996 are complex and highly technical. In order to offer clarity in what can be a challenging area of the law, it is important for us to examine quite separately the two distinct regimes. In so doing, we will focus on the following two issues:

- enforceability and the original parties to the lease
- enforceability and assignees of the landlord's reversion and tenant's leasehold.

We begin by considering how leasehold covenants are enforced in leases created before 1 January 1996.

---

[2] Fell, 604.   [3] Ibid.

[4] Law Commission Report No. 174 which recorded a widespread view that the pre-1996 law was deeply problematic and gave rise to 'justifiable shock, disbelief and outrage'.

12.3 The regime for leases granted pre-1 January 1996

For leases granted before 1 January 1996, the principles on the enforceability of leasehold covenants are an amalgam of common law rules and statutory interventions. As you will come to appreciate, the pre-1996 regime was regarded as giving rise to injustice, inconsistency in outcomes, and, more broadly, as generating unfairness. It was precisely these criticisms which led to the introduction of the 1995 Act which we consider in section 12.4. Sadly for us, the new regime ushered in by the 1995 Act is prospective only which means it applies only to leases created after the legislation came into force. We do, therefore, have to consider the principles governing the enforceability of leasehold covenants for leases granted before 1996. We examine these principles here.

12.3.1 The position as regards the original parties to the lease

For leases created pre-1 January 1996, the original parties to the lease are contractually liable for *all* leasehold covenants for the duration of the lease under the doctrine of privity of contract: *Stuart v Joy* (1904); *Allied London Investments Ltd v Hambro Life Assurance Ltd* (1984). This general position can be described as a 'continuing liability' as the original parties remain liable to each other even if both parties have assigned their interests (i.e. transferred or sold them) to a successor whether that be an assignee of the landlord's reversion or an assignee of the lease. Where, however, the landlord has assigned the reversion, the *benefit* of the covenants (the ability to sue) passes to the assignee under s. 141 of the LPA 1925 (see section 12.3.2.1). The effect, as confirmed in the case of *Re King* (1963), is that the landlord loses the right to sue on the covenants for breaches committed before the assignment.

On reflection, we can appreciate that the consequences of the continuing liability between the original landlord and original tenant (even in the event of assignment) can be severe and indeed this principle has been subjected to much criticism. Imagine a situation in which an original tenant assigns her leasehold interest to a third party who becomes the new tenant. If that new tenant fails to pay rent or breaches other tenant obligations contained in a leasehold covenant, the original landlord is fully entitled to sue the *original* tenant even though it is the new tenant who, in fact, committed the breach. In response to the perceived unfairness of this position, the 1995 Act abolished the 'continuing liability' principle. It does, however, still very much apply and bite in the pre-1996 leasehold context. In particular, it remains an important and fruitful avenue where the party in breach is insolvent and therefore a claim against the original tenant provides a way of achieving a meaningful remedy.[5]

The apparent harshness of the continuing liability principle was captured by Lord Nicholls in *Hindcastle Ltd v Barbara Attenborough & Associates Ltd* (1997):[6]

> [I]nsolvency may occur many years after the lease was granted, long after the original tenant parted with his interest in the lease . . . A person of modest means is understandably shocked when out of the blue he receives a rent demand from the landlord of the property he once leased.

---

[5] The principle of continuing liability was exploited to its full potential in this sense during the economically turbulent times of the 1980s and 1990s.

[6] *Hindcastle*, 83.

Unlike the landlord, he had no control over the identify of assignees down the line. He had no opportunity to reject them as financially unsound.

Fortunately, the harshness of the operation of the 'continuing liability' principle is mitigated in certain important circumstances. In the following instances the original tenant may be able to escape liability:

1. The original tenant will not be liable for an assignee's breach where the original parties to the lease have provided for an express limitation as to liability in the tenancy agreement. These clauses are, however, rare.

2. Under s. 145 and Sch. 25 of the LPA 1925, the original tenant will not be liable after an assignment of a perpetually renewable lease.

3. An original tenant is, equally, not liable for the breaches of the tenant's assignees where the original lease has been extended by operation of statute—for example, under the LTA 1954 where the breach is committed during the period of extension: *Fell*.

4. The original tenant may also, if sued as a result of a breach committed by an assignee, be able to rely on an indemnity covenant. An indemnity covenant may be expressly or impliedly undertaken by an assignee of the tenant's leasehold and acts so as to permit the original tenant to recover from that assignee any sums paid (damages or rent paid) in the event of the assignee's breaches.

   How does this indemnity obligation arise? First, an express indemnity covenant may be contained within the conveyance between the original tenant and the assignee (i.e. between the assignor and assignee) under which the assignee agrees to indemnify the assignor in the event of breach. If there are multiple assignments of the leasehold estate (i.e. the original tenant assigns his leasehold to an assignee who, in turn, assigns to another who subsequently assigns to another), a chain of indemnity covenants may develop which will allow the original tenant or 'assignor' to be indemnified so long as the chain remains unbroken. For this chain to exist, an indemnity covenant must be contained within each assignment. Secondly, where there is no express indemnity covenant, statute may nevertheless imply an indemnity covenant under s. 77 of the LPA 1925.[7]

   In the absence of an indemnity covenant, the original tenant may, in addition, be able to pursue a restitutionary action again the assignee in breach under the principle in *Moule v Garrett* (1872). As the court made plain in *Moule*, this action in 'restitution' will only be available to the extent of the assignee's liability and crucially it must be demonstrated that the assignee in breach has been 'unjustly enriched' at the original tenant's expense.[8]

5. Following the decision in *Friends Provident Life Office v British Railways Board* (1997) and now under s. 18 of the LTCA 1995 (one of the provisions of the 1995 Act that does have retrospective effect and applies to pre-1996 leases), the original tenant will not be held liable for any *increased* rent resulting from a variation of the terms of the original lease after the tenant's leasehold has been assigned. A variation here means a change in the rent as a result of an agreement reached between the landlord and the new tenant.

---

[7] You should note that the operation of s. 77 of the LPA 1925 is routinely excluded by the parties to tenancy agreements. See also Sch. 12, para. 20 of the LRA 2002.

[8] See *Re Healing Research Trustee Co.* (1992) for more on the operation of the *Moule* principle.

It must be right, on the basis of privity of contract, that the original tenant is not held liable as to terms negotiated under a variation to which he was not privy. There are two important caveats here that must be grasped. First, s. 18 concerns an *increase* in rent and, as such, the original tenant will remain liable as to the rent originally agreed. Secondly, it appears that the original tenant can be liable for the increase in rent if the increase results from the operation of an upward rent review clause which was a term of the original lease: *Centrovincial Estates plc v Bulk Storage Ltd* (1983).

6. Finally, under s. 17 of the LTCA 1995 (another provision which also has retrospective effect and applies to pre-1996 leases), where the original landlord wishes to recover a fixed sum (whether that be rent, service charges, or damages) from the original tenant, a statutory notice commonly referred to as a 'problem notice' must be served on that original tenant within six months of the sum falling due. The requirement of a statutory notice guarantees that the original tenant is informed early of the tenant's assignee's breach and, importantly, gives the original tenant the ability to take action to prevent further breaches. Where no statutory notice is served by the landlord, the original tenant will not be liable for the sums claimed. Where the original tenant complies with the statutory notice and pays the sums claimed, the original tenant is entitled to an 'overriding lease'[9] under s. 19 of the LTCA 1995, which takes effect as a statutory lease between the current landlord and the tenant in default. The effect is to parachute the original tenant back into the property as tenant of the current landlord and as landlord of the tenant in default. This means that the original tenant, now treated as 'tenant' of the current landlord, is able to bring an action against the tenant in breach such as forfeiture of the lease in order to recover the sums paid. The 'overriding lease' mechanism under s. 19 of the LTCA 1995 therefore serves to permit the original tenant to sue the tenant in default for the unpaid rent or in order to terminate the lease. The original tenant is entitled to seek an 'overriding lease' within 12 months of complying with the statutory notice under s. 17 of the 1995 Act and can protect the right to such a lease by entering a notice against a registered title under the LRA 2002 and by registration as a Class C(iv) land charge in unregistered land.

12.3.2 The position as regards assignees of the landlord's reversion and leasehold

We now turn to consider the question of the enforceability of leasehold covenants in pre-1 January 1996 leases where there has been an assignment of the landlord's reversion or an assignment of the tenant's leasehold. Here, the enforceability of leasehold covenants is determined by considering whether the benefit and the burden of those covenants has passed or, as we say, has 'run' with the reversion and the leasehold. In order to explore this further, it is helpful to split our discussion into two digestible parts:

1. where there has been an assignment of the landlord's reversion;
2. where there has been an assignment of the tenant's leasehold.

---

[9] This 'overriding lease' is in no way connected to overriding interests as understood in the registered land context and must be kept entirely separate.

12.3.2.1 Where there has been an assignment of the landlord's reversion

Here we are concerned with a situation where the original landlord assigns (i.e. transfers) her freehold reversion to a third party who becomes the new landlord, also called the landlord's assignee. Whether the landlord's assignee is free to enjoy the benefits of leasehold covenants and, at the same time, be bound by the burden of such covenants is determined by reference to the provisions of the LPA 1925. The key statutory provisions for these purposes are ss. 141 and 142 of the LPA 1925. Section 141(1) provides as follows:

> (1) Rent reserved by a lease, and the benefit of every covenant or provision therein contained, having reference to the subject-matter thereof, and on the lessee's part to be observed or performed, and every condition of re-entry and other condition therein contained, shall be annexed and incident to and shall go with the reversionary estate in the land, or in any part thereof, immediately expectant on the term granted by the lease, notwithstanding severance of that reversionary estate, and without prejudice to any liability affecting a covenantor or his estate.

Section 141(1) of the LPA 1925 provides that upon assignment of the landlord's reversion, the *benefit* of all covenants that have 'reference to the subject-matter' of the lease will run with the reversion. The 'benefit' of covenants reflects the ability of the landlord's assignee to sue on those covenants. What does this mean practically for the landlord's assignee, the new landlord? Section 141(1) operates so that the original landlord's assignee, the new landlord, has the right to sue the original tenant on the covenants in order to recover, for example, rent owed.

You may be wondering what is meant by 'reference to the subject-matter' of the lease. Under s. 141, only those covenants that have 'reference to the subject-matter of the lease' will run with the reversion. Another way of expressing this is that the provision applies only to covenants that 'touch and concern the land': *Spencer's Case* (1583). We are told that these two expressions can be taken as synonymous: *Caern Motor Services Ltd v Texaco Ltd* (1994). The applicable test here is that established in the case of *P. & A. Swift Investments v Combined English Stores Group plc* (1989) in which Lord Oliver noted:[10]

> Formulations of definitive tests are always dangerous, but it seems to me that . . . the following provides a satisfactory working test for whether, in any given case, a covenant touches and concerns the land: (1) the covenant benefits only the reversioner for time being, and if specified from the reversion ceases to be of benefit to the covenantee; (2) the covenant affects the nature, quality and mode of user or value of the land of the reversioner; (3) the covenant is not expressed to be personal . . . (4) the fact that a covenant is to pay a sum of money will not prevent it from touching and concerning the land so long as the three foregoing conditions are satisfied.

As Lord Oliver explained, formulating a definitive test of what constitutes 'touching and concerning' is challenging. As Gray and Gray note, 'it is notoriously difficult to propose a definition of "touching and concerning" which is not flawed by circularity'.[11] Plainly, as we saw in Chapter 11 on freehold covenants, of central importance is that the covenant benefits the land and not individuals.[12] References by Lord Oliver to the 'nature, quality and mode of user' again underscore the need for the covenant to be proprietary as opposed

---

[10] *P. & A. Swift Investments*, 642.
[11] K. Gray and S. F. Gray, *Elements of Land Law*, 5th edn (Oxford: Oxford University Press, 2009), [4.5.44].
[12] The 'touch and concern' test is applicable also to the law of freehold covenants explored in Chapter 11.

Table 12.1 Covenants that do and do not 'touch and concern land'

LEASEHOLD COVENANT	TOUCHES AND CONCERNS LAND?	CASE LAW
Covenant for quiet enjoyment	✓	*Spencer's Case* (1583)
Covenant for repairs	✓	*Matures v Westwood* (1598)
Covenant for the payment of rent	✓	*Parker v Webb* (1693)
Covenant for the payment of a deposit	✗	*Hua Chiao v Chiaphua* (1987)
Covenant to only sell landlord's products	✓	*Caern Motors v Texaco Ltd* (1994)
Covenant for non-competition	✗	*Thomas v Hayward* (1869)
Covenant of surety (i.e. promise to underwrite performance of the covenants)	✓	*Kumar v Dunning* (1989)
Covenant for option for tenant to purchase the reversion	✗	*Woodall v Clifton* (1905)
Covenant for the option to renew the lease	✓	*Phillips v Mobil Oil Co.* (1989)

to merely personal. For many covenants, the test has proved uncontroversial in its application. That said, and particularly in the commercial context, certain covenants have caused greater difficulty. This has led to apparently inconsistent results and, arguably, has given rise to 'arbitrary'[13] outcomes.

Consider Table 12.1 which lists a series of leasehold covenants and how the court has applied the Lord Oliver 'touch and concern' test to them. In short, under s. 141(1) of the LPA 1925, all proprietary covenants will run automatically with an assignment of the landlord's reversion with the result that the new landlord will be able to sue on those covenants: see Figure 12.3.

We have considered the position as regards the benefit of leasehold covenants but what about the burden? This is governed by s. 142(1) of the LPA 1925.

(1) The obligation under a condition or of a covenant entered into by a lessor with reference to the subject-matter of the lease shall, if and as far as the lessor has power to bind the reversionary estate immediately expectant on the term granted by the lease, be annexed and incident to and shall go with that reversionary estate, or the several parts thereof, notwithstanding severance of that reversionary estate, and may be taken advantage of and enforced by the person in whom the term is from time to time vested by conveyance, devolution in law, or otherwise; and, if and as far as the lessor has power to bind the person from time to time entitled to that reversionary estate, the obligation aforesaid may be taken advantage of and enforced against any person so entitled.

Section 142(1) of the LPA 1925 provides that upon assignment of the landlord's reversion, the *burden* of all covenants that have 'reference to the subject-matter' of the lease will run

---

[13] Gray and Gray, *Elements of Land Law*, [4.5.52].

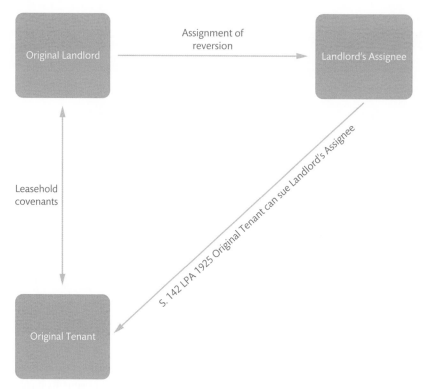

Figure 12.3 The operation of s. 141 of the LPA 1925 upon assignment of the landlord's reversion

with the reversion. The 'burden' reflects the obligation to perform the promises which are the substance of the leasehold covenants. Given that only those covenants that refer to the subject matter of the lease will run, Lord Oliver's 'touch and concern' test is again relevant. As noted in relation to s. 141 LPA 1925, s. 142 operates so that the burden of proprietary covenants will run automatically with the assignment of the landlord's reversion: see Figure 12.4.

12.3.2.2 Where there is an assignment of the tenant's leasehold

The position as regards the enforcement of leasehold covenants contained in pre-1 January 1996 leases where there is an assignment of the tenant's lease is again a question of the running of the benefit and the burden of covenants. In short, in order for the benefit and burden of leasehold covenants to run with an assignment of the lease, two elements must be satisfied: *Spencer's Case* (1583):

Element one: There must be privity of estate between the assignee of the lease (i.e. the new tenant) and the landlord subject to the benefits and burdens of the leasehold covenants

The requirement for privity of estate between the assignee of the lease and the landlord who is subject to the benefits and the burdens of the leasehold covenants can be seen as comprising two aspects:

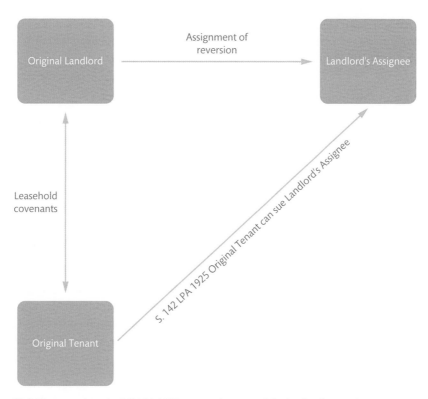

Figure 12.4 The operation of s. 142 LPA 1925 upon assignment of the landlord's reversion

(i) The assignee of the lease must stand in a landlord and tenant relationship with the land-lord that she is suing or by whom she is being sued. To explain this further, imagine, for example, a subtenant. No privity of estate exists between this subtenant and a landlord. Any privity of estate will exist between the subtenant and the sublandlord;

(ii) Privity of estate can exist only in relation to a legal lease and therefore does not arise where the lease is equitable in nature only. Additionally, any assignment whether of the reversion or the lease must also be legal. This means that an assignment must comply with the relevant formality requirements under s. 52 of the LPA 1925. This principle which originated from a time when the courts of law and equity were quite separate is easy to state but not easy to defend. Indeed, both commentators as well as the courts[14] have long criticized its operation. That said, as to pre-1996 leases, it endures.

Element two: The covenant over which enforcement is sought must 'touch and concern' the land

In addition to the requirement (element one) that there is privity of estate between the as-signee of the lease and the landlord, the covenant must also 'touch and concern the land'. As discussed in section 12.3.2.1, the appropriate test for 'touching and concerning' land is

---

[14] *Boyer v Warby* (1953), per Lord Denning.

again that laid down by Lord Oliver in *Swift*. As we encountered earlier in this section, the requirement ensures that the covenant is not merely personal in character but is proprietary and tied to the quality, nature and mode of user of the land.

12.3.3 Equitable leases and assignments

What is the position if the lease is equitable or, alternatively, where the lease itself is legal but the assignment of the landlord's reversion or assignment of the lease is equitable—for example, as a result of a failure to comply with the formalities for a legal assignment? In essence, many but not all of the rules outlined operate in the same way. First, the rules founded on privity of contract and the continuing liability of the original parties to the lease are entirely unchanged where the lease or assignment is equitable and operate precisely as outlined in this section. This was confirmed in *John Betts & Sons Ltd v Price* (1924). Secondly, ss. 141 and 142 of the LPA 1925 as discussed also apply equally to equitable leases and assignments. This was confirmed by Darling J in *Rickett v Green* (1910) and affirmed more recently by the Court of Appeal in *Scribes West Ltd v Relsa Anstalt (No. 3)* (2004).

Importantly, the rules outlined in *Spencer's Case* (discussed in section 12.3.2.2), which are historically founded upon the concept of privity of estate (traditionally regarded as a legal status), do not apply to equitable leases or equitable assignments of legal leases. Various mechanisms have, however, emerged to avoid the effects of the inapplicability of *Spencer's Case* to equitable leases and assignments including:

- implying a new and distinct contractual relationship between the assignee of the lease and the landlord giving rise to new contractual obligations between the parties;
- arguing that a legal periodic tenancy arises upon the payment of rent by the assignee of the lease once accepted by the landlord (under this legal lease, the leasehold covenants will be enforceable);
- where the covenants concerned are restrictive in nature, by relying on the principles in *Tulk v Moxhay* (1848);[15]
- under a further mechanism offered by Lord Denning in *Boyer v Warby* (1953), who argued that the burden of leasehold covenants that 'touch and concern land' should be taken to run where the lease being assigned was of a duration of three years or less. This, said Lord Denning, should be the result in a system where law and equity were fused. Respectfully, Lord Denning's proposed solution is best regarded as confined to the facts of *Boyer* itself and does rather overstate the impact of the Judicature Act 1871, certainly as far as concerns the law of leasehold covenants.[16] You should treat it with a large dose of caution.

12.3.4 Subleases

In Chapter 9, you were introduced to the possibility of a tenant creating a sublease carved from their own leasehold interest. A sublease creates subtenant and the original tenant becomes the subtenant's landlord. The sublease may very well—and, indeed, likely

---

[15] We discussed the important case of *Tulk* in section 11.6.1.

[16] For more on the ways around the unavailability of *Spencer's Case* in equity, see R. Smith, 'The Running of Covenants in Equitable Leases and Equitable Assignments of Legal Leases' (1978) 37 CLJ 98.

will—include leasehold covenants that operate according to the principles outlined. It is possible, however, that the actions of the subtenant constitute a breach of one or more of the leasehold covenants that exist between the original landlord and the original tenant. This is problematic for the original landlord as there will be no contractual relationship (privity of contract) nor landlord–tenant relationship (privity of estate) between the subtenant and the original landlord. How can the original landlord enforce the covenants against the subtenant?

Evidently, the landlord will struggle to enforce the covenants *directly* against the defaulting subtenant. There are, however, various indirect means by which those same covenants might, nevertheless, be enforced:

1. Section 1(1)(b) of the Contracts (Rights of Third Parties) Act 1999 might come to the aid of the original landlord to permit enforcement of a covenant in the sublease where a covenant in the sublease can be argued as being for the head landlord's benefit.

2. The landlord may be able to enforce negative covenants, so-called 'restrictive covenants' against the subtenant by seeking an injunction under the doctrine laid down in *Tulk*.[17]

3. A shrewdly drafted sublease should include a clause that requires the subtenant to comply with covenants contained within the headlease. Where a clause of this nature exists, the head landlord will sit in a relationship of privity of contract with the defaulting subtenant and will be able to ensure enforcement of the covenants.

4. In the event of breach by the subtenant, the head landlord retains the right to forfeit the headlease which will have the effect of terminating any subleases that exist: *Pennell v Payne* (1995). The subtenant will, however, be able to apply for relief from forfeiture.[18]

12.4 The regime for leases granted on or after 1 January 1996

The principles governing the enforceability of leasehold covenants were substantially reformed by the LTCA 1995 which gave rise to an entirely new statutory regime for leases granted on or after 1 January 1996. Before we examine how the post-1995 statutory regime operates, we begin this section by reflecting briefly on why the old law required reform and the proposals put forward by the Law Commission.

12.4.1 The old law: The impetus and recommendations for reform

It was argued that the old law generated unfairness, uncertainty, and inconsistency in the law. The Law Commission documented at length the many the problems surrounding the application of the old rules. In particular, the Commission identified the following areas of criticism:[19]

- It is 'intrinsically unfair' that an individual should bear a burden under a contract when they derive no benefit from it and over which they exercise no control.

---

[17] We discussed *Tulk* in section 11.6.1.
[18] We discuss relief from forfeiture in section 12.5.1.6.
[19] Law Commission Report No. 174, [3.1]–[3.3].

- The operation of the principle of continuing liability of the original tenant distorts and is out-of-step with public perception of the landlord and tenant relationship.

- The public do not realize that the original parties have a continuing liability and this liability is routinely not made plain on the face of most tenancy agreements.

- The original tenant may assume greater liability, for example for an increase in rent under a rent review clause, than she realized she was undertaking.

- Under the privity of contract principle, landlords are unduly privileged as to their ability to enforce obligations of the original tenant and the tenant's assignee.

- The original tenants against whom covenants are enforced are not adequately protected nor are they provided with sufficient means of reimbursement.

- While parties are free to negotiate the terms of any lease, there is an inequality of bargaining position by which tenants are disadvantaged and are more likely to lose out, feeling forced to agree to more onerous terms.

In consequence of the concerns identified, a radical reform programme (as opposed to merely 'tinkering with the [existing] law')[20] was proposed by the Law Commission which was to be guided by two fundamental principles:[21]

> First, a landlord or tenant of property should not continue to enjoy rights nor be under any obligation arising from a lease once he has parted with all interest in the property.

> Secondly, all terms of the lease should be regarded as a single bargain for letting the property. When the interest of one of the parties changes hands the successor should fully take his predecessor's place as landlord or tenant, without distinguishing between different categories of covenant.

The aim of these two central principles was that there should be a 'clean break' upon the transfer of leased property. The Commission was persuaded, however, after consultation, to stop short of recommending an absolute abolition of the privity of contract principle in the law of leasehold covenants. In summary, the Commission proposed that where the original tenant assigned the lease, he would be automatically released from all liability as to future breaches of leasehold covenants.[22] Additionally, it was proposed that the requirement, under the privity of estate principle, that covenants must 'touch and concern land' be abandoned. It was the firm view of the Commission that their recommendations should apply to both existing and new leases.

12.4.2 Scope of the LTCA 1995

The LTCA 1995, which emerged as a result of the work undertaken the Law Commission and will examined in the coming sections, represents, in many ways, a far more diluted instrument and contains far less radical reforms than those envisaged and proposed by the Law Commission in both scope and substance. In particular, the 1995 Act reflects a

---

[20] Ibid., [3.27].   [21] Ibid., [4.1].

[22] This was subject to an exception where assignment of the lease required consent of the original landlord. Here, the landlord would be entitled to require the original tenant to guarantee performance of leasehold covenants by the tenant's assignee. This would be limited to a single assignment, however.

greater compromise as regards the balancing of landlords' and tenants' rights than was rec-ommended. This was largely due to significant opposition to the Bill as it passed through Parliament.[23] For example, by way of s. 1(1), the LTCA 1995 applies only to 'new tenancies' which are defined as tenancies 'granted on or after the date on which this Act comes into force'[24] (i.e. on or after 1 January 1996). The new statutory code therefore does not apply to existing leases as the Law Commission had recommended. The provisions of the LTCA 1995 are, however, applicable to both legal and equitable leases: s. 28(1) defines a tenancy as including 'any lease' including 'an agreement for a tenancy'.

Though less radical than that proposed, the LTCA 1995 nevertheless introduced a new statutory code for leases granted on or after 1 January 1996. This statutory scheme will now be explored.

12.4.3 The position as regards the original parties to the lease

Under s. 5 of the LTCA 1995, the original tenant is released from contractual liability upon assignment of her lease:

(1) This section applies where a tenant assigns premises **demised** to him under a tenancy.

(2) If the tenant assigns the whole of the premises demised to him, he—

    (a) is released from the tenant covenants of the tenancy, and

    (b) ceases to be entitled to the benefit of the landlord covenants of the tenancy, as from the assignment.

Section 5 can be clearly contrasted with the pre-1996 position where contractual liability between the original tenant and the original landlord and his assignees survives assign-ments of the lease. Section 5 removes this continuing liability. The effect is that, on assign-ment, the original tenant will not be liable for default by the tenant's assignees whether that be non-payment of rent[25] or breaches of repair covenants.[26] As an exception to the opera-tion of s. 5, under s. 16 of the LTCA 1995, where a tenant is required to obtain the consent of the landlord in order to assign the lease,[27] a landlord is entitled to refuse consent unless the tenant enters what is called an 'authorized guarantee agreement' or 'AGA'. Under this AGA, the tenant guarantees the assignee's payment of rent and, furthermore, guarantees performance of the other leasehold covenants. Note that under s. 24(4) the tenant retains the right to sue in respect of breaches committed prior to any assignment.[28]

As regards the original landlord, there is no automatic release from contractual liability upon assignment of the reversion. The original landlord can, however, under s. 6 of the

[23] Incidentally, the 1995 Act was introduced to Parliament by way of a private members' bill rather than as a government bill largely due to significant opposition from landlords' pressure groups which made the Law Com-mission's recommendations controversial.

[24] LTCA 1995, s. 1(3).

[25] *RPH Ltd v Mirror Group Newspapers and Mirror Group Holdings* (1993).

[26] *Thames Manufacturing Co. Ltd v Perrots Ltd* (1985).

[27] The requirement for consent to assign is commonly seen in commercial leases but far less so in the residential context.

[28] LTCA 1995, s. 24(4) has the effect of reversing, for leases granted on or after 1 January 1996, the old law posi-tion as clarified in *Re King*.

LTCA 1995, request a release from contractual liability by serving a s. 8 notice on the original tenant within four weeks of the assignment of the landlord's reversion:

(1) This section applies where a landlord assigns the reversion in premises of which he is the landlord under a tenancy.

(2) If the landlord assigns the reversion in the whole of the premises of which he is the landlord—

(a) he may apply to be released from the landlord covenants of the tenancy in accordance with s. 8; and

(b) if he is so released from all those covenants, he ceases to be entitled to the benefit of the tenant covenants of the tenancy as from the assignment.

Under s. 8, where a landlord serves a notice requesting release and this request is refused by the tenant, a release can be granted by the county court if it is reasonable to do so. Under s. 25, the provisions of the 1995 Act can be neither varied nor excluded by the parties. The precise operation of s. 25 was considered in the leading case of *London Diocesan Fund v Avonridge Property Company Ltd*.

KEY CASE *London Diocesan Fund v Avonridge Property Company Ltd (2005)*

Facts: A lease contained a clause that the original landlord, Avonridge, would not be liable in the event of non-payment at the hands of an assignee of the lease. Avonridge assigned its reversion and the assignee fell into rent arrears. The headlease was forfeited on the basis of the non-payment of rent. The sublessees sought and were granted relief from forfeiture but were, nevertheless, required to pay the rent debt. The sublessees claimed that the clause limiting Avonridge's liability was void under s. 25 of the 1995 Act.

Legal issue: Did the clause limiting liability frustrate the operation of s. 25 of the 1995 Act?

Judgment: The sublessees claim failed. The limitation clause was valid and did not fall foul of the prohibition under s. 25 of the 1995 Act according to the majority of the House of Lords (Lord Walker dissenting). The majority held that the mischief at which the Act was addressed under s. 25 was the absence of any way out of liability. Lord Nicholls underlined that:

the mischief at which the statute was aimed was the absence in practice of any such exit route. Consistently with this the legislation was not intended to close any other exit route already open to the parties: in particular, that by agreement their liability could be curtailed from the outset or later released or waived. The possibility that by agreement the parties may limit their liability in this way was not, it seems, perceived as having unfair consequences in practice.

Lord Nicholls continued in holding that:

Section 25 is, of course, to be interpreted generously so as to ensure that the operation of the 1995 Act is not frustrated, either directly or indirectly. But there is nothing in the language of the scheme of the Act to suggest that the statute was intended to exclude the parties' ability to limit liability under their covenants from the outset in whatever way they agree. An agreed limitation of this nature does not impinge upon the operation of the statutory provisions.

According to the majority, this interpretation of the Act was entirely consistent with the 'thrust' of the Law Commission's Report No. 174 which was the forerunner to the 1995 legislation.

Lord Walker, dissenting, was not prepared to accept the majority's reasoning. For Lord Walker, s. 25 was: 'expressed in terms wide enough to interfere with the freedom of contract which was available to the parties in negotiating a tenancy'.

A 'get out' therefore does exist for the evasion of liability where an 'Avonridge clause' is included within a tenancy agreement. Where these clauses are included it will likely be at the insistence and for the benefit of the landlord (though they can equally operate in favour of tenants) given that landlords usually occupy the more influential bargaining position when it comes to negotiating the terms of a lease.

12.4.4 **The position as regards assignees of the landlord's reversion and leasehold**

The LTCA 1995 introduced an entirely new statutory code for the passing of the benefit and the burden of leasehold covenants. Essentially, s. 3 of the 1995 Act codifies the traditional common law rules as to privity of estate and governs what the provisions term 'landlord covenants' and 'tenant covenants'. It provides:

> (1) The benefit and burden of all landlord and tenant covenants of a tenancy—
>
> > (a) shall be annexed and incident to the whole, and to each and every part, of the premises demised by the tenancy and of the reversion in them, and
> >
> > (b) shall in accordance with this section pass on an assignment of the whole or any part of those premises or of the reversion in them.

The effect of s. 3(1) of the 1995 Act is the automatic passing of the benefit and burden of leasehold covenants upon an assignment of the reversion of the lease. There is no need to establish privity of estate and, moreover, ss. 141 and 142 of the LPA 1925 do not apply. The fundamental distinction between this statutory regime and the position under the old law is that, under the 1995 legislation, the 'touch and concern' test is no longer relevant. As a result, even the benefit or burden of those covenants that would not have satisfied the Lord Oliver test in *Swift*, will pass under s. 3. This position is subject, however, to the caveat contained in s. 3(6) of the 1995 Act:

> (6) Nothing in this section shall operate—
>
> > (a) in the case of a covenant which (in whatever terms) is expressed to be personal to any person, to make the covenant enforceable by or (as the case may be) against any other person . . .

Under s. 3(6), the benefit and burden of those covenants which are 'expressed to be personal' to a particular individual will not then pass upon an assignment of the reversion of the lease. This personal quality of a covenant must be identified and will not be implied from the general character of the covenant. The 1995 Act therefore represents a shift from the old law in that all covenants will be transmissible except those expressed to be personal. The operation of s. 3(6) was examined in the case of *Chesterfield Properties Ltd v BHP Great Britain Petroleum Ltd* in the Court of Appeal.

KEY CASE *Chesterfield Properties Ltd v BHP Great Britain Petroleum Ltd* (2001)

Facts: Chesterfield Properties, in a personal covenant contained within a lease granted to BHP over an office block, agreed to undertake work to remedy building defects. The covenant was expressly

→

→

stated to be personal in nature. Chesterfield subsequently assigned its reversion to an associated company. Therefore, Chesterfield served a s. 8 notice in order to seek release from its contractual liability on the covenant. BHP failed to respond to service of this s. 8 notice. BHP requested that Chesterfield carry out the repair works in line with the personal covenant.

Legal issue: Had Chesterfield been released from its contractual liability? What was the impact under the 1995 Act of the personal nature of the covenant to carry out works over the leased premised?

Judgment: The covenant was expressed to be personal and could not, therefore, constitute a 'landlord covenant' within the meaning of the 1995 Act as it did not fall within the statutory definition of a 'landlord' under s. 28(1) which provided:

the person who may *from time to time* be entitled to the reversion of the tenancy. [Emphasis added.]

A personal covenant does, said Jonathan Parker LJ, come within the statutory language here as that covenant does not fall to be performed by the person who may 'from time to time' be entitled to the reversion of the tenancy but by a particular legal person. It followed that the personal covenant was not a 'landlord covenant' and, accordingly, the s. 8 notice served was ineffective to release Chesterfield from its contractual obligations.

The decision in *Chesterfield* has proved controversial.[29] Slessinger, for example, has argued that it should be for the court to determine whether a covenant is personal rather than left to the parties to attach its own label.[30] For Slessinger, the ability of the court to look beyond labels chosen by the parties to a lease is already rooted in the law of leases and licences and should pose no challenge here. Slessinger asserts that there should be 'certain covenants which are essential to the lease and cannot be made personal'. The *Chesterfield* decision raises more fundamental questions as to the success of the 1995 Act to create an independent and effective statutory code for the enforceability of leasehold covenants. For Dixon, the Act fails in this task. Dixon observes that:[31]

[A] chance was missed, possibly deliberately, to establish the 1995 Act as a self-contained scheme free from the dictates of privity of estate and privity of contract. So it seems that, after all, the 1995 Act is another example of a piecemeal intervention . . . an intervention that can be sidestepped—in some circumstances—by careful draughtsmanship.

Under the 1995 Act, then, those with the money and inclination to seek professional legal advice as to the drafting of leases will be able to take advantage of the benefits and flexibility that the statutory language offers. We should be concerned that those most well-placed to do so will be wealthy landlords, already the more powerful in most landlord–tenant relationships.

12.4.5 The 1995 Act and subleases

The LTCA 1995 does little to change the principles governing the enforceability of leasehold covenants between a head landlord and a subtenant. Section 3(5) and (6) of the 1995 Act confirms the application to new leases granted on or after 1 January 1996, of the doctrine in *Tulk* which we explored in depth in Chapter 11 on freehold covenants.

---

[29] See P. H. Kenny [2007] Conv 1.
[30] E. Slessinger, 'Precedents Editor's Notes' [2007] Conv 198, 199.
[31] M. Dixon, 'A Failure of Statutory Purpose or a Failure of Professional Advice?' [2006] Conv 79.

12.5 The landlord's remedies for breach

Where there has been a breach of a leasehold covenant, from the landlord's perspective, three questions must be answered. First, does the landlord have the right to sue on the covenant (i.e. if necessary, has the benefit passed to that landlord)? Secondly, has the burden of the covenant passed to the would-be defendant so that the defendant is bound to comply with the obligation? Thirdly, what potential remedies are available to the landlord? The first and second questions have already been addressed in the previous sections. In this part, we are concerned with the third question, that of remedies. There are five potential remedies that a landlord might pursue in the event of a breach of covenant:

- forfeiture
- commercial rent arrears recovery (CRAR)
- action for rent arrears
- action for damages
- injunction and specific performance.

Each remedy will be considered in turn though, at the outset, be aware that the remedy of forfeiture is easily the most potent weapon in the landlord's arsenal when faced with a breach of covenant by a tenant. It is therefore with forfeiture that we begin.

12.5.1 Forfeiture

Forfeiture is the process under which a landlord is able to terminate a lease before expiry of an agreed leasehold term by exercising a 'right to re-enter' the leased premises. This is a drastic remedy and, as a result, its operation is highly constrained and bounded by statute. The remedy is extremely draconian as it can result in a tenant losing its entire leasehold interest as a result of a relatively minor breach of covenant. For many landlords, forfeiture, though evidently powerful in its effects, is therefore something of a remedy of last resort. As Clarke has argued:[32]

> Forfeiture displays the best and worst remedies of a self-help remedy . . . it can inflict loss on the tenant quite disproportionate to the blameworthiness of the breach, and it can produce a windfall profit for the landlord [by regaining the freehold now unencumbered].

As you will see, the severity of the remedy of forfeiture is, however, mitigated by the court's liberal approach to when the right to exercise the remedy is deemed to be waived by the parties and, additionally, by the intervention of statute which has limited its scope and availability. Forfeiture plays an important role as 'an essential management tool',[33] in commercial or long residential lease but can, theoretically, apply to any type of lease.

12.5.1.1 Availability of the remedy

Forfeiture is only available to a landlord faced with a tenant's breach and not available to a tenant facing a defaulting landlord. Forfeiture is also not available in the event of every breach of covenant. Forfeiture will only be available:

---

[32] A. Clarke, 'Property Law' (1992) 45(1) CLP 81, 104.
[33] N. Gravells, 'Forfeiture of Leases for Breach of Covenant' (2006) JBL 830.

1. where the lease contains an express forfeiture clause, or

2. where the covenant breached is formulated or drafted in the lease as a 'condition': *Doe d. Lockwood v Clarke* (1897), or

3. where a right to forfeit is implied into the lease[34]—for example, in the event that the tenant disclaims the landlord's title: *Clarke v Dupre Ltd* (1992).

Today, most leases will be drafted with the assistance of professional legal advice and, consequently, the vast majority of leasehold covenants will be drafted as 'conditions' as well as including a forfeiture clause within the express terms of the lease in order to ensure that forfeiture is available.

12.5.1.2 Waiver of the right to forfeit

A landlord can waive a right to forfeit a lease. Where the landlord has waived her right to forfeiture, the remedy will clearly not be available to her. The classic statement of waiver is contained in the decision of *Matthews v Smallwood* (1910) where Parker J noted:[35]

> Waiver of a right of re-entry can only occur where the lessor, with knowledge of the facts upon which his right to re-entry arises, does some unequivocal act recognising the continued existence of the lease.

What is crucial here is the landlord's knowledge of her right to forfeit the lease or the facts upon which that right arises. The most common instance of waiver occurs where, following a breach of covenant, the landlord continues to demand and accept rent from the party in default: *Segal Securities Ltd v Thoseby* (1963). The acceptance of rent provides evidence of the landlord's intention that the lease should continue despite the breach. There is, however, no requirement that the landlord *intends* to waive her right to forfeit: *Cornillie v Saha* (1996). Waiver may be express or implied from all the circumstances of the case and will apply only to the particular breach to which it relates and not more broadly to potential, future breaches of covenant: *Billson v Residential Apartments* (1992). With this in mind, it becomes important to draw a distinction between continuing breaches which take place each day (for example breaches of repair covenants) and one-off breaches. Where there is a continuing breach from day-to-day, the landlord may be able to withdraw the waiver and seek forfeiture: *Greenwich LBC v Discreet Selling Estates Ltd* (1990).

Smith has criticized the principles of waiver in that they operate to the disadvantage of landlords as: (1) rent is often accepted in error by the landlord or agents of the landlord from the party in default following a breach thereby waiving the right to forfeit; and (2) it seems not to matter at all that the tenant may be well aware that the landlord has no intention to waive the forfeiture.[36]

A landlord must, therefore, be prudent when faced with a breach of covenant not too readily to waive her right to forfeit the lease. Equally, it is surely fair that the courts apply strictly the legal principles outlined to avoid a landlord recovering rent and subsequently forfeiting the lease, thereby making a double gain.

---

[34] Note that such a term is implied into all equitable leases under *Shiloh Spinners v Harding* (1973).

[35] *Matthews*, 786.

[36] R. Smith, *Property Law*, 6th edn (London: Pearson, 2009), 408.

12.5.1.3 Exercise of the remedy

Where the remedy of forfeiture is available to the landlord, the remedy is exercised by the landlord re-entering the premises. This 're-entry' simply signifies the landlord's retaking of possession of the land. Re-entry can take place in two ways: either by peaceable physical entry into the premises or, alternatively, by initiating possession proceedings: *Billson*. Where forfeiture takes place, it is effective from the moment of re-entry and any tenant remaining in possession of the land will be committing a trespass.

As regards physical re-entry into possession, there are certain limitations on this forfeiture route:

1. If physical re-entry is the landlord's chosen mode of forfeiture, it must be peaceful in nature. The landlord must take care to avoid committing any criminal or other offence in law, in particular, under s. 6(1) of the Criminal Law Act 1977. Any use or threat of violence on re-entry will invalidate the forfeiture.

2. Physical re-entry is only possible in relation to commercial premises. Physical re-entry of residential premises is a criminal offence: s. 1 of the Protection from Eviction Act 1977.

3. Under s. 2 of the Protection from Eviction Act 1977, where property is 'let as a dwelling', a landlord is only entitled to forfeit the lease by means of court proceedings. To disregard s. 2 would be to render any forfeiture ineffective and may, additionally, result in criminal liability on the part of the landlord.

4. Any re-entry can, subsequently, be set aside by the court should the tenant apply for relief from forfeiture.[37]

In summary there are significant risks associated with a landlord exercising physical re-entry of leased premised. Lord Templeman echoed this in *Bilson*, describing forfeiture by physical re-entry as a 'dubious and dangerous method of determining a lease'. Far less risky is for a landlord to exercise forfeiture under the second 'route' by instigating possession proceedings in the county court.

12.5.1.4 Forfeiture for non-payment of rent

Forfeiture for non-payment of rent and forfeiture for non-rent breaches must be considered separately as different rules apply to each. Where the covenant breached concerns the payment of rent, a landlord wishing to forfeit the lease, must follow a series of steps: see Figure 12.5. To begin with, the landlord must make a formal demand for the rent owed. No formal demand is needed if the terms of the lease expressly exempt this requirement or the tenant is more than six months in arrears.[38]

Additional protections are provided under the Commonhold and Leasehold Reform Act 2002 (CLRA 2002) for long leases of dwellings.[39] Under the 2002 Act, a tenant is only liable for payment of rent upon the landlord serving a notice on the tenant detailing the sum and the date for payment,[40] and forfeiture for non-payment is only permitted where the sum

---

[37] We explore relief from forfeiture in section 12.5.1.6.
[38] Section 210 of the Common Law Procedure Act 1852.
[39] Defined under s. 76 of the CLRA 2002 as a lease granted for more than 21 years.
[40] Ibid., s. 166.

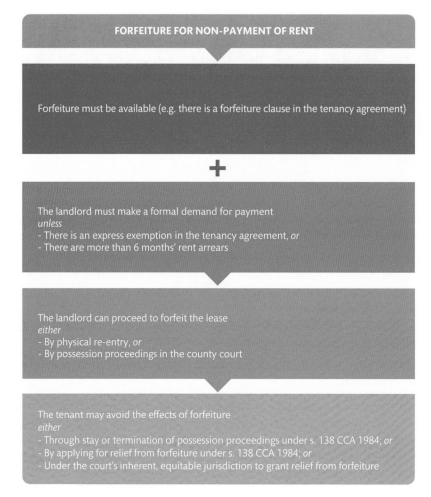

FORFEITURE FOR NON-PAYMENT OF RENT

Forfeiture must be available (e.g. there is a forfeiture clause in the tenancy agreement)

+

The landlord must make a formal demand for payment
unless
- There is an express exemption in the tenancy agreement, *or*
- There are more than 6 months' rent arrears

The landlord can proceed to forfeit the lease
either
- By physical re-entry, *or*
- By possession proceedings in the county court

The tenant may avoid the effects of forfeiture
either
- Through stay or termination of possession proceedings under s. 138 CCA 1984; *or*
- By applying for relief from forfeiture under s. 138 CCA 1984; *or*
- Under the court's inherent, equitable jurisdiction to grant relief from forfeiture

Figure 12.5 Forfeiture for breach of covenant as to non-payment of rent

owed exceeds a limit imposed by statute,[41] or has remained unpaid for a period prescribed by legislation.[42]

Where these obstacles are overcome, the landlord is entitled to forfeit the lease either by peaceful physical re-entry into the leased premises (only commercial premises) or by instigating possession proceedings in the county court (either residential or commercial premises). The tenant is, however, provided with several opportunities to avoid the effects of forfeiture:

1. Possession proceedings issued by the landlord in the county court will be stopped if the tenant is able to pay all the arrears plus court costs within the period up to five days before the case is due to be heard: s. 138(2) of the County Courts Act 1984.

---

[41] Ibid., s. 167, currently set at £350.   [42] Three years, at the time of writing.

2. The county court has the power to stay execution of a possession order for four or more weeks during which time the tenant enjoys an automatic right to relief from forfeiture upon payment of all arrears:[43] s. 138(3) of the County Courts Act 1984. The Court of Appeal in *Golding v Martin* (2019) reiterated the importance of upholding the operation of s. 138(3). A landlord of a flat had brought forfeiture proceedings and was awarded possession when its tenant had failed to pay a service charge under a long lease. The landlord gave the flat to his daughter who sold it. The tenant, who had been in Spain, discovered this and sought to have the possession order set aside. The Court of Appeal set aside the possession order on the basis that the court had not complied with s. 138(3). The Court of Appeal reiterated that, under this provision, a possession order may not take effect within four weeks of the date of the order and may not be unconditional. The order made by the county court had been immediate and unconditional. The issue in this case was 'no mere technicality' as 'where the forfeiture of a long and valuable lease is in issue it is plainly of the utmost importance that the lessee be given the right to pay', explained the Court of Appeal. It was, the court added, inconceivable that Parliament had intended that the safeguards for tenants could be bypassed by immediate and unconditional disposal of a claim to forfeit on the grounds of non-payment of rent. To attribute such an intention to Parliament would be to attribute an intention to legislate for 'an irrational scheme'.

3. Within six months of the landlord taking possession under a court order, the tenant retains the right to apply for relief from forfeiture, though this is strictly at the discretion of the court: s. 138(9A) of the County Courts Act 1984.

4. Where a landlord peacefully re-enters leased premises to effect forfeiture, the High Court has a power to grant relief from forfeiture to a tenant under its inherent jurisdiction: *Bland v Ingram's Estate Ltd (No. 2)* (2002). The county court enjoys a similar power under s. 139(2) of the County Courts Act 1984.

5. Finally, the court enjoys a general, equitable jurisdiction to grant relief from forfeiture where a tenant has paid all arrears plus costs and therefore has fully compensated the landlord: *Howard v Fanshawe* (1985); *Gill v Lewis* (1956).

12.5.1.5 Forfeiture for breach of covenants not concerning rent

Where the landlord seeks forfeiture in response to breach of a covenant other than as to the payment of rent, there must first be a right to re-entry in the lease (e.g. forfeiture clause in the tenancy agreement) and, secondly, the procedure provided for in s. 146 of the LPA 1925 must be followed (see Figure 12.6):

(1) A right of re-entry or forfeiture under any provision or stipulation in a lease for a breach of any covenant or condition in the lease shall not be enforceable, by action or otherwise, unless and until the lessor serves on the lessee a notice—

   (a) specifying the particular breach complained of; and

   (b) if the breach is capable of remedy, requiring the lessee to remedy the breach; and

---

[43] Arrears are calculated at the date of the possession order and not the date the action for possession was commenced: *Maryland Estates v Joseph* (1998).

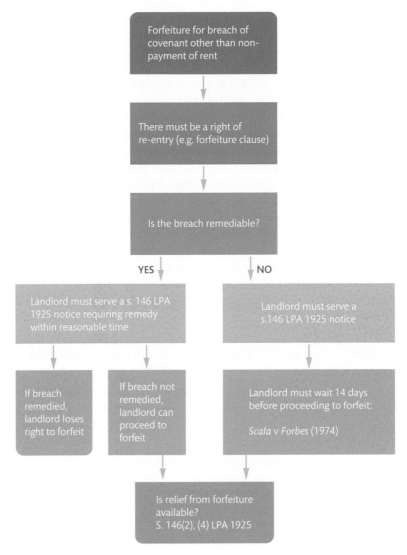

Figure 12.6 Forfeiture for breach of covenant other than for non-payment of rent

(c) in any case, requiring the lessee to make compensation in money for the breach;and
the lessee fails, within a reasonable time thereafter, to remedy the breach, if it is capable of remedy, and to make reasonable compensation in money, to the satisfaction
of the lessor, for the breach.

Under s. 146, a landlord believing that a breach of covenant (other than for non-payment
of rent) has occurred, must serve a notice (commonly called a 's. 146 notice') which:

- specifies the breach of covenant, and
- requests compensation is paid by the tenant (if the landlord so wishes), and
- if it is possible, requests that the tenant remedy the breach within a reasonable period.

The s. 146 procedure is designed to provide tenants in breach with 'one last chance'[44] to comply with their obligations under the lease and avoid the harsh consequences of forfeiture.

Where the notice served by the landlord does not fully comply with the provisions of s. 146, both the notice and any subsequent action on the part of the landlord to forfeit the lease will be void: *Glass v Kencakes* (1966); *Akici v L. R. Butlin Ltd* (2005). What is clear is that in drafting the s. 146 notice, it is vital that the correct breach is specified. This was made plain in the case of *Anders v Haralambous* (2013). Ms Anders was the tenant of a flat owned by Mr and Mrs Haralambous and had allowed language school students to use the premises. The matter came before the county court to determine if there had been a breach of any leasehold covenants prohibiting multiple occupation and subletting. The county court held that Ms Anders had breached the terms of her tenancy by allowing students to lodge in the flat on a commercial basis. Despite no findings being made of subletting, when Mr and Mrs Haralambous served the s. 146 notice on Ms Anders, the notice specified the breach as involving subletting to students and receiving payment. Possession proceedings were issued and the question arose as to the validity of the s. 146 notice. The matter ultimately reached the High Court which ruled the notice was void. The purpose of s. 146 notices was to inform the tenant of the breach and to allow remedy of that breach or to apply for relief from forfeiture if the breach could not be remedied. The notice in question wrongly specified the breach as subletting, which did not reflect the determination by the county court. Parting with possession (as Ms Anders had done) was quite different from subletting. Whilst Ms Anders knew what she had done wrong, nevertheless, the notice must specify the correct breach which it had not done and so was void.

Where, however, the landlord does comply with the requirements of s. 146, how long that landlord must wait before proceeding to forfeit the lease depends on the 'remediability' of the breach—by which we mean whether the breach is capable of being remedied. Section 146 expressly provides that if the breach is capable of remedy, the landlord must request that it be so remedied by the tenant. If remediable, the landlord must provide the tenant a reasonable period in which to remedy it and cannot forfeit during this time. Should the tenant remedy the breach as requested within this reasonable period, the landlord necessarily loses any right to forfeit the lease. If the breach is incapable of remedy, the landlord can proceed to forfeit either by peaceful, physical re-entry (in commercial leases) or by issuing county court possession proceedings (commercial and residential leases) after giving the tenant a reasonable time (usually 14 days) to consider her fate and decide whether or not to make an application for relief from forfeiture.[45]

The question of the remediability of a breach is therefore central to the nature and operation of the s. 146 notice. On one view, it might be thought that no breach of covenant is capable of remedy in so far as the clock cannot be turned back. This is not, however, the approach the court has taken. The traditional approach of the court is illustrated by the case of *Expert Clothing Service & Sales Ltd v Hillgate House Ltd.*

[44] *Expert Clothing Service & Sales Ltd v Hillgate House Ltd* (1986), per Slade LJ.
[45] As confirmed in *Scala House and District Property Co. Ltd v Forbes* (1974).

KEY CASE *Expert Clothing Service & Sales Ltd v Hillgate House Ltd (1986)*

Facts: Hillgate House was granted a lease over property which it was agreed Hillgate would convert into a gym, health club, or office space. The work to convert the premises was agreed to be completed in large part by 28 September. By the end of September, no work had been completed. The landlord served a s. 146 notice which stated that the breach by Hillgate was incapable of being remedied.

Legal issue: Was this breach of covenant remediable?

Judgment: The Court of Appeal held that the breach was capable of being remedied. According to Slade LJ, the question of remediability of breaches of covenants is to be determined by asking whether compliance with a s. 146 notice, coupled with appropriate compensation, could effectively rectify the *harm* or *damage* caused by the breach.

The Court of Appeal held that, when one considers remediability in this way, almost all positive covenants (i.e. covenants to actively do X or Y) will be capable of remedy. As to negative covenants (i.e. covenants to not do something), O'Connor LJ noted that:

> To stop what is forbidden by a negative covenant may or may not remedy the breach even if accompanied by compensation in money . . . to stop using [a] house as a brothel will not, because the taint lingers on and will not dissipate within a reasonable time.

Traditionally, then, the courts have drawn a sharp distinction between positive and negative covenants with the former being regarded as capable of remedy but not the latter. In line with this approach, the Court of Appeal in *Rugby School (Governors) v Tannahill* (1934) held that breach of a covenant not to use premises for an immoral purpose was irremediable in a case where leased property had been used as a brothel because the harm caused to the landlord's reputation could not be repaired. Interestingly, however, the Court of Appeal refused to accept the view of MacKinnon J at first instance who had found that all negative breaches were irremediable. Nevertheless, *Tannahill* established that breaches of covenant giving rise to stigma or reputation damage are likely to be incapable of remedy.[46] In *Scala House and District Property Co. Ltd v Forbes* (1974), the Court of Appeal held that breach of a covenant not to sublet premises was also incapable of being remedied.

Today, however, the positive/negative distinction as to remediability has been eroded. It is now widely acknowledged that it is not so simple or as binary. The modern approach is that certain negative covenants will be capable of remedy. Where, for example, a tenant uses premises as a residence in breach of a negative covenant (e.g. not to use property for a residential purpose), that residence can be brought to an end thereby remedying the breach: *Cooper v Henderson* (1982). Equally, a negative covenant not to keep sheep on land, if breached, can be remedied by removal of the sheep. In *Savva v Hussein*, the logic of the traditional positive/negative distinction was further challenged.

---

[46] See also *Dunraven Securities Ltd v Holloway* (1982) in which a breach of covenant whereby leased premises was used as a sex shop in Soho was held to be irremediable. Also, *Kelly v Purvis* (1983) involving the running of a brothel.

KEY CASE *Savva v Hussein* (1997)

Facts: Savva was the landlord of commercial premises in London leased to Hussein. The lease contained various covenants including a negative covenant to the effect that Hussein was not to erect signs or advertisements or carry out alterations to the property without Savva's express consent. Hussein, in breach of the negative covenants, changed the signs in front of the premises and altered the frontage to the property without securing Savva's consent. The landlord served on Hussein a s. 146 notice which stated that the breach was not capable of being remedied.

Legal issue: Was the breach of negative covenants not to erect signs or alter the leased property's fascia irremediable as the landlord suggested in the s. 146 notice?

Judgment: The Court of Appeal held that the breaches were capable of remedy and therefore, the landlord's s. 146 was invalid. According to Staughton LJ:

> When something has been done without consent, it is not possible to restore the matter wholly to the situation which it was in before the breach. The moving finger writes and cannot be recalled. That is not to my mind what is meant by a remedy, it is a remedy if the mischief caused by the breach can be removed. In the case of a covenant not to make alterations without consent or not to display signs without consent, if there is a breach of that, the mischief can be removed by removing the signs or restoring the property to the state it was in before the alterations.

Aldous LJ added that:

> There is in my view nothing in the statute, nor in logic, which requires different considerations between a positive and negative covenant although it may be right to differentiate between particular covenants.

The effect of the *Savva* decision is that the remediability of breaches cannot be determined according to a binary positive/negative distinction and each breach must be considered quite separately on its own facts. The test to apply is the practical analysis proposed in *Expert Clothing* as to whether the harm caused by the breach can be removed. The current approach to remediability was laid down by Neuberger LJ in *Akici* where breach of a covenant not to part with possession or to share possession of a property was held not to be irremediable (i.e. the breach was capable of remedy) where the breach fell short of creating or transferring a legal interest. Neuberger LJ noted that:[47]

> In principle . . . the great majority of breaches of covenant should be capable of remedy, in the same way as repairing or most user covenant breaches. Even where stopping, or putting right, the breach may leave the lessors out of pocket for some reason, it does not seem to me that there is any problem in concluding that the breach is remediable.

Neuberger LJ therefore confirmed the *Savva* rejection of the positive/negative remediability distinction, but, went on to note two breaches of covenant which will, nevertheless, remain irremediable:[48]

> [T]here are two types of breach of covenant which are as a matter of principle incapable of remedy. The first is a covenant against subletting: that is the effect of the reasoning of this court in the *Scala House* case (1974) . . . this is, I think, based on the proposition that one cannot, as it were, uncreate an underlease . . . the other type of breach of covenant which is incapable of remedy is

---

[47] *Akici*, 214.   [48] Ibid., 215.

a breach involving illegal or immoral use: see *Rugby School (Governors) v Tannahill* (1935). This has been justified on the basis of illegal or immoral user fixing the premises with some sort of irremovable 'stigma' which results in the breach being incapable of remedy.

In summary, after *Akici*, the starting point on remediability is that the majority of breaches will be capable of remedy except breaches of covenants not to sublet and those prohibiting illegal or immoral user. The *Expert Clothing* test remains in place: remediability is to be assessed by how far any harm or damage flowing from the breach can be removed or rectified. The *Savva* and *Akici* reasoning was most recently referenced in the Supreme Court in *Telchadder v Wickland Holdings Ltd* (2014), a case concerning eviction and the Mobile Homes Act 1983 where the court drew heavily on the s. 146 LPA 1925 jurisprudence. The Supreme Court held that the breach of a negative covenant not to commit antisocial behaviour was remediable if the mischief resulting from it could be redressed. Mr Telchadder had jumped out from behind a tree at residents on a mobile home site dressed in camouflage clothing with netting over his head and had also threatened other residents on occasions. Although the residents could not be 'unstartled' following Mr Telchadder's behaviour, the practical response was that his breach could be redressed by him not committing further breaches of the antisocial behaviour covenant for a reasonable period of time.

12.5.1.6 Relief from forfeiture

Once the obstacle of remediability has been overcome, the landlord may proceed to forfeit the lease. However, the tenant retains a right to make an application for relief from forfeiture whether under the court's equitable jurisdiction to order relief or under s. 146(2) of the LPA 1925. Section 146(2) provides:

> (2) Where a lessor is proceeding, by action or otherwise, to enforce such a right of re-entry or forfeiture, the lessee may, in the lessor's action, if any, or in any action brought by himself, apply to the court for relief; and the court may grant or refuse relief, as the court, having regard to the proceedings and conduct of the parties under the foregoing provisions of this section, and to all the other circumstances, thinks fit; and in case of relief may grant it on such terms, if any, as to costs, expenses, damages, compensation, penalty, or otherwise, including the granting of an injunction to restrain any like breach in the future, as the court, in the circumstances of each case, thinks fit.

The operation of s. 146(2) was considered extensively by the House of Lords in *Billson v Residential Apartments Ltd* (1992) which confirmed:

- Most tenants will make an application for relief from forfeiture upon the issuing of possession proceedings by their landlord.

- A tenant cannot apply for relief from forfeiture after a landlord has received judgment and has entered into possession under an order of the court.

- If a possession order is subsequently set aside or appealed, the court can consider a further application for relief from the tenant taking into account all circumstances including the conduct of the tenant and any delay.

- A tenant can make an application for relief where the landlord has peacefully re-entered the property without first securing a court order (though cases where no court order is sought will be increasingly rare).

Relief from forfeiture can be sought during possession proceedings instigated by the landlord or, alternatively, by means of an independent application to the court. Relief from forfeiture will be granted to a tenant who can show that she has, despite the landlord's claims, complied with the relevant leasehold covenants or, otherwise, where the court is persuaded that it is reasonable for the lease to continue in spite of the breaches: *Shiloh Spinners v Harding* (1973). The court's power to grant relief is broad and unfettered.[49] In considering whether to grant relief, the court will examine all the surrounding circumstances of the case but will attach particular weight to the following:

- the severity or negligibility of the breach of covenant;
- the conduct of the parties;
- the past performance of covenants;
- the intentions and motivations of the party in breach;
- the remediability of the breach;
- the draconian nature of forfeiture;
- the harm caused by the breach weighed against the value of the lease.

Relief is available in the event of breach of both positive and negative covenants (*Mount Cook Land v Hartley* (2000)) and, in *Patel v K. & J. Restaurants Ltd* (2010), relief was even granted where the covenant breached concerned immoral or illegal user on the grounds that the effects of forfeiture would be disproportionate to the nature and harm caused by the breach. Whether relief is granted is discretionary and thus, generally, relief will not be granted where the breach was committed intentionally by the tenant, where the breach cannot be remedied, or where the tenant has otherwise behaved inequitably: *Greenwood Reversions Ltd v World Environment Foundations Ltd* (2008); *Patel*. However, *Freifeld v West Kensington Court Ltd* (2015), is a rare example of relief granted in a case where the tenant had engaged in wilful and persistent breaches. A headlessee unlawfully and in breach of a covenant requiring the lessor's consent, sublet a restaurant. It admitted at trial that this had been a deliberate and cynical breach. The landlord forfeit the lease and the headlessee applied for relief. The headlease was worth between £1 million and £2 million and had a considerable period of time to run meaning that the landlord received a windfall. The trial judge, deeply unimpressed with the headlessee's conduct, refused to grant relief but, the Court of Appeal, allowed the appeal. Relief could be granted, it said, even in cases of deliberate and serious breaches. A landlord should not be entitled to keep a windfall where there has been no lasting damage to it from the breach. Relief was discretionary and so a tenant's conduct was highly relevant but the court had to consider whether depriving even a wilful defaulting tenant of a valuable asset was proportionate. The court reached a workable solution by granting relief for six months to allow the tenant to sell his interest and bring to an end the relationship with the landlord. Briggs LJ explained, however, that:

> This conclusion should not be misinterpreted as conferring carte blanche on tenants to disregard their covenants, wherever there is value in their leasehold interest which would be lost by an unrelieved forfeiture. In every case a balance will have to be struck, and there may well be cases where even substantial value has to be passed to the landlord, if no other way of securing the performance of the tenants' covenants can be found.

---

[49] *Rose v Hyman* (1912).

The leading case on the availability of relief is, however, *Ropemaker Properties Ltd v Noonhaven Ltd*:

KEY CASE *Ropemaker Properties Ltd v Noonhaven Ltd* (1989)

Facts: A lease over commercial premises provided that the property could be used only as a high-class eatery or nightclub. The lease contained a covenant under which the tenants agreed not knowingly to use the premises or permit them to be used for any illegal or immoral purpose. The premises were occupied by two nightclubs pursuant to an underlease and a licence. Both the sublease and licence agreements contained prohibitions against any illegal or immoral user. In breach of covenant, the premises were permitted to be used for the purposes of prostitution. Those managing the clubs knew very well that such activities were taking place.

Legal issue: Was the original landlord entitled to forfeiture of the lease? Was the court prepared to grant relief from forfeiture in the tenant's favour?

Judgment: The lease was forfeit but the court was prepared to grant relief from forfeiture. The availability of relief in cases of illegal or immoral user was, however, exceptional and would be granted only very rarely. Millett J noted: 'The mere fact that the breach in question involves immoral user does not in itself preclude the court from granting relief . . . It will, however, be only in the rarest and most exceptional circumstances that the court will grant relief in such a case, particularly where the breach of covenant has been both wilful and serious. The defendants' breaches in the present case were of the utmost gravity; they represented a deliberate and continuing disregard of their obligations under the lease. Despite the weighty considerations which tell against the granting of relief, however, I have come to the conclusion that this is an exceptional case in which relief should be granted.'

The factors identified by the court that rendered this case exceptional were as follows:

- The lease was of substantial value;
- The substantial loss that forfeiture would cause was disproportionate to the offence or any damaged caused by the breach;
- The immoral user has been brought to an end and was unlikely to recur;
- Any 'stigma' attaching to the premises was short-lived;
- Forfeiture of the lease and removal of the tenants would not assist in removing any stigma;
- Granting relief would not be to saddle the lessor with unacceptable tenants;
- The sole director of the tenant company was suffering from poor health;
- The tenant intended to dispose of the lease in any event.

Section 146(4) permits those with derivative interests (i.e. interests carved out of the original lease such as sublessees, mortgagees, or chargees)[50] to apply for relief from forfeiture even where the breach complained of was committed by the original tenant.[51] When a headlease is forfeit, the effect is to extinguish the headlease but also all those derivative interests springing from that lease. As a consequence, s. 146(4) is an important provision that offers a vital protection. Those with derivative interests may, however, also be able to bring an action under s. 146(2) (explored in section 12.5.1.6) as an alternative route for relief. The key difference between s. 146(2) and (4) appears to be that under s146(4) if ordered,

---

[50] Note, however, that equitable chargees are excluded: *Bland v Ingram Estates Ltd (No 2)*.
[51] *Bank of Ireland Home Mortgages v South Lodge* (1996).

relief will take the form of the grant of a new lease whereas, under s146(2), relief takes the form of a continuation of the existing lease.

Recall that the court also enjoys an inherent, equitable jurisdiction to grant relief from forfeiture quite independent of s. 146 of the LPA and independent of any statute.[52] This equitable jurisdiction was recently explored in *Pineport v Grangeglen* (2016). In this case, a tenant applied for relief from forfeiture under the court's equitable jurisdiction, some 14 months after the landlord had forfeited a long lease by peaceable re-entry when the tenant had failed pay to rent arrears of £2,155. The delay had resulted from the conviction and imprisonment of a director of the tenant company for MOT fraud conducted at the leased premises. The director was also suffering depression. The long lease had been valued at £275,000. The court, satisfied that funds could be made available to pay off the arrears within a reasonable period, granted relief. While granting relief in a case of enormous delay was a marked break from earlier case law (in which the maximum period after which relief was granted was six months), the court held the application had been made with 'reasonable promptitude' which, it was conceded, was an elastic concept. This elasticity could be stretched in this case on two grounds: (1) the value of the lease and the substantial premium for the lease paid by the tenant; (2) the director's personal circumstances which led to the delay. Equally, the landlord had not marketed the land after forfeiture and so relief would cause no prejudice to the landlord. *Pineport* therefore demonstrates the breadth and 'elasticity' of the court's inherent, equitable jurisdiction to grant relief.

12.5.1.7 Breach of covenants to repair

Where the breach committed by a tenant concerns a covenant of repair, the tenant is provided with additional statutory protections if the lease is for a period of more than seven years with at least three years left to run. You may wonder why Parliament specifically intervened in this context. The answer is simple. Parliament legislated to safeguard against unscrupulous landlords that might seize upon tenants' minor repair breaches in order to bring an otherwise valid, effective lease to an end. Under the Leasehold Property (Repairs) Act 1938, in the event of a breach of a repairing covenant, the landlord must serve a s. 146 LPA 1925 notice (as explored in section 12.5.1.5); however, the landlord must also inform the tenant in breach that she has 28 days within which to serve a 'counter-notice' claiming the protection of the 1938 Act. Upon service of this counter-notice, the landlord will be able to forfeit the lease only with leave of the court[53] and only in circumstances where one of the specified grounds for forfeiture in s. 1(5) of the 1938 Act is met.

12.5.1.8 Reform of the law of forfeiture

There has long been a clamour for reform to the law of forfeiture. The law of forfeiture has come to be seen as operating harshly and, in many cases, disproportionately to the loss caused by a tenant's breach. Equally, concerns have been expressed that the current law

---

[52] The existence of this separate, equitable jurisdiction was confirmed in *Billson*.
[53] As to when leave will be granted, see *Associated British Ports v C. H. Bailey plc* (1990).

enables dodgy landlords to intimidate and threaten their tenants into strict observance of covenants. The Law Commission has been working on reform proposals since 1968.[54] In 1985, it published its first report[55] which was heavily delayed as more headline-grabbing projects including land registration and the impact of the Human Rights Act took the limelight.[56] In spite of these important distractions, the Law Commission published a further report in 2006[57] after a positive response to its consultation on reform to forfeiture in 2004.[58] In its 2006 report, the Law Commission put forward proposals for a new scheme to entirely replace the current forfeiture regime. The most salient features of the new scheme are as follows:

- The current law of forfeiture would be replaced by an entirely statutory scheme.
- Non-payment of rent and other breaches would be treated in the same way.
- The new scheme would introduce the new concept of 'tenant default' which would reflect a breach by a tenant of a covenant or condition of the tenancy.
- There would be no need for a forfeiture clause or right of re-entry to be included in a tenancy agreement.
- Waiver of the right to forfeit would no longer be possible either intentionally or inadvertently.
- Under the scheme, a landlord faced with a tenant default would be required to serve a written notice, a 'tenant default notice', setting out the breach, remedial action, and date by which such action should be completed.
- If the tenant did not remedy the breach, the landlord could bring a 'termination claim' or apply under the speedier 'summary termination procedure'.[59]
- In considering the landlord's termination claim, the court would take all the circumstances into account and make such orders as it considered appropriate and proportionate. Orders available to the court would be: termination order (ending the lease); remedial order (requiring remedy by the tenant); order for sale; transfer order (transferring the leasehold interest to a particular party); or a new tenancy order (granting the applicant a new tenancy).
- Those with derivative interests would be permitted to respond to the landlord's termination claim.

Whilst progress towards implementation of the Law Commission's recommendations has somewhat stalled, the proposals are widely regarded as sensible, credible, and offering better protections to tenants than the current law while still guaranteeing landlords' ability to bring a lease to an end in the face of a breach of covenant.

[54] Law Commission Working Paper No. 16 (1968).
[55] Law Commission Report No. 142, *Forfeiture of Tenancies* (1985).
[56] This will be considered in Chapter 14.
[57] Law Commission Report No. 303, *Termination of Tenancies for Tenant Default* (2006).
[58] Law Commission Consultation Paper No. 174 (2004).
[59] The summary procedure would be for hopeless cases where the tenant has no prospect of resisting a termination of the lease or the premises have already been abandoned by the tenant.

12.5.2 **Commercial Rent Arrears Recovery**

Historically, in the event that a tenant fell into rent arrears, a landlord was permitted to enter the leased premises to seize and sell goods belonging to the tenant which were found in the property in order to satisfy the debt. This was called 'distress' and a landlord did not require a court order to pursue this self-help remedy. The law of distress and its application to leasehold land has long been criticized by the Law Commission as being, 'riddled with inconsistencies, uncertainties, anomalies and archaisms'.[60] In response, Part 3 of the Tribunals, Courts and Enforcement Act 2007 made provision for the abolition of distress for rent for all leases. Distress was to be replaced with a new system of 'Commercial Rent Arrears Recovery' (CRAR) which would to be limited to commercial leases. On 6 April 2014, this new scheme came into force.[61] CRAR does not apply where any part of premises is used for residential purposes and the scheme, which operates without involvement of the court, applies to pure rent only thus excludes service or insurance charges.

Under CRAR, a landlord must provide a tenant in arrears with at least seven days' notice before seizing goods and CRAR only operates where a tenant owes at least seven days' rent. Other limitations mean that only goods of the debtor (tenant in arrears) may be seized[62] and goods necessary for the debtor's business as well as personal and domestic items are excluded.[63] In addition, seizure of goods must be carried out by a certified agent and sale of the goods seized cannot usually take place for at least seven days. While CRAR clearly affords greater protections to tenants in arrears (excluded goods, seven days' notice etc.), it has proved controversial. This is largely due to concerns that the notice period will give tenants enough time to simply clear out the leased premises of any and all valuable items prior to any potential seizure by a landlord's agent.

For residential leases, the remedy of distress is no longer available and CRAR is inapplicable. A landlord must, therefore, take advantage of one of the other remedies available for breach; chiefly this will mean electing between suing for rent arrears or forfeiture.

12.5.3 **Action for rent arrears**

Other than forfeiture, an action for rent arrears is an extremely important remedy for landlords faced with defaulting tenants. Under s. 19 of the Limitation Act 1980, a landlord is not permitted to bring any action against a tenant for recovery of rent arrears 'after the expiration of six years from the date on which the arrears became due'. The effect of this is that a landlord is able to bring an action against a tenant in rent arrears for a maximum of six years' rent. The landlord will instigate proceedings for rent arrears in either the county court or the High Court dependent on the value of the claim. Importantly and unless expressly excluded in the terms of the lease, in any action for rent arrears, the tenant may be able to 'set off' any alleged breach of covenant by the landlord against the arrears claimed: *Smith v Muscat* (2003).

---

[60] Law Commission Report No. 194, *Landlord and Tenant: Distress for Rent* (1991).
[61] Under the Taking Control of Goods Regulations 2013, SI 2013 No. 1894.
[62] This was not the case under the old law of distress.
[63] Taking Control of Goods Regulations 2013, paras. 4 and 5.

12.5.4 **Action for damages**

For all breaches of covenant other than those of non-payment of rent, a landlord may bring an action against a tenant in breach for damages. In this action, the landlord is entitled to be put into the position as if the breach of covenant had not taken place. For breaches of repair covenants, the provisions of the Leasehold Property (Repairs) Act 1938 (discussed in section 12.5.1.7) still apply.[64] Under s. 1 of the LTA 1927, the amount of damages awarded for breach of a covenant to repair is limited to the diminution in value of the landlord's reversionary interest as a result of the breach.[65]

12.5.5 **Injunction and specific performance**

Finally, a landlord may be able to secure an injunction to prevent a tenant breaching a negative covenant contained within a lease. The availability of an injunction, as an equitable remedy, is however entirely at the discretion of the court. Beyond injunctions, the court has largely been reluctant to make orders for specific performance. In addition to concerns of fairness to the parties, the court has also been anxious as to how an order for specific performance would be supervised: *Co-Op Insurance Society v Argyll Stores* (1997). In particular regarding covenants of repair, the case of *Hill v Barclay* (1811) has long been followed as firm authority that the court would not order specific performance. In *Rainbow Estates Ltd v Tokenhold* (1999), however, Lawrence Collins QC held that an order for specific performance could be granted but only in exceptional cases, adding:[66]

> It will be a rare case in which the remedy of specific performance will be the appropriate one: in the case of commercial leases, the landlord will normally have the right to enter and do the repairs at the expense of the tenant; in residential leases, the landlord will normally have the right to forfeit in appropriate cases.

Under the authority of *Rainbow Estates*, specific performance may be available for breaches of repairing covenants where the landlord has no other remedy available and the court is able to closely define the order for specific performance to ensure it can be effectively supervised. Though not expressly disapproved by subsequent case law, *Rainbow Estates* remains a contentious decision in that it appears to afford landlords significant latitude in circumstances when they have not negotiated a forfeiture clause or provided for entry to the leased premises to carry out repairs at the expense of the tenant. Surely, a landlord so careless should not be entitled to an order for specific performance.

12.6 **The tenant's remedies for breach**

Compared to the position of the landlord, there are fewer remedies available to a tenant when faced with a landlord's breach of covenant. An important point to appreciate here is that a tenant is not able to forego performance of tenant obligations simply in response to

---

[64] The 1938 Act applies equally to forfeiture. [65] See LTA 1927; *Jones v Herxheimer* (1950).

[66] *Rainbow Estates*, 74.

a breach of covenant by the landlord. There are broadly four remedies available to a tenant faced with a landlord's breach of covenant:

- action for damages;
- injunction;
- specific performance;
- recouping the cost of repairs from future rent.

We will examine each in turn.

12.6.1 Action for damages

Confronted with a landlord's breach of covenant, a tenant is able to bring an action to recover damages for any loss caused. This action can be brought for breach of any leasehold covenant and, if successful, damages will be awarded to place the tenant in the position as if the breach had not been committed: *Calabar v Stitcher* (1984); *Wallace v Manchester City Council* (1998).

12.6.2 Injunction

At the absolute discretion of the court, a tenant may be able to secure an injunction to prevent an existing or anticipated breach of covenant at the hands of the landlord.

12.6.3 Specific performance

A tenant is able to seek an order for specific performance of a landlord's covenant provided that the court is satisfied of effective supervision of the order. In *Jeune v Queens Cross Properties Ltd* (1974), for example, a tenant was able to secure specific performance of a landlord's covenant to repair the leased premises.[67] In addition, under s. 17 of the LTA 1985, the court is given express statutory jurisdiction to order specific performance of landlords' repairing covenants in residential leases.

12.6.4 Recouping the cost of repairs from future rent

Where a landlord is in breach of a covenant to repair leased premises, a tenant is able to undertake the repair work herself and, subsequently, recoup the costs of the work from future rent payable to the landlord in breach: *Lee-Parker v Izzet* (1971). This course of action is only open to a tenant if she has served a notice on the landlord outlining the need for repairs to be completed. Tenants must be prudent when following this course of action and the *Izzet* authority, however, as in the event that too great a deduction from future rent is made, the landlord may subsequently seek forfeiture for a tenant's non-payment of rent.

---

[67] See also *Francis v Cowliffe* (1977).

12.7 **Future directions**

In this chapter, we have explored the content and enforcement of leasehold covenants, and the remedies available to landlords and tenants in the event of breach. This chapter has located and examined the complexity that exists in the law, how the courts and Parliament have intervened, and we have tracked the attempts of the Law Commission to clarify and simplify the law in certain fields (notably forfeiture). In looking ahead, this section focuses on the recently enacted H(FHH)A 2018 and the implications of this important new piece of legislation.[68]

The 2018 Act began life as the Homes (Fitness for Human Habitation) Bill 2017–19 and was introduced as an opposition Private Members' Bill into Parliament by Karen Buck, Labour MP for Westminster North. In offering the background to the Bill, Buck explained, 'tenants need greater protection, and . . . whilst having a stronger voice in decisions affecting them is vital, so too are clear, enforceable legal rights'. So what does the 2018 Act do? Well, the H(FHH)A 2018 promotes a startlingly simple objective: to ensure that rental properties in England are fit for human habitation and, should these properties not meet this standard, that tenants are able to force landlords to make improvements so that their housing is raised to meet the acceptable fitness standard. The H(FHH)A 2018 amends the LTA 1985 ss. 8–10 and, additionally, inserts new ss. 9A, 9B, and 9C into the LTA 1985. Section 9A(1) inserted into the LTA 1985 is the most important change introduced by the 2018 Act and implies into any applicable tenancy a covenant by the landlord that the dwelling:

(a) is fit for human habitation at the time the lease is granted or otherwise created or, if later, at the beginning of the term of the lease, and

(b) will remain fit for human habitation during the term of the lease.

This implied covenant cannot be contracted out or excluded by the landlord either at the time the tenancy is granted or subsequently and applies widely to all new tenancies of dwellings let wholly or mainly for human habitation of less than seven years' duration including new periodic tenancies granted on or after the commencement date (20 March 2019). Any attempt to exclude or limit the landlord's obligations under the implied covenant or impose on the tenant any penalty to cover any potential cost of the landlord's obligation will be void.

How is 'fitness for human habitation' determined under the new Act? One of the most significant aspects of the 2018 Act is its modernization of the categories that are used to determine whether a home is 'fit for human habitation'. Section 1(4) of the 2018 Act amends and extends the matters listed in the old s. 10 LTA 1985 under a new s. 10(2) LTA 1985 to include 'any prescribed hazard' as detailed in regulations made by the Secretary of State under s. 2 of the Housing Act 2004. What this means in practice is that the 2018 Act imports into the new s. 10 LTA 1985 the list of 29 hazards from the current Housing, Health & Safety Rating System (HHSRS) introduced by the Housing Act 2004 and will include any changes that may be made to the HHSRS following a review of the system to be completed in 2020.

---

[68] On which see generally: Bevan, 'Improving Housing Conditions in the Private and Social Rented Sectors'.

So, does it address the deficiencies of the current legal framework under which, it is accepted, far too many homes remain non-decent and unfit? Well, the position here is mixed. On one view, the 2018 legislation is a major step forward giving tenants in unsafe and dangerous housing conditions a right to a fit home that they can enforce. In 2017, an estimated 27 per cent of privately rented homes failed to meet the Decent Homes Standard in England. In view of this, the 2018 Act could genuinely transform tenants' lives and, in turn, the new obligations could force unscrupulous landlords to take pre-emptive steps to improve the quality of their rental properties to avoid legal action. However, we should not get carried away because the 2018 Act does nothing to address the broader structural problems in the housing market, the affordability crisis, the problem of poor housing supply in key parts of the country, and—often overlooked—the lack of legal aid for housing claims which has now slipped to near vanishing point. We wait to see how claims under the 2018 Act are litigated and the implications of this for housing stock in England but, in so far as it seeks to redress the power imbalance between landlords and tenants, many will and should welcome the new law.

Further reading

- C. Bevan, 'Improving Housing Conditions in the Private and Social Rented Sectors: The Homes (Fitness for Human Habitation) Act 2018—Fit for Habitation but Fit for Purpose?' (2019) 82(5) MLR 897.
- S. Bridge, 'Former Tenants, Future Liabilities and the Privity of Contract Principle: The Landlord and Tenant (Covenants) Act 1995' (1996) 55 CLJ 313.
- S. Bridge, 'Leases, Contract, Property and Status' in L. Tee (ed.), *Land Law: Issues, Debates, Policy* (Cullompton: Willan, 2002).
- A. Clarke, 'Property Law' (1992) 45(1) CLP 81
- M. Davey, 'Privity of Contract and Leases—Reform at Last' (1996) 59 MLR 78.
- N. Gravells, 'Forfeiture of Leases for Breach of Covenant' (2006) December, JBL, 830.
- P. Luxton, 'Waiver of Forfeiture: Time to Shake Away the Doctrine of Election' [1991] JBL 34.

Online resources

Access the online resources at www.oup.com/uk/bevan2e/ to test yourself with self-test questions and scenario problems. You can also view additional supporting material relevant to the topics in this chapter, including:

- *Videos*
- *Audio podcasts*
- *Maps, diagrams, and flowcharts*
- *Interactive exercises*
- *Examples of real-life legal documentation*

Mortgages

13.1 Introduction

It is difficult to overstate the importance of mortgages. When coming to the study of land law, it is often this topic which is of the greatest interest to students. Why? Well think about it, how often have you heard in the media about the difficulties of 'getting on the property ladder' or keeping up with mortgage payments? Practically, it is, for most of us, only with the help of a mortgage that we can ever hope to purchase our first home and get on that ladder. The vast majority of you reading this book will, therefore, seek a mortgage at some stage to raise the funds you need to purchase a home.

So, what is a mortgage? In short, a mortgage is a form of proprietary security interest for the advancement of a loan. A bank or lender advances a loan and in return they are granted a mortgage: an interest in the borrower's land. The uses to which mortgages can be put are not, however, confined to home ownership. Mortgages must be seen for the enduringly flexible devices that they are. Mortgages are therefore exploited in the residential and commercial sectors as well as being used for the purposes of property investment and capital financing. It really goes without saying that mortgages matter, but let's begin by unpacking a little further just why they hold such a prominent place in modern land law.

The numbers speak for themselves. According to the Bank of England,[1] at the end of March 2019 the total value of residential loans exceeded £1,461 billion. Mortgages represent the most important source of credit for individuals in the UK and evidently it is big business! In Chapter 6 we considered the central place of 'home' in land law and the deep attachments that we all have to it. Combine the impetus to own property with this attachment and we can see that the law of mortgages is more important than just providing capital—it gives individuals a chance to participate in the home-owning democracy. But we also know, beyond this, that land is not just a home but also an asset. Increasingly, land

---

[1] Bank of England, Mortgage Lenders and Administrators Statistical Release, September 2019.

is being mortgaged (and remortgaged) to release funds for a rainy day, to provide for retirement, or to finance a small or medium-sized business.

Against this backdrop, it is understandable that, for decades now, political parties of all stripes have heralded measures calculated to facilitate bank lending and advance a political narrative on the benefits of home ownership. Much of the political attention has focused on encouraging banks to lend money in the hope that burdens on the State, such as social housing and the expenditure on housing benefit, might be reduced. Home ownership is marketed as the 'aspirational' option, and as being superior to leasing property. In this narrative, mortgages are the key that unlock this aspiration. As Oldham explains:[2]

> The purchaser acquires a sense of belonging not only to the neighbourhood in which the house if located, but also to a larger group of homeowners generally. Home ownership signals respectability, responsibility and usually, also upward mobility. The particularly English ideology surrounding home ownership has had the result than non-homeowners have become almost second-class citizens.

The much-vaunted benefits of home ownership can only be accessed by the majority of us by borrowing money from lenders—via a mortgage. Mortgages therefore matter in as much as they are the conduit by which we, as citizens, gain the respectability, responsibility, and ownership status that Oldham identifies. Mortgages are therefore vital for home ownership but also for the growth of the small and medium-sized businesses often described as the engine of the British economy.

So far, so positive, but sadly the news is not all good, as mortgages carry risk. Mortgages played a central role in the financial woes of the early 1990s and in the Great Recession of 2008 with the sub-prime mortgage scandal. If anything, this serves to underscore the significance of the law of mortgages for the global economy. Mortgages have contributed to this country's most devastating financial crises. As Oldham argues:[3]

> [M]ortgages constitute a key economic institution—the means by which assets are mobilised, capital generated and productivity and the wider economy boosted. The mortgage is a mechanism that transforms 'passive' land value into 'active' value in that it allows the value of land to be released for other purposes while the freeholder or leaseholder is still able to enjoy the benefits of physical occupation or possession . . . From such a perspective, the stability of the entire economy of a country is dependent on a property functioning of the law of mortgages.

The State therefore has a keen interest in the functioning of the law of mortgages to ensure that the conditions necessary for the smooth running of the sector are maintained. This can be a fine balancing act between the interests of lenders and those borrowing money. The consequences of getting this balance wrong are obvious: too much regulation and over-zealous control of lending and lenders will stop advancing loans, to the detriment of the whole economy. Too little regulation and a lack of support for those borrowing money will lead to irresponsible lending and, ultimately, borrowers losing their homes as a result of defaulting on their mortgage payments. Mortgages carry great benefits and great risks and this central tension between lender and borrower forms the backbone of this chapter. We begin by exploring the essential nature of mortgages.

 Visit the online resources to watch a video on the often confusing terminology in the law of mortgages.

---

[2] M. Oldham, 'Mortgages' in L. Tee (ed.), *Land Law: Issues, Debates, Policy* (Devon: Willan, 2002), 172.
[3] Ibid., 169.

13.2 **The nature of mortgages**

Lindley MR in *Santley v Wilde* (1899) provided the classic definition of a mortgage in the following terms:[4]

> A conveyance of land . . . as security for the payment of a debt or the discharge of some other obligation for which it is given.

According to this traditional definition of a mortgage, the borrower[5] transferred his land to the lender as security for the loan money advanced, subject to a provision that the land would be retransferred upon repayment of the loan plus interest. A mortgage in this traditional and narrow sense therefore involved the actual *transfer* of the borrower's estate in land to the lender. Upon repayment of the loan, the borrower had the right to demand his property be returned to him. For as long as the debt remained outstanding, the lender enjoyed a proprietary status and could avail itself of proprietary remedies against the borrower. The result was that if the mortgage loan was not repaid, the lender would be able to sell or exploit the land for their own benefit.

The law of mortgages has moved on, however, and today in modern land law, a mortgage involving the transfer of the borrower's land to the lender is no longer possible over registered land.[6] Technically speaking, a distinction must therefore be drawn between the classic now defunct *mortgage* according to the *Santley* definition and the modern *charge* which takes centre-stage in today's law. Unlike a mortgage, a *charge* does not involve the transfer of any estate in land to the lender but instead confers on that lender certain rights over the borrower's land in order that the lender is able to secure repayment of the loan advanced.[7] Practically, this means that the lender is able to seek an order of the court that the borrower's land be sold, or to appoint a receiver so that income from the land can be used to satisfy the debt. When the debt is paid, the *charge* is automatically discharged.[8]

13.2.1 **Understanding the terminology**

Often the greatest challenge in studying land law is getting to grips with the terminology. The language used is often unfamiliar and obscure, and this is especially true in the law of mortgages. It is vital then that you appreciate that today when we speak of *mortgages* we use this term in two senses: first to describe the classic mode of security interest in land under which the borrower transferred his estate to the lender as security for a loan (just discussed in section 13.2), and secondly in a broader sense to refer to any borrower–lender relationship under which land is used as security for a loan today. Be aware that the terms *mortgage* and *charge* are often used somewhat interchangeably and indistinguishably, despite being technically distinct forms of security. The language has the very real potential to cause confusion and can make the law seem unduly complex when in fact the rules are

---

[4] *Santley*, 474.
[5] You should note it is also entirely possible for a person to mortgage property to cover someone else's debts.
[6] Section 23 of the LRA 2002.
[7] As explained by Scrutton LJ in *London County and Westminster Bank Ltd v Tompkins* (1918).
[8] Parallels can be drawn to the Roman Law concept of *hypothec*.

relatively straightforward. With this in mind, consider the following quick run-through of key terminology in this area:

- The 'mortgagor' or 'chargor': The landowner, person borrowing money and granting the mortgage.

- The 'mortgagee' or 'chargee': The person or financial institution (usually a bank) lending the money and to whom the mortgage is granted.

Coming to the subject for the first time, you might think that it is the bank or lender that grants the mortgage. This is not correct. It is actually the borrower or mortgagor that grants a mortgage to the lender or mortgagee by way of charge. The lender, in return, provides the loan monies. Note also that the mortgage describes the interest granted by the mortgagor to the mortgagee and not the money advanced.

13.2.2 **A brief historical overview**

History is not for everyone but it is crucial to understanding the law of mortgages. So bear with it. A concept of mortgage or, more accurately, the use of property as security for a loan, has existed in some form since Anglo-Saxon times. In large part, the mortgage developed as a reaction to the laws against usury, which prohibited the charging of interest.[9] As Baker traces:[10]

> From the earliest times, debtors have used property as security, or 'gage', for loans for money. In some early forms of gage no term was fixed: the gagee held the property until he was satisfied . . . if the gagee took the profits in reduction of the loan, this was known in early times as a living gage (*vivum vadium*) apparently because the property continued to work for the borrow; but if the lender took the principal as well as the profits, it was a dead gage ('mortgage') and the arrangement, though sinful as giving the lender a usurious return, was legally valid. By the fifteenth century, however, the name 'mortgage' has apparently come to be used for any arrangement whereby a loan was secured by a conveyance of real property . . .

The conveyance of the fee simple would contain a clause providing for redemption on a specific date, known as the 'legal date for redemption', on which the mortgagor would be required to repay the loan and would thereby be entitled to recovery of his land from the mortgagee. Upon conveyance of the fee simple by the mortgagor, the mortgagee was regarded, at least at common law, as the *owner* of the acquired freehold. Several consequences flowed from this position:

1. Having acquired the freehold, the mortgagee was entitled to enter possession of the property and to take any profits from the land. In the event that the profits extracted exceeded the sums owed by the mortgagor, the mortgagee was under no obligation to account to the mortgagor for that surplus.

2. In its characteristic manner, the common law held strictly to the 'form' of the mortgage arrangement in regarding the legal date of redemption as central to the operation of the

---

[9] The laws against usury were ultimately only abolished under the Usury Laws Repeal Act 1854.
[10] J. H. Baker, *An Introduction to English History*, 4th edn (Oxford: Butterworths, 2002), 311.

mortgage. As a result, if the mortgagor could not repay the loan on the precise date provided for in the mortgage, the right to redeem was lost and the mortgagor would not be able to demand reconveyance of his land. Crucially, the mortgagee was permitted to retain the freehold unencumbered by the mortgagor's interest even if the land's value exceeded the sums owed by the mortgagor. To boot, as Viscount Haldane LC confirmed in *Kreglinger v New Patagonia Meat and Cold Meat Storage Co. Ltd* (1914), whilst the right to redeem was extinguished, the debt owed by the mortgagor endured.

3. The result was to create something of a fiction:[11] what Maitland has called 'one long *suppressio veri* and *suggestio falsi*': Latin for a suppression of the truth, a statement of falsehood.[12] The air of unreality stems from the fact that the common law treatment of the mortgage arrangement did not truly reflect the interests of either party: neither the mortgagor, who regarded himself as the 'true' owner of the land even after the freehold had been conveyed to the mortgagee, nor the mortgagee itself, who was more concerned to guarantee security for the loan monies advanced and was not wanting ownership of the mortgagor's land.

The stage was set for equity's intervention. In the seventeenth century, equity began to scrutinize the operation of mortgages at common law. Taking a more flexible approach, equity was concerned to have regard to the substance and not the form of the mortgage arrangement. The effect was that equity would only recognize as having been granted to the mortgagee those rights necessary for the purpose of protecting its security. In equity, mortgagees taking profits from the mortgaged land were not permitted to retain sums in excess of the debt owed. Over time, ever greater proportions of mortgagors retained possession of the mortgaged land. In contrast to the common law's strict adherence to the legal date of redemption, equity established its own approach. The so-called 'equitable right to redeem' developed with the consequence that once the legal date of redemption had passed, and even where repayment of the loan was late, the mortgagor would be able to recover his property so long as the mortgage loan was repaid with interest and costs. The equitable right to redeem therefore arose only after the mortgagor's contractual right of redemption had been extinguished. This equitable right to redeem remains important today. Many mortgages still contain unrealistic, fictitious, contractual repayment dates fixed, for example, set at six months after the date of creation of the mortgage. In such cases, mortgagors will rely on equity once the legal date for redemption has passed.

Whilst Parliament has subsequently intervened, by way of the LPA 1925 and later the LRA 2002, to regulate how mortgages are created (discussed in section 13.3), as you will discover in this chapter, the fiction resting at the heart of the 'mortgage' in part survives. In its 1991 Report, the Law Commission highlighted the problems inherent in the law of mortgages and recommended the introduction of a new statutory form of security interest with clearly delimited rights and duties.[13] These proposals have yet to be taken up by Parliament. Mortgages are very much a product of their particular history and much of the current complexity in the law is a hang-over from earlier times.

---

[11] See G. Watt, 'The Lie of the Land: Mortgage Law as Legal Fiction' in E. Cooke (ed.), *Modern Studies in Property Law*, Vol. 4 (Oxford: Hart, 2007), chapter 4.

[12] F. W. Maitland, *Equity: A Course of Lectures* (Cambridge: Cambridge University Press, 2011), 182.

[13] Law Commission Report No. 204, *Transfer of Land: Land Mortgages* (1991).

13.3 The creation of mortgages

In this section, we consider how mortgages are created at law and in equity. At the outset, it is important to appreciate that a legal mortgage can only be created over land which is a legal freehold or a legal leasehold. Equally, where the interest to be mortgaged is itself equitable, an equitable mortgage only can be created.

13.3.1 Legal mortgages

It is necessary to draw a vital distinction between unregistered and registered land.

13.3.1.1 Legal mortgages in unregistered land

In unregistered land, under s. 85 of the LPA 1925, there are two methods for the creation of a legal mortgage: (1) the long lease method (mortgage by demise) and (2) the charge by way of legal mortgage.[14]

Creation of legal mortgages under either method constitutes a 'conveyance' under s. 205(1)(ii) of the LPA 1925 and therefore must be by deed.[15] Mortgages created by long lease (demise) give rise to a proprietary interest in the mortgagee's favour. The proprietary interest arising is a leasehold estate and lasts for 3,000 years. Upon repayment of the loan, the mortgagor enjoys an equitable right to redeem and the lease comes to an end (known as 'cesser on redemption' in s. 85(1)). Today, creation of a legal mortgage by long lease almost never happens, bowing to the increasing popularity of the second method: *charge by way of legal mortgage*. The charge by way of legal mortgage is a far less complex process, simpler in form,[16] and allows for the creation of mortgages of freehold and leasehold land in a single, unified transaction, rendering the charge by legal mortgage the key method by which legal mortgages are created today.

The charge by way of legal mortgage gives rise to what might be called a 'hybrid interest'. What we mean by this is that the mortgagee is granted a legal charge but, under s. 87(1), is said to enjoy 'the same protections, powers and remedies' as if the mortgagee held a lease of 3,000 years' duration. In this way, the vestiges of demise are not entirely banished. It was a clear policy objective of the 1925 legislation that the legal estate in mortgaged land should remain in the hands of the 'true' owner, the mortgagor. Therefore, mortgages created on or after 1 January 1926 no longer involve the transfer by the mortgagor of the legal estate in the land to the mortgagee. Instead, the mortgagor retains the legal estate subject to the legal charge granted in the mortgagee's favour.

Finally, be aware that the grant of a legal mortgage over unregistered land (either by way of demise or legal charge) will constitute a triggering event for compulsory first registration under the LRA 2002 bringing the land into the registered land regime.[17]

---

[14] The creation of legal mortgages over leasehold land is governed by s. 86 of the LPA 1925.
[15] Ibid., s. 52(1); s. 1 of the LP(MP)A 1989.   [16] Schedule 5 of the LPA 1925.
[17] Section 4(1)(g) of the LRA 2002.

13.3.1.2 Legal mortgages in registered land

Before the LRA 2002, legal mortgages in registered land were created according to the same two methods as those in unregistered land just outlined. The LRA 2002 changed this position, and today under s. 23(1) of the 2002 Act, the *only* method of creation of a legal mortgage in registered land is *the registered charge*: see s. 87 of the LPA 1925. Again, as in unregistered land, a legal charge by way of mortgage constitutes a conveyance under the LPA 1925 and, therefore, must be created by deed. In addition, under s. 27(2)(f) of the LRA 2002, the grant of a legal charge is a registrable disposition which cannot operate at law until it has been completed by registration in compliance with the relevant registration requirements.[18] Section 51 of the LRA 2002 confirms that once these registration requirements are met, the charge has effect as a charge by way of legal mortgage.

Where does this leave us? Well, charge by way of legal mortgage is now the predominant means by which legal mortgages are created in unregistered land and is the *only* means by which a legal mortgage can be created in registered land. Figure 13.1 depicts the necessary steps for the creation of a mortgage in registered land today.

Figure 13.1 Creation of a legal mortgage in registered land

---

[18] Ibid., s. 27(1), (2)(f), and Sch. 2, para. 8.

13.3.2 Legal mortgages and third parties

We consider the priority of mortgages in greater detail in section 13.7 but here, a summary is offered to give you an introduction to the issues. In registered land today, the enforceability of legal mortgages against third party transferees (i.e. those to whom the mortgaged land is conveyed) is determined by the rules of registration under the LRA 2002.

13.3.2.1 Legal mortgages and third parties in registered land

In *registered* land, a legal mortgage can only operate at law if it is duly completed by registration against the registered title.[19] The effect of this is that the legal mortgage constitutes a 'registered disposition' and will gain priority under s. 29 of the 2002 Act, subject to those interests protected by entry of a notice and overriding interests. The mortgagee will be registered as the proprietor of that legal charge. Where the mortgage is not properly registered, it cannot operate at law and takes effect only in equity and must be protected by entry of a notice if it is to bind third party purchasers of the mortgaged land.

13.3.2.2 Legal mortgages in unregistered land

In *unregistered* land, the grant of a first legal mortgage will trigger compulsory registration of title under s. 4 of the LRA 2002. If the unregistered estate owner does not comply and duly register as proprietor of the land, after a two-month period from the date of grant of the mortgage, the mortgagor has 'effect as a contract made for valuable consideration to grant or create the legal estate concerned': s. 7 of the LRA 2002. In essence, this means that either registration requirements are satisfied and the mortgage will become a registered charge or if not, after two months, it will take effect as an equitable mortgage only.

13.3.3 Equitable mortgages

We have seen how mortgages are created at law but what of the position in equity? Equitable mortgages give rise to equitable interests only. It is therefore crucial to know whether a mortgage is legal or equitable in nature as this can have serious repercussions for the protection of the mortgagor as well as determining the remedies available to the mortgagee. In essence, equitable mortgages arise in five principal circumstances:

1. Mortgages of equitable interests: This form of equitable mortgage is really quite simple. Where the borrower holds an equitable interest in land only (e.g. as a beneficiary under a trust), any mortgage of that interest will, by its nature, be an equitable mortgage. A mortgage of an equitable interest does not require a deed, and is created by an assignment of the equitable interest in writing to the lender, subject to reassignment to the borrower upon the repayment of the mortgage loan advanced.[20] Writing is required[21] as the assignment constitutes a disposition of a subsisting equitable interest under s. 53(1)(c) of the LPA 1925.

---

[19] A legal charge is a registrable disposition: ibid., s. 27.   [20] *William Brandt v Dunlop Rubber* (1905).

[21] Section 53 requires signed writing by the person disposing of the equitable interest or by an authorized agent.

2. 'Informal' or otherwise defective legal mortgages: Where there has been an attempt to grant a legal mortgage but the mortgage is defective either for want of a deed (as is required under s. 52(1) of the LPA 1925) or in registered land for want of registration (as is required under s. 27(1),(2)(f) of the LRA 2002), an equitable mortgage may arise under the doctrine of *Walsh v Lonsdale*.[22]

3. Mortgages where there is forgery: Where there is more than one *legal* owner, all must act together if they are to create a valid, *legal* mortgage. So, what if one forges the signature of the other legal co-owners? A purported legal mortgage will be ineffective at law where the mortgagor has committed a forgery or obtained by improper methods the signature of another for the purposes of a mortgage (for example, forging a partner's signature). However, in equity the circumstances might be construed as a contract for a mortgage of the forger's equitable interest.[23] In this scenario, an equitable mortgage will be generated.

4. Mortgages by deposit of title deeds: Before the enactment of the LP(MP)A 1989, an equitable mortgage could also be generated by the mortgagor depositing the title deeds with the mortgagee as security for a loan. This operated under the doctrine of part performance of an oral contract and the court would infer that the delivery of deeds was evidence of an intention to provide security.[24] Chadwick J in *United Bank of Kuwait plc v Sahib* (1997) confirmed, however, that s. 2 of the 1989 Act had effectively removed delivery of title deeds as a mode by which an equitable mortgage would arise.[25]

5. Mortgages arising under the doctrine of proprietary estoppel: In Chapter 8, we found that if a claimant establishes an equity by proprietary estoppel, the court moves to 'satisfy the equity' and in so doing seeks to award the minimum equity to do justice to the parties. It is therefore possible that the court might award an equitable mortgage as a remedy. One particular difficulty here is that it appears to entirely circumvent the formality requirements for the creation of mortgages. This issue was addressed head-on in the case of *Kinane v Alimamy Mackie-Conteh* (2005),[26] where the Court of Appeal held that an equitable mortgage arose by estoppel following a letter agreeing to provide a charge over property in return for the advancement of a loan despite failure to comply with the formality requirements of s. 2 of the 1989 Act. The Court of Appeal did not regard the claim to estoppel as side-stepping the formality requirements of s. 2 of the 1989 Act but rather construed the written letter as giving rise to the assurance, representation, or belief necessary to found the estoppel claim.

13.3.4 The equitable charge

The equitable charge is another form of equitable security and by far the most informal. The equitable charge requires no specific formalities for its creation beyond evidence of an intention that the land in question was to be charged as security for the loan: *Swiss Bank Corp. v*

---

[22] See also *Parker v Housefield* (1834); we considered the doctrine of *Walsh v Lonsdale* in Chapter 9 on leases.
[23] Subject to satisfying s. 2 of the LP(MP)A 1989; *United Bank of Kuwait plc v Sahib* (1997).
[24] *Thomas Guaranty Ltd v Campbell* (1985).
[25] This has since been confirmed by the Law Commission Law Report No. 204, [2.9].
[26] On which see S. Pulleyn, 'Equitable Easements Revisited' [2012] Conv 387.

Lloyds Bank Ltd (1982). The key distinction between the rather precarious equitable charge and the equitable mortgage is that a broader range of remedies is available for equitable mortgages not available to equitable charges—for example, the remedy of **foreclosure**.

13.3.5 Equitable mortgages and third parties

Equitable mortgages, just like other equitable interests in land we have encountered in this book, are exposed to the same risk of losing priority upon a conveyance of the land either in unregistered or registered land. As we found in Chapter 2 on registration, an equitable interest holder must take steps to protect their position. Figure 13.2 explores how an equitable mortgagee can protect itself in unregistered and registered land. We consider the priority of equitable mortgages in greater depth in section 13.7.

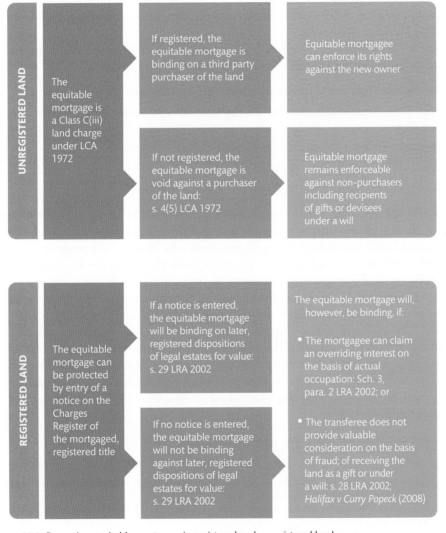

Figure 13.2 Protecting equitable mortgages in registered and unregistered land

13.4 The rights and powers of the mortgagor

In the first part to this chapter, you were introduced to the central tension of the law of mortgages: the balancing act between the interests of mortgagee and mortgagor. It is all too easy to characterize this struggle as a David and Goliath battle between big, bad banks and small, cowering, vulnerable borrowers. This is an oversimplification. Mortgages give rise to benefits and risks on both sides. That said, when things go wrong—say, when a mortgagor cannot meet mortgage instalments—how this power struggle plays out becomes pivotal. Where does the power lie in the mortgagor-mortgagee relationship? In this section, we consider the position of the mortgagor in this balancing exercise. As you will see, there has been a real attempt, often through the intervention of equity and Parliament, to strike a fair balance between the interests of the borrower and the lender. There is also an enormous raft of 'soft regulations' and 'guidance' documents governing mortgage lenders (for example, published by the Council of Mortgage Lenders) which have a real impact on the mortgage sector on the ground.[27]

In this part, we explore the mortgagor's rights, powers, and protections. There are five which we explore in this section:

- the equitable right to redeem and the 'no clogs or fetters' rule
- protection from unfair creditor–debtor relationships under the Consumer Credit Act 2006
- protection under the Financial Services and Markets Act 2000
- powers of the mortgagor to claim possession, to grant leases and seek an order for sale
- setting aside of the mortgage on grounds of undue influence.

As a first and fundamental point, you must recognize that despite the apparent strength in the position of the mortgagee, it is the mortgagor that remains the 'true' owner of the mortgaged land.[28] It is said that the mortgagor enjoys the 'equity' in the property, often described as the '**equity of redemption**', which represents the sum of the mortgagor's rights in relation to the mortgaged property minus the obligations owed by the mortgagor. In essence, the equity of redemption represents the continued right of ownership of the mortgagor over the land. This equity is a proprietary interest in itself and can be transferred or sold.[29] The equity of redemption is therefore synonymous with the mortgagor's residual bundle of rights in the property. Equity is prepared to intervene in a number of ways to prevent interference with these rights. Parliament has also legislated to further bolster the protections afforded to mortgagors, often in a bid to redress a perceived power imbalance in the mortgagee's favour. Let's take a look at the extent and scope of the rights and powers enjoyed by the mortgagor.

---

[27] See, for example, the newly named, *UK Finance Mortgage Lenders' Handbook* accessible from the Council of Mortgage Lenders website: www.cml.org.uk/policy.

[28] Unless and until the court orders that this position be altered or the land be sold, for example, in the event of default by the mortgagor.

[29] See *Casborne v Scarfe* (1738).

13.4.1 The equitable right to redeem: No clogs or fetters

The equitable right to redeem is, arguably, the most significant 'right' enjoyed by the mortgagor within its bundle of rights comprising the equity of redemption. The right to redeem means the right the mortgagor enjoys to repay the loan and for the mortgage to thereby be discharged from the land and for the mortgagor to get her property back unencumbered by any rights of the mortgagee. Redemption is therefore the process by which the land is released from the charge or mortgage.[30] In the introduction to this chapter, we discussed the contractual date for redemption and explored how equity had intervened to mitigate the harshness of the common law's strict adherence to this contractual date, rendering the contractual date, in almost all mortgages, entirely illusory. The equitable right to redeem only arises when the contractual right to redeem has passed. Today, it is upon the equitable right to redeem that mortgagors rely in seeking to discharge the mortgage. Equity will intervene to prevent interference with a mortgagor's equitable right to redeem to guarantee there are no 'clogs or fetters' stifling operation of the right. Equity's insistence that there be no 'clogs and fetters' on the mortgagor's equitable right to redeem has operated in five key ways, which are considered below.

13.4.1.1 Any term in the mortgage which purports to exclude or restrict the mortgagor's right to redeem will be void

Where a clause attempts to remove the right to redeem in its entirety such that, in effect, the mortgage is irredeemable, the term will be void: *Jones v Morgan* (2001). Similarly, a clause which restricts those individuals that are permitted to redeem the mortgage or the time for redemption will be struck out: *Re Sir Thomas Spencer Wells* (1933). Clauses which attempt to postpone the right to redeem are also likely to be void in circumstances where the result is to render redemption meaningless or illusory: *Fairclough v Swan Brewery*.

> **KEY CASE** *Fairclough v Swan Brewery* (1912)
>
> Facts: The mortgagor, Fairclough, held a tenancy over a hotel of which 17½ years of the term was still to run. The landlord, Swan Brewery, had loaned money to Fairclough with the lease as security for the money advanced. It was a term of the mortgage that redemption was not possible until six weeks before expiration of the lease.
>
> Legal issue: Was this postponement of the contractual date for redemption a clog and fetter on the equitable right to redeem or could it be enforced?
>
> Judgment: Lord Macnaghten held that the postponement of the contractual right to redeem was void as it made the equitable right to redeem illusory. Given that the equitable right only arose once the contractual date had passed, the mortgage was effectively irredeemable. The court held that Fairclough should be permitted to pay off the debt early and the clause postponing redemption was void.

Where, however, the postponement can be said to have been freely agreed and negotiated between the parties and it is not unconscionable, it will be valid: *Knightsbridge Estate's Trust Ltd v Byrne* (1939). In *Knightsbridge*, the mortgagor wished to alter an agreed mortgage

---

[30] In registered land, redemption is executed by way of a simple application in prescribed form lodged with Land Registry. In unregistered land, the process is governed by s. 115(1) of the LPA 1925 and requires a receipt be annexed to or 'endorsed' on the mortgage deed.

repayment plan and redeem the mortgage earlier than originally envisaged as a result of falling interest rates. The mortgagor argued that a clause in the original agreement providing for repayment over a 40-year period was void as a clog on the right to redeem. The court found the clause to be valid. This was a commercial context; the parties were of equal bargaining power; legal advice had been received and there was no evidence of oppressive or unconscionable conduct. Post-*Knightsbridge* and particularly in commercial big-business arrangements, the court will be slow to encroach on the parties' freedom to contract. Today, it is commonplace for lenders to offer favourable interest rates to mortgagors who, in return, agree not to redeem for a fixed period. In these circumstances, should the mortgagor redeem early, there may be provision for the payment of a 'redemption fee' or 'redemption charge'. Provided these fees have been fully explained to the mortgagor prior to the grant of the mortgage, they will be valid and will not fall foul of statutory protections.[31]

13.4.1.2 Any term in the mortgage which restricts or restrains the mortgagor's right to trade will be void

The rule against terms operating in restraint of trade seeks to achieve a balance between the freedom of contract and the wider public benefit of ensuring that trade is not hampered. A common example might be so-called 'solus agreements' which tie one commercial party to another—for example, under which one party agrees to purchase all stock from the other and not from competitors. The court will take account of the reasonableness of the term, the bargaining position of the parties and whether the term is unconscionable,[32] bearing in mind the nature, effect, and duration of the term in determining whether it constitutes an unreasonable restriction on the mortgagor's trade.[33]

13.4.1.3 A term providing for the transfer to the mortgagee of the mortgaged property may be void

A term in the mortgage which provides for the transfer to the mortgagee of the mortgaged property or affords the mortgagee an option to purchase the land may be void. These terms are entirely inconsistent with the fundamental nature of the contemporary mortgage as well as being incompatible with the equitable right to redeem and may be struck down. There is no need to demonstrate unconscionability for these clauses: *Samuel v Jarrah Timber & Wood paving Corporation Ltd* (1904).[34] A clause which provides that, on the occurence of a specified event, the mortgagee becomes absolutely entitled to the land is therefore void as the mortgagor is not free to repay the loan and redeem the property unencumbered.[35]

A clause may, however, escape being struck down if it is possible to construe the mortgage and the option to purchase as two distinct agreements or transactions. This is firmly a

---

[31] See sections 13.4.2 and 13.4.3.

[32] See, for example, *Esso Petroleum Co. Ltd v Harpers Garage (Stourport) Ltd* (1968) and *Texaco v Mulberry Filling Station* (1972).

[33] Much of the sting has been removed from the rule against restraint of trade as a result of the wealth of competition law legislation: see, for example, the Treaty on the Functioning of the European Union, Art. 101; *Courage (Ltd) v Crehan* (2001); N. Hopkins (1989) 49 NILQ 202.

[34] Here, a clause granting to the mortgagee an option to purchase 40 per cent of stock was held to undermine the mortgagor's equitable right to redeem.

[35] *Toomes v Conset* (1745).

question of substance and not one of form, and is rooted in the 'reality' of the agreement.[36] Identifying the true substance and reality of an agreement may not always be an easy task, however. It may, for example, be insufficient that the mortgage and option are contained within separate documents if this reflects mere artifice or a contrivance. In essence, it is only where the mortgage and options are truly independent of one another that the agreements will each be enforceable: *Jones v Morgan*.

13.4.1.4 Any term in the mortgage conferring collateral advantages on the mortgagee above and beyond repayment of the loan will be void

Terms conferring advantages on the mortgagee which go above and beyond the right to repayment of the loan may be void as being inconsistent with the mortgagor's right to redeem. These 'collateral advantages' are additional benefits provided to the lender by the mortgagor and might include the mortgagor undertaking further obligations such as promising to provide favourable treatment to the mortgagee's business or to buy only the mortgagee's goods.[37] Not every collateral advantage clause will fail, however.[38] In *Kreglinger*, the House of Lords emphasized that freedom of contract and equality of bargaining position between the parties would be relevant factors particularly in a commercial context.

KEY CASE *Kreglinger v New Patagonia Meat & Cold Storage Co. Ltd* (1914)

Facts: Kreglinger granted a loan to New Patagonia which was secured by means of a charge over all of the business' assets (a floating charge). Under the terms of the loan, New Patagonia was permitted to repay early. In addition, Kreglinger was provided a right of first refusal as to sheepskins made available for sale by New Patagonia. This right was to last for five years and guaranteed Kreglinger best market rate for the skins.

Legal issue: When the mortgagor, New Patagonia, subsequently repaid the loan early, the matter came before the court as to whether it was obliged to honour the right of first refusal granted to the mortgagee, Kreglinger.

Judgment: In the view of the House of Lords, the collateral advantage clause was valid and enforceable and the mortgagor could not escape the negotiated term. Lord Parker explained the approach of the court as follows:

> My Lords ... there is now no rule in equity which precludes a mortgagee, whether the mortgage be made upon the occasion of a loan or otherwise, from stipulating for any collateral advantage, provided such collateral advantage is *not either* (1) unfair and unconscionable, or (2) in the nature of a penalty clogging the equity of redemption, or (3) inconsistent with or repugnant to the contractual and equitable right to redeem.

The collateral advantage clause was not, in substance, a fetter on the exercise of the mortgagor's right to redeem but was in the nature of a collateral bargain negotiated by the parties in an equal bargaining position and at arm's length.

---

[36] *Reeve v Lisle* (1902).

[37] Many of the decided cases arise in the brewery, oil, or petrol industries—see *Noakes v Rice* (1901) and *Bradley v Carritt* (1903)—but are also observed in the commercial world of lending: see, for example, the recent Payment Protection Insurance ('PPI') scandal.

[38] See the change of approach of the court in cases beginning with *Biggs v Hoddinott* (1898) and *Santley*.

Post-*Kreglinger*, the court will therefore look to the substance and true character of the transaction and the bargaining position of the parties, and not simply its form, to consider whether the collateral advantage is genuinely 'collateral' to the mortgage and whether the term is unconscionable and repugnant to the equitable right to redeem.

13.4.1.5 Any term in the mortgage which is deemed to be oppressive or otherwise unconscionable will be struck out

Where a term is deemed oppressive or unconscionable, the court can, in its discretion, strike down either that single clause or the entire mortgage.[39] The test of what constitutes an oppressive or otherwise unconscionable term is a strict one. Mere unreasonableness will not suffice: *Multiservice Bookbinding v Marden*.

KEY CASE *Multiservice Bookbinding v Marden* (1979)

Facts: In 1966, Marden, a private individual, loaned £36,000 to Multiservice, secured by way of a mortgage on business premises. Clause 6 of the mortgage agreement linked repayment of the loan to the Swiss franc which, at that time, was worth just under 10p, with the aim of protecting against fluctuations in the exchange rate of the pound. In addition, the mortgage could not be redeemed for a period of ten years and interest was fixed at 2 per cent above the bank rate. When Multiservice wished to redeem the mortgage in 1976, the value of the Swiss franc had risen to around 25p, thereby trebling the sums owed by Multiservice on redemption to £133,000.

Legal issue: Could Multiservice avoid the effects of Clause 6 by arguing that it was (1) contrary to public policy, and/or (2) it was unconscionable and a clog and fetter on Multiservice's equitable right to redeem?

Judgment: The High Court held that the clause was neither contrary to public policy nor a clog on the equitable right of redemption. Browne-Wilkinson J explained that:

> to be free from the necessity to comply with all the terms of the mortgage, the claimants must show that the bargain, or some of its terms, was unfair and unconscionable: it is not enough to show that, in the eyes of the court, it was unreasonable. In my judgment a bargain cannot be unfair and unconscionable unless one of the parties to it has imposed the objectionable terms in a morally reprehensible manner, that is to say, in a way which affects his conscience.

Whilst this contract may have been unreasonable, it was not oppressive or unconscionable and the court would not rewrite an improvident contract. In particular, the court emphasized the equal bargaining position of the parties and that the mortgagor had taken the benefit of independent legal advice. Clause 6 was valid and enforceable.

To be oppressive or unconscionable, a term must therefore be 'imposed in a morally reprehensible manner' such that the mortgagee's conscience is affected and the court will have regard to: the equality of arms between the parties, whether the mortgagor could have refused to accept the deal, and whether the mortgagor received independent legal advice prior to granting the mortgage. If advice has been obtained, it will be difficult to argue that

---

[39] There is now also additional, statutory protection for mortgagors from unfair terms on which see sections 13.4.2 and 13.4.3.

the terms were oppressive or unconscionable.[40] In *Cityland and Property Holdings Ltd v Dabrah* (1968), a punitive interest rate in a case where there was no equality of arms between the parties was reduced to a reasonable rate. In *Paragon Finance v Nash* (2001), the court held that in circumstances where a mortgagee was permitted to increase the interest rate at its discretion, the mortgagee was subject to an implied term that the interest would not be 'set dishonestly, for an improper purpose, capriciously or arbitrarily'.[41]

So do we still need the rule against clogs and fetters? The rule developed during the nineteenth century and, arguably, had its high-water mark in the early twentieth century when it seemed that any clog or fetter on the mortgagor's right to redeem would be struck down. To continue the water metaphor, it could be said that the principle has been significantly watered down in more modern times particularly in commercial contexts where the parties are of equal bargaining power and have expressly and freely negotiated the terms of any agreement. There has been much criticism of its continued role by Thompson,[42] Duncan and Wilmott,[43] and others[44] who argue the principle has caused more problems than it has solved. According to Lord Phillips in *Jones v Morgan*:[45]

> [The] doctrine of a clog on the equity of redemption is . . . an appendix to our law which no longer serves a useful purpose and would be better excised.

This view was shared by the Law Commission in the early 1990s when, in its Report No. 204, it noted:[46]

> [T]here is some uncertainty over precisely which terms are not likely to be regarded as falling foul of the principle, and that, because it evolved over the nineteenth and early twentieth centuries in a very different commercial environment, the detailed rules are not always appropriate to modern conditions.

The Law Commission recommended replacement of the principle of clogs and fetters with a 'single new statutory jurisdiction' applicable to all mortgages, under which the court would be endowed with a discretion to alter or vary any term in a mortgage contract that would result in the mortgagee enjoying rights 'substantially greater than or different from those necessary to make the property available as security' or that would otherwise be unconscionable.[47] Parliament has not adopted the recommendations and for now, at least, the rule against clogs and fetters staggers on.

Watt goes even further arguing that the time has come to abandon the equity of redemption altogether:[48]

> Parliament has killed off the mortgage by conveyance and reconveyance of a fee simple, yet the courts have so far failed to acknowledge that the notion of the equity of redemption should

---

[40] *Jones v Morgan*.

[41] In *Paragon Finance v Pender* (2005), however, the court held that this implied term would not be breached if the mortgagee could point to a genuine, commercial justification for the interest rate rise.

[42] M. Thompson, 'Do We Really Need Clogs?' [2001] Conv 502.

[43] W. B. Duncan and L. Wilmott, 'Clogging the Equity of Redemption: An Outmoded Concept' (2002) 2 QUTLJJ 35.

[44] See, for example, A. Berg, 'Clogs on the Equity of Redemption or Chaining an Unruly Dog' (2002) JBL (September) 335.

[45] *Jones v Morgan*, D39.   [46] Law Commission Report No. 204, [8.2].   [47] Ibid., [8.4].

[48] Watt, 'The Lie of the Land: Mortgage Law as Legal Fiction'. See also D. Sugarman and R. Warrington, 'Telling Stories: Rights and Wrongs of the Equity of Redemption' in J. W. Harris (ed.), *Property Problems: From Genes to Pension Funds* (London/Boston: Kluwer Law International, 1997).

have died with it. They have failed to acknowledge that land subject to a registered charge is not 'redeemed' as was land conveyed under the classic form of mortgage rather the charge is simple discharged from the land upon repayment of the debt.

13.4.2 Protection from unfair creditor–debtor relationships

A mortgage is self-evidently a creditor–debtor relationship. Statutory protections shielding cash-strapped borrowers from ruthless money-lenders may therefore apply. One example is s. 140A of the Consumer Credit Act 1974, inserted by ss. 19 and 20 of the Consumer Credit Act 2006, which empowers the court to intervene if it finds the creditor–debtor relationship arising from a credit agreement to be unfair to the debtor.[49]

13.4.3 Protection under the Financial Services and Markets Act 2000

For mortgages granted on or after 31 October 2004, the protective regime under the Financial Services and Markets Act 2000 (FSMA 2000) will, in the majority of cases, also apply. Under the FSMA 2000, those providing 'regulated mortgage contracts' must ensure fair treatment and transparency to 'consumers'.[50] If any of the codes of practice are breached, the offending mortgagee can be required to pay compensation to the injured party.[51]

13.4.4 Powers of the mortgagor to claim possession, grant leases, and seek an order for sale

In addition to the rights already outlined in this section, the mortgagor also enjoys certain 'powers' under the mortgage which can be enforced by seeking an order of the court:

- The power to claim possession of the mortgaged property provided that no claim to possession has been made by the mortgagee: s. 98 of the LPA 1925.
- The power to grant a lease over the mortgaged property provided that it is not inconsistent with the terms of the mortgage: s. 99 of the LPA 1925.[52]
- The power to seek an order for sale of the mortgaged property: s. 91 of the LPA 1925.

It is important to note regarding this last power that, under s. 91, the mortgagor can seek an order for sale even if this is not desired by the mortgagee. Section 91 of the LPA 1925 gives the court the power to order sale and therefore to sanction sale even in cases of negative equity.[53] This power is therefore highly significant for the mortgagor, particularly if the mortgagor fears spiralling debt which they will be unable to pay. We consider s. 91 in greater detail in section 13.5.3.4 but it is worth noting that the 'unfettered discretion'[54]

---

[49] An analysis of these provisions is beyond the scope of this book, see *Woodroffe & Lowe's Consumer Law and Practice* (London: Sweet & Maxwell, 2016).

[50] Again, this regime is beyond the scope of this book, see *Blackstone's Guide to the Financial Services and Markets Act 2000*, 2nd edn (Oxford: Oxford University Press, 2010).

[51] Under FSMA 2000, s. 150.   [52] *Leeds Permanent Building Society v Famini* (1998).

[53] *Palk v Mortgage Services Funding plc* (1993); negative equity arises where the market value of the property has fallen below the outstanding amount of the mortgage secured against it.

[54] Ibid.

enjoyed by the court to order sale under this provision might be seen as undermining the value of the mortgagee's security or the freedom of the parties to contract.[55] Note the relationship between s. 91 of the LPA and s. 14 of TOLATA 1996, which we explored in Chapter 5. Section 91 permits applications for sale from 'any person entitled to redeem mortgaged property' and applies where there is *one mortgagor*. Where there is more than one, there will be co-ownership which necessarily operates under a trust of land and so applications for sale of mortgaged property will be brought under s. 14 of TOLATA 1996.

13.4.5 Setting aside a mortgage on the grounds of undue influence

In the previous sections, we considered the rights and powers enjoyed by a mortgagor. Here, we examine the effect of undue influence on a mortgage. Many of the principles in this area will be familiar to you from the law of contract. Put simply, where there is evidence that a mortgage has been procured as a result of undue influence, that mortgage may be set aside.

Let's take the most common example: imagine a family home shared by a husband and wife. The husband and wife hold both the legal and equitable title to the property in joint names. The husband seeks a loan secured against the family home by way of mortgage in order to finance a business venture. The consent of the wife will be required as she is a legal and equitable owner of the home. In order to procure the wife's consent to the mortgage, the husband exerts pressure on her. Subsequently, the husband defaults on repayments for the mortgage and the mortgagee seeks to enforce its interest by seeking an order of the court that the family home be sold. If it is shown that the wife was unduly influenced by her husband to grant the mortgage and that the undue influence is attributable to the mortgagee, the mortgage may potentially be set aside in its entirety, or in part, even though the undue influence was not exerted by the mortgagee itself.

In the mortgages context, it is routinely a wife (though could, of course, be a husband, civil or cohabiting partner) who claims that her spouse has exerted undue pressure on her to enter the mortgage and that, consequently, the mortgage lender is not entitled to enforce its security interest. The key question is whether the mortgagee has notice of the undue influence as was explained by the House of Lords explained in *Barclays Bank plc v O'Brien* (1994).

13.4.5.1 Establishing undue influence

Lord Hobhouse in the leading case of *Royal Bank of Scotland v Etridge (No. 2)* (2001) identified three questions that have to be answered in determining whether undue influence exists so as to vitiate a mortgage. There are therefore three distinct steps to any undue influence analysis: see Figure 13.3.

We will consider each step in turn.

---

[55] See *National Westminster Bank v Hunter* (2011) where the court refused to exercise its power to order sale under s. 91 of the LPA 1925 on the grounds that to do so would be to disturb the arrangements made for sale of the mortgaged property.

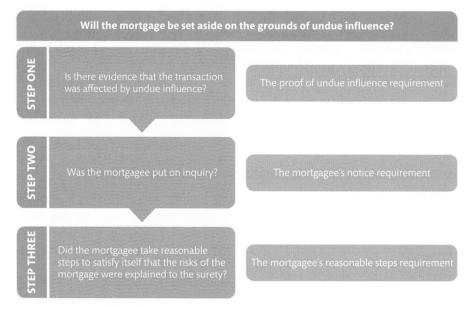

Figure 13.3 When a mortgage will be set aside on the grounds of undue influence

Step one: The proof of undue influence requirement

The claimant (i.e. the person alleging undue pressure has been exerted) must prove undue influence has tainted the mortgage transaction. The claimant can prove undue influence in two ways:

1. actual undue influence, or

2. presumed undue influence.

When claiming actual undue influence, the claimant must positively *prove* that the mortgage was procured by undue influence. This requires the claimant to point to evidence drawn from the particular facts of the case to establish that she was put under pressure either physical, or psychological to consent to the mortgage with the result that the claimant was not exercising her own independent will or free choice. This might range from evidence that a husband physically forced the claimant to consent by threatening violence, relationship breakdown, or otherwise intimated or repeatedly pestered the claimant so that she felt she had no option but to consent. Whatever evidence is adduced, the influence demonstrated must be 'actual' and 'undue'. A claim to undue influence will fail if there is evidence that the claimant was fully aware of the mortgage but subsequently regretted consenting: *Bank of Scotland v Bennett* (1998).

A more precise and comprehensive definition of actual undue influence, as noted by Lord Nicholls in *Etridge*, is impossible:[56]

> The law will investigate the manner in which the intention to enter into the transaction was secured: if the intention was produced by an unacceptable means, the law will not permit the

---

[56] *Etridge*, 794–5.

transaction to stand. The means used is regarded as an exercise of improper or 'undue' influence, and hence unacceptable, whenever the consent thus procured ought not fairly to be treated as the expression of a person's free will. It is impossible to be more precise or definitive. The circumstances in which one person acquires influence over another, and the manner in which influence may be exercised, vary too widely to permit of any more specific criterion.

As Lord Nicholls indicates, the key element is demonstrating that the claimant was not exercising free will in consenting to the mortgage. In *Stevens v Newey* (2005), the Court of Appeal explained that a mortgage was only entered into with consent if it could be said that the claimant knew not only what she was doing but also why she was doing it. In *BCCI v Aboody* (1991) the court had indicated that it required the claimant to prove that she had suffered manifest disadvantage as a result of the transaction. This requirement no longer applies to 'actual undue influence'.[57]

In certain circumstances, undue influence will be 'presumed'. As the court has clarified in *Etridge*[58] however, the expression 'presumed undue influence' is more accurately to be understood not as denoting any particular subspecies of undue influence but rather as a rebuttable, *evidential* presumption of undue influence which, if established, then shifts the burden to the alleged 'undue influencer' to prove that no undue influence was in fact exerted. There has, for some time, been debate as to precisely how this presumption operated. The Court of Appeal in *Aboody* established that undue influence could be proved according to the following classification:

- Class 1: By proof of actual undue influence.[59]
- Class 2A: Undue influence would be presumed where there existed a particular prescribed relationship: including that of parent–child, solicitor–client, doctor–patient.
- Class 2B: Undue influence would be presumed where there was evidence of a relationship of trust of confidence.

The *Aboody* classification was upheld and applied in the case of *O'Brien*. In *Etridge*, however, the House of Lords rejected this classification as unnecessarily rigid and mechanical and doubted the utility of subdividing class 2 into 2A and 2B. Lord Scott explained:[60]

In my respectful opinion [the decision in *O'Brien* as to classes 2A and 2B] at least in its application to the surety wife cases, has set the law on a wrong track. First, it seems to me to lose sight of the evidential and rebuttable character of the Class 2 presumption . . . [T]he presumption, if it arises on the facts of a particular case, is a tool to assist him or her in doing so. It shifts, for the moment, the onus of proof to the other side.

So, when will a presumption of undue influence arise? The House of Lords in *Etridge* engaged in an important and expansive reconsideration of the law of undue influence and, in particular, revisited the operation of the presumption. According to Lord Nicholls, the presumption of undue influence arises where two elements are satisfied:

1. where the relationship between the claimant and the alleged undue influencer is one in which the parties reposed trust and confidence in one another, and
2. where the transaction is not readily explicable by the relationship of the parties.

---

[57] *CIBC Mortgages v Pitt*; *Etridge*.   [58] See also *Turkey v Awadh* (2005).
[59] As discussed earlier in this section.   [60] *Etridge*, 841–2.

If one or both of these elements is not satisfied, the presumption of undue influence cannot operate and the claimant will only succeed in their action by proving *actual* undue influence. Where these two requirements are met, the evidential burden shifts to the defendant to prove that the claimant's consent to the mortgage was given freely. Certain categories of relationship, including doctor–patient,[61] parent–child,[62] solicitor–client,[63] spiritual advisor–devotee,[64] are irrefutably presumed to be relationships of trust and confidence. Where such a relationship is established all that is required is that the second element in Lord Nicholls' test be satisfied: a transaction calling for explanation. For all other relationships falling outside these recognized categories, the claimant must prove that a relationship of trust and confidence positively exists between the parties. Notable for its absence from this category of recognized relationships of trust and confidence is the relationship of husband–wife and same-sex spouses. In these relationships, the claimant must therefore expressly prove that a relationship of trust and confidence exists. Lord Nicholls in *Etridge* explained that:[65]

> There is nothing unusual or strange in a wife, from motives of affection or for other reasons, conferring substantial financial benefits on her husband. Although there is no presumption [of trust and confidence], the court will nevertheless note, as a matter of fact, the opportunities for abuse which flow from a wife's confidence in her husband.

Whilst no presumption exists, Lord Scott in *Etridge* noted that, in every case albeit subject to contrary evidence, he was prepared to regard a spousal relationship as one of trust and confidence with little difficulty:[66]

> For my part, I would assume in every case in which a wife and husband are living together that there is a reciprocal trust and confidence between them . . . I would not expect evidence to be necessary to establish the existence of trust and confidence. I would expect evidence to be necessary to demonstrate its absence.

In proving the existence of a relationship of trust and confidence, the court will look to the nature and length of the parties' relationship, the age of the parties, the character or personalities of each partner, any particular roles adopted by each partner, and cultural factors which might, for example, include distinct social or religious practices.[67] Whilst trust and confidence can arise in non-sexual, non-romantic relationships—for example, as between family members[68] and, exceptionally, even between employer and employee[69]—the court in *O'Brien* held that a finding of trust and confidence will most easily be reached in relationships involving 'sexual and emotional ties [which] provide a ready weapon for undue influence'.

It is fair to say that the second aspect, the requirement that the transaction is not readily explicable by the relationship between the parties, has caused the courts some difficulty. In *National Westminster Bank plc v Morgan* (1985), the House of Lords had held that the claimant was required to demonstrate that the transaction was to her 'manifest disadvantage' in that it offered no benefit to her. The courts began to regard any mortgage secured

---

[61] *Mitchell v Homfray* (1881).   [62] *Bainbrigge v Browne* (1881).   [63] *Wright v Carter* (1903).
[64] *Allcard v Skinner* (1887).   [65] *Etridge*, 797.   [66] Ibid., 799–800.
[67] This might include cultures in which women do not take the lead in financial matters.
[68] *Abbey National Bank plc v Stringer* (2006).   [69] *Credit Lyonnais v Burch* (1997).

against the family home to raise finance for a husband's business as being manifestly disadvantageous to a wife claimant. The result was a slew of undue influence cases. In *Etridge*, Lord Nicholls engaged in a close analysis of the 'manifest disadvantage' aspect and rejected this label:[70]

> This label has been causing difficulty . . . being understood and applied in a way which does not accord with the meaning intended by Lord Scarman, its originator [in *Morgan*]. In recent years, judge after judge has grappled with the baffling question whether a wife's guarantee of her husband's bank overdraft, together with a charge on her share of the matrimonial home, was a transaction manifestly to her disadvantage. In a narrow sense, such a transaction plainly ('manifestly') is disadvantageous to the wife. She undertakes a serious financial obligation, and in return she personally receives nothing. But that would be to take an unrealistically blinkered view . . . [I]n the case of husband and wife there are inherent reasons why such a transaction may well be for her benefit. Ordinarily, the fortunes of husband and wife are bound up together. If the husband's business is the source of the family income, the wife has a lively interest in doing what she can to support the business. A wife's affection and self-interest run hand-in-hand . . .
>
> Which, then, is the correct approach to adopt in deciding whether a transaction is disadvantageous to the wife: the narrow approach, or the wider approach? The answer is neither. The answer lies in discarding a label which gives rise to this sort of ambiguity . . . to adhere more directly to the test outlined by Lindley LJ in *Allcard v Skinner*.

The court in *Etridge* thus disapproved of the label of 'manifest disadvantage' and reinstated the test in *Allcard v Skinner* (1887) which considers whether the transaction entered into is 'readily explicable by the relationship' of the parties. In other words, as Lindley LJ explained in *Allcard*, the court is looking for a transaction which is:[71]

> not reasonably accounted for on the ground of friendship, relationship, charity, or other ordinary motives on which ordinary men act.

As Lord Nicholls explained in *Etridge*, the granting of a mortgage for the purposes of financing a husband's business endeavours may, in the particular relationship of the parties, be entirely explicable by reference to the relationship of the parties. Lord Nicholls explained that wives frequently enter similar transactions and may be enthusiastic about it or equally anxious. This is quite different from saying that these transaction call for explanation or are prima facie evidence of undue influence.

Lord Nicholls confirms that a wife consenting to the grant of a mortgage is indeed undertaking a serious financial obligation but she may equally acquire the benefit in so far as the loan may support the family home and husband's business which itself supports the upkeep of that home. Lord Nicholls expands on this position in identifying the 'obligation of candour and fairness' that exists in relationships of trust and confidence. Where this obligation is not discharged, said Lord Nicholls, the law would be defective not to recognize this. We see this obligation in action in the case of *Hewett v First Plus Financial Group plc* (2010). In *Hewett*, the Court of Appeal held that a husband's deliberate concealment of an extra-marital affair when urging his wife to consent to a mortgage over the family home was a breach of the parties' obligation of candour and fairness. The husband was found to have unduly influenced his wife.[72]

---

[70] *Etridge*, 842.   [71] *Allcard*, 185.   [72] See also *Royal Bank of Scotland plc v Chandra* (2010).

Clearly, in the circumstances, if the transaction is explicable by reference to the relationship of the parties, the presumption of undue influence will not arise. If, however, on the facts of the case, the transaction is not so explicable, the second of Lord Nicholls's requirements is met and the presumption of undue influence operates: *Turkey v Awadh* (2005). Before we turn to consider how this presumption can be rebutted, let us first consider some examples of presumed undue influence which fall outside the spousal context to illustrate the principles in action: *Abbey National Bank plc v Stringer* and *Awadh*.

KEY CASE *Abbey National Bank plc v Stringer* (2006)

Facts: A mother and son purchased property. The property was put into their joint names to enable the mother, who was 50 years old at the time, to obtain a mortgage. Some six years later, a second mortgage was granted to Abbey National Bank plc in order to finance the son's business venture. The mother, who could not read English, signed the relevant documentation, consenting to the grant of the second mortgage. The mortgage was not explained to her nor was it read to her. The son subsequently defaulted on the mortgage payments and Abbey National Bank plc sought possession of the property to satisfy its debt.

Legal issue: Had the mother been unduly influenced by the son to consent to the second mortgage?

Judgment: At first instance, the trial judge held that the mother's consent had been procured by the undue influence of her son. The court found that there was evidence of undue influence, either actual or presumed. The mortgage was therefore unenforceable against the mother. The judge held that there was no evidence that the son was to enjoy a beneficial interest in the property and therefore there was no interest against which the bank could assert an equitable mortgage. Abbey National Bank plc appealed.

In the Court of Appeal, Abbey National Bank plc argued:

1. The judge had made an error in law in finding that the son had no beneficial interest in the property.

2. There was no evidence of a relationship of trust and confidence between the mother and her son.

3. There was no evidence of actual undue influence.

4. Undue influence could not be presumed as the transaction was explicable on the basis of the parties' relationship in that the transaction represented nothing more than an act motivated by a mother's generosity.

The Court of Appeal dismissed the bank's appeal holding the judge had been justified in holding that, on the facts, the mother was to enjoy the entire beneficial interest in the property. The judge had been right to construe the relationship between the mother and son as one of trust and confidence. The transaction could not be explained simply by 'mother's generosity'. Lloyd LJ noted:

> The transaction involved putting her home at risk . . . in relation to a new business of which she knew nothing and from which she would obtain no benefit . . . she had no idea that by signing it she was putting her property up as security.

The mother was vulnerable as a result of her age and her lack of English. The son had particular influence over her as to financial matters. The presumption of undue influence arose and had not been rebutted. There was sufficient evidence that the mother would not have consented to the mortgage had she been aware of its nature and implications.

KEY CASE *Turkey v Awadh* (2005)

Facts: A father entered into a tenancy agreement with his daughter and son-in-law, under which the daughter and her partner rented a house owned by the father. The father agreed with the couple that he would pay the mortgage on the house if they agreed to grant a long leasehold interest in the house to him. The father advanced the money and cleared the mortgage and brought court proceedings to enforce the agreement.

Legal issue: Could the daughter succeed in arguing that the agreement be set aside on the grounds of undue influence?

Judgment: The trial judge held that the relationship between the parties was one of trust and confidence but that the transaction could be readily explicable by the relationship between the parties. No presumption of undue influence arose. The daughter and son-in-law appealed.

In the Court of Appeal, the appeal failed. The Court of Appeal held that the trial judge had been entirely justified in finding that the transaction was explicable by the relationship of the parties. While there was evidence that the daughter did rely on her father for financial advice and guidance, Buxton LJ held that it was apt for the court to look at 'what [the transaction] was trying to achieve for the parties'. Chadwick LJ confirmed that the transaction was not one calling for an explanation as:

1. The couple found themselves in financial difficulties and the transaction offered speedy 'cash in hand'; and

2. The transaction had 'important family elements in it' including the fact that 'nothing in real terms would change as far as use of the property was concerned'.

The presumption of undue influence did not therefore arise. The transaction was readily explicable according to 'the ordinary motives of the people concerned in the relationships in which they found themselves'.

The presumption of undue influence is not absolute and can be rebutted by evidence that the claimant (alleged victim of undue influence) acted freely and with independence in consenting to the grant of the mortgage.

KEY CASE *Royal Bank of Scotland v Etridge (No. 2)* (2001)

Facts: The case concerned a number of conjoined appeals by banks seeking possession of family homes in circumstances where a wife had consented to grant a mortgage in order to secure the business debts of the husband on those properties. The wives sought to argue that their signatures had been procured by undue influence and therefore the banks were not entitled to sale of the properties. The House of Lords offered a comprehensive review of the law on undue influence and restated or reframed some of the key principles. For present purposes, we consider the particular facts of Mr and Mrs Etridge. In 1987, a house was purchased and placed into Mrs Etridge's sole name. Subsequently, Mrs Etridge granted to the Royal Bank of Scotland a mortgage in the sum of £100,000 to secure an overdraft facility enjoyed by Mr Etridge linked to his business. The house was sold and a larger property purchased subject to a further mortgage of £100,000. Following default on the mortgage payments, the bank sought sale of the family home. Mrs Etridge claimed that the mortgages had been procured by undue influence exerted by Mr Etridge.

Legal issue: Could Mrs Etridge provide evidence of actual undue influence or, alternatively, did a presumption of undue influence arise?

→

→

Judgment: The House of Lords held that Mrs Etridge's appeal should be dismissed. Lord Scott noted:

> [Mr and Mrs Etridge's] relationship was, as one would expect of a married couple living together with the family income being provided by the husband's business activities and with financial decisions affecting the family being taken by the husband, a relationship of trust and confidence by her in him. But there was no evidence of abuse by Mr Etridge of that relationship, or of any bullying of Mrs Etridge in order to persuade her to support his decisions. Both the [mortgage] transactions under attack had been entered into in part in order to provide finance for the purchase of The Old Rectory and in part to obtain financial support for Mr Etridge in his business enterprises. Both had elements disadvantageous to her and elements that were to her advantage. To draw a distinction between the two charges as to inferences of undue influence that might be drawn was, in my opinion, unreal. In my view, the judge's conclusion that there had been no undue influence was well justified on the evidence. That conclusion should have been an end of the case.

In all the circumstances, there was no evidence from which either actual or presumed undue influence could arise. Mrs Etridge's appeal therefore failed.

The court in *Etridge* went on to discuss more generally how the presumption of undue influence can be rebutted. Of particular importance is the receipt of independent legal advice before agreeing to the grant of the mortgage. It is important to recognize, however, that the fact that legal advice is provided, does not operate to automatically rebut the presumption. This point was made plain by the Court of Appeal in *Pesticcio v Huet* (2004) which emphasized that only 'relevant and effective' independent advice informing the surety of the consequences of her actions will suffice. Lord Nicholls in *Etridge* identified that key factors included whether the legal advice: was competent; was impartial; was provided in an environment free from the pressure of the alleged wrongdoer; and was such that the consequences and risks of the mortgage were fully explored and explained to the alleged victim of undue influence. It is clear that advice given by members of the claimant's wider family, whilst a factor for the court to consider, will carry far less weight than independent legal advice.[73]

In summary the presumption of undue influence will be rebutted where there is evidence that the decision to grant the mortgage was that of the alleged victim, fully informed of the implications and exercised freely. Figure 13.4 provides an overview of the operation of the presumption of undue influence.

Step two: The mortgagee's notice requirement

Where there is no agency relationship between the mortgagee and the alleged undue influencer, the only way that the mortgagee will be affected by any undue influence is if that lender is taken to have notice of the undue influence. As Lord Browne-Wilkinson explained in *O'Brien*:[74]

> The doctrine of notice lies at the heart of equity . . . where a wife has agreed to stand surety for her husband's debts as a result of undue influence or misrepresentation, the [mortgagee] will take subject to the wife's equity to set aside the transaction if the circumstances are such as to put the [mortgagee] on inquiry as to the circumstances which she agreed to stand surety.

---

[73] See *Smith v Cooper* (2010): a case concerning advice given by the claimant's father.   [74] *O'Brien*, 195.

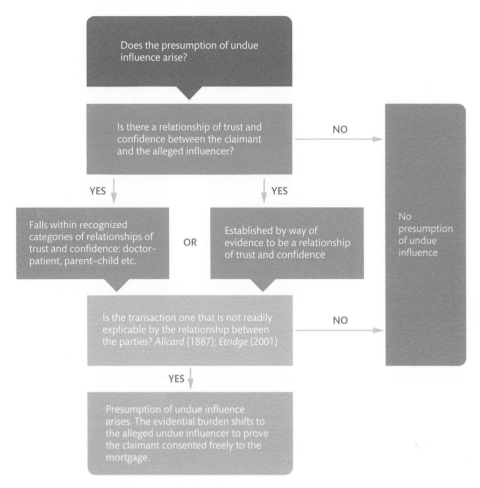

Figure 13.4 When the presumption of undue influence arises

The crucial question is: when will a mortgagee be 'put on inquiry' that the alleged influencer may be exerting undue pressure on the victim? According to the House of Lords in *Etridge*, a mortgagee will be 'put on inquiry in every case' where:

1. one party provides security for the debts of another, and

2. the relationship between the surety and the debtor is non-commercial.

A series of important points flow from this. A mortgagee will only be 'put on inquiry' where it is actually aware that the wife is acting as surety for her husband's debt: *Mortgage Business plc v Green* (2013). Further, a mortgagee will *not* be 'put on inquiry' where the loan is advanced to the husband and wife jointly for their mutual benefit: *Etridge*; *CIBC Mortgages plc v Pitt*. The bank *will* be put on inquiry where the mortgagee is advanced to the husband and wife jointly if it is aware that the loan is for the sole use of or is to be put to the purposes of just one party.

> **KEY CASE** *CIBC v Pitt* (1993)
>
> Facts: A husband and wife were the owners of a property which they occupied as a family home. The property was valued at £270,000 and there was an outstanding mortgage over the property of just under £17,000. The husband was keen to make business investments in stocks and shares, reportedly in a bid to raise the couple's standard of living. He exerted pressure on the wife until she agreed to consent to grant a second mortgage to CIBC plc in the sum of £150,000 secured on the family home. The wife did not read the legal documentation surrounding the charge, which stated that the second mortgage was sought for the purposes of purchasing a second property as a holiday home for the couple. The husband purchased shares but, as a result of the stock market crash of 1987, fell into arrears on the mortgage payments. CIBC brought proceedings seeking possession and sale of the family home.
>
> Legal issue: Was the wife able to raise the husband's undue influence as a defence to CIBC's possession claim?
>
> Judgment: At first instance and in the Court of Appeal, the wife's defence of undue influence failed. The wife appealed to the House of Lords where her appeal was dismissed. The court held that the alleged influencer (the husband) was not acting as the bank's agent and, moreover, the bank had no notice (actual or constructive) of the undue influence and was therefore not 'put on inquiry' as there was nothing to alert the bank that the mortgage loan advanced was anything other than for the mutual benefit of *both* parties. The bank was entitled to seek possession of the property.

Whether a mortgagee is 'put on inquiry' is treated differently if the relationship between the parties is a commercial one. As Lord Nicholls explained:[75]

> Different considerations apply where the relationship between the debtor and guarantor is commercial, as where a guarantor is being paid a fee, or a company is guaranteeing the debts of another company in the same group. Those engaged in business can be regarded as capable of looking after themselves and understanding the risks involved in the giving of guarantees.

Step three: The mortgagee's reasonable steps requirement

Simply because the mortgagee is 'put on inquiry' does not mean that the mortgage will be set aside. A mortgagee can avoid the mortgage being set aside by taking reasonable steps to bring home to the guarantor the risks she is running by standing surety for another's debts. In *Etridge*, the court reframed the reasonable steps a mortgagee should take and underlined that the guiding principle behind these steps was that the lender be concerned to minimize the risk that undue influence might have tainted the mortgage rather than as a means of discovery of any particular instance of undue influence.

Lord Nicholls laid down a series of 'reasonable steps'[76] to be taken by a mortgagee to avoid the setting aside of the mortgage: see Figure 13.5. The central pillar of the steps is the requirement that the wife (or other party standing surety) takes independent legal advice and that the lender receives written confirmation from the solicitor providing that advice that the nature and consequences of the transaction have been explained. The mortgagee must provide the solicitor with relevant financial information and any suspicions it may

---

[75] *Etridge*, 814.   [76] Sometimes referred to as 'the *Etridge* Protocol'.

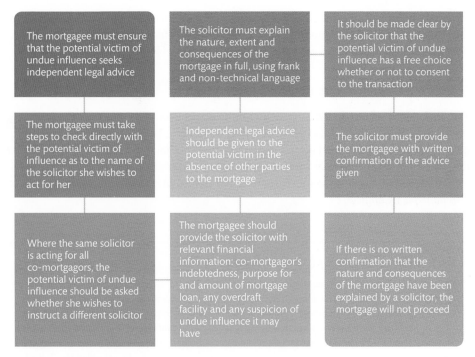

The mortgagee must ensure that the potential victim of undue influence seeks independent legal advice

The solicitor must explain the nature, extent and consequences of the mortgage in full, using frank and non-technical language

It should be made clear by the solicitor that the potential victim of undue influence has a free choice whether or not to consent to the transaction

The mortgagee must take steps to check directly with the potential victim of influence as to the name of the solicitor she wishes to act for her

Independent legal advice should be given to the potential victim in the absence of other parties to the mortgage

The solicitor must provide the mortgagee with written confirmation of the advice given

Where the same solicitor is acting for all co-mortgagors, the potential victim of undue influence should be asked whether she wishes to instruct a different solicitor

The mortgagee should provide the solicitor with relevant financial information: co-mortgagor's indebtedness, purpose for and amount of mortgage loan, any overdraft facility and any suspicion of undue influence it may have

If there is no written confirmation that the nature and consequences of the mortgage have been explained by a solicitor, the mortgage will not proceed

Figure 13.5 The *Etridge* 'reasonable steps' protocol

have as to any potential undue pressure exerted. Lord Scott in *Etridge* explained that, provided the mortgagee receives written confirmation that the wife has received legal advice, the lender is protected even if that advice was negligent. Any action by the wife in negligence will be against the solicitor and not the lender.[77]

The court in *Etridge* established that there was no requirement that a solicitor offering legal advice be acting for the wife alone. Lord Nicholls held that the issue of representation was to be left to each individual solicitor to decide as a matter of professional judgment:[78]

[I]n every case the solicitor must consider carefully whether there is any conflict of duty and interest and, more widely, whether it would be in the best interests of the wife for [the solicitor] to accept instructions from her . . . if at any stage the solicitor becomes concerned that there is a real risk that other interests or duties may inhibit his advice to the wife he must cease to act for her.

As to the substance of the advice that should be given by the solicitor, it should be delivered at a face-to-face meeting in the absence of any potential undue influencer, in non-technical language, explaining the nature and consequences of any documentation to be signed and, in particular, that the surety could lose her home. It should be underlined to the surety that it is her choice alone as to whether to consent. Finally, the solicitor should check whether

---

[77] Unless the mortgagee was aware of the inadequacy of the legal advice. For a case of solicitor negligence, see *Padden v Bevan Ashford* (2012).

[78] *Etridge*, 810.

the surety is content to proceed with the transaction and whether she gives authority for the solicitor to write to the mortgagee to confirm that the nature and risks of the transaction have been explained.

13.4.5.2 Effect of undue influence on the mortgage

The final aspect of our analysis on undue influence concerns its effect on the mortgage transaction. Where there is: (1) proof of undue influence; (2) the mortgagee is 'put on inquiry', and (3) has failed the take the reasonable steps outlined in Figure 13.5 to minimize the risk of undue influence, the mortgage may be set aside *in its entirety* even if there is evidence that certain parts of the mortgage were not tainted or procured by undue influence: *TSB Bank plc v Camfield*.

KEY CASE *TSB Bank plc v Camfield* (1995)

Facts: The Camfields were husband and wife and had agreed to grant a legal mortgage over their family home as security for loan facilities offered by the claimant, TSB Bank plc, to finance Mr Camfield's business endeavours. Mrs Camfield was misled into consenting to the grant of the mortgage after Mr Camfield had represented to her that her liability under the mortgage was limited to £15,000. The bank had failed to ensure that Mrs Camfield received independent legal advice regarding the nature and consequences of the mortgage. In reality, Mrs Camfield's liability was unlimited. TSB advanced various sums of money to Mr Camfield's business. When Mr Camfield's business failed, the bank brought possession proceedings against the family home and sought repayment of the sums advanced.

Legal issue: Could TSB enforce its security against Mrs Camfield to the sum of £15,000, that being the level of her anticipated liability under the mortgage? Alternatively, was the mortgage to be set aside in its entirety as against Mrs Camfield?

Judgment: The trial judge gave judgment in favour of TSB in the sum of £47,315 against the husband and in the sum of £15,000 as against Mrs Camfield. The judge made an order for possession over the family home subject to payment in full of the sums due within six months. The Camfields appealed.

In the Court of Appeal, the Camfields' appeal was allowed. Nourse LJ held that Mrs Camfield was entitled, on the basis of misrepresentation, to have the mortgage set aside. There was no authority known to the court to suggest that the mortgage could be partially enforced by the mortgagee against Mrs Camfield.

In spite of the decision in *Camfield*, there is also authority that, alternatively if, and so far as it is possible, to isolate a particular part or parts of a mortgage as being tainted by undue influence, the court may sever that tainted part, leaving the remaining untainted part of the mortgage intact: *Barclays Bank v Caplan* (1998). Whether the mortgage is set aside in its entirety (*Camfield*) or, alternatively, in part (*Caplan*) depends on the particular circumstances of the case before the court. Additionally, where the victim of undue influence has gained a benefit from the mortgage transaction, that party may only be entitled to have the mortgage set aside against her if restitution is made for the benefit received: *Dunbar Bank v Nadeem*.

KEY CASE *Dunbar Bank v Nadeem* (1998)

Facts: Mr and Mrs Nadeem entered a joint loan facility with Dunbar Bank for the purchase of a long lease of their family home in their joint names and granted a charge over the property as security for the loan. As a result, Mrs Nadeem gained a beneficial interest in the property for the first time. The loan was to cover Mr Nadeem's personal debts to the bank. Mr Nadeem defaulted on his loan repayments and Dunbar Bank brought possession proceedings over the property. Mrs Nadeem counterclaimed that the mortgage should be set aside on the grounds of undue influence.

Legal issue: The issue for the court was how far the mortgage could be set aside in circumstances where the victim of undue influence had received a personal benefit under the mortgage transaction.

Judgment: The trial judge held that Mrs Nadeem was able to establish presumed undue influence of which the bank had notice. However, the judge concluded that if the mortgage were to be set aside in its entirety, this would result in Mrs Nadeem being unjustly enriched as she had acquired a beneficial interest in the house as a result of the mortgage transaction for which she had contributed nothing financially. The judge therefore ordered that the mortgage would only be set aside on the proviso that Mrs Nadeem pay the bank £105,000 which represented 50 per cent of the money advanced for acquisition of the lease (plus interest). Mrs Nadeem appealed and the Bank cross-appealed arguing that the presumption of undue influence did not arise.

In the Court of Appeal, Mrs Nadeem's appeal failed, the Bank's cross-appeal was allowed and an order for possession was made. The Court of Appeal held that Mrs Nadeem was not able to demonstrate actual or presumed undue influence. Even in the event that Mrs Nadeem could prove undue influence, the judge at first instance had erred in holding that the setting aside of the mortgage was conditional on the repayment of 50 per cent of the monies advanced by the bank. Rather, Mrs Nadeem should have been required to restore her beneficial interest to her husband as her unjust enrichment related to her interest in the property and not in the money. Had Mrs Nadeem restored her beneficial interest to her husband, her personal liability would have been extinguished and the bank would have enjoyed a legal charge over the entire property.

As an alternative to the approaches taken in *Camfield*, *Caplan* and *Nadeem*, where there is a joint legal mortgage and that mortgage is set aside on the basis of undue influence, there may still be an effective, equitable mortgage of the undue influencer's equitable interest as a result of s. 63(1) of the LPA 1925. This important development was explained in the case of *First National Bank plc v Achampong*.

KEY CASE *First National Bank plc v Achampong* (2003)

Facts: The Achampongs, a married couple, granted a mortgage in favour of First National Bank plc against their family home, which was held in joint names. The mortgage was granted as security for a loan of £51,500 for the purpose of financing a family member's business venture. When mortgage repayments were not made, the bank issued possession proceedings. Mrs Achampong claimed that the mortgage should be set aside on the grounds of undue influence exerted on her by Mr Achampong.

Legal issue: Could Mrs Achampong make out her case of undue influence and, if so, what was the effect of this on Mr Achampong?

→

> →
>
> Judgment: At first instance, the court held that the entire mortgage be set aside on the basis of undue influence. First National Bank appealed. In the Court of Appeal, the bank advanced two grounds of appeal:
>
> 1. That it was unaffected by notice of any undue influence as Mrs Achampong had received independent legal advice, and/or
>
> 2. Under s. 63(1) of the LPA 1925, the bank enjoyed an equitable charge over Mr Achampong's beneficial interest in the property and it was entitled to an order for sale of the property under ss. 14 and 15 of TOLATA 1996.
>
> The Court of Appeal rejected the bank's first ground of appeal. It was quite clear that the reasonable steps outlined in *Etridge*, particularly as to independent legal advice, had not been followed. The bank succeeded on its second ground, however. According to the court, the effect of s. 63(1) of the 1925 Act was that an equitable charge arose in the bank's favour over Mr Achampong's beneficial half share of the property, severing the joint tenancy. Blackburne J explained:
>
>> In my judgment the legal charge, although ineffective as against Mrs Achampong, was apt to achieve two things: first, to create an equitable charge in the bank's favour over Mr Achampong's beneficial share in the property to secure, so far as the share was able, the bank's advance; and, second, as a consequence of the first and assuming that the Achampongs did not already hold as beneficial tenants in common, a severance of the beneficial joint tenancy subsisting in relation to the property.
>
> The court held that the bank was entitled under ss. 14 and 15 of TOLATA 1996 for an order for sale of the mortgaged property.

In summary, *Achampong* works as follows: where there is a joint legal mortgage, the mortgage will be set aside on the grounds of undue influence allowing the victim to escape liability, however, s. 63 of the LPA 1925 has the effect of severing the beneficial joint tenancy, giving rise to an equitable mortgage of the wrongdoer's equitable interest. This entitles the mortgagee to make an application for sale of the mortgaged property under ss. 14 and 15 of TOLATA 1996 to realize its debt. Whilst this may mean that the innocent victim loses their home, their equitable interest remains untouched and they will be able to keep their share in the property (in the form of money from the proceeds of sale). *Achampong* therefore affords mortgagees a vital means of realizing its debt against the wrongdoing undue influencer while protecting the victim.

13.4.5.3 Setting aside a mortgage on the basis of misrepresentation

Our discussion thus far has focused on mortgages tainted by undue influence. However, it is also possible for a mortgage to be rescinded following misrepresentation—for example, where a husband provides misleading information as to the extent or liability under a mortgage and thereby induces a wife to consent to the mortgage. This was the case in *O'Brien*.

> **KEY CASE** *Barclays Bank plc v O'Brien* (1994)
>
> Facts: Barclays Bank plc advanced a loan to Mr and Mrs O'Brien that was secured against the family home, for the purpose of financing the husband's ailing business ventures. Mrs O'Brien was persuaded to agree to the mortgage after her husband assured her that the charge was limited to £60,000, would last only a short few weeks and that Mr O'Brien's company would fail without the loan monies. This
>
> →

→

was a misrepresentation as the charge was neither limited in time nor in amount. The bank manager sent the relevant mortgage documents to the local Barclays branch along with clear instructions that Mr and Mrs O'Brien were to be made fully aware of the nature of the legal charge and that they should seek legal advice before granting the mortgage if they had any doubts. Unfortunately, these instructions, when received by a Barclays clerk, were not executed and Mrs O'Brien signed the mortgage deed without reading it or seeking legal advice.

Legal issue: Could the mortgage be set aside on the grounds of undue influence and/or misrepresentation?

Judgment: At first instance, the judge dismissed the wife's appeal as there was no evidence that Mr O'Brien, in deceiving his wife, had been acting on behalf of or as an agent for the bank and, consequently, the bank could not be held responsible for his misrepresentation. The court therefore held the mortgage was enforceable against the wife. Mrs O'Brien appealed.

In the Court of Appeal, Mr's O'Brien's appeal was allowed. The court held that she was entitled to the protection of equity as a result of her husband's misrepresentation and the mortgage was enforceable against her only to the extent of £60,000. Barclays appealed.

In the House of Lords, Mrs O'Brien was again successful and Barclays' appeal was dismissed. The mortgage was set aside against Mrs O'Brien a result of the bank's constructive notice of Mr O'Brien's misrepresentation of the extent and nature of the mortgage. The bank was held to have notice of the misrepresentation and it had failed to take reasonable steps to ensure the charge was obtained with the free consent of Mrs O'Brien and had not made Mrs O'Brien aware of the nature and consequences of the mortgage.

The essential point to grasp here is that whether a claim is made to set aside a mortgage on the grounds of misrepresentation or undue influence, for all intents and purposes, the same rules outlined in this chapter apply save that no presumption of misrepresentation operates. This was confirmed recently in the Court of Appeal in *Annulment Funding Company Ltd v Cowey* (2010) by Morgan J who noted:[79]

> It is clearly established that the principles which apply as to when a lender is put upon inquiry, and as to the reasonable steps it should take to avoid being affected by notice, apply equally to cases of misrepresentation and to other cases of undue influence.

13.5 The rights of the legal mortgagee

The previous sections have set out the mortgagor's position but what rights does a mortgagee enjoy? We turn in this section to consider the rights and remedies available to a legal mortgagee in the event that the mortgagor defaults on repayment of the mortgage. There are a number of avenues open to a mortgagee faced with default:

- the right to payment under the contract;
- the right to possession;

[79] *Annulment Funding Company Ltd v Cowey*, D58.

- the power of sale;
- the remedy of foreclosure;
- the power to appoint a receiver.

When assessing the scope and potency of these remedies, it is essential to remind yourself that it is in the very nature of the mortgage relationship that the mortgagee's right to repayment of the debt is secured against the property. Mortgages are therefore as advantageous to mortgagees as they are to mortgagors as mortgagees receive interest on the monies advanced. If the mortgagee did not have this right to charge interest and enjoy a range of rights and remedies, lenders would simply be unprepared to take the risk of lending money. Before we consider in greater detail the various avenues open to the mortgagee, three important preliminary points must be noted:

1. Whilst the gamut of remedies discussed in this section are *available* to a mortgagee, the mortgagee is under no strict *obligation* to exercise any of them even if the inaction of the mortgagee would result in loss to the mortgagor. This was best-expressed in *Silven Properties Ltd v Royal Bank of Scotland plc* (2003) by Lightman J:[80]

   > A mortgagee has no duty at any time to exercise his powers as mortgagee to sell, to take possession or to appoint a receiver and preserve the security or its value or to realise his security. He is entitled to remain totally passive.

2. Where, however, the mortgagee *does* decide to pursue remedies following the mortgagor's default, certain duties will apply. The precise nature of these duties will be explored further when we consider each distinct remedy. At a broad level, equity is prepared to oversee strictly that, in seeking a remedy, the mortgagee acts fairly and reasonably in the recovery of its debt and will not permit oppressive conduct by the lender. This was explained by Sir Donald Nicholls V-C in *Palk v Mortgage Services Funding plc* (1993):[81]

   > [A] mortgagee does owe some duties to a mortgagor . . . a mortgagee can sit back and do nothing. He is not obliged to take steps to realise his security. But if he does take steps to exercise his rights over his security, common law and equity alike have set bounds to the extent to which he can look after himself and ignore the mortgagor's interests. In the exercise of his rights over his security the mortgagee must act fairly towards the mortgagor. His interest in the property has priority over the interest of the mortgagor, and he is entitled to proceed on that footing. He can protect his own interest, but he is not entitled to conduct himself in a way which unfairly prejudices the mortgagor.

3. Which remedy the mortgagee elects in the event of mortgagor default is a matter for the mortgagee and will depend largely on the particular factual circumstances. By way of example, little would be gained by pursuing a personal action on the debt if the mortgagor has become bankrupt. Importantly, the remedies available to mortgagees can operate cumulatively. This means that a mortgagee may pursue an action for one remedy before moving to another and so forth until its debt is repaid.[82]

Let's consider each right and remedy in turn.

---

[80] *Silven Properties*, 1003.   [81] *Palk*, 337.   [82] *Alliance & Leicester v Slayford* (2001).

13.5.1 **The right to payment under the contract**

In every mortgage transaction, the mortgagor undertakes a personal contractual obligation to repay the loan advanced subject to the particular terms of the loan agreement. This is in the very nature of a mortgage: the advancement of loan monies by the mortgagee on the proviso that the money will be repaid with interest. So central is this contractual liability of the mortgagor to repay the loan that a term of repayment will be implied where there is no express term in the agreement[83] though almost all mortgage transactions today will include an express repayment clause.

The mortgagee can therefore bring an action in contract seeking repayment of the debt. What is the significance of this? The point is that the contractual liability of the mortgagor arises quite independently of the security (the charge on the mortgagor's land). The result is that the mortgagee may rely on the contractual liability of the mortgagor to 'top up' any deficit that may remain after other remedies have been pursued. Take an example: imagine a mortgagor defaults on mortgage payments and the mortgagee seeks sale of the mortgaged property but the sale does not generate sufficient funds to fully satisfy the debt. In these circumstances, the mortgagee may bring a contractual action to cover the shortfall.

There are, however, certain consequences flowing from an action on the contract. First, a claim on the contract is a personal action which will prove to be a blunt instrument if the mortgagor is bankrupt. Secondly, given that a mortgage is created by deed, there is an extended limitation period within which a mortgagee can bring an action: 12 years as opposed to the standard 6-year period for contracts for recovery of the deed debt.[84] The usual 6-year period applies, however, to recovery of any interest on the debt.[85] Whilst there is therefore a permissible 12-year statutory period for recovery of the deed debt, this has effectively been reduced to a 6-year period under the Mortgages Conduct of Business (MCOB) Rules[86] which were issued by the Financial Services Authority in 2013. The MCOB rules apply to 'Regulated Mortgage Contracts' entered into after 31 October 2014.[87]

The availability of a personal action in contract against the mortgagor for recovery of the debt is therefore of real significance to the mortgagee. It means, in effect, that even where the mortgaged property is sold, the mortgagee may still be able to chase the mortgagee some years later to recover any remaining sums owed to it.

13.5.2 **The right to possession**

Where a mortgagor is in default, a mortgagee may seek possession of the mortgaged property for two principal reasons.

First, a mortgagee may seek possession of the mortgaged property as a precursor to sale of the property to satisfy the debt. In this case, a mortgagee may seek possession before seeking an order for sale as the property will be more attractive to purchasers if there is vacant possession: in other words, where the mortgagor has been removed from the land.

Note that since 2008, there has existed the snappily titled 'Pre-Action Protocol for Possession Claims based on Mortgage or Home Purchase Plan Arrears in Respect of Residential Property' (updated in 2011) which provides steps that the court will expect a mortgagee to have followed

---

[83] *West Bromwich Building Society v Wilkinson* (2005).   [84] See ss. 8 and 20 of the Limitation Act 1980.
[85] Ibid., s. 20(5).   [86] MCOB 13.6.1 and 13.6.2.   [87] See MCOB 1.2.5.

before seeking possession including: providing key information to the mortgagor; considering rescheduling of the debt; accepting/giving reasons for refusing reasonable requests for a new payment plan; and seeking fair, open discussions as to settling the default out of court. The idea is that, as far as possible, an agreement may be struck without the need to go to court and that, if this fails, possession proceedings are a last resort. A Practice Direction provides for enforcement of the Protocol. Non-compliance with the Protocol can result in a delay to the mortgagee obtaining possession and costs orders against the lender, but possession itself will not be denied for failure to follow its steps.[88] In practice, the vast majority of mortgagees will abide by the Protocol if for no other reason than its requirements are far from onerous!

Secondly, a mortgagee may wish to take possession of the mortgaged property in order to manage the land in order to generate an income which can then be used to discharge the mortgagor's obligations such as mortgage repayments. In this scenario, the fact that the mortgagee takes possession does not necessarily mean the mortgage will be brought to an end though the mortgagee may very well proceed to seek sale if the land cannot be managed to guarantee sufficient income to its satisfaction.

There are ramifications for a mortgagee seeking to manage mortgaged land.

In particular, the mortgagee is under a strict equitable duty to account for all income received: *White v City of London Brewery* (1889). As explained in *White*, this means that the mortgagee has a duty to account for income actually generated but, additionally, for income that *should* have been generated but for the lender's 'wilful default'.[89] Whilst there has been a degree of uncertainty as to precisely what constitutes 'wilful default'[90] it seems the mortgagee will be held to a standard of reasonableness. The mortgagee will be liable to make up any shortfall between the actual income generated and that which should reasonably have been generated had the land been managed appropriately. The risks of taking possession for the purposes of generating income are seen as too great for most mortgagees who take this course of action only after considerable reflection or for a very short period of time.[91]

It often comes as something of a surprise to students of land law (and mortgagors too!) that a mortgagee is entitled to immediate possession of the mortgaged property. Technically, this arises from the operation of s. 87(1) of the LPA 1925 which, as we explored in section 13.3.1, entitles a mortgagee under a legal charge to 'the same protections, powers and remedies' as if the mortgagee held a lease of 3,000 years' duration. This includes enjoyment of immediate possession of the mortgaged property. In practice, of course, the right to possession is subject to the express terms of the mortgage which commonly provide that a mortgagee is not entitled to possession unless and until the mortgagor is in default. The mortgagee's immediate right to possession is encapsulated in the now infamous statement of Harman J in *Four-Maids Ltd v Dudley Marshall (Properties) Ltd* (1957):[92]

> [T]he right of the mortgagee to possession in the absence of some contract has nothing to do with default on the part of the mortgagor. The mortgagee may go into possession before the ink is dry on the mortgage unless there is something in the contract . . . whereby he has contracted himself out of that right.

---

[88] Paragraph 2.2 of the Protocol makes clear that 'This Protocol does not alter the parties' rights and obligations.'

[89] As to wilful default, see J. E. Stannard, 'Wilful Default' [1979] Conv 345.

[90] See S. Frisby (2000) 63 MLR 413.

[91] Mortgagees wishing for the land to be managed to generate income are far more likely to appoint a receiver for this purpose: see section 13.5.5.

[92] *Four-Maids*, 320.

While Harman J's statement is an accurate reflection of the law, it fails to fully reflect the modern reality of taking possession of mortgaged land. Today, there are a series of procedural safeguards as well as statutory and common law interventions which modify the position. These restrictions will be discussed in the next section. For present purposes, it suffices to note that in the vast majority of cases, mortgagees will seek possession by applying for an order for possession from a county court rather than taking it upon themselves to take possession by physical re-entry of the premises. Possession by re-entry runs the real risk of incurring criminal liability for assault or battery.[93] Executing possession under an order of the court is therefore the most common and evidently the safest route to possession unless the mortgaged property is empty.

Despite the mortgagee's immediate right to possession, certain restrictions exist to constrain this right, particularly as concerns domestic or residential property: see Figure 13.6. We consider them in turn here.

13.5.2.1 Duties on mortgagees taking possession

A mortgagee taking possession of mortgaged property is subject to certain duties which govern how a mortgagee must behave in relation to the land.

A mortgagee must seek possession bona fides and *reasonably* to protect its rights as a mortgagee (i.e. with a view to securing satisfaction of its debt): *Quennell v Maltby*. Lord Denning MR in *Quennell* explained:[94]

> A mortgagee will be restrained from getting possession except where it is sought bona fide and reasonably for the purpose of enforcing the security and then only subject to such conditions as the court thinks fit to impose.

The facts of *Quennell* demonstrate this duty in action.

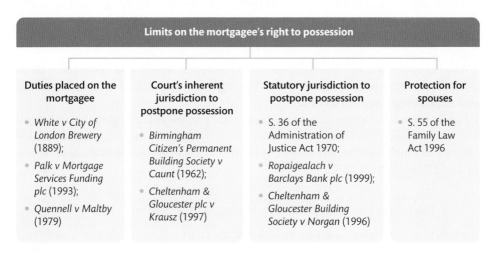

Figure 13.6 Limits on the mortgagee's right to possession

---

[93] Under either the Criminal Law Act 1977 or for harassment under the Protection from Eviction Act 1977.
[94] *Quennell*, 322.

KEY CASE *Quennell v Maltby* (1979)

Facts: In 1973, a landlord who owned a valuable property, leased the premises to university students for a year expiring on 31 December 1974. In August 1974, the landlord granted a mortgage to the bank in return for a loan of £2,500 secured on the property. It was a term of the mortgage that the property could not be leased without the consent of the mortgagee. On 1 December 1974, the landlord re-let the property to other students for one year without gaining the consent of the mortgagee and did so for another year after the expiration of this term. The tenants became statutory tenants and therefore enjoyed statutory protections from 1 December 1976. The landlord wished to evict the tenants in order to sell the house but was prevented due to the tenants' protected status. The landlord requested that the mortgagee exercise its right to possession and thereby evict the students. The mortgagee (bank) refused. The landlord therefore devised a plan to evict the students. The landlord's wife paid off the money owed to the bank under the mortgage and, on 17 January 1978, the benefit of the mortgage was transferred to the wife. As successor of the mortgagee, the wife then claimed a right to possession of the property.

Legal issue: Would the husband's ploy succeed? Was the wife entitled to exercise the right to possession and evict the students?

Judgment: At first instance, the judge made an order for possession. One of the tenants threatened with eviction appealed. In the Court of Appeal, the tenant succeeded. The court held that the wife was not exercising her powers as a mortgagee to protect or enforce her security interest but rather to further the scheme devised by her husband to evict the protected tenants. The wife was therefore acting on behalf of her husband and, given the husband landlord was not entitled to evict the students, neither was the wife. The action for possession had been brought for an ulterior motive and so the wife was not entitled to an order for possession.

Lord Denning in *Quennell* argued that equity had a broad discretion to intervene to prevent mortgagees acting other than in good faith. Whilst Smith[95] and others[96] have criticized this approach as affording too expansive a role to equity in supervising a mortgagee's right to possession, it has subsequently been followed by the court, most recently by the Privy Council in *Cukurova Finance International Ltd v Alfa Telecom Turkey Ltd* (2013).

Another duty is that when a mortgagee takes possession, it must take reasonable care as to the physical state of the property: *Palk*. A mortgagee is not entitled to act in a way that would drain the property of its value.

Finally, when a mortgagee takes possession for the purposes of managing the land, recall that the mortgagee is under an equitable duty to account for any income received and any income that should have been generated by the reasonable management of the land: *White*. We noted this in section 13.5.2.

13.5.2.2 The court's inherent jurisdiction to postpone possession

In addition to the duties placed on mortgagees, the court enjoys an inherent jurisdiction to grant temporary relief to a mortgagor by staying possession proceedings brought by a

---

[95] R. Smith [1979] Conv 266.
[96] R. A. Pearce, 'Keeping a Mortgagee out of Possession' (1979) 38(2) CLJ 257.

mortgagee to allow a mortgagor a short time to gather the funds to pay off any mortgage debt. This jurisdiction is limited in nature and the court has roundly rejected any suggestion of a broad equitable jurisdiction to postpone possession beyond 28 days: *Birmingham Citizen's Permanent Building Society v Caunt* (1962). This is far more constrained than the wider-ranging statutory jurisdiction under s. 36 of the Administration of Justice Act 1970 (AJA 1970) which we consider next in section 13.5.2.3. The court in *Caunt* confirmed that it had the jurisdiction to afford a mortgagor only a very limited opportunity to find means of paying off the mortgage debt. Equally, in *Cheltenham & Gloucester plc v Krausz* (1997), it was confirmed that the court's inherent jurisdiction to postpone is not available in cases of negative equity.

13.5.2.3 Statutory jurisdiction to postpone possession under s. 36 of the AJA 1970

Following *Caunt*, there were calls for a reconsideration of the breadth of mortgagees' right to possession particularly in relation to residential property.[97] Responding to this, Parliament intervened to provide for a broader, statutory jurisdiction to postpone possession proceedings concerning residential property under s. 36 of the AJA 1970. You should read this provision very closely. It is important to grasp what s. 36 does and does not allow a court to do. The provision does not allow a court to restrict the essential right of a mortgagee to possession but, rather, permits the court to either adjourn possession proceedings *or* stay or postpone execution of a possession order if it appears to the court that the mortgagor is likely to be able, within a reasonable period, to pay any sums due under the mortgage or to remedy any default. There are five aspects to consider regarding the operation of s. 36:[98]

- Are possession proceedings required?
- What is meant by 'dwelling-house'?
- What is meant by 'any sums due'?
- What is meant by 'reasonable period'?
- What is meant by 'such conditions . . . as the court thinks fit'?

A requirement for possession proceedings?

One key question of interpretation of s. 36 was whether the court's jurisdiction was available only where a mortgagee had commenced possession proceedings. Of course, as we have already noted, in the vast majority of cases, mortgagees seek possession by initiating court proceedings but what if the mortgagor is not occupying the land and so the mortgagee seeks possession without recourse to court? Does the s. 36 jurisdiction operate in these circumstances? The leading authority on this point is *Ropaigealach v Barclays Bank plc*.

---

[97] See, for example, the Payne Committee Report No. 3909 (1969).

[98] For a critique of s. 36 see R. Smith [1979] Conv 266; M. Haley, 'Mortgage Default: Possession, Relief and Judicial Discretion' (1997) 17 LS 483.

KEY CASE *Ropaigealach v Barclays Bank plc* (2000)

Facts: The Ropaigealachs granted a mortgage to Barclays Bank plc over a property which required substantial renovation works. The Ropaigealachs fell into arrears and Barclays made a final written demand for payment informing them of the significance of a failure to pay. No payment was made. Barclays again wrote to the Ropaigealachs informing them that the property was to be put up for sale by auction. The Ropaigealachs were not living at the property and so did not receive the letters. They learned of the completed sale from a neighbour. Upon hearing the news, the Ropaigealachs made an application for an injunction preventing sale. This was refused on the grounds that the sale had already been completed.

Legal issue: Were the Ropaigealachs entitled to a declaration that Barclays had not been entitled to act as it had without first obtaining a court order for possession? The Ropaigealachs argued that, in legislating under s. 36, Parliament intended that a mortgagor would be protected from ejectment and that this jurisdiction extended to cases where a mortgagee had not sought a court order for possession.

Judgment: The Court of Appeal refused to grant the Ropaigealachs the declaration sought and, in construing s. 36 in a literal manner, held that the provision only applied where a mortgagee had brought possession proceedings. In the present case, the section therefore had no application. The court reached this conclusion unanimously but with some reluctance, noting that it was 'very curious' that Parliament would intend protection to be afforded to mortgagors only in cases where the mortgagee had chosen to issue proceedings and not where the mortgagee simply chooses to re-enter the premises. In reaching its decision, the court highlighted that:

1. The statutory language made reference to 'where a mortgagee . . . brings an action in which he claims possession'. It was not permissible to conclude this extended to cases where no such action was brought.

2. Parliament had legislated in response to the decision in *Caunt* and the need to confirm the position where legal proceedings had been brought.

3. Some protection was afforded to mortgagors in a case where mortgagee took possession by re-entry under s. 6 of the Criminal Law Act 1977.

The Court in *Ropaigealach* confirms that the statutory jurisdiction under s. 36 is only available where the mortgagee has brought an action for possession of mortgaged land. The court in *Horsham Properties Group Ltd v Clark* (2009) identified another important exception to the application of s. 36. Where a mortgagee exercises a power of sale over mortgaged property without first seeking a court order for possession, the sale overreaches the borrower's equity of redemption and if the mortgagor remains on the land, he becomes a trespasser. Section 36 does not apply. It is surely concerning that the decision in *Horsham Properties* appears to provide an unscrupulous mortgagee with a means of avoiding the operation of s. 36 in this way. The court also rejected the suggestion that this contravened any rights under the ECHR.

Section 36 does apply, however, where a mortgagee seeks possession by initiating proceedings where there is no default on the part of the mortgagor.[99] Where proceedings for possession are issued by a mortgagee, the mortgagor wishing to rely on s. 36 must make an

---

[99] *Western Bank Ltd v Schindler* (1977).

application for relief under the provision. A mortgagee seeking a possession order is now obliged to send a notice of the proceedings to the mortgaged property so that any affected parties are made aware of the action and could initiate a s. 36 application.

'Dwelling-house'

Section 36 only applies to possession proceedings concerning mortgages that consist of or include a 'dwelling-house'. 'Dwelling house' includes premises where only part of the land is used as a dwelling, for example, where part of a commercial premises is used for a residence.[100] The dwelling-house in question need not therefore be the mortgagor's home. The question of whether the mortgage consists of or includes a dwelling-house is to be determined at the date of any possession proceedings as opposed to at the date of the grant of the mortgage.

'Any sums due'

Section 36 gives the court the power to adjourn possession proceedings or to postpone the execution of a possession order where there is evidence that, within a reasonable period, the mortgagor will be able to pay '*any sums due*' under the mortgage. But, what is meant by 'any sums due'? What might at first seem to be a rather innocuous provision has caused waves and even necessitated further intervention by Parliament. The problem arose as a result of default or acceleration clauses which are routinely included in mortgage agreements. Under these clauses, where a mortgagor defaults on mortgage repayments, the totality of the capital sum under the mortgage becomes payable plus outstanding interest. In *Halifax Building Society v Clark*, the court held in a case involving a default clause that 'any sums due' meant the *totality* of sums due under the mortgage.

KEY CASE   *Halifax Building Society v Clark* (1973)

Facts: A mortgagor defaulted on mortgage repayments over a dwelling-house. Under a 'default clause' in the mortgage, in the event of default, all sums under the mortgage became immediately due. The bank applied for possession of the mortgaged property.

Legal issue: On the mortgagee's application for possession, could the mortgagor rely on s. 36 of the AJA 1970 to postpone the execution of the possession order?

Judgment: At first instance, a possession order was granted but suspended on terms that the mortgagor would pay a certain sum each month. On appeal, the High Court held that, on a true construction of s. 36, the court had no power to postpone possession unless it could be shown that the mortgagor could, within a reasonable period, pay off *all that was owing* under the mortgage. In this case, 'any sums due' meant the totality of the debt under the mortgage plus interest and not just the outstanding arrears. On the particular facts, Pennycuick V-C held:

> I conclude that since, on Mrs. Clark's own evidence, there is no likelihood of Mr. Clark as mortgagor or herself . . . being likely, within a reasonable period, to pay the redemption moneys under the mortgage—and it being conceded that 'any sums due under the mortgage' must mean the redemption moneys—the condition in section 36 (1) is not satisfied. Therefore, the court has none of the powers expressly conferred by subsection (2).

---

[100]   *Bank of Scotland v Miller* (2001) where land was used partly as a nightclub and partly as a residential flat.

The effect of *Halifax Building Society v Clark* was to stultify the central purpose of s. 36 of the AJA 1970 for if a mortgagor has defaulted on mortgage repayments, it is fair to assume she will not be able to repay the totality of the capital debt within a reasonable period. The essential aim of the provision is therefore frustrated. Parliament's responded to *Halifax Building Society v Clark* by legislating to reverse the effect of the decision and to restrict 'any sums due' to the payment of arrears: s. 8 of the AJA 1973. This is a rather odd and obscurely drafted provision. The effect of s. 8 is that where a 'default clause' exists 'any sums due' under s. 36 of the AJA 1970 is to be interpreted as referring to those sums which the mortgagor 'would have expected to be required to pay if there had been no such provision for earlier payment'. In short, 'any sums due' covers arrears and not the totality of the capital debt.[101]

'Reasonable period'

The Payne Committee and Parliament in legislating intended that s. 36 of the AJA would afford only a short period of perhaps one to two years for the mortgagor to get their act together, to settle and stabilize their financial position after a redundancy or job loss, perhaps, or following a period of ill-health.[102] However, the Court of Appeal in *Cheltenham & Gloucester Building Society v Norgan* gave a far broader interpretation of 'reasonable period'.

KEY CASE *Cheltenham & Gloucester Building Society v Norgan* (1996)

Facts: Mrs Norgan borrowed £90,000 from Cheltenham & Gloucester Building Society secured against her house. Under the terms of the agreement, Mrs Norgan was to repay the loan in monthly instalments over a period of 21 years. It was a standard term of the contract that if any instalment was not paid, Cheltenham & Gloucester would be entitled to possession of the property. Mrs Norgan fell into arrears and Cheltenham & Gloucester sought a possession order. The order was suspended on various occasions to enable Mrs Norgan to pay off certain arrears and interest instalments but this was not done and the debt remained high. Cheltenham & Gloucester applied to the court for the possession order to be executed.

Legal issue: Under s. 36 of the AJA, what was to be regarded as a 'reasonable period' in which Mrs Norgan could repay the arrears?

Judgment: The first instance judge held that four years was a 'reasonable period' within which to repay the arrears. On the basis that there was no evidence that Mrs Norgan could settle the outstanding arrears within this period, the judge held that the possession order should be executed. Mrs Norgan appealed.

In the Court of Appeal, allowing Mrs Norgan's appeal and relying on earlier cases of the court (*First Middlesbrough Trading and Mortgage Co. Ltd v Cunningham* (1974) and *Schindler* (1977)), Waite LJ held that:

> The court should take as its starting point the full term of the mortgage and pose at the outset the question: 'would it be possible for the mortgagor to maintain payment off of the arrears by instalments over that period'.

→

---

[101] It is now established that s. 8 applies to repayment mortgages: *Centrax Trustees v Ross* (1979), endowment mortgages: *Bank of Scotland v Grimes* (1986), but not to mortgages payable on demand: *Habib Bank Ltd v Tailor* (1982).

[102] As explained in *Royal Trust Co. of Canada v Markham* (1975).

→

Evans LJ laid down a series of 'considerations' to be taken into account by the court in determining what would constitute a 'reasonable period':

(a) How much can the borrower reasonably afford to pay, both now and in the future?

(b) If the borrower has a temporary difficulty in meeting its obligations, how long is the difficulty likely to last?

(c) What was the reason for the arrears which have accumulated?

(d) How much remains of the original mortgage term?

(e) What are the relevant contractual terms and what type of mortgage is it (i.e. when is the principal sum due to be repaid)?

(f) Is it a case where the court should exercise its power to disregard any accelerated payment provisions (s. 8 of the AJA 1973)?

(g) Is it reasonable to expect the lender, in the circumstances of the particular case, to recoup the arrears of interest (1) over the whole of the original term, or (2) within a shorter period, or even (3) within a longer period (i.e. by extending the repayment period)? Is it reasonable to expect the lender to capitalize the interest or not?

(h) Are there any reasons affecting the security which should influence the length of the period for payment?

The Court of Appeal noted that determination of what constituted a 'reasonable period' required a detailed analysis of the mortgagor's budgets and a discussion of future financial projections. The case was remitted to the county court for determination of what would constitute a reasonable period in Mrs Norgan's particular circumstances.

The decision in *Norgan* represented a significant break from the more restrictive approach taken in the Payne Report and from that intended by Parliament. Interestingly, there is a growing body of evidence, as Whitehouse has identified,[103] that the court is increasingly prepared to determine 'reasonable period' as constituting a far shorter period than the entire term of the mortgage.

A mortgagor may well feel that she is in a better position to sell the mortgaged property and receive a higher price than could be obtained by the mortgagee. Properties are often regarded as more 'saleable' with occupants still in possession of the property. Equally, purchasers aware that a mortgagee is forcing sale may be put off from going ahead. Where a mortgagor applies under s. 36 for a stay to possession proceedings in order to seek a sale of the mortgaged property herself to discharge the debt, additional factors will be relevant to the court when determining 'reasonable period':

1. The adequacy of the property as security for the debt and the length of time it will take to sell the property are key considerations. The court in *Krausz* clarified that it has no power to suspend possession proceedings to allow a mortgagor to sell the property where the proceeds of sale would be insufficient to discharge the debt. The

---

[103] L. Whitehouse, 'Longitudinal Analysis of the Mortgage Repossession Process 1995–2010: Stability, Regulation and Reform' in S. Bright (ed.), *Modern Studies in Property Law*, Vol. 6 (Oxford: Hart, 2011), 163.

court in *Bristol & West Building Society v Ellis* (1997) held that the mortgagor must provide:[104]

> [E]vidence, or at least some informal material . . . of the likelihood of a sale the proceeds of which will discharge the debt and of the period within which a sale is likely to be achieved.

2. The mortgagor must be able to adduce clear and specific evidence of a proposed sale of the property before the court will suspend possession proceedings: *National & Provincial Building Society v Lloyd* (1996). In *Lloyd*, the court held that the mortgagor's desire to sell the mortgaged property itself was founded more in hope than reality.

3. Merely pointing to evidence or opinion from estate agents that a property will command a particular sale price will be insufficient without further evidence of steps towards an actual, proposed sale: *Ellis*.[105]

4. Where the mortgaged property is already on the market and there is evidence from an estate agent that an offer on the property has been received, this may justify a short suspension of a possession order: *Target Home Loans Ltd v Clothier* (1994).[106]

'Such conditions . . . as the court thinks fit'

Under s. 36(3), the court—when adjourning possession proceedings or suspending or postponing execution of a possession order—has the power to attach conditions as it thinks fit as regards payment of any sum under the mortgage. This aspect of s. 36(3) was considered in the case of *Bank of Scotland v Zinda* (2012). In *Zinda*, the court suspended a possession order imposing conditions on Mr Zinda, the mortgagor, that he pay off his mortgage arrears by way of monthly instalments in addition to his current instalment payment schedule. Subsequently, Mr Zinda and the mortgagee, the Bank of Scotland, agreed to consolidate the arrears into the capital sum payable under the mortgage. When Mr Zinda again fell into arrears, the court held that the bank was entitled to execute its possession order. The court underlined that in circumstances of a suspended possession order and where conditions imposed upon the suspension were not met, the possession order would be executable without the need for a further court hearing. This outcome may seem harsh against Mr Zinda, but note that s. 36(4) does give mortgagors the power to make an application to vary or revoke any court-imposed conditions. Faced with difficulty in complying with such conditions, an application should be made to avoid the result in *Zinda*.

As a final note, do not forget the 'Pre-action Protocol for Possession Claims' that we discussed briefly in section 13.5.2. The Protocol provides:[107]

> If a borrower can demonstrate that reasonable steps have been or will be taken to market the property at an appropriate price in accordance with reasonable professional advice, the lender

---

[104] *Ellis*, 287.

[105] In *Ellis*, the court refused to suspend a possession order where there was insufficient evidence that the mortgagor could sell the property within three and five years in circumstances that could discharge the debt.

[106] In *Clothier*, the court postponed execution of the possession order for three months to allow the mortgagor to secure a sale of the property.

[107] Pre-Action Protocol for Possession Claims based on Mortgage or Home Purchase Plan Arrears in Respect of Residential Property (2011), para. 6.2.

must consider postponing starting a possession claim to allow the borrower a realistic period of time to sell the property.

The Protocol therefore comes to the mortgagor's assistance as an additional tool to s. 36 of the AJA 1970. Arguably, the Protocol is more favourable here than the 1970 Act which requires the mortgagor to point to strong likelihood of sale before the court will postpone possession proceedings.

13.5.2.4 Protection for spouses under the Family Law Act 1996

Where a mortgagee seeks possession of mortgaged land, it is required to serve notice on any spouse who has registered his or her occupation rights under the Matrimonial Homes Act 1983. Additionally, under s. 55 of the Family Law Act 1996, where mortgaged land consists of or includes a dwelling-house and a mortgagee makes an application to enforce its security, a spouse is entitled to be made a party to the proceedings. This permits a spouse to play a more active role in any application under s. 36 of the AJA. In the case of a joint mortgage, the mortgagee is required in any event to inform both parties of impending possession proceedings.

13.5.3 The power of sale

The power to seek sale of mortgaged property is the most muscular of the mortgagee's remedies when facing default by the mortgagor. Sale, if realized, means that a mortgagee is ultimately able to enforce its security and have the mortgage debt repaid. Recall that in a co-ownership scenario where there is more than one co-owner, a mortgagee will rely on the provisions of TOLATA 1996 in seeking sale. In this section, however, we are concerned with the specific statutory powers of sale provided by the LPA 1925.

There are several important aspects to the mortgagee's power of sale which need to be unpacked:

- When does the power of sale arise and, once arisen, when is that power exercisable?
- What is the effect of sale and how are the proceeds of sale applied?
- To what duties is the mortgagee subject on sale?

13.5.3.1 When will a power of sale arise and when is it exercisable?

The mortgagee will enjoy either an express power of sale under an express term of the mortgage or by implication under s. 101(1)(i) of the LPA 1925. In the event of an express power of sale, the mortgage agreement will govern how and in what circumstances the power will operate. If the lender relies upon the implied power of sale, the power of sale must both *arise* under s. 101 and be *exercisable* under s. 103 of the LPA 1925. You should keep these two stages separate in your mind: see Figure 13.7.

All mortgages that satisfy the requirements in s. 101 will benefit from the implied power of sale except in so far as the power is modified or excluded by the terms of the mortgage. Once *arisen*, the next question becomes whether that power is *exercisable* under s. 103 of the LPA 1925. When any of the three conditions in s. 103 is satisfied, the power of sale becomes exercisable and the mortgagee need not seek a court order to effect sale of the

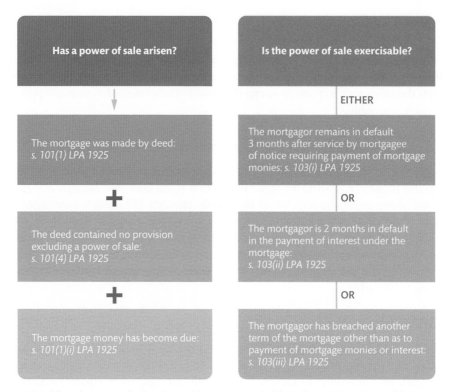

Figure 13.7 When the power of sale arises and becomes exercisable under ss. 101 and 103 of the LPA 1925

mortgaged property. Of course, in the vast majority of cases, the mortgagee will have already sought a court order to secure vacant possession of the property. Strictly speaking, no court order is required in order to exercise a mortgagee's power of sale. There are, however, two important scenarios which require further thought:

- What if a mortgagee sells the mortgaged property before the power of sale has arisen? The purchaser will receive the mortgagee's interest in the land only. The mortgagor will not be affected by the sale. In practice, the effect is that the purchaser now sits in the same position as the mortgagee with the mortgagee's rights but nothing more.

- What if the mortgagee sells the mortgaged property once the power of sale has arisen but where the power has not yet become exercisable? The purchaser will take the land free of the mortgage. The mortgagor will be entitled to have the sale set aside, however, if and only if the purchaser had notice of the mortgagee's improper exercise of the power of sale: s. 104 of the LPA; *Cuckmere Brick Co. v Mutual Finance* (1971).

Haley has observed that the effect of s. 36 of the AJA 1970 in a case of a mortgage of a dwelling-house is to erode the true value of the power of sale under ss. 101 and 103 of the LPA 1925, which envisages the power of sale arising and becoming exercisable relatively quickly upon the mortgagor's default.[108] Any suspension or delay occasioned by s. 36 of the

---

[108] M. Haley, 'Mortgage Default: Possession, Relief and Judicial Discretion' (1997) 17 LS 483.

1970 Act could therefore, according to Haley, be seen as diluting the potency of the mortgagee's remedy of sale. There is, on this view, a strong case for reforming both the mortgagee's right to possession and sale in order to recalibrate and clarify the law.

13.5.3.2 The effect of sale and application of the proceeds of sale

Section 88(1) of the LPA 1925 provides that the sale vests legal title in the purchaser. Section 104 of the LPA 1925 confirms that the purchaser acquires the fee simple free from all estates, rights, and interests to which the mortgage had priority but the purchaser will be subject to all estates, interests, and rights which took priority over the mortgage. The sale serves to overreach the mortgagor's interest (in other words, the mortgagor's equity of redemption) which then sounds in the proceeds of sale.[109] On sale, the mortgage and any subsequent charge is extinguished.[110] A measure of protection is afforded to purchasers of mortgaged land under s. 104(2) of the LPA 1925. Under this provision, whenever mortgaged land is sold, the purchaser will get good title and its title is unimpeachable even in the event that the mortgagee did not, in fact, enjoy an exercisable power of sale. Rather, the mortgagee will be liable to pay damages to any person suffering loss as a result of the improper exercise of the power.

This just leaves one fundamental question: once sold, how are the proceeds to be divvied up between the relevant parties? This question of the distribution of proceeds is governed by s. 105 of the LPA 1925, which sets out a hierarchy or an order in which the proceeds are to be paid:

1. to discharge any prior incumbrances including any prior mortgage;
2. to discharge the costs of sale of the mortgaged property;
3. to discharge the sums owed to the mortgagee which sold the property;
4. any balance remaining to be paid to any subsequent mortgagee and, if none, to the mortgagor.

In applying the proceeds under this provision, s. 54 of the LRA 2002 provides that the mortgagee is 'taken to have notice of anything in the register immediately before the disposition on sale'. The onus is therefore on the mortgagee to make the necessary searches of the register before sale.

13.5.3.3 Duties on the mortgagee in conducting the sale

In light of s. 105 of the LPA 1925, it is clear that the mortgagee but also the mortgagor has an interest in how the sale is conducted. It would be quite unfair to the mortgagor if, on sale, the mortgagee was not required to act fairly and in good faith. The mortgagee wants its debt paid but also given that any remaining sums following the sale of mortgaged land are to be paid to the mortgagor, the borrower too is concerned that the sale is conducted in the most effective manner to secure the greatest return. In view of this, a series of duties have been recognized through case law to guarantee a fair balance between the interests of the mortgagee and the mortgagor in the conduct of the sale. The leading case here is *Cuckmere*.

---

[109] Section 2(1)(iii) of the LPA 1925; *Horsham Properties*.   [110] Section 88(1)(b) of the LPA 1925.

> **KEY CASE** *Cuckmere Brick Co. v Mutual Finance* (1971)
>
> Facts: Cuckmere owned land over which there was planning permission to build 100 flats. Cuckmere granted a mortgage over the land to Mutual Finance in return for a loan of £50,000. Subsequently, Cuckmere gained planning permission to build 35 houses on its land. Some two years later, the mortgagee's power of sale arose and became exercisable. Mutual Finance entered into possession of the land and instructed auctioneers to conduct the sale by way of public auction. Advertising the sale, the auctioneers drew the attention of potential buyers to the permission to build 35 flats but made no mention of the permission to construct 100 flats. Cuckmere informed Mutual Finance of this but the mortgagee refused to postpone the sale. The auctioneers agreed to mention at the auction the issue of the 100 flats. The land was sold for £44,000. Cuckmere brought proceedings against Mutual Finance arguing that a price of around £75,000 should have been obtained and argued the mortgagee ought to account for the difference between this sum and the price actually received.
>
> Legal issue: Was the mortgagee subject to a duty to publicize fully the planning permission over the relevant land? If so, had that duty been breached?
>
> Judgment: The Court of Appeal held that Mutual Finance owed Cuckmere:
>
> - a duty to act in good faith in the conduct of the sale
> - a duty to take reasonable care in the conduct of the sale
> - a duty to obtain a fair and proper price for the land.
>
> Mutual Finance had breached this duty as a result of the inadequate advertisement of the planning permission obtained over the land and by refusing to postpone the sale.

Some important observations can be made about the mortgagee's duties in conducting the sale:

- The duties owed by a mortgagee in conducting the sale are not tortious in nature but arise in equity as a result of the relationship of mortgagee and mortgagor: *AIB Finance Ltd v Debtors* (1998). It is not accurate therefore to speak of a mortgagee's duty of care in negligence. The duties owed by mortgagees extend to the mortgagor only and not to others—for example, beneficiaries under a trust of which the mortgagor was a trustee.[111]

- A mortgagee is under a duty to act in good faith and obtain a true market value for the mortgaged land at the time of the sale. That said, the mortgagee can choose when and if it sells the land at all. In this sense, the mortgagee is entitled to take its own interests into account. There is no obligation on a mortgagee to wait for an improvement in the market value of the land: *Cuckmere*. If and when it does choose to sell, however, it is then under a duty to obtain a proper price for the land. If it fails to do so, it may have to account to the mortgagor for any shortfall between the price obtained and the true market value. A mortgagee is entitled to sell mortgaged property at a market undervalue if the informed consent of the mortgagor is obtained: *Mercantile Credit Co. v Clarke* (1996). The High Court in *Philbin v Davies* (2018) reaffirmed that the burden of proof in establishing a breach of duty to obtain a proper price is firmly on the mortgagor.

---

[111]   *Parker-Tweedale v Dunbar Bank plc* (1991).

• In obtaining a proper price for the land, the mortgagee is not entitled to 'sell hastily at a knock-down price sufficient to pay off his debt'.[112] A mortgagee will be in breach of its duties if it sells property which has not been on the market for a reasonable period of time: *Predeth v Castle Phillips Finance Co. Ltd* (1986),[113] or where the property is sold to a neighbouring landowner rather than being placed on the open market: *Skipton Building Society v Stott* (2000). The mortgagee is not required, however, to incur expenses or take positive action to secure a higher price for the land—for example, by actively pursuing planning permission applications (*Silven Properties*) but must advertise planning permission if it has already been granted (*Cuckmere*). Even if embarked upon, any positive steps can be abandoned without breach of any mortgagee's duties.[114]

• A particular issue concerns the possibility of a sale to a person associated with the mortgagee. Clearly this may give rise to a conflict of interests. In *Tse Kwong Lam v Wong Chit Sen* (1983), the Privy Council held that a mortgagee cannot sell to itself or its agent[115] but is able to sell mortgaged property to an associated person or company even if the mortgagee has a substantial shareholding in that associated company. It will be the mortgagee who bears the burden of proving that it acted in good faith and without fraud. Where there is a sale to a person or company associated with the mortgagee, the court will scrutinize closely the nature of the sale and a heavy burden of proof falls on the mortgagee to show the sale was fair (*Philbin v Davies*). Lord Templeman explained in *Tse Kwong Lam* that:[116]

> The sale must be closely examined and a heavy onus lies on the mortgagee to show that in all respects he acted fairly to the borrower and used his best endeavours to obtain the best price reasonably obtainable for the mortgaged property.

In *Tse Kwong Lam*, a mortgagee sold mortgaged property by auction to his wife who was acting on behalf of a company owned by the mortgagee and his family. The court held that the mortgagee had not used best endeavours to obtain the highest price and an auction was not the most appropriate means of selling the property.

• Where a mortgagee breaches any of its duties in conducting the sale, the mortgagor can seek an order of the court that the sale be set aside or, alternatively, seek an order that the mortgagee account for the shortfall between the price paid and the price reasonably obtainable for the land. A sale will, however, only be set aside where there is a degree of impropriety such as fraud. Even if fraud or impropriety is proved, a court will refuse to set aside a sale where the mortgagor has itself caused 'inexcusable delay'[117] or where to do so would cause undue hardship.[118] Where there is a breach of duty falling short of impropriety, liability to account will be the more appropriate remedy.

---

[112] *Palk*.

[113] At first instance, the judge found that the property should have been advertised for sale with local estate agents for a period of at least three months.

[114] *Silven Properties*.   [115] See also *Farrars v Farrars Ltd* (1889).   [116] *Tse Kwong Lam*, 1355.

[117] *Tse Kwong Lam v Wong Chit Sen* (1983): court refused to set sale aside in light of mortgagor's nine-year delay in bringing its claim.

[118] *Corbett v Halifax Building Society* (2002).

13.5.3.4 **Sale by the mortgagor**

In certain circumstances, it may in fact be the mortgagor who wishes for the mortgaged property to be sold. We encountered earlier, in section 13.4.4, that a mortgagor may feel she is best-placed to sell the property and, vitally, best-placed to secure the highest price. A mortgagor can sell its mortgaged land in two principal ways: either with the consent of the mortgagee or, if consent is not forthcoming, the mortgagor can seek an order for sale under s. 91 of the LPA 1925. Section 91 endows the court with a wide discretion to order sale at the request of any 'person interested either in the mortgage money or in the right of redemption'. The leading case on the operation of this provision is *Palk* and it is well-worth reading in full.

KEY CASE *Palk v Mortgage Services Funding plc* (1993)

Facts: The mortgagor owed £358,000 and wished to sell the mortgaged property to reduce this indebtedness. The mortgagor had negotiated a sale of the property at £283,000. The mortgagee re-fused to consent to the sale and wished to lease the property and wait for an increase in house prices. There was evidence that any rent that could be generated would not cover the interest payments on the debt, giving rise to a £30,000 shortfall each year. Without a strong upturn in the housing market, the mortgagor was faced with spiralling debts.

Legal issue: In the circumstances, was the mortgagor entitled to an order for sale under s. 91 of the LPA 1925 against the express wishes of the mortgagee?

Judgment: The Court of Appeal held that it had an 'unfettered discretion' under s. 91 and an order for sale was made. The fact the mortgagee was not in breach of any of its duties was just one factor to be taken into account. To order sale was just and equitable as otherwise unfairness and injustice would follow in view of the prospect of the mortgagor's increasing indebtedness.

Note that the decision in *Krausz* to the effect that the court will not allow a suspension of possession proceedings under s. 36 of the AJA in a case of negative equity does not over-rule the authority of *Palk*. *Palk* was followed in the case of *Polonski v Lloyds Bank Mortgages Ltd* where the court was prepared, under s. 91 of the LPA 1925, to take account of all the mortgagor's circumstances both financial as well as social and lifestyle factors.

KEY CASE *Polonski v Lloyds Bank Mortgages Ltd* (1997)

Facts: A single parent mortgagor wished to sell her property in order to move to another area offering

better prospects for her own employment and schooling options for her children. The mortgagee did not consent to the sale, arguing that sale would result in a £12,000 shortfall that the mortgagor could not presently meet.

Legal issue: Was the mortgagor entitled to an order for sale of the property under s. 91 of the LPA 1925? The mortgagee argued that a sale could only be ordered in cases of extreme social need.

Judgment: The court applied the decision in *Palk* noting the wide discretion it enjoyed under s. 91 of the LPA 1925. In considering application of the provision, the court was permitted to take into ac-count non-financial matters such as social factors. The mortgagor had shown good reasons why she wished to move areas. In addition, there was nothing in her past financial conduct that suggested she was anything other than financially responsible. The order for sale was made.

13.5.4 **The remedy of foreclosure**

Foreclosure is a process under which the mortgagor's equity of redemption is completely extinguished by an order of the court and the mortgagor's estate vests in the mortgagee. The consequence is that the mortgaged property is transferred to the mortgagee free of all rights of the mortgagor and any rights of the mortgagor are brought to an end.[119] The landlord's remedy of foreclosure is plainly an extremely potent and draconian one. It has the effect of extinguishing the rights of the mortgagor, yes, but also rights of subsequent mortgagees under mortgages created after the mortgage subject of the foreclosure action. Importantly, where an order of foreclosure is granted, even the mortgagor's contractual obligation to repay the loan is brought to an end which means the mortgagee loses the right to initiate an action for any remaining sums owing. Under s. 91(2) of the LPA 1925, in an action for foreclosure brought by a mortgagee, the mortgagor is entitled to seek an order for sale in lieu of foreclosure. This has led to a dramatic decline in the number of foreclosure orders granted by the court. A mortgagee can bring an action for foreclosure at any time after the contractual date for redemption has passed though usually does so only in the event of default or breach of other mortgage terms by the mortgagor.

Today, foreclosure is seen as an overly technical and particularly dramatic remedy and is therefore rarely used in practice. As Sir David Nicholls noted in *Palk*:[120]

> [F]oreclosure actions are almost unheard of today and have been so for many years. Mortgagees prefer to exercise other remedies.

The Law Commission has recommended that the remedy be abolished largely due its disuse and be replaced with a broader power for the mortgagee to sell the property.[121] Other criticisms can be made of foreclosure. First, the process is lengthy and burdensome and, secondly, despite its powerful effects, it can actually prove to be rather uncertain in operation as foreclosure orders may, in certain circumstances, be reopened by the court at some later time to allow the mortgagor to redeem the mortgage: *Campbell v Holyland* (1877).

13.5.5 **The power to appoint a receiver**

The final remedy available to a mortgagee is the power to appoint a receiver. A receiver acts as a manager or administrator of the mortgaged land. This power is important if the mortgagee does not want the hassle of taking possession or does not yet wish to realize its security.

A power to appoint a receiver will be provided for expressly as a term of the mortgage or will otherwise be implied into the mortgage under s. 101 of the LPA 1925. Under s. 101 and 103 of the LPA 1925, the power to appoint a receiver arises and becomes exercisable in the same circumstances as the power of sale. The power to appoint a receiver is often used in place of the remedy of sale or in conjunction with it.[122] Typically, the receiver is appointed to 'receive' rents or profits generated from the mortgaged land and harness this income to repay sums owed under the mortgage. Under an express term of the mortgage, a receiver may also enjoy a right to sell the property.

---

[119] LPA 1925, s. 88.   [120] *Palk*, 336.   [121] Law Commission Report No. 204, [7.27].
[122] *Horsham Properties*.

The benefit of the mortgagee appointing a receiver as opposed to taking possession of the land is that the receiver is treated as the agent of the mortgagor. Should the receiver be found to have acted negligently in the management of the land, liability will not fall on the mortgagee. The receiver, in a similar manner to that of a mortgagee selling the mortgaged land, is subject to certain duties of proper management of the land. The court in *Medforth v Blake* (2000) noted that the receiver must act with due diligence subject to a primary obligation of paying down the mortgage debt. In *Blake*, the court found the receiver to have breached its duty when, in managing a pig-farming business, it failed to negotiate readily available price reductions on pig feed which, as the principal cost for the business, had significantly impacted on the profitability of the venture. A receiver with a power of sale is not, however, required to take positive steps to increase the value of the land such as seeking planning permission: *Silven Properties*.

13.6 The rights of equitable mortgagees and equitable chargees

The rights and remedies available to an equitable mortgagee are similar in certain respects to those of a legal mortgagee but sufficiently different in others to warrant a brief discussion here. Thus, for example, an equitable mortgagee has the same right to bring an action on the contract for repayment of the sums owed under the equitable mortgage and can seek foreclosure and the appointment of a receiver as is the case for legal mortgages. However, unless the equitable mortgage is created by deed, the equitable mortgagee will not enjoy an implied power of sale under s. 101 of the LPA 1925. Where no deed is used, equitable mortgagees will, nevertheless, still be able to rely on the court's discretion to order sale of mortgaged property under s. 91 of the LPA 1925.

As to equitable chargees, they do not have the right to possession nor a right to seek foreclosure as they do not enjoy any estate in land. The power of sale and to appoint a receiver is only available to an equitable chargee where the charge was granted by deed. Where an equitable charge is not granted by deed, the equitable chargee would need to apply for sale under s. 91 of the LPA 1925 and for the appointment of a receiver under s. 37(1) of the Supreme Court Act 1981.

13.7 The priority of mortgages

It is entirely possible for a landowner to grant more than one mortgage over her land and thereby secure more than one loan against the property. If the value of the mortgaged property is equivalent to the total of the loan monies secured against the land, very few problems arise as, in the event of default, the property can be sold and all the lenders' debts repaid. Where there is insufficient value in the property to satisfy the total lenders' debts, it becomes crucial to determine which mortgage takes priority. This is particularly important where the mortgagor is in default, the land is sold, and the question arises as to the order in which each mortgagee is to be paid from the proceeds. The rules governing the issue of priority are largely matters of overreaching, registration, and notice. The applicable principles can at first seem complex and so this section aims to offer as clear as possible an overview.

13.7.1 Priority of mortgages in registered land

13.7.1.1 Priority of legal registered charges

As we noted earlier in this chapter, mortgages of registered land constitute registrable dispositions under s. 27 of the LRA 2002 and therefore cannot operate as legal mortgages unless and until they are registered. Where there is more than one registered charge over the same parcel of land, s. 48(1) of the LRA 2002 provides that priority is to be governed by the order in which the charges were registered. Once registered, a legal charge takes priority over subsequently granted mortgages.

Under s. 29(1) of the LRA 2002, a registered legal charge will take priority over any pre-existing interests in the land which were not protected by way of a notice in the register and which do not constitute overriding interests under Sch. 3 of the LRA 2002. The result is that a registered legal mortgage will enjoy priority over prior, unprotected interests including unprotected equitable mortgages. Note, however, that a registered legal mortgage will lose priority where a beneficial interest-holder is in actual occupation of the land and overreaching has not taken place: *Williams & Glyn's Bank v Boland* (1981).

A registered legal charge is also capable of overreaching pre-existing equitable interests in the land such as beneficial interests under a trust provided the requirements for overreaching are satisfied.[123] Overreaching can take place even if a beneficial interest holder is in actual occupation[124] and where the grant of mortgage does not generate capital monies.[125]

13.7.1.2 Priority of equitable mortgages

Where more than one equitable mortgage exists over registered land, the starting point under s. 28 of the LRA 2002 is that priority is determined according to the order in which the mortgages were granted.[126] This is, of course, subject to the exception in s. 29. An equitable mortgage, as we discovered in section 13.3.3, is capable of being protected by the entry of a notice in the Charges Register. If so protected, the mortgage will take priority over any subsequent interest created in the land if there is a registered disposition of a registered estate for valuable consideration completed by registration.[127]

13.7.2 Priority of mortgages in unregistered land

The rules as to the priority of mortgages in unregistered land are fast becoming obsolete. This is because the grant of a legal mortgage over unregistered land is a triggering event under s. 4 of the LRA 2002 for compulsory registration of land.[128] Where a first mortgage is granted in unregistered land the rules of first registration therefore govern the priority of mortgages.[129] On first registration, the Registrar is required to enter a notice in the register as to any interest which appears from his examination of the title to affect the registered estate.[130] The result will be that any existing mortgages will be take priority over subsequently granted mortgages.

---

123 Sections 2(1), 27 of the LPA 1925. 124 *City of London Building Society v Flegg* (1988).
125 *State Bank of India v Sood* (1997). 126 *Halifax plc v Curry Popeck (A Firm)* (2008).
127 Under s. 29(1) of the LRA 2002. 128 Ibid., s. 4(1). 129 Ibid., ss. 11 and 12.
130 Land Registration Rules 2003, r. 35(1).

Outside first registration, the priority question in unregistered land is determined according to whether there was a deposit of the title deeds or not.[131] In brief, a mortgage protected by the deposit of title deeds takes priority over all other interests created subsequently to the mortgage unless otherwise provided for in the mortgage instrument. Where a mortgage is not protected by the deposit of title deeds, the mortgage is registrable either as a Class C(i) (legal) or Class C(iii) (equitable) land charge under s. 2(4) of LCA 1972. If not = registered, the mortgage will be void as against a subsequent purchaser of the land or any legal or equitable interest in the land made for valuable consideration under s. 4(5) of the LCA 1972.

13.7.3 Modification of the priority rules: Express and implied postponement of interests

The court has been prepared to modify the priority rules discussed in the previous sections to allow a mortgage to take priority over a pre-existing interest which would otherwise enjoy priority where it can be shown that there is either an express or implied postponement of the priority of that pre-existing interest to the mortgage.

13.7.3.1 Express postponement of pre-existing interest to the mortgage

As established by the case of *Boland*, the interest of a person in actual occupation is capable of constituting an overriding interest which is binding on a mortgagee. Mortgagees were not altogether too pleased. As a result, mortgagees now routinely insist that an express term of waiver or postponement be included in the mortgage contract which has the effect that the interests of any person occupying or intending to occupy the mortgaged property with the mortgagor are postponed (i.e. lose priority) to the interests of the mortgagee.

13.7.3.2 Implied consent to postponement of pre-existing interest to the mortgage

Postponement of a pre-existing interest to the interest of the mortgagee can also be implied in certain circumstances in relation to acquisition mortgages (i.e. mortgages granted to fund the initial purchase of a property). Postponement by implication was first observed in the case of *Bristol & West Building Society v Henning* (1985). In *Henning*, a couple purchased a house with the assistance of a loan secured against the property by way of charge with the intention that each party enjoy a 50 per cent share of the property. The mortgage was in Mr Henning's name only, and he subsequently defaulted on the mortgage payments. The lender sought possession of the land. Mrs Henning resisted. The Court of Appeal held that Mrs Henning knew or ought to have known about the mortgage and therefore any interest she had in the property had been impliedly postponed to that of the mortgagee. This is sometimes referred to as 'imputed consent'. The mortgagee's interest therefore took priority. *Henning* was followed in *Abbey National Building Society v Cann*.

[131] These rules are complex and need not be covered here in great detail: for further detail see C. Harpum, S. Bridge, and M. Dixon, *Megarry & Wade: The Law of Real* Property, 8th edn (London: Sweet & Maxwell, 2012), chapter 12.

> **KEY CASE** *Abbey National Building Society v Cann* (1991)
>
> **Facts:** Mrs Cann lived in a property, on South Lodge Avenue, purchased in the name of her son, Mr Cann. The purchase price was raised, in part, by a mortgage loan from Abbey National Building Society with the remainder supplied from the proceeds of sale of a different property in which Mrs Cann had a beneficial interest. Mrs Cann understood that a loan would be needed in the sum of £4,000 but unbeknown to her, in fact, the amount of the loan secured against the property was £25,000. Mr Cann defaulted on the mortgage repayments and Abbey National sought to have Mrs Cann (and her husband) removed from the property in order to sell the house with vacant possession.
>
> **Legal issue:** Did Mrs Cann's knowledge of the mortgage loan (albeit she believed it was in the sum of £4,000) mean that the mortgagee's interest took priority?
>
> **Judgment:** The House of Lords stated, obiter, that Mrs Cann's rights were postponed to the full extent of the mortgage (£25,000) even though she had believed the loan to be in the sum of £4,000. Mrs Cann had impliedly consented to the postponement of her rights in favour of the mortgagee's interest taking priority.

What about the position of non-acquisition mortgages (i.e. subsequent mortgages)? Priority here is governed by issues of overreaching, notice, registration, and actual occupation. One interesting caveat here, however, comes from the case of *Equity and Law Home Loans Ltd v Prestidge* (1992). The Court of Appeal held that where a property is purchased and mortgaged in the name of one party only (party A) but with the consent of another (party B) and party A subsequently remortgages the property at a higher amount without party B's knowledge, party B will be taken to have impliedly consented to the remortgage in the original sum, giving the mortgagee priority over party B's beneficial interest in the property up to but not exceeding that original sum. This may sound very little technical and obscure so let's consider the facts of *Prestidge*. In *Prestidge*, Keith and Ivy lived together and were unmarried. They purchased a house. Ivy contributed £10,000 to the purchase price thereby gaining a beneficial entitlement in the property. The remainder of the purchase price was provided by way of a mortgage loan of £30,000. The house was in Keith's sole name. Keith subsequently remortgaged the property in the sum of £43,000 without Ivy's knowledge. Keith defaulted on the mortgage and the mortgagee issued possession proceedings. The Court of Appeal held that despite Ivy's lack of knowledge of the remortgage, her consent to postponement of her interest to the mortgagee would be implied up to the original amount (£30,000) but not to the £43,000. The consequence of this was that the mortgagee's interest took priority over Ivy's beneficial interest up to the amount of the original mortgage.

Implied consent to postpone an interest to that of the mortgagee has proved controversial[132] and the decided cases could be explained variously as resting on a foundation of implied consent, imputed consent, or agency. Is the mortgagee afforded too great a protection as a result of these decisions? Most recently, in the case of *Wishart v Credit & Mercantile plc* the Court of Appeal appears to have broadened the principles of implied consent still further. In short, the court held that where an equitable owner has given authority to another party to deal with the property on their behalf and has failed to bring any limitation on that authority to the attention of a mortgagee, that equitable owner will be unable to assert her equitable right against the mortgagee:

---

[132] See, for example, R. Smith (1990) 109 LQR 545.

KEY CASE *Wishart v Credit & Mercantile plc* (2015)

Facts: Mr Wishart and Sami were friends and had been involved in property development projects together. As it transpired, Sami was a fraudster. In May 2010, a company controlled entirely by Sami, Kaymuu Ltd, purchased a property (Dalhanna), and Kaymuu Ltd was registered as the legal owner of the property, though it was understood that the land was being acquired for both Mr Wishart and Kaymuu Ltd. In June 2010, Kaymuu Ltd granted a mortgage in favour of Credit & Mercantile plc in return for a loan of £500,000 secured on Dalhanna by way of mortgage. The charge was duly registered. Mr Wishart was in occupation of the land at the time. Sami subsequently took the mortgage monies and blew the entire sum on gambling. Sami was declared bankrupt and disappeared. Kaymuu Ltd defaulted on the loan repayments. The lender obtained possession of the land and sold the property.

Legal issue: Was Mr Wishart entitled to the proceeds of sale as a result of a beneficial interest in the property? In other words, could Mr Wishart assert priority over the mortgagee as a result of his overriding interest?

Judgment: The trial judge held that Mr Wishart enjoyed a beneficial interest under the principles in *Pallant v Morgan* (1953) and that Mr Wishart was in occupation of the land at the date the charge was registered and his occupation was discoverable. However, Mr Wishart's interest did not qualify as overriding according to the 'Brocklesby principle' taken from the case of *Brocklesby v Temperance Permanent Building Society* (1895). The *Brocklesby* principle provides that where a person has allowed another to manage its asset, any limitation on the powers of this manager must be brought to the clear attention of a third party (for example, a mortgagee) if the owner is to be able to establish an interest against that third party. By way of illustration, if an equitable owner permits the legal owner of land to deal with that land, the equitable interest cannot amount to an overriding interest against the mortgagee (even where the requirements of LRA 2002 Sch. 3 are satisfied).

At first instance, the lender's charge took priority and the mortgagee was entitled to the sums claimed. Mr Wishart appealed, primarily, as to the proper application of the 'Brocklesby' principle.'

The Court of Appeal dismissed Mr Wishart's appeal holding that the trial judge had been right to apply the *Brocklesby* principle as he did. Mr Wishart had left the acquisition of the property, Dilhanna, entirely in the control of Sami. Mr Wishart exercised no supervisory function over Sami. Practically speaking, the result was that Mr Wishart had allowed Sami to hold himself out as the true beneficial owner of the property and so grant a mortgage to Credit & Mercantile. Mr Wishart was therefore unable to assert a beneficial interest that was overriding on the duly registered mortgage.

There may be potentially wide-ranging ramifications in light of the decision in *Wishart*[133] in so far as the court, in effect, appears to afford primacy to the bona fide purchaser test in the registered land context, a context which makes no provision for the application of these principles. Is the case wrongly decided or confined to its particular facts? It must be questioned whether the decision would survive an appeal to the Supreme Court. We reflect upon the implications of *Wishart* in greater detail in the next section as we consider the direction of travel for the law of mortgages.

---

[133] M. Dixon, 'The Boland Requiem' [2015] Conv 285–90.

13.8 Future directions

This chapter has demonstrated both the importance of the law of mortgages and the fine line that the law is required to tread between ensuring mortgage lenders continue to lend whilst offering sufficient protections to mortgagors whose homes are at stake. Mortgages reach into our everyday lives in a more profound way than most other aspects of the land law course. But where is the law of mortgages headed?

In section 13.5.2.1, we noted the limits placed on a mortgagee's right to possession. What we did not consider is how far the mortgagee's right to possession might be susceptible to a human rights challenge. Might it be open, for example, to a mortgagor to argue that a mortgagee's right to possession violates Art. 1 of Protocol 1 as to enjoyment of one's possessions or Art. 8 of the ECHR which guarantees respect for home and family life? Human rights arguments seem plausible but, as we will discover in Chapter 14, the wind does not appear to be blowing in this direction. In addition, we might reflect on whether the court's exercise in discretion under s. 36 of the AJA 1970 is human rights compliant. Under s. 3 of the Human Rights Act 1998, the court is called upon to interpret statutory provisions in compliance with the ECHR. When we consider s. 36 more closely, there are grounds for concluding that the provision is not human rights compliant. First, in determining whether to postpone possession, the court is focused on the financial position of the mortgagor and whether she can pay all sums due within a reasonable period. No discretion is given in the statutory language to the court to consider wider considerations such as the mortgagor's personal or non-financial circumstances. No provision is made for how possession might impact upon any relevant children of the mortgagor. This may very well not be a sufficiently robust examination and exercise of judicial discretion to ensure compatibility with the provisions of the ECHR.

Nield has argued that the mortgagee's right to possession more broadly may infringe Arts 1 of Protocol 1 and 8 of the ECHR:[134]

> Proportionality calls for an examination of the process by which a legitimate aim is achieved. So that, even though repossession to ensure the efficient repayment of debts is a legitimate aim, the means by which that repossession is obtained is a vital consideration under both Articles 1 and 8. The possibility that the lender may obtain possession without some form of judicial consideration over its exercise must tip the fair balance that lies at the heart of proportionality [and] provides the strongest argument that the right to possession conferred by sub-section 87(1) is incompatible with the [Human Rights Act 1998] and thus should be amended.

The human rights jurisprudence is by far one of the fastest-moving and liveliest areas of the law. We watch this space with interest to see how far it impacts on our land law.

The law of mortgages has been the source of political interest in recent years particularly in the light of the Great Recession of 2008 which led to a significant increase in the number of mortgaged properties being repossessed. The government in the wake of the 2008 downturn instigated a number of interventions in an attempt to assist mortgagors facing financial difficulty (often as a result of losing their jobs and not being able to meet mortgage payments). The Mortgage Rescue Scheme and The Homeowners Mortgage Support

---

[134] S. Nield, 'Charges, Possession and Human Rights: A Reappraisal of Section 87(1) Law of Property Act 1925' in E. Cooke (ed.), *Modern Studies in Property Law*, Vol. 3 (Oxford: Hart, 2005).

scheme are two such initiatives. Indications from the National Audit Office suggested that the schemes were not as successful as intended. The Rescue Scheme, for example, prevented fewer than 2,600 households avoid repossession and homelessness and cost over £240 million. It had been expected to assist over 6,000 homes at a cost of £205 million. The Homeowners Mortgage Support scheme was intended to encourage lenders to defer mortgage payments for up to two years. This scheme, too, is now closed. What these schemes demonstrate is the intense tussle between mortgagor and mortgagee, the importance of the law of mortgages and the need to strike the right balance between encouraging lenders to keep lending while protecting vulnerable homeowners.

And so the call for changes to the law continues. In 2010, a Private Members Bill, 'the Secured Lending Reform Bill' was presented to Parliament which called for an end to a mortgagee's right to peaceable re-entry and measures to ensure, on an application for possession, a mortgagor is given adequate time to prepare their defence and any counterclaim. In addition, the Bill proposed a new power be provided to the court to vary the terms of any mortgage including interest rates, payment schedule, and scale of payments where justice required it. Finally, the Bill sought an enlargement of the powers under s. 36 AJA 1970 to allow applications to be made over any property and not only dwelling-houses. The central impetus for the Bill was the protection of mortgagors who find themselves in severe financial hardship. The Bill ran out of time in the 2010 parliamentary session and has yet to be resurrected but it provides us with a reason to reflect. Is this where the law of mortgages is headed? Are we set to see greater protections for mortgagors which will shift the balance in borrowers' favour? What might be the consequence of this for the alignment of the law?

Finally, we return to the recent Court of Appeal decision in *Wishart*. Just how significant a decision is it? You will recall that the Court of Appeal in *Wishart* established that an equitable owner, who might otherwise have an overriding interest binding on a mortgagee, will be taken to have authorized the legal owner to grant a mortgage and therefore lose priority to the mortgagee even where the equitable owner knew nothing of the mortgage. On one view, this is a staggering result and one which presents a direct challenge to the essential nature of our land registration system. Moreover, if correctly decided, it would mean that Mrs Boland would not have been able to rely on an overriding interest as she would have been taken to have authorized her husband's mortgaging of their home despite her never knowing of his actions. What are we to make of the decision? It seems we have three options. First, we might conclude that the decision is wrongly decided and will be assigned to history should the issue come before the Supreme Court. Secondly, we might confine the decision to its particular and very narrow facts. It does present an unusual set of circumstances involving a very complex business relationship and perhaps it is to be seen as an unusual case where, all things considered, Mr Wishart ought to have protected his position and done more. As he took no steps, he is taken to have impliedly authorized the actions of his agent. The problem with this interpretation is that it carves out an exception to the clear statutory language of the LRA 2002. Thirdly, we could accept the decision in *Wishart* as a redrawing of the boundaries of our land registration system. This latter interpretation must be untenable given the clarity of the statutory language and the reasoning in the House of Lords' decision in *Boland*. This is a view shared by Televantos who advocates departing from the decision in *Wishart*:[135]

> The question of whether a purchaser *actually* had any way of knowing the extent of a [legal owner's] authority should be irrelevant to this inquiry. *Wishart*, by transplanting an agency doctrine into [land and] trusts law, by the back door re-introduces the doctrine of notice into priorities disputes concerning registered land. The reasoning is inconsistent with both the nature of the rights of trust beneficiaries and the aims of the LRA 2002, and so should be departed from by later courts.

How do you assess the significance of the decision?

Further reading

- M. Conaglen, 'Mortgage Powers Rhetoric' (2006) 69 MLR 583.
- M. Dixon, 'The Boland Requiem' [2015] Conv 285.
- W. Duncan and L. Wilmott, 'Clogging the Equity of Redemption: An Outmoded Concept' (2002) 2 QUTLJJ 35.
- M. Haley, 'Mortgage Default: Possession, Relief and Judicial Discretion' (1997) 17 LS 483.
- Law Commission Report No. 204, *Transfer of Land: Land Mortgages* (1991).
- S. Nield, 'Charges, Possession and Human Rights: A Reappraisal of Section 87(1) Law of Property Act 1925' in E. Cooke (ed.), *Modern Studies in Property Law*, Vol. 3 (Oxford: Hart, 2005).
- S. Nield, 'Mortgage Market Review: Hard-Wired Common Sense?' (2015) Consumer Law and Policy Online.
- M. Oldham, 'Mortgages' in L. Tee (ed.), *Land Law: Issues, Debates, Policy* (Devon: Willan, 2002).
- S. Pulleyn (2012), 'Equitable Easements Revisited' [2012] Conv 387.
- A. Televantos, 'Trusteeship, Ostensible Authority, and Land Registration: The Category Error in *Wishart*' [2016] Conv 181.
- M. Thompson, 'Do We Really Need Clogs?' [2001] Conv 502.
- A. Wallace, '"Feeling Like I'm Doing It on My Own": Examining the Synchronicity between Policy Responses and the Circumstances and Experiences of Mortgage Borrowers in Arrears' (2012) 11 Social Policy and Society 117.
- G. Watt, 'Mortgage Law as a Legal Fiction' in E. Cooke (ed.), *Modern Studies in Property Law*, Vol. 4 (Oxford: Hart, 2007).
- L. Whitehouse, 'Longitudinal Analysis of the Mortgage Repossession Process 1995–2010: Stability, Regulation and Reform' in S. Bright (ed.), *Modern Studies in Property Law*, Vol. 6 (Oxford: Hart, 2011).

---

[135] A. Televantos, 'Trusteeship, Ostensible Authority, and Land Registration: The Category Error in Wishart' [2016] Conv 181.

Online resources

Access the online resources at www.oup.com/uk/bevan2e/ to test yourself with self-test questions and scenario problems. You can also view additional supporting material relevant to the topics in this chapter, including:

- *Videos*
- *Audio podcasts*
- *Maps, diagrams, and flowcharts*
- *Interactive exercises*
- *Examples of real-life legal documentation*

14

Land Law and Human Rights

14.1 Introduction

It is now quite impossible to undertake any law degree without encountering human rights considerations and exploring the implications of the ECHR on our laws. The protections of the ECHR are said to have been brought 'home'[1] into our domestic law via the HRA 1998. As the then Prime Minister, Tony Blair, argued in 1997:

> It takes on average five years to get an action into the European Court of Human Rights once all domestic remedies have been exhausted; and it costs an average of £30,000. Bringing these rights home will mean that the British people will be able to argue for their rights in the British courts—without this inordinate delay and cost.

As we have moved through the substantive chapters of this book, where human rights issues have arisen, we have considered them. In this chapter, we do something a little different. We ask, at the broader level, how do land law and human rights interact? From a distinctly land law perspective, the human rights discourse has given rise to much debate which, today, continues to fuel significant academic commentary. We therefore begin this chapter by examining the relationship between land law and human rights. This, as you will see, is not altogether an easy relationship and remains something of a contested issue which persists in engaging and vexing lawyers almost 20 years after the HRA 1998 came into force.

 Visit the online resources to watch a video on the judgment of the Supreme Court in the *McDonald v McDonald* case.

---

[1] The Human Rights Bill was introduced to the British Parliament as part of a package of 'bringing rights home': see *Bringing Rights Home* (1997) CM3782.

14.2 The relationship between land law and human rights

It is fair to say that land law and human rights are not natural bedfellows.[2] Why is this? This apparent discommunion stems from the inherent nature of property rights versus human rights: see Figure 14.1.

At their core, property rights (and, in particular, rights in land) are concerned with self-serving notions and instincts including possession, ownership, appropriation, and that resounding retort 'this is *mine* and not yours'. In this way, entitlement in land law stems from an assertion of superiority of one's rights to property over another. Land law is centred on determining claims of one party's rights or priority over those of another. In this way, we might conceive of property rights as being self-centred, self-serving, and concerned with one's own individual status vis-à-vis others. As we encountered in Chapter 1, land law is largely preoccupied with the so-called 'priority question'; in other words, where there is a multitude of competing interests in land, whose interest takes priority in this enforceability battle or, put bluntly, who wins? This analysis remains central to the operation of land law and how property law disputes are resolved by the court today.

Human rights, on the other hand, might be seen as operating at the opposite extreme of the spectrum. Human rights, at their core, are concerned with universal, global notions of human freedoms, human dignity, and equality. These are not immediately discernible as central impulses in the operation of the principles of land law. There is, unsurprisingly, no mention of dignity in land law statutes from the LPA to the LRA 2002.[3] Human rights protect fundamental human values where land law is transaction-focused—dependent not on fundamental freedoms but on freedom of the parties to contract and on the primacy of administrative practices such as registration to ensure the free alienability of land. Property rights afford a distinctly, though not exclusively, financial[4] benefit and are often enforced to support a party's economic position. By contrast, human rights appear to occupy a higher

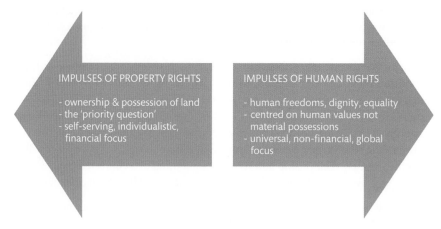

IMPULSES OF PROPERTY RIGHTS

- ownership & possession of land
- the 'priority question'
- self-serving, individualistic, financial focus

IMPULSES OF HUMAN RIGHTS

- human freedoms, dignity, equality
- centred on human values not material possessions
- universal, non-financial, global focus

Figure 14.1 The apparent divergence of property rights versus human rights

---

[2] See generally K. Gray, 'Land Law and Human Rights' in L. Tee (ed.), *Land Law: Issues, Debates, Policy* (Devon: Willan, 2002), 211.   [3] Perhaps there should be!

[4] Consider the importance of land as 'home' as explored in Chapter 6.

moral status or irreducible core of rights that reach beyond any monetary consideration, embracing ideas of respect, privacy, and fairness. Lord Macnaghten famously noted that a landowner concerned to protect his position is free to act in a manner calculated as being, 'churlish, selfish and grasping'.[5] In clear contrast, Lord Hoffmann has explained that human rights are:[6]

> rights which belong to individuals simply by virtue of their humanity, independently of any utilitarian calculation.

How far is this apparent dislocation of property rights and human rights, however, open to challenge? Gray argues that, while land law certainly does respond to different impulses and has a distinct historical foundation quite apart from human rights discourse, nevertheless, the alienation of the two disciplines must not be exaggerated:[7]

> [T]he assumed dissociation of land law and human rights has always been one of the larger (but no less insidious) myths of the law. The law of property silently betrays a range of value judgments about the 'proper' entitlements of human and other actors. These value judgments reflect a complex picture of social relationships and rankings, each casting a shadow on some extra-legal index of freedom, dignity and equality.

This chapter will focus on the key ECHR rights incorporated into domestic law by the HRA 1998—namely, Art. 1 of the First Protocol to the ECHR and Art. 8 of the ECHR. In section 14.6 we identify other Convention rights which exert an influence on land law. However, before we turn to explore these provisions in greater detail, we begin with a brief summary of the broader machinery of the HRA 1998, much of which you will be already familiar with from your Constitutional or Public Law courses.

14.3 The HRA 1998 machinery

You will have encountered the HRA 1998 machinery already as part of your wider study of law. There is little value, then, in rehearsing in detail the position here. It suffices to say that the HRA 1998 incorporated the ECHR[8] into domestic law in England and Wales and that a claimant wishing to bring a claim in the domestic court arguing that the UK has breached the ECHR, is required to jump through certain essential hoops:[9] see Figure 14.2.

Once a claimant has established a route by which the breach is relevant to the domestic courts under the HRA 1998 and demonstrated that the State's liability is engaged (i.e. there is an actionable breach) the enquiry shifts to the 'justification exercise'. Figure 14.3 depicts the hurdles that must be overcome for an interference with a qualified Convention right to be justified.[10]

---

[5] *Bradford Corporation v Pickles* (1895), 601.

[6] *R (Alconbury Developments Ltd) v Secretary of State for the Environment, Transport and the Regions* (2001), 1411. [7] Gray, 'Land Law and Human Rights', 212.

[8] The UK became a signatory to the ECHR in 1951.

[9] See A. Goymour, 'Property and Housing' in D. Hoffmann (ed.), *The Impact of the UK Human Rights Act on Private Law* (Cambridge: Cambridge University Press, 2011).

[10] See dicta of Lord Hodge in *R (on the application of ZH and CN) v London Borough of Newham and London Borough of Lewisham and Secretary of State for Communities and Local Government* (2014).

Figure 14.2 Mounting a claim for breach of a Convention right in the domestic courts

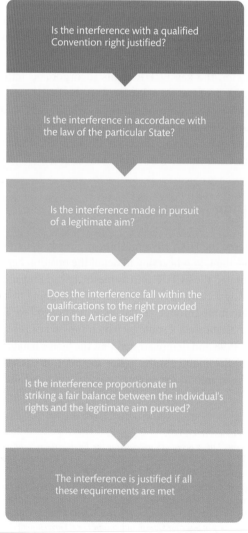

Figure 14.3 Justifying an interference with a qualified Convention right

A consideration of the intricacies of the 'justification exercise' fall outside the scope of this book, but one key issue that does warrant some further thought is the matter of horizontal effect.

We know that the HRA provides for 'vertical effect' (i.e. individual citizens have a right to bring a direct action against public authorities and the State),[11] but how far does the 1998 legislation operate 'horizontally' as between private individuals?[12] For land law, this matters as horizontal effect has the potential to 'throw off balance a system, which, whilst not perfect, has been in place in some of its parts for hundreds of years'.[13] The Supreme Court in *Manchester City Council v Pinnock* (2010) had refused to offer a view on the issue of horizontal effect and until the recent case of *McDonald v McDonald*, there was no settled position. In *McDonald*, however, the Court of Appeal, then the Supreme Court and most recently the European Court of Human Rights addressed head-on (in a direct, property law context) whether the HRA 1998 could operate horizontally. The *McDonald* litigation is well-worth a read.

KEY CASE *McDonald v McDonald* (2014–16)

Facts: The McDonalds had a daughter, Fiona, who suffered from a mental disorder which meant that she became upset by changes in her environment. As such, the McDonalds decided to buy a house for Fiona and raised the money by way of a mortgage from Capital Homes Ltd. They leased the premises to Fiona, using the rental income to meet the mortgage repayments. Subsequently, the McDonalds fell into arrears with their mortgage repayments. Capital Homes Ltd therefore appointed receivers who, acting as agents for the McDonalds, issued a notice to quit under s. 21 of the Housing Act 1988 (HA 1988) and brought possession proceedings against Fiona. Given the nature of Fiona's tenancy, the court had no discretion as to whether a possession order was made. At first instance, the judge therefore made an order for possession and Fiona appealed.

Legal issue: Fiona argued that the mandatory grounds on which possession was sought by the receiver constituted a disproportionate interference with her rights under Art. 8 of the ECHR on the basis that the court was not provided with an opportunity to conduct the proportionality exercise. Could this Art. 8 argument succeed in possession proceedings between two private individuals?

Judgment: In the Court of Appeal, Arden LJ delivering the leading judgment with which Tomlinson and Ryder LJJ agreed, accepted that Art. 8 was engaged but on the issue of horizontal effect, dismissed Fiona's appeal holding that:

1. There was no 'clear and constant' jurisprudence of the Strasbourg court that the proportionality test implied into Art. 8(2) applied in a case involving a private landlord.

2. Even if the proportionality test had applied in this case, the court would still have made a possession order.

3. In any event, the court was bound by *Poplar Housing and Regeneration Community Association Ltd v Donoghue* (2002) which held that s. 21 of the HA 1988 was compatible with the ECHR. This precluded the court from holding that the proportionality test applied.

4. In the circumstances, the question of interpreting s. 21 of the 1988 Act to conform to Convention rights did not arise.

→

---

[11] Where a public authority is found to have acted unlawfully under s. 6(1), the court can award a remedy as is 'just and appropriate' under HRA 1998, s. 8.

[12] See generally M. Hunt, 'The Horizontal Effect of the Human Rights Act' (1998) (Autumn) PL 423; N. Bamforth, 'The Application of the Human Rights Act 1998 to Public Authorities and Private Bodies' (1999) 58 CLJ 159; R. Buxton, 'The Human Rights Act and Private Law' (2001) 116 LQR 48.

[13] J. Howell, 'The Human Rights Act 1998: Land, Private Citizens, and the Common Law' (2007) 123 LQR 618.

➡

Arden LJ also rejected Fiona's second ground of appeal that the receivers did not have the authority to serve the s. 21 HA 1988 notice to quit. The receivers enjoyed powers to do anything necessary to realize the mortgaged property 'in an orderly and efficient way' and this included serving a s. 21 notice in order to secure vacant possession and sell the property. The matter proceeded to appeal in the Supreme Court. In the Supreme Court, there were three issues to be considered:

1. Whether a court, when considering a claim for possession by a private sector owner against a residential occupier, should, in light of s. 6 of the HRA 1998 and Art. 8 of the ECHR be required to consider the proportionality of evicting the occupier.

2. Whether, if the answer to question 1 was yes, the relevant legislation, in particular s. 21(4) of the 1988 Act, could be read so as to comply with that conclusion.

3. Whether, if the answers to questions 1 and 2 were yes, the trial judge would have been entitled to dismiss the claim for possession in this case, as he said he would have done.

It was Fiona's argument that the judge should have taken into account the proportionality of making an order for possession for Art. 8 purposes and, on that basis, could have refused to make an order for possession despite the apparently mandatory terms of s. 21(4) of the 1988 Act. The Supreme Court unanimously dismissed Fiona's appeal, Lord Neuberger and Lady Hale delivering the only judgment, with which the other justices agreed. The court's reasoning was as follows:

1. It was well-established that it is open to an occupier to raise the question of the proportionality of making an order for possession where the party seeking possession is a public authority within the meaning of s. 6 of the HRA. This was the effect of *Pinnock*. The court in *Pinnock*, however, made clear that nothing in its judgment was intended to bear on cases where the person seeking possession was a private landowner.

2. It was the court's 'preliminary view' that it was not open to the tenant to contend that Art. 8 could justify a different order from that which is mandated by the contractual relationship between the parties, at least where there are legislative provisions through which the democratically elected legislature has balanced the competing interests of private sector landlords and residential tenants. Were it otherwise, the ECHR could be said to be directly enforceable as between private citizens so as to alter their contractual rights and obligations.

3. The court then considered the Strasbourg authorities. It was apparent that the decisions of *Di Palma v UK* (1988) and *Wood v UK* (1997) were inconsistent with the appellant's claim to horizontal effect. The impact of these decisions was that Art. 8 was not engaged where there was an 'exclusively private law relationship between the parties'. While subsequent authorities provided a measure of support for the notion that Art. 8 was engaged on the making of the order for possession against a residential occupier, there was no support for the proposition that the judge could be required to consider the proportionality of the order which he would have made under legislation such as the 1980 and 1988 Acts.

Fiona's appeal was therefore dismissed. The court offered obiter comments as to Fiona's second and third grounds of appeal. As to the second ground, had the court been persuaded that Art. 8 operated horizontally, it would not have been possible to read s. 21(4) of the 1988 Act compatibly with Art. 8. Rather, a declaration of incompatibility under s. 4 of the HRA would have been the only remedy. As to the third ground, in those rare cases where a court is required to assess the proportionality of making a possession order, its powers to suspend or postpone the effect of that order are severely limited by s. 89(1) of the Housing Act 1980. The cases in which it would be justifiable to refuse, as opposed to postpone, a possession order must be very few and far between and could only be cases in which the landlord's interest in regaining possession was heavily outweighed by the gravity of the interference in the occupier's right to respect for her home. On the facts of the present case, it seemed likely that the most the appellant could have hoped for on a proportionality assessment would have been an order for possession in six weeks' time, the maximum permitted by s. 89(1) of the 1980 Act.

The judgment of the Supreme Court is emphatic in holding that the HRA 1998 does not have horizontal effect and is a well-supported judgment drawing widely on Strasbourg jurisprudence. Fiona subsequently took her case to the European Court of Human Rights which affirmed and reiterated the domestic courts' stance: *FJM v UK* (2018).[14] In *FJM*, the Strasbourg court restated that the loss of one's home is the most extreme form of interference with the right to respect for the home under Art. 8 but, relying on the case of *Vrzic v Croatia* (2018), confirmed that the ECHR did not operate between a private landlord and its tenant. The court reiterated that eviction proceedings brought by private parties were 'distinguishable' from those involving social landlords because private proceedings concern private property rights arising from contractual relations entered into voluntarily by the parties. The court found that the HA 1988 reflected the State's assessment of the balance to be struck between the rights of private landlords under Art. 1 of the First Protocol and their tenants under Art. 8. It was important to note, held the court, that a private tenant, by agreeing to enter a private tenancy, voluntarily agrees to the terms by which such a tenancy could be brought to an end under the relevant legislation. To allow a proportionality assessment to be conducted by the courts in this private context would lead to unpredictable and potentially damaging consequences for the private rental sector. In any event, the Strasbourg court noted that some protection was afforded to private tenants under the HA 1988 in that, in cases of 'exceptional hardship', standard 14-day possession orders could be postponed for up to six weeks. The court expressed its sympathy for Fiona's plight but, falling in line with the Supreme Court's domestic decision, held that an Art. 8 complaint could not be raised against a private sector eviction.

Where does the *McDonald* litigation leave us? Well, for now at least, it seems to settle the argument on the issue of horizontality of the ECHR. The Strasbourg court reiterated the position that it was for Parliament through legislation to make any change to the balance of rights and protections between private landlords and their tenants. It is, however, very unlikely that this will be the final say on the issue. Nield writing after the Court of Appeal judgment, for example,[15] heavily criticized the reasoning of Arden LJ, branding the Court of Appeal pronouncement:[16]

> . . . a weak decision. The reasoning is poor and at times simply inaccurate. *McDonald* is a weak decision. In this author's view the reasoning is incomplete in failing to fully address incompatibility in the context of horizontal effect. Furthermore, at times it is unconvincing. Accordingly, if the horizontal effect of the HRA upon private parties is to rest on this decision, then it will be on unstable foundations.

Nield argued, in particular, that there was a lack of engagement by the Court of Appeal in *McDonald* with the different ways in which horizontal effect might operate.[17] Leigh,[18] on whom no court in *McDonald* drew, had identified six separate ways in which private

---

[14] For a discussion of the decision of the Strasbourg court, see J. Boddy and L. Graham, 'FJM v UK: The Taming of Art. 8' (2019) 2 Conv 166.

[15] But prior to the matter coming before the Supreme Court.

[16] S. Nield, 'Thumbs Down to Horizontal Effect of Article 8' [2015] Conv 77, 88.

[17] See also E. Lees, 'Horizontal Effect and Article 8: *McDonald v McDonald*' (2015) 131 LQR 34.

[18] I. Leigh, 'Horizontal Rights, the Human Rights Act and Privacy: Lessons from the Commonwealth?' (2009) 48 ICLQ 57.

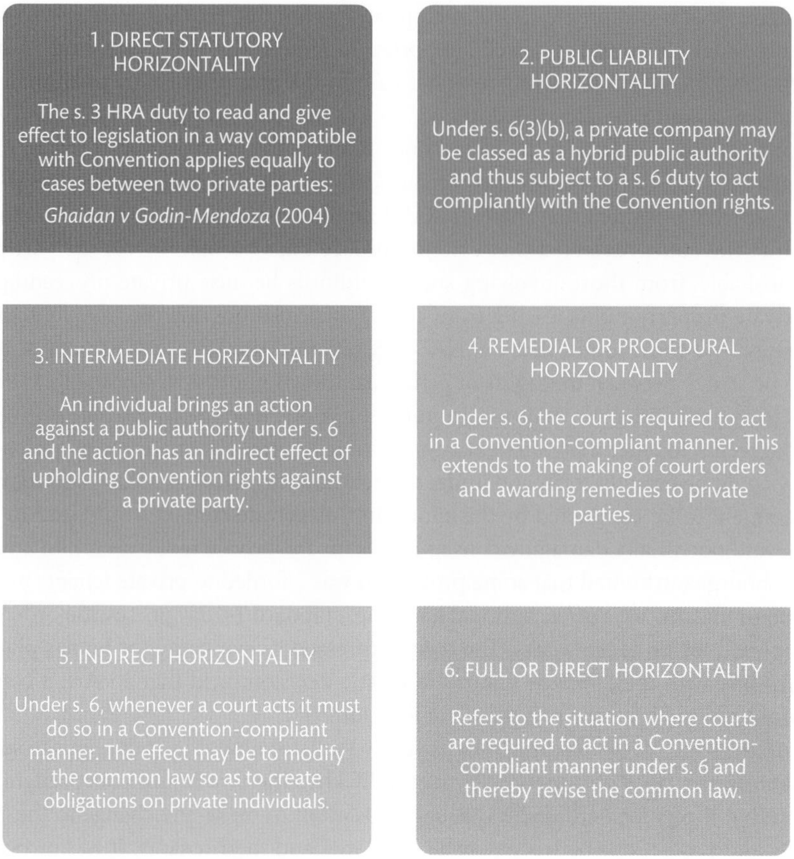

1. DIRECT STATUTORY HORIZONTALITY

The s. 3 HRA duty to read and give effect to legislation in a way compatible with Convention applies equally to cases between two private parties: *Ghaidan v Godin-Mendoza* (2004)

2. PUBLIC LIABILITY HORIZONTALITY

Under s. 6(3)(b), a private company may be classed as a hybrid public authority and thus subject to a s. 6 duty to act compliantly with the Convention rights.

3. INTERMEDIATE HORIZONTALITY

An individual brings an action against a public authority under s. 6 and the action has an indirect effect of upholding Convention rights against a private party.

4. REMEDIAL OR PROCEDURAL HORIZONTALITY

Under s. 6, the court is required to act in a Convention-compliant manner. This extends to the making of court orders and awarding remedies to private parties.

5. INDIRECT HORIZONTALITY

Under s. 6, whenever a court acts it must do so in a Convention-compliant manner. The effect may be to modify the common law so as to create obligations on private individuals.

6. FULL OR DIRECT HORIZONTALITY

Refers to the situation where courts are required to act in a Convention-compliant manner under s. 6 and thereby revise the common law.

Figure 14.4 Leigh's six modes of horizontality

parties could be impacted by Convention rights: see Figure 14.4. Set against a backdrop of 'housing crisis' in the UK and with the private rental sector expanding at a vastly greater pace than the social sector, the decision in the *McDonald* litigation that the ECHR provides no protection to private tenants facing eviction might be considered particularly troubling. Certainly, this is an area of the law on which to keep a very close eye!

We now turn to consider in sharper focus the most important rights of the ECHR from a land law perspective: Art. 1 of the First Protocol and Art. 8.

14.4 Article 1 of the First Protocol to the ECHR

This article states:

> Every natural or legal person is entitled to the peaceful enjoyment of his possessions. No one shall be deprived of his possessions except in the public interest and subject to the conditions provided for by law and by the general principles of international law.

The preceding provisions shall not, however, in any way impair the right of a State to enforce such laws as it deems necessary to control the use of property in accordance with the general interest or to secure the payment of taxes or other contributions or penalties.

Article 1 of the First Protocol guarantees peaceful enjoyment of one's existing possessions and 'in substance guarantee[s] the right of property'.[19] It does not, however, guarantee a positive right to actually receive property. The protection of one's existing property is a qualified right and the provision goes on to provide for circumstances when a deprivation of one's own property will be justified. The European Court in *Sporrong and Lönnroth v Sweden* (1983) explained that Art. 1 must be read as containing three distinct but necessarily interrelated[20] rules:[21]

The first rule, which is of a general nature, announces the principle of peaceful enjoyment of property; it is sets out in the first sentence of the first paragraph. The second rule covers deprivation of possessions and subject it to certain conditions; it appears in the second sentence of the same paragraph. The third rule recognises that the States are entitled . . . to control the use of property in accordance with the general interest, by enforcing such laws as they deem necessary for the purpose; it is contained in the second paragraph.

The Court must determine, before considering whether the first rule was complied with, whether the last two are applicable.

Article 1 therefore comprises three rules:

- Rule 1: peaceful enjoyment of property
- Rule 2: deprivation of possessions
- Rule 3: control of possessions by the State.

In analysing Art. 1, Protocol 1, and a potential infringement of the provision, we can therefore adopt the approach summarized diagrammatically in Figure 14.5.

14.4.1 When will Art. 1 of the First Protocol be engaged?

Article 1 will be engaged where 'possessions' have been affected and this constitutes an 'interference' which falls under one of the three forms of interference (Rules 1–3) identified in section 14.4. But what do we understand as 'possessions' and 'interference'?

14.4.1.1 'Possessions'

Clearly the definition of 'possessions' is vital to the operation of Art. 1.

'Possessions' is afforded an 'autonomous meaning' in the jurisprudence of the European Court. This means that the Court develops its own construction of what constitutes 'possessions' and, whilst the Strasbourg Court does have regard to the position in Member

---

[19] *Marckx v Belgium* (1979), [63]; *Sporrong and Lönnroth v Sweden* (1983), [57]; *James v UK* (1986), [37] (1986); *Banér v Sweden* (1989), [138].   [20] *James v UK.*

[21] *Sporrong and Lönnroth v Sweden*, [61].

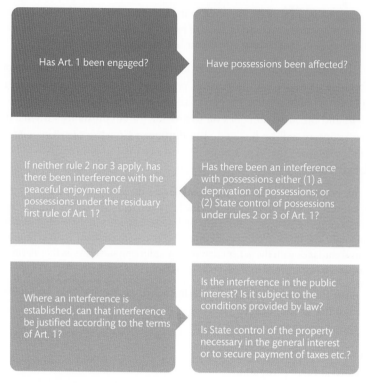

Figure 14.5 Analysis of a potential action under Art. 1, Protocol 1

States' domestic legal systems, it is free to adopt a different interpretation.[22] As the Court explained in *Broniowski v Poland* (2005):[23]

> The concept of 'possessions' in the first part of Art. 1 of Protocol No. 1 has an autonomous mean-ing which is not limited to the ownership of material goods and is independent from the formal classification in domestic law. In the same way as material goods, certain other rights and in-terests constituting assets can also be regarded as 'property rights', and thus as 'possessions' for the purposes of this provision. In each case the issue that needs to be examined is whether the circumstances of the case, considered as a whole, conferred on the applicant title to a substantive interest protected by Art. 1 of Protocol No. 1.

For the purposes of Art. 1, the meaning of 'possessions' has been given a broad interpre-tation by the European Court and extends beyond merely tangible goods. Clearly, land is covered by the definition. Yet, possessions are not restricted to merely physical goods or property and also encompass intellectual property and contractual rights (those rights arising under contract and under statute). Other examples include:

[22] See T. Allen, 'The Autonomous Meaning of "Possessions" under the European Convention on Human Rights' in E. Cooke (ed.), *Modern Studies in Property Law*, Vol. 2 (Oxford: Hart, 2003).

[23] *Broniowski*, [129].

- patents[24]
- shares[25]
- licences, for example, to sell alcohol[26]
- ownership of debt[27]
- interests under pension schemes.[28]

To qualify as 'possessions' under Art. 1, there must, however, be a discernible and associated economic value. An expectation of future property or future inheritance does not constitute a 'possession' for the purposes of Art. 1[29] but the court in *Kopecky v Slovakia* (2005) held that the term 'possessions' does include:[30]

> Claims, in respect of which the applicant can argue that he or she has at least a 'legitimate expectation' of obtaining effective enjoyment of a property right.

Land is clearly captured by the broad interpretation given to 'possessions' but what about where a parcel of land is burdened by proprietary rights such as covenants or easements? Are covenants and easements 'possessions' in their own right? It is now clear that these rights do not constitute distinct 'possessions' under Art. 1 and are treated as forming part of the land which they encumber.[31]

14.4.1.2 'Interference': The three rules

Once it has been established that possessions are affected, you must demonstrate that what has taken place in relation to those possessions constitutes an interference.

'Interference' is given a broad interpretation and signifies an activity which, as Gardner explains,[32] serves as a 'restriction on the normal exercise of your rights associated with the "possession" in question'. As Gardner and MacKenzie illustrate, the passage of a new high-speed railway through the countryside may very well constitute an interference with possessions. Landowners may either lose their property entirely or, less dramatically, may have difficulty in selling or developing their land as a result of the new infrastructure project.

In our discussion of 'possessions' we noted that encumbrances such as easements and covenants are not regarded as separate 'possessions' from the land which they burden. As to the issue of 'interferences', it is also now clear that where land is acquired which is already subject to such pre-existing burdens, this burden will not constitute an interference.[33] It is therefore important to those acquiring land to identify which encumbrances burdening land existed prior to that acquisition. Let's imagine you purchase land which is already subject to an easement in favour of a neighbour giving a right of way. This easement will not constitute an interference under Art. 1 of the First Protocol. If, however, after

---

[24] *Smith Kline and French Laboratories Ltd v The Netherlands* (1990).
[25] *Bramelid & Malmstrom v Sweden* (1982).   [26] *Tre Traktorer Aktiebolag v Sweden* (1989).
[27] *Agneesens v Belgium* (1998).   [28] *Wessels-Begervoet v The Netherlands* (1986).
[29] *Marckx v Belgium* (1979).   [30] *Kopecky*, [35].
[31] *Antoniades v UK* (1989); *Scott v UK* (1984).
[32] S. Gardner and E. MacKenzie, *Introduction to Land Law* (Oxford: Hart, 2015), 33.
[33] As explained by the Lower Chamber of the European Court of Human Rights in *J. A. Pye (Oxford) Ltd v UK* (2006).

you acquired the land, a neighbour subsequently begins using a track across your land believing they have a right of way, this could very well constitute an interference under Art. 1. Whether the **encumbrance** existed prior to the acquisition is therefore crucial.

In *Aston Cantlow Parochial Church Council v Wallbank* (2004), Mr and Mrs Wallbank acquired freehold land to which liability to repair a church chancel was attached under domestic law. The Aston Cantlow Parochial Church Council sought to enforce this liability in the sum of £100,000 against the Wallbanks who argued this amounted to a disproportionate interference with their Art. 1 rights. Three of the four judges in the House of Lords noted (obiter) that seeking to enforce the chancel liability did not constitute an interference with the church's Art. 1 rights as the land had been acquired subject to the pre-existing obligation to repair.[34] Article 1 of the First Protocol was not engaged. Lord Nicholls explained:[35]

> I recognise that Mr and Mrs Wallbank may well need to draw on their personal funds to discharge the liability. But they are not being deprived of their possessions or being controlled in the use of their property, as those expressions must be understood in the light of the general principle of peaceful enjoyment set out in the first sentence of article 1 of the First Protocol. The liability is simply an incident of the ownership of the land which gives rise to it. The peaceful enjoyment of land involves the discharge of burdens which are attached to it as well as the enjoyment of its rights and privileges. I do not think that in this case the right which article 1 of the First Protocol guarantees, read alone or in conjunction with article 14 of the Convention, is being violated.

As we have already noted, the Strasbourg Court regards Art. 1 as comprising three distinct rules of interference. Importantly, the court in *Sporrong and Lönnroth v Sweden* treated Rule 1 (peaceful enjoyment) as only engaged where neither Rule 2 nor 3 applied: see Figure 14.5. Rule 1 is therefore residual and our analysis should begin by considering whether the alleged interference falls within Rule 2 or 3. Let's look at the rules in this order and in more detail:

- Rule 2: Deprivation of possessions: A deprivation of possessions involves an expropriation or change in ownership—for example, where the government compulsorily purchases land,[36] nationalizes a business,[37] or seizes the proceeds of crime.[38] There will be no deprivation if the property owner retains some use of the possessions in question.[39]

- Rule 3: Control of possessions by the State: Control of possessions by the State will most usually be engaged where planning laws operate so as to prevent development of a parcel of land or require specific consent from a local authority.[40] Further examples include restrictions on rights of fishing or hunting[41] and on who can actually enter and make use of land.[42]

- Rule 1: Peaceful enjoyment of possessions: Any other activity which serves to restrict the exercise of rights as to possessions not covered by Rule 2 or Rule 3 should fall under Rule 1. *Sporrong and Lönnroth v Sweden* itself illustrates the Court's approach here.

---

[34] For a discussion of the breadth of this principle see Goymour, 'Property and Housing'.
[35] *Aston Cantlow Parochial Church Council v Wallbank* (2004), 573.
[36] *Howard v UK* (1987).   [37] *Lithgow v UK* (1986).
[38] *R v Ahmad* (2014).   [39] *Sporrong and Lönnroth v Sweden*.
[40] *Pine Valley Development Ltd v Ireland* (1992).   [41] *Baner v Sweden* (1989); *Chassagnou v France* (2000).
[42] *Gillow v UK* (1989).

KEY CASE *Sporrong and Lönnroth v Sweden* (1983)

Facts: Sporrong and Lönnroth, the complainants, were served with expropriation permits by the Swedish State. These permits operated so that the parties' land could, at some later time, be seized for the purposes of redevelopment and, in the interim, the complainants were barred from themselves building or redeveloping their own land. The permits remained in place over the land for many years and, ultimately, the complainants challenged the permits on the basis that they constituted an infringement of Art. 1 of the First Protocol.

Legal issue: Did the expropriation permits constitute an interference with possessions for the purpose of Art. 1 of the First Protocol?

Judgment: The Court began by identifying the three different 'rules' of interference contained within the article and explaining that Rules 2 and 3 should be considered before turning to Rule 1. The Court held that the long-term expropriation orders did not constitute deprivation of possessions (Rule 2) as there had been no formal deprivation per se as the complainants remained able to make use of, dispose of, and even mortgage their properties. Equally, the permits did not fall within Rule 3 as control of possessions. Rather, they served as an interference with the complainants' peaceful enjoyment of their possessions (Rule 1). The Court held that:

> Although the expropriation permits left intact in law the owners' right to use and dispose of their possessions, they nevertheless in practice significantly reduced the possibility of its exercise.

This interference, said the Court, could not be justified and the complainants therefore succeeded in demonstrating that the expropriation permits violated Art. 1 of the First Protocol.

There is undoubtedly scope for overlap between the rules and identifying the boundary between deprivation and control (Rules 2 and 3) appears particularly problematic. Does it really matter whether an interference comes under Rule 2 or Rule 3? Well, in fact, it matters quite a lot as the principles as to the justification of an alleged interference differ for Rule 2 and Rule 3. We will examine this more closely in the next section. For now, we will reflect a little further on the intersection between Rules 2 and 3. This overlap is epitomized by the decision of the Grand Chamber of the European Court in *J. A. Pye (Oxford) Ltd v UK*. You will recall this vital case from our discussion of adverse possession in Chapter 4.

KEY CASE *J. A. Pye (Oxford) Ltd v UK* (2006)

Facts: Pye was the proprietor of development land which adjoined a farm owned by the Grahams. The Grahams had purchased the farm in 1982 and a year later, in 1983, had entered into a short grazing agreement to make use of the development land in return for £2,000 paid to Pye. Pye subsequently refused to renew the grazing agreement, wanting to apply for planning permission and taking the view this would be readily granted if the land was not in use. Pye requested that the Grahams vacate the land and cease using it for the purpose of grazing. The Grahams persisted in their occupation and use of the land and did, for a time, make repeated requests for renewal of the grazing agreement. When there was no correspondence from Pye, the Grahams nevertheless continued to use the land as they had previously. The land was enclosed by a series of hedges and accessed via a gate for which only the Grahams had a key. The Grahams maintained the hedges, boundary fencing, and ditches every year.

→

→

In 1999, Pye issued legal proceedings seeking possession of the land. The Grahams claimed adverse possession of the land. The House of Lords, ultimately, accepted the claim to adverse possession and held that the Grahams were entitled to be registered as the new proprietors.

Pye brought an action in the European Court alleging that the law of adverse possession as it operated in English and Welsh law was incompatible with the ECHR and violated, in particular, Art. 1 of the First Protocol.

Legal issue: Was the law of adverse possession incompatible with the Convention and constituted an interference under Art. 1 of the First Protocol? The UK government argued that the Convention was not engaged and there was no positive duty on the State to protect citizens from the consequences of their own inattention. If, alternatively, the Convention was engaged, the law of adverse possession promoted a legitimate objective, land was a limited resource and it was therefore in the public interest that time limits for the recovery of possession from squatters were set by law and were finite. The absence of a regime for compensation for those losing land under the law of adverse did not render the law disproportionate.

Judgment: The Grand Chamber accepted that Art. 1 of the First Protocol was engaged but dismissed Pye's complaint and found in favour of the UK government by a majority of 10:7. The majority of the Grand Chamber in examining interference under Art. 1 held:

> The statutory provisions which resulted in the applicant companies' loss of beneficial ownership were thus not intended to deprive paper owners of their ownership, but rather to regulate questions of title in a system in which, historically, 12 years' adverse possession was sufficient to extinguish the former owner's right to re-enter or to recover possession, and the new title depended on the principle that unchallenged lengthy possession gave a title. The provisions of the 1925 and 1980 Acts which were applied to the applicant companies were part of the general land law, and were concerned to regulate, amongst other things, limitation periods in the context of the use and ownership of land as between individuals. The applicant companies were therefore affected, not by a 'deprivation of possessions' within the meaning of the second sentence of the first paragraph of Art.1, but rather by a 'control of use' of land within the meaning of the second paragraph of the provision.

The Chamber therefore identified the interference as falling within Rule 3 (control of possessions) rather than Rule 2 (deprivation of possessions). Having identified an interference with possessions under Art. 1, the Chamber went on to consider whether this interference was justified. It held that:

1. Ordinarily, the loss of land without payment of compensation would be a disproportionate interference with a landowner's rights which could not be justified under Art. 1 of the First Protocol.

2. However, the rules contained within the Land Registration Act 1925 and the Limitation Act 1980 had been in place long before Pye acquired the land. It was not, therefore, open to Pye to assert that it was ignorant of the legislation. In particular, very little action or steps were required by a landowner to stop the adverse possession clock running.

3. The lack of a compensatory regime in the event that land is lost as a result of the law of adverse possession did not render the law unfair. Such a regime would, rather, sit quite uncomfortably with the essential purpose of limitation and limitation periods whose objective is to provide legal certainty by barring parties from launching legal action after a prescribed date.

4. The law of adverse possession therefore struck a fair balance and any interference with Art. 1 of the First Protocol was justified.

Gardner and MacKenzie question the reasoning of the Grand Chamber as to the nature of the interference with Art. 1. They note that:[43]

> This analysis serves very well to highlight the problem in question. The fact is that the two descriptions ('intended to deprive paper owners of their ownership', rather to regulate questions of title') are not antithetical, as the court pretends; some interferences—such as the impact of adverse possession—clearly 'deprive paper owners of their ownership' within the second rule, at the same time as they can *also* be perfectly accurately said to 'regulate questions of title' for the third.

> Matters become worse still, of course, when we remember that there is also the first rule to be factored in. This requires us to be able to say, with fair assurance, that a particular event *is* (for example) a (mere) 'control of use', and *is not* a 'deprivation' *or indeed* 'some other kind of interference'. Sometimes perhaps we shall be able to; but often enough we shall not.

Gardner and MacKenzie argue, as a result of the confusion that may arise distinguishing Rules 2, 3, and 1, that a far more practicable approach would be to move away from the three-rule classification altogether:[44]

> No one, certainly not the Strasbourg court, has ever successfully explained why the three-rule categorisation is either theoretically meaningful or practically helpful. It would be better to recognise that interferences come not in discrete categories, but in all sorts of forms and degree of intrusiveness; quite simply, that interferences come in all shapes and sizes, but nonetheless ultimately remain . . . interferences.

14.4.2 When will an infringement of Art. 1 of the First Protocol be justified?

Once we have established that possessions have been affected and that this activity involved an interference under Art. 1, the final question to be addressed is whether this interference is justified. A close reading of the text of Art. 1 suggests that there are differences as to how interferences are justified, in particular, between Rules 2 (deprivation) and 3 (control):

- As to deprivation of possessions, Art. 1 provides that no one shall be deprived of his possessions 'except in the public interest and subject to the conditions provided for by law and by the general principles of international law'.

- As to control of possessions, Art. 1 provides that State control can be justified by reference to 'laws as [the State] deems necessary . . . in accordance with the general interest or to secure the payment of taxes or other contributions or penalties'.

Strictly speaking, therefore, under Rule 2, an interference can be justified by reference to the 'public interest' and under Rule 3 by reference to the 'general interest'. In the case of *James v UK* (1986), however, the Court appeared to accept that there is no meaningful distinction to be drawn between 'public' and 'general interest'. Importantly, as to Rule 1 (peaceful enjoyment), Art. 1 makes no reference whatsoever to either public or general interest. The Court in *James v UK* held that whichever rule of interference is engaged, the starting point test for justification is therefore the same.

---

[43] Gardner and MacKenzie, *Introduction to Land Law*, at 37.   [44] Ibid., 38–9.

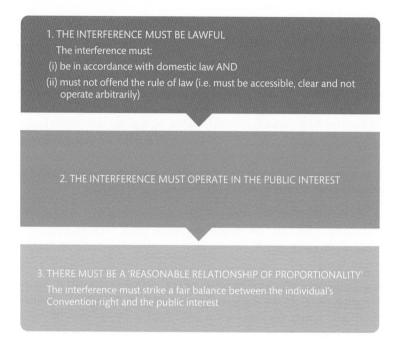

Figure 14.6 Justifying an interference with possessions under Art. 1 of the First Protocol

Where does this leave us and how is an interference with possessions under Art. 1 justified? Figure 14.6 depicts diagrammatically the steps that must be taken if an interference under Art. 1 (of either Rule 2, 3, or 1) is to be justified.

Of the three steps of justification, the first two are self-explanatory and have been touched upon earlier in this chapter. It is most certainly the third requirement, 'the proportionality exercise', which has proved to be the most difficult to pin down and to articulate. Unfortunately, the Strasbourg Court has not helped this situation by failing to engage in a clear and robust analysis. Goymour and others have sought to make sense of the approach of the Court but sadly the Court does not adopt a well-defined or consistent approach to the issue of proportionality. Proportionality essentially signals that the ends justify the means or what Hickman has described as a cost–benefit analysis. Lord Reid in the case of *Bank Mellat v HM Treasury (No. 2)* (2014) explained that the proportionality exercise was 'relatively broad-brush' and set out a structure for approaching the issue drawing on decided case law.[45] Lord Reid explained that it was necessary to determine:[46]

1. whether the objective of the measure is sufficiently important to justify the limitation of a protected right;

2. whether the measure is rationally connected to the objective;

---

[45] Points 1–3 draw on the judgment in *De Freitas v Permanent Secretary of Ministry of Agriculture, Fisheries, Lands and Housing* (1999). Point 4 is a reworked criterion from dicta of Lord Wilson in *Huang v Secretary of State for the Home Department* (2007).

[46] *Bank Mellat v HM Treasury (No. 2)*, 790–1.

3. whether a less intrusive measure could have been used without unacceptably compromising the achievement of the objective;

4. whether, balancing the severity of the measure's effects on the rights of the persons to whom it applies against the importance of the objective, to the extent that the measure will contribute to its achievement, the former outweighs the latter.

In addition to Lord Reid's helpful guide to proportionality, we can identify factors to which the Court routinely has regard in considering whether a 'reasonable relationship of proportionality'[47] exists:

- the State's margin of appreciation;
- the provision of compensation;
- procedural safeguards.

14.4.2.1 The State's margin of appreciation

In considering whether the interference strikes a 'fair balance' between the individual's Convention right and the wider, public interest, the European Court appears to place particular emphasis and weight on the State's margin of appreciation: *Sporrong and Lönnroth v Sweden*. The breadth of the margin of appreciation is demonstrated by the decision of the Court in *James v UK*.

KEY CASE *James v UK* (1986)

Facts: The claimants were trustees of a large estate comprising around 2,000 houses on land which had become one of the most desirable residential areas in London. Under the provisions of the Leasehold Reform Act 1967 as amended, tenants residing in houses under 'long leases' at 'low rents' enjoy the right to acquire by compulsory purchase the freehold of the leased properties. In this case, the claimant trustees had been deprived of their ownership of a number of the properties on the estate when the tenants of the same properties became entitled to purchase the freehold. The claimant trustees challenged the 1967 Act in an action against the UK government in the European Court arguing that it violated their Art. 1, Protocol 1 rights as it deprived them of their property rights when the tenants were given the power to purchase the freehold reversion.

Legal issue: Was Art. 1 engaged and, if so, was the interference justified?

Judgment: The Court held that:

1. Article 1 of the First Protocol was indeed engaged and the claimants had, through the operation of the Leasehold Reform Act 1967, been deprived of their possessions for the purposes of Art. 1.

2. In turning to consider whether the interference was justified, the Court focused primarily on the question of 'public interest' and the margin of appreciation. In this regard, the Court noted that:

   Because of their direct knowledge of their society and its needs, the national authorities are in principle better placed than the international judge to appreciate what is 'in the

   →

---

[47] *James v UK*.

→

public interest'. Under the system of protection established by the Convention, it is thus for the national authorities to make the initial assessment both of the existence of a problem of public concern warranting measures of deprivation of property and of the remedial action to be taken. Here, as in other fields to which the safeguards of the Convention extend, the national authorities accordingly enjoy a certain margin of appreciation.

Furthermore, the notion of 'public interest' is necessarily extensive. In particular, as the Commission noted, the decision to enact laws expropriating property will commonly involve consideration of political, economic and social issues on which opinions within a democratic society may reasonably differ widely. The Court, finding it natural that the margin of appreciation available to the legislature in implementing social and economic policies should be a wide one, will respect the legislature's judgment as to what is 'in the public interest' unless that judgment be manifestly without reasonable foundation.

3. Applying this wide margin of appreciation to the 1967 legislation, the Court continued that:

The aim of the 1967 Act, as spelt out in the 1966 White Paper, was to right the injustice which was felt to be caused to occupying tenants by the operation of the long leasehold system of tenure . . . The Act was designed to reform the existing law, said to be 'inequitable to the leaseholder', and to give effect to what was described as the occupying tenant's 'moral entitlement' to ownership of the house (ibid.). Eliminating what are judged to be social injustices is an example of the functions of a democratic legislature. More especially, modern societies consider housing of the population to be a prime social need, the regulation of which cannot entirely be left to the play of market forces. The margin of appreciation is wide enough to cover legislation aimed at securing greater social justice in the sphere of people's homes, even where such legislation interferes with existing contractual relations between private parties and confers no direct benefit on the State or the community at large. In principle, therefore, the aim pursued by the leasehold reform legislation is a legitimate one.

The provisions of the 1967 did not therefore violate the Convention and any interference with the claimants' Art. 1, Protocol 1 rights was justified.

In *James v UK*, the Court underlines just how wide is the margin of appreciation and discretion afforded to States to determine what is 'in the public interest'. In addition, the decision confirms that the actions of the State will be respected unless 'manifestly without reasonable foundation'. The effect of this is that the 'fair balance' scales are very much skewed in favour of finding an interference to be proportionate. There is a significant degree of deference paid to the activities of national legislatures in choosing to act in the manner which gave rise to the interference. The result is that the proportionality exercise (step 3 in our analysis in Figure 14.6) is not to be regarded as a particularly onerous hurdle to overcome and is, in many cases, easily satisfied.

14.4.2.2 The provision of compensation

Where an interference falls under Rule 2 of Art. 1 as a deprivation of possessions, this interference will not usually be justified under the proportionality exercise unless those deprived are provided with compensation. This is so even though, unlike other Convention rights, Art. 1 is silent on the matter. The Court in *James v UK* held that:[48]

---

[48] *James v UK*, [54].

> [T]he taking of property without payment of an amount reasonably related to its value would normally constitute a disproportionate interference which could not be considered justifiable under Article 1 Protocol 1.

The word 'normally' in this passage is important as there are exceptions. Where an interference arises in relation to significant constitutional changes taking place domestically, less than full compensation may nevertheless satisfy the proportionality test: *Former King of Greece v Greece* (2001); *Jahn v Germany* (2006). These cases have, however, been described as truly exceptional.[49]

As regards Rules 1 and 3 as to interference with peaceful enjoyment and control of possessions, the availability of compensation is but one factor and does not operate according to the same presumption as to Rule 2 just outlined. As we discovered earlier—for example, in *J. A. Pye (Oxford) Ltd*—in a case of control of possessions, the absence of a compensatory regime did not prevent the law of adverse possession being justified as proportionate. The differentiation in treatment between 'deprivations' and 'control' cases here underscores the importance of how a case is argued before the Court and how it is subsequently analysed. Should so much turn on a slender distinction between deprivation and control? Surely the distinction is simply a matter of degree. Could it be said that a deprivation of possessions is essentially a more serious example of control of possessions?

14.4.2.3 Procedural safeguards

One final important factor taken into account by the Court in conducting the proportionality exercise is that of process or, put differently, procedural safeguards. As the Court made plain in the decision in *Zehentner v Austria* (2011):[50]

> [A]lthough Article 1 of Protocol No. 1 contains no explicit procedural requirements, the proceedings at issue must afford the individual a reasonable opportunity of putting his or her case to the relevant authorities for the purpose of effectively challenging the measures interfering with the rights guaranteed by this provision. In ascertaining whether this condition has been satisfied, the Court takes a comprehensive view.

In *Zehentner*, the Strasbourg Court found that the judicial sale of the applicant's property for non-payment of a debt was an interference with her Art. 1, Protocol 1 rights that could not be justified. The sale was disproportionate largely on the basis of a failure to provide procedural safeguards. First, the debt was a comparatively minor sum and the Court doubted whether this had been taken into consideration. Secondly and crucially, the applicant lacked legal capacity and, despite the Austrian government's assertions that a fair procedure for challenging the sale was in place, the Court disagreed:[51]

> The [Austrian] Government pointed out that the applicant, represented by her guardian, had obtained a finding that the payment orders underlying the judicial sale were not enforceable due to her lack of legal capacity. Subsequently, she would be able to obtain a review of the proceedings on the merits and, if they resulted in her creditor's claims being dismissed, she could claim reimbursement of the amounts which had been paid to them from the proceeds of the judicial sale.

---

[49] *Scordino v Italy* (2009).   [50] *Zehentner*, at [73].   [51] Ibid., [77]–[78].

However, the Court is not convinced that this procedural mechanism, which requires conducting a number of consecutive sets of proceedings against each of the applicant's creditors, offers adequate protection to a person lacking legal capacity.

14.5 Article 8 of the ECHR: The right to respect for private and family life, and home

Now we turn to Art. 8, perhaps the most recognizable human rights provision of the Convention and one that is particularly pertinent to land law:

1. Everyone has the right to respect for his private and family life, his home and his correspondence.

2. There shall be no interference by a public authority with the exercise of this right except such as is in accordance with the law and is necessary in a democratic society in the interests of national security, public safety or the economic well-being of the country, for the prevention of disorder or crime, for the protection of health or morals, or for the protection of the rights and freedoms of others.

Article 8 provides a right to respect for private and family life and the home. Article 8 does *not* guarantee a right to a home nor a right to have your particular housing needs met.[52] Equally, if you find yourself homeless, Art. 8 will be of no use to you. Rather, Art. 8 guarantees respect for an *existing* home. Protection for the home as a human right is unsurprising given that few things are more key to the enjoyment of human existence than having a safe, secure and settled place to live.[53]

14.5.1 When will Art. 8 be engaged?

Article 8 is engaged when there has been an interference with 'respect' for 'home'. That much is simple but what do we mean by 'home' and 'respect' in this context?

14.5.1.1 'Home'

The term 'home', just like 'possessions' under Art. 1 of the First Protocol, is given an autonomous meaning under the ECHR.[54] A person need not enjoy a right of occupation in domestic law for a property to constitute a 'home' for the purposes of Art. 8. What is required is that an individual can point to 'sufficient and continuous links' with the property or place in question. The sufficient-link test was laid down by the European Court in *Gillow v UK* (1989) and has since been applied and discussed in much subsequent case law.[55] Despite this, the test is not always easy to articulate. It is clear that the length of time a person

---

[52] *Chapman v UK* (2001).

[53] For discussion of the value and importance of 'home' see L. Fox O'Mahony, *Conceptualising Home* (Oxford: Hart, 2007); C. Bevan, 'Challenging Home as a Concept in Modern Property Law Post-*Stack* and *Kernott*' in W. Barr (ed.), *Modern Studies in Property Law*, Vol. 8 (Oxford: Hart, 2015), chapter 11.

[54] *Buckley v UK* (1997).   [55] *Harrow LBC v Qazi* (2004); *Hounslow LBC v Powell* (2011).

has spent residing in a particular property and any ties to the land will be important factors. A very brief temporal connection to a property seems to be fatal to a finding of 'home'. By way of example, in *Leeds City Council v Price* (2006) travellers occupying a site for just two days were held to have demonstrated insufficient ties to the land after only a very brief period of occupation.[56] As Lord Bingham explained in *Harrow LBC v Qazi* (2004):[57]

> [U]se of the expression 'home' appears to invite a down-to-earth and pragmatic consideration whether [the property] is where a person 'lives and to which he returns and forms the centre of his existence'.

> The general approach of the Strasbourg institutions has however been to apply a simple, factual and untechnical test, taking full account of the factual circumstances but very little of legal niceties.

The test of 'home' is therefore not one founded on domestic or international property law conceptions but rather a broad, factual enquiry into an individual's use of and connection to land over time. As if to underline this point, it is clear that the lawfulness of an individual's occupation is relevant only at the justification stage and not in determining whether the property was being occupied as a 'home'. One consequence of this non-legalistic interpretation is that the term has been construed expansively.

In *Niemietz v Germany* (1993), the Court went as far as acknowledging that even business premises could constitute 'home' for the purposes of Art. 8. It is often said that this wide interpretation stems from the French version of the text which makes reference to a right to '*respect de sa vie privée et familiale, de son domicile et de sa correspondance*'. The French text's reference to 'domicile' is said to bear a wider interpretation than the term 'home'. This may have influenced the Court's consideration of the issue. As Nield has explored,[58] the term 'home' has also been construed as embracing the psychological notions of identity and self-determination, as well as a place where relationships are formed and maintained.[59]

14.5.1.2 Interference with 'respect' for home

Establishing that Art. 8 has been infringed requires demonstrating (1) that the property in questions is a 'home', and (2) that there has been interference with respect for that home. In fact, demonstrating an interference with Art. 8 respect for home proves relatively easy to do and the courts have construed many different scenarios as constituting interference. You must remember that, at this first stage of the enquiry, we are not concerned with whether an interference is justified but rather whether any interference in fact arises. The following are examples where the Court has found Art. 8 to have been engaged and an interference to exist:

- compulsory purchase of land: *Howard v UK* (1987);
- eviction from land: *Cyprus v Turkey* (1976);
- exercising a right to possession: *Pinnock* (2010); *Hounslow LBC v Powell* (2011);
- preventing occupation of land: *Gillow v UK* (1989);

---

[56] See also *O'Rourke v UK* (1997).   [57] *Qazi*, 990.
[58] S. Nield, 'Article 8 Respect for the Home: A Human Property Right' (2013) 24 KLJ 149.
[59] See discussion in *Connors v UK* (2005).

- pollution and noises affecting amenity of land: *Hatton v UK* (2003);
- road maintenance and construction near land: *Khatun v UK* (1998).

Once engaged, the next issue to be considered is whether the interference with Art. 8 is justified.

14.5.2 When will an infringement of Art. 8 be justified?

Figure 14.7 depicts the justification exercise for Art. 8. In summary, restrictions on respect for one's home will be justified if they are in accordance with the law, necessary in a democratic society in response to a pressing social need and are proportionate to the legitimate social aim pursued.

The first step, that the interference must be lawful (i.e. in accordance with domestic law and the rule of law), is self-explanatory. It is the second and third steps in Figure 14.7 which have proved the more contested. Once it is established that the interference is lawful, it must then be shown (1) that the measure is 'necessary in a democratic society',[60] and (2) the measure is proportionate to the legitimate aim pursued.

14.5.2.1 Proving that the measure was 'necessary in a democratic society'

This involves pointing to one of the legitimate aims listed in Art. 8(2) and demonstrating a 'pressing social need'. The listed legitimate aims include:

- the interests of national security
- the interests of public safety or the economic well-being of the country

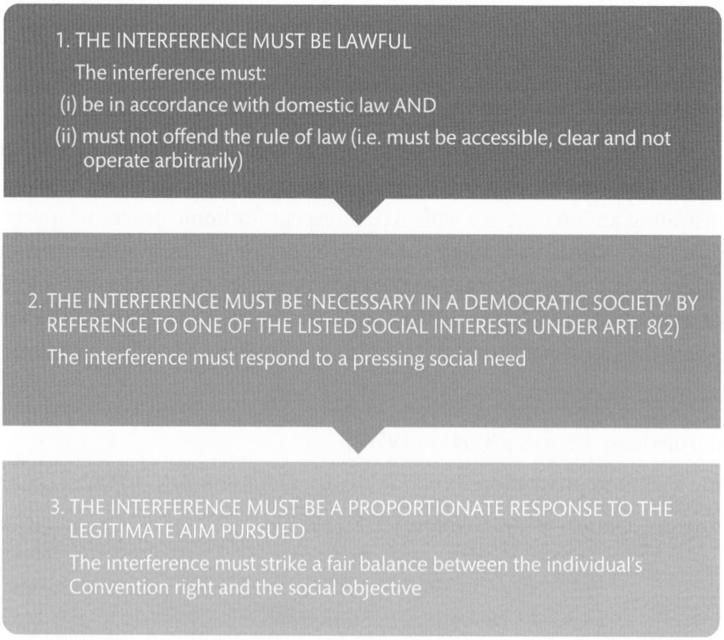

> **1. THE INTERFERENCE MUST BE LAWFUL**
> The interference must:
> (i) be in accordance with domestic law AND
> (ii) must not offend the rule of law (i.e. must be accessible, clear and not operate arbitrarily)

> **2. THE INTERFERENCE MUST BE 'NECESSARY IN A DEMOCRATIC SOCIETY' BY REFERENCE TO ONE OF THE LISTED SOCIAL INTERESTS UNDER ART. 8(2)**
> The interference must respond to a pressing social need

> **3. THE INTERFERENCE MUST BE A PROPORTIONATE RESPONSE TO THE LEGITIMATE AIM PURSUED**
> The interference must strike a fair balance between the individual's Convention right and the social objective

Figure 14.7 Justifying an interference with Article 8

---

[60] ECHR, Art. 8(2).

- the prevention of disorder or crime
- the protection of health or morals
- the protection of the rights and freedoms of others.

In pursuing one or more of these legitimate aims, the measure taken must respond to 'a pressing social need': *The Sunday Times v UK* (1979). Note the sheer breadth of these legitimate aims—in particular, 'economic well-being' which could doubtless be used in almost every case in which Art. 8 is engaged!

14.5.2.2 Proving that the measure is proportionate to the legitimate aim pursued

A measure will be proportionate if it strikes a fair balance between that individual's Convention rights and the pressing, social need pursued by the measure in question. As with Art. 1 of the First Protocol, the State is afforded a wide margin of appreciation under Art. 8.

From a land law perspective, the Art. 8 case law surrounding the provision of social housing and possession proceedings launched by social landlords has proved to be the most fruitful. The approach of the Strasbourg Court to the proportionality exercise in this context is summarized by the Court in *Kay v UK* (2012):

> In making their initial assessment of the necessity of the measure, the national authorities enjoy a margin of appreciation in recognition of the fact that they are better placed than international courts to evaluate local needs and conditions . . . The Court set out its approach in *Connors*, cited above, § 82, in which it stated:
>
> > ' . . . The margin will tend to be narrower where the right at stake is crucial to the individual's effective enjoyment of intimate or key rights . . . On the other hand, in spheres involving the application of social or economic policies, there is authority that the margin of appreciation is wide . . . The Court has also stated that in spheres such as housing, which play a central role in the welfare and economic policies of modern societies, it will respect the legislature's judgment as to what is in the general interest unless that judgment is manifestly without reasonable foundation . . . Where general social and economic policy considerations have arisen in the context of Article 8 itself, the scope of the margin of appreciation depends on the context of the case, with particular significance attaching to the extent of the intrusion into the personal sphere of the applicant . . .'
>
> [It] is clear . . . that the requirement under Article 8(2) that the interference be 'necessary in a democratic society' raises a question of procedure as well as one of substance. The procedural safeguards available to the individual will be especially material in determining whether the respondent State has, when fixing the regulatory framework, remained within its margin of appreciation.
>
> As the Court emphasised in *McCann*, the loss of one's home is the most extreme form of interference with the right to respect for the home. Any person at risk of an interference of this magnitude should in principle be able to have the proportionality of the measure determined by an independent tribunal . . .

This last paragraph is crucial as it underlined that Art. 8 required that courts have the power to engage in a proportionality exercise whenever asked by a local authority to make an order for possession of a person's home. The decision of the Strasbourg Court in *Kay v UK* followed that in *Connors v UK* (2005) and *McCann*[61] and, at the time, stood in direct contrast

---

[61] *McCann v UK* (2008).

to the position adopted in a series of decisions of the then House of Lords in the domestic courts: *Qazi*, *Kay v Lambeth LBC; Leeds City Council v Price*, and *Doherty v Birmingham City Council* (2008). The House of Lords in this trio of decisions reached an entirely different conclusion to the Strasbourg Court on precisely the same issue. In what has been variously described as a 'battle' and a 'dialogue' with the European Court, the House of Lords resisted attempts to allow human rights to intrude into possession proceeding disputes.

Harrow LBC v Qazi

In *Qazi*, by a bare majority, the House of Lords refused to allow a husband's Art. 8 defence to possession proceedings brought by Harrow London Borough Council when his wife had passed away. Lord Hope explained that contractual and proprietary rights to possession could not be defeated by a defence based on Art. 8. The result was, effectively, to hold that all possession claims were compatible with Art. 8 and the Convention was irrelevant in these proceedings.

Kay v Lambeth LBC; Leeds City Council v Price

In the conjoined appeal of *Kay; Price*, the House of Lords was called upon to revisit the *Qazi* decision following the Strasbourg decision in *Connors* in which travellers who were evicted from local authority land successfully established that the eviction violated their Art. 8 rights. In *Kay*, the local authority sought to recover possession from a tenant whose (*Bruton*) tenancy had been lawfully terminated. In *Price*, the local authority sought possession occupied by travellers. Both defendants argued that their Art. 8 rights had been infringed. The House of Lords found that the travellers had only occupied the land for two days and this was an insufficient connection with the land to engage Art. 8. In *Kay*, the House of Lords was concerned by the 'colossal waste of time and money' that Art. 8 claims would incur. The majority (4:3) therefore set out two circumstances when a defence could be raised to a possession claim. These later became known as the two 'gateways'.[62]

> Gateway (a): This would be a seriously arguable challenge under Art. 8 to the law under which the possession order is made, but only where it is possible (with the interpretative aids of the HRA 1998) to adapt the domestic law to make it more compliant.
>
> Gateway (b): This would be a seriously arguable challenge on conventional, judicial review grounds (rather than under the HRA 1998) to the authority's decision to recover possession.

The effect was that, according to the majority, human rights arguments could only be raised under gateway (a) but were irrelevant under gateway (b) when seeking judicial review of a local authority's decision to evict an occupier. The minority argued that Art. 8 was applicable to both gateway (a) and (b).

In *McCann*, a decision of the Strasbourg Court handed down after *Kay; Price*, it was held that any occupier at risk of losing their home should be entitled:

> [T]o have the proportionality of the measure determined by an independent tribunal . . . notwithstanding that, under domestic law, his right of occupation has come to an end.

---

[62] *Doherty v Birmingham City Council* (2006), per Carnwath LJ in the Court of Appeal; Lord Hope in the House of Lords.

Subsequently in *Kay v UK*, the Strasbourg Court held that the approach to Art. 8 adopted by the domestic House of Lords in *Kay* had been too restrictive. Kay's Art. 8 rights should have been considered by the domestic court, this had not been done and this constituted a violation of Art. 8. The Strasbourg and domestic courts were diametrically opposed in their view of the application of the Convention right to possession proceedings.

Doherty v Birmingham City Council

In Doherty, another case in which the local authority sought possession of a site previously occupied by travellers, despite the strength of the Strasbourg position, the House of Lords held firm to its view that gateway (b) had 'nothing to do'[63] with Art. 8 considerations. Prior to the decision of the Supreme Court in *Pinnock*,[64] which we will discuss next, the domestic courts:[65]

> clung to their view that the Convention should rarely—and only via gateway (a)—upset established domestic property law principles. As such, the law of property retained strong—albeit not complete—fortifications against human rights challenges.

These fortifications were well and truly demolished by the Supreme Court in *Pinnock* and this position was confirmed in *Powell*.

Manchester City Council v Pinnock; Hounslow LBC v Powell

In *Pinnock* and followed in *Powell*, the domestic courts, at last, acceded to the Strasbourg Court's long-held, consistent approach (and the minority view in *Kay; Price*) to the application of Art. 8 in possession proceedings. Whilst strictly speaking obliged only to 'take into account' the decisions handed down by the Strasbourg Court, the domestic court held that where there was a clear and consistent line of European jurisprudence 'whose reasoning does not appear to overlook or misunderstand some argument or point of principle' it was 'wrong' for the court not to follow that line of authority.

KEY CASE *Manchester City Council v Pinnock* (2010)

Facts: Mr Pinnock lived in a property owned by Manchester City Council for over 30 years with a partner. From time to time, one or more of their shared five children would also reside in the premises. Due to a series of incidents of serious antisocial behaviour by various members of the Pinnock family (though not Mr Pinnock himself), the Council served notice on Mr Pinnock seeking possession of the property. A possession order was granted to the Council. Mr Pinnock contended that the possession order violated his Art. 8 right to respect for his home and was disproportionate.

Legal issue: Was Art. 8 engaged in possession proceedings and was it open to the court to undertake a proportionality review?

→

---

[63] Per Lord Walker in *Doherty* (2008).

[64] For a discussion of the case, see S. Bright, '*Manchester CC v Pinnock* (2010)—Shifting Ideas of Ownership in Land' in N. Gravells (ed.), *Landmark Cases in Land Law* (Oxford: Hart, 2013), chapter 11.

[65] Goymour, 'Property and Housing', 267.

➜

Judgment: Both the county court and the Court of Appeal rejected Mr Pinnock's Art. 8 submissions on the grounds of the established position in the previous line of House of Lords authorities (*Qazi, Kay; Price, Doherty*) that it was not open to the court to engage in a proportionality review under Art. 8 in such possession proceedings.

On appeal, the Supreme Court departed from the approach adopted by the courts below it and the previous decisions of the House of Lords. Lord Neuberger delivering the unanimous judgment of the Supreme Court held that:

> [I]f our law is to be compatible with Article 8, where a court is asked to make an order for possession of a person's home at the suit of a local authority, the court must have the power to assess the proportionality of making the order, and, in making that assessment, to resolve any relevant dispute of fact.

Lord Neuberger went on to explain the influence on the domestic court of the European jurisprudence in the following terms:

> This court is not bound to follow every decision of the European court. Not only would it be impractical to do so: it would sometimes be inappropriate, as it would destroy the ability of the court to engage in the constructive dialogue with the European court which is of value to the development of Convention law . . . Where, however, there is a clear and constant line of decisions whose effect is not inconsistent with some fundamental substantive or procedural aspect of our law, and whose reasoning does not appear to overlook or misunderstand some argument or point of principle, we consider that it would be wrong for this court not to follow that line.

The court set out the following propositions as to the application of Art. 8 which it identified as established principles in the Strasbourg Court jurisprudence:

(a) Any person at risk of being dispossessed of his home at the suit of a local authority should in principle have the right to raise the question of the proportionality of the measure, and to have it determined by an independent tribunal in the light of Art. 8, even if his right of occupation under domestic law has come to an end.

(b) A judicial procedure which is limited to addressing the proportionality of the measure through the medium of traditional judicial review (i.e. one which does not permit the court to make its own assessment of the facts in an appropriate case) is inadequate as it is not appropriate for resolving sensitive factual issues.

(c) Where the measure includes proceedings involving more than one stage, it is the proceedings as a whole which must be considered in order to see if Art. 8 has been complied with.

(d) If the court concludes that it would be disproportionate to evict a person from his home notwithstanding the fact that he has no domestic right to remain there, it would be unlawful to evict him so long as the conclusion obtains—for example, for a specified period, or until a specified event occurs, or a particular condition is satisfied.

The Supreme Court did, however, place certain restrictions on the availability of an Art. 8 defence. Lord Neuberger identified a series of 'general points' as to the role and operation of Art. 8 and the proportionality exercise:

1. Article 8 is only engaged when a person's 'home' is involved.

2. As a general rule, the proportionality of seeking a possession order will be considered *only* if the point is raised directly by the occupier.

➜

→

3. Any Art. 8 claim raised should (initially at least) be considered summarily.

4. Even where an outright order for possession is justified under domestic law, Art. 8 may nevertheless (in exceptional circumstances) warrant granting an extended period for possession, suspending any possession order, or refusing an order altogether.

5. The conclusion that the court must have the ability to consider the Art. 8 proportionality of making a possession order may require certain statutory and procedural provisions to be revisited.

6. The Art. 8 proportionality exercise is more likely to be relevant in respect of occupiers who are 'vulnerable'.

Applying these principles to the instant case, the Supreme Court held that Art. 8 was engaged but Mr Pinnock's eviction was proportionate in view of the series of antisocial incidents carried out by his sons.

Despite not reaching the result Mr Pinnock had wanted, the decision of the Supreme Court in *Pinnock* is an extremely important one for its alignment of the domestic court's approach to Art. 8 with that of the Strasbourg jurisprudence bringing the decade-long, troubled relationship between Strasbourg and the domestic courts to an end. A unanimous Supreme Court in *Powell*, which is regarded as the 'sequel' to *Pinnock*, albeit concerning a homelessness context, subsequently confirmed the approach taken in *Pinnock*.

After *Pinnock* and *Powell*, occupiers threatened with eviction and defending possession proceedings issued by a public authority are able to request that a court consider the proportionality of the proposed eviction. This will surely encourage public authorities to give greater thought to the basis upon which they instigate possession proceedings than was previously the case. In addition, *Pinnock* and *Powell*, confirm that the arbitrary distinction between gateways (a) and (b) taken from the case of *Kay; Price* has been swept aside ensuring greater application of Art. 8 Convention arguments.

Whilst welcome for its opening of the door to greater application of Art. 8 in property law disputes, the Supreme Court in *Pinnock* and *Powell* nevertheless laid down a series of what could be called 'counterweights' to offset the potential burden on the judicial system of a flood of human rights arguments:

• It was made plain in *Pinnock* that the Supreme Court's decision extended to the vertical application of Art. 8 only and the court was not addressing the horizontality issue:[66]

> We emphasise that this [judgment] relates to possession proceedings brought by local authorities. As we pointed out at para 4 above, nothing which we say is intended to bear on cases where the person seeking the order for possession is a private landowner. Conflicting views have been expressed both domestically and in Strasbourg on that situation . . . But it is preferable for this Court to express no view on the issue until it arises and has to be determined.

The Supreme Court and Strasbourg Court have since expressed a clear and unanimous view on horizontality in *McDonald* as we discussed in section 14.3.

---

[66] *Pinnock*, 126.

- The effect of the decisions in *Pinnock* and *Powell* is that an Art. 8 argument will only be considered by the court if the point is raised directly by the occupier. Courts are not expected to consider Art. 8 arguments off their own bat. This places the responsibility firmly with the party facing eviction to seek proper legal advice. Those occupiers who do not avail themselves of legal advice will find themselves barred from later relying on the Art. 8 guarantees.

- Just because an Art. 8 argument is *possible* in possession proceedings issued by public authorities evidently does not mean that the argument will succeed.

Regarding this final argument, in *Pinnock* the court noted that:[67]

> [I]n virtually every case where a residential occupier has no contractual or statutory protection, and the local authority is entitled to possession as a matter of domestic law, there will be a very strong case for saying that making an order for possession would be proportionate.

Whilst Lord Neuberger rejected that only in 'very highly exceptional cases' would an order for possession be held to be disproportionate, it is quite plain that it will only be in a rare case that an occupier will succeed under the proportionality review. Why is this? Lord Neuberger explained that the question was always whether the sought eviction was a proportionate means of achieving a legitimate aim. In an action by a social landlord for possession, the proportionality of making an order for possession is likely to be supported, said the court, on two bases:[68]

> [First] the fact that it would serve to vindicate the authority's ownership rights. It will also, at least normally, be supported by the fact that it would enable the authority to comply with its duties in relation to the distribution and management of its housing stock, including, for example, the fair allocation of its housing, the redevelopment of the site, the refurbishing of sub-standard accommodation, the need to move people who are in accommodation that now exceeds their needs, and the need to move vulnerable people into sheltered or warden-assisted housing. Furthermore, in many cases (such as this appeal) other cogent reasons, such as the need to remove a source of nuisance to neighbours, may support the proportionality of dispossessing the occupiers.

Lord Neuberger continued by emphasizing that:

> Unencumbered property rights, even where they are enjoyed by a public body such as a local authority, are of real weight when it comes to proportionality. So, too, is the right—indeed the obligation—of a local authority to decide who should occupy its residential property. As Lord Bingham said in *Harrow v Qazi* [2004] 1 AC 983, 997, para 25:
>
> > '[T]he administration of public housing under various statutory schemes is entrusted to local housing authorities. It is not for the court to second-guess allocation decisions . . .'

The court will therefore attach very significant weight to the public authority's vindication of its property rights and, additionally, to the very difficult task of social housing management in which they must engage. This point was amplified yet further in *Powell* where Lord Hope explained:[69]

> In the ordinary case the relevant facts will be encapsulated entirely in the two legitimate aims that were identified in *Pinnock*, para 52. It is against those aims, which should always be taken for

---

[67] Ibid., 127.   [68] Ibid., 126–7.   [69] *Powell*, 208.

granted, that the court must weigh up any factual objections that may be raised by the defendant ... It is only if a defence has been put forward that is seriously arguable that it will be necessary for the judge to adjourn the case for further consideration of the issues of lawfulness or proportionality. If this test is not met, the order for possession should be granted. This is all that is needed to satisfy the procedural imperative that has been laid down by the Strasbourg court.

Lord Hope in *Powell* therefore goes further than the court in *Pinnock* in indicating that only where an occupier facing eviction can point to a 'seriously arguable' Art. 8 submission should the court adjourn proceedings to conduct the proportionality review and where such an enquiry is undertaken, the twin aims of vindicating property rights and management of social housing stock will, in most cases, prove decisive of the issue. The public authority should, it seems, presumptively be taken as acting in accordance with these legitimate aims. Additionally, as we already noted, the Supreme Court was concerned with the procedural difficulties that might be caused by a slew of Art. 8 claims in possession proceedings. The court was clearly at pains to keep within limits the effect of these claims.

It might be said that in *Pinnock* and *Powell*, the court gave with one hand and took away with the other. The result is a pre-weighting in the proportionality exercise in favour of the property right, in favour of the public authority.[70] It will be challenging indeed for a social housing tenant facing eviction to overcome this heavy presumption. And so it has proved. There are only a very small number of cases where an Art. 8 defence to possession proceedings has succeeded. One example is *Southend-on-Sea v Armour* (2014) where Mr Armour, who had Asperger's and depression, successfully defended local authority possession proceedings brought against him for his antisocial behaviour. Mr Armour could point to over 12 months of good behaviour and, on this basis, the court found it would not be proportionate to grant the authority an order for possession.[71]

Successful Art. 8 defences of the kind in *Armour* are rare. For some, this may be troubling. For others such as Goymour the decision in *Pinnock* serves as a welcome acknowledgement of the status of property rights in the face of Art. 8's potential destabilizing influence and offers a harmonious and 'eminently sensible' balance of principle and pragmatism to the proportionality test.[72] Might we, however, bemoan the absence in the Supreme Court's analysis of a meaningful engagement with the more subjective considerations of 'home' (as discussed in Chapter 6 on interests in the home) and Mr Pinnock's psychological attachment to his property?[73] Without a consideration of the more subjective, home-centric concerns of the case, the scales are tilted even more markedly in favour of public authorities and against the occupier in the Art. 8 analysis.

14.5.3 Article 8 and procedural safeguards

The interplay between Art. 8 and procedural safeguards warrants special mention. Lord Neuberger in the Supreme Court in *Pinnock* made express reference to the need for adequate procedural safeguards to be in place when considering the proportionality exercise

---

[70] Gardner and MacKenzie, *Introduction to Land Law*, 47.

[71] The Court of Appeal rejected an appeal by the local authority, upholding the decision of the lower court.

[72] See Goymour, 'Property and Housing', 294.

[73] A point made by Bevan in 'Challenging Home as a Concept in Modern Property Law Post-*Stack* and *Kernott*'.

under Art. 8. This has been an area of much recent judicial activity as the courts grapple with the question of how far an absence of procedural safeguards constitutes a violation of Art. 8. In the important judgment in *R (on the application of ZH and CN) v London Borough of Newham and London Borough of Lewisham and Secretary of State for Communities and Local Government* the Supreme Court addressed this question head-on in a case concerning homelessness duties.

KEY CASE *R (on the application of ZH and CN) v London Borough of Newham and London Borough of Lewisham and Secretary of State for Communities and Local Government* (2014)

Facts: Two single mothers were provided temporary accommodation under s. 188 of the Housing Act 1996 (HA 1996) by their respective local authorities while further enquiries were made as to whether they were deemed statutorily homeless and therefore entitled to further housing assistance. Each mother occupied this temporary accommodation under a licence granted on a nightly or day-to-day basis. Both Newham and Lewisham London Borough Council concluded that the mothers were intentionally homeless and therefore asked them to leave the temporary accommodation. Subsequently, both mothers brought claims for judicial review of the authorities' decisions and the matter ultimately was appealed to the Supreme Court relying chiefly on s. 3 of the Protection from Eviction Act and Art. 8. Section 3 of the 1977 Act provides:

> Where any premises have been let as a dwelling under a tenancy which is neither a statutorily protected tenancy nor an excluded tenancy and

(a) The tenancy (in this section referred to as the former tenancy) has come to an end, but

(b) The occupier continues to reside in the premises or part of them,

> it shall not be lawful for the owner to enforce against the occupier, otherwise than by proceedings in the court, his right to recover possession of the premises.

Legal issue: The Supreme Court was asked to address two central legal questions:

1. Under s. 3 of the Protection from Eviction Act 1977, is a local housing authority required to obtain a court order before taking possession of interim accommodation?

2. Does a local authority which evicts a person without obtaining a court order where a duty to provide temporary accommodation has come to an end, violate that person's Art. 8 rights?

Judgment: The mothers' appeals were dismissed. The Supreme Court held that:

1. The local housing authorities did not need to obtain a court order under s. 3 of the 1977 Act to evict the mothers as the mothers did not occupy the temporary accommodation 'as a dwelling' as s. 3 requires. The words 'live', 'reside', and 'dwell' were ordinary words and should not be given a technical meaning. The word 'dwelling' in s. 3 suggested a greater degree of permanence and settled occupation than mere 'residence' and should therefore be equated with a person's home. Occupation under a licence was not occupying the premises 'as a dwelling'. Important in reaching this decision were the following factors: (i) the duty of a local authority to provide temporary accommodation could involve very short periods of time and different locations; (ii) those residing in temporary accommodation could be required to move to alternative accommodation at very short notice; (iii) requiring local authorities to seek court orders to evict those in temporary accommodation would impose a significant burden on authorities and hamper the statutory

→

➙

scheme as to homelessness under the HA 1996. Regard must also be had to the policy underlying the statute. Lord Neuberger and Lady Hale dissented, arguing that the word 'dwelling' was as wide as 'reside' and the purpose of s. 3 was to protect those lawfully living in premises. S. 3 should be given a broad interpretation.

2. Although Art. 8 was engaged, eviction from temporary accommodation provided under s. 188 of the HA 1996 did not violate Art. 8 as there were sufficient procedural safeguards in place including under the HA 1996, the Children Act 1989 (which requires an assessment be made of the needs of any relevant children and duty to safeguard the welfare of such children), and the availability of judicial review of the authorities' decisions to ensure compliance with Art. 8. Lord Hope noted that:

> In my view, when one looks at the procedures as a whole, the procedural safeguards contained in the 1996 Act, the procedures available under the Children Act 1989 and the possibility of judicial review of the authority's s. 2 of the Housing Act 1996 decision by a court with enhanced powers are sufficient to comply with article 8 of ECHR in this context. See paras 70 and 71 below. Article 8's procedural guarantee does not require further involvement of the court in granting an order for possession. The interim accommodation which an authority provides under section 188 of the 1996 Act is but transient accommodation, a stop gap pending the completion of inquiries and a decision on the scope of the authority's duties towards a homeless person. As I have set out above, domestic law requires less formal procedures at the final stage of the recovery of possession in such circumstances than when the occupier has a more substantial and long-term connection with the accommodation ... Having regard to the proceedings as a whole, there are several opportunities for the applicant to involve himself or herself in the decision-making process and also procedures by which an independent tribunal can assess the proportionality of the decision to re-possess the accommodation and determine relevant factual disputes. In my view there are sufficient procedural safeguards to satisfy the applicant's article 8 rights. The article 8 challenge therefore fails.

As such, though engaged, Art. 8 had not been violated. The termination of the mothers' occupation licences was:

(i) in accordance with the law

(ii) in pursuit of a legitimate aim to allow the accommodation to be made available to other applicants entitled to temporary accommodation, and

(iii) recovery of that temporary accommodation was proportionate to the legitimate aim pursued and necessary in a democratic society.

The message from the Supreme Court is loud and clear: an Art. 8 argument will fail where there are adequate procedures in place which:

• permit individuals affected by eviction or termination of accommodation to be involved in the decision-making process, and

• permit those individuals to seek review of any decisions reached by a local authority as to termination of accommodation, and

• permit an independent tribunal to assess the proportionality of the decision to evict (for example by way of judicial review).

14.5.4 **Article 8 and vulnerability: A special case?**

As we have seen, it has proved challenging to persuade a court that an order for possession sought by a local authority is disproportionate. This argument is far more likely to succeed where the claimant is vulnerable, whether that be as a result of mental illness, old age, or disability. In *Pinnock*, Lord Neuberger acknowledged the vulnerability issue:[74]

> The suggestions put forward on behalf of the Equality and Human Rights Commission, that proportionality is more likely to be a relevant issue 'in respect of occupants who are vulnerable as a result of mental illness, physical or learning disability, poor health or frailty', and that 'the issue may also require the local authority to explain why they are not securing alternative accommodation in such cases' seem to us well made.

Lord Neuberger's comments reflect a growing body of case law of the Strasbourg Court which has acknowledged that States are under a positive duty towards vulnerable groups.[75] We know therefore that those who are vulnerable as a result of mental illness, disability, and age are more likely to succeed in persuading a court that actions by a local authority do not satisfy the proportionality test. Recall our discussion of *Armour* in section 14.5.2.2. Mr Armour's mental illness was a key factor in the court's reasoning. The difficulty is determining when and what measure of vulnerability will result in a finding that possession sought by a local authority is disproportionate. Nield has explored the issue of vulnerability and explains that:[76]

> Vulnerability must be seen in the context of the eviction, in the sense that the vulnerability will be exacerbated by the eviction. In *Bjedov* [*v Croatia*] there was evidence that the health of the 78 year old Mrs Bjedov would have been seriously affected by her eviction. By contrast in *Corby v Scott* a murderous assault on the occupier was discounted because it was unconnected with the eviction.

The courts appear to be reticent to lay down any particular definition of vulnerability for the purposes of the proportionality exercise. It has, however, been suggested in the domestic courts that any vulnerability could be mitigated and any disproportionality thereby avoided by the provision of support services or alternative accommodation.[77]

14.6 **Other ECHR provisions exerting an influence on land law**

We have spent the bulk of this chapter considering Art. 1 of the First Protocol and Art. 8 but there are two further areas for discussion which may exert an influence on land law: Art. 6 and Art. 14.[78]

---

[74] *Pinnock*, 129.

[75] See, for example, *Winterstein v France* (2013), *Bjedov v Croatia* (2012), *MSS v Belgium and Greece* (2011), *Kiyutin v Russia* (2011), *Alajos Kiss v Hungary* (2010), *D. H. and Others v the Czech Republic* (2007).

[76] Nield, 'Article 8 Respect for the Home: A Human Property Right', 163.

[77] See, for example, comments in *Kay v Lambeth LBC*, [38], per Lord Bingham; for a discussion of the concept of vulnerability in Strasbourg jurisprudence see: L. Peroni and A. Timmer, 'Vulnerable groups: The Promise of an Emerging Concept in European Human Rights Convention Law' (2013) 11(4) Int J Const Law 1056; A. Timmer, 'A Quiet Revolution: Vulnerability in the European Court of Human Rights' in Martha Fineman and Anna Grear (eds.), *Vulnerability: Reflections on a New Ethical Foundation for Law and Politics* (Farnham: Ashgate, 2013).

[78] Article 10 (right to free expression) and Art. 11 (right to free association) may also be more indirectly engaged with issues pertaining to property law; beyond Art. 14, in domestic law, there is now the additional protection offered by the 'public sector equality duty' under s. 149 of the Equality Act 2010.

14.6.1 Article 6 of the ECHR

Article 6 guarantees a fair hearing before an independent, public, and impartial tribunal within a reasonable time unless exceptions apply. The protection under Art. 6 extends to disputes that concern *criminal or civil rights*. Importantly, the delivery of a judgment by the court is itself regarded as part of the 'hearing' for the purposes of Art. 6.[79] This means that the State is required to put in place a system for the effective enforcement of judgments which functions fairly and without delay.[80]

14.6.2 Article 14 of the ECHR

Article 14 of the ECHR provides for the right against discrimination but is parasitic—in other words, it does not provide a stand-alone cause of action; rather, a claimant can only rely on Art. 14 where another Convention right is engaged. This might give the impression that Art. 14 offers little protection. That would be quite wrong. In practice, even where the substantive Convention right is not found to be engaged, the court is still able to proceed to consider whether Art. 14 has been violated. The elements necessary to prove an infringement of Art. 14 were explained by Baroness Hale (as she then was) in *Ghaidan v Godin-Mendoza* (2004):[81]

> It is common ground that five questions arise in an article 14 inquiry, based on the approach of Brooke LJ in *Wandsworth LBC v Michalak* [2003] . . . The original four questions were:
>
> (i)   Do the facts fall within the ambit of one or more of the Convention rights?
> (ii)   Was there a difference in treatment in respect of that right between the complainant and others put forward for comparison?
> (iii)   Were those others in an analogous situation?
> (iv)   Was the difference in treatment objectively justifiable? I.e., did it have a legitimate aim and bear a reasonable relationship of proportionality to that aim?
>
> The additional question is whether the difference in treatment is based on one or more of the grounds proscribed—whether expressly or by inference—in Article 14.

In *Ghaidan*, the House of Lords held that Sch. 1, para. 2 of the Rent Act 1977 (which provides for the succession to a protected tenancy of the surviving spouse living in that property) did indeed extend to same sex couples. The House of Lords in *Fitzpatrick v Sterling Housing Association Ltd* (2001), a case decided before the coming into force of the HRA 1998, had held that Sch. 1 did not apply to same sex couples. In *Ghaidan*, the court found that Sch. 1, para. 2 violated Art. 14 of the ECHR taken together with Art. 8 and that there was no justification for the difference in treatment of heterosexual couples vis-à-vis same sex couples. Under s. 3(1) of the HRA 1998, Sch. 1, para. 2 of the Rent Act 1977 was to be interpreted in a manner compliant with Convention rights. In so doing, the difference of treatment between opposite and same sex couples was eliminated.

---

[79]   *Pelipenko v Russia* (2013).
[80]   Art. 6 is often advanced as a secondary argument to the primacy of Arts 1 and 8 as it was in the case of *Mullen v Salford City Council* (2010).   [81]   *Ghaidan*, 605.

14.7 **Future directions**

It remains for us to reflect on just how significant human rights arguments are and might become for the development of modern land law. The domestic courts have, thus far, largely seen off calls for wholesale engagement with human rights arguments and the proportionality exercise in property law disputes but, after *Pinnock* and *Powell*, it is becoming ever more difficult for the courts to shrug off human rights considerations. Property law and land law in particular has long been wedded to the attraction of clear and certain rules but human rights arguments threaten to shake up the established order by importing greater discretion, subjectivity, and proportionality into the mix. So far, land law has seen less impact from human rights than many other areas of the law but it is intriguing to consider how human rights arguments might already be operating in our land law.

One key thinker in this area is Allen, who has examined the potential impact that human rights arguments might exert on the development of property rights. According to Allen,[82] this question can be answered in one of two ways: either we accept that the fundamental rights and freedoms of the ECHR are *already* embedded within our established land law principles in which case human rights arguments will have little impact or, alternatively, human rights arguments will give way to a *new* balancing exercise in which competing interests in land are to be weighed against one another. This balancing exercise will require courts to assess the proportionality of measures as against the aims being pursued. If this latter vision proves to be accurate, we can expect an increasing influence of human rights arguments in property law disputes. This does not, however, necessarily mean that these arguments will succeed.

Certainly, as things currently stand, Art. 1 of the First Protocol offers little protection and has had little impact in matters of domestic land law. Allen has described the provision as 'a very conservative element in the protection of human rights'.[83] As Goymour noted in 2011,[84] there was no known area of property law which has been shown to violate Art. 1. That is not to say that it will not happen one day but, as yet, the effect of Art. 1 is not being felt in land law circles.

The position as regards Art. 8 appears somewhat different, far more vibrant and dynamic. If there is one right with the potential to disturb the apple cart of land law it is likely to be Art. 8. It is now apparent, following *Pinnock* and *Powell*, that Art. 8 does afford a degree of potential protection to those social tenants facing possession proceedings albeit subject to the caveats the court was at pains to lay down and only in the 'vertical' context. Article 8, once engaged, requires the court to see land as more than an asset but as a 'home' and to attach weight to more subjective notions of privacy, dignity, and vulnerability. This is a change for land law! However, we must not get carried away. The deference paid by the Supreme Court to local authorities' twin aims of vindicating property rights and managing their cash-strapped and finite resources remains very strong and there is no reason to suspect that this deference will change anytime soon. Unless and until the Supreme Court signals a more liberal approach, it will only be the exceptional possession cases that succeed on Art. 8 grounds.

---

[82] T. Allen, *Property and the Human Rights Act 1998* (Bloomsbury, 2005).

[83] T. Allen, 'The Autonomous Meaning of "Possessions" under the European Convention on Human Rights', 69.

[84] Goymour, 'Property and Housing', 286.

Whilst the Supreme Court in *Pinnock* would not be drawn on the horizontal application of Art. 8, there are indications in a series of cases that demonstrate the court's willingness to at least recognize the *potential* implications of the Convention right in private disputes, albeit ultimately in each case domestic law was found to be compatible or the discussion was obiter only:

- where a court considers whether co-owned property is to be sold under ss. 14 and 15 of TOLATA 1996 and s. 335A of the Insolvency Act 1986: *Barca v Mears* (2004);[85] *Donohoe v Ingram* (2006); *Putnam v Taylor* (2006); *National Westminster Bank plc v Rushmer* (2010)[86]

- where repossession and sale of mortgaged property is sought by secure creditors: *Horsham Properties Group Ltd v Clark* (2009)[87]

- where beneficiaries' interests have been overreached in the secured creditor context: *Birmingham Midshires Services Ltd v Sabherwal* (2000); *National Westminster Bank plc v Malhan* (2004).[88]

These cases must now, of course, be seen in light of the Supreme Court's rejection of horizontal effect in *McDonald* and the Strasbourg Court's judgment in *FJM v UK*; discussed in section 14.3.

So, is Art. 8 changing the land law discourse? Art. 8 requires the court to engage in a more subjective analysis of the circumstances and impact that, for example, a possession order may have on a given individual in their own particular circumstances. In this way, an argument can be mounted that Art. 8 has changed the traditional approach of land law and marks a move away from a fixation on the objective assertion of clear property rules. In this way, as Nield has observed, Art. 8 has been interpreted not as introducing a new property right per se but as ushering a new property dynamic:[89]

> Article 8 has . . . changed the property landscape, but it might be misleading to think in terms of a 'new equity'. *Pinnock* is undoubtedly a landmark judgment in recognising a new source of protection for the home, flowing from the respect for the home demanded by Article 8. This protection is not a traditional property right. It does not attach to property in the sense of binding purchasers or third parties . . . this protection springs from the corresponding duty imposed upon public authorities under the HRA 1998 . . . the protection is thus enduring . . . it governs the relations between parties according to an individual's rights, derived not from recognised property rights, but from their deep connection with a certain physical shelter . . . By affording the home a distinct form of protection, Article 8 introduces a new dynamic into rights to possession of the home which could provide a greater voice to home values.

---

[85] Nicholas Strauss QC noted (obiter) that the presumption in favour of sale one year after the grant of a bankruptcy order under s. 335A may infringe Art. 8.

[86] The court in *Rushmer* held that the s. 15 factors were sufficient to enable the court to balance creditor's rights with the Art. 1 and Art. 8 rights of those affected by the sale. On the facts, due regard had therefore been given to the occupier's Convention rights.

[87] The court considered but rejected arguments based on Art. 1 of the Convention advanced by the occupier. It was said the Art. 8 argument would also fail.

[88] Both *Sabherwal* and *Malhan* were decided before the HRA 1998 came into force and comments are therefore obiter. In *Sabherwal*, the court reached the conclusion overreaching would be a proportionate interference with Art. 8, while the opposite view was adopted in *Malhan*.

[89] Nield, 'Article 8 Respect for the Home: A Human Property Right'.

Where does this leave us? Well, the courts have long been grappling with the 'human rights question' and there is no likelihood this will change in the near future as claimants continue to advance novel arguments based upon their Convention rights. It is important, however, not to overstate the role and significance of human rights, particularly for land law. As Baroness Hale noted in *Kay v Lambeth LBC*:[90]

> The Convention began life as a code of individual civil and political rights, not a code of social and economic rights.

The Convention was therefore designed neither to give rise to new property rights nor to reform the principles of property law and we must take account of this. Howell has urged property lawyers to strongly resist the seductive effects of human rights:[91]

> Land law must, it is suggested, keep to the narrow stony path. Land law is essentially pragmatic and practical and, most importantly, has consequences for third parties: certainty is almost always justice ... The introduction of human rights values is a wild card which is wholly unpredictable ... parties will not enter into agreements over land if they cannot be sure of their effect, and practitioners will not be able to advise them.

Whether you agree with Howell's rather pessimistic perspective on the impact of human rights on land law, it is difficult to disagree with Nield who concluded (even before the judgments of the Supreme Court and Strasbourg Court in *McDonald/FJM* were handed down) that the courts have thus far adopted a very conservative approach:[92]

> Certainty is a quality beloved of property lawyers and discretion smacks of uncertainty. First, the nature of any discretion must be justified by clear policy, in which the judiciary ... will wish to defer to Parliament. Secondly, the exercise of any discretion must be guided by avoidance of a disproportionate outcome ... proportionality concentrates its attention on the vulnerability of the occupier whose personal circumstances are pushed beyond the acceptable by the repossession. Although judges are used to making these judgments, only time will tell how far their sympathy will extend. Initial signs are that the quality of their mercy will not often be strained.

As we reach the end of both this chapter and indeed the book, it seems that a bald assertion of a property right of itself may not be sufficient to succeed in a property law dispute where other competing interests such as 'home' and the 'peaceful enjoyment of possessions' are *potentially* in play. Deciphering exactly what this means for the modern land law landscape remains somewhat elusive, however, as the precise boundaries of this relatively immature human rights jurisdiction continue to take shape. For you, as students of land law, just one question to end on: how far should land law stick to a narrow and stony path, as Howell has argued? Or, should it instead embrace a new and evolving human rights dynamic?

---

[90] *Kay v Lambeth LBC*, 537.
[91] Howell, 'The Human Rights Act 1998: Land, Private Citizens, and the Common Law', 634.
[92] Nield, 'Article 8 Respect for the Home: A Human Property Right', 171.

Further reading

- T. Allen, Property and the Human Rights Act 1998 (Oxford: Hart, 2005).

- T. Allen, 'The Autonomous Meaning of "Possessions" under the European Convention on Human Rights' in E. Cooke (ed.), *Modern Studies in Property Law*, Vol. 2 (Oxford: Hart, 2003), at 69.

- C. Bevan, 'Challenging Home as a Concept in Modern Property Law Post-*Stack* and *Kernott*' in W. Barr (ed.), *Modern Studies in Property Law*, Vol. 8 (Oxford: Hart, 2015), chapter 11.

- S. Bright, '*Manchester CC v Pinnock* (2010)—Shifting Ideas of Ownership in Land' in N. Gravells (ed.), *Landmark Cases in Land Law* (Oxford: Hart, 2013), chapter 11.

- D. Cowan, L. Fox O'Mahony, and N. Cobb, Great Debates in Property Law (Basingstoke: Palgrave, 2012), chapter 8.

- D. Cowan and C. Hunter, '"Yeah But, No But": *Pinnock* and *Powell* in the Supreme Court (2012) 75(1) MLR 78.

- S. Gardner and E. MacKenzie, *Introduction to Land Law* (Oxford: Hart, 2015).

- A. Goymour, 'Property and Housing' in D. Hoffmann (ed.), *The Impact of the Human Rights Act on Private Law* (Cambridge: Cambridge University Press, 2011), at 286.

- K. Gray, 'Land Law and Human Rights' in L. Tee (ed.), *Land Law: Issues, Debates, Policy* (Devon: Willan, 2002), at 211.

- J. Howell, 'The Human Rights Act 1998: Land, Private Citizens, and the Common Law' (2007) 123 LQR 618.

- S. Nield, 'Article 8 Respect for the Home: A Human Property Right' (2013) 24 KLJ 171.

- S. Nield, 'Thumbs Down to Horizontal Effect of Article 8' [2015] Conv 77.

- L. Peroni and A. Timmer, 'Vulnerable Groups: The Promise of an Emerging Concept in European Human Rights Convention Law' (2013) 11(4) Int J Const Law 1056.

- A. Timmer, 'A Quiet Revolution: Vulnerability in the European Court of Human Rights' in Martha Fineman and Anna Grear (eds.), *Vulnerability: Reflections on a New Ethical Foundation for Law and Politics* (Farnham: Ashgate, 2013).

Online resources

Access the online resources at www.oup.com/uk/bevan2e/ to test yourself with self-test questions and scenario problems. You can also view additional supporting material relevant to the topics in this chapter, including:

- *Videos*
- *Audio podcasts*
- *Maps, diagrams, and flowcharts*
- *Interactive exercises*
- *Examples of real-life legal documentation*

Glossary

Absolute title The 'gold standard' of title available to registered proprietors of estates in land.

Adverse possession A doctrine allowing acquisition of title to land owned by someone else by possessing it continually for a required period without the owner's permission.

Alienation/alienability Transferring/ability to transfer property to another.

Animus possidendi Intention to possess—one requirement for the acquisition of title by adverse possession.

Appurtenant Belonging or pertaining to land e.g. an easement attaching to a parcel of land.

Assign To transfer rights or benefits in land to another.

Assignment The process by which one person, the assignor, transfers rights or benefits in land to another, the assignee—most commonly a leasehold interest.

Beneficial interest Interest of a beneficiary—the right in equity to the benefit of land as distinct from a legal right in land.

Beneficiary A person with an equitable interest in land or property held under a trust as distinct from the legal owners (trustees).

Bona fide 'In good faith'.

Cestui que trust Another name for beneficiary under a trust.

Charge Interest granted to secure payment of money. Common example: charge by way of legal mortgage where mortgage lender advances money to borrower/mortgagor in return for interest in the mortgagor's land.

Chattel Moveable items of personal property that are not land and not attached to land as distinct from fixtures.

Common intention constructive trust An implied trust arising from an express or implied agreement between parties to share ownership of property.

Co-ownership Simultaneous ownership of land by two or more people.

Constructive trust A form of trust that arises by implication and operation of law rather than expressly.

Conveyance The legal process of transferring land or property rights to another; also refers to the formal legal document transferring title.

Corporeal hereditaments Tangible and visible items or rights in relation to land or property that can be inherited, e.g. buildings, trees, coal as distinct from intangible incorporeal hereditaments.

Covenant A promise made in a deed to do or not do something on land.

Covenantee The person benefiting from a promise made in a covenant, i.e. the person to whom the promise is made.

Covenantor The person burdened by a promise made in a covenant, i.e. the person making the promise.

Deed A formal, legal document which complies with the requirements of s. 1 of the Law of Property (Miscellaneous Provisions) Act 1989.

Demise Transfer of land to another either by lease or under a will.

Disposition The creation or transfer of an interest in land.

Dominant tenement Land benefiting from or having the advantage of a right, e.g. an easement.

Easement A right of one landowner over land belonging to another e.g. a right of way over neighbouring land.

Encumbrance A right or burden affecting land.

Equitable right A right that operates in equity only in contrast to a legal right.

Equity of redemption Rights enjoyed by a mortgagor and, specifically, the right to recover full, unencumbered use of the mortgaged land on repayment of all mortgage monies owing.

Equity's Darling A bona fide purchaser of a legal estate for value without notice.

Estate An interest in land that allows the interest holder rights of use and possession of that land for a particular duration.

Estate contract A contract for the sale or creation of an interest in land.

Exclusive possession The key ingredient of a lease; amounting to territorial control i.e. the ability of tenants to exclude others from the land.

Express trust A trust created in express terms usually involving the use of writing as distinct from implied (constructive or resulting) trusts.

Fee simple absolute in possession One of two recognized legal estates in land (the other being leasehold). The closest thing to outright ownership of land recognized in English & Welsh land law.

Fixture An object or item affixed, attached to land so that it is taken as forming part of that land as distinct from chattels.

Foreclosure Draconian remedy in the law of mortgages involving the outright transfer of the mortgagor's land to the mortgagee.

Forfeiture The right of a lessor (landlord) to re-enter leased land in the event of a breach of covenant by the lessee/tenant.

Freehold An estate in land with an uncertain (potentially unlimited) duration which can be passed on to heirs; term often now used interchangeably with fee simple absolute in possession.

Headlease A lease out of which is carved a leasehold estate of shorter duration.

Implied trust A trust not created by express terms or statute but by operation of law.

In gross Refers to a right, e.g. a *profit à prendre*, that exists over servient land but without being tied to any benefited, dominant tenement.

Incorporeal hereditaments Intangible or non-visible rights in relation to land, e.g. easements or *profits à prendre* which can be inherited.

Injunction A remedy of the court ordering a person to do or not to do some identified activity.

Ius accrescendi Another name for the right of survivorship in the context co-ownership.

Joint tenancy A type of co-ownership under which co-owners are all wholly entitled to the land in contrast to tenancy in common.

Land charge Interests in unregistered land that can be protected by registration under the Land Charges Act 1972.

Leasehold/lease Also called term of years absolute in possession, the second and lesser of the two estates capable of existing at law (the other being freehold). Involves a time-limited right to exclusive possession of land.

Lessee Another name for a tenant in the leasehold relationship.

Lessor Another name for a landlord in the leasehold relationship.

Licence A personal permission (i.e. non-proprietary right) to enter another's land.

Mortgage A security interest in land under which the mortgagor grants to the mortgagee an interest in her land in return for the payment of loan monies.

Mortgagee Another name for the lender; the person to whom the mortgage is granted.

Mortgagor Another name for the borrower; the person creating the mortgage.

Notice (doctrine of) Now of very marginal application only, a principle which determined whether a purchaser of an unregistered legal estate for value took title to the land free of any equitable interests. Three forms of notice were recognized for this purpose: actual, constructive, and imputed.

Notice (entry of under LRA 2002) Entry of a notice on the Charges Register at Land Registry is a means of protecting the priority of an interest in registered land.

Notice to quit A means by which a landlord or tenant can bring a periodic tenancy to an end.

Option to purchase An equitable interest which allows a prospective purchaser the right to buy a parcel of land within a given time period, at an agreed price or on the occurrence of specified events.

Overreaching A doctrine or 'device' provided for by statute under which equitable interests are detached from the land and translated into the proceeds of sale; operates in both unregistered and registered land.

Overriding interest Interests in registered land which, whilst not protected by an entry on the register, are capable of binding third parties acquiring rights in the land.

Personalty Personal property (e.g. cash, clothes) as distinct from realty.

Periodic tenancy A lease/tenancy for a specified period which runs from period to period continually (whether that period be weekly, monthly, yearly) until it is terminated by service of a notice to quit by the landlord or tenant.

Personal rights Rights only binding on parties to the arrangement/relationship, e.g. rights under a contract in contrast to property rights.

Prescription A means of acquiring an easement by long user.

Profit à prendre A right to take something from land belonging to another, e.g. fish or timber.

Property rights/proprietary rights Rights capable of binding third parties in contrast to personal rights.

Proprietary estoppel An equitable doctrine which allows for a claimant to acquire rights in land despite a lack of formality. Where a claimant reasonably relies to her detriment on a representation that she is to have an interest in land and it would be unconscionable for the person making the representation to resile from it, that representation will be enforced.

Puisne mortgage A legal mortgage over unregistered land (typically a second or subsequent mortgage) not protected by deposit of title deeds; must be protected by registration as a Class C(i) land charge under the Land Charges Act 1972.

Quasi-easement A right that is in the nature of an easement except that the dominant and servient tenements are owned by the same person and would amount to an easement if the dominant and servient tenements were separately owned.

Realty Another name for land or real property as distinct from personalty.

Rectification Correction of a mistake on the register held at Land Registry which prejudicially affects the title of the registered proprietor and may give rise to an indemnity.

Register The official record of title ownership and registered interests affecting registered land held at Land Registry.

Registered land A system under which title to land is proved by reference to entries on a State-guaranteed and maintained register. Governed in England and Wales today by the Land Registration Act 2002 and controlled by HM Land Registry.

Rent Payment made by a tenant under a lease to a landlord.

Rentcharge A sum of money paid annually by a freehold owner to a third party who usually has no interest in the land.

Restrictive covenant A covenant which is negative in character, i.e. a promise in a deed not to do something on land.

Resulting trust An implied trust arising in favour of a party who advances funds towards acquiring a property or, alternatively, where a party transfers property to an intended legal owner but the transfer fails for some reason; the legal owner is taken as holding the land on resulting trust for the transferor.

Reversion In the leasehold relationship, the right of the landlord to retake possession of the land.

Servient tenement Land subject to or burdened by a right such as an easement.

Severance The process by which a joint tenancy is converted into a tenancy in common in equity.

Specific performance A remedy of equity whereby the court orders one person to fulfil her obligations to another under a contract previously concluded between the parties.

Sublease Also called a subtenancy; refers to a lease carved out of a larger leasehold: the headlease.

Tenancy Another name for a lease.

Tenancy in common A type of co-ownership under which co-owners each enjoy a share and separately transferable interest in the property in contrast to joint tenancy.

Tenant A person who occupies another's land (the landlord) for a defined period of time, usually paying rent, with exclusive possession. Also known as a lessee.

Tenure Tenure describes the basis on which land is held. Ultimately all land in England is held from a lord; generally, the Crown. Today, the doctrine has little practical significance but is still used in the leasehold context.

Term of years absolute Another name for a lease or leasehold estate.

Title Title describes the right to an estate, to ownership of land and serves as proof of that right.

Trust A device of equity which permits the division of ownership into legal ownership and equitable ownership. The legal owners (trustees) and equitable owners (beneficiaries) may be different people (though commonly will be the same). The legal owners (trustees) hold the land on trust for the beneficiaries who have an equitable right to benefit from and enjoy the land.

Trustee The legal owners of land under a trust.

Trustee in bankruptcy A person or entity in charge of administrating the estate of a person who is made bankrupt.

Trust for sale A trust under which property is held by trustees with a duty to sell the land. This duty of sale is immediate but can be postponed by the trustees. Under the LPA 1925, virtually all co-ownership took place under a trust for sale. Today, co-ownership operates under trusts of land and not trusts for sale: s. 1 of the Trusts of Land and Appointment of Trustees Act 1996.

Trust of land Any trust of property which consists of or includes land: see s. 1(1)(a) of the Trusts of Land and Appointment of Trustees Act 1996; replaces the old trust for sale.

Unregistered land A system governing land not covered by the registered land scheme under the LRA 2002; of dwindling significance in contemporary land law.

Waiver A voluntary act (express or implied) relinquishing or abandoning a right.

Writ A formal document used (largely historically) to initiate proceedings in court; today proceedings are almost universally commenced by claim forms or applications.

Index